THE MONEYCHANGERS

By the same author

DO YOU SINCERELY WANT TO BE RICH?
(With Bruce Page and Godfrey Hodgson)

SLATER WALKER

Charles Raw

THE MONEYCHANGERS

HOW THE VATICAN BANK ENABLED
ROBERTO CALVI TO STEAL
$250 MILLION FOR THE HEADS OF
THE P2 MAŞONIC LODGE

HARVILL
An Imprint of HarperCollins*Publishers*

First published 1992 by
Harvill
An imprint of HarperCollins*Publishers*,
77/85 Fulham Palace Road,
Hammersmith, London w6 8jb

1 3 5 7 9 8 6 4 2

ISBN 0-00-217338-7

A CIP catalogue record for this title is
available from the British Library.

The author asserts the moral right to be
identified as the author of this work.

Photoset in Linotron Ehrhardt
by Rowland Phototypesetting Ltd,
Bury St Edmunds, Suffolk
Printed and bound in Great Britain by
HarperCollinsManufacturing, Glasgow

CONTENTS

CONTENTS

ACKNOWLEDGEMENTS

This book has been some years in the making and during this time a number of people have helped me in one way or another, mostly translating Italian for me – until I mastered the ability at least to read the language – and carrying out research for me in Italy. I am grateful to all of these but I must single out Philip Willan who has worked doggedly on my behalf.

This is a long, detailed and complicated book and I wish to thank the friends who encouraged me to persevere and my publishers for their patience. I am also particularly grateful to Alison Macleod, once of the *Daily Worker* but more lately of *Euromoney*, for her labours with me in getting the text into final shape, and for her work on the index.

I must also thank Carlo Calvi for providing me with the papers from his father's safe in the Bahamas, without which it would not have been possible to reconstruct what happened. Carlo and his mother helped in other ways, such as providing photographs and other documents, and I should like to emphasize that they have never attempted to influence what I have written.

My own investigations were, of course, conducted in parallel with many others, in particular those of the magistrates, police and liquidators in Italy, of the magistrates in Switzerland, and of the liquidators in Nassau and in Luxembourg (for whom I worked as a consultant). The great bulk of the material uncovered is now in the public domain in one place or another, usually in evidence in criminal or civil actions around the world, and I should like to mention the meticulous work of Geoffrey Robinson of Touche Ross, who headed the research team of the Luxembourg liquidators. Another important source of information was the many volumes of evidence published by the Italian Parliamentary commission on the P2 affair. While I have conducted a considerable number of interviews, I have relied for the most part on this documentary evidence. I have not, however, attempted to provide a list of specific sources as this would have been of inordinate length.

THE MONEYCHANGERS

ONE

The Villain in the Affair

"I will be remembered as the villain in the Calvi affair," said the American archbishop Paul Casimir Marcinkus, when he retired from the presidency of the Vatican bank known as IOR, in the autumn of 1990. "It is always going to be that way. There is no way that is going to be wiped off."

Marcinkus regards it as a stain on his name that in 1984 the Vatican made his bank pay $240,822,222.23 to the creditors of the bankrupt Banco Ambrosiano. In 1988 he said: "I told them right from the beginning: 'You're crazy! Don't even open up that conversation,' I said. 'If we're not guilty, we don't pay. And we're not guilty.'"

This book will show that he was guilty. Using documents never before made public, I shall prove that Marcinkus was indeed "the villain in the Calvi affair" – not, indeed, the only villain, but the crucial accomplice who made the fraud possible. He thereby cost shareholders, creditors and the Italian taxpayer over a billion dollars.

It is no part of my case that Marcinkus made anything for himself. The main beneficiaries of the fraud were the heads of the P2 masonic lodge, Licio Gelli and Umberto Ortolani. I am going to show, for the first time, how they and their friends got something like a quarter of a billion dollars. There is no reason to believe that Marcinkus knew this.

But he provided the mechanism which enabled Calvi to divert this money. I am going to trace the series of secret agreements he made with Calvi – agreements which began earlier, and ranged more widely, than has ever before been suspected. His role as a director of the Cisalpine Bank, always ignored by Vatican apologists, is vital to my story. I shall show that he misled his fellow-directors on twenty separate occasions, and that he lied deliberately to the auditors of the bank. Marcinkus has avoided every criminal court, because of the Vatican's immunity from Italian law, and has not even tried to defend his conduct in the civil courts of the Bahamas.

Roberto Calvi was found hanging under Blackfriars Bridge early in the morning of 18 June 1982. For eighteen months afterwards the Vatican refused to admit that it had any responsibility to his creditors. The Pope

3

himself joined in the cover-up. But the Vatican did eventually pay, and, as Marcinkus himself points out, the payment was an admission of guilt.

But it was less than half of what Marcinkus cost the Catholic Church. IOR stands for Istituto per le Opere di Religione (Institute for Religious Works) and it was the job of Marcinkus to use the money entrusted to him by the faithful for the building of hospitals, orphanages and schools. As it is a secretive institution, and issues no balance sheet, we do not know what proportion of the money he used to finance Calvi's fraudulent schemes.

When Marcinkus retired at the end of October 1990, he issued a written statement, expressing his gratitude to the Pope for having accepted his request to be released from the service of the Holy See and to return to the United States.

"The forty years that I have spent far from my Diocese – in the diplomatic service, collaborating on the preparation and the undertaking of the papal journeys, serving at the Institute for Religious Works and at the governor's office – have enriched my priesthood and have given me a clearer and deeper perception of the Unity and Universality of the Church."

However it may have enriched his priesthood, it impoverished the Church. I am going to show that Marcinkus cost the Vatican a total of half a billion dollars. Sensibly invested, that sum could have relieved the Holy See from all financial anxiety.

It is true that, as the Vatican apologists have contended, Marcinkus did not know until July 1981 the size of the hole in Calvi's accounts. Even then, he may not have known where all the money had gone.

But his conduct after that became so indefensible that those appointed to defend it have tried to conceal the documents. I shall show that Marcinkus did not denounce the fraud, but instead issued "letters of patronage" which enabled Calvi to keep his own executives quiet for almost another year. (See Appendix A) At the same time he extracted from Calvi a "letter of indemnity" which is blatant evidence of a conspiracy between himself and Calvi to deceive third parties. (See Appendix B(vii)) I shall examine its contents in due course.

The case that can be proved against Marcinkus is weighty enough; I shall not contend, and do not believe, that he had Calvi murdered. It has been many times alleged that some of Calvi's associates killed him to save themselves from scandal. As I am going to show, Marcinkus was admitting, the day before Calvi died, that the scandal was inevitable.

If Calvi's death was suicide, however, Marcinkus was among the foremost of those who made him suicidal. He had imposed on Calvi a deadline for repayment – 30 June 1982 – which could not possibly be met. Yet there is evidence that Calvi, almost to the last, thought or fantasized that he could meet the deadline.

Calvi was not a brilliant man. He made relatively little out of his own fraud. By my reckoning, he left his family about $30 million. Less than half of that was directly embezzled; most of the rest was accounted for by an uncharacteristically successful property development.

But this is not a book about clever financiers, making far-sighted plans. Calvi never could admit that he had made a bad investment; in the struggle to cover up his losses, he lost more and more. That he kept his fraudulent edifice looking good for ten years proves only that a number of people round him had poor eyesight. Among the blindest were some of the world's famous banks.

These banks, which had been happily lending to Calvi until a year before the crash, found that the Italian Government was not going to reimburse them, unless they had lent directly to the Ambrosiano in Milan. Those who had lent to Banco Ambrosiano Holding, the Luxembourg company through which the Ambrosiano held its foreign subsidiaries, or directly to those subsidiaries were left to recover their money as best they might.

Eighty-eight of the creditor banks formed a committee. (Though, as it proved, there were more than a hundred creditor banks all told.) It was this committee which insisted on a payment from the Vatican, and which eventually got that $240 million.

The payment was made after a remarkable agreement, finalised on 25 May 1984 in Geneva with the officials winding up the affairs of the Ambrosiano in three centres: Milan, the home of the parent bank, Luxembourg, the base of its international arm, and Nassau in the Bahamas, where Calvi's relationship with Marcinkus had begun in earnest thirteen years before.

The signing was a very discreet occasion. Marcinkus did not attend. He had signed the day before, in front of his lawyers in the Vatican. The agreement carried a preamble, in which the IOR, having reiterated its claim that it had no responsibility for the Ambrosiano crash, in which it had found itself "involuntarily" involved, had nevertheless "by reason of its special position alone, stated that it is prepared to make a voluntary contribution". The agreement, the preamble concluded, had been made "in a spirit of mutual reconciliation and collaboration".

The Vatican amplified this in its own newspaper, *L'Osservatore Romano*, on 4 June 1984. The "voluntary contribution" had been made to "facilitate a comprehensive solution, and also to help restore international relations". The statement ended with the hope that what had been done "at much sacrifice" would also serve to alleviate the consequences of the collapse to all who had suffered from it.

This was a face-saving formula, and a lie. The payment was not a contribution, since the IOR was alone in handing over such a sum. Nor was it voluntary, since it was made only after a combination of pressures. The fiercest fighters were the banks, which had lost some $600 million in the crash. Two British banks, the Midland and the National Westminster, led the campaign. These creditors were content to let the IOR save its face, in return for $240 million.

This was not a simple repayment. The Vatican did make money out of its association with Calvi, largely by special commissions, premium interest rates and profits from the illegal export of currency. By my estimate, all this came to no more than $25 million. Against this, even before the payment, it had lost, as I am going to show, ten times as much. If it had been an innocent dupe of Calvi, it could have pleaded its losses and queued up with the creditors. But it had in fact, though not in words, abandoned its plea of innocence.

Marcinkus began denying his responsibility for the crash even before it happened. Calvi disappeared from Italy on 11 June 1982. His deputy, Roberto Rosone, attempted to avert the crash. Rosone had not recovered from being shot in the leg on 27 April – an episode which then seemed a complete mystery. Calvi had told him that he had undertaken to repay $400 million of the bank's debts by 30 June. Was there anything to pay it with? At the Luxembourg office Angelo de Bernardi, whose job it was to keep in touch with the IOR, produced the "letters of patronage" (also called "letters of comfort") dated 1 September 1981, and signed by Luigi Mennini, second in command of Marcinkus. These purported to show that the IOR controlled a group of companies with addresses in Luxembourg, Liechtenstein and Panama, and that it was "aware" of their debts. De Bernardi knew the figures; the debts of these companies to Ambrosiano's foreign subsidiaries totalled $1.3 billion. If the Vatican paid even a quarter of them, that would stave off the immediate problem.

De Bernardi and Rosone went to Rome to see the heads of the IOR. They took with them Michel Leemans, an unflappable Belgian, who was head of La Centrale, the holding company for Calvi's Italian subsidiaries. He told Rosone: "You'll have to call in Grandmother." (The Bank of Italy.)

But not, surely, if the Vatican paid up? On the morning of 16 June 1982 Rosone went in alone to see Mennini and the IOR chief accountant, Pellegrino de Strobel. He confronted them with the "letters of patronage". This was when Rosone first learned that the IOR had written these because, the previous August, Calvi had asked for them. In exchange, Calvi had given the IOR his own letter of indemnity. He was not going to hold Marcinkus to any obligation which might be thought to arise from these letters of patronage.

Calvi was thus making it clear that the aim of the letters of patronage was to deceive someone. (His own employees, as we shall see later.) By doing what Calvi asked, Marcinkus was taking part in the deceit.

Calvi's "letter of indemnity" contained a deadline, which was imposed on him by the IOR. The arrangement was to run only until 30 June 1982. Then he would have to pay the Vatican some $300 million, which would extricate the IOR from its involvement with Calvi. This deadline was a fortnight from the day on which Rosone was talking to Mennini.

When he knew that the IOR had a letter, signed by Calvi, to back its claim that it had no responsibility, Rosone called in Leemans and de Bernardi to join the discussion. Leemans proposed various expedients to avoid the crash, none of them acceptable to the IOR. Rosone went back to Milan. At noon the following day, 17 June, he told an emergency board meeting that the board would have to dissolve itself and ask the Bank of Italy to put in commissioners. The meeting lasted five hours, largely because of the protests of a new board member, Orazio Bagnasco. Calvi had brought him in at the end of January 1982, and his companies had spent something over $20 million on Ambrosiano shares, all of which was now about to be lost.

That morning, Leemans had made a last approach to Marcinkus, pointing out that the impending crash meant a scandal which would involve the IOR. He said: "You realise what this means? When I leave this room I go straight to the telephone, and let the Ambrosiano board meeting know that there's nothing else for it; they'll have to call in the Bank of Italy. That means that everything about these letters of patronage will come out."

Marcinkus replied: "I realise I'm going to have to pay a high price for that, personally. I made a mistake. I was convinced of the validity of that friendship." (His friendship with Calvi.)

Leemans pleaded: "Don't you at IOR want to save your own faces?"

"Whatever happens to our faces," Marcinkus said, "we just haven't got that kind of money."

The Ambrosiano board dissolved itself, and called in the Bank of Italy, at five that afternoon. Calvi was then hiding in London. There is reason to believe that he learned through a phone call of the board's decision. If so, who was on the Milan end of the phone?

There is no evidence that Calvi knew of his secretary's suicide, which took place about two hours after the board meeting.

7

Calvi's body was found the next morning, 18 June. As the passport in his pocket bore a false name, the news of his death did not reach Italy until the evening. By that time the Bank of Italy had already put in a temporary special commissioner to run the bank, until three independent commissioners could be appointed.

The three took over on 21 June, and at once learned of the letters of patronage. They saw Marcinkus on 2 July. He made it clear that he was not going to pay. That day the Treasury Minister, Beniamino Andreatta, made a statement in Parliament calling on the IOR to accept its responsibilities.

Quite apart from the sum covered – or, rather, not covered – by the letters of patronage, the IOR appeared to owe a total of $213 million to two of the Ambrosiano's foreign subsidiaries, Banco Andino in Peru and Banco Ambrosiano Overseas in Nassau. (The bank in Nassau was still remembered by its former name, the Cisalpine, and I shall be calling it that from now on.) On 13 July the manager of the Cisalpine, Pierre Siegenthaler, was lunching at the Hôtel du Rhône, Geneva, with a Cisalpine director, Count Luciano della Porta. Angelo de Bernardi (the man who had brought the letters of patronage from Luxembourg) was a director of the Andino. He, too, was at the lunch table. So were two lawyers, and Graham Garner of Coopers and Lybrand, auditors of the Cisalpine. Garner had earlier tried to discover the truth about the Cisalpine, and Marcinkus had misled him, as I shall show later.

These six people drank five bottles of wine; the bill came to 789 Swiss francs. After lunch Siegenthaler and della Porta rang up Marcinkus, and asked him to repay what he owed the Cisalpine, $88 million. He replied that the money was not really owing. That was the last lunch party charged up to the Cisalpine.

The Andino then telexed the IOR asking for its $125 million. By telex, the following day, the IOR informed the Andino that the loans were, "as you are aware", the "counterpart" of sums lent to United Trading Corporation and that, therefore, the "amounts in question are not due by us".

United Trading Corporation was one of the companies mentioned in the letters of patronage, and the managers of both the Andino and the Cisalpine by this time had some reason for suspicion. However, Marcinkus had been a director of the Cisalpine from August 1971 until Calvi's disappearance, when he hastily resigned. Never, in all that time, had he suggested that the IOR was not the real borrower of the loans it had received.

Marcinkus was, in theory, answerable to an IOR supervisory commission of five cardinals. One of them was Agostino Casaroli, who, as Vatican

Secretary of State, was the most powerful official in the Holy See. Casaroli and Marcinkus were believed not to be friends. And Marcinkus was thought to have a direct line to the Pope, bypassing the cardinals.

Nevertheless, Casaroli now acted. On 13 July he announced the appointment of a committee of three experts – who at once became known to the press as "the three wise men" – to produce an "objective" report on the relationship between the IOR and the Ambrosiano. The three were: Joseph Brennan of the Emigrant Savings Bank of New York; Carlo Cerutti, the retired head of the state-owned telecommunications corporation, STET; and Philippe de Weck, a former chairman of the Union Bank of Switzerland. It later emerged that this was the bank through which many of the Ambrosiano's missing millions were channelled.

The appointment of these investigators was a great shock to many Catholics, who had been trying to believe that there was nothing to investigate.

On 23 July a London inquest found that Calvi's death was suicide. Why there had to be a second inquest I shall explain later. On 6 August the Italian Government put the Ambrosiano into compulsory liquidation. The good business was transferred to a new bank, the Nuovo Banco Ambrosiano. It had to be underwritten by the government, at a potential cost to Italian taxpayers of more than 1,000 billion lire ($700 million). The taxpayers blamed the Vatican.

And the Italian authorities revived an old complaint. Italy, like many other countries, thought the health of its currency demanded strict laws to prevent its citizens from taking their money abroad. But, unlike any other country, it had in the heart of its capital city a foreign state, the Vatican, which was not bound by its laws. Easily accessible to Italian banks and citizens, the IOR provided an obvious route for the currency smuggler.

On 13 September *Time* Magazine published a story headed: "Trouble at the Pope's bank." It dug up an American friend of Marcinkus who said: "There are two things he is not: dumb or crooked."

That same day, Licio Gelli was arrested in Geneva. He had fled from Italy in the spring of 1981. Magistrates had raided his house and office at Arezzo, and removed the membership list of his secret Masonic lodge, P2. (The P stands for Propaganda.) Calvi's name was on the list. So were the names of many people in the highest circles – business, military, political and even judicial.

Gelli had taken much of his money to Uruguay, and put it into a bank owned by his friend Ortolani, Bafisud. Perhaps Gelli lost confidence in Bafisud. (With reason; Bafisud ran into such difficulties that Ortolani is believed to have pumped in millions to save it from liquidation. He eventually sold it, for a nominal dollar, to a Dutch bank.) Gelli unwisely brought most of his money back to Switzerland, and was arrested at the Union Bank of Switzerland, attempting to withdraw deposits totalling $55 million. He had on him a number of documents, including a cryptic *tabella* or table, which could be deciphered to show that Calvi had paid him and Ortolani well over $200 million. These crucial documents were not passed on by the Swiss to the Italian investigators for nearly four years.

By the autumn of 1982 Marcinkus and his senior colleagues at the IOR, Mennini and de Strobel, were wanted for questioning by the public prosecutor in Milan. The IOR men stayed in the Vatican. They said they did not come under Italian jurisdiction. Marcinkus engaged a Roman lawyer, Adolfo Gatti.

The IOR and its lawyers had been quietly working away on its own internal report. A version was leaked to the press. This was at first reported to be the work of the "three wise men". On 17 October, however, *L'Osservatore Romano* said that the report was the IOR's own. It gave a five-point summary.

1. The Institute for the Works of Religion has not received either from the Ambrosiano Group or from Roberto Calvi any funds, and, therefore, does not have to refund anything.
2. The foreign companies indebted to the Ambrosiano group have never been run by the IOR, which had no knowledge of the operations carried out by the same.
3. It is established that all the payments made by the Ambrosiano Group to aforementioned Companies were made in the period prior to the so-called "letters of comfort".
4. These letters, by their date of issue, have not exercised any influence on the said payments.
5. In any future checking of the facts, all the above will be proved to be true.

That first assertion was a deliberate lie. The IOR was at that very moment repaying its Italian currency debts to the Ambrosiano Group banks. With interest, the sum repaid eventually came to 137 billion lire (about $99 million).

The Bank of Italy commissioners had discovered that, in addition to the $213 million that the IOR appeared to owe the Cisalpine and the Andino, it owed the Ambrosiano in Italy 55.6 billion lire at the time of the crash. It began to repay this on 11 August 1982, and by early 1983 had repaid a total of over 65.5 billion, including interest at 20 per cent. It owed a subsidiary, the Banca Cattolica del Veneto, 43.35 billion lire, and it started repaying this even earlier, on 15 July. Eventually, with interest, it repaid the Banca Cattolica just over 49 billion. It also owed another subsidiary bank, the Credito Varesino, just under 19.9 billion lire. These debts, too, it began repaying in July and by mid-September 1982 it had repaid the total, plus almost 2.5 billion of interest, bringing the total to 22.4 billion. So its total repayment to all three banks was 137 billion.

These lira debts resulted from a secret arrangement between Calvi and the IOR, parallel to the arrangement which resulted in the $213 million of debts outside Italy. Yet the IOR, while refusing to pay the dollar debts, did not refuse to pay the lira ones.

Why? Probably because, if the lira debts had not been repaid, the Italian Government's burden would have been greater, and its hostility stronger. By making the repayment, the IOR appears to have bought the Italian Government's silence. The foreign creditors were never told of the repayment of the lira debts. Only in 1984, when the Italian Parliament was informed of the creditors' deal with the IOR, were the lira debts mentioned in passing. Later I shall be giving the first full account of how they arose.

The only public explanation of his relationship with Calvi which Marcinkus gave at the time was an interview with *Il Sabato*, a small-circulation Catholic paper which, though not owned by the Vatican, had close ties with it. Asked if he had been aware of the operations carried out by Calvi through the Ambrosiano's foreign associates, Marcinkus replied: "The IOR is and was unrelated to all the operations carried out in the past by all the companies controlled by the Ambrosiano group. Can one say more than this?"

Then the allegation was put to Marcinkus that the IOR operated as "a safe channel for exporting capital out of Italy". He replied: "There are no grounds whatever for this statement. The IOR has always gone about its business to deal with the requirements of the Church's work in all parts of the world. That is what it has done; and only that."

In reality, some 20 billion of the lira debts that the IOR was at that very moment quietly repaying had been created in order to enable Calvi to take money illegally out of Italy, the lire having been converted into dollars by the IOR and taken out of the country through a bank the IOR controlled in Lugano, Switzerland: the Banco di Roma per la Svizzera.

By making public the defiant statement of his lawyers, and giving the *Sabato* interview, Marcinkus was going out on a limb. The Pope and Casaroli now had either to disown him or back him.

The IOR had had its critics inside the Vatican since 1974, when the financier Michele Sindona spectacularly crashed. Marcinkus publicly denied all business dealings with him. In 1978, when Albino Luciani was elected Pope as John Paul I, after the death of Marcinkus's great patron Paul VI, it was Vatican insiders who spread the story that Marcinkus was going to be sacked. After one month, John Paul I was found dead in bed, and the story that he was poisoned also came from within the Vatican. Marcinkus survived that crisis, largely because of the election of the Polish Karol Wojtyla as John Paul II. Like Marcinkus, he was an outsider in a Curia dominated by Italians, and the two seem to have found a great deal in common.

In the autumn of 1982, yet another investigation of the IOR-Ambrosiano affair was supposed to be taking place within the Vatican. A committee of fifteen cardinals had been set up the year before, to study the "organizational and economic questions of the Holy See". The fifteen – there were, curiously, no Italians among them – would have a chance to discuss the affair with their colleagues from around the world when the Sacred College of Cardinals met for its three-year plenary meeting on 23 November.

There were four topics on the agenda for the three-day meeting. The first two concerned the Curia and canon law. The last two were financial: the balance sheet of the Holy See and the relationship between the IOR and the Ambrosiano.

The financial position of the Vatican had been worsening. It was now revealed that income for 1981 had exceeded outgoings by only 4.8 billion lire. This was after the inclusion of St Peter's Pence – the annual collection made for the Pope in every Catholic Church throughout the world – and other donations. Without these, there would have been a deficit of nearly 24 billion lire (more than $13 million) and it would be larger in 1982.

The result was not quite as bad as had been feared. Nevertheless, the Pope announced that 1983 would be another Holy Year, in which Catholic pilgrims are encouraged to come to Rome. This yields the Vatican – and Italy – valuable tourist income. The last Holy Year, not a great financial success, had been in 1975. Normally, the next should not have been held for another twenty-five years.

None of the figures given to the cardinals mentioned the cost of the Ambrosiano affair. Marcinkus had told *Il Sabato* that the IOR had "suffered losses", but did not specify them.

What the fifteen cardinals had to say about the affair, if anything, has never been made public. The Pope told the final session of the meeting that it was "a delicate and complex matter which has to be considered in all its details". Clearly the Pope and Casaroli had decided that they must close ranks behind Marcinkus.

That day the Vatican put out a special communiqué on the Ambrosiano affair. After saying that the situation called for "painstaking" inquiry to establish "objectively" what had happened, it reiterated the conclusions of the IOR's lawyers. These blatant lies were now being endorsed by the Vatican.

What, then, had happened to Casaroli's "three wise men"? The communiqué revealed that they had delivered the result of their inquiry at the beginning of September. It "did not yet have a completely conclusive character". However, the communiqué went on, it had recommended a joint investigation by the Vatican and the Italian government, to be conducted "on the basis of the documents in the possession of the two parties, in order subsequently to draw from them consequences that seem legitimate".

That was the last major contribution of the three wise men, though they were asked to stay on as consultants to the IOR, along with a fourth man, Hermann Abs, a Catholic and the former chairman of Deutsche Bank, who was 81.

It would have been hard for the Vatican to resist the suggestion of a joint commission, put forward by its own wise men. So the communiqué confirmed the Holy See's "full readiness to cooperate with the Italian authorities for the purpose stated". The Pope himself told the assembled cardinals that the Vatican was "willing to complete all the steps that are necessary for an agreement by both parties so that the entire truth may be brought to light". He added: "In this issue too, the Holy See's only desire is to serve the cause of love."

The Pope also told the cardinals that the communiqué had given them "an adequate explanation". In fact it had given a fantastic rigmarole. The IOR had, it explained, "for many years maintained a connection with the Banco Ambrosiano Group, traditionally considered in Italy as a Catholic bank and one of proven seriousness".

So far, so truthful, though the Anglo-Saxon reader may wonder how a bank can be Catholic. A bank is not a church. But the expression means a great deal in Italy, as we shall see in the next chapter.

The communiqué went on to say that the relationship had been "marked by a total trust in the ends pursued by the Group in its, until recently, unquestioned solidity, and trust in the persons who, in the course of time, have directed it".

But, after the crash: "It became clear that the name of the Institute had been used for the carrying out of a hidden project, which, without the knowledge of the Institute itself, linked together for one purpose operations which, if considered separately, had the appearance of being regular and normal."

Here it must be repeated that the letters of patronage, and the simultaneous disclaimer from Calvi, had not the appearance of being either regular or normal.

The communiqué then became technical, not to say obfuscatory. "The Institute, following upon banking operations that were themselves normal, found that it had the ownership and therefore the juridical control of two companies, and, without its knowledge, indirect control of another eight companies linked to the first two. Since the Institute has never administered any of these companies, it has not even had knowledge of the operations that were carried out by each of them." Only in July 1981 did the IOR discover that "through a direct or indirect link, it had attributed to it juridical control of *all* the said companies".

No other group of educated men would have accepted this. The cardinals seem to have failed even to ask the obvious questions. What companies, exactly? And when did the IOR discover that it owned the first two, if it was in July 1981 that it found it owned them all?

On other matters cardinals may be astute. But many of them are affected by the medieval view that banking is usury and by its nature a sin. Therefore, when banks are mentioned, they stop thinking.

Only men determined not to think could have swallowed what the communiqué said about the letters of patronage. Having discovered that it owned the companies, the IOR "thought it opportune that, at least, the indebtedness of the companies should remain for the time being blocked, until such time as the attribution of juridical control of them should cease". So it signed the letters dated 1 September 1981 "whereby direct or indirect control de facto juridically existing was confirmed".

The claim that, nevertheless, the IOR had no liability was repeated. The letters "did not go beyond a declaration of the existence of a direct or indirect control of the companies listed and a mention of the enclosed balance sheets". So the IOR "did not assume direct obligations or obligations of a fiduciary guarantee". The letters, therefore, "both by the juridical value proper to them, and by their concrete content, did not create, nor could create, in conformity with the common doctrine and usual banking practice, legal obligations for the Institute".

The cardinals allowed the Vatican to endorse the IOR's claim that it had no financial responsibility for the Ambrosiano crash. By doing this before the joint inquiry with the Italian government had even been set up, the

Vatican was ensuring that it would fail. Those it appointed would either have to toe the line or tell the world that the Pope had been talking nonsense – an act requiring considerable courage.

The Vatican and the Italian Government established the joint commission by international treaty on Christmas Eve. It was given a deadline of March 1983. But the Vatican appointees toed the line, and this led to disagreements. The report, finally produced in November 1983, was divided and did not establish the truth.

But it did give so much new information that the Vatican refused to allow its release even to interested parties. The Italian Government had promised not to release it unilaterally. However, its findings leaked out, and will be described in Chapter 4.

These findings added to the pressures that forced the Vatican into its about-turn. Every fact that emerged led up to that day in 1984, when over $240 million was transferred from the IOR's main bankers in New York, Manufacturers Hanover Trust, to an account at the Union Bank of Switzerland, for distribution among the delighted creditors.

Where did the money come from? According to a Vatican announcement, when the committee of fifteen cardinals met in March 1985 they were told that the cost "was covered entirely by the Institute itself without contributions from the Holy See and without drawing on the funds entrusted to the administration of the Institute".

We have already seen what standards of truthfulness the Church thinks good enough for its own cardinals. We also have the remarks of Marcinkus about this $240 million, made to the author John Cornwell, when he was writing *A Thief in the Night*. (It was for this book that Marcinkus uttered the words we have already quoted: "If we're not guilty, we don't pay.") After expressing his annoyance that the payment was made at all, Marcinkus said: "It didn't kind of clear us out completely; we had to kind of lower our capital level. But it kills me, because of the problems of tomorrow. I'm not thinking of the covering up of the deficit; that's secondary. It's tomorrow, your pensions and stuff . . ."

The suggestion that "the covering up of the deficit" is a mere secondary part of a banker's life is breathtaking, though it was indeed part of Calvi's life. Cornwell, who did not know the extent of the IOR's losses, did not press the point. But the words of Marcinkus could be taken to mean that the IOR was, in effect, bankrupt, and kept in being only by the loyalty of its depositors. It is possible for a bank to stagger on for years like this – as, indeed, the Ambrosiano did.

The losses that Marcinkus had to cover, besides the $240 million repayment and the $99 million cost of the lira repayments, included the IOR deposits with the Cisalpine. They stood at $69.3 million and the IOR claimed this, plus $5.2 million of unpaid interest – a claim abandoned in the Geneva agreement. It may, however, have got some compensation from a small Swiss bank, the Banca del Gottardo, which secretly owed $8.5 million of this. If they split the loss between them, the IOR's loss on the Cisalpine deposits would have been just over $70 million.

In addition, Marcinkus had advanced a further $65 million to BA Holding and Andino, plus unpaid interest of $6.4 million – another claim he had to abandon. On the shares the IOR owned in the Ambrosiano it lost, by my reckoning, $24 million. It also owned shares in BA Holding, on which it lost $6.6 million; on its shares in the Cisalpine $2.2 million.

So the loss totals $510 million. Legal costs after the crash have added several further millions. We will be looking later at what assets the IOR could sell to offset this. Marcinkus was later to claim that the IOR covered all its losses. We shall see whether this could possibly be true.

Nothing could offset the damage done to the Vatican's reputation. How did this disaster happen?

TWO

Who Owed What to Whom

Roberto Calvi had few social graces. There was about him not a hint of the charm and assurance which enabled his friend Sindona to get away with so much for so long.

What Calvi had, nevertheless, was a matchless ability to deceive. He did it by stonewalling. Sitting across from him at the lunch table, a man would ask him some pertinent question about the bank. Calvi would not reply. The man would ask him again. It would be as if Calvi had not heard. And, somehow, it would be the questioner who became embarrassed.

For ten years, Calvi was able to find money to finance the ever-expanding demands of his "hidden project". He persuaded some of the world's most important banks to lend money to the Ambrosiano. Again and again he survived crises which made exposure seem certain.

The strain got to him. We now know that, in the last year of his life, Calvi was turning this way and that, finding expedients which only hastened his ruin. Yet in public, almost to the end, he presented the Ambrosiano as the epitome of a sound, solid Catholic bank.

What is a Catholic bank? During the burst of prosperity which followed the unification of Italy in 1870, banks were founded from the Alps to Agrigento. Many of them are still in existence. But there were some scandalous crashes. Some Catholics took this as proof that banking was a dirty business, fit for Freemasons, atheists, Protestants and Jews.

But other Catholics insisted that a sound bank would be a great thing for the Church. With the backing of some wealthy Milanese Catholics, the Ambrosiano was founded in 1896 by Monsignor Giuseppe Tovini. He took the name from St Ambrose, patron saint of Milan. The intention of its founders was that it should not be taken over by Freemasons or atheists. Nobody could buy more than five per cent of its shares, and initially an intending purchaser had to have a certificate of Catholic baptism. This requirement was later abandoned, but the board of directors kept the right to veto any shareholder (a right seldom used in later years). A register of shareholders was kept.

17

Several other Catholic banks were founded on the same lines at about the same time. Some failed; some prospered. The Credito Romagnolo was perhaps the most successful. But not one found the rules watertight.

The shares were not bought or sold on the main stock exchange, but on the *mercato ristretto*, or unlisted securities market. This was suspended for three years in the mid-seventies, and the transfer of shares was in effect in the hands of the bank, that is, in the hands of Calvi. The five per cent rule did not prevent him from accumulating, and hiding abroad, 10.65 per cent of the shares.

The existence of 38,000 small shareholders did not make the bank demo-cratic. A strong and wealthy shareholder, with a big stake in the bank, was capable of challenging Calvi – as we shall see – but the small shareholders never did. Some of them, from time to time, threatened to make trouble at the annual general meeting, but Calvi seems to have bribed them to stay away.

The ultimate irony was that this Catholic head of a Catholic bank secretly joined a Masonic lodge – a mortal sin. (Not until after Calvi's death did the Church decree that this was a sin no longer.) The P2 list, with Calvi's name on it, came to light in May 1981. Stonewalling, he denied that he did belong to P2. Called before the parliamentary commission on P2, he admit-ted his membership – and then, in the last press interview of his life, denied it again.

The great expansion of Ambrosiano, from its heartland in Milan to the rest of Italy, had already begun when Calvi joined the staff in 1947. During the ten years – 1972 to 1982 – while he was at the helm, first as managing director and then also as chairman, the bank's capital rose from 5 billion lire to 50 billion lire. It employed 4,115 people and had 107 branches throughout Italy, bringing in clients' deposits of nearly 3,700 billion lire (about $2.6 billion). Only the state-owned banks were bigger.

There were, by modern standards, too many employees. But automation had not yet reached Italy. By the standards of Milan, the Ambrosiano was doing well.

So were its Italian subsidiaries. Through its holding company, La Cen-trale, acquired in 1972, the Ambrosiano controlled the Banca Cattolica del Veneto and the Credito Varesino, which between them employed another 4,716 people in 252 branches, with deposits of 5,160 billion lire (about $3.7 billion). Also through La Centrale, it owned a prosperous insurance company, Toro Assicurazione.

From the point of view of Calvi's own interests, all his frauds, all the lies and deceits which to this day are being unravelled, were unnecessary. If he had, at the start, decided to run an open, honest bank, concentrating on business in Italy, he might have reached an honoured retirement, to receive a pension perfectly adequate to his tastes (which were not luxurious). A good part of his Italian business was perfectly sound, even at the end. The disasters were hidden abroad. What the Bank of Italy commissioners found is shown in the chart (see pages 20 and 21). This shows that the Ambrosiano owed more than $1.2 billion in short-term foreign currency loans to overseas banks and that it had re-lent nearly $700 million – twenty times its capital – to its overseas subsidiaries: BA Holding in Luxembourg, Cisalpine in Nassau, Andino in Peru, and Banco Comercial in Nicaragua.

Much of the parent bank's lending was done in the last few months of Calvi's life, as the more sophisticated foreign bankers, realising that something was wrong, stopped lending to him. There were, even then, still foreign banks willing to act as intermediaries. Of the $694 million lent by the parent bank to its children, $228.5 million had been channelled through these intermediaries, half of it through the Banco de la Nación. It worked like this. The parent bank made deposits with foreign banks, in the course of its perfectly legal interbank business. The foreign banks then lent the money on to BA Holding and Andino at slightly higher interest rates, the difference being their "turn" or reward. Such operations are known to bankers as "back-to-backs". Some bankers claim they have legitimate uses, but it is hard to see what they are. Calvi's purpose was to disguise the extent of his lending to his overseas subsidiaries.

At the moment of the crash, the parent bank owed an extra $70 million to foreign banks. This does not figure in the chart, because it was repaid at once by the Bank of Italy commissioners. Then the foreign banks which had acted as intermediaries began to ask for their money back, and the "back-to-back" arrangements came to light. The commissioners then stopped repayments.

The chart on pages 20 and 21 shows that $60 million had been lent by Banca Cattolica and Credito Varesino to the Banco Andino in Peru, via the Banco de la Nación, the central bank of Peru. The Banca Cattolica and the Varesino could lose that without going bankrupt. It was the parent bank which was in trouble.

The short-term borrowings of the Ambrosiano represented only a part of the group's total debts abroad. As we shall see, the main means by which Calvi financed the fraud at its height, between 1978 and 1981, was borrowing through BA Holding. By using this Luxembourg company he could borrow for up to five years. Under Italian law he could not do this through the parent bank, since the money was not for use in Italy. Indeed,

Table 1: The debts of the Ambrosiano group and the secret network at end June 1982

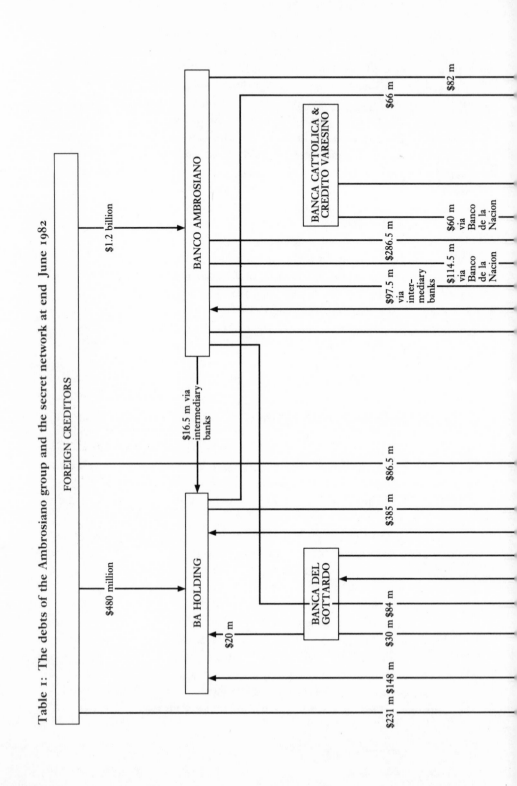

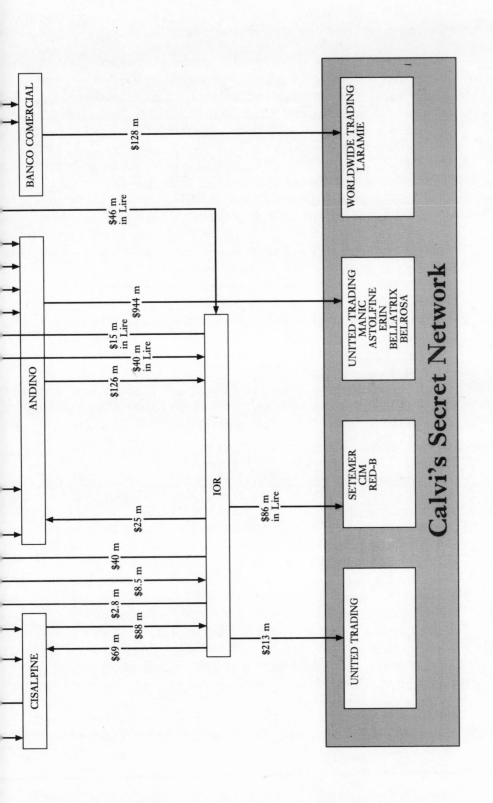

Calvi's Secret Network

the parent bank was not even allowed to guarantee the loans raised in Luxembourg. Yet many banks with famous names were willing, either singly or in groups, to pour some $460 million into BA Holding; and when BA Holding could borrow no more because it had reached the limit permitted by the Luxembourg authorities, these obliging creditors lent another $86.5 million directly to Andino.

Only Banco Comercial in Nicaragua had no direct debts to foreign banks. Its role in the fraud was financed by loans within the group.

The dual role of the Vatican as creditor and debtor is shown by the chart on pages 20 and 21. In 1980 the IOR had made $100 million of fixed-term loans to the Ambrosiano's overseas subsidiaries and it had a further $39.3 million in deposits at the Cisalpine. It emerged that, for about $8.5 million of this, it was acting as a "back-to-back" intermediary for the Banca del Gottardo, which, with its help, was evading Swiss regulations. So, against the $213 million the IOR appeared to owe *to* the group, it was owed, more than $134 million *by* it. (The IOR also had at least $2.8 million on deposit at the Gottardo, but the Italian commissioners did not know about that.)

Banco Comercial in Nicaragua and Banco Andino in Peru were bankrupt. The chart shows that Banco Comercial had lent $128 million to two of the companies covered by the letters of patronage, and that Andino had lent $944 million to letters-of-patronage companies and $126 million directly to the IOR.

The Cisalpine – the one where Marcinkus was a director – was not in such poor shape. This was the only one of the foreign subsidiaries which had a substantial level of personal deposits. It had solicited customers in South America, as well as opening illegal accounts for Italian citizens who had smuggled their money abroad. The chart shows Cisalpine as owing $69 million to the IOR, as against $88 million owing from the IOR, and also as owing about $231 million to other banks and depositors. The Cisalpine had made no direct loans to letters-of-patronage companies. Many of the loans it had made were to genuine commercial companies, and seemed recoverable. Two loans had gone bad – $15 million advanced in early 1980 and $14 million paid out in February 1982. It might have written these off, and survived. But what sealed the fate of the Cisalpine was that it had lent $148 million to its parent, BA Holding; and BA Holding could not repay because of the bankruptcy of its other subsidiaries.

So it all came back to the $1,072 million of loans to the letters-of-patronage companies and the $213 million that had disappeared into the IOR – which, it was to emerge, had also gone into Calvi's secret network. The shares pledged as security for these loans would not cover a tenth of the debt. Prime among them were 5.3 million shares in the Ambrosiano itself – 10.65 per cent of its entire capital.

After the crash these shares were virtually worthless. At their peak they were worth $250 million. But the *mercato ristretto* was a somewhat distorted market, and Calvi had distorted it further by illegally using the bank's money to buy its shares. Ambrosiano shares were not quoted on the main stock exchange of Milan until 5 May 1982. They immediately plunged, though Calvi tried to keep up the price by continuing his illegal purchase of shares. At their best, they never quite touched $30 each. That would have made the hidden 5 million shares worth less than $150 million. And yet, a month before the crash, Calvi was telling Rosone and other colleagues that he had found an Arab-American consortium willing to pay $200 each for the shares – in round figures, $1 billion for the 10 per cent he had. Was he so far out of touch with reality as to believe what he was saying? There is conflicting evidence even in his private papers.

If the bank had been as outwardly respectable in May 1982 as it had been a year before, $250 million might have been a possible price. But there never was a time when Calvi or Marcinkus could honestly have regarded 10 per cent of Ambrosiano as adequate security for a billion dollars, or even half a billion.

Also pledged as security was a block of shares in La Centrale, amounting to just over 5 per cent of its capital. These were eventually to fetch about $7 million.

The most valuable of the shares was an investment of 7.67 per cent in the Banca del Gottardo in Switzerland, worth about $17 million. The Gottardo was not a full Ambrosiano subsidiary, since BA Holding had only 45 per cent of it. But, because of this secret block, it had in fact been under Calvi's control.

Also held as security were 189,000 shares in Rizzoli, of dubious value. This company, as the full extent of its dependence on the Ambrosiano came to light, was put into the hands of special commissioners. Then there was a controlling interest in a television paper, *TV Sorrisi e Canzoni*. This was a going concern, but it was now part of the Rizzoli empire. There were shares in Montreal Holding, which owned a building in Buenos Aires (a real one, but immensely overvalued).

And there were 2,000 shares in a Rome-based construction company, Vianini, known to be an investment of the Vatican. The IOR's pleas of innocence looked weaker than ever when it emerged that these shares were not, after all, available as security for the loan. The IOR had been paid $20 million for them, but nevertheless kept them locked up in its own safe.

Since the assets would hardly begin to cover the debt, the Ambrosiano could not expect to get much of its $700 million back. The Bank of Italy commissioners realised that they could not keep the bank going in its existing form. Confidence had evaporated. There was no panic in the streets, because Italian law guarantees bank depositors against loss. Only the 38,000 shareholders found themselves, to quote a headline of the time, "seduced and abandoned". But most of the shareholders *were* depositors. They did not want to leave what money they still possessed in a bank which had just deprived them of their life savings. The Ambrosiano's deposits were halved in a few weeks.

A rescue plan was devised. Seven banks were called together: three state-owned, three private and one co-operative. With a government guarantee against loss, they formed the Nuovo Banco Ambrosiano.

On 6 August three liquidators were appointed to the old Ambrosiano. Two days later, all its business, branches and staff – except for some senior men under investigation for their part in the fraud – were transferred to the new bank. Also transferred were most of the old bank's assets and nearly all its liabilities.

Among the assets not transferred were the Italian debts, totalling more than 61 billion lire, that the IOR was about to start repaying. (It made the first repayment five days later.) Not transferred, either, was the $700 million owed by the overseas subsidiaries, and the old bank's 69 per cent share in BA Holding. (Most of the rest of BA Holding was held by the IOR, either as Calvi's nominee or on its own account, but this was not known then.)

The Nuovo Banco Ambrosiano eventually did well. Even the "seduced" shareholders got something; in May 1985 "Operation Warrant" allowed them to buy shares in the new bank at a concessionary price, and 98 per cent of them (including the IOR) accepted. The IOR thus recouped about $1 million of its loss.

Automated, well capitalised and profitable, the bank is now back in the private sector. Having merged with the Banca Cattolica, it is known as the Ambroveneto.

But it had a difficult first quarter. The foreign banks which had lent directly to the parent bank in Milan were free to withdraw their money, and they did withdraw more than $1 billion in the first three months of the new bank's life, putting it under such a strain that the Treasury had to advance it more than 500 billion lire ($350 million). The Italians claimed that in this way they were "safeguarding the reputation of the Italian banking system".

What did not safeguard anyone's reputation was the treatment of those who had lent to the foreign part of Calvi's empire. It was now clear that they were to get no help from the Italian Government.

The creditors were furious. They would have been even more so, if they had understood how the government had sidestepped a confrontation with the IOR. The foreign creditors did not know that the IOR was repaying the lira debts recorded in the Ambrosiano books. Or that, in return, the Italian authorities had refrained from freezing some 21 billion lire ($15 million) of credit balances that the IOR held at the Ambrosiano. Like other depositors, the IOR could now transfer this money to the new bank.

The Italian liquidators now had no direct cause for action against the IOR. They retained an interest in the eventual settlement, because of their claim against BA Holding.

In Luxembourg, BA Holding did not at once go into liquidation. It had been placed under the control of court-appointed commissioners, who nominated their own directors to the board. The commissioners retained Touche Ross, the London-based firm of international accountants, to investigate the tangle of loans we have seen on the chart. This might have seemed odd, because Touche Ross had an associated company in Luxembourg, Fiduciaire Générale, which had been the auditor of BA Holding, and might therefore be regarded as in some degree responsible. However, two partners of Touche Ross, Brian Smouha and Gerald Paisley, were appointed liquidators, along with a Luxembourg lawyer, Paul Mousel. Three years later Brian Smouha was to get a standing ovation from a creditors' meeting, when he announced that $417 million had been recovered by July 1985, and that there was more to come. The following year, 1986, he was able to put the proportion recovered at 68 per cent. As I write, the liquidators have not yet finished their task. It has been a hard-fought battle from the beginning.

The creditor banks formed a steering committee under the joint chairmanship of Michael Connolly of the International Westminster Bank and Claude Eric Paquin of Midland's French subsidiary. The two British banks had been the most prominent in leading syndicated loans for the Ambrosiano. (A syndicated loan is one raised by a number of banks acting together. The lead manager is the bank which does the organizing.)

At first 88 creditor banks were known, but the number turned out to be 109. Besides European banks, American, Japanese and Arab banks had joined the queue to lend to Calvi. There were even Italian-owned banks. Indeed, two Italian groups turned out to be the largest creditors. Not everyone thought them entitled to take part in the eventual share-out; their reasons for lending to Calvi were mysterious.

The biggest creditor was ENI – Ente Nazionale Idrocarburi – Italy's state-owned oil corporation. Through Tradinvest, a bank it owned in Nassau, it was owed over $90 million by BA Holding and Andino. ENI also had a financial subsidiary at Curaçao in the Netherlands Antilles, and another in the Cayman Islands. These two were owed another $45 million. Tradinvest had also lent $25 million to the Cisalpine. In all, ENI was owed, with interest, some $170 million.

The ENI loans to Calvi will be examined later. What the creditors knew at the time was that there had already been a scandal, and that this had led to the resignation of ENI's vice-president, Leonardo Di Donna, and its financial director, Florio Fiorini. Di Donna was a member of P2, and documents about him were found in Gelli's files. The ENI executives were later cleared by magistrates in Rome.

The next largest creditor was the state-owned Banca Nazionale del Lavoro, biggest of Italian banks. Through two subsidiaries, it had lent more than $70 million to BA Holding. Lavoro's managing director at the time, Alberto Ferrari, was also in P2. Lavoro, under new management, was one of the seven banks recruited to found Nuovo Ambrosiano. The creditors felt this gave it a foot in both camps.

Some creditors argued that both ENI and Lavoro should be excluded from the settlement. But this might have meant that there was no settlement.

The third largest creditor was the Banca del Gottardo, which was owed some $20 million by BA Holding and another $30 million by the Cisalpine. The Gottardo was not in liquidation; it was still being run by its chairman Fernando Garzoni and its general manager Francesco Bolgiani, both of whom had been there throughout the eleven years of transactions between the IOR and Ambrosiano, handling many deals about which the creditors would have liked to know more.

As the Gottardo's role emerged, it was suggested that it should be sued for damages. But this idea was soon abandoned. The Gottardo had developed a good business unconnected with Calvi. If it could survive the crash, it would be BA Holding's most valuable asset. And so it proved. In 1984 all the shares – the known 45 per cent plus the secret block – were sold for $144 million to a Japanese bank, Sumitomo.

To what extent was the creditors' plight their own fault? Shouldn't they all have been suspicious? Throughout the 1970s, any client of Mediobanca (Italy's only merchant bank) was privately warned to stay away from Calvi, because of his association with the financier Michele Sindona.

After the event, the creditors reproached the Bank of Italy, for not having given them a hint about the adverse report of its inspectors on Calvi's foreign dealings, made in 1978. Yet, if they had been in touch with Milan financial circles, they would have heard about it. Just before Christmas 1978 the weekly paper *L'Espresso* published a well-informed article, pointing out that the Vatican was involved. In October 1979 Calvi was summoned for questioning by an examining magistrate, and once again *L'Espresso* carried the news. All the foreign banks' lending to Calvi took place after these events.

On 20 July 1981 Calvi, having been found guilty of currency offences, was sentenced to four years' imprisonment and fines of 16.5 billion lire, or nearly $14 million. He had been in prison throughout the trial; now he was released, pending appeal.

Now, at last, some foreign banks got the message. Midland had agreed to another syndicated loan in April 1981: $25 million to Andino. But it postponed this after Calvi's arrest, and then cancelled it. BA Holding and its subsidiaries found it difficult to raise funds. The parent bank did not have the same trouble; it could get short-term loans abroad. So, in the following months, Calvi borrowed in order to lend more and more to his overseas subsidiaries.

Those foreign banks which went on helping Calvi with back-to-back arrangements, even after he had been found guilty of breaking his country's laws, could argue that he was still, after all, the chairman of Italy's largest private bank. How could he have been allowed to keep that job?

The Bank of Italy did suggest to him that, pending his appeal, he should step down. But it had no power to make him do so. And he was under no pressure from his shareholders. Even if they thought him guilty, they did not think his guilt disgraceful.

The currency laws had an effect on Italian life like that of prohibition on America. They made law-breaking respectable. Until May 1979, many British citizens went on holiday with £5 notes in their socks; for nearly ten years longer, many Milanesi were taking the train to Lugano with lire lining their underwear. Italy is not a land without good guys. But the good guys devoted far too much energy to the enforcement of currency laws, and thereby made life easier for the bad guys. One reason why Calvi got away with it for so long is that many people thought he was merely smuggling currency, like everybody else.

To do the Italian authorities justice, they had intended to charge Calvi not only with currency offences but also with fraud. However, the Swiss authorities did not provide the information which, by their international agreements, they should have given the Italians. This was largely because of the obstacles put in their way by the Swiss banks. Only the crash, and the investigations of the creditors, have made the Swiss carry out their obligations. To this day, there are secrets not divulged, as we shall see.

THREE

The Spirit of Lucca

The Italian Government was on shaky legal ground, when it refused to pay the creditors of Calvi's foreign empire. The creditors pointed to an international agreement on the supervision of banks, reached after the Sindona crash. The heads of the central banks of ten industrialised countries meet regularly in Basle, Switzerland. In 1975 they agreed that the authorities in a bank's home country should be responsible for the supervision of that bank's subsidiaries in other countries.

But the concept of a group was somewhat looser in Italy than in Britain or America. The Ambrosiano had never been obliged to produce consolidated accounts covering all the banks in the group, though it would have had to do so if it had survived its quotation on the Milan stock market.

The Italians tried to suggest that BA Holding had a life of its own, separate from that of the Ambrosiano in Milan. But in reality the parent bank had taken all the decisions for BA Holding. The creditors knew this, because they had negotiated the loans for BA Holding with the Milan management.

From Germany, the Hessische Landesbank wrote to Carlo Ciampi, Governor of the Bank of Italy, suggesting that, if the debts of BA Holding were not met, there would be serious consequences for Italy's financial relations with other countries. Ciampi replied that the Ambrosiano had no legal obligation for the debts of BA Holding, which it had not guaranteed, and that the moral obligation ceased when it became bankrupt. He saw no reason to think this would reflect adversely on Italy's relations with other countries.

But Italian borrowers were already being asked to pay higher interest rates. The Luxembourg Banking Commission insisted that other Italian banks must guarantee their local subsidiaries. And the creditor banks resolved to boycott all syndicated loans for Italian borrowers.

The creditors were also discussing legal action. But against whom? The Nuovo Banco Ambrosiano? The three liquidators of the old bank? Perhaps even the Bank of Italy itself? Or the IOR?

In the eyes of the creditors, the Italian Government and the IOR were equally guilty. But this did not bring these two powers any closer together. The Treasury Minister, Beniamino Andreatta, reiterated in October 1982 his earlier demands that the IOR should repay all the $1,287 million which was now known to be the size of the deficit. He did not mention the repayment of the lira debts, which is odd, since Andreatta's reputation was for frankness, even tactlessness. When he called on the Pope personally to intervene in the affairs of the IOR, some Christian Democrats were outraged at this "insult" to the Holy Father. Though the new Prime Minister, Spadolini, was a Republican, not a Christian Democrat, he relied on the support of that party. Andreatta himself was a Christian Democrat, but he belonged to "the lay wing". Pressure from "the clerical wing" forced Andreatta, an excellent Treasury Minister, to resign in November 1982.

Once the government had agreed to the setting up of the joint commission with the Vatican, it could plead that it must await the outcome before making any further pronouncements. But Spadolini took a further step; he suspended the talks that had been going on with the Vatican to reformulate the 1929 Concordat which the Church had made with Mussolini. This was not a dramatic measure, as the talks had been dragging on for some fifteen years. But it showed the isolation of the Vatican.

Marcinkus was now within the Vatican walls, where he had had an apartment of his own since the autumn of 1981. That was when he was made an archbishop, and pro-president (or deputy governor) of the Vatican City State.

Marcinkus was considered a virtual prisoner within the Vatican, since the Milan magistrates were expected to issue an arrest warrant against him. In fact they had issued only a *comunicazione giudiziaria*, indicating that they wanted to question him. But through his lawyer, Gatti, he disputed their right to do this. In fact he continued to circulate freely in Rome, and was often to be seen entertaining his friends in good restaurants. He had no difficulty in returning to his home town, Chicago, for Christmas 1982. He was still an object of reverence there – the son of a Lithuanian window-cleaner, who had become a prince of the Church.

On 18 January 1983 the steering committee of the creditor banks formally discussed the possibility of suing the IOR. It looked as if the spectacular fraud would end in a spectacular lawsuit.

Then, on 17 February 1983, came the first peace feeler. The committee received a message from a lawyer, Pasquale Chiomenti. Clearly, this was important. Chiomenti had been appointed by the Italian Government to be chairman of its three representatives on the joint commission of inquiry with the Vatican.

It so happened, Chiomenti indicated, that he would be in Paris the following Sunday. He would like to take the opportunity to put a proposal to the representatives of the banks. Could they meet at the Hotel Lotti in the Place Vendôme?

Chiomenti, a tactful man with a quiet voice (who died in 1990) was known to have advised many great companies, and the Bank of Italy. But his reputation was as a mediator.

There was an air of mystery about him, at that first meeting. For whom was he speaking? He said he had come in a personal capacity. He could arrange for the banks' loans to BA Holding to be bought out at 30 per cent of their face value – about $180 million. In exchange, the banks would have to sign over all their claims against BA Holding. They would also have to agree not to sue the Nuovo Ambrosiano or the liquidators. He did not mention the IOR.

The creditors thought he was representing a group of Italian banks, probably acting with a government guarantee. The proposal was, therefore, not well received. The creditors were still insisting that they should be paid in full. Giving up their claims against BA Holding would mean that its realisable assets would go to repay the Italians.

So the creditor banks rejected the proposal. They filed a writ against the Nuovo Ambrosiano on 28 March 1983. The writ claimed that the new bank had assumed the obligations of the old.

The liquidators of the old bank then filed writs against those foreign banks which, by taking part in the "back-to-back" operations, had helped Calvi to conceal the true size of his debts. But not one of these banks was also a creditor. Hence the writ was not much of a counter-attack. More to the point was the writ the liquidators issued later against Andino in Peru, demanding the return of nearly $300 million.

The opening shots in the court war having been fired, the creditors got in touch with Chiomenti again. They would not yet abandon their demand for 100 per cent reimbursement. But it need not be paid in cash all at once. Existing loans could be "rescheduled" to later payment dates. There might even be new loans on favourable terms.

The National Westminster's London solicitors, Wilde Sapte, now took the leading role in the negotiations. Wilde Sapte sent its senior partner, Ted Sturmer, to meet Chiomenti in Milan on 5 May.

Chiomenti made it clear that there could not be 100 per cent repayment, however it was dressed up. But the 30 per cent cash offer was still open, and this might be increased by a contribution from the IOR. It was the first time the possibility had been mentioned.

Chiomenti knew that the banks had begun to examine ways of suing the IOR. One idea was to sue for the return of the $125 million which the IOR appeared to owe to the Andino. But in March 1983 Touche Ross discovered details of the Vianini deal. This looked even more promising.

In December 1980 the Banco Comercial in Nicaragua had lent $20 million to one of the letters-of-patronage companies, Laramie, which then paid the money to the IOR for two million shares in the construction company Vianini. Laramie had also contracted to buy two further blocks, each of two million shares, in Vianini. But it had not done so. The IOR had kept the first block of shares *and* the $20 million. There was thus a clear claim for the return of the $20 million. The IOR was refusing to return it, on the grounds that it had been damaged by Laramie's failure to buy the other two blocks. If the case came to court it would publicly disprove the brazen statement of the Vatican lawyers. It showed that the IOR had received money from the Ambrosiano group, and that it did know of the existence of Laramie before the summer of 1981.

This discovery strengthened the creditors' determination that the IOR should not escape responsibility. They were waiting to start legal action until the joint commission had reported. But the commission's original deadline, the end of March 1983, had been twice postponed. Chiomenti, as the Italian joint chairman, was interested to learn what Touche Ross was uncovering, but he was discreet about the commission's own inquiries. The creditors could now see that he was representing the old bank's liquidators. But clearly he was in touch with other interested parties. He seemed to know that the IOR might pay something. The question was: how much?

In June 1983 Chiomenti reported that the liquidators might be able to increase their offer, because they believed the IOR might pay them up to $75 million. The banks were not told that the IOR had already paid back lira debts to the Ambrosiano, the Cattolica and the Varesino, at a cost equivalent to $99 million.

The legal case against the IOR was getting stronger. The creditors had discovered letters from the IOR to a Calvi company based in Luxembourg, Ambrosiano Services. The IOR was asking Ambrosiano Services to manage on its behalf the ten companies named in the letters of patronage, plus Zitropo. The IOR wrote that Ambrosiano Services should accept instructions on its behalf from its "attorney in fact", who was named as Calvi. Under Luxembourg law, a person who gives a mandate of this kind to another nevertheless retains a duty to supervise the other person. The

IOR had given a mandate to Calvi, knowing that he had mismanaged the companies previously – mismanagement it had ratified with the letters of patronage – and it had then failed to supervise him. To plead that it had been duped by Calvi would not be an adequate defence.

It would be possible, too, to produce such witnesses as the executives of the Andino, who would say they had been deceived by the letters of patronage into believing that the companies were solvent, whereas they were bankrupt, as the IOR knew. It was beginning to look like a strong case, in which the IOR could be sued for the full amount of the debts. A judgment in the Luxembourg courts could be enforced anywhere in the European Community, by the seizure of the IOR's assets.

But the case against the Italians was not so clear. A negotiated settlement would be better, and the creditors could now see that they were not going to get it if they insisted on 100 per cent repayment.

By July 1983 the Italians were offering *either* 30 per cent (about $175 million) plus a half share of whatever could be extracted from the IOR, *or* 40 per cent in full and final settlement. The Italians were still expecting to take over the assets of BA Holding, now reckoned at about $200 million. The creditors made a counter-proposal, that the $200 million of controversial claims by ENI and the Banca Nazionale del Lavoro should be dropped.

Negotiations became tense. The Italians accused the banks of "blackmail", and said they had only themselves to blame; they should have taken more care. The banks retorted that they had been deliberately misled. By early August it looked as if the talks had broken down.

Then Chiomenti and Sturmer decided on a last meeting in a country house near Lucca, where Chiomenti was spending the summer. On the first day, 10 August, both sides repeated the old arguments. But, that evening, Sturmer and his assistant drafted a document embodying what came to be called: "The spirit of Lucca". It opened with a declaration; the parties accepted "that they were all victims to a greater or lesser extent of a deliberate conspiracy and fraud". Therefore they now agreed "to co-operate fully on a basis of non-culpability" to achieve certain ends. The first of these was that the assets of BA Holding should be realised for the greatest possible amount. The second was "to maximise the contribution from the IOR". The third was that the proceeds of the first two should be applied, first, to repaying the banks 70 per cent of what they were owed, and then that any subsequent shortfall would be borne equally between the banks and the Italians. (The 70 per cent was afterwards reduced to 66.67 per cent.)

33

The essence of Sturmer's proposal was that the creditor banks and the Italians should stop warring with each other, and concentrate on making the IOR yield as much as possible. The inducement to the IOR was that it would not be sued, or even publicly blamed. It was, though, implicit that the creditor banks and the Italians would share information that could be used to embarrass the IOR.

Chiomenti broke off his holiday to consult the Italian liquidators and "others indirectly involved". This obviously meant the Bank of Italy and the government. By the end of August it emerged that they had reacted favourably.

There had been two changes of government since the crash. Spadolini's government fell in late 1982, and was replaced by a coalition of familiar appearance, led by Christian Democrats. But in the election of summer 1983 the Christian Democrat vote fell to its lowest level since the war. In July a new coalition government was formed under the Socialist leader Bettino Craxi. It was anxious to complete the renegotiation of the Concordat. Its left-wing supporters wanted to diminish the role of the Church in Italian life. Its right-wing supporters wanted more state money to pay the stipends of priests. Both of these the new Concordat was expected to provide. Talks were quietly restarted.

The first encounter between the new government and the Vatican on the Ambrosiano affair took place in September 1983. Cardinal Casaroli told a government representative that the Pope wanted an amicable settlement, in which there must be no implication of blame. A payment would be made, but the amount must be "bearable". The IOR had itself lost money in the crash. It had assets: gold bullion worth perhaps $40 million, its majority holding in the Banco di Roma per la Svizzera and shares in the Cattolica and the Varesino. So the IOR might be able to raise $150 million.

The creditor banks had already calculated that the IOR contribution would have to be much higher than that. The Italian liquidators were still owed over $700 million by the overseas part of Calvi's empire. Besides, there was the cost to the Italian taxpayer of the help provided to the Nuovo Ambrosiano. A year earlier Andreatta had demanded that the IOR should repay $1,287 million. That was now seen as unrealistic. But the Italian share would have to be substantial, or the government would look foolish.

In October it began to look like deadlock. To show they meant business the banks, with the approval of the Italian liquidators, decided to prepare a writ against the IOR in Luxembourg. They also indicated that some among them were getting restless, and might start individual actions against the IOR.

At the end of October the Vatican let the banks and the liquidators know that it had appointed a team to discuss a final settlement with them. It would contribute $150 million, and this was "not negotiable". The team was to consist of Carlo Cerutti, the only Italian among the "three wise men", Adolfo Gatti, the lawyer handling the defence of Marcinkus, and one of the three Vatican appointees to the joint commission. (All these Vatican appointees, it was now known, had insisted that the IOR had done no wrong.)

A meeting was due on 15 December, but this had to be postponed, because a strike at Milan airport, followed by a snowstorm, prevented the liquidators from reaching Rome. On 14 December *La Repubblica* published a summary of the joint commission report (officially still a secret). It revealed that the commission had been split. Reports also appeared that the Craxi government was anxious to sign a new Concordat with the Vatican, but would not do so until the Ambrosiano affair had been settled.

So the creditors knew that the Vatican was under some pressure from the Italian Government. It was under pressure, too, from the Milan magistrates, who wanted to question Marcinkus and his colleagues, with a view to levelling charges of fraudulent bankruptcy. Under Italian law, those who have suffered damage in such a case can join the magistrates' action as civil parties. On 19 December the magistrates invited the liquidators to file a complaint. The liquidators declined, on the grounds that this would prejudice the chance of a settlement. But, if there were no settlement, they might change their minds. Then it might be possible to get a court order freezing IOR assets in Italy.

So, when the meeting with the Vatican team took place on 21 December, it was known that the IOR was on the defensive. The negotiators met in the office of the lawyer Gatti. Besides Gatti and Cerutti, there was Agostino Gambino, the Vatican co-chairman of the joint commission. He was reputed to be a brilliant lawyer – the youngest man ever appointed as professor of commercial law at Rome University.

The Vatican team offered a "voluntary contribution" of $160 million in cash. In return, it wanted an all-embracing release from legal liability.

The other side said it could not ensure that nobody would ever sue the IOR. The banks and liquidators could speak only for themselves. (Three years later the accountants Coopers and Lybrand, auditors of the Cisalpine, found that it was actually quite simple to sue the IOR. They took out writs against the IOR and against Marcinkus personally, not only because he had been a director of the Cisalpine but because he had lied to the auditors, on an occasion which we shall describe in due course. The writs were served on the lawyer whom the IOR had retained in Nassau. Coopers and Lybrand had themselves been sued for negligence by the Cisalpine liquidators.)

But the banks and liquidators were willing enough to undertake that they themselves would not sue. It had long been clear that they would do all they could to get the IOR off the hook, in return for money. But it had to be enough money. The proposed $160 million was not enough; they wanted $250 million. Gambino said it was "not negotiable". The IOR owed nothing. The meeting broke up.

Over Christmas, the Vatican capitulated. On 4 January 1984 the creditors and the liquidators met Chiomenti in Milan, and heard that the Vatican had agreed in principle to pay $250 million. What led to this climb-down? The decision was almost certainly taken by the Pope and Casaroli, not by Marcinkus. He was known to be arguing that they should "tough it out" and pay nothing. (Later he said so to John Cornwell, as we have seen.)

But the talks on the Concordat were close to agreement. So there was more at stake, perhaps, than another $90 million. (The creditor banks had agreed that $90 million of the $250 million should go to the Italian liquidators.)

The Vatican negotiators had been told that they would be able to pay the $250 million over a period of time. Instead, they suggested making a "prompt" payment of $230 million. When interest was taken into account, they argued, this would amount to the same thing. The reason for the prompt payment, it emerged, was that the Pope did not like to hear of "financial engineering" – methods proposed by the banks to make the payments easier.

Then it emerged that Marcinkus himself wanted to talk about "financial engineering". He would not see a direct representative of the creditor banks. So an intermediary was found, the London merchant bank Morgan Grenfell, which had worked with the Vatican for years.

The diaries of Cecil King, former head of the Mirror group of newspapers, record a dinner in July 1973 with John Stevens, a former director of the Bank of England who had become chairman of Morgan Grenfell. King wrote that Morgan Grenfell "are the financial agents of the Vatican in this country. They have dealings with the Vatican over two funds: one presided over by a Monsignor of the greatest culture and discretion, a real eighteenth-century figure; the other run by an American bishop, of Lithuanian origin, from Chicago. Of the two, Stevens thought the first the better financial man." King continued that Stevens "has had to transact business in the financial departments of both the Vatican and the Kremlin. The setting in both cases is remarkably similar – austere, bare rooms and a green baize-top table with a carafe of water. The main difference was that the only picture was in one case of the Pope, and in the other of Lenin."

On the morning of 26 January 1984, as the headlines proclaimed the overwhelming approval by Parliament of the new Concordat, two representatives of Morgan Grenfell passed through the Angel's Gate to meet Marcinkus in the Vatican. One was an Englishman, a director of the bank, the other a young Italian employee.

Marcinkus, who was accompanied by Mennini and de Strobel, asked what the banks proposed. The Englishman replied that there were no proposals; they had come as neutrals, to listen.

This was followed by a long silence. The Englishman finally said that he understood the IOR would pay $250 million. Marcinkus said it was the first time he had heard of such a figure. Turning to Mennini, he said: "We have heard of $210 to $230 million."

The Englishman said the only figure he knew of was $250 million. He understood that the IOR had certain assets which could be sold, but that there was a gap. Marcinkus asked if there were any suggestions how such a gap might be financed. "We are talking of a figure of between $50 and $90 million, are we not?" he asked. Presumably he meant the difference between the December offer of $160 million and the $210 million he had just mentioned, or between that and the $250 million the creditors wanted.

There followed a discussion of what terms might be available for borrowing the $50 to $90 million. The Morgan Grenfell men pointed out that the IOR's credit rating was now poor. A loan would have to be covered by guarantees from the Vatican, or by collateral, presumably also from the Vatican. Marcinkus made a witticism: "What about the Pietà of Michelangelo?"

Later that day Marcinkus called the Morgan Grenfell men, to say that the IOR had arranged "other financing".

After that meeting there seems to have been a conflict within the Vatican. But on 29 January the message came that the definitive offer was $160 million, to be paid within 90 days, plus another $70 million by 31 December 1985. This added up to $230 million. The Italian liquidators wanted to accept. But the banks held out for $250 million, and on 8 February they got it, though the timing of the payment was slightly extended. On 18 February Craxi and Casaroli signed the new Concordat.

Even after Marcinkus had signed, the banks feared that the money might not actually turn up. But on the due date, the first working day after 30

June 1984, not just the first instalment but the whole amount was paid over, with a discount deducted, quite legally, for the interest the IOR lost by paying the last $90 million early. Hence the odd figure: $240,822,222.23.

The payment was a serious reversal for Marcinkus. He was passed over for promotion, and never has become a cardinal. Yet he remained head of the IOR until March 1990; and as pro-president of Vatican City, he did take some steps to repair the damage he had done to the Vatican's finances.

The repayment of the lira debts was in part offset by the sale of a holding of 3,040 shares in a company called Setemer. This was one of a number of securities held by the IOR as a result of its Italian dealings with Calvi – the only one to retain any value after the crash. In April 1985 it sold these shares to Setemer's parent, Ericsson of Sweden. To judge from Ericsson's accounts, it received about $10 million. The IOR had probably pocketed the Setemer dividends, which totalled about $3 million during the period when it held them.

To meet its main dollar commitments, the IOR sold some Daimler-Benz shares, and in the spring of 1984, its investment in Vianini, the company about which the creditors had been prepared to sue. (It was still hanging on to the $20 million it had received from Calvi for one third of this.) The price of Vianini was never announced, but I estimate it at $25 million. In July 1986 the IOR sold its 51 per cent interest in the Banco di Roma per la Svizzera to the Union Bank of Switzerland. The price is not known but it was probably about $100 million

The IOR does not publish a balance sheet, but some figures are known for the Vatican as a whole. At the time of the Ambrosiano crash the Vatican's deficit was running at about 35 billion lire a year. This went up to about 66 billion lire in 1985. Most of this was covered by St Peter's Pence. America and Germany are the two largest contributors, and their money bought increasing amounts of lire. In 1981 St Peter's Pence of $24 million bought about 29 billion lire; in 1984 $26 million bought 49 billion. However, this was not so helpful as it seems, because what weakened the lira was Italian inflation, which added to the Vatican's expenses.

The lira began to strengthen early in 1985. That year $28 million of St Peter's Pence produced nearly 48 billion lire, but the following year $32 million bought only 43 billion lire, falling well short of the deficit of nearly 77 billion.

The Vatican made a special appeal in the autumn of 1986. In 1987 St Peter's Pence jumped to nearly $50 million (though this was not enough; it bought only 59 billion lire). In the autumn of 1987 the Vatican issued a warning: "Reserves have now been almost completely exhausted."

Wearing his other hat, however, Marcinkus has been helpful. As pro-president of the *Governatorato*, the body responsible for administering the Vatican City State, he must be credited with the jump in its income from a negligible amount to some 8 billion lire a year. This comes from the tourists, who pay for admission to the Vatican museums, buy Vatican stamps and visit the coffee shop on the roof of St Peter's. There was also the sale to Nippon Television of the right to film the cleaning of the Sistine Chapel. Without pawning the Pietà, Marcinkus is believed to have contributed 15 billion towards the Vatican deficit in his last year, 1990. However, the deficit had climbed to 102 billion lire in 1989, and was expected to reach 5 billion more than that in 1990. St Peter's Pence has stabilised at about 60 billion lire.

The creditor banks of BA Holding have, as I write, recovered more than 70 per cent of what was owing to them. The creditors of the Cisalpine are likely to get every penny of the $300 million due. Only the Vatican is broke. And the IOR? The statement made to the cardinals in March 1985 was that the payment to the creditors "was covered entirely by the Institute itself, without contributions from the Holy See and without drawing on the funds entrusted to the administration of the Institute". The cardinals were almost certainly not told that the full loss to the IOR was more than double the contribution. But the implication was that the full $500 million had been met out of the IOR's reserves. There is no evidence that, when it was set up in 1942, the IOR was endowed with any capital. If it had really been able to accumulate such reserves, this would have been a remarkable feat.

When the IOR was reorganised after the scandal, the new directors were all laymen. The chairman was Angelo Caloia, head of Mediocredito Lombardo. Philippe de Weck, one of the original three wise men, was a director. There were three more directors: Thomas Pietzcker, a director of Deutsche Bank, Thomas Macioce, an American businessman, and Jose Sanchez Asiain, president of Banco Bilbao-Vizcaya.

The new general manager, Giovanni Bodio, had to help the directors to wrestle with the consequences of "the covering up of the deficit". Bodio was the same age as Marcinkus – sixty-eight. He was formerly the managing director of the Mediocredito Lombardo, which presumably pays him a pension. Perhaps the Vatican cannot afford to employ anyone but a pensioner.

Preaching at an open-air Mass in the Swiss village of Flüeli, birthplace of Saint Nicholas, on 14 June 1984, the Pope said: "You must watch vigilantly over all that goes on in this world of money. The world of finance, too, is a world of human beings, our world, subject to the consciences of all of us. Ethical principles apply to it too."

The Pope is said to have summoned Marcinkus to discuss the IOR on 24 January 1983, just after the setting up of the joint commission of inquiry. They are believed to have met again on 13 June 1983. If the Pope had the chance to question Marcinkus about his conduct, that is more than the joint commission had, when it tried to establish the truth.

FOUR

The Secret Letters

The legal adviser to the liquidators of the Cisalpine in Nassau got a present from his wife – a parrot named Marcinkus, because it would not talk.

Marcinkus has consistently refused to discuss the details of the IOR's involvement in the Ambrosiano affair. His blanket denials to *Il Sabato*, quoted in Chapter I, can scarcely be considered a discussion. In March 1983 he told the *Chicago Tribune*: "Some day I'll be judged by my Maker on what I've done; and I'm ready to be judged right now. I did nothing wrong. I'm not losing any sleep. I can still look at myself in the mirror each morning. I have a clean conscience. It's just a matter now of standing firm and doing battle."

His sister, then still living in Chicago, explained to the *Tribune*: "His way is to tough it out, to let people think what they want, as long as he knows in his heart what the truth is. He's not the kind of person who defends himself when he knows there's nothing to defend."

Marcinkus has spoken to a number of journalists on an unattributable basis, and he gave two unprecedented interviews to John Cornwell, whom I have already quoted. Cornwell could not be put off; he had – literally – the Pope's blessing for his enterprise, which was to rebut the thesis of David Yallop's book *In God's Name*, that Pope John Paul I had been murdered. In the event, Cornwell's book, *A Thief in the Night*, cannot have been what the Pope envisaged. Cornwell gave a picture of the Vatican as a hotbed of spiteful, unreliable gossip. He suggested that John Paul I was not murdered, so much as allowed to die for want of medical care, denied an autopsy for reasons that remain mysterious and buried with a death certificate which, in England or America, would not have been legal.

Even with the officially approved Cornwell, Marcinkus did not allow himself to be drawn into detail. After his giveaway phrase about covering up the deficit, he rambled on about pensions. "And once you're trying to run everything out of ordinary administration, that's when you get killed. If your company had used over the years the money for the pension fund, then they'd go broke. You've got to have the pension fund set aside."

What did this mean? The Vatican has no pension fund. It deducts a percentage from current salaries which goes directly to retired staff, but it is not enough to cover the full pension bill. The remainder comes out of the Vatican's income, and that comes mainly from the investments of its other financial institution, APSA, as we shall see in the next chapter. Perhaps the IOR is responsible for the pensions of its own employees. That might explain their extreme reluctance to retire.

Reporters without the Pope's blessing get little out of Marcinkus. The powerful American TV current affairs programme, *Sixty Minutes*, was reduced to filming its reporter vainly phoning the office of Marcinkus, to be given a polite brush-off by his intensely loyal secretary.

I, too, was initially given the same treatment by his secretary. But in November 1984 I wrote to Marcinkus, explaining that, unlike other journalists, I had seen Calvi's own working papers. Therefore I knew that the key company, in the early days of Calvi's relationship with the IOR, was a Liechtenstein corporation called Radowal. I hoped, I wrote, that he would be willing to give me his side of the story.

Weeks later, having had no reply, I rang his office. This time his secretary said he would talk to me. He apologised for not having replied. He was not averse, he said, to giving me the information I wanted, but he knew nothing about me. So I sent him a long biographical letter, and some examples of my work. I had no reply. After some weeks I rang again. Again he apologised. But he said his "people" – it was clear he meant his lawyers – had advised him not to get involved. Shortly before he left the Vatican, I made another attempt. His secretary promised faithfully to ring me back. She never did.

Many people do not want to talk to journalists. But Marcinkus, with remarkable arrogance, refused to be interviewed by the joint commission set up at the instigation of the Vatican itself. Cardinal Casaroli said in November 1982 that the Holy See had confirmed its own full readiness to cooperate with the Italian authorities for the purpose of "ascertaining the truth". Yet here was the man who knew the truth refusing to cooperate. Mennini and de Strobel also indicated that they were "unavailable for interview", as the joint commission politely reported.

Whether the Pope and Casaroli endorsed the IOR's refusal to give oral evidence remains unclear. This may have been what the Vatican meant when it said that the inquiry would be carried out "on the basis of the documents in the possession of the two parties".

But, even when it came to documents, the commission was not permitted to go through the IOR records. It had to rely on those documents the IOR chose to produce, and the IOR took its time.

On 3 March 1983 the joint commission got eleven files of documents, and some short memoranda about the IOR's relationship with the letters-of-patronage companies. There were also some letters from Calvi to the IOR. Over the following weeks the IOR produced further documents, in response to requests by the commission. There was an important session on 16 June 1983 – three days after the interview between Marcinkus and the Pope. Gambino, the Vatican-appointed joint chairman, produced a further batch of letters from Calvi to the IOR. The other commissioners were allowed to examine these and copy them by hand, but not photocopy them.

The first of these – and the most damaging – was Calvi's letter of indemnity, dated 26 August 1981. This, as we have seen, clearly established that the IOR had deceitfully issued the letters of patronage after receiving Calvi's secret assurance that it would not be held to account.

The letter of indemnity referred to seven previous letters. The IOR had already handed over copies of four of these. The commissioners were now allowed to see the other three. The most important of these, dated 9 November 1978, set out the arrangements under which the IOR had accumulated its lira debts to the Ambrosiano, the Cattolica and the Varesino. The letter said that the debts were all for the Ambrosiano's purposes, and that the IOR was merely an intermediary. These were the lira debts that the IOR had nevertheless repaid.

The other two letters produced that day were dated 8 and 15 October 1981. In the first, Calvi confirmed his letter of indemnity, and asked the IOR to write to Ambrosiano Services in Luxembourg, asking it to manage the letters-of-patronage companies, plus a further eleven, the first of which was Zitropo. In the second letter, Calvi asked the IOR to appoint him as its "attorney in fact". The IOR responded to both of these as requested; hence the letters which the creditors discovered in Luxembourg.

But the originals of the letter of indemnity, and of the letters dated 8 and 15 October 1981, have remained in the Vatican. If Calvi kept copies, they have not been found. Only in the course of the Ambrosiano trial in 1991 did a copy of the letter of indemnity finally turn up. If it had been available earlier it would have been most useful to the creditors, reinforcing their case that the IOR had empowered Calvi to act for it after it had, by its own account, discovered for the first time the extent of the debts he had accumulated in its name.

Nineteen letters from Calvi to the IOR were labelled by the commission the "parallel" documentation. Calvi wrote the letters either as chairman of the Cisalpine, or as chairman of the Ambrosiano (with one exception which he signed as a director of the Gottardo) but not one of them was to be found in the records of these banks. They formed the core of the evidence that secret arrangements had been made between Calvi and the IOR. The commission had been given another four letters which fell into the same category, but which they omitted from their list, possibly because they related to Zitropo, a company which was not named in the letters of patronage. The "parallel" and other secret letters written by Calvi to the IOR which have emerged are listed and their contents summarised in Appendix B. Some of the letters are then reproduced in full, like the letter of indemnity (B(vii)).

The commissioners knew that these letters were not in the records of Calvi's banks, because the IOR had written to all the banks concerned, releasing them from the obligations of confidentiality, and asking them to help the joint commission. The banks were all members of the Ambrosiano group – with one exception, the Kredietbank of Luxembourg, where the IOR kept an account which featured in its dealings with Calvi.

The commissioners did not find all the banks equally cooperative. They were able to get what they wanted from the liquidators of the Cisalpine in Nassau, and from the Kredietbank and the Ambrosiano group banks. The liquidators of the old Ambrosiano in Milan said that they were prepared to provide whatever documents could be found at the bank, but could not help in tracing others. As the senior executives who worked for Calvi had left the bank, they did not know where to look.

The commissioners' most serious problem was with the Gottardo – where, as they soon realised, many of the answers lay. On 19 February they called on its executives, Garzoni and Bolgiani, in Lugano, to ask for the relevant documents. Some details of the IOR accounts held at the Gottardo were indeed sent to them, and some details of the accounts of two letters-of-patronage companies which had been administered by the Gottardo, United Trading Corporation and Nordeurop.

But the commissioners had great difficulty in extracting further information. The Gottardo men avoided further meetings and did not answer letters, and the commissioners had to complain to the Swiss Banking Commission, the self-regulatory body which oversees the conduct of Swiss banks. After "repeated and insistent" requests the Gottardo gradually yielded more information during the summer of 1983. But some of its versions of events were inconsistent with the versions given by the IOR and others.

For all the volume of paper the commission had amassed, there was little that shed light on the IOR's motives. The "parallel" correspondence was all one way; Calvi wrote to the IOR, but what did the IOR write to Calvi?

This remains a mystery. The commissioners did not have access to Calvi's own working papers. About 1,500 pages of them were kept in a safe in the Roywest Bank in Nassau. There they were frozen, along with papers relating to Calvi's personal affairs, by court order, but Calvi's son Carlo was allowed to have copies. When I went through them I found Calvi's own copies of some of the "parallel" letters, though not of the three written in 1981. What I did not find was one private or personal letter from Marcinkus or any other IOR executive to Calvi. There were, however, copies of financial statements which, I was later able to deduce, were drawn up by the IOR itself. And on two of the letters about Zitropo is the IOR stamp, and the initials of Marcinkus under his handwritten comment: "OK." (See Appendix B(ii))

After the commission had twice postponed its original deadline, Marcinkus did produce a written memorandum in Italian, 22 pages long, dated 1 July 1983 – within three weeks of his discussion with the Pope. It was much better and more precise to do it in writing than orally, Marcinkus wrote. The memorandum purported to be a "detailed description of the relationships at issue", written in order to "complete" the IOR's "collaboration in the work of the commission". A shorter memorandum containing much the same account later went to the Milan magistrates: it was apparently with this that the copy of the letter of indemnity was enclosed – possibly by mistake.

Clearly vetted closely by the Vatican lawyers, the memorandum nowhere explains the reasons for the transactions it describes, or even what the IOR believed to be the reasons. In one respect (which we shall come to later) it is seriously misleading. It maintains the defiant tone of the IOR's original statement, and concludes: "With all that has now been done, this Institute believes that it has fully complied with the request, received from the Holy See, to give its collaboration to the commission promptly and fully. Furthermore, the writer is not in a position to add to what has already been copiously described and documented."

Marcinkus having thus firmly shut the door, the commission was left groping in a half-light. It said in the preamble to its report: "What has emerged is a complicated web of facts, documents and opinions, from which it was extremely difficult to distinguish truth from falsehood." All the commissioners could do was try to reconstruct "the most probable course of events".

The events they were trying to reconstruct did not cover all aspects of the relationship between the Ambrosiano and the IOR. The commission's terms of reference were quite narrow. It had to concern itself with the operations of the companies named in the letters of patronage, and any obligations that might arise as a result of these letters. It had also to inquire into the $213 million of debts which the IOR had refused to repay to the Cisalpine and the Andino.

In effect the commission was being asked only to look into the allegations that the IOR was liable for $1,287 million. It need not, and did not, concern itself with other matters crying out for explanation, such as the operations which led to the lira debts. The commissioners were certainly aware of the lira debts, because they were shown the "parallel" letter about them.

By the time the commissioners came to write their report – it was delivered in late October 1983 – the IOR had conceded that it would pay its "voluntary contribution", and only the amount was in dispute. So none of the interested parties wanted to go into the legal arguments on liability.

Therefore the commissioners did not go directly into the question of liability. Nor did they examine the main plank of the IOR's defence in the autumn of 1982 – that it had never received any money from Calvi or the Ambrosiano. They concerned themselves, rather, with the ownership of the companies, and how much the IOR might have known of what Calvi was doing through them.

In the communiqué thought good enough for the cardinals, in November 1982, the IOR had said it had not known it was involved in Calvi's illicit activities, until, "following upon" normal banking operations, it had "found" that it had the ownership of two of the companies.

The two companies were not named, but the communiqué seemed to mean Manic, another company listed in the "letters of patronage", and United Trading. Now documents produced by the IOR for the commission, including some of the "parallel" letters, showed beyond doubt that the IOR had known of the existence of both these companies from their earliest days. It was evident from the documents that the IOR had known of Zitropo shortly after its operations began in 1972. And the documents all showed that the evidence that the IOR might be said to own these companies had been in existence and known to the IOR for some time.

It was evident, too, that the IOR had known, for much of the period of the fraud, not just of the existence of the companies but also of the arrangements which could be said to constitute its control of them. The IOR had claimed that this control was "juridical", by which it appeared to mean that it was not their real owner, but was merely holding them on trust, or as a nominee, for someone else. It claimed that it had nothing to do with their management, and knew nothing of their operations. The commissioners devoted much of their report to these claims.

Two of the Italian Government's appointees to the commission, the lawyers Alberto Santamaria and Mario Cattaneo, could not accept that the IOR had no knowledge at all of what Calvi was doing through the letters-of-patronage companies. These two concluded: "The IOR's knowledge of the decisions and arrangements adopted . . . was both continuous and constant." As for ownership, they said the question had not been decisively resolved, but the evidence that the IOR was the real owner was stronger than the evidence that it was merely holding the companies for someone else. They regarded that question as secondary; the "parallel" documents showed that Calvi had enjoyed "an important and close association with senior officials of the IOR in the management of these so-called protected companies".

Santamaria and Cattaneo, then, were saying that the IOR (and the Vatican) had not told the truth the previous year. Chiomenti, whose hopes were pinned on the settlement he was then arranging, was more cautious. He was careful to qualify the conclusion that the IOR knew what was going on. According to Chiomenti, the letters which the IOR had produced for the commission demonstrated that the IOR "was well aware – *or should have been aware according to the criteria with which one normally judges the actions of those who preside over the destiny of an important financial institution* – that its conduct provided Roberto Calvi with the means to accomplish operations which it would not have been possible for him to carry out openly". (My italics.)

Chiomenti thought that only Zitropo could "be said to have effectively been owned by the IOR". This was a bizarre conclusion, since there was no intrinsic difference between IOR's role in Manic and in Zitropo. But Zitropo was deemed to be outside the commission's terms of reference; therefore Chiomenti did not have to elaborate.

What had emerged – "and of this there is not the slightest doubt," Chiomenti said – was that "by 1974 at least there was evidence of a very strong link between Roberto Calvi and the IOR, the object of which, *or at least the result of which*, was to provide a cover for certain of Calvi's somewhat unorthodox operations . . ." (My italics.)

The three Vatican men on the commission, who like the Italian Government's men were all lawyers – Professor Gambino, Pellegrino Capaldo and Renato Dardozzi – backed the IOR by insisting that it was not the real owner of the companies. They had to concede that the IOR must have known of the existence of Manic and United Trading before the summer of 1981, but asserted that it knew of them "merely by name". They then undermined their own assertion, by pointing out that the IOR had been sent the Manic balance sheets for the years up to 1976. But they ingeniously argued that, if the IOR had owned Manic and United Trading, it would have insisted on more information. They ignored the fact that the IOR was also sent the Manic balance sheet for 1980 in May 1981, a matter of some significance, as we shall see later.

As for the other letters-of-patronage companies, the three Vatican men maintained that the IOR did not know of their existence, let alone their operations, before the summer of 1981. Again, they undermined their own argument, by admitting that there was an exception – Laramie, to which the IOR had sold the two million Vianini shares in December 1980. The evidence before them also proved that the IOR knew of the existence of two other letters-of-patronage companies, Astolfine and Belrosa, from June 1978.

Last, the commissioners looked at the $213 million that the IOR appeared to owe the Cisalpine and the Andino. These were the debts it had repudiated in its telexes of 14 July 1982, when it claimed that they were the counterpart of sums owed to the IOR by United Trading.

These debts arose because of what were called by Calvi and the IOR *in conto deposito* operations. The arrangement had come to light in one of the "parallel" letters, dated 24 November 1976 and written by Calvi as chairman of the Cisalpine. The IOR had not only produced this for the commission; it had filed it with the courts in the Bahamas, in order to rebut the claims of the Cisalpine liquidators.

It was quite a simple arrangement. Whenever the Cisalpine placed a deposit with the IOR, the IOR was to make a corresponding deposit in the account of United Trading at the Gottardo. For this service it would be paid 0.0625 per cent (one sixteenth of a percentage point) more interest by United Trading than it had to pay the Cisalpine. (This "turn", or profit, was the only financial benefit to the IOR from its association with Calvi that the commission identified.) The arrangement was transferred to the Banco Comercial in Nicaragua by a "parallel" letter dated 24 October 1978. Then, a year later, it was transferred to the Andino.

The arrangement was very much like the "back-to-back" deposits that Calvi had made through a dozen foreign banks in the last months of his life. The aim was to deceive the Italian authorities about his use of the group's Italian banks to finance its foreign subsidiaries. But the *in conto deposito* arrangement with the IOR was not exactly a back-to-back. The

IOR did not deposit the money it received with another bank in the group. It passed it on to the bank account of a "brass plate" company – that is, one with no physical presence in the form of offices or employees. Further-more, the IOR itself could be said to be the company's owner. The arrange-ment was considerably more incestuous than the banking back-to-backs.

Marcinkus wrote in his memorandum of 1 July 1983 that the *conto deposito* operations with United Trading had begun in December 1974. He did not explain why it was not until two years later that Calvi had written to formalise the arrangement. Furthermore, Marcinkus was misleading the com-missioners about the origin of the operations. Although it was strictly true that December 1974 was the month of the first advance to United Trading by the IOR of money it had previously received from the Cisalpine, the system had already been in continuous operation for two and a half years. The first *conto deposito* financing had taken place in May 1972, though the recipient of the first deposit was not United Trading, which had not then been formed, but the Liechtenstein corporation Radowal.

The commissioners knew of the existence of Radowal; it was mentioned in the documents provided by the IOR. But they did not look into its activities, possibly because it was not mentioned in the letters of patronage, having long since been liquidated. So they never became aware of the importance of Radowal in the origins of the relationship between Calvi and the IOR. They concentrated, instead, on the question – when the IOR took part in these back-to-back arrangments, was it acting on its own account, or on behalf of someone else?

The Italian Government's men pointed out that there was nothing in the Cisalpine records to show that the IOR was not the real recipient of the money. Pierre Siegenthaler, the general manager of the Cisalpine through-out its life, told the commission that he had never seen or heard of the arrangement, or of the letter in which Calvi set it up, until after the crash. Other Cisalpine executives agreed.

The Vatican men again came down firmly on the side of the IOR. They maintained that it was just an intermediary – as, indeed, the "parallel" documents seemed to show. They also argued that Calvi's closest collabor-ators in Milan, such as his joint general manager for international business, Filippo Leoni, and the head of the foreign department, Giacomo Botta, must have known that this was the IOR's true role. The telex messages the commission had studied seemed to reinforce this view.

But none of the commissioners raised the most important question about the *conto deposito* arrangement. If the IOR was not the true recipient of the money, and was not liable to repay it, why had not Marcinkus, as a director of the Cisalpine, ensured that its executives knew this and its books recorded it? Far from being an innocent dupe, Marcinkus helped Calvi to deceive others and keep the *conto deposito* arrangement secret.

To do better than the commissioners did, we have to look again at the documents they unearthed, together with the documents from Calvi's safe and what has emerged from the investigations in Italy, Luxembourg, the Bahamas and Switzerland, and see what they reveal of the origins of the relationship between Calvi and the IOR.

To see how the arrangement arose, we have to look at what was happening inside the Vatican.

FIVE

Hell? It's a Limited Company

By the late 1960s a nightmare had come to haunt Paul VI and those connected with Vatican finance: that St Peter's Square would be flooded with workers demonstrating against the Vatican in its role as employer. It controlled a number of disastrous companies at a time when the worst thing an Italian capitalist could do was give anyone the sack. It was his plain duty, in the eyes of the press, to keep an overstaffed, old-fashioned firm running at a loss.

At this time the press attacks on the Vatican centred, not on the IOR, but on its other financial institution, APSA. The initials stand for *L'Amministrazione del Patrimonio della Sede Apostolica*, which means that it administers the property of the Holy See.

APSA has an "extraordinary" section which holds its investments. These arose after the Vatican made its 1929 Concordat with Mussolini. It then received 1,750 million lire (then worth about $90 million) in compensation for Vatican property in Rome, seized by the state nearly fifty years before, when Italy was unified. A separate department, the Special Administration, was set up to look after this money, under a lay banker, Bernadino Nogara, the brother of a bishop. He built up substantial holdings in Italian companies. His first investment was a construction company, Società Generale Immobiliare. By the 1960s this had become a great international group. It had built the Watergate building in Washington, the Montreal Stock Exchange and the Pan Am building in Paris. But its work nearer home brought embarrassment to the Vatican. It built the new Rome airport, Fiumicino, on land that seemed unsuitable. Some papers alleged that it was trying to increase the value of land it owned nearby. It also built the Hilton Hotel, spoiling the look of a hill just outside Rome. This and other developments in the pine woods led to a protest campaign. The chairman of the firm, Count Enrico Galeazzi (a former Governor of the Vatican City) and the general manager, Aldo Samaritani, sued *L'Espresso* over a particularly virulent article. They won. But the Vatican had become associated in the public mind with unscrupulous property development.

51

Other allegations against the investments of APSA concerned the arms trade and a chemical company said to be making a birth control pill. It was never proved either that the Vatican owned the company or that the pill was a contraceptive. But the Vatican did own Ceramica Pozzi, a porcelain firm run by Nogara's son. The firm was losing money heavily, but the necessary cuts led to a strike of employees. It was this that led to the fear of a demonstration in front of St Peter's. A pasta firm, Pantanella, was also losing money. The Vatican had either to sack the workers, or pump in money to keep it going.

But the Vatican had little spare money to pump in. The Pope at the time, Paul VI, was Giovanni Montini, whose background should have given him a good knowledge of the financial world. His father had been a businessman in Brescia in northern Italy, involved in banking and agricultural enterprises. He had also published a Catholic local newspaper and had, for a time, been a member of the Italian Parliament. Montini rose quickly in the Curia, but had some disagreements with the then Pope, Pius XII. He was said to have criticised nepotism and some irregularities in the Vatican finances which concerned the Pope's relations, the Pacelli family. In 1954 he was sent to Milan as its archbishop, and he remained in the business capital of Italy until he was elected Pope in 1963, and took the name Paul VI.

As Pope, Montini made a number of speeches calling for a "just distribution" of wealth and a better deal for developing countries, most notably in his 1967 encyclical "Populorum progressio", in which he also attacked laissez-faire capitalism. This only fuelled the general accusations of hypocrisy, based on the Vatican's reputed wealth.

Most of the wealth in fact was tied up in works of art and historic buildings. Montini could see a shortage of cash ahead. Income was falling and expenditure was rising. Montini may have been brighter than his predecessor, the "peasant Pope" John XXIII, but he had nothing like the same charm. The contributions of the faithful were falling off.

The new Pope had long been determined to reform the administrative structure of the Church, and in 1967 he announced some important changes. This was when APSA took its present form, absorbing the Special Administration. Archbishop Sergio Guerri became its secretary.

At the same time the Pope set up a new Prefecture for Economic Affairs to coordinate all the main financial and administrative offices of the Vatican. At its head he placed Egidio Vagnozzi, a strong, sensible cardinal, who was by Vatican standards remarkably open and accessible to the press. Unfortunately, the Pope exempted the IOR from Vagnozzi's control. Vagnozzi was not even one of the cardinals who theoretically supervised it.

The origins of the IOR lie in a commission of cardinals set up in secret in 1887 by Pope Leo XIII, the commission *ad pias causas* (for holy causes). It seems to have been created because of the continuing threat of expropriation of Church property. It converted the gifts of the faithful into shares, creating a fund of liquid assets. Its existence came to light a few years later, after the theft of a strongbox containing many of these shares. In 1904 it was renamed the Commission for Religious Works by Pius X. Four years later it was downgraded from a cardinals' commission and renamed the Prelate's Administrative Commission for the Works of Religion.

In the 1930s this body called in, as its investment advisor, Prince Massimo Spada, a layman. He was both a lawyer and a stockbroker.

In 1934 Pius XI approved a statute which made it possible for the Administrative Commission to turn into something more like a bank, accepting deposits from lay clients, and acting as a banker to other departments of the Vatican. According to an interview which Spada gave to *L'Espresso* in February 1975, the time of the new body's greatest expansion was between 1935 and 1945. While Italy was at war the Vatican was neutral, and an attractive financial haven. Not that anyone could say so at the time; Mussolini's laws included the death penalty for the export of capital. Even thirty years later, Spada did not mention the point. But he did tell *L'Espresso* that the IOR sought deposits, not only from religious bodies, but also from laymen, "provided that there was a destination, *even if only partial or in the future, for religious works*." (My italics.) *L'Espresso* gave this interview the headline: "Hell? It's a limited company."

Spada was quoting the statutes of the IOR. In 1941, when it was restored to cardinals' status, the Administration (as it then still was) got a new set of statutes, one of which had an article declaring that it would not accept on deposit any money unless it was destined for "the works of religion and Christian piety". But the crucial words "at least partial or in the future" were inserted. The deposits of cardinals, bishops and other ecclesiastics resident in the Vatican or Rome were to be accepted whatever their destination.

In January 1942 the cardinals themselves decided that the new constitution was unsatisfactory. They needed a body more clearly distinguished from the other offices of the Holy See. On 27 June 1942 Pius XII issued a six-point charter, establishing the IOR.

The first clause gave the IOR its own "juridical personality". Did anyone understand what this meant? In its November 1982 statement, the Vatican, in its own English, said that this clause was to show "the responsibility proper to the administration of the Works of Religion, as expressly separate and distinct from that of the Offices of the Holy See, through the creation of an instrumental entity in relation to the general functions of the Apostolic See . . ." This hardly suggests that the Vatican understood what sort of financial animal it had created.

The 1942 charter made it clear that the IOR would take real estate, as well as shares and cash, and that such property could be entrusted to it by "physical or juridical persons". This is the Vatican's English, translating an Italian term which includes any person or body with a legal status, including companies, state corporations or charities. It was to preserve the confidentiality of its dealings with such clients that the IOR, in 1967, insisted that it should not be subject to the Prefecture for Economic Affairs.

On 24 January 1944, when Monsignor di Jorio took over as president of the IOR, a new Papal edict laid down the all-important procedures for supervision. The supervisory commission of cardinals was to be responsible for the appointment of the president and secretary and all senior officials. This commission was to nominate "two ordinary auditors, of proven ability in the field". These auditors, besides their ordinary tasks, had the job of preparing annual reports for the cardinals' commission.

This procedure became a formality. The names of the two auditors were not listed in the Vatican's directory, the *Annuario Ponteficio*, which does list the IOR executives. The cardinals' commission did meet to be given the annual balance sheet, but it is not clear whether any of the cardinals knew how to read a balance sheet.

Marcinkus himself told FBI agents in 1973 (in what circumstances we shall see) that his operations were only "theoretically" directed by the cardinals.

The cardinals' duty was to represent those to whom the IOR was financially accountable. But who were they? The managers of most companies and banks are responsible to the shareholders. But, according to the Vatican statement of 1982, the IOR has no shareholders. There are financial institutions without shareholders, such as the trustee savings banks in Britain before they were privatised. Such institutions usually regard themselves as accountable, instead, to the customers who provide them with their resources.

But the Vatican does not regard the IOR as that sort of financial institution. "It is not a bank in the common sense of the term," said the Vatican statement of November 1982. Marcinkus took a similar line in his interview with *Il Sabato*. "In Italy everybody considers us to be a bank. In reality we are an institute which operates with its own procedures." He did not say what those procedures were. They have never included distributing balance sheets to depositors.

But if the IOR is not run primarily for the benefit of its depositors, and feels entitled to make a profit from using their money, for whom is it doing this? Before the Ambrosiano crash, in May 1982, *Panorama* quoted Marcinkus as saying: "Any profits made by the IOR are placed at the disposal of the Pope. He uses these funds not to cover deficits, but for direct activities that do not come under the Holy See's budget." A Papal slush fund? The Vatican itself put the matter more discreetly. Profits were used "in favour of works of religion", as the bank's name implied.

Both statements contradicted a widespread belief that the IOR was an important contributor to the mainstream of the Vatican's income. The Vatican statement implied, moreover, that not all the IOR's activities were profitable; it could make loans, presumably for religious projects, on concessionary terms.

But what about losses? Banks which have no shareholders, or no risk capital, must invest with extreme caution, at least at the outset. They have nothing to meet losses with, except their customers' deposits. Reserves may be built up over the years, out of income and the capital appreciation of investments. The Vatican has never disclosed whether the IOR, on its establishment in 1942, was endowed with any reserves. Forty years later, when the Ambrosiano crash came, the figure most widely accepted for the IOR's "own" money, as distinct from that of its clients, was $150 million. This figure was used by the *Chicago Tribune*, to whom Marcinkus had spoken at length. This would be small in relation to the clients' deposits, then believed to total $2 billion. In the absence of a balance sheet, all these figures must be treated with caution.

The IOR found that, on the back of the financial status it acquired by handling large sums of other people's money, it could start borrowing and investing in its own name and on its own account. Whatever resources it used, immediately after the Second World War the IOR embarked on a vigorous policy of investment. Marcinkus played no part in this. The man who built up the investments was Prince Massimo Spada.

He liked the IOR to acquire outright control. A cotton manufacturer, Maino, handed over his business in exchange for an annuity for life. It was later resold to the textile giant Snia Viscosa. The IOR acquired a property company, XX Settembre, of which more will be heard, and the construction company Vianini. Sometimes Spada took a minority investment, as in Italcementi, whose head, Carlo Pesenti, was a personal friend.

In 1946 he bought the IOR's first bank. This was Banca Cattolica del

Veneto, one of the earliest Catholic banks, founded in 1878. It had run into difficulties in the 1930s, been rescued by the government, and survived to become the leading provincial bank in the Venice region. Now it returned to the Church. Some of the shares were taken up by local bishops, though they soon sold them on to the IOR.

The IOR then bought 51 per cent of the Lugano-based Banco di Roma per la Svizzera. The other 49 per cent belonged to the Banco di Roma, a state-owned bank.

It bought its first Ambrosiano shares in 1952. By the end of the sixties it still owned only 6,181 shares, or a little over 0.2 per cent of the capital.

The first of Spada's investments to cause public scandal were the Banque de Financement (Finabank) in Geneva, and a small Milan bank, the Banca Unione. These led to the IOR involvement with Michele Sindona.

Unlike most of the people in this book, Sindona talked freely to journalists. He talked to me, while he was in prison in the United States. At a time when he was telling fantastic stories to many people, I was surprised by his willingness to discuss financial details which were by no means always to his credit. However, I had one example of his ability to distort facts, after I wrote to him saying that I had evidence to support some of his statements but not others. Sindona then told the Italian court which tried him for murder in 1985 that I had documents that would help him prove his innocence.

Michele Sindona was born in 1920 in Patti, Sicily, to a father who could not settle to a steady job, and a mother who soon became an invalid. He was brought up mainly by his grandmother. The Sindona family had come down in the world; Sindona's grandfather had been a prosperous merchant until his sudden death in 1914. Some of the relations were still doing well; one was a lawyer. Sindona, as a boy, helped in the lawyer's office and decided he liked the life. In 1938 he went to study law at Messina University, working his way through college with a part-time job at the local tax office. He got a good degree in 1942.

In 1943 the allied armies landed. Sindona made money from barter deals with the Americans. But more than simple black marketeering was going on. The Americans allowed the revival of the Mafia (which Mussolini had suppressed) because the Mafia could give Palermo to them, without the loss of a single American life.

Sindona set up his own tax consultancy business in Messina. Two years later, taking with him letters of introduction from the Archbishop of Messina, Sindona moved to Milan. He went briefly into partnership with an established lawyer, and then set up on his own, specialising in tax consultancy. Soon he was doing business deals with his clients, or accepting payment in the form of shares in the clients' companies. According to Sindona, his initial money was made in property speculation.

In 1958 Sindona achieved an introduction to Spada. Then, the following year, he registered his main holding company, Fasco AG, in Liechtenstein, and his relationship with Spada produced its first results. Through Fasco, he bought the Banca Privata Finanziaria in Milan. This was a small bank with a good industrial clientele, including the textile company Snia Viscosa.

The IOR almost certainly took up a stake in the Banca Privata at the same time, but no shares were ever registered in its name. It may have used nominees. It resold the shares in circumstances that remain mysterious.

Mystery also surrounds the circumstances in which Spada left his full-time post with the IOR in 1962. He told *L'Espresso* that it was "on reaching the limits of age". Those must be elastic limits. Spada was only 57 at the time, five months older than Pellegrino de Strobel, who until 1990 continued as the IOR's chief accountant. Luigi Mennini, who stepped into Spada's shoes as administrative secretary, and a year later became managing director, also remained in his post until 1990. He is only three years younger than Spada.

The break is all the more mysterious because Spada maintained close links with the Vatican. He accepted a seat on the board of the Banca Privata, and on some of Sindona's other companies.

If the IOR had a disagreement with Spada, it was not over Sindona. In 1964 the IOR was happy to sell to Sindona a majority stake in the Banque de Financement (Finabank) in Geneva. The IOR retained 29 per cent of the shares, and thereby accepted Sindona as its partner. And in 1968 it became a partner in yet another bank, when Sindona bought a controlling stake in the Banca Unione, in which the IOR already had a minority interest. Mennini sat on the board.

Sindona is said to have enjoyed excellent relations with Giovanni Montini, while he was still Archbishop of Milan. When Montini became Pope Paul VI in June 1963, this may have been good news for Sindona. It was certainly good news for Spada, who had come to know Montini well in the Vatican, before he became Archbishop of Milan.

Sindona, while making powerful friends, made a powerful enemy. Enrico Cuccia, head of the merchant bank Mediobanca, had among his clients one who consulted him about buying a company from Sindona. After the sale Cuccia alleged that he and his client had been deceived. Two years later he was justified, when a court of arbitration ordered Sindona to pay the purchaser $800,000. From that time onwards, Cuccia devoted himself to frustrating every grandiose scheme attempted by Sindona.

Most people in Milan went right on doing business with Sindona as if nothing had happened.

In 1965 Sindona set up Moneyrex, a firm whose one purpose was foreign exchange dealing. To run it, he put in Carlo Bordoni, who had been sacked from Citibank for going over his trading limits. Sindona knew this. True, he had every reason to want a reckless trader in charge of a firm which was soon to specialise in reckless trading. But why did it never occur to Sindona that Bordoni might ignore his instructions, as he had ignored those of his old boss?

Sindona, by his own later account, was warned not to hire Bordoni by a new friend, David Kennedy, chairman of Continental Illinois. Sindona sold 22 per cent of Banca Privata to Continental Illinois, and another 22 per cent to Hambros, the London merchant bank. With such respectable partners, Sindona seemed a suitable associate for both the Vatican's financial institutions, IOR and APSA. In 1968 Sindona bought a majority stake in the Banca Unione in which the IOR already held a minority stake and of which Mennini was an executive director.

The same year Pope Paul VI decided on a new investment strategy. The embarrassing and loss-making investments would be disposed of, and the Vatican would pursue a more diversified policy, reducing its stakes in individual companies to a level at which it could not be accused of having control, and ceasing to appoint Vatican representatives to their boards. He now had reasons for the change, more urgent even than the threat of demonstrations of redundant workers outside St Peter's. In 1962 the Italian Government had imposed a withholding tax on dividends. The Vatican had claimed exemption under the terms of the Lateran pacts, though it was willing to concede that the IOR should pay the tax. The government appeared to accept this. But in 1968 a new government, under Aldo Moro, was relying on Socialist Party support, and in order to get this it had to require the tax in full from the Vatican, including arrears – a total of 6.5 billion lire. It fell to Guerri to carry out the new policy which was the Vatican's response to this crisis. Guerri asked Spada for his advice and Spada suggested that he should consult Sindona.

By the spring of 1969, Sindona had agreed to buy the bulk of APSA's holding in Generale Immobiliare (allowing APSA to retain a small stake as an investment). He also bought the bulk of another construction company, Condotte d'Acqua. For a nominal sum, he relieved the Vatican of the loss-making Ceramica Pozzi. And he found a buyer for the loss-making

Pantanella. (The buyer was an American insurance company, Equity Funding, which collapsed in 1973 after a spectacular fraud by its management. Pantanella was back in Italian hands by then. We shall see the name again; it was used by Calvi as a vehicle for share manipulation.)

Before the deal could be signed, Guerri was made a cardinal, and his job at APSA was taken over by Archbishop Giuseppe Caprio. Caprio faced some doubters within the Vatican, who raised the question of Sindona's ability to pay. They might well have worried. Sindona did pay – about $50 million, spread over two years – but only by making a remarkable deal with Hambros. The London merchant bank agreed that, with Sindona's holding company, Fasco, it should form a joint Luxembourg holding company called Distributor. It was joint in the sense that it was managed by Sindona but financed by Hambros. Many of the Generale Immobiliare shares ended up in this company. Hambros then discovered that Sindona had agreed to pay the Vatican twice the market price for them. Not that Sindona got all the $50 million from Hambros; he diverted a good deal of it by means of fiduciary deposits made by the Banca Privata. This was similar to the back-to-back system, afterwards perfected by Marcinkus and Calvi. Deposits were made by the Banca Privata with one of Sindona's banks abroad. Sindona could then use the money in any way he liked, including the payment to the Vatican.

Sindona resold a block of Generale Immobiliare shares to the American conglomerate Gulf and Western (owners of Paramount and financiers of the film *The Godfather*). The chairman of Gulf and Western, Charles Bludhorn, handed over to Sindona in exchange all the shares of Commonwealth United, a record and film distribution company that was close to bankruptcy. The Securities and Exchange Commission in the US later charged both men with trading worthless stocks to and fro in order to create a false market.

At about the time he bought the APSA companies, Sindona met Marcinkus, who has often been associated with this sale, but in fact had nothing to do with it. He had been making his way up a different ladder.

Marcinkus was born on 15 January 1922, the fifth child of Lithuanian immigrants who had settled in Cicero, a suburb of Chicago where there was a large Lithuanian community. His father worked as a window cleaner – a secure job, which he held right through the depression. Lithuanian social life centred round the local Catholic churches, and the priests were a dominating influence on the boyhood of Marcinkus. He was a bright schoolboy, but is remembered largely for his ability at every kind of sport. Throughout his career, he was to remain an enthusiastic golfer.

His decision to train as a priest was unexpected by his family. At thirteen he went to Quigley Preparatory Seminary. In 1940 he moved to the major seminary of St Mary of the Lake in Mundelein, Illinois. He was ordained on 3 May 1947. He worked briefly as a curate in a Chicago parish. In 1949 he took the first step in his ecclesiastical career; he was appointed to the matrimonial tribunal of the Chicago archdiocese, where he processed petitions to have marriages annulled. The following year he went to Rome to study canon law at the Pontifical Gregorian University.

During his second year he was asked to take a temporary job at the Vatican Secretariat of State. In his 1983 interview with the *Chicago Tribune*, he recalled: "I was at the British Museum doing research for my doctorate when I got a letter asking if I could fill in there, so some other priests could take their summer vacations." That led to a permanent job, and also to his friendship with Montini, who was then Undersecretary of State at the Vatican. Marcinkus told the *Chicago Tribune*: "I used to see him walking around the grounds and I'd give him a lift in my car. We got along well. We both left the Vatican about the same time. I went to Bolivia and he went to Milan."

Marcinkus was secretary of the Papal Nuncio in Bolivia from January 1955 to September 1956, when he was transferred to the Vatican delegation in Ottawa. He returned to the Vatican three years later to take up a post in the English section of the Secretariat of State.

Marcinkus began to make his mark during the Second Vatican Council, when he ran a service bureau for the American bishops attending it. He organised travel, accommodation, sightseeing and "any other service a bishop might need", as he told the *Chicago Tribune*. He then successfully organised the building of a residence for American priests working in Rome. It was named the Villa Strich after the Cardinal Archbishop of Chicago (then recently dead) who had first given Marcinkus permission to work in Rome.

When Montini became Pope Paul VI, he at once called on the services of Marcinkus, who was fluent in Italian, French, Spanish and Lithuanian. Marcinkus became the Pope's personal interpreter, and a close friend of the Pope's secretary, Pasquale Macchi.

This was the first Pope to make those spectacular journeys abroad, which are now part of the job. His first trip, to Israel in 1964, was badly organised, and he found himself in danger from uncontrolled crowds. Marcinkus was asked to plan the next papal journey, to Bombay. It was a success. From that time on Marcinkus planned all the Pope's journeys, and was always by his side, as interpreter and also as a sort of unofficial bodyguard. His height and athletic build enabled him to keep away the reporters, who called him "the gorilla".

For these tasks he may have been admirably suited, but it came as a surprise, even to Marcinkus himself, when the Pope appointed him to the vacant post of secretary of the IOR in December 1968. By his own account he resisted initially; as he told *Il Sabato* after the Ambrosiano crash: "I have never been a businessman. I would not know where to begin. I am above all a priest."

He was persuaded to begin, presumably by the Pope himself, since he, rather than the cardinals' supervisory commission, seems to have made this curious choice. It was part of the Pope's campaign to break with the dubious business associations of the past, and to bring in new blood.

When Pope Paul VI died in 1978, he did not know that he had brought about the greatest financial scandal of the century, costing the Vatican a sum which, properly invested, would have solved its whole financial problem.

SIX

The Growth of the Secret Network

It was typical of Sindona that he boasted of being the first to present Calvi to Marcinkus. Sindona said he asked the Vatican "to look favourably upon" Calvi.

In fact the Ambrosiano group was already close to the IOR. Under a contract between the IOR and the Gottardo, dated 30 October 1967, the IOR authorised the Gottardo to manage a company called Intermax. The purpose of Intermax has never come to light.

This contract, signed by de Strobel and Monsignor Donato de Bonis, who later became secretary of the IOR, was made more than a year before Marcinkus joined the IOR. It shows that he inherited the situation. So did Calvi.

Calvi, like Sindona, was born in 1920. His father, Giacomo Calvi, worked for the Banca Commerciale Italiana in Milan, respectably but without rising beyond middle management ranks. Roberto Calvi studied economics at the Bocconi University, and wrote for the student Fascist newspaper. So did his friend Giuliano Magnoni (who afterwards introduced him to Sindona).

Before Calvi could take his degree, Italy entered the war on the German side. Calvi, regarded by other students as reserved and taciturn, showed a dashing streak by joining an aristocratic cavalry regiment, the Novara Lancers. From May 1942 to April 1943 he served as a lieutenant on the Russian front. Later he recalled that Russian winter, when he carried a live chicken under his coat to keep his hands from freezing.

On his return to Italy, his father found him a job in the Banca Commerciale. But he had to go to its Bari branch. In Bari he joined the newly formed Socialist Party. It was later alleged that he carried his new Socialist Party card in one pocket, and his old Fascist Party card in another, so as to be ready for anyone he might meet. However, he seldom talked politics.

In 1947 Calvi returned to Milan, and began his career at the Ambrosiano as a clerk in the foreign department. In those days the bank's chairman was not a professional banker. (From 1953 to 1965 it was Duke Tommaso Gallarati Scotti.) He presided over a non-executive board, consisting largely of industrialists. The man who actually ran the bank was the general manager. He had a deputy, and under them was the central directorate of the bank. The head of this, in 1947, was Carlo Canesi.

It was Canesi who took Calvi up. Calvi became his personal assistant. And when Canesi was made general manager in 1955 Calvi began to rise rapidly.

He was now married to Clara Canetti, a beautiful girl he had met on the beach at Rimini. Displaying, once more, his dashing streak, he won her in spite of her engagement to another man. They took a flat in Via Frua, and never moved out of it, though they enlarged it later by taking over an adjoining flat. Their country home at Drezzo in the Alps – near the ancestral village of the Calvi family – was not ostentatious. Calvi never showed the least inclination to riotous living. He disliked parties and loathed casinos. Not one of his tastes or habits went beyond what could be indulged on a rapidly rising middle-class income.

Calvi was happiest in his country home, with his wife, his son Carlo and his daughter Anna. There he could indulge his liking for carpentry. This would have been considered normal in England, but not in Italy. When Calvi cut his index finger at his bench, one weekend, and came to the bank on Monday morning with a bandaged hand, his business associates laughed behind his back. This was the scar that Calvi's brother spoke of, when he identified the body.

At the Ambrosiano, devious activities were beginning. In September 1956, when Canesi was general manager, a company called Lovelok was registered in Liechtenstein. They used the services of Walter Keicher, a local lawyer who has acted for many of the world's richest and most secretive men. He was the man who formed the mysterious Intermax for the IOR.

Lovelok was secretly linked with the Ambrosiano. It was probably used in the formation of the Banca del Gottardo in April 1957, and it may have controlled the Gottardo until the Ambrosiano openly acquired 40 per cent of its capital in 1960.

In May 1963 Lovelok formed a new subsidiary in Luxembourg: Compendium, later BA Holding. Lovelok put up 80 per cent of the initial capital. The rest came from a Gottardo nominee company, Etablissement pour les Participations Internationales, registered in Liechtenstein.

Compendium was set up to buy Ambrosiano shares – the shares which the founders of the bank had intended for small savers with certificates of Catholic baptism. Over the next three years Compendium acquired nearly 8 per cent of the capital of the bank. The cost, over 15 million Swiss francs, was provided by Lovelok. Lovelok borrowed the money from the Ambrosiano itself, or from the Gottardo.

The records show that Calvi was involved with Compendium from the beginning. But he cannot have acted without the approval of Canesi and his other superiors. Why did they want a secret holding of Ambrosiano shares? They may simply have regarded them as a good buy. Or they may have wanted to make it easier for shareholders to sell. A substantial part of Compendium's holding was bought from one seller, the Missionary College, further evidence of the bank's long association with the church. This form of incestuous investment is highly dangerous, which is, no doubt, why it was done in this furtive way. Many of these shares were to resurface in the United Trading block fifteen years later.

In early 1965 Duke Scotti retired as chairman of the Ambrosiano. Canesi was elected in his place. So, for the first time, the Ambrosiano had a professional banker as chairman. Canesi's post as general manager went to Ruggiero Mozzana, a man already in his sixties; Calvi moved up into a senior post, but not yet into one worth mentioning in the bank's annual report.

In 1968 Compendium began to resell its Ambrosiano shares, completing the process early in 1970. Most of the shares, however, remained under the control of the Ambrosiano. They were acquired by a nominee company, Locafid, formed by the Gottardo. Lovelok formed yet another subsidiary: Ultrafin, a Swiss merchant bank based in Lugano. Calvi was appointed to its board.

By this time Calvi already knew Luigi Mennini, managing director at the IOR, and "the only competent man there", as Sindona afterwards told me. He was described as "shrewd, diligent, discreet" by the magistrates who charged him with knowing, when he was a director of the Banca Unione, that Sindona was diverting its deposits. Apart from denying this and all other charges, Mennini has kept his mouth shut. All that is known of him for certain is his devotion to the Church. Of his fourteen children, one is a Jesuit and another a nun.

Mennini used to visit the Calvi family at Drezzo, where he and Calvi would converse in low tones as they strolled together in the garden. The Ambrosiano's links with the Church, always close, grew closer; the body which administers Milan Cathedral took a stake in the bank. Marcinkus was later to tell *Panorama* that he did business with Calvi because he was recommended by the Curia in Milan. Carlo Calvi remembers that an old Lancia was kept specially for visiting ecclesiastics.

In 1969 the Ambrosiano hired one of Mennini's sons, the 31-year-old Alessandro, as an assistant manager in the foreign department. He had no previous banking experience. According to a colleague, Giacomo Botta, he was hired because of the IOR's influence. Filippo Leoni had just been appointed as head of the foreign department, which was being extended. Botta was moved into the foreign department at about the same time; a dinner was held in a restaurant to mark the appointments. Leoni and Botta became close collaborators of Calvi. Alessandro Mennini played an important role in raising money from foreign banks, but the others believed that he was never taken into Calvi's confidence.

It was probably in 1968 that Calvi first met Sindona. Calvi's college friend Giuliano Magnoni had a son, Pier Sandro Magnoni, who worked for Sindona and married his daughter. But it was not until 11 May 1970 that Compendium bought a block of shares in Sindona's Banca Unione. Four days later the IOR more than doubled its investment in the Ambrosiano, buying 10,000 shares. Marcinkus had by then been secretary of the IOR for over a year.

On 1 July 1970 Calvi was promoted again, becoming head of the central directorate. The bank's links with Sindona and with the IOR grew stronger. Compendium took its holding in Sindona's Banca Unione to 100,000 shares, over 7 per cent. Sindona, using a Swiss company called Valiana, started to buy shares in the Ambrosiano. The IOR, too, was investing in the Ambrosiano. It acquired over 40,000 more shares, to bring its total holding to 56,972 shares, or 1.14 per cent.

Calvi, with the help of Leoni, set about bringing Compendium out of its shadowy existence, and making it the spearhead of the Ambrosiano's foreign interests. In June 1970 Compendium formed another investment banking operation under the name Ultrafin, this time based in New York. The Swiss Ultrafin moved from Lugano to a more important financial centre, Zürich. At the end of 1970 the Ambrosiano bought 40 per cent of Compendium from the shadowy Lovelok, and the Gottardo acquired another 20 per cent. The remaining 40 per cent went to a nominee.

On 1 January 1971, Marcinkus, not yet forty-nine, succeeded the eighty-seven year old di Jorio as president of the IOR. He had been a bishop since January 1969. Sindona told me that he used to meet Calvi and Marcinkus for lunch at the Grand Hotel in Rome. Sindona said of Marcinkus: "He was greedy; he wanted the IOR to make large profits so that he could give the Pope a lot of money for his religious works, and create a base for him to become a cardinal."

It was also in January 1971 that *Institutional Investor* published an article on the Vatican's finances by Paul Horne. Cardinal Vagnozzi told him: "When the Pope said we need more money and are a poor church, he meant exactly that." The Vatican no longer controlled any companies,

Vagnozzi said, and was getting away from the practice of having its own men on the companies' boards. It could simply "not afford primary responsibility for business failures requiring transfusions of capital." He added: "It wouldn't do for the Church to lose its capital in speculation."

The article did mention that Vagnozzi had no jurisdiction over the IOR. Marcinkus refused to see Paul Horne and would only say, on the phone, that it would take time to make changes at the IOR.

In fact he was about to plunge the IOR into just the type of financial adventure that Vagnozzi had said the Church must not undertake.

Calvi's plan was that Compendium should form a new subsidiary bank at Nassau in the Bahamas. With Garzoni of the Gottardo, he went to the Bahamas early in 1971. They were taken with Nassau, not only as an offshore banking centre with little tax and less regulation, but as a warm place with deep-sea fishing. Calvi and Garzoni applied for a banking licence and hired a Swiss manager, Pierre Siegenthaler.

At the Ambrosiano, Calvi became general manager on 10 February 1971. One of the documents from his safe records what must have been his first major deal after that promotion. It is a brief agreement (reproduced opposite), made in Milan on 8 March 1971, between Calvi and his superior Mozzana on the one hand, and Jocelyn Hambro (Sindona's backer) on the other. The Ambrosiano (in the form of Ultrafin) was joining Hambros and an unnamed third partner in a takeover bid for a company known as Bastogi.

Italiane Strade Ferrate, familiarly called Bastogi after its founder, was a large holding company with interests in the chemical firm Montedison, the cement firm Italcementi and many others. The anonymous third partner was Sindona. He had already formed a Luxembourg company, Colias, with which to start building a secret stake in Bastogi. It was a costly enterprise. The support of the Ambrosiano gave Sindona the help he needed. By the end of March Colias had bought, or undertaken to buy, over 7 per cent of Bastogi's shares, at a cost of over $15 million.

Calvi's new bank in Nassau, the Cisalpine, was registered on 23 March 1971. Its first board meeting took place the same day, in Milan. Calvi was chairman. The other directors were: Garzoni of the Gottardo, Ned Feldman, an American who ran Ultrafin in New York, and Count Luciano della Porta Rodiani Carrara, who had been in the cavalry with Calvi. Another aristocrat was there too: Cesare di Montemozolo, who helped Ned Feldman in New York. Much of the new bank's business was expected to come from the United States. Siegenthaler was there as general manager. It was decided that Calvi could sign for the bank on his own, and that business would start on 21 April.

ULTRAFIN AG Zurigo

Partecipazione con Hambros Bank, Londra ed altro partner,
per il quale Hambros agisce come fiduciario, ad un terzo
di una operazione di acquisto del controllo della Bastogi .
L'intervento si manifesta mediante depositi alla Hambros,
procurati da Ultrafin AG, pari ad un terzo del finanziamento
de l'operazione, sempre fronteggiati da pegno sui titoli
acquistati sotto la responsabilità della Hambros.
La finalità é di poter intervenire in una nuova formulazione
del potere nell'ambito della Bastogi, per trasformarla in
uno strumento finanziario attivo su piano europeo.
Scadenza 31 dicembre 1971.
Milano 8 marzo 1971.

The initial share capital of the Cisalpine was $2.5 million, composed of 15,000 A shares of $100 and 1,000 B shares of $1,000 each. Compendium subscribed for 10,000 of the A shares. The other 5,000 were secretly acquired by the IOR.

Marcinkus, in his memorandum to the joint commission, wrote: "In 1971, on the establishment of the Cisalpine Overseas Bank for the operations of the Ambrosiano group, the IOR decided to participate, with a minority stake, in the capital of this bank. To this end, on 21 April 1971, the IOR acquired 5,000 category A shares with a nominal value of $100 each . . ."

He then described how the IOR had taken up new issues of shares over the years, bringing the IOR's holding to 16,667 shares, "equal to a participation of 8.3 per cent in the capital of the Cisalpine". This was, he wrote: "an investment based on the good prospects of return on the capital which the company offered".

The IOR's shares were held through a Panamanian company, Cisalpine Inc. This company also held the 1,000 B shares. The real owners of these have never come to light. Sindona afterwards claimed that his Finabank had 2.5 per cent of the Cisalpine.

Whoever held the B shares, they had only one vote each for their $1,000, whereas the owners of the A shares had one vote for their $100. So Compendium had 62.5 per cent of the votes at the outset, and the IOR 31.25 per cent, while the holders of the B shares had only 6.25 per cent. By the end, the IOR's 16,667 shares may have been only 8.3 per cent of the capital, but that meant 26 per cent of the votes.

The IOR had more at stake in the Cisalpine than its equity investment. Right at the start it placed the equivalent of nearly $16.5 million on deposit, mostly in dollars but also in Swiss francs and German marks. A further $70.5 million of deposits came from the Ambrosiano itself. The money bought a ready-made portfolio of loans and investments, most of it from Lovelok. It was quite a respectable portfolio, with loans to such international companies as Burroughs and AEG, as well as the Italian chain store Rinascente and the textile firm Snia Viscosa. There was a loan of $1 million to Sindona's Banca Unione and one of $2,750,000 to the building firm Sindona had bought from the Vatican, Generale Immobiliare, but alarm bells were not yet ringing at loans to Sindona.

In May 1971 one of Sindona's clients alleged that people who thought they had money in the Banca Unione found that what they had instead were shares in Sindona's companies. Ugo de Luca, managing director of the bank, publicly blamed Sindona for this. Sindona fired him, but with a golden handshake of $1.3 million. Then he bought the news agency which had spread the story.

Another board meeting of the Cisalpine was held, this time in New York, on 26 April 1971. The directors accepted that the ultimate decision on any loan would be made by Calvi. On 14 May the Cisalpine lent 11,520,000 Swiss francs to Lovelok, which immediately passed the money on to Compendium, which used it to finance the purchase of 7,200 shares in Sindona's Finabank.

In this, Calvi was clearly doing Sindona a favour, since Sindona paid him a commission of 75 francs a share, or 540,000 francs. The money was paid out of Sindona's private account at the Finabank, known as Mani 1125 – from the names of his children, Maria and Nino – and paid to an account Calvi had opened in the Swiss Credit Bank in Zürich in the names of "Mr C. Ralrov and Mrs K. Ralrov".

This is the first evidence that Calvi took a bribe. This payment from Sindona was followed by others. That was how Sindona came to know the figures with which he blackmailed Calvi in 1977.

Calvi seems not to have got any personal benefit from the money. He used that first 540,000 francs to buy some Swiss shares. These shares were then sold to the Cisalpine, and the proceeds were not paid into the Ralrov account. They disappeared into the Gottardo, and may have been used to fund the secret parallel structure that Calvi was already building.

In the summer of 1971, Hambros Bank bought a large block of Ambrosiano shares, and Calvi sent his son to Hambros in London as a trainee for a few months. In June, acting together, Hambros, Calvi and Sindona took over an important holding company, La Centrale. Hambros, acting for all three, bought a controlling stake from the previous owners, principally Pirelli. The origins of La Centrale were in the electrical and telephone industries, and it still held a minority interest in an electronics company, Setemer, which was controlled by the Swedish Ericsson.

Calvi and Sindona became directors of La Centrale on 5 August. The same day another appointment went unnoticed; Marcinkus became a director of the Cisalpine. A discreet letter from the Cisalpine to the Bahamian registry of companies reported the appointment of "Mr Paul C. Marcinkus".

Why did Marcinkus become a director? Sindona said he fancied playing at international banker. Marcinkus, in his memorandum to the joint commission, wrote that he was invited to join the board "in relation to" the IOR's shareholding. But the timing was almost certainly related to the secret deal he had just signed.

This was the sale to Calvi of the major part of the IOR's controlling interest in the Banca Cattolica. Some aspects of this deal remain mysterious, partly because of Sindona's conflicting stories. In his more extreme versions he claimed that he had negotiated an option to buy the Banca Cattolica, and that he had then resold this right to Calvi. Or, at least, he was responsible for persuading Marcinkus to sell to Calvi. There is, however, no hard evidence that he had anything to do with it.

On strictly commercial principles, Marcinkus did right to sell the Cattolica. It had deposits of over $700 million, but it had difficulty in putting them to profitable use. There was then a shortage of good industrial customers in the Veneto region. And its other customers, religious bodies, expected to borrow on concessionary terms. The IOR was earning an income on its investment equivalent to about $700,000 a year. Yet bank share prices were beginning to soar on the markets, thanks to the activities of Sindona. If the IOR could sell at even the quoted price of Cattolica shares it could realise over $40 million. Placed on deposit, that could earn an income many times larger.

Yet it was not easy for the Church to sell a bank whose very name proclaimed it to be Catholic. Marcinkus consulted Pope Paul VI. Or so

Calvi said. In his last months, the secretive Calvi chose as his companion
Flavio Carboni, not knowing that Carboni sometimes tape-recorded his
remarks. (Why? To prove that he was not blackmailing Calvi, Carboni
explained.) Calvi said that Marcinkus had arranged a private audience for
him with the Pope. When the secret agreement was drawn up, it stipulated
that the "high social, moral and Catholic aims" of the bank would be
maintained.

The Ambrosiano was willing to pay over the market price. A note in
Calvi's files shows that on 15 July 1971 Canesi and Mozzana authorised
him to pay up to 1,900 lire a share, a premium of some 35 per cent. It tells
us something about their respective bargaining powers that when Marcinkus
signed the deal with Calvi he had parted with the shares for 1,600 lire each.

Yet the price Calvi paid for 50 per cent of the bank (the IOR kept a small
stake) was, by British or American standards, enormous. It came to $46.5
million, which meant valuing the bank at nearly sixty times profits – perhaps
five times higher than would be normal in London or New York. It was to
be paid in five instalments: $12 million on 5 August, then three instalments
of $10 million each on 24 September and 8 and 22 October, and the final
$4.5 million on 29 October. (The contract is reproduced in Appendix C.)

Calvi signed on behalf of Compendium, but it was not Compendium that
paid. It is still not clear which company paid the first $12 million on 5
August, the day Marcinkus joined the Cisalpine board. It was probably
Lovelok. The IOR put $12 million on deposit in the Cisalpine that day –
probably the same $12 million it had just received from the sale.

In September a Liechtenstein company called Vertlac was formed. On
each due date the Cisalpine made a $10 million loan to Vertlac, which paid
the money to the IOR – which immediately put it on deposit at the Cisalpine.
The final $4.5 million was probably paid by the Ambrosiano itself, but again
the IOR put the money on deposit in the Cisalpine, which used it to reduce
its debts to the Ambrosiano.

Each IOR deposit at the Cisalpine was for six months, and the interest
rate averaged 7.4 per cent, though on some deposits the IOR was paid an
extra three-eighths of a percentage point. Its annual return from the $46.5
million was about $3.44 million, so by selling the Cattolica it had increased
its income almost fivefold.

On the other hand it was putting many of its eggs in one basket. It had
been increasing its deposits in the Cisalpine even before the sale of the
Cattolica; when the sale was complete it had $73.5 million there. Did
Marcinkus join the board so as to look after the IOR's money?

At this time the IOR retained considerable security, since it kept physical possession of the Cattolica shares. On 29 October 1971, the day of the last instalment, Marcinkus himself sent a statement to Compendium to say that the 18,060,000 shares had been placed for it in account 90521 at the IOR. We shall hear more of this account.

Marcinkus attended his first board meeting on 5 November 1971 in New York. Over ten years later he told *Panorama* that he saw Calvi only at Cisalpine board meetings, "no more than four times a year, and often I am not even present because of commitments elsewhere". In fact, in the eleven years that Marcinkus was a director there were twenty-two board meetings, in New York, Nassau, London, Paris, Zürich and Geneva. Marcinkus missed only one.

If he did not meet Calvi at other times, when did they discuss the deals between them? They were never discussed at board meetings. Indeed, Calvi and Marcinkus were silent about them even when they were vital to the working of the bank.

At the first board meeting Marcinkus attended, the most important matter discussed was the transfer of the bank's accounting records from Milan to Nassau. The role of the Cisalpine in financing the acquisition of the Cattolica, involving $30 million of loans to an obscure Liechtenstein company, was not mentioned. Nor did Calvi mention the opportunities opening up before him – opportunities that could be seized only by committing the Cisalpine to further enormous loans.

These opportunities had arisen out of a setback. Since the secret agreement between Sindona, Calvi and Hambros Bank, Sindona had been quietly buying Bastogi shares through his Luxembourg company, Colias. By September 1971 he had accumulated about 12.5 per cent of the capital, at a cost to the three partners of over $26 million. Sindona, on the advice of Hambros Bank, imported a technique hitherto unknown in Italy – a public offer for the shares. It was launched over the weekend of 10 to 13 September. The offer was made in the name of a German bank, the Westdeutsche Landesbank. Shareholders would get a price of about 20 per cent above the market level, provided that acceptances for at least 20 million shares had been received by 8 October.

It was known that Sindona and Hambros were behind the offer, though the Ambrosiano's role was a secret. There were by this time some influential people – with Enrico Cuccia at their head – who had seen through Sindona. The Bank of Italy thought poorly of Sindona's banking methods. Most of the Bastogi shares were held by banks, and the banks understood that the Bank of Italy would not be pleased if they accepted Sindona's offer. So the bid was a failure.

This was when Hambros Bank began to lose its illusions about Sindona. It wanted to pull out of both Bastogi and La Centrale. (The original plan had been to merge the two.) Sindona had no desire to retain his stakes, either. So Calvi had the opportunity, which he embraced, to take over the entire holdings in Bastogi and La Centrale.

There was a problem. Italian law did not allow banks to take controlling interests in commercial companies. They could hold shares; otherwise there would have been practically no stock market. But was it legal for them to have large stakes in holding companies like Bastogi and La Centrale?

And there was a special problem with Bastogi. The Ambrosiano had not been publicly associated with the bid that failed. Calvi had to hide the Bastogi shares. On 18 November 1971 Sindona's Liechtenstein company, Colias, passed its 7.5 million shares to another Liechtenstein company, Radowal, which Calvi had formed three weeks before. Radowal borrowed $28 million from the Cisalpine to pay for them.

On the same day that Radowal was formed, 29 October 1971, the Gottardo set up another Liechtenstein company, Cimafin. Calvi seems to have intended this to buy La Centrale. Then he found there was no need for secrecy. The Ambrosiano was already known to be interested in La Centrale, and the Bank of Italy had not taken any action. So La Centrale was openly bought by Compendium, a final block of 1,246,600 shares being acquired on 1 December 1971 from Hambros and Sindona. The total cost was $43 million. Like Radowal, Compendium borrowed all the purchase money from Cisalpine.

The decision to put La Centrale into Compendium led to another change of plan. Compendium would not, after all, take over the Cattolica. The Cattolica shares were quietly reallocated to Radowal.

No money had to change hands, but Radowal accepted liability to repay the loans that had been created in the Cisalpine's books to match the $46.5 million of IOR deposits.

So Radowal, a little company with a capital of only 20,000 Swiss francs, had suddenly acquired nearly $75 million of assets and liabilities. Who owned it? As it was registered in Leichtenstein, it did not have to say. Its directors were Garzoni and Bolgiani of the Gottardo, who have never willingly said anything about Radowal. Sindona got to hear of Radowal, in spite of the secrecy with which Calvi surrounded it, and formed the impression that it belonged to Calvi. This is possible, or it may have been the joint property of Calvi and his immediate superior, Mozzana. On 20 October 1971, nine days before Radowal was formed, Calvi and Mozzana formed a Luxembourg company called Anli, with themselves – not the Ambrosiano

– as owners. This was done through a Swiss bank account in the joint names of Calvi and Mozzana; the account was number QLZ 6278 at the Kredietbank in Geneva, an affiliate of the Kredietbank in Brussels.

Anli, named after an employee of the Kredietbank, Annie Lippert, immediately formed a subsidiary in Milan, Suprafin. Its purpose, as the Bank of Italy inspectors later discovered, was to deal in shares, including those of the Ambrosiano itself.

These companies formed the embryo of Calvi's secret network. Soon Radowal became crucial in his dealings with the IOR. It was the forerunner of United Trading. Documentary evidence proves that the IOR was aware of Radowal's existence by March 1972. It may even have owned Radowal. But no management contract between the IOR and the Gottardo concerning Radowal has ever been discovered, though the contract concerning United Trading has been found. The contract concerning the mysterious Intermax, as we have seen, was signed before Marcinkus came to IOR. Intermax was still active at this time. On 16 November 1971 its name was changed to Timaring, and a few weeks later the IOR confirmed the management contract with the Gottardo.

Whoever owned Radowal, its function was to serve as a sort of limbo, into which shares could be put without ever appearing in the books of Ambrosiano group companies. The shares could then be sold to the group, and perhaps later bought back from it, as if the transactions were normal. Thus profits could be created, either secretly for the network, or publicly for the Ambrosiano.

But who was to benefit? At the start, Calvi seemed concerned to plough money back into the system. His "Ralrov" account was credited with two further sums from Sindona: $1,350,000 in late November and $632,000 in early December 1971. Sindona explained these to me by saying that he and Calvi had entered into an agreement to buy Ambrosiano shares jointly. It is true that yet another Liechtenstein company, Supply Point, associated with Calvi and the Ralrov account, did buy 100,000 Ambrosiano shares at this time. But it did so with a loan from the Cisalpine. During the 1977 blackmail campaign, Sindona represented these payments as kickbacks from the Bastogi deal. One of the sums mentioned in the blackmail campaign, $2.7 million, was not paid *to* Calvi but *by* him, out of the Gottardo to Sindona. It probably represented Sindona's profits on La Centrale shares bought by Compendium, which he then shared with Calvi. (Hence the $1,350,000 paid into the Ralrov account.) The other payment into the Ralrov account, $623,300, was a half-dollar-a-share premium on the 1,246,600 La Centrale shares bought by Compendium on 1 December.

That is, the Ambrosiano group had paid too much for these shares, and Calvi and Sindona were dividing the spoils.

But Calvi did not salt the money away; he used it to reduce Radowal's debt to the Cisalpine to $26 million.

At the Ambrosiano Mozzana, at least, was fully aware of the activities of Anli and Radowal. He must have approved of them, since Calvi was appointed to the Ambrosiano board on 17 November, and made managing director on 15 December 1971.

He still had a problem. The Cisalpine's vast loans to Compendium and Radowal had been financed mainly by deposits from the Ambrosiano in Milan. This would make the year-end figures for both banks look bad. The IOR came to the rescue; on 16 December it made a Swiss franc deposit, equivalent to more than $37 million, at the Cisalpine. The deposit was for five years at the excellent rate of 8.5 per cent. This brought its total deposits to some $112.5 million. So Marcinkus had more reason than ever to be a vigilant director of the Cisalpine.

He was at its board meeting in Nassau on 28 December 1971. Calvi pointed out to his fellow-directors that deposits from the Ambrosiano had been reduced – without saying that this was thanks to the IOR. A 10 per cent dividend was proposed. And nobody mentioned the loans to Radowal, Vertlac or Supply Point. Nor did anyone say that the bank had bought from Compendium its 7,200 shares in Sindona's Finabank.

SEVEN

The Birth of the Back-to-Backs

Calvi's next big secret deal, in February 1972, brought him control of the Credito Varesino, a small but successful bank in the province of Varese, north-west of Milan.

Calvi's methods of acquiring this bank, and his manipulation of its shares, have been investigated by the Bank of Italy, the Guardia di Finanza, and various magistrates. None of these have got to the bottom of the IOR's role in the affair. This is what I shall now attempt.

The people who owned a large stake in the Varesino at the beginning of 1972 were Anna Bonomi, aged 60, and her son Carlo Bonomi, aged 32. Anna has been twice married, but she is seldom known as Signora Campanini or Signora Bolchini. The name of Bonomi cost her so much trouble to acquire that she has kept it throughout her adult life. Her son, born Carlo Campanini, has also chosen to be known by it.

Anna was brought up in the porter's lodge of a block of flats; her mother was at the beck and call of every tenant. Her mother's husband, whom she considered her father, was a carpenter. Only as she grew up did she realise that a wealthy tenant who ordered her mother about was her real father. He was one of the four Bonomi brothers who developed substantial parts of Milan between the wars. As he grew richer, he became less and less able to conceal his paternal pride in the little girl. Eventually he adopted her and made her his heir. Anna had to fight his scandalised relations in the courts, to establish her right to what had become a splendid inheritance.

She consolidated her business interests in a company called Subalpina Investment. As the Milan Stock Exchange began to rise in 1971 she became, along with Sindona and Calvi, one of its leading operators, or *golpisti*. (The word means people who take part in a military coup.)

The Bonomis built up their stake in Varesino in late 1971, borrowing heavily to do so. On 22 February 1972 they opened a "riporto", usually translated by an old-fashioned stock market phrase, a contango, with the Ambrosiano. This meant that the Ambrosiano advanced Anna Bonomi and her company some 8.9 billion lire, equivalent to $15.3 million, on the security of a forward contract of sale of 2.1 million Varesino shares at 4,240 lire each for maturity on 6 April. The price was 20 per cent below the market level of 5,300 lire.

But this deal was only a feint. The real deal was signed in Lugano the following day. The Bonomis agreed to sell Calvi the shares, not for 4,240 lire éach but for 8,500 lire. The difference was to be paid in Switzerland, in Swiss francs, which made the deal illegal for Italian citizens. At the same time the Bonomis agreed to sell Calvi a further 1.1 million Credito Varesino shares which were "circulating abroad" – that is, held legally outside Italy – for an average price of just over 7,718 lire, again to be paid in Switzerland. The total price for the 3.2 million shares – over 53 per cent of the Varesino's capital – came to 116 million Swiss francs, equivalent to about $30 million.

The company Calvi chose to make the acquisition was Cimafin, the one he had formed at the same time as Radowal. Naturally, it borrowed from the Cisalpine, which lent it over 90 million Swiss francs. (Where Calvi found the remaining 26 million Swiss francs is not known.) Thus the Cisalpine was making yet another huge loan to a tiny Liechenstein company.

The loan was for six months. Calvi may have had some scheme for dealing with the debt by August 1972. But at the beginning of March he was jolted into a change of plan.

The international firm Price Waterhouse audited both the Cisalpine in Nassau and Compendium in Luxembourg (through its Zürich office). The Compendium auditors found that, even after talking to Calvi, they could not satisfy themselves either of the correctness of the price Compendium had paid for La Centrale, or of the value of its underlying investments, and on 2 March they made a report saying so.

The annual meeting of the Ambrosiano was due on 4 March, and Price Waterhouse attended in case any questions were asked about Compendium. But the Ambrosiano shareholders never did ask awkward questions. Soon afterwards, Price Waterhouse ceased to be Compendium's auditors, and were replaced by Fiduciaire Générale, then the largest independent Luxembourg firm. (It became part of the group headed by Touche Ross of London in 1979.)

Calvi's real problem was not in Luxembourg but in Nassau. There, Price Waterhouse's men had not yet signed the Cisalpine's 1971 accounts. These auditors were in touch with their colleagues in Europe. They were confronted with the $43 million loan to Compendium, and some $59 million of loans to Radowal, Vertlac and Supply Point. To these had been added a $12.5 million loan to Lovelok, and now the loan of 90 million Swiss francs ($23 million) to Cimafin.

There was also the question of security. When Marcinkus made his helpful deposit of $37 million just before the end of 1971, he enabled Calvi to turn $35 million of the Compendium advance into a debenture. This meant that the Cisalpine had first call on Compendium's assets – those very assets the Price Waterhouse men in Europe had said they could not value. The security for the Radowal and Lovelok loans was a letter from the Gottardo, saying it held the Bastogi shares. There was also a letter from Compendium indicating that the Banca Cattolica shares were available as security. (When the letter was written, the shares were still with the IOR.) The Supply Point and Cimafin loans appear to have been unsecured.

If the auditors had qualified the accounts, it would have been more serious for the Cisalpine than it had been for Compendium. The Cisalpine was trying to attract deposits from other banks, and from the public. In the event, Price Waterhouse in Nassau signed the accounts on 14 March with no serious qualification. The auditors merely appended a note pointing out that a $35 million debenture had replaced part of the $43 million loan to an "affiliated company" – which they did not name.

The partner in charge of the audit is now dead. What discussions he had with Calvi, before he signed the accounts, we do not know. But we can guess, from what Calvi did next, that he had been told to improve the quality of the Cisalpine balance sheet.

So, by the end of April 1972, Calvi brought about a dramatic change in the situation. All the Liechtenstein companies repaid their loans except Vertlac, which reduced its debt to $20 million. The debenture to Compendium was reduced by $10 million.

How did Calvi do it? He used two methods, for both of which the IOR's help was essential.

The first method involved the shares of Banca Cattolica. On 30 March 1972 it was disclosed that La Centrale, now a known member of the Ambrosiano group, had bought 13.5 million shares – 37.4 per cent of Banca Cattolica – for 27 billion lire. For the public, and for the authorities, *this* was the sale by the IOR to Calvi. In fact, as we have seen, the IOR had secretly sold 50 per cent of the Cattolica the previous July to *Compendium*, which then passed the shares to Radowal. So it was Radowal which sold the 13.5 million shares to La Centrale. The IOR may not have been fully aware of this. On that same day, 30 March, it sent a statement to Compendium to inform it that the shares had been removed from account 95201 at the IOR. The statement, however, went on to say that the remaining 4,560,000 Banca Cattolica shares were now held in the account for Radowal. The financial arrangements behind the transaction also suggest that the IOR knew full well that the secret Liechtenstein company was involved.

What happened, in effect, was that the IOR swapped most of the $46.5 million Calvi had secretly paid it for the 27 billion lire he was now openly paying it. But there was an important difference. The secret deal was for half of Cattolica; the public deal was for not much more than a third of it. (The secret deal was for 18,060,000 shares; the open deal for 13,500,000.)

On 4 April 27 billion lire were credited to IOR account number 10841 at the Ambrosiano. At about the same time the IOR started withdrawing deposits from the Cisalpine and paying the principal to Radowal's account and other accounts at the Gottardo, while keeping the interest for itself. Most of the deposits withdrawn were those created to make up the original purchase price. A total of about $44 million was in this way made available to Radowal and the other companies in the secret network, enabling them to reduce their debts to the Cisalpine, while the IOR had, instead, 27 billion lire on deposit at the Ambrosiano.

Radowal had bought the Cattolica shares for 1,600 lire each, and it sold them to La Centrale for 2,000 each, profiting by about $9.3 million. The losers were La Centrale, which did not realise what was happening, and the IOR, which did. But the IOR did not object, because it got a substantial slice of the profit. The conversion of the $44 million into 27 billion lire was at an exchange rate of 616 lire to the dollar, whereas the market rate was about 580. That gave the IOR a profit of about $2.5 million.

This was the price for that service which, according to Marcinkus, the IOR did not render to its Italian clients – currency smuggling. The Italian authorities have always suspected that this was how the IOR made a large part of its income. Certainly it was to make millions in this way from Calvi.

The swapping of the $44 million for the 27 billion lire marked the completion of the first stage in the bolstering of the Cisalpine balance sheet. (Reproduced opposite is the IOR's own reconciliation of the figures for the the transaction, adjusted for costs, commissions, and so on, and clearly showing the exchange rate used.) The IOR was helpful in the second stage too, because it continued to make the 27 billion lire available for Calvi's use.

To raise the rest of the money he needed, Calvi did a deal with Sindona over the Credito Varesino shares. On 18 April 1972 Cimafin sold to a Sindona company called Mabusi the 1.1 million Credito Varesino shares "circulating abroad", and the right to buy the other 2.1 million shares before 20 October for 11,130 million lire, or 5,300 lire each, the current market quotation. The total price for this package was 138 million Swiss

```
30/3/1972   accredito (rif.to 13.500.000)     L.                      27.000.000.000
            addebito -comm.ni                 L.      13.500.000
            addebito -bolli                   L.       4.050.000
            accredito :
            div. : 18.060.000 x 14            L.                         252.840.000
20/4/1972   addebito ( 2.100.000 x 15)        L.      31.500.000
            addbito -bolli                    L.       3.339.500

            addbito - a pareggio:
              ctv.$USA 44.156.575 a 616       L.27.200.450.500
                                              ─────────────────
                                              L.27.252.840.000    27.252.840.000
                                              ════════════════    ══════════════

30/3/1972   ctv L.27.200.450.500 a 616 c.s. USA$                        44.156.575
• 31/3/1972  addebito -bonifico               "       10.000.000 ✓
. 10/4/1972✓      idem                        "       10.000.000 ✓
. 12/4/1972✓ addebito -bonifico :
             Frs.sv.10.000.000✓a 3,8461       "        2.600.000 ✓
• 14/4/1972✓ addebito -bonifico               "        1.000.000 ✓
• 24/4/1972      idem                         "       10.000.000 ✓
• 28/4/1972 ✓    idem                         "        4.500.000 ✓
• 28/4/1972 ✓ addebito -bonifico:
             D.M. 10.000.000✓a 3,1645         "        3.160.000 ✓
. 28/4/1972✓ addebito -bonifico✓              "        2.500.000 ✓
  5/5/72. ✓  addebito-bonifico  a saldo✓      "          396.575 ✓
                                              ──────────────────
                                        USA$   44.156.575          44.156.575
                                              ════════════════    ══════════════

                          +++++•+++++

DI 90521

10/4/1972   addebito ( N° 500.000 a 1750)     L.     875.000.000
                                              ════════════════    ══════════════


   2/5/72
```

francs, which put a value on the Varesino shares of 10,000 lire each, taking into account the 11,130 million lire to be found before 20 October.

The IOR's role in the operation concerned the way the 11,130 million lire would be financed in the meantime. The original forward contract taken out by the Bonomis was due to mature on 6 April, but on that day it was renewed until 19 May. Then, on 18 April, the day of the deal with Sindona, it was prematurely closed, not at the original price of 4,240 lire but at the market price of 5,300 lire, so that the total was 11,130 million lire. The shares were transferred to Giammei, a Rome stockbroker much used by the IOR. This made everyone think that the IOR was the buyer.

What really happened was that a new forward contract was made, this time with the IOR. That is, it advanced 11,130 million lire out of its account at the Ambrosiano, until the maturity date of 19 June, against the security of the forward purchase of the shares at 5,300 lire each.

But with whom did the IOR make this contract? Documents from Calvi's safe suggest that the IOR may have believed the Cisalpine would be the eventual buyer. In reality it was Radowal, or Cimafin acting for Radowal.

What actually happened to the 11,130 million lire? The proceeds of Calvi's sale to Sindona ostensibly belonged to the Bonomis, as the 5,300 lire price represented the publicly known price of the sale of their Credito Varesino shares in Italy. But, because of the secret agreement they had made in Lugano, only 8.9 billion of the proceeds was theirs – the amount they needed to extinguish the loan from the Ambrosiano. There was thus a profit, after cost and interest, of some 2.3 billion lire (nearly $4 million). Who got it? The Bank of Italy subsequently discovered that at least 1,750 million lire made its way back to the IOR, by a circuitous route involving the issue of 155 cheques. At the IOR, as so often, the trail ended. It is, however, unlikely that the IOR kept it. Calvi's papers suggest that half this sum may have been used to buy another 500,000 Banca Cattolica shares for Radowal.

The 138 million Swiss francs that Cimafin received from Sindona enabled Calvi to reduce still further the debts of his Liechtenstein companies to the Cisalpine. It is unlikely that Sindona ever intended to take over the Credito Varesino. Almost certainly, he had agreed to step in temporarily while Calvi reorganised his finances. Sindona had by this time given up trying to expand in Italy. Hambros Bank had told him to go away. It had discovered that Sindona had committed their partnership company, Distributor, to paying the Vatican seller APSA twice the market price for the last block of Generale Immobiliare shares. Besides, he had dumped on it a disastrous textile company, Rossari & Varsi.

Jocelyn Hambro, the innocent taken in by Sindona, retired. John Mc-Caffery, the Hambros Bank representative in Italy, who had been a Special Operations Executive during the war, had been Sindona's friend and confidant in a plan to defeat the Communist danger in Italy by means of a military coup. McCaffery now retired.

Charles Hambro, cousin of Jocelyn, gave Sindona an ultimatum. Either he was to buy back the Hambros Bank stake in Banca Privata, or Hambros would sell it to the highest bidder. Sindona bought it back by a roundabout route, which disguised the fact that he was using money diverted from the bank's depositors. In search of people who had not seen through him yet, Sindona was living in Geneva, and negotiating to buy the Franklin National

Bank in the US – a bank which was already in such trouble that the American authorities ought not to have let anyone buy it. It would have been inconvenient for Sindona to have his 138 million Swiss francs tied up for long. (The Ambrosiano had lent him 40 million of this.)

On 25 April 1972 Calvi was in New York for a Cisalpine board meeting, attended, as usual, by Marcinkus. The board approved the raising of $5,250,000 of new capital by the issue of a further 3,500 of the $1,000 B shares at a premium of 50 per cent. The IOR did not take any of these.

The audited accounts for 1971 were approved. But the minutes reflect some concern by the directors that they would have to be improved next time. It was noted that the total of loans and deposits had fallen since the year-end. A point was made of the fact that all new loans were guaranteed by major banks or industrial companies, or else covered by security.

In spite of Calvi's great power as chairman – and there are signs of concern about this too – he was faced with the fact that he could not go on using the Cisalpine as he had used it in its first year. But if he could no longer make unlimited loans, without proper security, to obscure Liechten-stein companies, his ability to complete the deals already in the pipeline would be endangered. And how could he embark on new ones? The secret network would become useless almost before it was in place. What Calvi needed was to find a way round the tedious scrutiny of auditors, directors and others who might want to ask embarrassing questions about published accounts.

Marcinkus enjoyed freedom from such petty hindrances, and it was to Marcinkus that Calvi looked for a solution to his problem. It must have been shortly after that board meeting that Calvi and Marcinkus agreed on their *in conto deposito* (or back-to-back) operations. The first such loan by the Cisalpine to the secret network, by way of the IOR, was made on 17 May 1972. No documentation about the agreement has ever come to light. It may well have been reached orally. A cryptic note in Calvi's papers hints that this happened on 9 May.

The arrangement worked like this: instead of lending directly to Radowal, or other companies in the secret network, the Cisalpine would deposit the money with the IOR, and the IOR would secretly pass it on to Radowal. So the secret network's borrowings would not appear in the books of the Cisalpine, and would be hidden from auditors and directors. The manager, Pierre Siegenthaler, afterwards claimed that he knew nothing of it, though he at least had some reason for suspicion.

There would also be no problems of putting up security, for the money would appear as an interbank deposit with the IOR, and who could doubt the IOR's ability to repay?

The arrangement had yet another advantage. Though the Bahamas had a more liberal financial régime than Italy, there were some rules. One was that banks must show a certain proportion of their assets as liquid and sound. For this purpose, deposits with the IOR would count.

Two directors of the Cisalpine knew of the agreement: Calvi and Marcinkus. As Marcinkus, on becoming a director of the Cisalpine, had accepted the responsibilities of that post, he had no right to conspire with another director to falsify the Cisalpine balance sheet.

What made him do it? Marcinkus himself has never offered any account – let alone explanation – of the origin of these back-to-back operations. In his memorandum to the joint commission he wrote misleadingly that they began in December 1974. His lawyers protected him – just – from telling an outright lie, by slipping in the words: "with UTC". This made the statement true, to the extent that December 1974 was when the first back-to-back loan was made to United Trading, Radowal's successor. So the joint commission, along with most other investigators in Italy, remained unaware that the real beginning was over two and a half years earlier.

By remaining silent, Marcinkus has saved himself the trouble of working out an innocent explanation. He would have to present himself as hood-winked by Calvi – the IOR's line when the scandal broke – and at the same time show that he fulfilled his duties as a director of the Cisalpine. If Calvi gave him some plausible explanation, for example by saying that the operation was just a technical device, why did Marcinkus keep it secret from the other directors?

It would be almost as hard for Marcinkus to convince his colleagues in the Vatican that the scheme worked for their benefit. The IOR's investment in the Ambrosiano was concentrated in the Cisalpine, and it was not, therefore, to the IOR's long-term advantage to by-pass the mechanisms designed to protect the interests of shareholders and depositors. What the IOR got out of the back-to-back operation, at the outset, was a quarter of one percentage point of all money it passed on. This was afterwards to be reduced to one-sixteenth. It was easy money, for which the IOR had virtually nothing to do, except make the occasional in and out entries in its books. However, if Marcinkus made his decision for the sake of that gain, it looks like a bad case of what financiers call "short-termism". The Church calls it sin.

That first *conto deposito* loan on 17 May 1972 was for 50 million Swiss francs, and was a "call" loan, which meant it was repayable on two days' notice. During the following week a further 60 million Swiss francs was advanced to Radowal through the IOR in four instalments, the loan this time being for six months. Another six-month loan, this time for 20 million Swiss francs, was made at the end of June. The total was equivalent to more than $34 million.

The main purpose of these loans was to provide capital for Calvi's secret network, and to finance its holdings of Ambrosiano group shares. Calvi had clearly decided that Radowal would be the key company in the secret network. The other Liechtenstein companies – Cimafin, Vertlac and Supply Point – now became nominees for it, protecting its identity. So did two new companies, Tufnell and Fabiar.

The first thing Radowal seems to have done with its new funds was to acquire an 11 per cent stake in the Gottardo and 40 per cent of Compendium, at a cost of some 22 million Swiss francs. These shares were probably already under the Ambrosiano's control, possibly through Lovelok, the old secret company. Lovelok's activities were being run down and transferred to Calvi's new parallel structure.

Compendium, now known as BA Holding, badly needed to increase its capital. Luxembourg law required that capital should grow in line with assets and liabilities. Since Compendium/BA Holding had acquired La Centrale, there had been a bad imbalance. Now the capital was increased threefold, to 45 million Swiss francs. The Ambrosiano subscribed 40 per cent of this from Milan. Because of the currency laws, it had to obtain the permission of the Ministry of Foreign Trade for this. But Radowal did not have to tell anyone that it was subscribing for its share of the capital increase by using 12 million Swiss francs, provided unwittingly by the Cisalpine through the IOR. Radowal subsequently sold most of its shares in Compendium/BA Holding to the Luxembourg company Anli, as it had done with its Gottardo shares. We have seen that Anli was set up by Calvi and his superior Mozzana, acting in concert. It seems to have been designated as the long-term holding company for such group investments.

Anli had now become a subsidiary of Radowal. Indeed, Radowal used its new Swiss franc borrowings to take over Anli and increase its capital from 1 million to 10 million Swiss francs. Some of this money was needed to increase the capital of Anli's subsidiary Suprafin, which was now actively dealing in Ambrosiano shares in Milan. Radowal also provided Anli with further funds to finance the Gottardo and Compendium/BA Holding shares, and to take up some of the new B shares issued by the Cisalpine itself.

Radowal's final use of the Swiss franc back-to-back loans was to subscribe for 55 million of new Swiss franc debentures issued by Compendium/BA Holding. These replaced $13 million of the original $35 million issue which Radowal had bought from the Cisalpine. This time they were 10-year debentures.

Calvi's use of the short-term back-to-back loans to make such long-term investments would suggest that, from the start, the IOR had committed itself to a continual renewal of the back-to-back loans as they fell due. The built-in instability of Calvi's structure was thus concealed, thanks to the IOR.

Sindona was now in America, concluding negotiations for the control of the Franklin National Bank. By the end of June 1972 he was close to a deal to acquire 22 per cent of the bank for $40 million. He therefore wanted, not only to retrieve the 138 million Swiss francs he had put up to finance the acquisition of the Credito Varesino, but to raise further money. He and Calvi now hatched a complex plan, the purpose of which was to make substantial sums available to Sindona, while enabling Calvi to make huge secret profits from the manipulation of the Credito Varesino shares. The cooperation of the IOR was, once more, essential.

The centre of the operation was another Luxembourg company, Zitropo, formed by Sindona on 9 June 1972 with a capital of $100,000. Into this company were to be transferred two main assets. One was the controlling interest in an Italian group named Pacchetti. Sindona had acquired this former leather company a couple of years before. Having installed Prince Massimo Spada as its chairman, he set about turning it into a conglomerate, along the lines then fashionable in America. Pacchetti bought up businesses in, for example, agricultural machinery and electrical engineering. Its share price went rocketing up on the Milan Stock Exchange.

The other asset transferred into Zitropo was the interest in Credito Varesino, which Sindona's company Mabusi had bought.

Mabusi, let us recall, had bought more than the 1.1 million Varesino shares "circulating abroad". It also had the right to buy the 2.1 million Varesino shares in Italy before 20 October 1972, at 5,300 lire each. This was the price used for the forward contract taken out with the IOR for 11,130 million lire on 18 April and due to expire on 19 June. On that day, however, the IOR agreed to open a new forward contract, this time for maturity on 31 March 1973 at 10,000 lire a share.

That is, the IOR was agreeing to lend another 9,870 million lire (about $17 million) at 9 per cent, against the security of the forward sale of the shares at a price which, in spite of the rapidly rising market, was still 20 per cent above the current quotation.

Perhaps because of the risk it was taking, the IOR had the share certificates delivered to the Vatican, where they were deposited in account 90521, along with the remaining Banca Cattolica shares.

The net amount of the IOR's new loan was just over 9.5 billion lire, after interest and costs on the original loan had been deducted. The IOR received over 175 million lire (more than $300,000) in interest. Costs included a lump sum of 150 million lire (nearly $260,000). This was, almost certainly, a special commission to the IOR – the first of a number of such payments from Calvi. However, this was not the only way in which the Vatican was to profit.

Documents from Calvi's safe suggest that the IOR may have believed that the Cisalpine was at the other end of the contract – that if nobody else would pay the 10,000 lire a share, the Cisalpine would. But it was not to the Cisalpine that the IOR paid the 9.5 billion lire. That went to two bank accounts in the name of Zitropo, at the Luxembourg offices of the First National City Bank and the Kredietbank. It was paid in dollars, and the IOR itself made the conversion. This is how it made the rest of its profit. The lire were converted, not at the official rate of about 581 lire to the dollar, but at an average of over 613 to produce exactly $15.5 million. That gave the IOR a further profit of nearly $860,000 on the deal. (The document showing the IOR's calculations is reproduced on page 86.)

In Zitropo's books, the $15.5 million was entered into a special "partners' account". The "partner" was almost certainly Calvi. Although Sindona had set up Zitropo, Calvi had agreed to provide it with the bulk of its financial needs. In addition to the $15.5 million, he now poured a further $60 million into the company. It was all lent to Zitropo by Radowal, and Radowal got it all from the Cisalpine.

The first $30 million was lent directly by Cisalpine to Radowal, without using the back-to-back arrangement. It is not known why. Calvi was careful to set the unusual term of five months for this loan, so that it could be repaid before the balance sheet had to be drawn up. There seem to have been problems over security. The Gottardo wrote an extraordinary letter to the Cisalpine, with the assurance that an unnamed "third party" had deposited with an unnamed "first-class bank" a block of shares quoted on the Milan Stock Exchange, whose value was well over $30 million. If this referred to the Credito Varesino shares, they were in the IOR, acting as security for its loan.

Radowal's next two loans to Zitropo had no such problems; they were made by the back-to-back arrangement, through the IOR.

```
= saldo conto riporto val. 19/6/72                          9.544.702.500

= commissioni           12.600.000
 - bolli (4)            12.600.000
                                            25.200.000

= commissioni            8.400.000
 - bolli                 6.300.000
                                            14.700.000
                                                            39.900.000
                                                            _____

                    = residuo netto                       9.504.802.500
                                                          ==============



= 20/6 - US$ 7.000.000 (606)            4.242.000.000
= 10/7 - US$ 3.500.000 (618)            2.163.000.000
= 24/7 - US$ 1.500.000 (618)              927.000.000
= 31/7 - US$ 3.500.000 (620,80)         2.172.802.500
                                        _____

                                        9.504.802.500
                                        =============
```

The $75.5 million Calvi provided for Zitropo was not enough. Sindona sold to Zitropo 40 million Pacchetti shares for $48,315,517. He also extracted $37,134,539 to cover the 138 million Swiss francs he had put up to finance the Varesino operation, plus interest. That left $9,950,056 owing to Sindona, or rather to one of his companies, Steelinvest, which had sold most of the Pacchetti shares.

On 20 July 1972 Sindona got control of Franklin National. He paid with two remittances of $22 million and $18 million from the Banca Privata and the Banca Unione. Years later, when he was charged with fraud in the US, Sindona denied that he had stolen the money from the depositors of those banks. He said he had used money he got from Calvi.

In 1979 the liquidator of Sindona's Italian empire, Giorgio Ambrosoli, accepted that the Zitropo/Pacchetti deal had made it possible for Sindona to buy Franklin National. But he made a deposition that "not a single dollar" from Calvi had been used directly in the acquisition of Franklin.

At his trial in 1980 in the United States, Sindona was convicted and.

sentenced to 25 years in prison. What seems to have weighed most heavily with the court was that Sindona had made a false statement to the US Securities and Exchange Commission, saying that he was buying Franklin with his personal resources. This cannot have been true. On the day he made the statement, 24 July 1972, Zitropo still belonged to him, or rather to his holding company Fasco. Therefore Pacchetti still belonged to him.

In early August 1972 Sindona paid Radowal $6,557,377.04. Ambrosoli, in his deposition almost seven years later, said that this had been "probably paid as a commission to an American bishop and a Milanese banker". Who told Ambrosoli this, and what the commission was for, he would doubtless have explained. But as he returned home at midnight from making his deposition, on 11 July 1979, he was confronted by Joseph Aricò, known in New York, where Sindona had hired him, as "the exterminator". Aricò said: "Are you Doctor Ambrosoli?" "Yes," replied Ambrosoli. Aricò said: "Excuse me," and shot him. Ambrosoli died on the way to the hospital, in the first minutes of 12 July 1979.

EIGHT

I Never Did One Bit of Business with Calvi

Even seven years after the murder of Ambrosoli, there were people who dreaded the completion of the investigations that he began. In February 1986 I got a phone call from a man with an Irish accent, who said I would find myself lying on a mortuary slab. I did not connect the call with the Ambrosiano until I learned that crosses and the initials of the Italian liquidators of the Ambrosiano had been cut in the paintwork of their official car a few days before, and that the same had been done to the car of their lawyer the very day of the phone call. Sindona died shortly after these events.

The liquidators continued their task, and so did I. To clear up some of the puzzles Ambrosoli left behind, we have to look again at that strange amount, $6,557,377.04. It was treated in Zitropo's books as a repayment of a loan from "shareholders" – in fact from Radowal. What happened to it later we shall see, but at first Radowal used it to reduce its one direct loan from the Cisalpine. Shortly afterwards that loan was paid off entirely, with the help of a new $25 million loan, made to Radowal by the Cisalpine but disguised, in what had now become the usual way, by the back-to-back arrangement with the IOR. Though Radowal was in fact borrowing more than ever, it had, by August 1972, disappeared from the books of the Cisalpine.

The sale of Zitropo to Calvi (or rather to Cimafin acting for Radowal) took place at the end of August 1972. Calvi paid 1,100 lire for each Pacchetti share, which meant valuing the company at nearly $80 million. Subtracted from this was the amount already paid to Sindona for Pacchetti shares, but added back was the strange $6,557,377.04. With interest, the sum Calvi had to find was more than $44.3 million, to be paid by 23 February 1973.

Calvi was thus agreeing to pay a further $27 million for Pacchetti, over and above the price fixed in July. Moreover Pacchetti was to cost Calvi nearly $14 million more, because its capital was later increased. The loss lay at the core of the Ambrosiano deficit ten years later.

Why should he make such a vast overpayment? Was Sindona, as he afterwards suggested, expected to buy Ambrosiano shares? Or was Sindona already blackmailing Calvi?

We have seen that, when the Cattolica was openly sold to Calvi, a huge block of the shares acquired in the secret sale remained with Radowal. Now Radowal sold 10 per cent of Cattolica, or 3,612,000 shares, at 2,300 lire each, 44 per cent above the price the IOR had been paid. Marcinkus does not seem to have resented that. The IOR took $900,000 of the profits, by its device of converting lire into dollars at 621, against the market rate of about 582. However, Radowal was left with a profit of $3.5 million.

Who bought this 10 per cent of Cattolica? Nobody has ever found out. It may have been the Bonomis. Calvi and Anna Bonomi were at this time so friendly that she took a one third interest in Suprafin (which does not prove that she knew it was part of the secret network). Her companies also bought shares in BA Holding.

Though Calvi had found a home for the bulk of the Cattolica shares, he was still, in September 1972, undecided about the Varesino shares. He had 1.1 million of them in the nominee company Locafid (but held on behalf of Zitropo) and another 2.1 million lodged at the IOR. On 14 September, writing as chairman of the Cisalpine, he suggested to the IOR that it should buy for itself a million shares at 10,000 lire each, while the Cisalpine agreed to buy them back, either at 11,000 lire each in a year's time, or at 12,000 lire each in two years' time. In the event this deal was annulled. But it shows that Calvi led the IOR to believe the Cisalpine was the real owner of the shares the IOR was holding under the forward contract.

If Marcinkus had mentioned the matter to his fellow directors, Calvi's deceptions might have been uncovered. But he said nothing about it at the board meeting on 27 October 1972 at Claridge's Hotel in London. Nor did anyone mention the huge deposits the Cisalpine had made with the IOR. Shutting the stable door after the horse had bolted, the board passed a resolution restricting Calvi's powers. His ability to make unlimited secured loans, or deposits with other banks, was confirmed. But his authority to make unsecured loans without reference to another director was cut back to a limit of $10 million. Only Calvi and Marcinkus knew that the back-to-back arrangements had already made this constraint useless.

By late November 1972 Calvi had decided what to do with the Varesino shares. On 20 November he wrote to the IOR to confirm arrangements that must already have been made orally. The million shares the IOR had, in September, been planning to keep for itself for another year or two had been lumped back with the others in the forward contract. This contract would now be closed before 23 November. On its closure the IOR, which

CISALPINE OVERSEAS BANK LIMITED

> Spett.le
> ISTITUTO PER LE OPERE DI RELIGIONE
> CITTA' del VATICANO

Con riferimento alla nostra lettera del 14 settembre 1972 ,alla Vostra pari data n.578103/4773 ed alle successive intese ci pregiamo confermarVi che l'operazione oggetto delle citate lettere ,relativa a n.1.000.000 azioni Credito Varesino viene ,d'accordo,nuovamente de= terminata quale operazione di Riporto ,valuta 19 giugno 1972 ,scaden= za indicata 31 marzo 1973,conglobandosi con il Riporto di n.1.100.000 azioni dette ,di cui alla Vs/ lettera 14 settembre 1972 n.578102/4773, di modo che il Riporto in parola concerne complessivamente n.2.100.000 (duemilionicentomila) azioni Credito Varesino a Lit.10.000 (diecimila) ciascuna con valuta 19 giugno 1972 ,scadenza indicata 31 marzo 1973, tasso 9% annuo.

Questa Banca intende provvedere alla chiusura della operazione entro il : *23-11-1972-*

In relazione questa Banca verserà a codesto Istituto l'importo di Lit.10.000 per ciascuna delle 2.100.000 azioni e gli interessi al tassp del 9% annuo dal 19 giugno 1972 alla data di estinzione della operazione.

Questa Cisalpine Overseas Bank Ltd corrisponderà altresì a co= desto Istituto l'importo di Lit.700.000.000 (settecentomilioni) in relazione alla chiusura ,come determinata,della operazione in oggetto.

Distinti saluti

20.11/72

was forgoing future profits of at least a billion lire by dropping the September arrangement, would be paid instead 700 million lire. (See letter reproduced above.)

The operation was not in fact completed until 27 November, when all the 2.1 million Varesino shares had been resold – at 14,000 lire each. La Centrale bought 1.6 million; the Bonomi company Subalpina bought the other half million. The proceeds of the sale were 29.4 billion lire, of which 21 billion reverted to the IOR as repayments of its two original loans. From the gross profit of 8.4 billion lire were deducted various duties and costs, totalling about 80.5 million lire. The IOR's interest, at 9 per cent, came to nearly 834 million lire. Then the IOR's special payment of 700 million lire, equivalent to about $1.2 million, was deducted. So there was just under 6.8 billion lire left for Calvi. To this was added a separate profit of just over 200 million lire from the resale on the market of the half million Banca Cattolica shares bought in April. (The stock market was still rising.) So the IOR had just under 7 billion lire to distribute. It was paid out in instalments over the coming weeks to Radowal – in dollars. Again the IOR performed the conversion at its own rate. This time it averaged nearly 50 lire more than the going rate. So the IOR made a further profit on the deal of some $930,000. That still left more than $11 million for Radowal, which used $7 million to repay back-to-back loans.

On the day of the closing the IOR lent 50 billion lire to Italmobiliare, a company owned by Carlo Pesenti. Such was Pesenti's reputation that, when he repaid the loan seven years later, two small shareholders of Italmobiliare tried to prove that the loan had never existed. This was widely believed by people who thought Pesenti was under some sort of pressure to pay the IOR a large lump sum. Why, the small shareholders asked, had the loan never been mentioned in any Italmobiliare balance sheet, until it appeared in the 1979/1980 balance sheet as repaid? Why had Pesenti, notoriously keen on dodging taxes, not claimed exemption from tax for the amount paid in interest, as he was entitled to do? The matter came to court and Pesenti was handicapped by the IOR's usual reluctance to hand over documents. After the case had been dragging on for months, the IOR produced a typewritten document, with a place and date scrawled underneath. "Città del Vaticano 24 novembre 1972." It appeared to be signed by Pesenti and Marcinkus. This was an unauthenticated photocopy. Another court declared the 1979/1980 balance sheet of Italmobiliare invalid on other grounds, and the matter was still undecided when Pesenti died in 1984. The IOR was finally cleared of wrongdoing.

What made people suspicious about the loan was that both interest and capital repayments, though in lire, were linked to the Swiss franc. The more the Swiss franc went up against the lira, the more Pesenti had to repay. So, by November 1979, the amount had quadrupled, to more than 200 billion lire (about $154 million).

One sign that the loan really was made was that Pesenti's company was able to buy the Bastogi shares that Calvi had been hiding since the failed takeover bid. Radowal may not have made much profit on them, but the proceeds enabled it to repay another $10 million of back-to-back loans.

On 30 November 1972 Calvi, writing as chairman of the Cisalpine, asked the IOR for a six-month loan of $43.5 million. The letter (reproduced in Appendix B(i)) implied that the Cisalpine would be the borrower. But it specified that the money was to be paid into an account named *zeta*, or Z, at the Gottardo. The IOR would get 8 per cent, and on top of that a lump sum, described as an *una tantum* commission, of 200 million lire. Security would be 20,000 shares of Zitropo, deposited in an account at the Krediet-bank of Luxembourg. This letter was produced for the joint commission, and would have been reckoned the first of the "parallel" letters, if the Vatican side of the commission had not decided to ignore Zitropo.

Calvi wanted the money to settle with Sindona. When the IOR advanced it, on 4 December, $27.1 million was passed on to Sindona's company, Steelinvest, at his Zürich bank, Amincor. The remaining $16.4 million was paid to Zitropo, which used it to repay the two debts to Sindona still standing in its books: the $9.95 million outstanding from the purchase of the Pacchetti shares and the odd $6,557,377.04.

Did Marcinkus know what the loan was for? In his memorandum to the joint commission, he conveyed the impression that he believed the loan was for the Cisalpine. But the IOR had made many deposits with the Cisalpine, and none of them involved special Z accounts. Besides, if he were doing his duty as a director of the Cisalpine, he would have looked at its books and seen that the money was not there.

And, if he did not know that there was something peculiar about the loan, why did he accept a commission of 200 million lire? The innocent explanation does not stand up.

But the guilty explanation also looks odd. If Marcinkus made the loan knowing all about Zitropo, he was very rash. Zitropo's assets consisted of its investment in Pacchetti. Its books were strangely kept. The $16.4 million that went to Zitropo was not entered on its books as a loan. The bulk of it, $15.4 million, was treated as equity investment, and converted into 3,080,000 new Zitropo shares, which in due course were deposited in the IOR account at the Kredietbank. The $27.1 million paid direct to Sindona did not feature in the books at all; so far as Zitropo was concerned it had simply disappeared.

The IOR's loan had financed the return to Sindona of the $6,557,377.04.

There is a possible explanation for the amount. At the exchange rate used by Calvi and Sindona in the summer of 1972, it works out at exactly 95 lire for each Pacchetti share.

When Sindona was blackmailing Calvi in 1977, he named exactly half that sum, $3,278,688.52, as having been paid to Calvi at an account in the Swiss Credit Bank in Zürich in the name of Ehrenkreuz, as a "premium" on the Pacchetti shares. After Ambrosoli's death, other investigators found that this was true. Sindona had transferred the money from the sums paid into Amincor Bank, first to Finabank and then to the Ehrenkreuz account, which had been set up by Calvi personally.

What about the evidence that the other half went to Marcinkus? The story was first put about by Carlo Bordoni, who in 1972 was still managing director of Sindona's Banca Unione. Four years later he told L'Espresso that Marcinkus and Calvi had been paid $7 million over the Pacchetti/Zitropo deal. But four years after that, in 1980, he told a parliamentary commission on the Sindona affair that the money was split, not between Marcinkus and Calvi, but between Marcinkus and Archbishop Caprio of the Vatican's other financial institution, APSA. Besides being inconsistent, this is the evidence of a self-confessed scoundrel.

Bordoni was the man Sindona hired in the knowledge that he had been sacked from Citibank. Bordoni's own story was that, when he discovered how Sindona was robbing the clients of Banca Unione, he began to rob Sindona. He put $25,223,301 in a bank account in his wife's name in Chiasso. This is the Swiss town nearest Milan; it has figured in more than one scandal. The name means "uproar". Its charm, for the Italians, is that almost every building in the main street is a bank.

Apart from Bordoni's first version, there is no evidence that Marcinkus got the money. Why Ambrosoli believed he did is not known.

That Calvi got his half we know. Self-enrichment was not, at this point, his main aim. From the "Ehrenkreuz" account, $2 million was paid to Radowal. Then $1,250,000 was transferred to account QLZ 6278, the one Calvi had opened jointly with his superior, Mozzana. From there $575,000 was paid out, over a period, to other accounts. Probably some of these were for the personal use of Calvi and Mozzana. The last $675,000 was paid out in the summer of 1973 to Professor Ravello.

We shall meet him again. Professor Fiorenzo (or Florent) Ley-Ravello, a former teacher, had moved to Lausanne, where he set up a company, Alphom, apparently to administer funds smuggled out by rich Italians. Calvi, through Radowal, bought shares in Alphom in late 1973. The money may have been intended for this purpose. Carlo Calvi, however, remembers his father going to see Ravello in Lausanne in connection with the purchase of apartments. After the crash the shares in Alphom were found in Calvi's secret network. They proved unsaleable. The Calvi family could find no trace of the apartments. So that part of the money was lost.

By the end of 1972 Calvi had made, or promised, at least 1.05 billion lire in ethically dubious commissions to the IOR. In addition, the IOR had made $5.2 million out of Calvi in its currency-changing racket. Besides, Calvi paid it above average interest rates. All this may have blinded Marcinkus to the risks he was running.

Besides, there were such advantages as a winter holiday in the Bahamas. The first time the Calvi family indulged in this new luxury, at Christmas 1971, they took a small villa and Marcinkus had to stay in town. But for Christmas 1972 they rented a large villa at the Lyford Cay Club, where they could entertain visitors. First Sindona and his wife joined them. After the Sindonas had gone, Marcinkus arrived for a couple of days.

He was more than vague about this visit, when John Cornwell questioned him in 1988. "People say I knew Calvi. I met him two or three times. I had lunch with him once, I blessed a building of his once, but I never knew him or spent any time with him; I never visited his house or anything. I couldn't have spent more than nine hours with him in my whole life. Maximum!"

At his second interview with Cornwell, Marcinkus made the startling statement: "I never did *one* bit of business with Calvi." (John Cornwell's italics.) "But my office did. Deposits with his bank, made loans to his bank. And maybe we were too trustful . . . Maybe I should have known the man personally . . . I didn't even know where Calvi lived . . . I never sought him out. I met his wife and kids on one or two occasions, I think, in the Bahamas back in 1974. I met her again, went back for a meeting, never saw her again in my life." This is an odd way of saying that he stayed with the Calvi family twice.

The excuse for this first visit was another board meeting of the Cisalpine, held on 5 January 1973 at the bank's office. And a sorry excuse the board meetings had become. As usual, there was no discussion about what was being done with the bank's money. Marcinkus does not seem to have raised the question of the $43.5 million which (he later claimed) he thought the bank had just borrowed from the IOR. There was some vague talk about expanding into South America.

The one matter of importance at that meeting was brought up, not by any of the directors, but by Price Waterhouse, the auditors. They had expressed their concern at Calvi's wide powers, even after the limitations imposed at the previous meeting, and had suggested that his decisions should be countersigned by another director. The directors present – Calvi, Marcinkus, Garzoni and Feldman – unanimously decided that they were satisfied with the existing procedures. Marcinkus remained silent.

Calvi's family says that Calvi and Marcinkus did not discuss business in the house. But they discussed it somewhere, for in January 1973 two more deals highly profitable for the IOR came to completion.

First came the final distribution of the Banca Cattolica shares. Radowal still held 948,000 of these in account 90521 at the IOR. As a result of a rights issue, these grew to 1,264,000 by the end of 1972. On 26 January 1973 they were all sold – to Pacchetti, whose role in Calvi's scheme was to be yet another share-dealing company in Italy.

The proceeds of the sale were just under 2.8 billion lire. From this were deducted various sums. First there was the cost of the new shares in the rights issue: 62 million lire. Then 200 million lire (more than $340,000) were removed. To judge from Calvi's notes, this was the commission he had agreed to pay on the loan to account Z, although it was not due until June. Finally another 50 million lire (more than $85,000) was deducted. Against this Calvi marked: "SS". If that stands for *Santa Sede* – Holy See – this looks like another lump sum commission to the IOR.

The remaining 2.5 billion lire were converted into dollars at a premium over the official rate of some 60 lire per dollar. So the IOR's exchange rate gain was more than $400,000. Its total profits from the conversion of lire for Calvi now added up to nearly $5.6 million in seven months. From special lump-sum commissions, over the same period, it had earned nearly $2 million.

Radowal now also resold its last Credito Varesino shares. It had bought 800,000 of the block "circulating abroad" from Zitropo in December 1972 at 11,700 each. Then it subscribed 416 million lire to a new issue of shares, which doubled Credito Varesino's capital. The Bonomis acquired another 250,000, to bring the total to over 50 per cent. In February 1973 Calvi and the Bonomis signed an agreement to exercise joint control of Varesino. Anna Bonomi later alleged that there had been from the start an oral agreement between them, by which Calvi would at some point pay her part of the huge profit. The Milan magistrates declared that there was no evidence of this. Yet Calvi certainly paid her something, as we shall see.

By disposing of its last Cattolica and Varesino shares, Radowal brought the first phase of its career to an end. No formal, audited accounts were ever kept for Radowal, nor for its successor, United Trading. But Calvi kept his private ones at least from December 1972, the earliest to be found among his papers. They were either roughly typed or handwritten, and I found them hard to identify, since they carried no distinguishing marks except, occasionally, an "R" scribbled in the corner. The entries, too, were not always easy to identify. Calvi used abbreviations, or sometimes a mere initial. But these balance sheets, once deciphered, are crucial to the story of Calvi's fraud. Although they were drawn up at irregular intervals, they provide a more or less continuous account of Calvi's main secret company until the end of 1980 – his last visit to the Bahamas.

Some of the early balance sheets carry Mozzana's signature as well as Calvi's. Mozzana, then, must have approved of what Calvi was doing.

Reproduced opposite is Radowal's balance sheet, drawn up on 29 January 1973. It shows the investment in shares and debentures of Anli – "A" – and in the debentures of BA Holding/Compendium – "C" – and the expected proceeds from the final sales of Banca Cattolica – "BCV" – and Credito Varesino – "CV" – shares, which had not yet reached Radowal's bank account. The Cattolica proceeds have been converted into dollars at 640 lire, though the official rate was 580. Presumably the IOR could charge what rate it liked, and Calvi did not know what it would do.

The figure for the proceeds of the Varesino sale is puzzling. It shows only the original cost of the shares, not what La Centrale paid for them on 5 February – about $14 million. It is possible that the profit on the resale, about $5.5 million, did not go to Radowal, but to some unidentified beneficiary. Could this have been the share Anna Bonomi claims that she was promised? Even without this, Radowal had made profits of more than $25 million from the Cattolica and Varesino operations – reflected in the surplus of assets over liabilities of more than $30 million.

The liabilities consist exclusively of back-to-back loans from the Cisalpine by way of the IOR. The total had been reduced to $69.4 million. Besides repaying the dollar loans in late 1972, Radowal had been able to repay loans totalling 15 million Swiss francs. This was because Anli had reduced its borrowing to the 3 million Swiss francs shown, having raised some outside money in the form of a loan from the Kredietbank. Radowal's Swiss franc loans were about to be further reduced, as a result of a new major financing operation that Calvi had just agreed with the IOR.

On 27 January 1973 Calvi wrote another letter to the IOR, on the headed notepaper of the Cisalpine. This, though similar to the other "parallel" letters, was not produced by the IOR for the joint commission. Nor did Marcinkus mention it in his memorandum. Yet the transaction it described was one of the most important deals between Calvi and the IOR.

The letter (listed in Appendix B) laid out the terms on which the IOR

29 gennaio 1973   US $
—————————

2.788 az. A a $ 1.000   2.788.000
3.000.000 nom.obbl.A.5% 72/82 =   frs.3.000.000   818.553,66
55.000.000 nom.obbl.C 5% 72/82 = frs.55.000.000   15.006.821,28
8.100.000 nom.obbl.C 8 ½% 72/77   8.100.000
1.000.000 nom.obbl.G.SouthWest   500.000

Anticipi

Z 6 7/8% scad. 2 gg.v.   13.442.622,96
  7 1/4% scad. 2 gg.v.   20.000.000
  7 1/4% scad. 2 gg.v.   10.000.000

Crediti
per vendita n' 2.500 az A a 250%   6.250.000
   "   " 1.264.000 az BCV = 2.481.020.975/   3.876.595
   "   " 1.000.000 az CV   10.188.467

Banche

BdG 2 gg. v. tasso 5 ½%   8.000.000
c/c R $ 530.055,10
c/c R frs   frs. 1.689.916,72   459.185
c/c L c/o Generalux rubr.f.o. frs   2.669,47   728

                                                           ————————————
                                                             99.961.028
                                                           ================

Passivita'   US $

IOR cto dep.

    3 1/4% scad. 2gg.v.   frs. 45.000.000   12.278.308
    5%   scad. 2gg.v.   frs 20.000.000   5.457.026
    6 1/4% scad. 20/2/73   frs 50.000.000   13.642.564
    5 3/4% scad. 2 gg.v.   15.000.000
    5%   scad. 2 gg.v.   20.000.000
    5 3/4% scad. 2 gg.v.   3.000.000

                                                           ————————————
                                                             69.377.898
                                     Surplus   30.583.130

                                                             99.961.028
                                                           ================

Cambi applicati : $/frs 3,6650

was to take up debentures to be issued by BA Holding and repayable in five years' time, to a total value of 85 million Swiss francs (about $24 million).

These terms demonstrate how Calvi wooed the IOR, by offering an income it could not have obtained from conventional investments. The IOR was to receive 7.75 per cent interest on the debentures. But BA Holding's records made no mention of such a rate. The debentures were publicly described as "participating" debentures. That is, the rate of interest would be related to the profits of the company, though there was a yearly minimum of 5 per cent. In the event, although BA Holding's profits were continually rigged in ways which will be described, it paid only 5.5 per cent in 1973, 6 per cent in 1974 and 5 per cent for the last three years of the debentures' life. The difference between what BA Holding paid and what the IOR got was secretly made up, first by Radowal and then by its successor United Trading. Out of the IOR's total interest income, over the five years, of more than 30 million Swiss francs, nearly 7 million represented the premium Calvi had offered to induce the IOR to produce the money.

Calvi's letter said that payment of both capital and income on the debentures would be guaranteed by the Cisalpine. Here we leave innocent explanations behind, and have to choose between two guilty explanations. Either Marcinkus believed that the guarantor really was the Cisalpine, in which case, as a director of it, he should have ensured that such a large contingent liability was recorded in its books. Or he knew that the real guarantor was Radowal. In that case he knew more about the secret network than he admitted to the joint commission.

The second explanation is the more likely. The IOR knew that Radowal was involved, since it paid the 85 million Swiss francs not to BA Holding but to Radowal. Radowal passed on only 30 million of this to BA Holding, which used it to buy some convertible notes in an American bank, the Union Commerce Bank of Cleveland, Ohio, which Calvi had his sights on at the time. The other 55 million Swiss francs were treated by Radowal as repayment of the BA Holding debenture it had taken up the previous summer, with the first batch of back-to-back loans. It now repaid a similar amount of those loans, the money being channelled back through the IOR's account at the Gottardo.

But for whose benefit was Calvi running Radowal? For what purpose had its secret surplus been accumulated? There is no evidence that the IOR shared it, though it made a generous income out of commissions, extras on the interest rate and the currency racket.

Indeed, there is not much evidence of personal gain for anyone. We have seen that Calvi and Mozzana paid money *into* Radowal. There is only one example of a payment *out* that was clearly designed for personal enrichment. In February 1974 Radowal paid $450,000 to account AEQ 6546 at the Swiss arm of the Kredietbank – an account in the joint names of Calvi and Mozzana. Calvi appears to have kept $200,000 of this and Mozzana $125,000. The remainder went to Swiss bank accounts, whose holders have never been identified.

If that was all Calvi and Mozzana took for themselves they might, like Warren Hastings, stand astounded at their own moderation. It would seem that the main purpose of Radowal, at least in the early days, was to make dealing profits out of share transactions with official Ambrosiano companies, and then to act as a storehouse for those profits, which could be reinjected into the official companies as and when required. It was mainly the new overseas companies that needed the money. In 1972 Radowal had paid over $3.3 million to Panamanian subsidiaries of BA Holding, which passed much of their money on to their parent in the form of "dividends". Without this, BA Holding would not have been able to declare a profit of more than 800,000 Swiss francs (nearly $220,000) in 1972.

Then, in February 1973, Radowal paid $3,646,000 to the Cisalpine. The payment was disguised as a loss by Radowal on a currency transaction with the Cisalpine. Why did the Cisalpine need this artificial boost? It declared a gross profit of $1.9 million in 1972, and out of this it paid a dividend of $600,000. (The IOR's share of this was $50,000.) But, for the sake of Calvi's prestige, it had to show increased profits for 1973. He arranged yet another injection of artificial profits: Zitropo secretly sold 40 million Pacchetti shares to the Cisalpine for $52.5 million, and bought them back again for the equivalent of more than $58.5 million. It was only thanks to this deal that the Cisalpine could return a profit of $4.9 million in 1973, and pay its 10 per cent dividend. The IOR's share that year was $75,000, because it had subscribed for a further 2,500 A shares.

To finance its loss, Zitropo borrowed another 25 million Swiss francs from Radowal, which in turn borrowed the money through a back-to-back loan by way of the IOR, from the Cisalpine. This manufacture of artificial profits became more frequent after the market crash of 1974. The debts the process created, hidden by the back-to-back arrangement with the IOR, were to form a substantial part of the Ambrosiano deficit.

It should now be clear that Calvi was not a good banker. People who are good at making real money do not have to resort to such crude falsification. And there is evidence that, right from the start, Radowal was used not only to hide artificial profits, but to hide embarrassing real losses. The early

Radowal balance sheets carried a cryptic item shown usually as "GS", but a couple of times as "Great S" and once, in the balance sheet shown on page 97, as "G SouthWest". This was an American corporation, Great Southwest. At the end of the 1960s it was a subsidiary of the ill-fated railway, Penn Central. Great Southwest was a conglomerate with interests in property, mobile homes and amusement parks. Like its parent, it succeeded in raising large loans in Europe just before the Penn Central collapse in 1970. The Ambrosiano, through Ultrafin, was one of about twenty banks which subscribed to a $25 million short-term loan for Great Southwest in May 1970.

The Ambrosiano's $1 million slice of this loan was put into the Lovelok portfolio. But, when most of that portfolio was made over to Cisalpine in April 1971, Great Southwest was in trouble over its repayments. Calvi's solution seems to have been to hide the loan in Radowal. He entered it in his accounts as being worth half the original $1 million. It stayed hidden until 1978, when Great Southwest succeeded in repaying most of it.

Towards the end of Calvi's life, when he was unwittingly talking into Carboni's tape recorder, he said that one of the first investments he made with Marcinkus and the IOR was in silos along the Mississipi.

Radowal had more and more losses to hide as time went on. If there was a company in the secret network designed to make personal fortunes it was Radowal's Luxembourg subsidiary, Anli. Its principal investment was in the Milan share-dealing company Suprafin. But it also had shares in the Gottardo and in BA Holding. In early 1973 Anli's capital was reorganised, and Radowal sold 2,500 Anli shares, almost half its holding, at two and a half times their nominal value. (The expected proceeds are included in the balance sheet on page 97.) The shares went to nominees, who cannot be positively identified. They probably represented Calvi and his closest colleagues. Close colleagues were also allowed to take shares in BA Holding itself; Anli sold off parcels to various groups, including Alphom (the company of Professor Ravello in Lausanne) and Anna Bonomi's Subalpina. The IOR bought 3,000 BA Holding shares on 18 April 1973 for 7.5 million Swiss francs, equivalent to $2.3 million.

At this time the dealings between Calvi and the IOR were secret. It was known that Calvi had bought control of the Banca Cattolica from the IOR – but not that he had done it secretly, over seven months earlier than the public acquisition. It was known that the IOR had common interests with Sindona in the Banca Unione and Finabank. But Sindona had not yet crashed. Nothing was known that brought the IOR into disrepute. Only in 1973 did the revelations begin.

NINE

Answerable Only to the Pope

On 2 March 1973 the *Wall Street Journal* ran an article headed: "Vatican identified as big Vetco investor: adviser to stop dealing in firm's options." The adviser, Irving Eisenberger, had run into trouble with the watchdog of the US stock markets, the Securities and Exchange Commission (SEC). Eisenberger had been trading in the shares of Vetco Offshore Industries, a firm which made equipment for oil and gas companies.

Eisenberger, a former liquor salesman, had become an investment advisor, operating through a Los Angeles broking firm, William O'Neill. He had bought, or acquired options to buy, 27 per cent of Vetco for himself and his clients. US law requires that any group which, acting together, holds over 5 per cent of a company's capital, has to tell the SEC who they are and what they are doing. Eisenberger had not done this. The authorities stopped all trading in Vetco shares. They discovered that one of Eisenberger's principal clients was a Liechtenstein company, Fiduciary Investment Services, which was acting for the IOR.

Fiduciary Investment Services was a Sindona company, operating from his office in Rome. When I saw Sindona he denied that he had provided the IOR's link with Eisenberger. He added, loftily, that he had warned Marcinkus against doing business with small-time advisers.

It turned out that Eisenberger had been dealing wildly in Vetco stock and options for about two years, and had bought and sold some $35 million worth. He agreed that he would cease to act as an investment adviser without the SEC's permission. He and his clients would buy no more Vetco stock, and would dispose of what they had.

The dealings in Vetco had breached more than disclosure requirements. There was another SEC rule, which said that anyone who owned more than 10 per cent of a company was an "insider". Insiders who had speculated in a company's shares were obliged to hand over the profits to that company. Fiduciary Investment Services – that is, the IOR – had to pay more than $300,000 to Vetco. Scarcely had that been settled, when Marcinkus became entangled in an even stranger affair.

In late April 1973 a team of investigators from the US Department of Justice and the Federal Bureau of Investigation arrived in Rome to ask the IOR what it knew about a conspiracy to circulate counterfeit bonds.

In the late 1960s there was an invasion of Europe by American swindlers with Mafia connections. They engaged in every sort of financial crime, including a traffic in stolen and forged securities. One Mafia boss, Vincent Rizzo, was followed to Munich by a New York police sergeant, Joseph Coffey, who enlisted the aid of the German police and the CIA to bug his room. They heard Rizzo's German confederate, Winfried Ense, say: "I learned they had a deal in Rome; this deal would be made with his people in the Vatican . . ."

The plotters apparently planned to order $950 million of forged bonds in America, but the investigations concentrated on an initial batch of $14.5 million which had already been printed and had made their way to Europe. An Italian, Mario Foligni, had deposited $1.5 million of them with the Handelsbank in Zürich in July 1971, naming a Vatican lawyer, Monsignor Mario Fornarsari, as owner of the account. He deposited a further $2.5 million of bonds with the Banco di Roma in Rome in September.

Tests by the banks quickly established that the bonds were forged. Foligni, a Roman businessman, claimed that he had been innocently duped into trying to raise money against the bonds. He had helped to unmask the forgers, he pleaded, by cooperating at once with the authorities.

Foligni alleged that Marcinkus and Sindona had wanted forged bonds for the attempt to take over Bastogi. He also alleged that Marcinkus had secret bank accounts in the Bahamas, set up by Sindona.

On 25 April 1973 the American investigators were received in the Vatican by Archbishop Giovanni Benelli, under-secretary of state. The following day they were allowed to meet Marcinkus. According to the FBI note of the interview, Marcinkus took the allegations seriously. He said that he and Sindona had known each other for years, but that he had had "only very limited financial dealings with him". He described Sindona as a man "well ahead of his time as far as financial matters were concerned". (Sindona had just bought a financial company called Talcott, by diverting $27 million from the depositors of his Italian banks.)

Marcinkus then denied that he had any bank accounts in the Bahamas, though he did mention that the IOR had an interest in a bank there, "a business transaction similar to many others". Marcinkus went on to boast to his fellow-countrymen that he was the first American to rise to such a powerful position in the Vatican. He thought this had caused a certain amount of hard feelings towards him among other people in responsible positions there. He said his operations were "theoretically" directed by a group of cardinals, who met on occasion and acted generally as overseers of the IOR. But, the FBI note recorded: "His position is completely unique." He was "answerable only to the Pope".

Marcinkus, who had met both Fornarsari and Foligni, outlined his dealings with them. Fornarsari had approached him on behalf of an American businessman who wanted to raise lire against his interest in a chain of hotels in the United States. Marcinkus said he turned the deal down. He had been involved in two transactions with Foligni. The first, in 1971, was a proposition on behalf of Foligni's own companies for a $100 million project for the benefit of the Diocese of Rome. Marcinkus said the deal never got beyond the paper stage, because Foligni's companies did not check out. The second, in March 1972, was, according to the FBI note, a proposition that the IOR should finance Carlo Pesenti to the tune of $300 million. Foligni had apparently managed to get a letter from Pesenti about the proposal directly to Paul VI, who had then asked Marcinkus to look into it. Marcinkus was angry with Pesenti and Foligni for going direct to the Pope. But he agreed to meet them. He did not like this deal either, and turned it down. He said that Foligni was spreading rumours against him, because he would have been rewarded with a substantial commission if the deal had gone through.

The American investigators had seen Fornarsari, who told them that he had approached Marcinkus on behalf of Foligni, to see if he would make him a loan against American bonds, but that Marcinkus was not interested. Marcinkus told the investigators that he did not recall discussing bonds with either Fornarsari or Foligni, and that he knew nothing of the deposits at the Handelsbank or the Banco di Roma.

The investigators gave Marcinkus a list of the bonds being forged, and told him that if he found any at the IOR he could contact the US legal attaché in Rome so that their authenticity could be checked.

In America, those in charge of the investigation decided that the IOR angle should not be pursued. On 11 July 1973 a press conference was held to announce that sixteen people, including Foligni, had been charged with conspiring to try to cash the $14.5 million of counterfeit bonds, plus another $3.4 million of stolen ones. The IOR was not mentioned. But the following day the *Wall Street Journal* carried, in some editions, this addition to the story: "Sources close to the investigation in Europe said a man of the cloth within the Vatican was suspected."

The source was the police sergeant, Joseph Coffey, who did not agree with his superiors' decision. His story was turned into a book, *The Vatican*

Connection, by Richard Hammer, published in 1982. It concludes that the Vatican was involved in the conspiracy and that Coffey's investigation was blocked to cover this up. There is little hard evidence for either contention. Hammer suggests that the IOR wanted $950 million of forged bonds as security for loans. But, at the time, the IOR was trying to lend money, not borrow it.

Nevertheless, there are oddities about the behaviour of Marcinkus. He did not, apparently, tell the investigators that, even if he had not lent Pesenti $300 million in March 1972, he had lent him 50 billion lire (about $85 million) in November 1972. Foligni has since claimed that he was involved in that loan.

Nine years after the counterfeiting case – that is, just before the publication of *The Vatican Connection* – the *Wall Street Journal* ran two articles about the suspected role of the Vatican. In the second Marcinkus was quoted as saying that he "had never heard of any of the names" of those involved. Yet he had told the FBI men that he did know Foligni and Fornarsari. Foligni, who cooperated with the American investigators, was never extradited to stand trial in the US. He has always claimed he was duped into trying to cash the securities.

It was discovered only after Marcinkus had been questioned that the forgers were in touch with another cleric in the Vatican, Monsignor Barbieri, later defrocked.

By coincidence, the Cisalpine also found itself at risk as the result of a major fraud. At the next board meeting, which took place in London on 22 May 1973, at Calvi's favourite hotel, Claridge's, Marcinkus asked about the Cisalpine's position with the Bishops Bank. This was not a bank for bishops but a small bank in Nassau, with which the Cisalpine had done business. Marcinkus, alert to the affairs of the Cisalpine when somebody else might be defrauding it, had been keeping in close touch with events. The Bishops Bank was owned by the American insurance company Equity Funding, which had acquired the pasta company Pantanella from the Vatican's other financial institution, APSA. In April news had broken of a huge fraud at the company; executives had been swindling reinsurance companies by fabricating false life policies. Fortunately, the Cisalpine was secured and did not lose.

This appears to have been the main issue discussed. There was, as usual, no mention of the real business between the Cisalpine and the IOR, though the $43.5 million loan to account Z was due for repayment on 4 June. The matter was clearly discussed in private by Calvi and Marcinkus the following week, for on 29 May they reached a new agreement.

In Calvi's safe were two letters dated 29 May 1973, written by himself as chairman of the Cisalpine to the IOR. (See Appendix B(ii)) Marcinkus had dealt with them personally; he had initialled each in the bottom left-hand corner the following day, with the comment: "OK." These letters did not appear in the files of the Cisalpine, and should therefore have been included among the joint commission's "parallel" documents, but were not.

The first letter confirmed that, as agreed, the $43.5 million would be repaid on 4 June with interest of $1,814,312.50 and the *una tantum* commission of 200 million lire – although, as we have seen, this had almost certainly been paid or set aside in January. The second letter outlined a new deal. The IOR would advance $25,350,000 on the undertaking of the Cisalpine to buy back from it in a year's time 1,500,000 shares of Zitropo at $16.90 each. For this arrangement the IOR later used the old-fashioned term "contango". The IOR would be paid interest at 8 per cent, but this time there was no special commission.

At this stage Pacchetti shares were still riding high in the market, and Zitropo was showing a surplus of $37 million on its investment. Calvi reached the $16.90 value for Zitropo shares by adding this surplus to Zitropo's capital of $15.5 million and dividing it by the 3.1 million issued shares. With the exception of ten shares held by Zitropo's directors – nominees who rubber-stamped whatever Calvi did – all these shares were in an IOR account at the Kredietbank in Luxembourg as security for the $43.5 million loan. As the new loan was only against 1.5 million shares, the rest could have been removed. But they stayed where they were. The IOR, in documents filed in the Bahamian litigation in October 1982, wrote: "The party entitled to these shares did not request their withdrawal."

Who was that party? More to the point, who did the IOR think it was? Marcinkus, if pleading innocence, would have to say the Cisalpine. But, as a director of the Cisalpine, he knew that Zitropo shares never appeared in its portfolio.

In Calvi's mind, Zitropo was clearly a subsidiary of Radowal. Yet he dithered when it came to recording the 1.6 million shares in his private Radowal balance sheets. He first put them in at $16 a share, and then left them out altogether. At the end of 1973, when the Pacchetti share price had fallen sharply in the market, he entered them at their nominal value of $5 each – and there they stayed till the bitter end.

What Calvi omitted to do, however, was to enter the $25,350,000 as a liability of Radowal. Since it was neither a true liability of the Cisalpine, nor of Zitropo itself, it was thus brushed aside, if not forgotten. This may be an early example of Calvi fooling himself.

Radowal did repay the $18.15 million balance it owed the IOR – that is the original $43.5 million loan less the new loan. Radowal could do this because it had received money from Zitropo in payment of debts, and Zitropo could pay the debts because it had borrowed $20 million from an outside source, the Kredietbank, on the security of the Pacchetti shares.

In May 1973, with the stock market still booming, Calvi embarked on something even more ambitious than the Cattolica and Varesino operations. He was now trying to take over one of Italy's leading insurance companies, Toro Assicurazioni, based in Turin. Its largest shareholder was the Zanon family, whose fortune had been made in wool. Giuseppe Zanon, chairman of Toro, entered into negotiations with Calvi in late 1972. The family's hold on Toro was vulnerable, and Zanon hoped to maintain control by forming an alliance with the Ambrosiano.

Calvi began to dabble in the shares in March 1973. In May the Cisalpine bought 110,500 Toro shares, paying 14.6 million Swiss francs (equivalent to just over 24,000 lire each). Calvi then began ramping the share price. The Cisalpine resold the shares at the end of the month to Zitropo for 30,000 lire each, giving the Cisalpine a profit of more than 2.5 million Swiss francs. At the same time Zitropo bought another 65,000 Toro shares at an average of just over 28,600 lire each.

This was the wrong time to start a series of stock market manipulations. Early in July a new Italian Government took office. Giulio Andreotti, who had always supported Sindona, ceased to be Prime Minister. His place was taken by another Christian Democrat, Mariano Rumor, who appointed as his Treasury Minister Ugo La Malfa.

La Malfa, the leader of the small Republican Party, was respected by everyone who wanted to bring some law and order into the financial jungle. Throughout the intrigues we have been following, there was another Italy, the Italy which believed that the way to make money was to manufacture things that people would buy. It was this Italy that La Malfa represented. He was determined to reverse the easy money policy which had encouraged the market boom.

La Malfa disliked stock exchange speculators. It was he who first called them *golpisti*, naming Calvi, Sindona and Anna Bonomi. As soon as he took office, there was a sharp fall in share prices, and it was sharpest in the companies connected with *golpisti*. The price of Ambrosiano shares dropped by over a third in a month. Nevertheless Calvi signed an agreement with the Zanon family on 10 July. His subsequent manipulations of the Toro share price were all the more remarkable in view of the slump in the market.

Giuseppe Zanon signed the agreement in Lugano with Ultrafin (acting for Calvi) and the details were kept secret. As the signing of secret agreements in Lugano was an evasion of Italian currency laws, this figured in the 1981 trial of Calvi. Zanon was charged along with Calvi, but did not appear in court, having stayed outside Italy. Even that court did not establish what the agreement said.

Calvi kept a copy in his safe, though. From this it is clear that the Zanon family agreed to sell to Ultrafin, "or other entities of its group", two blocks of Toro shares. One block of 325,000 shares was to be sold for cash, in dollars, at the equivalent of 40,000 lire each. The other block, of 336,042 shares, was to be exchanged for 672,084 La Centrale shares, whose market price at the time was about half that of Toro's. This would still leave the Zanon family with a substantial holding of Toro. The agreement stipulated that a syndicate would be formed between the two parties in late November, in which the Zanon and Ambrosiano stakes would be pooled for control of Toro, although further shares would have to be acquired to reach a majority holding. Similarly the Zanon family would commit their shares in La Centrale to a syndicate, to maintain control over La Centrale.

The agreement also contained what was to be a costly clause for Calvi. If, by the end of 1978, the syndicate had not been renewed, each participant was entitled to sell back his shares in Toro or La Centrale to the other, at *either* the average ruling market price over the last six months of 1978 *or* at 40,000 for each Toro share and 20,000 lire for each La Centrale share, whichever was the higher. That is, Calvi had guaranteed the Zanon family against a fall in share prices.

It was the Cisalpine which acquired the first block of Toro shares, paying the Zanon family more than $21 million. But it was Radowal which fulfilled the second half of the deal. It had considerable liquid assets, because BA Holding had recently doubled its capital to 90 million Swiss francs, and had used its new funds to repay the last of its dollar debentures held by Radowal. This money, supplemented with a further $4 million back-to-back loan, enabled Radowal to buy La Centrale shares from Pacchetti, which had been building up a stake since it came under Calvi's control six months earlier. These shares were now passed on to the Zanon family.

The Bonomis, too, were brought into the deal. They had 550,000 Toro shares, which they now undertook to sell to La Centrale at 47,000 lire each, using the proceeds to buy another 1.5 million La Centrale shares from Pacchetti.

The Cisalpine also bought a further 170,075 Toro shares from other large holders. By the end of August Calvi had accumulated over a million shares, representing nearly 17 per cent of Toro's capital, using the

Cisalpine, Zitropo and Radowal to do so. Then the somewhat overburdened La Centrale was made to buy most of these shares at 43,000 lire each. Zitropo sold all its 175,000 for a profit of about $4 million; Cisalpine sold 295,075 to make over $1.5 million; Radowal sold 29,425 on which it gained about $300,000. With the shares bought from the Bonomis, La Centrale held, at the end of its financial year on 31 October, 1,159,750 shares, over 19 per cent of Toro's capital but nearly 28 per cent of the voting stock.

These arrangements become clearer if we recall that La Centrale was in the public part of Calvi's empire. It had small shareholders of its own, and the 38,000 small shareholders of the Ambrosiano had an indirect financial interest in it. It was the small shareholders (with or without certificates of Catholic baptism) that Calvi was rooking when he made La Centrale buy shares in Cattolica or Varesino or Toro from the secret parts of his empire at inflated prices.

It showed how little he cared for the shareholders that, even before 31 October, he had made La Centrale resell some of its Toro shares, without making a profit on them. They disappeared into various Liechtenstein nominee companies, and, even at Calvi's trial, their destination remained secret. Calvi had decided to keep a secret stake in Toro outside Italy, and these shares were acquired by the third main Luxembourg holding company of his secret network, Manic.

Manic was formed in 1973, with an initial capital of $50,000, which probably came out of the account jointly held by Calvi and Mozzana, QLZ 6278 at the Swiss Kredietbank. Manic, taking its example from Anli, was named after two Kredietbank employees, Marie-Christine van Mechelen, and Nicole Mathie Davos. It is clear that, like Anli and Zitropo, it was intended to come under the umbrella of Radowal. For the first few months of its life it engaged only in minor dealing, but in late October 1973 it undertook to buy 413,150 Toro shares, for nearly $31.2 million.

On 10 October Calvi wrote to the IOR, again in his capacity as chairman of the Cisalpine, asking it to advance $45 million "to the Cisalpine Overseas Bank Limited in favour of Manic SA Holding". Again, no record of this letter went into the Cisalpine's files. So it is one of the "parallel" letters – the earliest one the joint commission included in its list. (See Appendix B(iii)) The letter added that the Kredietbank in Luxembourg would make available shares and debentures of Manic totalling $45 million, which would revert to the Cisalpine when the loan was repaid. The initial period of the advance would be one year, although the letter mentioned that it might be extended for a further six months. The rate of interest would be 10 per cent, and on top there would be an *una tantum* commission of 200 million lire.

The IOR duly came up with the money, paid in instalments in October and November, with the last $2 million not arriving until February 1974. To finance this $45 million loan, the IOR withdrew $36 million of deposits from the Cisalpine. This conversion of short-term deposits into a long-term loan was clearly advantageous to Calvi. In Manic's books the money served to increase the share capital to $5 million in 5,000 shares of $1,000 each, and to finance the issue of $40 million of five-year debentures. The latter were placed in the IOR's account at the Kredietbank in January and February 1974. It is odd that the 5,000 ordinary share certificates were sent to the Gottardo in Lugano, and were not returned to the IOR account until a year later. This may indicate sloppiness on the part of the IOR. If so, it was uncharacteristic; the IOR was as a rule pernickety about the fine print of its deals, however misconceived their substance.

On 29 November 1973 Calvi signed the syndicate agreements about the shares in La Centrale and Toro. The Zanon family had acquired more of La Centrale; their 1,020,084 shares, plus the stake held by BA Holding, gave Calvi just under half the votes. He could, however, count on the Bonomis, with their holdings of 1.5 million shares. Besides, he had accumulated a secret holding of 880,000 shares through Anli.

As for Toro, the Zanon family brought 717,000 shares to the syndicate, while La Centrale had increased its holding again, to 1,479,750 shares, giving the partners a joint holding of over 52 per cent of the voting stock.

The extra 320,000 Toro shares acquired by La Centrale comprised the remaining 306,617 of the block Radowal had originally acquired from the Zanon family, plus 13,383 bought back from Manic. This left Manic still with 399,767 Toro shares, and the Cisalpine still held 200,000, so that Calvi had 14.3 per cent of the voting stock hidden abroad. The Cisalpine sold these shares in early 1974 at well over 50,000 lire a share; Manic bought 155,700 of them for $12.8 million, so that it then held 555,467 shares. This block was repurchased by La Centrale in 1975, in a deal which formed the basis of one of the charges against Calvi and his fellow-directors of La Centrale in 1981. (By that time the directors included Zanon.)

Radowal sold its remaining shares to La Centrale, but not directly. It first passed them at cost to Zitropo, which resold them at about 45,000 lire each to La Centrale, thus making a profit of $2.2 million, to add to the $4 million it had already made out of Toro shares. This particular bit of price rigging was done because Calvi badly needed Zitropo to show profits. The market value of its principal investment, Pacchetti, had now fallen sharply.

Since Calvi had taken Pacchetti from Sindona, it had bought and sold in rapid succession large numbers of shares in La Centrale, Cattolica, Varesino and Toro. It had also acquired, for longer-term investment, shares in two Bonomi companies, a property firm called Beni Immobili Italia and Saffa, a company making chemicals. Its share price was thus particularly vulnerable to La Malfa's discouragement of speculators; it had fallen from 800 lire to 460. At this level, Zitropo's holding was worth $12 million less than its cost. With Zitropo's expenses and financing charges running at some $6 million a year, a large income had quickly to be generated, if it were not to record a huge loss. On top of the artificial Toro profit, Calvi created another $6.5 million on 3 December 1973 by a simple device. He made Zitropo buy Radowal's shares in Anli at $2,500 each, and sell them back the same day for $3,600. Most of the remainder was made up by the arbitrary revaluation of shares Zitropo had acquired in Beni Immobili Italia. It also made a small profit by selling Cattolica shares to Suprafin, which sold them on to Toro.

Thus Zitropo recorded an illusory profit for 1973. As a Luxembourg company, it had to file summary accounts with the authorities there, and comply with regulations governing the size of its capital and its borrowings. When Marcinkus wrote his memorandum for the joint commission, he did not mention ever receiving accounts for Zitropo. If Marcinkus did not make inquiries about the financial health of the company whose shares were acting as security for the IOR's $25,350,000, it would show an extraordinary degree of negligence.

Within a year of Calvi's decision to pay Sindona a huge premium for Pacchetti, it was proving a weak link in his chain of interlocking shareholdings. Yet his main public investments in Italy were sound. Cattolica, Varesino and Toro did well, and continued to do well for several years.

The growth in the profits and dividends of the Cattolica was particularly marked. But the increase in rates charged to its old customers, particularly those connected with the Church, was unpopular locally. This was why the Patriarch of Venice, Albino Luciani, went to Rome to remonstrate with Marcinkus over the change in control. Some reports say that Marcinkus was brusque with him. (Luciani outranked Marcinkus; for historical reasons Venice has a patriarch, but he is equivalent to an archbishop.) However, Luciani's secretary is on record as saying that he was civilly received. But his visit was in vain. Soon, as we shall see, Calvi and Marcinkus came to an agreement in which the Cattolica's funds were used in a most questionable manner.

The IOR still had about 6 per cent of the Cattolica. La Centrale held just over 37.5 per cent at the end of 1973. Other blocks of Cattolica shares were being traded to and fro among Calvi's companies, open and secret.

In two years the Ambrosiano group had become one of the most powerful financial forces in Italy. It could not have achieved this without the backing, largely secret, of the IOR. By the end of 1973 Marcinkus had committed nearly $170 million of the savings of the faithful to Calvi.

The IOR held 125,298 shares in the Banco Ambrosiano, 1.25 per cent of the capital, valued at about $5 million. (The IOR sold a few shares as the market fell in the second half of 1973.)

It owned 7,500 shares in the Cisalpine, having just subscribed to an increase in its capital. These brought 25.6 per cent of the votes, and had cost $875,000.

It held 4,300 shares in BA Holding, at a net cost of $2.3 million.

It had taken up BA Holding debentures worth 85 million Swiss francs (about $26.15 million).

It had an outstanding loan of $25,350,000 against shares in Zitropo.

It had committed $45 million to Manic by way of a loan secured on its shares and debentures.

Finally, at the end of 1973 it had over $63 million on deposit at the Cisalpine.

Little was known of this huge commitment at the time. Calvi would occasionally murmur to those he wanted to impress that he had the Vatican's backing. But even Sindona knew so little about it that, during his blackmail campaign, he urged the authorities to investigate where Calvi got "$200 and more million" to buy shares which did not appear in the group's balance sheets.

At the end of 1973 the money the IOR had with the Cisalpine represented 18 per cent of all Cisalpine deposits (which totalled $350 million). The secret lending to Radowal represented 30 per cent of the Cisalpine's total loans. But, since the money did not appear on the balance sheet as a loan, but as a deposit with the IOR, it was 37 per cent of "deposits with banks". The Cisalpine annual report declared: "We have been able to expand our loan portfolio without compromising our conservative credit standards." (On pages 112 and 113 are two charts showing the structure of the "official" Ambrosiano group on the one hand, and of the secret empire on the other.)

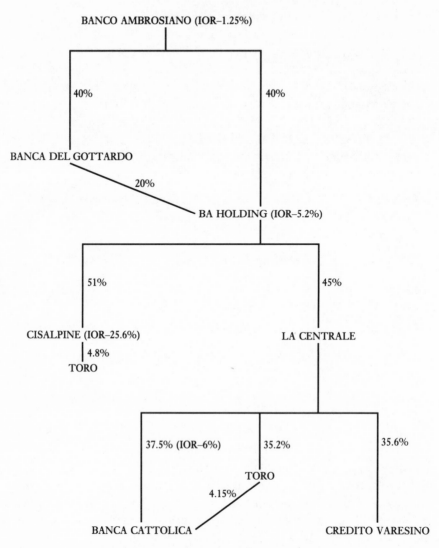

Table 2a: The "Official" Ambrosiano Group, 1973

The Calvis hired another large villa at Lyford Cay that year, this time
one overlooking the ocean. Marcinkus joined them there again; Clara Calvi
remembers him singing, as he arrived: "Arrivederci Roma". He attended
two board meetings on 4 January 1974. At the first, little business of importance was done. But the second meeting decided what the directors should
be paid. Calvi was to get $50,000 for 1973, and the other directors $4,000

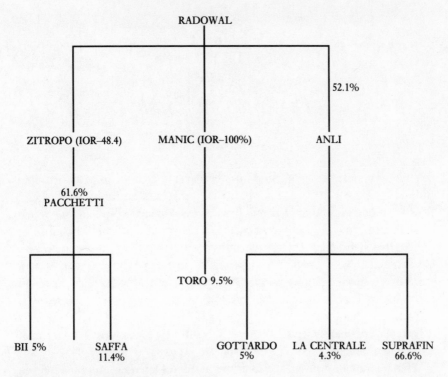

RADOWAL

52.1%

ZITROPO (IOR–48.4) MANIC (IOR–100%) ANLI

61.6%
PACCHETTI

TORO 9.5%

BII 5% SAFFA GOTTARDO LA CENTRALE SUPRAFIN
        11.4%   5%   4.3%   66.6%

Table 2b: The Secret Network, 1973

each. In future they would get $4,000 whether or not they came to board meetings, with an additional $1,000, plus expenses, for each meeting they attended.

It was to be the last Cisalpine board meeting held in the warm Bahamas. The oil price had just quadrupled and markets around the world were beginning to crumble. Calvi's empire survived, thanks to the IOR. Sindona's did not.

TEN

The Sindona Crash

By the summer of 1973 Sindona's apparent success in America had emboldened him to return to Italy. He still had his two banks there, Banca Unione and Banca Privata, besides his property company, Generale Immobiliare. Now he pulled off a remarkable coup, by gaining control of Edilcentro-Sviluppo, a company with property and industrial holdings. He merged it with Generale Immobiliare to form a huge and powerful group. As a parliamentary commission was later to put it, he seemed on the point of important financial initiatives, and capable of constructing a powerful magnet for attracting private capital into Italy.

In reality his banks were already insolvent. His plans were not so much great new financial initiatives as desperate attempts to survive.

What Sindona proposed was that the merged Generale Immobiliare and Edilcentro-Sviluppo should be taken over by a shell company, Finambro, which had been formed the previous year by a former furniture dealer, with a capital of a million lire. Little Finambro would have its capital increased to 160 billion lire, and the new shares would be sold off.

The last stage of the capital increase was approved by the company on 3 August 1973. The same day, Sindona went to see Guido Carli, then Governor of the Bank of Italy, whose permission was required for the capital increase. Carli and his deputy, Paolo Baffi, wanted to know who would subscribe for the shares. Sindona said that they would mostly be taken up by non-residents, bringing a huge inflow of money to Italy. The shares would not be sold on the stock exchange.

The Bank of Italy referred the matter to La Malfa, who had already said that, as part of his measures to tackle inflation, he would not allow increases in the capital of financial companies. Sindona began a campaign to bring political pressure on him. As La Malfa himself wrote afterwards, "half Italy" wanted the operation to go ahead. But La Malfa did not consult half Italy. He consulted Enrico Cuccia, the man who had been tricked by Sindona into deceiving his client.

If Sindona had been allowed to deceive a host of new shareholders, he could have kept his balloons dancing unsupported in the air a little longer.

But La Malfa, acting on Cuccia's advice, was determined not to let Sindona loose on the savings of the public. The Inter-Ministerial Committee for Credit and Savings, which had to take the decision, was full of Christian Democrat supporters of Sindona. Knowing this, La Malfa simply refrained from calling it together.

While Sindona was negotiating to buy the Franklin National Bank, ABC Television in the United States broadcast a programme called "Hot Dollars". In this Jack Begon, an American journalist working in Rome, accused Sindona of recycling Mafia money, and gave details of a Mafia meeting in Palermo in 1957. But there was then no independent confirmation of the story, and the US authorities allowed Sindona to buy Franklin National.

On 22 July 1973 Jack Begon was kidnapped in Rome. The Mafia held him for four weeks, trying to find out the source of his information. The Rome police asserted that Begon had engineered his own disappearance, in order to steal the petty cash in the office safe. When he was released in the streets of Rome by the kidnappers, the police arrested him for wasting their time with such an absurd story.

In September 1973 Andreotti made a speech in New York, hailing Sindona as the saviour of the lira. (In fact the lira had remained strong in spite of, not because of, his speculations.) In October the Bank of Italy allowed Sindona to go ahead with his plan to merge the Banca Privata and the Banca Unione into a single new bank, though this plan, like the Finambro one, required a large increase in capital.

Under the terms of the issue, the capital of the Banca Unione was to be increased six times, from 2.52 billion lire to 15.12 billion. BA Holding no longer had an interest in the Banca Unione, having sold its holding a couple of years before. (The shares had been held in the name of a Liechtenstein company, Inparfin.) The IOR still held about 16 per cent of Unione, and could have subscribed for nearly 1.6 million of the new shares. But it appears to have taken up only about a quarter of them, selling the rights to the remainder, for after the issue its shareholding had fallen to 5 or 6 per cent. (Ambrosoli later said 6 per cent; the IOR itself said 5 per cent.) The price at which the IOR sold its rights is not known, but if it was only at the nominal value of the shares – 1,250 lire – it probably received enough to cover, not just the cost of the new shares it did buy, but of the whole remaining investment. This, at the still vastly inflated market quotation of some 30,000 lire, was worth well over 20 billion, or about $33 million.

This refusal to take up all the shares issued by his friend Sindona showed

Marcinkus acting as a shrewd and alert operator, even if he did it only because this was a good moment to cut down on equity investments.

That October, even as Sindona got his permission to raise new capital for the Banca Unione, the Franklin National Bank in New York came close to not paying its third quarter dividend. A $2 million profit on foreign exchange dealing saved the day. This profit never existed. Franklin National bought currencies from Sindona's bank in Switzerland, Amincor, and sold them back at $2 million profit, the rates of exchange being rigged in both directions.

In December 1973 a Rome court exonerated Jack Begon, accepting that he really had been kidnapped. This raised suspicions against Sindona. Why would anyone bother to kidnap a reporter, unless what he reported was true?

Yet Sindona continued to be taken at his own valuation. In January 1974, at a lunch in the Grand Hotel, Rome, the American ambassador, John Volpe, presented Sindona with a trophy as "Man of the Year, 1973". Those present would have done better to honour the memory of a policeman, Angelo Sorino, who had just been shot dead in the street in Palermo because the Mafia thought he was the source for Jack Begon's story.

In February 1974 La Malfa was forced to resign from the government. His austere economic policies had made him unpopular. The new Treasury Minister was a Christian Democrat, Emilio Colombo. Sindona thought he would now get permission for the Finambro deal.

But it was too late. In the first few months of 1974, Sindona and Carlo Bordoni (still his right-hand man) had been speculating on currency movements on a vast scale. Their speculations always proved to be in the wrong direction. When they backed the dollar to rise, it fell. (It should once more be stressed that this is not a story about clever people, good at making money.) By the beginning of March Deutsche Bank was refusing to clear either spot or future contracts for Franklin National. Two of Sindona's New York henchmen flew to Germany to argue with Deutsche Bank. Then they hurried round to other banks, pleading with them not to follow Deutsche Bank's lead.

On 3 April the American bank Manufacturers Hanover lent Franklin National $30 million, to tide it over what were then presented as temporary difficulties. So the facade of the Sindona empire was still outwardly intact in April 1974, when he arranged a capital increase for the other bank he controlled with the IOR as a minority shareholder, the Finabank of Geneva.

This was a relatively modest capital increase, the capital being doubled from 20 to 40 million Swiss francs (about $13.5 million). The IOR owned just over 29 per cent of the capital, and it could have subscribed for 11,666 new shares. In fact it took up only half that number, selling the rights on the other half to cover the cost of the new shares. It was thus left with 22 per cent of the increased capital.

Calvi chose this moment to dispose of the 7,200 Finabank shares – 18 per cent of the capital – that he had bought three years before. This ought to have been a wise move. But unfortunately he did it in such a way that he found himself lending Sindona the money to buy them back.

The Finabank shares had been on a three-year voyage around both Calvi's empires, the official one and the secret one. BA Holding bought them in May 1971. It sold them in December 1971 to the Cisalpine, which sold them in March 1972 to Centralfin. In December 1973 Centralfin sold them to Manic; on 19 April 1974 Manic sold them to Zitropo, which disposed of them the same day. On each resale a profit was recorded; the total gain came to 9.5 million Swiss francs ($8.3 million).

The final buyer was part of Sindona's empire, Edilcayman, a subsidiary of Edilcentro-Sviluppo, but registered in the Cayman Islands. Calvi caused the Cisalpine to lend 25 million Swiss francs to Edilcayman, not only to buy the shares but to subscribe to the new issue. He also secretly lent a further $2.2 million through Radowal, to enable Edilcayman to buy the rights to the new issue which the IOR, and some other shareholders, did not want. The following year Calvi wrote that loan down to zero, and the money was never recovered.

Sindona had been playing with another scheme. He wanted Franklin National to buy his 1.5 million shares in Talcott, the financial company he had bought the previous year. His proposition was that Franklin National should pay him the $27 million the shares had cost him (or cost his Italian depositors, if the truth were known) plus another $3 million for his expenses. The Federal Reserve Bank, America's central bank, if it had been doing its job, would never have allowed Sindona to buy Franklin National. Now, at last, it interfered. It pointed out that Sindona was proposing to charge his own bank $30 million for shares whose current market value was $7.6 million. On 1 May 1974 the Fed publicly announced that it had forbidden the plan.

Events moved rapidly. On 3 May the National Westminster Bank refused to clear foreign exchange contracts for the Franklin National, whose large depositors then began to pull out. On 10 May the Franklin National announced that it was not paying its quarterly dividend. On 11 May the SEC suspended trading in the bank's shares.

And yet Sindona staggered on through the summer, persuading people who should have known better that his difficulties were temporary. The day after the SEC suspended trading, Manufacturers Hanover offered him a merger. Sindona refused. He would raise $50 million in fresh capital from his shareholders, he said. He was given permission to do this on the same day, when he met representatives of the Fed and of the SEC, besides his constant friend, James E. Smith, Comptroller of the Currency. All these people agreed that, though Franklin National had lost $40 million, the loss had been sustained entirely in the current year. After the meeting James E. Smith announced that Franklin National was solvent.

But in Italy, on 14 May, the newspapers reported Franklin National's foreign exchange losses, and added that Edilcentro-Sviluppo had been taking part in fraudulent currency deals with Franklin National, both ends of the transaction being controlled by Bordoni. Depositors began to pull out of Sindona's Italian banks. Shares on the Milan stock exchange (which had risen when La Malfa resigned) fell faster than ever.

What now loomed ahead for Calvi was 4 June 1974, when the IOR's $25,350,000 loan was due to be repaid. This was the loan made against 1.5 million shares of Zitropo. The shares of Zitropo's principal investment, Pacchetti, were falling as fast as any. Yet Calvi continued to record them at cost *in his private accounts*. This is another sign that he had begun to fool himself.

On 29 May he wrote to the IOR asking for a renewal of the loan, but for a reduced amount, $20 million (see Appendix B). It was to be repaid on 5 April 1975, and the rate of interest would be 10 per cent. If the loan were renewed again, for a further six months, the IOR would receive another *una tantum* commission of 200 million lire.

The letter was obviously a formality. Marcinkus must already have agreed. Calvi had to find $5.35 million for his part-repayment, and $2.15 million interest to pay to the IOR. The money came from Radowal, although he had never entered the original loan in Radowal's books. He used Radowal's cash reserves, plus another back-to-back loan of $4.5 million from the Cisalpine, by way of the IOR.

On 17 June Sindona won a respite for himself in Italy. An old friend of his, Mario Barone, had recently been appointed managing director of the Banco di Roma, and the Banco di Roma now lent him $100 million. But in America the authorities, making a belated inspection of Franklin's books, decided that its deficit was considerably more than Sindona's estimate of $50 million. The bank's own management announced on 20 June that losses amounted to $65 million. Officials from the office of James T. Smith – the man who had said the bank was solvent – now declared that it was not.

On 1 July Bank of Italy inspectors went into Sindona's two Italian banks. On 19 July the Banco di Roma, which had taken charge of the two banks, imposed a *cordon sanitaire* around them. That is, the two banks and their close associates were forbidden to repay deposits between each other, so that whatever resources they had would be available to meet the claims of third parties.

The IOR was included in this freeze, being an associate, but on 23 July Luigi Mennini, managing director of the IOR, succeeded in extracting $5 million of IOR deposits due for repayment. This breach of the rule afterwards caused a furore. The same day, Mennini gave notice that he wanted to withdraw a further $41 million of IOR deposits as they fell due for repayment in the ensuing months.

On 26 July the Bank of Italy inspectors reported that both Sindona's banks had been "emptied" and that $293 million was missing. (Sindona said his enemies had taken it.) The inspectors found that most of the money had gone to Sindona's companies abroad, or had been used for speculation on the stock exchange. It had been secretly extracted from Italy by means of fiduciary deposits; that is, the depositors' money had gone into Swiss bank accounts.

Two Milan magistrates, Guido Viola and Ovilio Urbisci, made further inquiries and reckoned that the amount missing was $386 million. Viola afterwards spoke of Carli's "indecision in applying the law".

Carli still hoped that the Banco di Roma might mount a rescue operation. That was why, even after his inspectors had made their interim report, he allowed the merger of Sindona's two banks to go ahead.

The man who put a stop to the rescue operation was one of Sindona's old associates, Giuseppe Petrilli, then head of IRI (the state-owned body for industrial reconstruction). What Petrilli said went, because IRI owned the Banco di Roma. Petrilli was by no means a man of unblemished reputation. But he had been quicker to see through Sindona than Carli had.

By this time La Malfa was talking about the attempts made to bribe him into supporting Sindona's plans. It was known in financial circles in Milan that Sindona must crash. And the word went round: "Calvi's in this up to his neck."

Calvi stonewalled. If he had not, if he had called the shareholders together, and told them that the Ambrosiano had in fact sustained little direct loss from its dealings with Sindona, he might have averted his own fate. But such openness was not in his nature.

The crash came first in Italy. On 27 September 1974 the Bank of Italy put Sindona's bank into liquidation, and appointed as liquidator a lawyer specialising in company law, Giorgio Ambrosoli. On 8 October the Franklin National crashed, costing the Federal Deposit Insurance Corporation – that is, the American people – $2 billion. It was the biggest banking crash in American history up to that moment. (There have been bigger ones since.) On the same day, Sindona fled from Switzerland, having been warned by his friend Licio Gelli that there was a warrant out for his arrest. He did not stop running until he arrived in Taiwan. Bordoni fled to Venezuela, where he was later arrested.

Who had lost what? For months rumours went round of the losses sustained by the Vatican. Some people confused the IOR with the Vatican's other financial institution, APSA. As we have seen, APSA had not lost, but gained, by Sindona's extravagance. True, he was being extravagant with money belonging to Hambros Bank. But APSA remained so grateful that, when Sindona was on trial in the United States in 1980, two cardinals wanted to be character witnesses for him. They were Cardinal Guerri (who had opened the negotiations for the sale of APSA's embarrassing investments to Sindona) and Cardinal Caprio (who had concluded them).

That the IOR had lost something was known. The weekly magazine *Europeo* put it at $750 million. But Prince Massimo Spada told *L'Espresso* the following February that it was not more than 35 billion lire, or a little over $50 million at the exchange rate ruling at the time of the collapse. Spada's estimate was very roughly made; he took 10 per cent of what was itself a rough estimate of the Vatican's total wealth. The Vatican press office put out a denial.

Marcinkus gave an account of the IOR's relations with Sindona to an American journalist, Paul Horne, for an article published in *The Times* on 4 June 1975. Horne pointed out that the IOR had had interests in both Banca Unione and Finabank. He added: "Bishop Marcinkus noted that these holdings were acquired before he was at the Institute, and predated Signor Sindona's takeover of both banks."

Briefed by Marcinkus, Horne put the cost of the original Banca Unione stake at a modest £105,000. This would appear to have been based on the nominal value of the IOR's 16 per cent holding. Horne continued: "When Marcinkus arrived, he reduced the equity to only 5 per cent which represents the Institute's potential loss. Basically a loss of paper profit, the equity might have been worth £4 million – £6.2 million when the bank stock was at its peak."

This conveys a misleading picture. As we have seen, it was in late 1973, nearly five years after Marcinkus joined the IOR, that the IOR "reduced" its holding – by taking up only a quarter of its entitlement to new shares.

True, its loss was only a paper one, since the amount it realised by the sale of its rights almost certainly covered the whole cost of its subsequent holding.

Horne wrote that Marcinkus had also "reduced" the IOR's holding in Finabank from 30 to 22 per cent. "Again the loss would be the value of the equity in the small bank."

This "reduction", actually from just over 29 per cent, was made at the last minute, when the IOR took up only half its rights in the new issue. In this case the rights sold would not have covered the cost of the original investment, which was probably about 6 million Swiss francs ($2 million).

As for the IOR's deposits with these banks, Horne pointed out that the Italian Government had guaranteed those in Italy. Marcinkus was expecting the deposits in Finabank to be covered by the Swiss.

And foreign exchange losses? Marcinkus, Horne wrote, "insists that not only was the institute not a net loser in foreign exchange, but also that it did not speculate in currencies".

But the Pesenti loan was a very successful speculation on the weakening of the lira. So was the loan of 85 million Swiss francs to BA Holding.

Marcinkus, who told the FBI investigators in 1973 that he had "only very limited financial dealings" with Sindona, was reported by Horne in 1975 as saying that he had had "no business dealings with Sindona".

It was true that the Italian Government had guaranteed Sindona's depositors against loss, but there was a certain embarrassment over $17 million which the IOR claimed, but which Ambrosoli did not feel certain belonged to it. The ownership had been remarkably well disguised, and it was believed that this was done so that Bordoni could use it for currency speculation. Certainly Bordoni said so. Bordoni also said that the IOR was not only an eager, but an insatiably greedy currency speculator. Bordoni's remarks, here as elsewhere, must be treated with reserve. The IOR did get its mysterious $17 million back, three years after the crash.

So the IOR's losses in the Sindona crash were modest. And one rumour which became current then certainly had no foundation. It was thought that Marcinkus turned to Calvi as a partner only after Sindona crashed, in order to recoup huge losses. But we have seen that there had been three years of close and profitable dealing between Marcinkus and Calvi. This now continued.

A Cisalpine board meeting took place in New York on 25 September 1974 – two days before Sindona's bank crashed in Milan, but several days after the crash was seen to be inevitable. It was reported that the Cisalpine had only a small deposit with that bank. Besides the 25 million Swiss francs the Cisalpine had lent to Edilcayman, it had lent some $4 million to Edilcayman's parent, the combined property group that Sindona had formed out of Edilcentro and Generale Immobiliare.

This began an argument that went on for years. The property group did not go into liquidation with Sindona's banks, but was taken over by the Banco di Roma, whose $100 million loan had been secured on its shares. A consortium of property companies was organised to run it, so that the creditors did not suffer. But the Cisalpine loan to Edilcayman had been made so that Edilcayman could buy the Finabank shares from Calvi. The new managers of the property group disputed the validity of this loan, and stopped paying interest on it. Calvi, to take the disputed loan off the books of the Cisalpine, got a company from the secret network, Starfield, to take it over. In 1979 the property group settled the loan by transferring to Starfield a residential building in Montreal, Port Royal Apartments. By the time of Calvi's own crash, the sale of individual apartments had recouped some of the loan and accumulated interest. Directly, the Sindona crash contributed only about $10 million to the Ambrosiano deficit.

Indirectly, the effect was long-lasting and serious. Because Calvi was known to have joined Sindona in speculative dealing on the stock exchange, Ambrosiano shares fell. In the ten days before Sindona crashed the shareholders took fright en masse. The price, which had been 31,000 lire each in the spring, fell to 18,500. Calvi thereupon embarked on a desperate and illegal support operation, with the help of the IOR.

The Milan dealing company Suprafin was not known to belong to Calvi's secret network. It began buying Ambrosiano shares, and kept on buying until it had spent 15 billion lire.

To begin with, Suprafin drew on its account at the Ambrosiano. But this was just a temporary measure. It was never authorised to overdraw large sums. If the Ambrosiano had closed its 1974 accounts with a 15 billion lire overdraft for Suprafin, it would have been obvious even to the least attentive auditor that the bank was buying its own shares with its own money.

In fact Suprafin was buying the shares for Radowal, which bought large blocks from it, and Radowal was able to do this because of back-to-back loans from the Cisalpine, arranged through the IOR.

Suprafin sold the first block to Radowal in July: 50,000 shares for $1.84 million – about 23,000 lire each – financed by a $2 million increase in the back-to-back loans. They were not registered as belonging to Radowal, but to a Gottardo nominee company, Etablissement pour les Participations Internationales (EPI). In September Suprafin sold another 120,000 shares to Radowal at about 19,400 lire each, a total of more than $3.5 million.

Again they were registered as belonging to EPI. In October Suprafin passed on 170,000 shares it had acquired in Milan at 19,500 lire each, or a total of nearly $5 million; these were registered in the name of a Liechtenstein nominee company, Ulricor. The following month a block of 175,000 were registered in yet another name: Rekofinanz. They had cost 19,800 lire each in Milan, so the price was recovering slightly. They totalled more than $5.2 million.

More than 6 per cent of the Ambrosiano's capital – over 600,000 shares – was already held outside Italy, by shareholders who hid their identity in the Gottardo nominee company Locafid. Many of these holders also wanted to sell, and in the autumn of 1974 Radowal bought 88,930 of these shares for over $2.6 million.

So, by mid-November, Radowal owned 604,930 Ambrosiano shares, which had cost it $18.3 million, financed entirely by back-to-back loans.

This was the origin of the 10.65 per cent of the Ambrosiano which, by the time of the crash, Calvi had accumulated outside Italy. It looked then as if he had been trying to become the bank's owner, instead of merely its best-paid employee. No doubt he would have liked to be its owner, but it was not his original motive for the frantic buying of 1974. That slackened when the Ambrosiano share price began to improve, and the worst effects of Sindona seemed to be over.

ELEVEN

A Back-dated Contract?

Calvi still had the company Sindona had lumbered him with, Pacchetti. A special audit of Pacchetti's books revealed that the accounts from 1969 to 1973 (for most of which time it was under Sindona's control) had concealed a deficit of over 4.2 billion lire. The share price fell 72 per cent, to 160 lire. Zitropo owned 67 per cent of Pacchetti's capital, and at this level the investment was worth little more than $20 million, rather than nearly $64 million, as Calvi had it in his Zitropo balance sheets. Zitropo had outstanding debts of $40 million: $20 million of debentures (of which Radowal held $13 million and Manic $7 million) a $5 million short-term loan from Radowal, and $15 million borrowed from Kredietbank. Therefore Zitropo was bankrupt. But Calvi could not let it be bankrupt; that would have threatened the whole group.

A secret injection of money was arranged – so secret that Calvi did not even put it through Radowal. It was done directly by the IOR. The Cisalpine made a $12 million deposit with the IOR, which then passed the money on, through accounts at Chase Manhattan in New York and the Banco di Santo Spirito in Rome, to Zitropo. Zitropo then paid $6.4 million to Pacchetti in Italy to plug the hole in its accounts, and used most of the rest of the money to reduce its loan from the Kredietbank. In Zitropo's books the debt was later, in March 1975, converted into equity capital by the issue of 2.4 million new shares, which were deposited in the IOR's account at the Kredietbank, along with the rest of the Zitropo shares. But that still left a $12 million liability to the Cisalpine, concealed, along with the back-to-back loans, as deposits with the Vatican bank.

At the end of November 1974 Calvi removed Radowal from the apex of his secret trading network and replaced it with United Trading Corporation, registered in Panama. Probably this was done because Sindona knew the name Radowal. Until December 1974, when Sindona turned up in America to contest the charges against him, nobody knew where he was, or what he might say. Calvi put Radowal into liquidation, along with other companies that Sindona might know – Cimafin, Lovelok, Vertlac, Tufnell and Fabiar.

United Trading had been formed in February 1974 by the Panamanian consul in Zürich, Dr Arthur Wiederkehr, who was promoting the attractions of Panama's corporate secrecy, in competition with Liechtenstein. The Gottardo acquired it from him in November; Garzoni became its president and Bolgiani its vice-president. Calvi went to Lugano to oversee the transfer from Radowal to United Trading. He drew up a schedule of Radowal's assets and liabilities, which (according to Bolgiani) he then took away with him. There is no copy of it in his safe in the Bahamas. But it can be reconstructed.

Radowal's most important assets were the 604,930 Banco Ambrosiano shares, which had cost $18.3 million. Then there were 10,781 Anli shares. Radowal's holding in those had risen because of another increase in Anli's capital in the summer of 1974. Calvi valued this, too, at over $18 million. Radowal's 1.6 million shares in Zitropo, which Calvi consistently, if irrationally, valued at $8 million, were transferred. So were the $13 million of debentures. United Trading also renewed the short-term loans to Zitropo. The $1.5 million of BA Holding debentures, which Radowal still held, were also transferred.

Radowal's other investments included the $1 million of Great Southwest stock and two or three oddities, such as a $30,000 investment in a new advertising agency in Milan, Ufficio Pubblicità. Then there was the $2.2 million loan to Edilcentro to enable it to buy the unwanted rights of the IOR and others to the Finabank issue the previous April. This never was repaid. There was also a loan of $5 million made in September 1974 to Anna Bonomi personally. The loan was supposedly made so that she could repay certain lira debts to the Ambrosiano, incurred on her behalf by her front man Giuseppe Marinoni. But the money was not used to repay these debts. Nor was the loan ever repaid to the UTC, as we shall see.

The total value Calvi would have put on the assets transferred was about $80 million. The liabilities can be more precisely determined. They con-sisted almost entirely of back-to-back loans from the Cisalpine by way of the IOR. The dollar loans now stood at $80.5 million. Counting a loan of 24 million Swiss francs, the total was about $88 million. Thus, even on Calvi's reckoning, Radowal's surplus had gone, to be replaced by a deficit of $8 million. In fact it was more, since Zitropo's shares were not worth anything. Besides, Calvi persistently ignored, in his balance sheet, that he would have to find $20 million to buy the other Zitropo shares back from the IOR. To that he should have added another $12 million, to reflect the new shares Zitropo was about to issue. Then there was the liability to buy back the 5,000 Manic shares, which were in part securing the IOR's $45 million loan. But that problem had been pushed into the future. In October 1974 the IOR had, at Calvi's request, renewed the loan for three years. On 6 November the Manic share certificates were deposited, a year late, in the IOR account at the Kredietbank in Luxembourg.

The schedule of Radowal's assets and liabilities was not the only document Calvi took away with him from Lugano. According to a letter from Bolgiani to the joint commission, Calvi took the single share certificate representing United Trading's capital of 500 bearer shares, issued on 21 November 1974. Moreover he took a standard management form, the one clients used to sign when asking the Gottardo to manage companies on their behalf. It was just like the one dated 16 January 1972, which had been signed on behalf of the IOR by de Bonis and de Strobel, confirming instructions to the Gottardo to continue managing the mysterious company Timaring, after it had changed its name from Intermax.

The contract concerning United Trading is illustrated on pages 127 and 128. Under its terms, the United Trading shares ought to have been left with the Gottardo, but, according to Bolgiani, the certificate was given to Calvi "taking into consideration the particular relationships existing", so that he could forward it to the "principals". But Calvi hung on to both the share certificate and the contract for three years. He probably kept them in a safe at Ultrafin in Zürich, where he had another hoard of papers. After that, de Bonis and de Strobel signed it for the IOR. The joint commission had before it two versions of that event. The memorandum from Marcinkus implied that the form the IOR signed was undated, and was then backdated to 21 November 1974 by the Gottardo – an abuse of the IOR's trust. But Bolgiani's account implied that he and Garzoni had already signed and dated the contract when Calvi took it, and that the IOR, whenever it signed the form, knew it had been operative since that date.

According to Marcinkus, it was not until 26 July 1977 that the IOR was asked to hold the capital of United Trading in its name "on a fiduciary basis". The IOR produced the letter in which Calvi made this request. (See Appendix B(v)) It is probably the most significant of the "parallel" letters. Like the others, it is not addressed to anyone in particular at the IOR, and it is signed off even more impersonally than the others, with Calvi's abbreviated signature scrawled under "Banco Ambrosiano spa", along with the date in Calvi's handwriting. It opens by stating clearly that the Ambrosiano is asking the IOR to acquire and hold the 500 shares of United Trading on its behalf. It continues: "It is agreed that the possession of these shares (and they constitute the entire capital of United Trading

CONTRATTO DI GESTIONE

Fra la BANCA DEL GOTTARDO, Via Canova 8, Lugano (in seguito chiamata Banca)

e Il(i) Signor(i)
(in seguito chiamato(i) Mandante(i):

ISTITUTO PER LE OPERE DI RELIGIONE —CITTA' del VATICANO

premesso che:
A) Come da istruzioni ricevute, la Banca ha provveduto alla costituzione della Società

UNITED TRADING CORP. S.A.
Panama

B) Amministratori della Società citata sono i Signori

F.Garzoni , O.Husi , F.Bolgiani

il(i) proprietario(i) dell'atto di cessione rappresentativo i diritti di fondatore della
è(sono) il(i) Signor(i)

ISTITUTO PER LE OPERE DI RELIGIONE —CITTA' del VATICANO

D) Il(i) Mandante(i) si impegna(no) a depositare presso la Banca del Gottardo, Lugano, l'atto di cessione rappresentativo i diritti di fondatore della società suddetta.

Si stipula il seguente CONTRATTO DI GESTIONE:

1) La Banca, e per essa gli Amministratori citati alla lettera B), assumono il mandato di amministrare la Società di cui alla lettera A) e la sua rappresentanza di fronte ai terzi. In tale qualità la Banca funge da intermediaria con le Autorità, gli organi fiscali e i terzi.

2) Salvo il caso di rappresentanza di fronte alle Autorità in generale e quelle fiscali in particolare, gli Amministratori potranno creare obbligazioni e impegni per conto della Società soltanto se muniti di una istruzione scritta da parte del(i) Mandante(i). In casi particolari tali istruzioni potranno essere accettate anche verbalmente.

3) Il(I) Mandante(i) s'impegna(no) a rispondere personalmente sia nei confronti della Banca che degli Amministratori e dei terzi, per gli impegni di qualsivoglia natura che potranno derivare alla società dall'esecuzione di istruzioni sue o dei Mandanti elencati al punto 4.

4) Viene esplicitamente dichiarato che le persone sotto designate possono in modo particolare:
   — effettuare operazioni sia sui conti correnti sia sui depositi titoli ordinari della società
   — dare istruzioni per l'acquisizione di nuove operazioni, e analogamente per la chiusura di operazioni preesistenti.

Nome e Cognome, Indirizzo	Diritto di firma (individuale, collettiva)
come da elenco firme	

5) La Banca dà atto che modifiche al modulo delle firme autorizzate nonché cambiamenti aventi per oggetto la proprietà dell'atto di cessione rappresentativo i diritti di fondatore potranno avvenire unicamente con la firma della persona indicata alla lettera «C» della premessa. Nel caso in cui vi fossero due o più aventi diritto le istruzioni dovranno essere impartite in modo concordante da tutti gli aventi diritto stessi.
Queste istruzioni sono accettate dalla Banca solo se impartite a mezzo lettera raccomandata.
La Banca declina ogni e qualsiasi responsabilità per errori o disguidi dovuti alla mancata osservanza di questo articolo.

6) La Banca riceverà a titolo di compenso per la sua funzione una indennità annuale di Fr.   pagabile anticipatamente. Tale importo è comprensivo delle indennità agli Amministratori e di domicilio. Eventuali spese vive nonché prestazioni professionali, spese di trasferta, ecc. dovranno essere solute a parte, così come i pubblici tributi.

7) Il(I) Mandante(i) dichiara(no) espressamente che non eseguirà(anno) nessuna operazione per conto della Società se non per il tramite della Banca. Questa declina già sin d'ora ogni e qualsiasi responsabilità per le conseguenze, specialmente d'ordine fiscale, che potrebbero derivare dalla mancata osservanza di quanto sopra.

8) Il(I) Mandante(i) si impegna(no) a fornire alla Banca tutta la documentazione, relativa alle operazioni eseguite, che dovesse essere richiesta dalle Autorità fiscali o altre.

9) Il(I) Mandante(i) dichiara(no) di aver preso conoscenza delle condizioni generali della Banca, allegate, e di accettarle in ogni sua parte.

10) Il presente contratto, allestito in due esemplari (uno per ciascuna parte), sottoposto al diritto svizzero, può essere disdetto in ogni tempo da ciascuna delle parti, mediante lettera raccomandata con preavviso di un anno.

11) Le parti riconoscono competente, per ogni contestazione che dovesse sorgere, il Foro di Lugano.

BANCA DEL GOTTARDO

Lugano, 21/11/1974

Il(I) MANDANTE (I)

ISTITUTO PER LE OPERE DI RELIGIONE
Città del Vaticano

Corporation) will be held by the Institute solely as a fiduciary for the account of the Ambrosiano."

Thus the letter makes it plain that United Trading's activities were not carried on for the benefit of the IOR. But it goes on to say that the Ambrosiano would be responsible for any consequences for the IOR that might result from the fact that it appeared to be the owner of United Trading so far as third parties were concerned. It assures the IOR that the company's affairs will be conducted in a proper manner, but absolves the IOR of any responsibility for those affairs and those of its subsidiaries, and promises to indemnify the IOR against any costs it may incur as a result of being the fiduciary owner.

This letter, then, is spelling out that the IOR is to act as a front for the Ambrosiano, but it also recognises that others may be deceived and damaged by this device. It shows that the IOR was fully aware that its secret arrangements with Calvi were questionable and could have serious consequences.

That same day, Calvi wrote a second, shorter letter to the IOR, again on Banco Ambrosiano headed paper, rather than, as usual, on Cisalpine paper (see Appendix B). In this second letter Calvi undertook to indemnify the IOR for all actions and decisions taken in respect of "Intermac" – the correct name was Intermax – which had changed its name to Timaring. It remains unknown what Timaring had been up to.

Both letters were, to judge from their contents, written at the IOR's request. It looks as if Marcinkus had been seeking assurances from Calvi that would apply retrospectively, as well as into the future. Nobody has yet found a letter asking Calvi to indemnify the IOR for anything Radowal did.

As we shall see, there was a great increase in the IOR's activities on behalf of Calvi in the summer of 1977, and this was probably why the IOR asked Calvi to write these two letters. Neither Calvi nor the IOR seems to have regarded the matter of the United Trading share capital as urgent. As Marcinkus put it in his written memorandum to the joint commission, Calvi's letter about it, dated 26 July 1977, "remained without result" until the following February. Then Calvi "asked the IOR to issue fiduciarily a management contract relative to" United Trading. Marcinkus continued: "The Institute agreed to sign the contract form, which, signed as a true copy by the Banca del Gottardo, together with the bearer share certificates for the whole capital of United Trading, carrying the date 21.11.74, were returned to the Institute on 1 and 9 March 1978."

The contract form, Marcinkus went on, carried the same date, 21.11.74. It stated that the Gottardo had constituted United Trading on instructions from the IOR, and that its nominees to the board were authorised to administer and represent the company. Marcinkus then complained that, under the terms of the contract, the directors were not supposed to have taken on loans or other commitments without instructions from the principals. The IOR, he wrote, "never gave any instructions connected with the operations of UTC".

It is understandable that Marcinkus did not appear in person before the joint commission to be questioned about this story. How was Calvi's request made in February 1978? How did the IOR receive the contract form to be signed? No letter of the time from Calvi was produced. Did Calvi, then, come in person to the IOR with the form, and was it then signed at once by de Bonis and de Strobel? And how did these two people – normally sticklers for detail – come to leave the date blank? If the Marcinkus version is correct, the form would then have been handed back to Calvi, who would have had to take it or send it to the Gottardo for the details to be filled in, including the 24.11.74 date. A copy would then have had to be sent back to the IOR. There is no doubt that the IOR received it a second time through the post; it showed the envelope to the joint commission. It was posted on 27 February 1978, but not in Lugano – in Zürich. The envelope containing the share certificate, posted on 7 March 1978, also came from Zürich.

If the Bolgiani version were correct – and he repeated his denial of any backdating to the Milan magistrates in 1987 – then the form required only the IOR signatures to be complete. In that case the IOR could have taken a copy when its two men signed. Calvi would then have taken the original away, to be returned to the Gottardo, and there would have been no need to post a copy back to the IOR.

So Bolgiani's version must be treated with caution. On the other hand the Marcinkus version makes no sense. He did not claim to have remonstrated with Calvi or the Gottardo when the contract, back-dated by more than three years, turned up in its envelope at the IOR, apparently without a covering letter.

Bolgiani had to amplify his version in January 1989, when the two Milan magistrates finally obtained access to the IOR accounts at the Gottardo after a court ruling. He said then that Marcinkus had told him that Calvi had been mandated by the IOR to act on its behalf. In his evidence to the joint commission six years earlier he said that he had met Marcinkus only once, in the company of Calvi, but did not say when, or what they talked about.

It is evident from documents produced by the IOR itself that it knew

United Trading was accumulating debts. The back-to-back operation was transferred without a break from Radowal to United Trading, which, as we have seen, took over the $80.5 million debt and the 24 million Swiss franc loan. In December 1974 a further $17.85 million of dollar loans were put through from the Cisalpine, as well as the 31.2 million new Swiss franc loan which Marcinkus described in his memorandum as initiating the operations with United Trading. (Even there he was inaccurate; the first United Trading loan was $6 million, put through on 23 December 1974.)

It looks as if the IOR was not informed at once of the substitution of United Trading for Radowal. It continued to use the name Radowal on bank instructions until late February 1975. But then it must have been told about United Trading, since it started using the new name, and adjusted its books retrospectively. The IOR produced for the joint commission the statements of accounts it kept for the United Trading back-to-back operation: account 051 6 04436 for the dollars and account 053 6 00617 for the Swiss francs. (The IOR used the prefix 051 for dollars, 053 for Swiss francs and 001 for lire.) These accounts opened with the correct balances transferred from Radowal, and included the new loans put through in December.

Marcinkus and Calvi must have discussed the back-to-back arrangements in February 1975. It was probably when they met for the Cisalpine board meeting held on 12 February 1975 at the Ultrafin offices in Zürich. Naturally the matter was not raised *at* the meeting, which was principally concerned with the Cisalpine's loans to Generale Immobiliare, and with approving another $50,000 for Calvi. This was almost certainly when Calvi introduced Marcinkus to Bolgiani, since Bolgiani had been invited to attend the Cisalpine board meeting.

Calvi now negotiated a change in the terms of the back-to-back arrangement. From the end of January 1975 the IOR's "turn", or profit, went down from a quarter of one percentage point to a sixteenth, or 0.0625 per cent. How did Calvi persuade Marcinkus to agree to this? Perhaps he pointed out how fast the total amounts were growing. In January a further 16 million Swiss francs and $9 million had been lent to United Trading, so that its total borrowing from the Cisalpine had reached nearly $134 million. On top of this, there was the $12 million which the IOR had passed directly to Zitropo. Even at the reduced rate, the IOR's income for entering a few figures into an account ledger was running at over $90,000 a year.

On top of this the IOR had, at the end of October 1974, embarked on yet another back-to-back operation, this time with the money going the other way, *into* the Cisalpine. The funds came from the Gottardo in Lugano, and also from a branch the Gottardo had opened in Nassau. Both placed deposits with the IOR, with instructions to pass them on to the Cisalpine. This was done to get round Swiss regulations. The Cisalpine relied heavily on the Gottardo as a source of funds, but the Swiss imposed limits on the amount that any bank deposited with another, so that no bank should put all its eggs in one basket. The Gottardo could now safely exceed the limit, because the excess appeared in its books as deposits with the IOR.

The *conto deposito* arrangements remained oral for another couple of years. Not until 24 November 1976 were they finally put into writing. What caused the IOR and Calvi to choose that moment to make the agreements more formal remains unknown, but on that day Calvi sent two letters to the IOR. One (see Appendix B(iv)), signed by Calvi as chairman of the Cisalpine, confirmed the basic agreement: that, for every sum deposited in the Cisalpine's account at the IOR, the IOR was to make a corresponding deposit in United Trading's account at the Gottardo, and said that the Cisalpine "approves what has been done in this regard up to now". The IOR's turn of one-sixteenth of a percentage point was restated, and the IOR was given the right to "extinguish" the operations at fifteen days' notice, by debiting the Cisalpine account with the amount. If this had been done, it would have forced the Cisalpine either to find another intermediary or to enter the United Trading loans directly on to its books.

The second letter, also signed by Calvi, but written on Gottardo paper, outlined the same terms for the Gottardo back-to-back arrangement.

Marcinkus mentioned the back-to-back arrangement with the Gottardo in his written memorandum, but gave no reason for it. He did not mention that the IOR also started a back-to-back operation between its own Swiss subsidiary, the Banco di Roma per la Svizzera (Svirobank) and the Cisalpine, though on a smaller scale.

The total of these reverse operations, conducted in dollars, Swiss francs and German marks, had already reached nearly $40 million by the end of January, and rose to about $50 million later in 1975, before falling to about $30 million in 1976. The IOR collected its one-sixteenth on these operations too, so that it was getting a further $25,000 to $30,000 for doing little more than lend its name.

To judge from Calvi's papers, the IOR also started passing deposits to the Cisalpine from the Ambrosiano itself in 1975. His United Trading balance sheets usually had a list of the IOR deposits, identifying those made on behalf of the Gottardo and the Svirobank, and including also an item, mostly stable at $8 million, for "Ba". It has not been possible to reconstruct this operation completely, but it may provide the answer to the mystery of some billions of missing lire, to be considered later (see page 171).

With the exception of this last arrangement, all the IOR's back-to-back operations went through an account at the Gottardo, number 958 360 20. This was divided into three sub-accounts, with the suffix 01 for Swiss francs, 02 for dollars and 03 for German marks. The money destined for United Trading was then transferred to its own account at the Gottardo, before being paid out for whatever purpose Calvi had in mind. Thus the IOR would not have been able to see, from its own bank statements, how the money was being used.

At the end of 1974 the Cisalpine loans to United Trading and Zitropo, appearing in the Cisalpine's books as deposits with the IOR, amounted to 73 per cent of what the published balance sheet called "cash and deposits with independent banks". If the auditors had spotted what was going on, they would have told the Cisalpine that it could survive only by getting United Trading to repay what it had borrowed. And United Trading would have been unable to repay.

What was Calvi doing with the money? Moving it around, so that companies which had to produce balance sheets would look all right the day the auditors came in, even if they were empty the following day. Calvi constantly sought new loans to pay the interest on the existing ones, and to pay the interest due to the IOR, such as the $4.5 million due to it in October 1975. Anli's balance sheet would have shown a huge deficit, because the price of La Centrale shares had fallen, but some shares were parked with United Trading while the year-end accounts were done.

Then United Trading incurred over $15 million of expenditure as a result of dealings between Calvi and his curious associate, Professor Ley-Ravello. Calvi bought back the 8,000 BA Holding shares Ley-Ravello had acquired, and also 100,000 shares in a Spanish bank, Banco Occidental – an investment which proved worthless when Banco Occidental had to be bailed out of bankruptcy in 1981.

But United Trading's largest burden was its holding in the Ambrosiano. Suprafin continued to buy shares in Milan, though not as fast as in the immediate aftermath of the Sindona crash. On 30 December 1974 United Trading bought from it another block of 70,000 shares, this time registered in the name of Sektorinvest. United Trading paid 23,000 lire a share, against a market price of 19,150, the total cost being $2.5 million, financed out of the back-to-backs. Why the inflated price? Because the proceeds enabled Suprafin to close its 1974 accounts with only a small loss, and to eliminate its overdraft at the Ambrosiano. However, Suprafin was left with 99,032 shares at the end of the year, and in January 1975 it was once more dealing in both Ambrosiano and La Centrale shares, going into the red again.

It was illegal for the Ambrosiano to buy its own shares at that time. But the law in Italy, as in other countries, had a grey area. If a bank lent money to a customer, who then bought the bank's shares with it, was this illegal? The usual answer was: not if the loan had been made in the ordinary course of business, and not specifically for the purpose of buying the shares. If, however, the bank had made the loan to a company over which it exercised control or influence, and that company bought its shares, it was a different matter.

So it was important to Calvi to make Suprafin look as if he did not control it. In January 1975 one third of Suprafin's capital was registered in the name of a company known to be associated with Anna Bonomi. Two thirds was in the name of Anli. Of Anli's capital, 54 per cent was owned by United Trading, but the shares were registered in the name of a Kredietbank company, Finimtrust.

This was not quite obfuscation enough. Hence a letter from the IOR to the Ambrosiano, dated 20 January 1975 and signed by de Bonis and de Strobel. "With this letter we refer to the portfolio of shares in existence at 31 December 1974 concerning the company Suprafin spa, Milan, in the pertinence of this Institute, and we ask you please to carry out in the most appropriate manner the management and administration of the portfolio in question, looking after all suitable operations of investment or disinvestment. Would you please inform us periodically of the situation of the portfolio and of the relevant operations." (The letter is reproduced in Appendix D.)

This letter was found by the Bank of Italy inspectors in 1978. By then Suprafin's capital was registered in the names of two Liechtenstein nominee companies, Inparfin and Teclefin, but these were just acting for United Trading, which had bought both the Bonomi and the Anli shareholdings in the spring of 1975, to take full control of Suprafin. The inspectors were told, however, that Inparfin and Teclefin were IOR companies, and the IOR's letter seemed to confirm that. The inspectors were sceptical, and papers in Calvi's safe indicate that in the autumn of 1978 he was seriously worried about possible legal action over Suprafin. But the IOR letter seems to have worked.

That letter is another piece of evidence that the IOR knew of Calvi's secret network, and, furthermore, that it was happy to fulfil its own role in that network, which was to be passed off as owner when officials came snooping.

Marcinkus did mention this letter when he submitted his memorandum to the joint commission. The IOR, he wrote, "was already interested in a certain investment in the bank". It sent the letter about the shares "for the purpose of the management and administration of these shares that was to be carried out by the Banco Ambrosiano". Nothing came of it, he added, "because the shares subsequently left the Suprafin spa portfolio". It is hard to make sense of this. Perhaps it suggests that the IOR was going to buy the shares but that they were sold elsewhere. True, the market in Ambrosiano shares improved briefly in February, and Suprafin was able to sell more than it bought. But the IOR chose the opportunity to dispose of 4,200 Ambrosiano shares that month. Then, in the course of the rest of the year, Suprafin accumulated a large new holding.

The suspicion later arose that the letter had been written specially for the Bank of Italy inspectors, and back-dated three years. But each IOR letter carried a reference number, and the one on this letter, 634792, looks more appropriate to 1975 than to 1978. It may have been written to reassure the Ambrosiano's own auditors.

But it remains an oddity. As a rule it was the IOR which insisted that Calvi should put on record that he absolved it from responsibility. The first such letter was written in May 1975, about Manic.

The events which led up to that one are complex. On 28 March 1975 Garzoni of the Gottardo wrote to Luigi Mennini at the IOR about a forth-coming meeting of Manic shareholders on 22 April. Garzoni wrote that a change in the capital structure of Manic had taken place; $40 million of debentures had been repaid and 40,000 new $1,000 shares issued in their place. The IOR would shortly be receiving documents to formalise this from the Kredietbank in Luxembourg. Garzoni enclosed the documents for the shareholders' meeting: the balance sheet and statement of profit and loss for Manic as at 31 December 1974. He asked Mennini to have them signed and returned "as a sign of agreement and ratification of our actions".

The balance sheet was the minimum required by Luxembourg law, and contained virtually no breakdown of assets and liabilities, which totalled $88.4 million. The IOR was already aware that $45 million of these were represented by the capital and debentures. Marcinkus, as a director of the Cisalpine, would probably also have known that Manic had borrowed $35 million directly from Cisalpine. It had needed the money to buy the

Cisalpine's Toro shares in early 1974, and also to acquire Zitropo's large holding in the property company Beni Immobili Italia.

These investments had naturally suffered in the market crash, but they were valued at cost. Nevertheless, the Manic profit and loss account showed that it had a deficit in 1974 of $5.7 million. The change in the capital structure, of which the IOR was obviously already aware, was designed to reduce this loss, as Manic would no longer have to pay $4 million a year in interest on the debentures. But the change was purely cosmetic. Under Calvi's secret agreement with Marcinkus, the IOR would still receive its 10 per cent on the full $45 million loan, paid in future entirely by United Trading, Manic's true parent. There would thus be no saving to Calvi's secret network.

On 1 April the Kredietbank duly sent the papers about the capital increase to Mennini, asking him to sign and return them. In fact the capital increase had taken place, and the new shares had been issued and registered, as were the original 5,000, in the name of the Kredietbank nominee, Finimtrust. The forms the IOR was asked to sign were not strictly necessary, but would have made it clear that Finimtrust was holding Manic's shares on behalf of the IOR.

Having had no reply by 5 May, the Kredietbank wrote again. But the IOR neither signed documents nor wrote, either to the Gottardo or the Kredietbank. Marcinkus wrote in his memorandum that the IOR had not replied because it thought it had been sent the papers for information only. This could not be true unless Mennini had not bothered to read the covering letters. It is more probable that the IOR had decided not to sign documents so closely associating itself with Manic.

This would account for the letter Calvi wrote on 13 May 1975, as chairman of the Cisalpine (see Appendix B). It asked the IOR to comply with the formalities, but went on to assure it that whatever it did was exclusively for the benefit of the Cisalpine, which "assumed full responsibility, exonerating the Institute from each and every charge and responsibility".

In spite of this, the IOR never did send the papers back to the Kredietbank. It did not make much difference. The new shares were issued, and eventually placed in the IOR's account at the Kredietbank. The Gottardo never got a signed balance sheet from the IOR. It sent Manic balance sheets for 1975 and 1976 to the IOR, but for information only, with no request that they should be signed and returned. After that the IOR received no further Manic balance sheets until May 1981 – a significant date, as we shall see.

On 13 May 1975 Calvi wrote to the IOR about Zitropo. The $20 million loan had been due for repayment on 5 April, but had not been paid. The letter formalised what must have been an oral agreement to extend it to 5 October 1975 at 9 per cent. The IOR had never been asked to sign anything which would have established it as the owner of Zitropo's shares, and Calvi's letter contained no such assurances as he had given in the Manic letter. He owed the IOR a 200 million lire commission – about $314,000 – which United Trading paid on top of interest. Further renewals of the $20 million loan must have been agreed orally; there were no further letters about Zitropo until October 1978.

Clearly this episode does not show any serious disagreement between Marcinkus and Calvi, since on 24 April 1975 the IOR bought 345,000 Ambrosiano shares at 31,000 lire a share, nearly 10,000 lire above the market price. These were the shares previously parked with United Trading, in the names of Ulricor and Rekofinanz. Thus, at a total cost of $16.8 million, it brought its holding up to 4.6 per cent of the bank.

Why? Marcinkus did not mention this in his written memorandum. It might have been another "contango" deal – that is, Calvi might have undertaken to buy the shares back at some fixed price at some future date. But no documents to support this theory have emerged. So it looks like an outright investment by the IOR, though an extremely expensive one.

The IOR paid by removing deposits from the Cisalpine (though it still had $100 million there). United Trading sent much of the money back to the Cisalpine, by repaying $11 million of the back-to-back loans. These had grown to over $93 million by early 1975, largely because United Trading had lent money to Manic so that Manic could start repaying its $35 million direct loan from the Cisalpine. United Trading had also lent nearly $10 million to BA Holding, as BA Holding had to repay a loan from the Kredietbank. BA Holding was badly in need of some income; United Trading paid it a secret "commission" of $5.4 million on the sale of the Ambrosiano shares.

The IOR's purchase had been helpful indeed. But Calvi now needed help of another kind.

TWELVE

The Protection of P2

On 24 January 1975 a sharp note went to the Ambrosiano from the enforcers of the currency laws, the Ufficio Italiano dei Cambi, or UIC. The Cisalpine, said the UIC, was a financial company rather than a correspondent bank. If the Ambrosiano were to continue dealing with it, it must get authorisation.

The stern tone was the result of the Sindona crash. Italian banks had, until then, been fairly free in their dealings with banks abroad. Now it was clear that Sindona's Italian banks had deposited money with his Swiss banks, by the system of fiduciary deposits, and that Sindona had then used the funds for his various other projects. Suspicion naturally fell on those who dealt with their own overseas associates, rather than with independent correspondent banks. The authorities wanted to make sure that other banks were not doing the same as Sindona, and a new directive had been issued, requiring permission to be sought in such circumstances.

The Ambrosiano replied on 29 January, pointing out that the Cisalpine had obtained a Bahamian banking licence on 6 May 1971, was under the supervision of the Bahamian authorities and was developing an ordinary credit business. The Ambrosiano's dealings with it were currency "swap" operations – that is, short-term deposits covered by forward currency sales, so that there was no exchange risk.

Leoni, of the Ambrosiano's foreign department, and a legal adviser, Dr Zoffoli, went to Rome to see two officials of the UIC. Their arguments did not convince the officials, who thought that the continual renewal of the swaps made them, in effect, permanent funding. Theoretically the Ambrosiano could ask for special authorisation from the Ministry of Foreign Trade (known as the Mincomes). But Dr Manciotti, central manager of the UIC, did not think that such an application would be successful.

Zoffoli then broke the news to Calvi, and made a note of their talk, a copy of which Calvi kept. Calvi, wrote Zoffoli, "expressed his keen regret".

No wonder. The UIC's fears were fully justified. It had not been convinced by seeing a 1973 balance sheet of the Cisalpine, even though this was, as usual, grossly misleading. During 1974 the disguised back-to-back loans to United Trading had risen from $48.3 million to more than $132 million. Most of the increase was financed by deposits from Ambrosiano group companies and banks, which rose by nearly $100 million to $162 million. It is not possible to say which deposits were from which banks. A substantial part certainly came from the Gottardo (which, being Swiss, did not have to obey the UIC) but the Ambrosiano, the Cattolica and the Varesino between them probably had nearly $100 million with the Cisalpine. If Calvi had to withdraw all this money the Cisalpine would collapse, because United Trading could not possibly cut its borrowing.

Calvi had a breathing space; the UIC had said that existing contracts would be allowed to run to maturity. During this period the reverse back-to-backs began. As we have seen, the Gottardo, Svirobank and perhaps the Ambrosiano itself were feeding deposits into the Cisalpine by way of the IOR. But Calvi knew that, ultimately, he would have to secure Mincomes permission to go on dealing with the Cisalpine. During the summer of 1975 he sought a new kind of help – the help of people with political influence.

There are conflicting accounts of Calvi's first meeting with Licio Gelli and Umberto Ortolani. Calvi himself, interrogated after his arrest in 1981, said: "If I remember well I knew Ortolani around 1976/77, through Dr Cosentino, then secretary-general of the Chamber of Deputies . . . Ortolani succeeded little by little in gaining my confidence . . . It was he who introduced me to Gelli."

Ortolani, on the other hand, said it was Gelli who introduced him to Calvi. In an interview in *L'Espresso* in December 1983, he said he met Calvi in 1974 at the Intercontinental Hotel in Geneva. "Between me and Calvi a bond of mutual sympathy and trust was quickly established."

Gelli himself originally said that he first met Calvi at a reception in the Grand Hotel in Rome in 1975 – although, when I interviewed him, he insisted it was 1976. He went on saying that, even when I showed him the evidence of his dealings with Calvi in 1975. Certainly Calvi's date of 1976 or 1977 is wrong. It was in the summer of 1975 that the association between Gelli, Ortolani and Calvi blossomed – shortly after Gelli had been made Venerable Master of the P2 lodge.

That P2 was a conspiracy is clear. What it was a conspiracy to do is less clear, even after the monumental work of the P2 Parliamentary Commission. The Commission suggested that Gelli might be the tool of sinister political forces. It put forward the image of a double pyramid, one inverted at the top of the other, with Gelli at the meeting point, answerable upwards to unknown powers, whose orders were passed down through the ranks of P2.

Certainly some of those taking part were hoping to bring fascism back to Italy. But whether Gelli was involved in acts of terrorism to destabilise the democratic state remains to this day unresolved: after he was initially cleared of trying to frustrate the inquiries into the Bologna station bombing on 2 August 1980, in which 85 people died, the appeal court ordered in 1991 that his role should be reexamined.

It looks as if many people joined P2 merely to advance their careers. The general untidiness of the conspiracy became evident in 1977, when one P2 member, Sindona, was blackmailing another P2 member, Calvi, and a third P2 member, Mino Pecorelli, was blackmailing everyone in sight.

To judge by their actions, the overwhelming motive of Gelli and Ortolani – from the time they met Calvi, at least – was greed for money. From the autumn of 1975 to the spring of 1981 they got some $250 million out of Calvi. How they did it I am now going to show, using the details Gelli was trying to cover up, when he obscured the date of his first meeting with Calvi.

Gelli was born in 1919 in Pistoia (where the pistol was invented). His father was a miller. At seventeen, already an enthusiastic fascist, Gelli volunteered to fight for Franco in the Spanish Civil War. When Italy entered the Second World War, he was posted to Albania, and then to Yugoslavia. Back in Italy in July 1943, after Mussolini had been overthrown, he worked with the Germans, as a liaison officer with the SS. (It was that or being deported to Germany, according to his own account.) He helped to round up escaped British prisoners and anti-fascists.

The new Italian Government in Rome signed an armistice with the Allies in September 1943. The Germans still held northern Italy, but Gelli began to hedge his bets. While still wearing German uniform, he provided the Partisans with information, and even joined in an attack on Pistoia prison, to release Partisans and Jews. After the liberation of Pistoia in September 1944 he was publicly branded a collaborator, but managed to secure declarations in his favour from the head of the local National Liberation Committee.

Arrested by the Allied military police in 1945, released; arrested again under a warrant issued by the Pistoia prosecutor's office, provisionally released in March 1946, arrested again for his handling of British prisoners, finally released by the appeal court in Florence in January 1947 . . . So far the story is that of many an Italian who, at the end of the war, tried to fight on both sides at once.

But the story took on a new twist when Gelli, now 26, tried to become a businessman. He set up as a wire manufacturer; then he turned to dealing in books, then razors and typewriters. In 1950 the secret services put a note on their files. Gelli was suspected of being an agent for the Eastern Bloc, and his business trips were considered a cover for spying. The Parliamentary Commission on P2 was later to spend a great deal of time over this. Perhaps Gelli really was spying for the Communists? Or perhaps he was working for the Italian secret services, and they put that suspicion on his file in case they wanted to have something to use against him later? In Italy the word "Machiavellian" is a compliment.

Whatever else he was doing, Gelli was building up his business career. He was taken up by a Christian Democrat deputy, Romo Diecidue, for whom he appears to have worked as a sort of general factotum, learning his way around the political corridors of Rome. Through Diecidue he met Giovanni Profferi, owner of a company called Permaflex, which had developed a new kind of mattress. Profferi took Gelli on as a salesman, and he spent the next few years selling mattresses to the army, convents and other large institutions. He was promoted to be general manager of a new Permaflex factory at Frosinone, between Rome and Naples.

In 1967 Gelli left Permaflex, because Profferi would not make him a full partner, and returned north. In Arezzo he set up a rival business, Dormire, with the backing of two brothers called Lebole, who ran a ready-to-wear suit business. Dormire itself was not a great success, but the association with the Lebole brothers was fruitful. In 1970 Gelli helped them to negotiate the sale of the suit business to ENI, the state oil corporation, which wanted to integrate it with a clothing business it already owned. In gratitude, the Lebole family allowed Gelli to buy from them a villa in Arezzo. He named it Villa Wanda, after his wife.

The Lebole brothers set up a new clothing firm, Giole, and this took over the ailing Dormire. Gelli was appointed managing director of the whole business, but with only a small shareholding. According to his friend Francesco Cosentino, he bought cheap Romanian suits, brought them to Italy, had "Made in Italy" labels sewn on, and resold them for three times the price in America.

As one magistrate's report put it at the time: "Undoubtedly Gelli has put together over the course of a short period a fair personal wealth and a sound financial position. Nevertheless, it would seem that he cannot be considered an 'economic power', not even at local level."

It is possible that, all this time, Gelli had mistaken his vocation. In October 1990 he won a prize in a poetry competition, set by the municipality of Riolo, near Ravenna. He had submitted three poems anonymously. There was uproar on the town council (dominated by Communists) when the name was revealed. One of the judges declared that they were good poems, "even if Beelzebub wrote them".

But, since he had decided to be a businessman, Gelli needed to look like a successful one. He had to keep up, socially, with the new friends he had made when he joined the Freemasons. He applied to join in 1963, and was admitted into a Rome lodge called Romagnosi in 1965. There he came to the attention of Roberto Ascarelli, an associate Grand Master, and head of a secret lodge called Hod. Ascarelli was impressed with Gelli's account of his business. (He was running Permaflex in Frosinone at the time. "An enormous establishment," wrote Ascarelli. "Sales of 3,000 mattresses a day.") Besides, Gelli had contacts in Florence, a stronghold of Free-masonry. Ascarelli recommended Gelli directly to Giordano Gamberini, the Grand Master of the Grand Orient of the Palazzo Giustiniani, the principal lodge of one of the two rival branches of Freemasonry in Italy.

In 1966 Gelli moved to the Propaganda Due (P2) lodge. It could trace its origins back to the nineteenth century, but had dwindled to a handful of members. It seems he was entrusted with special tasks by Gamberini, who wanted to bring the rival grand lodge, based at the Palazzo del Gesù in Rome, under his control. If Italian Freemasonry were unified, it might win recognition from Freemasonry's top body, the Grand Lodge of England.

In 1970 Gamberini was succeeded as Grand Master by Lino Salvini, a professor of medicine from Florence. In June that year Salvini gave Gelli the first written instructions about P2. This document, produced by the P2 Commission, merely asks Gelli to look after the administration of the lodge. What Salvini had in mind is now hard to discover, because after the P2 scandal broke official Freemasonry tried to distance itself from Gelli. Politics is theoretically a forbidden topic at gatherings of respectable Free-masons, and any official backing for political activity would have precluded recognition by the Grand Lodge of England.

In 1970 Salvini set up a P1 lodge, which Gelli was also to run, along with a Florentine businessman, Alessandro Del Bene. We shall meet Del Bene again, but no more was ever heard of P1.

Whatever his instructions, Gelli seems to have made the attraction of joining P2 a political one. Matters to be discussed included the danger that the Communist Party, in alliance with clerical forces, might seize power. Freemasonry had traditionally been anti-clerical in the Catholic countries; that was why the Church declared it mortal sin to join. Gelli strangely combined the traditional enemy – the political power of the Church – with the new enemy, Communism. He denounced "the clerico-communists".

This distinguished him from other neo-fascists. But he was like them in deploring the weakness of the "forces of order", the lack of a governing class and the inability of the government to carry out necessary reforms.

All this was commonplace. For many years after the Second World War, it was by no means clear that Italy was a stable democracy. The referendum which abolished the monarchy, on 2 June 1946, was orderly, and the King went quietly. But right up to the day it happened, monarchists were secretly calling on the "forces of order" to ban the newspapers, prevent public meetings, impose a curfew and set up military tribunals.

The Communists, on their side, kept the secret stores of weapons they had accumulated in the wartime struggles against Mussolini. Sometimes, in private, they would remind each other of this. Civil war was a possibility, and the neo-fascists were still saying so in the 1970s.

Gelli was driving a coach and horses through the rules of Freemasonry, not only by making his lodge a political one, but by running it in a fascist way. The election of leaders is fundamental to Freemasonry, but nobody elected Gelli. The members never met, though select groups of them did, when Gelli chose to call them together.

While this was going on, Salvini and the Grand Orient achieved unification with the rival lodge in 1973. Two senior officials from the Grand Lodge of England, James Stubbs and Jeremy Pemberton, visited Florence and were entertained by Salvini and Del Bene (the man who ran the theoretical P1 lodge).

But already a number of "democratic" Freemasons had become alarmed at Gelli's activities. Formal complaints began to reach the Grand Orient. At first these were dismissed. Gelli intensified his political activities, which culminated in a meeting of senior military figures at the Villa Wanda, to discuss the unstable political situation. News of this meeting leaked out; the Grand Orient began to distance itself from Gelli. In December 1974, at a meeting at the Naples lodge, a resolution was passed to "demolish" P2.

But Gelli was now too influential to be cast off. His lodge included powerful figures in the armed forces and the secret services. And his influence extended to South America. In 1971 he had been introduced to the exiled dictator of Argentina, Juan Peron, in Spain. When Peron returned to Argentina the following year, Gelli went too. He founded a local branch of P2 there. In 1973 he was made honorary consul-general for the Argentine in Florence.

In May 1975 Salvini and Gamberini agreed to the secret reconstitution of P2, and promoted Gelli to *Maestro Venerabile*. But the ties with official Freemasonry were loosened. Although Gelli remained answerable to the Grand Master, he would not belong to any college of venerable masters; and P2 members were relieved of the obligation of performing the masonic rituals.

Probably Salvini and Gamberini told Gelli to cool it, politically; the P2 Commission did not find any documents for this period as inflammatory as those produced before the meeting of the military leaders. And the emphasis on recruitment seems to have switched to industrialists and financiers. With this change of emphasis we come to the role of Ortolani, known to his friends as *Il Baffino* – the little moustache.

In 1975 Ortolani was sixty-two. The P2 Commission did not delve into his early life as it did into Gelli's. Ortolani himself, when he issued a *curriculum vitae* through his lawyer, did not mention his family or his early life. He is said to be the son of the stationmaster at Viterbo, a fine mediaeval city 50 miles north of Rome. There is a story that the stationmaster went to America, and came back rich enough to buy his son a good education.

Nobody has disproved Ortolani's claim that he supported the anti-fascists from 1939 onwards, and was "arrested, tortured and tried by the SS in the Via Tasso prison" in Rome.

Ortolani was a lawyer, and in 1946 he joined the Rome bar. He also qualified as a civil servant, and joined the association of journalists. But what he did for a living was run the Rome office of a Genoa shipping company, Villani & Fassio.

Ortolani seems to have given this job up after a couple of years, to work as a consultant and director of various companies. He acquired a small news agency, Agenzia Italia, which he built up to be one of the leading agencies. The Christian Democrats took a 10 per cent stake in it. He then sold it to ENI, and bought another news agency, Agenzia Stefani, once associated with the fascists. Ortolani was a strong supporter of a Christian Democrat politician, Ferdinando Tambroni, who briefly formed a government in 1960 in partnership with the Movimento Sociale Italiano (MSI) – known to everyone but itself as the neo-fascist party. This government was quickly swept away on a tide of popular demonstrations. The episode seems to have cost Ortolani a great deal of money – all his money, according to Sindona, as quoted by Nick Tosches in his book *Power on Earth* (Arbor House, New York, 1986). That may be an exaggeration. But Sindona knew something about the affairs of Ortolani, who had an account at the Banca Privata. It was always overdrawn, Sindona told me in 1984.

Ortolani had numerous other interests. He was chairman of the "Organizing Committee and World Congress" of the Italian overseas press, and president of the National Institute for the Housing of State Employees. In that capacity, he is said to have had a hand in the building of Rome's Olympic Village. His public work earned him the distinction of *Cavaliere di Gran Croce* – Knight of the Grand Cross. Through his friendship with Cardinal Giovanni Lercaro, he became a member of the Pontifical Household. He was also appointed to the Sovereign and Military Order of the Knights of Malta.

His business interests led him to South America, which he first visited in 1958. His first venture was a plastics business in Brazil. Then he bought a small bank in Montevideo, the Banco Financiero Sud Americano, or Bafisud. Two of his sons, Mario and Piero, moved to Uruguay to run it, as it expanded into Brazil and Argentina. His eldest son, Amedeo, stayed in Italy and ran a Rome-based radio manufacturer, Voxson, owned by the British firm EMI. Ortolani also acquired Italian publications in South America, including the *Corriere degli Italiani*, based in Buenos Aires.

Here we have to introduce Mino Pecorelli, the blackmailer of Rome. He ran a scandal sheet called *OP* (Osservatore Politico) which people paid to be kept out of. One week, when he had nothing special to put in the paper, he seized on the name of a Christian Democrat politician, about whom he knew nothing. After giving the name, he asked simply: "How long does this man expect to get away with it?" The politician rang him up in a panic, begging him to say no more.

In 1973 *OP* carried an article suggesting that Argentina's problems would be solved if certain named Italians were removed, including the Ortolanis. Ortolani was concerned for the safety of his sons. This was how he first came to meet Gelli. Knowing that Gelli had influence in Argentina, he got in touch with him, and the attacks decreased. Such, at least, was the story Ortolani told *L'Espresso* ten years later. But it seems to be a bowdlerised version. It leaves out the fact that Gelli was closely connected with *OP*. He had wanted its editor-in-chief, Nicola Falde, to be the press officer of P2 – a proposal blocked by an influential member, General Siro Rosseti.

After the P2 scandal erupted, Ortolani denied being a member. In November 1981 he said he was a "practising Catholic" and so "never became a Mason". But by 1983 he had to admit to *L'Espresso* that he had joined P2. It had been a "very delicate question" for him, because of his faith, but he had finally given in to pressure from Gelli. He salved his conscience by entrusting to his lawyer a declaration that he had joined the Freemasons under compulsion. To *L'Espresso* he added: "I never attached much importance to P2 as such. For me it was a list of 900 people, some of whom, among other things, did not even know each other. The P2 never existed as a structure and organisation."

According to General Rosseti, who already knew Ortolani, it was about the middle of 1974 that he joined P2. Rosseti said, in an official interrogation, that he was surprised to see Ortolani "descending to the level of Gelli, and certainly he was from a superior class".

Nevertheless, they soon formed a formidable partnership, with Gelli as the salesman and Ortolani as the financial brain.

Nobody has ever clarified the circumstances in which Ortolani's eldest son, Amedeo, the 36-year-old president of Voxson, was kidnapped in June 1975. He was released after eleven days, and it was reported that a billion lire had been paid. If so, it did not come from Voxson, which was in dire straits at the time. Four men were arrested, but not the two suspected of being behind the plot: Jacques Berenguer, a Marseilles gangster, and his partner Albert Bergamelli. It was afterwards said that another man was involved, one we shall meet again. His name was Danilo Abbruciati.

At about this time Ortolani formed another important association. An old acquaintance, Andrea Rizzoli, owner of the Rizzoli publishing group, introduced Ortolani to his son Angelo, the company's managing director, and to their financial manager, Bruno Tassan Din. They asked Ortolani's advice on raising money for the group – a problem which they were to solve, at least for the time being, when they met Calvi.

We have Calvi's own word for it that Ortolani was more important to him than Gelli. When interrogated by the magistrates in July 1981, he said that Ortolani had introduced him to political and financial circles in Rome. "It was he who introduced me to Licio Gelli, and I began a friendship with both of them. To be correct, my relationship was particularly close to Ortolani; he boasted friendships in all circles, even internationally, and in particular with the London masons. I repeatedly had occasion to notice that Ortolani really had friends in high places, even ecclesiastical circles, being an ambassador of the Order of the Knights of Malta. It was Ortolani who gradually made me understand that, in my position, I had particular need of protection and backing on a political, financial and administrative level, which he said that he and Gelli would be able to guarantee me. In time, Ortolani managed to involve himself more and more in my activities as a banker, at times proposing operations and agreements with other financial groups to me. He also persuaded me to finance the Rizzoli group. He, too, led me to understand that I could benefit from financial operations in favour of political parties."

It seems to have been soon after the kidnapping of Amedeo that financial dealings between Calvi and Ortolani began. It is even possible that Calvi paid the ransom. There are signs that certain payments in lire were made to Ortolani in July and early August 1975. But the first payment Calvi made to Ortolani out of United Trading was on 7 August 1975, when $750,000 was transferred to an account in Ortolani's name at the Union Bank of Switzerland in Geneva.

The reason for this payment cannot be established with certainty. Among Gelli's papers, found at Castiglion Fibocchi, there is a handwritten schedule (reproduced on page 148) relating to this period, which meant little to the Italian investigators. It is still highly cryptic, but I have been able to identify certain financial operations, which, as we shall see, throw light on the relationships between Calvi, Gelli and Ortolani. The first payment seems to have something to do with the Toro insurance company.

Calvi cemented the relationship by joining P2. To judge from Gelli's notes, this happened in Geneva on 23 August 1975. Another banker, Alberto Ferrari, managing director of the Banca Nazionale del Lavoro, joined on the same day.

According to Gelli's schedule, there were a couple of smaller transactions in late August and early October, but the next important deal took place in mid-October. It concerned a news agency, Radiocor, in which Sindona had a controlling interest. It had escaped the notice of the liquidator, Ambrosoli. The exact nature of the deal remains unclear, but it seems to have been designed to raise money for Sindona against his 60 per cent stake in Radiocor. Calvi got United Trading to pay out $4.4 million, most of which probably went to Sindona. But Ortolani, who was to become president of Radiocor, received $534,000. Whether Calvi expected to get the money back one day is not known. Perhaps not; he did not enter Radiocor as an asset in his United Trading balance sheets. Certainly none of it ever was recovered.

Thus Ortolani had begun to amass a tidy sum from Calvi. Whether he shared any of these first payments with Gelli is not known. These direct payments were not the only way that Calvi helped the Ortolani family. In September 1975 the Cisalpine bought a 5 per cent stake in Bafisud for $150,000. Also in September 1975, EMI tired of its loss-making investment in Voxson, and decided, in effect, to give the company away. It was acquired by a Liechtenstein company, Electronic General. The Ortolani family must have been behind this, for Amedeo continued as president. Moreover, Calvi came to its rescue, causing the Ambrosiano and other banks in his group to make huge credit lines available to finance a reconstruction plan.

RIPORTO 194.152

22-4-76
O. CATTOLICA N°50/900   45.000
239.152

24-8-76
billions Au.vun 6:   5.000

24-8-76
_____ 50-   20.000
264.152

15-8-75
O. Toro N°40/680   27.000

29-8-75
O. Jasini   10.000

7-10-75
O. Depos. INT. al 18.9-   6.552

10-10-75
O. Radiocor. N°36/7.5   27.000

16-10-75
O. Cisalpina N°50/7   35.000

10-11-75
O. Latina-Yares.nD-50/7   35.000

18-11-75
Rizzo-Visita   10.000

12-12-75
O. Silc-parciale   10.000
160.552

1976
10-1- O. Az.Ambrosia.Rizzo
F. 18.000   12.600

3-2-76-Az.Ambros.Rizzo   21.000

A RIPORTARE 194.152

In order to make the Radiocor payment, United Trading borrowed, on 10 October, a further $5 million from the Cisalpine through the IOR. After the substantial repayments of back-to-back loans made possible in April by the IOR's acquisition of Ambrosiano shares, the total had been edging up again in the summer. This new loan brought the amount outstanding to some $148 million, stretching the Cisalpine's resources to the limit. But by now Calvi almost certainly knew that the crisis caused earlier in the year by interfering officials was over. The Ambrosiano had applied to the Mincomes for permission to extend a credit line of $50 million to the Cisalpine, and on 15 October the Mincomes gave its consent.

On 22 October the Mincomes let it be known that it would look with favour on similar requests from other banks. The Cattolica and the Varesino immediately applied for permission to extend credit lines of $75 million each to the Cisalpine. On 8 November the Mincomes approved the Cattolica and Varesino applications. The ten-month crisis was over.

But the price was high. On 16 and 17 October Calvi made United Trading pay 900,000 Swiss francs (about $327,000) and $3 million to an account at the Union Bank of Switzerland in Geneva in the name of Ortolani's daughter-in-law, Marcella Cicchitti, and on 12 November he had a further $3 million transferred to another account at the same bank, in the name of Ortolani's son Piero.

These payments were the price for the role of Ortolani and Gelli in securing the permissions. The operations are listed in the schedule in Gelli's handwriting. One interpretation of the figures he entered against them is that the commission was 7 per cent, or a total of $7 million.

This is what Calvi meant when he told his interrogators in July 1981: "Many times, I must say, Ortolani pointed out to me the necessity of having proper introductions and contacts with the Bank of Italy, the UIC, and, most importantly, the Mincomes."

THIRTEEN

Their Man at the Ministry

How did Ortolani and Gelli do it? Not by going to the Minister for Foreign Trade. Ministers come and go often in Italy; by the time you got one on your side he might have made way for the next. At this time the minister was Ciriaco de Mita, later leader of the Christian Democrat Party, and, in 1988, Prime Minister in Italy's forty-eighth government since the war. It was his name that went on the authorisations of Mincomes.

But the man who advised the minister whether to grant the authorisations, the man who was there all the time as the ministers came and went, was the civil servant Ruggiero Firrao, director general for currencies. This was the man Gelli had recruited into P2.

Clara Calvi called Gelli and Ortolani the fox and the cat, after the characters who stole the gold pieces from Pinocchio. She has recalled the occasion when she first met them, at a dinner in the Grand Hotel, Rome, probably in late 1975. After the dinner the gathering was joined by three men: Aladino Minciaroni, a director of the Ambrosiano, Francesco Cosentino, the secretary-general of the Chamber of Deputies (who, Clara said, used to advise her husband on political matters) and Ruggiero Firrao.

Cosentino was not advising anyone on political matters much longer. Early in 1976 he had to resign, after it was revealed that the American aeroplane manufacturer Lockheed had a slush fund for bribing politicians. But Firrao went on being important for another five years.

Angelo Rizzoli, when officially interrogated in 1983, said that Ortolani and Gelli had told him Firrao was "their man" at the Mincomes. "Ortolani brought Firrao to my house and told me to turn to him whenever I needed to. I know that Ortolani often went to him for various needs because I overheard many telephone calls, even though I could not repeat what was said because they used esoteric language."

The Ortolani family accounts which received Calvi's $6 million and the 900,000 Swiss francs were just staging posts; the money was immediately paid out again. To whom? Some details emerged in 1987, in the course of litigation brought by the liquidators of BA Holding to recover money from the Calvi family.

The extraordinary thing is that some of the money was paid back to Calvi. In October 1975 Gelli and Calvi opened consecutive bank accounts at the Union Bank of Switzerland in Geneva, 593 607 ZC and 593 608 ZD. Out of the original sums, $1 million was paid to Gelli and $900,000 to Calvi. Besides, each of them got 140,000 Swiss francs. Another $1.9 million and 285,000 Swiss francs were paid to account 591 969 PE at the same bank. The name of the owner of that one was not revealed in the legal documents. The remaining $2.2 million and 335,000 Swiss francs were passed on to various Ortolani accounts, suggesting that he got the lion's share.

The briber does not usually share in the bribe. Calvi could have helped himself when he liked from the secret network he had created. Why did he take money in this way, through Ortolani, rather than by paying it directly to himself?

In late 1975 he was not hard up. His principal source of income was probably the $50,000 a year he was drawing as chairman of the Cisalpine. What he earned from the Ambrosiano itself is not on record, but to the Italian tax authorities he declared an income of 25 million lire in 1973 – about $40,000. After renting villas at Lyford Cay for successive Christmases, he had bought one, North Point, as well as a number of building plots. These would probably have cost him about $500,000. In Italy he had the double apartment in Via Frua, and the country property at Drezzo.

Such assets were not abnormal for the managing director of a substantial bank. What was not generally known was that in 1974 Calvi had acquired property in Canada: a 4,500-acre ranch at the foot of the Rockies, and a large office development, the Rocky Mountain Plaza, in Calgary. Anna Bonomi had introduced Calvi to some businessmen from Calgary; she had met them in Mexico, where she owned a substantial property.

The Calvi family inherited the ranch after Calvi's death. But the asset was found by the liquidators of BA Holding; hence the lawsuit in which the details of the 1975 payments were made public. The office development had been completed and sold shortly before Calvi's death, producing a gain of some $18 million. Only half of this went to Calvi, because he had sold a half interest at cost to a fellow-director of the Ambrosiano.

Where Calvi got the money to buy the Canadian property is not clear. It was fashionable at the time for rich Italians to invest in Canada, and as it could be done only by breaking the currency laws the transactions were always veiled in secrecy. It is clear that Calvi borrowed some of the original cost, but it seems that he had to produce $3 or $4 million in cash.

The sums he had illicitly received through the Ralrov account and the Ehrenkreuz account may have helped to finance the purchases. But they would not have been enough, and there is little evidence to suggest that he personally benefited from payments out of Radowal and United Trading, apart from the $450,000 payment to the AEQ 6546 account in January 1974, most of which he appears to have shared with Mozzana. Yet suddenly, in October 1975, we find him pocketing some $950,000. Why the onset of greed?

One possible answer is that this was the moment when Calvi found himself without an overseer. In the autumn of 1975 the 73-year-old Mozzana decided to retire as chairman of the Ambrosiano. He was succeeded by Calvi, who also retained his post as managing director, so that he now had complete control of the bank.

Mozzana, as we have seen, was aware of the secret network and, on at least one occasion, had shared in the gains. Nevertheless, he may have been a restraining influence on Calvi.

But this does not explain why Calvi should have paid money to Ortolani, only to be handed some of it back. It is probable that Ortolani and Gelli insisted on this arrangement. This would give them a hold over Calvi. The payments to them could be explained as fees for "services rendered" – an argument much used after the crash. But the payments to Calvi himself, through bank accounts whose numbers they knew, would enable them to prove him guilty of embezzlement.

Calvi might have avoided such a trap by quietly repaying his share to United Trading. He had fed most of the Ralrov and Ehrenkreuz money back into Radowal. Yet he kept this money for himself. If he had paid it back to United Trading, he might have been able to prove himself not guilty of embezzlement – but only at the cost of revealing the existence of United Trading.

Did Calvi realise that he had compromised himself? He could hardly have foreseen that, once he had done so, the greed of his new associates would far exceed his own. Over the following six years, out of the $250 million or so that he channelled into Ortolani-controlled accounts, the sum channelled back to him was about $9 million – large in absolute terms, but making him a minor beneficiary of his own fraud. He used the Union Bank account only for the early payments. His private affairs were in the main handled by Crédit Suisse, until about the end of 1976, when he moved his business to the Geneva private bank Lombard Odier. In Nassau, from about the same time, he entrusted his affairs to the Roywest, a bank then owned by the National Westminster and the Royal Bank of Canada. Roywest administered three companies for him: Butric, Lomand and Waylet. Through these his assets outside Europe and Canada were held.

From 1977 to 1981 Calvi paid a further $3.3 million into the account of Butric, and this money did not come through Ortolani. Some of it represented his pay as chairman of the Cisalpine; the sources of some other payments cannot be identified. He did benefit from two or three small sums – $100,000 to $250,000 – paid out illicitly through a company called Palmetto, which was set up in 1976 for the purpose of paying various expenses that Ambrosiano executives wanted to keep out of the audited books. "Other small presents not able to be passed through official accounts," one of them explained. It was not used by Calvi for the more serious bribery. All the Roywest accounts were frozen after his death.

The main beneficiaries of the fraud – Gelli, Ortolani and their associates – must have known that the money came from the Ambrosiano group in one way or another. But there is no evidence that they understood the mechanism by which Calvi extracted it – the feeding of United Trading from the Cisalpine, by way of the back-to-back arrangement with the IOR. They may well not have known of the existence of United Trading. Nothing in Gelli's papers, and nothing said afterwards by Gelli or Ortolani, suggests that they knew. Calvi seems to have been careful not to tell them too much detail.

To finance the payments to the Ortolani accounts, United Trading borrowed another million Swiss francs, plus $3 million, on 16 October 1975, and a further $3 million on 12 November 1975 – channelled, of course, through the IOR. Two days later it borrowed yet another $5 million, this time in order to pay the IOR the $4.5 million interest due on the Manic loan. This brought United Trading's debts to $161 million – excluding the $12 million direct back-to-back loan made the previous year to finance Zitropo's capital increase. These increased liabilities were faithfully entered in Calvi's private balance sheets for United Trading. But there was nothing for him to enter against them; no assets had been acquired. So the deficit was further inflated.

The Mincomes authorizations, for which Calvi had paid so heavily, removed the threat that the Italian banks might have to withdraw the money they had on deposit with the Cisalpine. But they did not allow for much extra money to be fed in. The credit limits granted were not much above the sums the group's Italian banks had been lending to the Cisalpine when the UIC started all the trouble. Furthermore, there was a rebellion by some of the Varesino directors. They were worried by the size of the proposed advance to the Cisalpine, and the risks involved, and they forced the board to postpone a final commitment. So there was no great increase in the money available to the Cisalpine, and what extra there was had been used in the payments to the Ortolani accounts. By late November Calvi was again looking for ways of raising funds. The solution he found was to be a thorn in his side; it was the basis of one charge against him at his trial in 1981.

Probably the soundest investment of Calvi's secret network at this point was Manic's holding of shares in the Toro insurance company. True, the market price had fallen back to about 14,000 lire a share. As a result of a capital increase earlier in the year, Manic owned 1,110,934 Toro shares. On 20 November 1975 it sold them all to La Centrale – at 35,000 lire each.

It was hardly surprising that this payment of more than double the market price should have caught the attention of the Bank of Italy inspectors three years later. It caused huge losses for La Centrale when the investment had to be written down to market levels. The inspectors could not make out who reaped the benefit. They knew nothing of Manic. The Toro shares had been registered in the names of Liechtenstein companies. The inspectors, and subsequently the court, believed that the transaction was just a means for La Centrale to export capital illegally. They rejected Calvi's explanation that it was a genuine transaction, and that the high price was justified because it gave La Centrale voting control of Toro.

The court was right to conclude that it was not a genuine transaction, but wrong to think that the money remained under the control of La Centrale. If it had, it would have been only a breach of the currency laws, instead of what it really was – the robbery of La Centrale shareholders.

All $56.6 million of the money La Centrale paid for Toro went flowing back to Manic. Knowing more than the inspectors knew, we can now see that Calvi probably resorted to this deal for two main reasons.

One was to enable Manic to record a profit. In spite of the replacement of the $40 million of debentures with equity capital, its interest costs were still outrunning its income. But its profit of $12.6 million on the Toro shares enabled it to record a profit for 1975 of $6.6 million. This must have reassured the IOR when the Gottardo sent it a copy of the Manic accounts – for information only – early in 1976.

The second, and perhaps more important, reason for the Toro sale was to raise money for the secret network. With the proceeds of the sale Manic was able to repay $16 million of the money it had borrowed from United Trading, thus enabling United Trading to repay $15 million of back-to-back loans. This injection of liquidity was badly needed. As the year-end approached, Calvi faced a familiar problem: an embarrassing excess of Banco Ambrosiano shares.

Since March 1975 Suprafin had been continuing to buy Ambrosiano shares, without being able to resell more than a handful. By late 1975 it had accumulated about half a million shares. These were financed by short-term borrowings; therefore the shares had to be resold quickly. So, at the end of November 1975, Suprafin sold 450,000 shares to Manic. They were registered in the nominee names of Lafidele, Finprogram, Finkurs and Sansinvest. Manic paid 21,000 lire each for them, whereas the market price was 18,000 lire. Suprafin was therefore able to register a profit. The cost was nearly $14 million, which Manic financed with what was left of the proceeds of the Toro sale, plus a new $9 million loan from United Trading, which in turn borrowed the money from the Cisalpine by way of the IOR.

United Trading, too, had been buying Ambrosiano shares. Together with the remainder of the shares it had bought from Suprafin the previous year, it now owned some 400,000 shares. So Calvi, yet again, needed to find a home for a large block of shares. Did he think of asking the IOR to add to the 345,000 it had so obligingly bought in April? In the event his new P2 friends came up with a buyer – the Rizzoli family.

In the closing weeks of 1975 Ortolani cemented the relationship he had formed with Angelo Rizzoli and Bruno Tassan Din during the summer. In November he introduced them to Gelli at his office in the Via Condotti in Rome. The ostensible reason for the meeting was to consult Gelli about Argentina. The Rizzolis had acquired a small publishing business there, Anesa. They were thinking of merging it with a locally owned firm, Julio Korn. Gelli did later play a role in the Rizzoli operations in South America, with disastrous results. But his first move was to convince Angelo Rizzoli and Tassan Din that he could be of wider use to them if they joined P2, because of its influential membership. At about Christmas he introduced them to some of his important banker members: Ferrari of the Banca Nazionale del Lavoro, Giovanni Cresti of the Monte dei Paschi di Siena, and, of course, Calvi.

The Rizzoli story is one of "clogs to clogs in three generations", as they say in the North of England. (The old man, who used to go to work in clogs, builds up a business; the son spends the money; the grandson loses everything and has to go to work in clogs again.) Rizzoli Editore was founded in 1911 in Milan by Angelo's grandfather, a jobbing printer also called Angelo. In 1927 he moved to a new factory, which he equipped with a rotogravure printing plant. He began to print weekly and monthly magazines, four of which he published himself. In 1939 he expanded to Rome. The business continued to thrive after the war, both by investing in new technology and by acquiring other publishers. It grew particularly fast during the 1960s, when turnover rose almost five times and the number of employees reached 3,600.

Throughout this expansion old Angelo kept full control of the company. When he died in 1970 he left 70 per cent of it to his son Andrea, and 30 per cent to his daughter Giuseppina. Andrea, whose passion was gambling, seems to have had little interest in the day-to-day running of the business. In December 1971 he made his son Angelo managing director. His younger son, Alberto, was also employed in the business. Andrea continued to guide the firm's policies, and the expansion continued, although with signs of financial strain. To help young Angelo, Tassan Din was hired from Montedison in September 1973.

The head of Montedison, Eugenio Cefis, persuaded Andrea Rizzoli to buy the *Corriere della Sera* in the summer of 1974. The paper had for years been owned by the Crespi family, but they had recently brought in outside shareholders, including the Agnelli family of Fiat and an oil company, Moratti, which was thought to represent the state-owned oil giant, ENI. With no outright proprietor, and with a strong editor, Piero Ottone, the *Corriere* was much respected for its independence. However, it was losing money heavily, and was up for sale.

The price Andrea Rizzoli had to find was 49.6 billion lire (about $75 million). He got almost half of this, 24 billion lire, as direct finance from Montedison. Then there was a loan from the Credito Commerciale. The Agnelli family agreed to wait for their share of the price, 13.5 billion lire, until June 1977. But the money had to be indexed to the cost of living. Like the gambler he was, Andrea took on these commitments without working out how he was going to meet them.

The deal became even more expensive when his sister objected to it. She could not see why he had undertaken to buy the Agnelli stake in the *Corriere*. Without that, he would still have had two thirds of the capital – enough to exercise control. Andrea bought out her 30 per cent of the family business, for about 25 billion lire. After that, as Tassan Din said later, Andrea's personal resources "dropped to zero".

With the *Corriere* losing about 12 billion lire a year, the Rizzolis were soon desperately looking round for money. It was this search that took them to Ortolani in the summer of 1975. But Ortolani did not then have access to the Ambrosiano. In August 1975 the Rizzolis came to an extraordinary secret agreement with Montedison. It would pay the Rizzolis 2.5 billion lire in 1975, 2 billion in 1976, 2 billion in 1977, and further sums to be agreed later. In return, the Rizzolis would ensure that the *Corriere* should support

Montedison's economic and political policies, and give the company favourable publicity. It seems that Cefis had all along been using the Rizzolis as a means of trying to secure covert influence over the newspaper. Thanks to the editor, Ottone, these attempts were largely thwarted.

When Angelo Rizzoli and Tassan Din met Calvi in December 1975 the immediate financial crisis had been averted. But they were always on the lookout for new sources of money. Calvi immediately opened a line of credit for them at the Ambrosiano, so that they could draw up to 3 billion lire. Tassan Din said later: "Once we got to know Calvi, it was marvellous. Getting money was like turning on a tap."

At first, though, they had to do something for it. They were persuaded to help Calvi with his problem of the surplus Ambrosiano shares. The family owned a Luxembourg holding company, Rizzoli International, and in December 1975 and January and February 1976 this bought a total of 510,000 Ambrosiano shares.

The first 150,000 cost $6.16 million, about 50 per cent above the market price. They came from United Trading's holding on 29 December. But first, that same day, United Trading sold them to Cisalpine at their cost of $4.4 million, so that Cisalpine made an instant profit of $1.76 million. This accounted for nearly 70 per cent of Cisalpine's profits for that year, enabling it to pay a dividend of $900,000, of which the IOR received $75,000.

The other 360,000 shares came from Manic's holding, and cost $14.24 million, but Manic first passed the shares to United Trading for $11.7 million, so that it could take the profit to help finance the Ortolani payments.

The Rizzolis did not have to find any cash to pay for the shares. Calvi provided credit, mostly in the form of loans from the Cisalpine to Rizzoli International. As security for these loans, the Rizzolis put up assets they owned – not the Ambrosiano shares. The advantage for Calvi was that apparently genuine third party loans appeared in the books of the Cisalpine. Calvi assured the Rizzolis that the shares would be bought back from them at some future date, and that they would not lose by the transaction. (In the event they lost $7 million.)

A note about this deal in Calvi's papers indicated that "related payments" of $1,452,500 were added to the cost of the shares. Undoubtedly these represented "commissions". The placing of the Ambrosiano shares with the Rizzolis also appears in Gelli's schedule of operations for this period. Indeed, the cryptic figures in the schedule suggest that the payments may have been even higher. Clearly, Ortolani and Gelli pocketed substantial sums for their role. Possibly Calvi took a lesser share back from Ortolani.

So the first big deal between Calvi and the Rizzolis was for his benefit, rather than theirs. At the outset Calvi and his P2 friends do not seem to have been much interested in the Rizzoli publishing company. Their main energies went into setting up a share dealing operation based in Rome. Rizzoli Finanziaria was established at the end of 1975, and began operations early in 1976. It acquired a large stake in an insurance company, Savoia, in conjunction with a political friend of Ortolani's, Giuseppe Battista, who had also joined P2. (Battista became assistant to another P2 member, Gaetano Stammati, who, as we shall see, was Minister for Foreign Trade at a crucial time in 1979.) The Ambrosiano cut back the credit line it had opened for Rizzoli Editore, in order to make a 3 billion lire advance to Rizzoli Finanziaria.

This was the beginning of a vast and systematic manipulation of shares, in particular the shares of insurance companies and banks, which was to last several years. These fraudulent dealings were the first to catch the attention of the authorities; they were being investigated long before the Ambrosiano crash. The investigators found that some 7 billion lire of secret profits had been illicitly removed from Rizzoli Finanziaria, and this led to the issue of warrants for the arrest of Ortolani, Gelli, Tassan Din and Battista on 11 June 1982, six days before Calvi's death.

Throughout 1976 Montedison continued to be much the most important source of funding for Rizzoli Editore. In March Montedison made a further 9 billion lire available, concealed by a back-to-back arrangement with the Banca Commerciale. In September a further secret contract was signed in Switzerland. Montedison agreed to provide $29 million. Three months later Rizzoli made its first drawing of $11.8 million on this new line of credit. The money was channelled through the Rothschild Bank of Zürich, so that the true source remained hidden. The choice of bank was probably made by Andrea Rizzoli, who had transferred some of the Rizzoli share capital to Rothschilds. Two Rothschilds' representatives, Gilbert de Botton and Walter Stiefel, were invited to join the Rizzoli board.

But it is clear from Calvi's papers that he was taking a close interest in the way Montedison was financing Rizzoli. Ortolani, who had experience with newspapers, may already have been awaiting his opportunity.

The key to such ambitions lay in Tassan Din, the financial manager. He owned no shares, and was not even on the Rizzoli board. But he was a stronger character than Angelo Rizzoli, with more business sense; he was also much more deeply involved in the Rizzoli Finanziaria manipulations, which drew him closer to Ortolani, Gelli and Calvi.

At first Calvi was quite happy to deal with Angelo Rizzoli (according to Angelo Rizzoli). Calvi even asked Angelo to arrange a dinner, so that he could meet a high Vatican official, Agostino Casaroli, then deputy secretary of state for foreign affairs. But by the autumn of 1976 Calvi had begun to ignore Angelo, insisting that he would communicate only with Tassan Din. There is evidence that Tassan Din received about $1 million at this time.

It was probably before the end of 1976 that the P2 men realised that an opportunity lay ahead which, if exploited correctly, would give them a real hold over the Rizzolis. The coup they pulled off in July 1977 was one of the most important chapters in the Ambrosiano story, for it was eventually to make Rizzoli the centrepiece of the fraud. It was in this deal that the affairs of Calvi's two sets of associates – the IOR and the P2 – became most closely intertwined.

To understand what happened we first have to look at another aspect of the Ambrosiano's dealings with the IOR, one which was ignored entirely by the joint commission (though its members were aware of it) and which was, therefore, not mentioned in the written memorandum by Marcinkus. This aspect, although touched on briefly by the magistrates investigating the crash, was largely left out of their inquiries.

Yet the operations we are about to describe cost the Vatican nearly $100 million, for they led to the lira debts that the Vatican, after the crash, quickly and quietly agreed to repay. As we have seen in the first chapter, the probable motive for the repayment was to prevent further investigation. Unlike all its other dealings with the Ambrosiano, these transactions appear to have involved deception by the IOR, not for Calvi's benefit, but for its own.

FOURTEEN

Back-Scratching in Italy

Calvi kept his private papers in various places outside Italy, secure from the prying eyes of the Italian authorities – at the Ultrafin offices in Zürich, and at the Gottardo in Lugano. Many of those at the Gottardo have never come to light. The largest known cache is in Nassau.

When Calvi was in Nassau he would often visit the Roywest, where he was called: "Mr Butric" – the name of the chief company it managed for him. The senior executives knew perfectly well who he was, though the bank charged him a hefty fee for "confidentiality". Calvi would bring the papers back to his villa at Lyford Cay. In his living room, which was hung with tapestries designed by a Nicaraguan friend, he would spread his papers out on the deep-pile carpet. He would sift through them, perhaps rearranging them, adding some documents or removing others. Then he would put the papers back into black plastic bags and seal them with sticky tape before returning them to the safes.

Calvi kept an index to the papers, of a kind, in a little black book. This was handwritten, and many of the entries are indecipherable. Those entries referring to particular stacks of papers dealing with Rizzoli proved easy enough to identify. Even in these, though, there are no direct references to Calvi's dealings with Ortolani and Gelli.

The papers from the Nassau safe alone total 1,500 pages. The liquidators of the Cisalpine got an injunction to prevent the removal of the originals, but Calvi's son Carlo was allowed to take photocopies, of which he gave me a set. I found many of them infuriatingly hard to interpret, but I eventually worked most of them out. They shed new light on Calvi's relationship with the IOR. As I have shown, Calvi kept private accounts for Radowal and United Trading, supplemented by the accounts he kept for other secret network companies, such as Zitropo and Manic.

There was also another collection of documents which appeared to concern Calvi's dealings with the IOR. Carlo had the impression that these were particularly important. He saw his father examining them several times, not only in the Bahamas but also at Drezzo.

One of these documents is reproduced on page 162. It contains two lists of six accounts. The top list, headed "Funds", refers to loan accounts with the Ambrosiano group. According to the inspectors from the Bank of Italy, who arrived at the Ambrosiano in April 1978, and stayed for three months, these accounts were in the name of the IOR. There were accounts R, S and R-1 with the Banco Ambrosiano, or "BA". There were accounts R and B with the Banca Cattolica del Veneto, or "BCV". And there was an account with the Credito Varesino, or "CV".

According to the list, therefore, the IOR owed or appeared to owe the Ambrosiano group banks nearly 140 billion lire – about $165 million at the exchange rate ruling at the end of 1978.

The second list, headed "Uses", carries numbers typical of accounts at the IOR, with the prefix 001 indicating that they are in lire. The list, then, appears to show how the money has been used. Yet there is no direct correlation between the sums the IOR apparently owed to the Ambrosiano group and the sums owed to the IOR. Nor do the totals match.

The letters against the numbers stood for names. SET stood for Setemer, the telecommunications company controlled by Ericsson of Sweden, in which La Centrale, even before it was acquired by the Ambrosiano, had a substantial minority holding.

The two accounts designated with a C represented a company called CIM – Grandi Magazzini, and XX meant a company called Società Immobiliare XX Settembre. RED meant Rizzoli Editore. RED-B might also be thought to have something to do with Rizzoli. But, as we shall see, no clear connection has emerged.

These accounts represent a back-to-back operation in lire, between the Italian part of Calvi's empire and the IOR. It was run in parallel with the dollar/Swiss franc back-to-back arrangement between the Cisalpine and the IOR. The mechanism, however, was different. It had to be, because, inside Italy, Calvi could not have secret companies like Radowal or United Trading. So the IOR drew money out of the Ambrosiano banks and paid it into accounts it held at other Italian banks, where it mingled with other IOR funds and became difficult to trace. But Calvi kept a record, so that he knew there was a pool of lire he could use when he needed them, without the knowledge of auditors or inspectors.

The IOR kept records too, although it has never produced them. Some of the documents in Calvi's safe are clearly copies of those drawn up by Pellegrino de Strobel, the IOR's chief accountant. The joint commission did not inquire into the back-to-back lira loans; hence there is little information from that source. The Bank of Italy discovered the existence of the

SITUAZIONE AL 31 DICEMBRE 1978

(senza conteggio interessi)

FONDI		Lit.
B.A.	c/ "R"	28.956.929.206
B.A.	c/ "S"	27.948.456.034
B.A.	c/ "R-1"	9.704.270.533
B.C.V.	c/ "R"	20.009.897.387
B.C.V.	c/ "B"	26.958.138.906
C.V.		26.382.638.889
	Totale	139.960.330.955

UTILIZZI		
001 6 02505	"SET"	31.207.293.565
C01 6 02535 ·	"C"	11.360.708.399
001 6 02536	"C"	99.101.981
001 6 02550	"XX"	48.951.826.228
C01 6 02553	"RED"	24.918.042.745
001 6 02559	"RED-B"	21.299.391.287
	Totale	137.836.364.205

Residuo   2.123.966.750

12.1.1979

debit accounts in the course of the 1978 inspection, and the bank statements for them were eventually published in the mass of P2 Commission evidence. But they go no further than March 1978. Little information about the back-to-back lira loans has emerged since, and the investigating magistrates did not look into them in detail. But they did commission a Guardia di Finanza report. This was far from comprehensive. But, largely with the help of Calvi's documents, I have been able to reconstruct events up to the collapse.

The latest of Calvi's documents on the lira back-to backs is dated 24 April 1980. The IOR then owed 173.4 billion lire, or more than $200 million, to the Ambrosiano group banks.

Shortly after that, the debts rose to a peak of just over 180 billion lire. But in the last year and a half of the Ambrosiano's life there was a substantial reduction. After the crash the IOR was found to owe, before interest, about 119 billion lire – $86 million – on the six special accounts. It was these debts, together with interest amounting to a further $13 million, that the IOR quietly and quickly repaid in the months following the crash.

This repayment suggests that the IOR knew it would be foolish to deny responsibility, as it did for its debts to the Cisalpine under the dollar/Swiss franc back-to-backs. Yet the IOR had in its possession a letter from Calvi saying that the debts were counterparts of debts between the Ambrosiano group banks and the IOR, which arose out of operations "pertaining to" and "arranged by" the Ambrosiano. That is, the operations were not for the IOR's benefit. This letter might have been produced, as Calvi's letter covering the Cisalpine back-to-backs was produced, in support of a claim that the IOR did not have to repay the money. (No photocopy of this important back-to-back letter has ever surfaced, and so, although it is listed in Appendix B, it cannot be reproduced separately: but its contents are known.)

The letter about the lira back-to-backs was written by Calvi on behalf of the Ambrosiano, not the Cisalpine, and was dated 9 November 1978. It was mentioned only in passing, and without explanation, in the joint commission's report. The joint commission listed it with the other "parallel" letters, because it had been attached to the famous letter of indemnity. As with that letter, the joint commission was allowed to examine it and make notes, but not to take a photocopy.

Like the other "parallel" letters about operations which had been going on for years, this one looks as if it had been written at the IOR's request. Why should the IOR have wanted it in November 1978? One possibility is that the IOR had heard that the Bank of Italy inspectors were asking why there was no proper documentation of the accounts (though there is, as we shall see, a more probable explanation). There were neither formal agreements at the time the accounts were opened, nor any subsequent files of correspondence.

Letters have also appeared, one to each of the three lending banks, from the IOR. The letters merely confirmed that the banks had "deposits" with the IOR, averaging 50 billion lire from the Ambrosiano, 35 billion from the Cattolica and 25 billion from the Varesino. The Ambrosiano board was formally to raise the IOR limit to 75 billion three months later, but the debts to the Cattolica were already above the "average", and were to rise much higher. The mystery about these three letters is that they are all dated 3 January 1978. Yet they were never mentioned by the Bank of Italy inspectors, who went into the Ambrosiano in April 1978. Perhaps they were written later, and backdated.

More serious than the lack of documentation was the fact that the accounts were a breach of the currency regulations. The IOR was a foreign bank. Yet the Ambrosiano banks had not sought permission to lend it money, or make deposits with it. Acting on information from the Bank of Italy, the UIC wrote to the Ambrosiano group banks in September 1978, pointing this out.

The Ambrosiano group applied to the Mincomes for the necessary authorisations – and got them. The Mincomes conceded that the IOR was a special case, in the light of the treaties with the Vatican. At this time the Minister for Foreign Trade was Rinaldo Ossola, not a politician but an old Bank of Italy man, and one of the most honest men who have ever held office in Italy. But the civil servant who advised him, the director general of currencies, was still Gelli's friend, the P2 member Firrao.

The letter sent by Calvi secretly to the IOR, shortly before the Mincomes permissions were granted, cannot have been intended to safeguard the IOR against the Bank of Italy, the UIC, or the Mincomes, since none of these Italian authorities had any power over it. Indeed, if any of them had known of the letter, Calvi could scarcely have got his authorisations, because it proved that the advances to the IOR were not, as he had claimed, ordinary interbank deposits. Calvi, therefore, was taking a risk when he wrote it.

Marcinkus must have asked for the letter because his own position in the Vatican was threatened. Pope John Paul I had died suddenly after a reign of one month, and Karol Wojtyla had been elected as Pope John Paul II on 16 October. It was a moment when Marcinkus might well have needed Calvi's letter, to explain the IOR's apparent huge debt to the Ambrosiano banks.

The letter contained no reference to any reward to the IOR. But clues to the IOR's gains are to be found in Calvi's papers. There is a calculation of the interest on the accounts for 1979. It shows that the IOR had to pay a commission of a quarter of a percentage point – 0.25 per cent – to the Ambrosiano banks on top of interest, which at that time was 11 per cent, rising to 12.25 per cent on 1 November 1979. But on the other side a mark-up of half a percentage point was added – as a rule, at least – to the interest due on the matching IOR accounts. In addition the IOR received a further "turn" on three of the six accounts: three-quarters of a percentage point – 0.75 per cent – on Setemer, and 0.25 per cent on XX Settembre and "RED-B".

Calvi's papers show that the total extra accruing to the IOR accounts in the second half of 1979 was over 620 million (about $775,000), so that its return on the lira operations was considerably larger than on the foreign currency back-to-backs. But the interest on the foreign currency loans was regularly paid out; the interest on the lira operations was "rolled up" – that is, added to the total due, either at the end of the year or at the end of each half-year. Banks may legitimately treat such rolled-up interest as income. But it would only be on the ultimate repayment of all the accounts that the money could be regarded as safely earned. Calvi's letter, in effect, recognised this, because he wrote that the Ambrosiano banks undertook to meet any difference between the total owed to the IOR and the total owed by it.

The most extraordinary aspect of Calvi's letter was the statement that the amounts apparently owed by the IOR were counterparts of sums owed to the IOR *by the Ambrosiano banks*. This was not true, as Marcinkus must have known. There were no matching credit accounts in the name of the IOR at the Ambrosiano banks, and it would have been impossible for the IOR to exercise its right to end the agreement on 15 days' notice, as stipulated in the letter. Certainly the IOR had other accounts at these banks; it had a current account no 42800 and a deposit account no 42801 at the Ambrosiano branch in Piazzale Gregorio VII, just outside the Vatican walls. It had various accounts at the Ambrosiano in Milan, including account 10841, used in the Banca Cattolica/Credito Varesino operations in 1972, and an account at the Banca Cattolica.

At the end of March 1978, just before the Bank of Italy inspection began, these credit balances totalled only about 4 billion lire, but a document among Calvi's papers shows that they stood at 35.4 billion lire in October 1979. At the time of the crash the IOR's credit accounts had fallen to about 21 billion lire. It also had some 20 billion lire in a credit account at the

Cattolica, and the IOR may well have used this money to help pay off the lira debts.

Although, as we shall see, some of these accounts were involved for a period in the lira back-to-back operations, they were in no way matching accounts securing the IOR's debts. Again, Calvi was writing to Marcinkus with the intention of deceiving some third party, and on this occasion it must have been someone within the Vatican.

The letter was misleading in another way, too. The implication that the lira debts had been amassed for the benefit of the Ambrosiano was not true. Some of the money was used for the IOR's objectives, rather than for Calvi's; so the IOR had no claim to be an innocent intermediary.

Working out how the money was used has proved particularly difficult, and nobody has ever attempted as detailed a reconstruction as I have. I have to say that not all the money can be accounted for. Nor is it possible to find out what the IOR's interest was in certain transactions. The Bank of Italy inspectors examined the operations behind the Setemer account, which turned out to be relatively simple, and those leading to the XX Settembre account, which were a great deal more complicated. Some aspects of this are still baffling.

The inspectors also touched briefly on the CIM operation, but the payments that led to the "RED" and "RED-B" accounts escaped their attention entirely. While Calvi was alive, nobody saw his notes except himself. The inspectors were not aware that the IOR accounts were used for the illegal export of lire to Calvi's secret network, and to Ortolani's bank accounts. Even after the crash, the magistrates do not seem to have followed up the preliminary investigations of the Guardia di Finanza.

The lira back-to-backs began on 22 July 1974, when the IOR sent instructions to the Cattolica to transfer 1.3 billion lire (about $2 million) to a fiduciary company, Italtrust, owned by La Centrale. The Cattolica was to debit the sum to "our separate account B". The money was paid a week later to an Italtrust account at the Banco Ambrosiano. From there (the Bank of Italy men established) it was transferred to the capital account of the company CIM. Six months later the IOR drew a further 900 million lire out of "account B" (which was also called no 188) and this was also paid to Italtrust, which passed it on to CIM with the description: "Funds pertaining to capital increase." The IOR opened an account, no 001 7 55000, to reflect the money received. It was later replaced by the two accounts shown in the document on page 162.

The army of Victor Emmanuel entered Rome by the Porta Pia on 20 September 1870. Hence the road from there to the heart of the city is called the Via XX Settembre. The date marked the end of the Papal States, and the shrinking of the Pope's temporal power to the Vatican City. It is odd that it came back to haunt the Vatican's business affairs.

On the corner of the Via XX Settembre and the Via Pastrengo stood the "glass palace", the Palazzo di Vetro, the biggest store belonging to CIM – Grandi Magazzini. This huge concrete and glass building, with 27,420 square metres of floor space in two basement levels and nine floors above ground, was designed as a store in the late 1930s. It was completed in 1942, and first put to use as a recreation centre for the troops. But in 1944, when Rome was in the hands of the allies, the building was returned to its original owners, the Marziale family.

This family had set up CIM (Consorzio Italiano Manufatti) in 1927. Besides the Palazzo di Vetro, CIM owned three other shops in Rome, one in Genoa and one in Reggio di Calabria. Long before the time of Marcinkus, the IOR took (or perhaps was bequeathed) a stake in this company. By 1955 Prince Massimo Spada was a director of it. So was Luigi Mennini. Pellegrino de Strobel was a *sindaco*, one of the three auditors required by Italian law to look after the interests of the share-holders.

In 1970 the trading activities of the company were merged with those of another company, Cinco. The new company became CIM – Grandi Magazzini. Spada and Mennini were on the board of that too; de Strobel was once more a *sindaco*.

But the old company had not completely disappeared. It had changed its name to Società Immobiliare XX Settembre. It had no activities, except to own the Palazzo di Vetro. As the landlord, it signed a formal agreement with CIM, the tenant.

The capital of XX Settembre was only 1.2 million lire, divided into 600,000 shares. What proportion the IOR owned is not known, but it had a substantial, probably a controlling, interest. CIM's capital was increased in 1970 to 900 million lire, divided into 180,000 shares. Again, the exact number owned by the IOR is not known, but it seems to have had a controlling interest. The running of both companies, however, was under-taken by members of the Marziale family. Antonio, the founder of the business, was managing director of XX Settembre. His son, Giuseppe, was president of CIM.

In September 1971 Antonio Marziale died. The following May the whole board of XX Settembre resigned, including Spada and Mennini, and a sole director was appointed to run the company. This, however, did not mean any loosening of the company's ties with the IOR. De Strobel continued in his post. And the new sole director, Antonio Falez, was an old friend of Marcinkus.

Falez, born in Yugoslavia, came to Rome as a refugee. He later went to work for the Catholic Relief Service in Geneva, and he is believed to have met Marcinkus there. Marcinkus was sometimes sent to Geneva on Vatican business, when he worked for the Secretariat of State.

The two men began working together during the Second Vatican Council, when Marcinkus ran the service bureau for the American bishops. Falez had started a travel agency, Catintours, which was used by Marcinkus in making travel arrangements for the visiting Americans. The agency did well, and opened an office in Chicago, where Matilda, the sister of Marcinkus, worked for a time. But, after Falez had sold his interest in 1975, Catintours denied strongly that it had any close links with the Vatican. Long before that, Falez had developed other business interests, particularly in property. He had been involved with the construction of Rome's Holiday Inn. So he was not without qualifications to run XX Settembre.

The company was losing money, and it was recognised that much better use could be made of the Palazzo. CIM did not need the whole building, but a full internal reconstruction could not take place while it was the main tenant. Some improvement work was carried out, to create more lettable space, and CIM was confined to the two basement floors and the first four floors above ground. The other five floors were let, for the most part, to the Ministry of Labour. XX Settembre returned to profitability in 1972 and 1973, but by the end of that year rising costs were beginning to catch up.

CIM presented a far more serious problem. It had been losing money since the reorganisation in 1970. In 1973 the losses totalled 776 million lire, bringing the accumulated deficit to over 810 million lire by the end of that year. By then the economic crisis caused by the fourfold increase in oil prices had begun to make its mark on retail sales. In 1974 CIM lost nearly 2 billion lire more (about $3 million).

The 2.2 billion lire of back-to-back loans from the Cattolica to the IOR were made to finance most of these losses. In order to deal with the accumulated deficit in the 1973 balance sheet, on 12 August 1974 the nominal value of the 180,000 shares was reduced from 5,000 lire to 500, so that a total of 810 million lire was wiped off the capital of the company. Then, in two stages, the capital was increased again, to 1 billion lire, by the issue of 1,820,000 new 500-lire shares. The existing shareholders – probably for the most part the IOR – had the option of subscribing for the new shares. In reality the 910 million required came from the 2.2 billion lire provided by the Cattolica. The remaining 1,290 million was recorded in CIM's accounts as a payment made "by the shareholders as a whole". The remainder of CIM's losses came from the company's last reserves.

So 2.2 billion lire of Cattolica funds went into the ailing CIM. It was clearly done to suit the IOR, since there is no evidence that Calvi had any previous interest in either CIM or its landlord XX Settembre.

Why didn't the IOR use its own money to support CIM? Almost certainly, because Marcinkus wanted to declare maximum profits to the Pope. If the payments to the CIM had come out of IOR funds, the gift of 1.29 billion lire "from the shareholders" would have had to be treated as a loss, and the payment for the new CIM shares could hardly have been regarded as a sound investment. By the back-to-back device, the IOR avoided any adverse effect on its earnings.

How did the IOR treat the transaction in its own books? It must have recorded the debt to the Cattolica among its liabilities, but what did it record as the corresponding asset? To judge from Calvi's letter it looks as if the IOR may have entered the money it passed on to CIM – and indeed all the money shown under the "uses" column in the document we have reproduced – as advances repayable by the Ambrosiano group. This would have been false.

The IOR did have security of a kind for these notional advances, to judge from another document from Calvi's safe, which, like the first, is dated 31 December 1978. This (reproduced on page 170) is a schedule of all the securities held either at the IOR or in IOR accounts at other banks, as a result of all the back-to-backs – both the lira ones and the foreign currency ones – and of the contango loans financing Zitropo and Manic. It can be seen from this list that all two million CIM shares had been deposited, along with some CIM effetti, or loan notes. It is not clear whether all the previous CIM shareholders had been bought out; the 2,020 shares held at the IOR itself would appear to be held for third parties, and the 1,997,980 held at the Credito Commerciale in Milan are designated "Estero" – foreign. These were held by two Swiss nominee companies. A director of one was Marco Gambazzi, a Lugano lawyer whom we shall meet again. In effect the lira back-to-backs had created a limbo in Italy, equivalent to United Trading abroad, enabling the IOR to disclaim ownership of CIM and conceal this disastrous investment in its books.

The IOR opened its second and third loan accounts for the lira back-to-backs in August and September 1974. The first was with the Ambrosiano itself: account 3000, designated R. The next was a second account at the Cattolica: number 189, also labelled R. By the end of September the IOR

Posizione titoli al 31 Dicembre 1978

90521 - 90532 - 90618

			loco:
MANIC HOLDING - Luxembourg -	Azioni	45.000	Krediet Bank-Luxembourg-
UNITED TRADING CO. - Panama -	Azioni	500	I.O.R.
ZITROPO HOLDING S.A.	Azioni	5.499.990	Krediet Bank-Luxembourg-
BANCO AMBROSIANO HOLDING	Azioni	53.133	Banca Gottardo -Lugano-
EFFETTI C.I.M.	Lire	1.150.000.000	I.O.R.
PLICHI CHIUSI B.A. C/ RED.	N°	2	I.O.R.
C.I.M. c/ Terzi	Azioni	2.020	I.O.R.
C.I.M. Estero	Azioni	1.997.980	Crecom - Milano -
SETTEMBER	Azioni	3.040.000	I.O.R.
SOC.IMMOBILIARE XX SETTEMBRE	Azioni	1.320.000	I.O.R.

=========================

had been debited with 12 billion lire at the Ambrosiano and 6 billion lire on the second Cattolica account. During the rest of the year there were both substantial credits and further debits to the Ambrosiano account, which ended the year 5.5 billion lire in the red. The Cattolica account remained 6 billion lire overdrawn. So, at the end of the year, the IOR owed, or appeared to owe, 11.5 billion lire on these two accounts.

It is not possible to trace 3.5 billion lire (about $5.4 million) of this. Some of it may have been converted into dollars and deposited with the Cisalpine. But 8 billion lire has been accounted for; it was used for operation Setemer, which the Bank of Italy was able to reconstruct. This was a device to enable Calvi artificially to inflate the profits of La Centrale.

Setemer was the telecommunications company controlled by Ericsson of Sweden, which owned 51 per cent of the capital. The remaining shares were quoted on the *mercato ristretto*. In the early 1970s a large block of 2,265,858 shares, or nearly 32 per cent of the company, was owned by La Centrale. In September 1974 the price of Setemer shares was about 5,080 lire each, and at this price they were carried in La Centrale's books. Then, on 23 September, La Centrale sold 1.2 million of its Setemer shares for 6,484 lire each. The profit was about 1.7 billion lire – some 27 per cent of La Centrale's profits for that financial year, which ended on 31 October. The shares were initially bought by the Ambrosiano itself, but it quickly resold them for 6,666.5 lire each, a total of just under 8 billion lire.

The shares were traced by the Bank of Italy's men to Giammei, the stockbrokers known to act for the IOR. The inspectors made the connection with the loans from the Ambrosiano and the Cattolica to the IOR, but they drew the wrong conclusion. They thought the shares really still belonged to La Centrale, and had merely been parked with the IOR. They knew nothing of the back-to-back operations, by which Calvi and the IOR had been able to consign the shares to limbo.

The following year, 1975, much the same thing happened again. La Centrale's remaining holding of Setemer shares had risen to 1,600,000, as a result of a new issue and of purchases in the market. In October the IOR drew 6 billion lire out of the two accounts labelled R at the Ambrosiano and the Cattolica, and shortly before the year-end La Centrale sold all its remaining Setemer shares for a total of 12 billion lire. La Centrale thus made a profit of 4.8 billion lire, without which it would have had to report a loss at the year-end. Again the shares were acquired through Giammei.

With the earlier new issue, there were now 3,040,000 Setemer shares in limbo. Physically, it is clear from Calvi's schedule that they had been sent to the IOR, presumably as security for the 20 billion lire liability (plus interest) that it had incurred by the transactions. The benefit to Calvi is clear; by an apparently genuine sale of the Setemer shares he had been able to rig the profits of La Centrale in Italy, to offset the raids he had made on its resources for the benefit of his secret network.

The benefit to the IOR is less clear. The market price of Setemer shares fell, and it must soon have realised that the liability could never be covered by the sale of the shares alone. However, it was on this account that the IOR received, in addition to the standard half per cent mark-up, the extra three-quarters per cent. Its biggest reward was probably the 4 billion lire of dividends paid on the Setemer shares while it held them.

On the day the stockbroker Giammei bought the second batch of Setemer shares, 22 October 1975, the same firm bought from La Centrale a block of 400,000 Credito Varesino shares, for 2.9 billion lire. Calvi's notes indicate that these, too, were acquired through the back-to-back lira operation. There were plenty of lire in the pool at that time; in addition to the 12 billion lire needed for the Setemer shares, the IOR had withdrawn, in July and August, 4.5 billion lire from account 3000 R at the Ambrosiano. The Varesino shares were, however, held only briefly by the IOR. In December they were bought back by La Centrale, through a newly acquired subsidiary, Pantanella. This was the ailing pasta firm once owned by the Vatican's other financial institution, APSA. Sindona had arranged its sale to Equity Funding in the United States. Equity Funding had gone bankrupt in its turn; now Pantanella was sold to La Centrale by an Italo-American businessman, Roberto Memmo. Calvi was not, of course, interested in making pasta. He wanted another vehicle for share dealing.

Since the IOR did not repay anything to the Ambrosiano group banks on the resale of the Varesino shares, the 3 billion lire proceeds went into the back-to-back pool. These and the other 1.5 billion lire drawn out in the summer of 1975 have not been accounted for conclusively, but there are clues. This is where Calvi got bogged down deeper in the ill-omened XX Settembre, and the still more troubled CIM.

FIFTEEN

How the IOR Smuggled Calvi's Money Out

The affairs of CIM and its landlord XX Settembre came to a crisis in the autumn of 1975. The modifications to the Palazzo had not increased rental income enough to cover the rising costs of XX Settembre, which had lost 39 million lire in 1974. Its capital was only 1.2 million lire. So this was now increased to 450 million lire, divided into 30,000 shares. Who paid up? Presumably the IOR, which was also providing all its short-term borrowings – more than 1.5 billion lire.

CIM's rent could not be raised to a realistic level; its 1970 contract was not due to expire until the end of 1980. Besides, CIM could hardly pay what it owed already. Probably some of the untraceable sums from the back-to-back operations went towards covering its deficit.

The obvious answer was for CIM to move out of the Palazzo, so that it could be converted into smaller units and relet. In October 1975 Falez made a deal with CIM (still being run by Giuseppe Marziale) under which it undertook to leave the building by 30 November 1976.

As it was thus forfeiting four years of occupation, CIM was entitled to some compensation. What XX Settembre paid it was 600 million lire in November 1975 and another 600 million lire in February 1976. The deal seems to have been somewhat generous to CIM, which was now being supported by the Ambrosiano by way of the IOR. XX Settembre was being supported directly by the IOR.

The IOR's best course would have been to shut down CIM at once. But the late-sixties' nightmare of workers demonstrating in St Peter's Square lingered on. Businesslike solutions to economic problems could always bring bad publicity to the Church. This was just the sort of situation that Pope Paul VI had been trying to avoid, when he got APSA to dispose of its embarrassing investments.

As for XX Settembre, the payments to CIM had sharply increased its losses, and it still had to face the costs of the conversion. This was when the Ambrosiano came into its affairs. Calvi extended it a 3.5 billion line of credit to finance the work.

But this was not the only use for the secret pool of lire created by the back-to-backs. Another 1.5 billion lire almost certainly became $2 million, paid into Zitropo to make the accounts look better. We have seen that Zitropo was, in effect, bankrupt after the Sindona crash, because its assets consisted of shares in the company Sindona had unloaded on to Calvi, Pacchetti.

Zitropo had no income out of which to pay interest on its $30 million of short-term debts, now owed entirely to United Trading, and its $20 million of debentures, of which United Trading held $13 million and Manic $7 million. As a result, Zitropo had lost $7.3 million in 1974. In 1975 Calvi decided to do something about this. He arbitrarily reduced the interest rate on the debentures from 11 per cent to 2 per cent, but that still left financial charges running at some $3.5 million a year. So, at the end of 1975, Calvi decided that he would simply inject lump sums from time to time into Zitropo. To give them some sort of disguise, Zitropo formed a Panamanian subsidiary, Lepartner, which opened an account at the Gottardo. Into this came money from an account at the Crédit Suisse in Lugano. The money was then paid to Zitropo as "dividends".

In 1975, 1976 and 1977 Zitropo received a total of $16,065,000 from Lepartner in this way. Calvi's papers throw no light on the first payment – $2 million on 31 December 1975. But some of the other payments can be identified in his notes. It can be seen that they originated with the lira back-to-back operation. The IOR drew on the lire made available by the Ambrosiano group banks, converted them into dollars and then had the money paid into Lepartner's account at the Gottardo. There is no information about the exchange rate used for the first transaction, but there is reasonably clear evidence that, on the other payments, the IOR charged a substantial premium over the official rate. It was charging more, even, than on the illegal exports of lire in 1972 and 1973.

Calvi also used the lira back-to-back operations to pay Ortolani and Gelli. The role of the IOR in helping Calvi to remove money fraudulently from his Italian banks, and then to export it illegally from Italy, would have attracted more attention from the authorities after the crash, if the IOR had not repaid the resulting debt so quickly.

The Italian investigators did come across one transaction in Switzerland which led them back to the IOR. They did not fully appreciate the nature of the arrangement, but their inquiries have helped me to reconstruct the mechanism used by Calvi and the IOR to take money out of Italy.

The investigators found that on 4 September 1981 two sums, of $1.9 million and $1.4 million, were paid into an account at the Banque Bruxelles

Lambert in Lausanne. The money was for Francesco Pazienza, a larger-than-life character whose role in the Calvi story we shall consider later. Here we are looking only at the route the money took. It came, like the payments to Lepartner, from an account at the Crédit Suisse in Lugano. This account had received $3.5 million the previous day from the IOR's subsidiary in Lugano, the Banco di Roma per la Svizzera (Svirobank).

It is an illusion that Swiss banking secrecy protects everybody. It protects many tax-dodgers, and all breakers of currency regulations. But, once given evidence that shareholders have been defrauded, the Swiss authorities are supposed to order any bank to open up its books. They have not always complied with their obligations, as we shall see, but since the Ambrosiano crash they have, for the most part, cooperated with the Italian authorities.

So the Italians were able to discover that the owner of the account at the Crédit Suisse was the Lugano lawyer, Marco Gambazzi, whom we have already met as director of a nominee company which held shares in CIM. He was interrogated on 29 October 1986 about the money going to Pazienza through his account at Crédit Suisse. He said the credit to his account had been by order of "a client" of Svirobank. He had been asked to undertake the operation by "a functionary of an Italian bank belonging at the time to the Pesenti group". This man told him that the funds were "of Vatican origin", but that he did not know who was the beneficiary.

Gambazzi made it clear that this was not the only payment of its kind. "Already, at a time before this operation, this functionary had told me that the principal of this type of operation was the IOR's Mennini, a person I did not know. At this point I should specify that on other occasions, always by the same route, this functionary had asked me to execute operations of this type, that is to receive particular sums on my account and immediately to pay them out to other accounts which were from time to time indicated to me, always at Swiss banks."

Gambazzi admitted that, clearly, his role in the operation was to hinder any reconstruction of the movements of the funds. He would not give the name of the Italian functionary or the bank. This, he said, would breach his obligations of secrecy.

(Gambazzi was a good man for secrecy; he was custodian of the secret agreement signed in Lugano on August 6 1975, when the Rizzolis agreed that Montedison should get favourable mentions in the *Corriere*.)

Still, the investigators had the clue that the "functionary" came from a bank which had been owned by Pesenti at the time. There were three of those. One was Credito Commerciale. They interrogated both its general manager, Giuseppe Lazzaroni, and the manager of the Milan branch,

Raffaello Bartolomasi. Both admitted their dealings with the IOR. Bartolomasi had been in regular contact with Mennini. They recalled a phone call from Mennini, about the transfer of funds "from one foreign account to another with the interposition of a third party". They were not absolutely sure whether Gambazzi's name had come from them or from Mennini.

According to Bartolomasi, this happened several days before the September 1981 operation, and was the only occasion on which Gambazzi was contacted "for this type of operation requested by Mennini". Gambazzi, as we have seen, said it happened several times. They cannot both be right, and the Credito Commerciale officials may have been trying to protect the IOR. But it is also possible that Gambazzi had been approached by more than one functionary on behalf of the IOR. Credito Commerciale was only one of a number of banks with IOR accounts containing back-to-back lire. They included the other two Pesenti banks, the Banca Provinciale Lombarda and the Istituto Bancario Italiano.

It is clear that at least from December 1975, if not earlier, a route had been established by which lire were illegally exported from Italy and converted into dollars by the IOR. The lire originated from the Ambrosiano group banks, being debited to the special IOR accounts; they were then transferred to IOR accounts at other Italian banks, from which they would be moved, presumably at Calvi's request, to the IOR-controlled Svirobank in Lugano, being converted into dollars at a premium rate in the process. Then the dollars were transferred to the Crédit Suisse in Lugano, to be passed on to whatever account Calvi had designated.

The lira back-to-back operation also became an integral part of Calvi's overseas operation. Whenever the Cisalpine's resources were under pressure, and it was difficult for Calvi to feed United Trading by way of the foreign currency back-to-backs, he could resort to this illicit supply of lire. It was expensive, because of the premium the IOR charged for the exchange conversion, but it was a useful emergency supply.

I have estimated that, between the end of 1975 and September 1981, Calvi illicitly took about 50 billion lire from the Ambrosiano group banks, and exported them through his lira back-to-back arrangement with the IOR. Using the exchange rate ruling at the time of each payment, the total is equivalent to about $50 million. To judge from Calvi's notes, the IOR usually charged a premium of 25 to 30 lire more than the official rate (although sometimes it may have been considerably higher) and so the IOR's income from these exchanges must have totalled 1.25 billion lire.

Of this $50 million, $16 million went to Zitropo and another $5.6 million to Calvi's other offshore companies – the bulk of it to Palmetto, which paid the minor bribes. Then there was the $3.5 million paid to Pazienza. Much of the rest was also used for payments to Calvi's close associates, distributed through accounts controlled by Ortolani. About $8.5 million cannot be accounted for.

All this money was, in reality, lost the moment it was paid. It should have been recorded as an expense. Instead, it was recorded in the books of the Ambrosiano group banks as advances to, or deposits with, the IOR. In the strange accounting between Calvi and the IOR for the lira back-to-backs, the sums were also added to the notional amounts owing *to* the IOR. The sums seem to have been somewhat arbitrarily allotted to the CIM, Setemer or XX Settembre accounts. But in late 1977 the "RED-B" account was opened. This seems to have been done specifically to reflect a sudden steep rise in the use of lira back-to-backs for the illegal export of currency.

On 4 February 1976 Marcinkus attended his tenth Cisalpine board meeting. This one was in Geneva. Calvi disclosed to the board that the Cisalpine now had a 5 per cent interest in Ortolani's bank, Bafisud. It was resolved to increase the paid-up capital from $9 million to $12 million, which meant a further investment of $375,000 on the part of the IOR, bringing its total commitment to $1 million. Yet Marcinkus must have known that the solvency of the Cisalpine depended entirely on the ability of United Trading to repay the dollar and Swiss franc back-to-back loans. At the end of 1975 these totalled $175.3 million (including the $12 million for Zitropo's capital increase). All this was still appearing on the Cisalpine balance sheet as deposits with independent banks. It accounted for 78 per cent of them.

By the time of the board meeting, Calvi had succeeded in reducing the total by $7.5 million, largely as a result of the sale of the Ambrosiano shares to the Rizzolis. But the following day another 35 million Swiss francs went into United Trading – and straight out again. It was paid to a subsidiary of La Centrale based in Nassau, La Centrale Finance. This company seems to have accumulated vast losses through speculation, though it is not clear how. Calvi decided the loss had to be concealed. He clearly considered the money irretrievably lost. The 35 million Swiss franc payment was noted in his United Trading balance sheets, but no value was attributed to it, so that United Trading's deficit went up to some $57 million. A further $5.9 million was paid to La Centrale Finance and written off in the same way a few months later.

So the foreign currency back-to-back mechanism was under pressure. Calvi turned again to the lira mechanism. On 19 February 1976 a fourth IOR debit account was opened, "R-1" or no 3001, at the Ambrosiano in Milan. From this 2 billion lire went into the IOR's account at the Banco di Santo Spirito in Rome. This money has not been traced, but it seems probable that it was transferred abroad. Indeed, the account was labelled an "external" lira account, which implied that permission had been granted to place it with a foreign bank. Calvi was later to claim that this label was an administrative error. But there seems little doubt that the money was paid to Switzerland, where it would have been converted into about $2.6 million. It was then almost certainly paid to Ortolani-controlled accounts.

This can be deduced from the fact that more money went through accounts for the benefit of Ortolani, Gelli and Calvi than can be accounted for by the sums known to have been paid out of United Trading.

Indeed, United Trading made only one payment to an Ortolani-controlled account in 1976. On 9 April it paid $1.8 million to a new Ortolani account at the Union Bank, 594 427 60R, and from there $400,000 was transferred to a new Union Bank account opened for Gelli, 594 616 AW, while $350,000 went to Calvi's account, 593 608 ZD. Ortolani appears to have kept $625,000 of the remainder. And $425,000 went to the unidentified account 591 969 PE.

This payment was clearly linked with P2 influence at the Mincomes. Three days earlier, that ministry had granted permission for the Banca Cattolica to increase its credit line to the Cisalpine from $25 million to $50 million. Calvi needed this because he had not been able to persuade the rebellious directors at the Varesino to approve that bank's $25 million facility to the Cisalpine. On the contrary, the bank had told the Mincomes that it was allowing the authorisation already given to lapse.

The price of the permission given to Cattolica was clearly listed in Gelli's schedule. It is hard to make sense of the figures entered against it, but they may mean that a total of $4.5 million was to be paid. This would suggest that the $1.8 million from United Trading was not enough, and that the balance had come from the 2 billion lire removed by way of IOR account "R-1". The P2 men were now rewarding themselves with staggering sums. Ortolani seems to have appreciated that this might lead to trouble. On 5 April 1976 he quietly established himself as an official resident of Brazil.

In the first four months of 1976, the value of the lira fell by more than 30 per cent against the dollar. The Italian Government decided that this was because too many people were taking their money out of Italy. So they may have been, but what was there in Italian life that frightened them? Instead of coping with the country's economic problems, the government brought in tougher currency regulations, enacted on 30 April as Law 159. There was an amnesty for those who would admit that they had previously taken money out of Italy, but for those who did not own up the penalties could be applied retrospectively. (This was why Law 159 was later applied to La Centrale's purchase of Toro shares in November 1975.) The penalties now included imprisonment, and fines related to the sums involved.

The small fry, the people with lire lining their underwear, became a little more careful. They sewed the notes in better, so that they did not rustle. But the big fish, for whom the new net was designed, did not believe that anything could catch them. Calvi did not change his methods in the least. Within weeks of the new law he embarked on the deal which was to form the basis of the second main charge against him at his trial five years later.

Calvi had intended to gain complete control of the Credito Varesino in 1972. But, as we have seen, he still had rebellious directors to contend with. La Centrale did not own a majority of the shares. Calvi had exercised control by his pact with Anna Bonomi. But since early 1975 they had been disentangling their joint arrangements. Calvi had already bought back the Bonomi interest in Suprafin and La Centrale. On 9 February 1976 the pact for control of the Credito Varesino was confirmed in a note between the parties. But both clearly wanted to cut the link. On 27 May a deal was done over the Bonomis' Varesino shares. The main part of this was straightforward. La Centrale would buy, in instalments between June and November, 2.4 million Varesino shares – enough to give it outright voting control – at 10,000 lire each.

The directors who had supported the Bonomis were replaced at once. In July the Varesino reapplied to the Mincomes for authorisation to advance $25 million to the Cisalpine. This was immediately granted.

But the Bonomis owned another 900,000 Varesino shares. They sold these on 31 May, ostensibly to a Lugano bank, the Banca della Svizzera Italiana, at 8,100 lire each, or a total of 7,290 million lire. As a result of a rights issue, this block increased in number to 1,350,000 and in cost to 7,340 million lire. It was then sold to La Centrale (or, more accurately, to a subsidiary, Sparfin) on 29 November.

Sparfin paid 7,100 lire a share, against a market level of 4,850. The total, with costs, was 9,569 million lire. When the Bank of Italy inspectors tried to make sense of this transaction, they came to the conclusion that the shares had really been under La Centrale's ownership all along. They thought the difference between the 9,569 million lire La Centrale paid, and the 7,340 million the shares cost – 2,229 million lire – had been illegally exported. Calvi could not very well explain, either to the Bank of Italy or to the court which tried him, what had really happened. It was not the Swiss bank but the secret network company Anli which had bought the shares at the end of May. And it had paid, not 8,100 lire each, but 10,000. Who got the difference? Certainly not Calvi; probably the Bonomis. Anli still made a profit of some 500 million lire when it resold the shares to La Centrale.

It was at this point that Calvi's relations with the Bonomis began to deteriorate. Anna Bonomi still maintains that Calvi had promised to pay her half the profits made on the Credito Varesino operations in 1972. But Anna Bonomi owed United Trading $5,518,670.47 – the original $5 million loan made in the autumn of 1974 plus accrued interest. On 18 November 1975 she gave Calvi a *cambiale*, or promissory note, for this amount. Calvi clearly expected this to be paid one day, since he continued to enter it in his United Trading balance sheets.

She borrowed a further 3.25 billion lire from Calvi in Italy, pledging as security jewels held by the Rome jeweller Bulgari.

Calvi had some cause for optimism in the spring of 1976. His support operation for Ambrosiano shares was no longer necessary. In the first three months of the year the market price rose by more than 20 per cent, without any help from Suprafin. Calvi took immediate advantage. At the annual meeting of Ambrosiano shareholders on 27 March, a plan to double the bank's capital was announced. Shareholders were offered one new 1,000 lire share free for every two they held, but were asked to pay 4,000 lire for another new one, so that 40 billion lire would be raised for the bank. Of this, 10 billion lire would go to double its capital; the extra 30 billion would go to reserves.

This involved the offshore network in some expense. United Trading had to take up its allotment, bringing its holding to 530,280 shares. The Rizzolis' holding also had to be increased, to 1,020,000 shares. As the Rizzolis had no money, they had to be lent some.

In Italy, Suprafin had to take up some 86,000 unwanted options, and then buy in the market to prevent the price from dropping back. However, the issue was reasonably well taken up, and the worst of the crisis was over. Calvi may have hoped that one day the price would rise to a level which would enable him to wipe out the United Trading deficit.

The IOR took up all the new shares to which it was entitled, both for the holdings in its own name and for those in the names of Ulricor and Rekofinanz, bringing its total holding to 917,076 shares, at a cost, with expenses, of more than 933 million lire. Half the new shares due to the two Liechtenstein nominee companies were put directly into the IOR's name, so that its known holding rose from 113,538 shares to 399,576. Its true percentage stake remained constant at just under 4.6 per cent. There was clearly no flagging in its support for the Ambrosiano. True, the IOR deposits at the Cisalpine had fallen by about $14 million since late in 1975, to about $92 million. But, with the loans to the secret network, and the debenture loan to BA Holding, the IOR was still supporting Calvi with more than $190 million.

Some of its other attempts at investment were equally unwise. In late 1975 a small American bank, Security National Bank of New Jersey, got into the papers because of a strange takeover bid.

Joseph Dunn, a lawyer, founded his bank in 1966. In 1969 he had what seemed a good idea at the time. If he specialised in loans to Federal Bureau of Investigation agents, he would not need to spend any money or time in checking their creditworthiness, because every FBI agent is by definition respectable. When the FBI agents discovered that Dunn's little bank would hand over unsecured loans of up to $25,000, and charge them only 8 per cent when the going rate was 11 or 11.25 per cent, they were delighted. By the end of 1975, some 300 FBI borrowers owed the bank a total of over $1 million, or more than a third of the bank's net worth.

Unfortunately their respectability did not make all of them good payers. The bank's net income declined from a peak of $176,775 in 1970 to a deficit of $40,000 in 1975. The Federal Court of New Jersey began to hear allegations by Dunn that there had been a conspiracy against him; that some of his employees had ganged up with borrowers who were not really FBI men.

In the midst of this case, Dunn became aware that someone was trying to take over the bank, and was offering $28 each for shares worth only $17. Why would anyone want to pay so much for a rapidly failing bank? The suggestion has been made since that the bank's list of 300 FBI agents, with details of their personal financial difficulties, would be useful to the Mafia.

However, there is no evidence that the man making the takeover bid knew about the list of FBI agents. Dunn's troubles with his employees were not reported in the New York Times or the Wall Street Journal. Besides, the would-be buyer seemed respectable. He was John J. Fedigan, head of the Fiduciary Investment Company (which had no connection with Sindona's Fiduciary Investment Services). This company had no other business than to administer fiduciary funds of $4 million for the Passionist Fathers of New Jersey, who owned six old people's homes and ran them at a profit. The Passionist Fathers had also invested $500,000 dollars in non-voting shares of the Fiduciary Investment Company. "As good as General Motors," explained the treasurer of the Passionist Fathers, when he was questioned about this in the Federal Court of New Jersey.

Dunn, resisting the takeover, filed a complaint against Fiduciary and against Fedigan personally, alleging, among other things, that Fedigan had not disclosed who his backers were.

In subsequent depositions to the court, reported in the *New York Times* the following April, Fedigan revealed that the Banco di Roma per la Svizzera (Svirobank) had invested $1 million in non-voting Fiduciary stock early in 1975. The investment had come about because he was a friend of Marcinkus, whom he had met in his previous job working for the Bessemer Trust, where he handled the portfolios of two religious bodies, the Carthusian Order of Monks and the Eastern Province of Passionists. The friendship blossomed and they played golf together whenever they could. When Fedigan decided to set up on his own, with the backing of the Passionists, Marcinkus "said he was going to do everything he could to help me", according to Fedigan. That help came when Marcinkus got Mennini, as a director of Svirobank, to arrange the investment. Evidently Svirobank did whatever Marcinkus wanted, even handing over $1 million to a golfing companion.

No sooner had the name of Marcinkus been mentioned in public than the offer to take over Dunn's little bank was withdrawn. Dunn himself died five weeks later. The matter attracted no attention in Italy at the time. But later, when the Italian authorities were hoping to bring Marcinkus before a court of law, this was one of the episodes they began to study closely.

Undeterred by his setback in New Jersey, Marcinkus was setting up another deal with Calvi, the details of which, to this day, have not fully come to light. The deal involved that other friend of Marcinkus, Stefano Falez. Calvi had decided that his expanding Ambrosiano group needed grand new offices in Rome. And what could be more suitable than XX Settembre, with its Palazzo di Vetro? It did not deter Calvi that he would have to take over not only the building, but also its debts.

SIXTEEN

Sit-in at CIM and RED for Rizzoli

In late April 1976 the board of the Ambrosiano formally decided to buy XX Settembre from the IOR. The Palazzo was valued at 27.5 billion lire (about $32 million) and its acquisition would be completed within a year. But the takeover of the debts was immediate. The Ambrosiano paid 1.8 billion lire into the IOR's main account, 42800 at the Ambrosiano branch in the Piazzale Gregorio VII, Rome.

Surely this deal at least could be straightforward. The Ambrosiano was legally and openly buying a new office in Rome. Yet the story became so convoluted that the Bank of Italy inspectors were baffled.

On 3 May, a few days after the Ambrosiano's undertaking to buy the company, XX Settembre held its annual general meeting. Nobody mentioned the Ambrosiano. De Strobel was reappointed auditor for another three years. His superior at the IOR, Luigi Mennini, not previously an auditor, was now appointed one for three years.

Four days after that meeting, on 7 May, the Ambrosiano credited the IOR's account 10841 at the bank's head office in Milan with 22,085,159,997 lire. It was described as a *deposito cauzionale* – a down payment guaranteeing the deal. The strange figure was reached by deducting the total of XX Settembre's bank debts from the original 27.5 billion lire.

What happened to this money? According to the bank statement of account 10841, which was obtained by the Bank of Italy inspectors and published in the P2 Commission documents, 20 billion lire of it was paid into the IOR's account 42800 in Rome, from which it was immediately transferred to deposit account 42801. There it remained untouched until December, while a little more than 2 billion lire, still in account 10841 in Milan, also remained untouched for the time being.

But among Calvi's papers are two handwritten notes (one of which is reproduced on page 185) clearly showing the 22,085,159,997 as broken down into eight constituent parts. The largest component, 8.65 billion lire, carried no form of identification. On one of the notes the other items carry various cryptic marks. In both notes, Calvi wrote against the second largest lira sum another figure – 4,625,000.

This can be identified. On 19 May 1976 Lepartner, Zitropo's subsidiary, received $4,625,000 from the Crédit Suisse in Lugano, which it paid on to its parent as a "dividend". Thus Calvi's notes clearly show that part of the down payment was in reality allocated for conversion into dollars and removal from Italy by way of the IOR-Svirobank-Crédit Suisse route.

But the lire could not have been at the same time in the IOR accounts and in Switzerland. So it looks as if Calvi and Marcinkus had agreed on yet another back-to-back arrangement. Leaving the down payment intact, the IOR used other lire it held at other accounts to effect the payments Calvi asked it to make.

It seems likely that more lire were converted into dollars, for on 11 June Lepartner received another $440,000 from the Crédit Suisse. And Palmetto – the one for the minor bribes – also got $440,000.

Calvi's lists also suggest that 2.9 billion lire went to repay the original CIM back-to-back account no 001 7 55000 at the IOR. This would simply have meant wiping the debt off the Calvi-IOR secret accounting system; the IOR made no corresponding repayments to the Banca Cattolica account B, or any of the other special debit accounts, and the funds would thus have remained within the pool of back-to-back lire, free to be used for some other purpose.

Were any of the lire designated for the IOR itself? Probably the 8.65 billion lire represented money owed to the IOR for the majority holding in XX Settembre. On 29 May 1976 control of the company clearly passed to the Ambrosiano. Falez resigned as sole director, to be replaced by Leo D'Andrea, a former employee of the Bank of Italy. He had inspected the Ambrosiano in 1970, when the great fraud was not in operation. On his retirement D'Andrea became a consultant to the Ambrosiano group. When he took up this new post at XX Settembre, de Strobel and Mennini resigned their recent appointments as auditors, to be replaced by known Ambrosiano associates.

At the end of June 1976 Calvi modified his plans. XX Settembre would be acquired, not by the Ambrosiano itself but by another company in the group. He chose the pasta manufacturer, Pantanella, now owned by La Centrale. The down payment was now switched into Pantanella's name, and there was a curious retrospective adjustment of the books, in which the original 22,085 million lire credit to the IOR's account 10841 was reversed, and instead it was put into a special IOR account, no 10843. But the

21.500.000.000
5.414.840.003
—————————
22.085.159.997

22.085.159.997
14.106.744.877
—————————
7.978.415.120

3.650.000.000
1.553.944.785   F2
x 2.902.800.092   e
1.000.000.000   St
14.106.744.877

1.500.000.000   c
844.000.000   T2
—————————
2.000.000.000
500.000.000   Pol
2.500.000.000
5.478.415.120   F2   4.625.000
7.978.415.120

x   1.000.000.000
569.049.265
—————————
1.569.049.265
1.000.000.000
—————————
569.049.265
500.000.000   T2
—————————
69.049.265

2.902.800.092   x
1.000.000.000
—————————
3.902.800.092

200.000.000   g?
200.000.000
—————————
1.800.000.000
300.000.000   b
1.500.000.000

Ambrosiano still intended to make the Palazzo into its Rome office. That ambition was frustrated by the shopworkers of Rome.

On 8 September a special meeting of CIM shareholders was called. Three of the five directors were present: Giuseppe Marziale, Maurizio Bossini and Mario Davoli (a known associate of the Ambrosiano). Mennini and Spada did not attend, but de Strobel was there in his capacity as auditor.

Marziale reported that the accounts up to 30 June showed losses of 930 million lire – virtually the entire capital. These losses would have to be covered by reducing the share capital from 1 billion lire to 70 million lire. Attempts to restructure had been aggravated by the refusal of the workers to cooperate in a voluntary reduction in numbers; the various "institutes of credit" were making continuous and pressing requests.

The meeting decided that there was no alternative but to put the company into liquidation the following day. Two liquidators were appointed, one of whom was the managing director, Bossini. They dismissed the company's 370 employees and closed the stores with effect from the end of the week.

This caused an immediate storm of protest. On the night of Saturday 11 September the sacked workers occupied both the Palazzo di Vetro and the company's other large Rome store, in the Piazzale del Radio. There were demonstrations in Genoa and Reggio di Calabria, where the other CIM stores were.

The workers' representatives had heard about the plan for the Ambrosiano to take over the Palazzo di Vetro. They argued that the company's public explanations for the closure were merely an excuse. Supported by the unions representing distribution workers, they called for the intervention of the Minister of Labour. This was Tina Anselmi, the lady who was later to head the parliamentary commission of inquiry into P2. Her ministry, as it happened, was the other main tenant of the Palazzo.

She asked her undersecretary, Giacinto Bosco, to talk to both parties. After five days he secured a truce. The company would remain in liquidation, but the stores would reopen, to give the government and the company time to find a solution which would ensure jobs for the employees. Effectively, CIM had given in. That is, the IOR had. Nobody had yet spotted that the IOR owned the company; those well-known figures Mennini and Spada had stayed away from the final shareholders' meeting. But the Vatican connection would inevitably have come out, if the dispute had continued.

The climb-down was costly. In the second half of 1976 CIM lost some 3.8 billion. Where did the money come from? From the Ambrosiano group banks, by way of the lira back-to-backs. The original CIM account, as we saw, had probably been paid off out of the down payment on XX Settembre.

Subsequently two new CIM accounts were opened, 001 6 02535 and 001 6 02536, shown in the document on page 162. The small account probably reflected the CIM's reduced capital of 70 million lire, with accumulated interest. The operative one was clearly the larger account. As far as CIM's balance sheet was concerned the money seems to have been entered in its liabilities under the vague heading of "correspondents". This item had soared to nearly 1.4 billion lire by the time liquidation was decided, and by the end of the year it had nearly doubled. It was probably mainly to finance this that the IOR borrowed another 2 billion lire from the Cattolica on 27 October.

It was not until early 1978 that alternative employers had been found for all the CIM staff and the company was able finally to cease operations. By the end of that year accumulated losses had reached 8 billion lire (about $9.6 million), almost entirely financed by "correspondents" of 7.9 billion. The CIM account stood at 11.36 billion lire; some of the difference was accounted for by accumulated interest, and it is possible that some of the lire paid to Switzerland had been added to this account.

The IOR had not handled the matter exceptionally badly, by the standards of Italy in the 1970s. At that time trade union power made it virtually impossible for a business which was losing money to sack its workers. It was not until 1980 that, during a confrontation at Fiat, the workers defied their own unions and returned to work.

Before that, the state could often be forced into bailing out threatened firms. The IOR had no need to ask for Italian government money; it could use the Ambrosiano. But the money had been irretrievably lost. CIM shares and promissory notes held by the IOR were worthless. By the device of the lira back-to-backs, the loss was hidden, appearing in the books of the Ambrosiano group as deposits with the IOR. How the IOR presented the matter in its own books we do not know for sure. If it was shown as a debt from the Ambrosiano, this would have been false.

Once CIM had agreed to reopen the store, it could not honour its agreement with its landlord, XX Settembre, to leave the Palazzo by 30 November 1976. It had already been paid 1.2 billion lire in compensation, but it was not in a position to give that back. It did not even pay the rent it owed for 1976. While it was still occupying the building, conversion work could not be started. Besides, during the dispute the government had indicated that it would not allow a change of use for the building. So it could not become the Ambrosiano's Rome base.

Calvi and Marcinkus appear to have renegotiated the arrangements over XX Settembre. On 1 December 1976 the fifth IOR lira back-to-back account, no 3003 "S", was opened at the Ambrosiano in Milan. In the first three days of the month 23 billion lire ($26.6 million) were debited to it and transferred to IOR accounts at six other banks.

The Bank of Italy inspectors did not mention this huge payment in their attempt to unravel the XX Settembre operation, but there can be little doubt that it was an important part of it. If the analysis of the original down payment suggested by Calvi's notes is correct, this new account would probably have reflected a decision to refinance the sum through the back-to-backs. That is, the 23 billion would enable the IOR to repay the down payment to Calvi (or rather to Pantanella) and XX Settembre would disappear into the back-to-back limbo, allowing both the IOR and the Ambrosiano to disclaim responsibility for it in their books.

But, if that was the plan behind the 23 billion advance, it was not carried out. Calvi and Marcinkus embarked on a new operation, designed, it would seem, to create the opportunity of removing even more money from Italy by the Svirobank/Crédit Suisse route.

A small bank in Florence, the Banca Mercantile, had been chosen as a target for manipulation by Rizzoli Finanziaria, the dealing outfit set up by Ortolani and Tassan Din. In June 1976 the Savoia insurance company, then controlled by Rizzoli Finanziaria, acquired a controlling interest in Banca Mercantile at 11,000 lire a share. Savoia increased its holding to 666,300 shares, and in November 1976 it sold them to La Centrale's subsidiary, Sparfin, at 14,000 lire each. Investigators later found that 1 billion lire of this profit had gone to Calvi. It seems he used most of it to reduce Anna Bonomi's debts to the Ambrosiano by 744 million lire. Why he did this remains unclear, since he had already advanced her considerable sums. She claims the sum represented money Calvi owed her for a deal in a block of Toro insurance company shares.

On 17 December 1976 Sparfin resold the Banca Mercantile shares at 14,350 lire each. They were bought through the brokers Giammei – that is, they seemed to have been bought by the IOR. As Calvi's papers make plain, it was another back-to-back operation. The IOR opened another account, no 001 6 02545, to reflect the total cost of the shares – 9,561 million lire. However, the IOR appears to have used 8 billion lire of the 20 billion it had held since May in its account 42801 to pay most of this money, rather than drawing funds from the new debit account. Which funds the IOR used for which operations was unimportant, so long as it kept track of the total amounts.

That was the last back-to-back lira operation for six months. In the meantime, Calvi had to clear up the Palazzo di Vetro business. At the end of March 1977 he sold the pasta company Pantanella. The buyer was the Rome construction group Genghini, whose owner, Mario Genghini, had joined P2 at about the same time as Calvi. Genghini had plenty of money; he got it from the Ambrosiano. It was lending him $60 million, to be spent on Italian plant and goods for a major construction project in Saudi Arabia. About $17 million of this was now diverted into buying Pantanella from La Centrale.

Presumably Genghini was assured that the down payment of 22 billion lire made to the IOR in May 1976 would be repaid. This had still not been done. It looks as if Calvi and Marcinkus had not yet made up their minds what to do when the XX Settembre shareholders met on 28 April 1977. The documents recorded that there were two shareholders (presumably the Ambrosiano and the IOR). D'Andrea made a report in which he ascribed the company's misfortunes largely to CIM; XX Settembre had made the "useless sacrifice" of paying it 1.2 billion lire. Moreover the company's other main tenant, the Ministry of Labour, was ignoring notices to bring its tenancy to an end, and not paying the full rent it owed.

Then another shareholders' meeting was called, on 23 June. D'Andrea reported that CIM's problems might take another year to resolve. So XX Settembre must find other means, "in the financial field", of making ends meet. The capital would be doubled, to 900 million lire, and he would cease to be sole director. He was joined by a president, Luigi Landra (an Ambrosiano man) and three other directors.

On 29 June this new board of directors resolved that XX Settembre should take a controlling interest in a bank – none other than the Banca Mercantile. That same day it bought the 666,300 shares in the IOR back-to-back account for 26,000 lire each – a total of 17,323,800,000 lire. Thus the price had been inflated by over 80 per cent in six months. The deal was wholly artificial, since the shares were being transferred from one of Calvi's pockets to another, but the IOR had played its part in making this look like a genuine sale.

Who got the 7.8 billion lire profit? On the face of it, the IOR. The Bank of Italy inspectors concluded that most of it was needed to pay interest on the 22 billion lire down payment of the previous year.

Again, Calvi's papers show what really happened. There is a note in his own handwriting (reproduced on page 190) giving a breakdown of the 17,323,800,000 lire. Over 10.5 billion represented the repayment, with interest, of the 9.5 billion lire advanced to the IOR under account 001 6 02545, which was then closed. The profit, after interest, was thus only 6.8 billion.

S   23.738.074.163

6.848.313.665		3040	1500	
30.086.387.828				
				306
71.645.000	⋎	34265	1" sem	227

20
	22.085.159.997	407
	5198.547.333	
ex 22.585.000.000	27283.707.337	
	2345.045.476	
	19.912.700 diff	
	28.918.739.451	

C   p^m

3902.680.092	306
3823.444.213 /	137
84.741.898	

17.323.800.000
   60.633.420
10.582.121.124
   200.000.000
   459.000.000 —
   500.000.000   548.000
  2736.000.000   3/
   500.000.000
14978.758.528₄

17 séi

24.848.744.347

Of this the largest component was a sum of 2,736,000,000 lire, against which Calvi wrote: "3". This, it can reasonably be deduced, represented $3 million paid to Lepartner from Crédit Suisse in Lugano on 15 July 1977. Against another 500,000 lire Calvi wrote: "548,200". This clearly corresponds to $548,200 which reached Palmetto on 19 July 1977.

One thing Palmetto needed the money for was a payment of $100,000 to Calvi himself. This was less than the $120,000 the IOR would have made out of converting the lire into dollars at 30 lire above the market rate.

Of the remainder of the Banca Mercantile profit, 450 million lire was allotted to pay for the capital increase of XX Settembre. Then there were two items of 200 million and 500 million which cannot be identified. That still left 2,345 million lire, and this was used to help pay the interest on the 22 billion lire down payment. For on 29 June 1977, the same day that XX Settembre bought the Banca Mercantile shares, it also repaid the down payment to Pantanella, together with 5.2 million in interest and commissions owed to La Centrale. From Calvi's papers it can be seen that a new back-to-back account, no 001 6 02550, was opened for XX Settembre. Its starting balance was just over 24.9 billion, made up of the repayment of the 22,085 million and the 5,200 million, less the 2,345 million remaining profit on the Banca Mercantile shares.

Thus, although the IOR made the repayment out of its account 42801, it is clear that it was deemed to have been financed from the pool of back-to-back lire it had withdrawn from its special debit accounts with the Ambrosiano group banks. The puzzling aspect of the deal, from the IOR's point of view, is that it seems to have exchanged an asset – its interest in XX Settembre – for a liability. Calvi's figures appear to show that the IOR had removed at least 8,650 million lire from the pool for itself. But XX Settembre might turn out to be worth more than that. However, the deal freed IOR money which had been tied up in an asset producing no income.

It also freed the IOR from the burden of having to finance XX Settembre, which was now buying further Banca Mercantile shares in addition to the original block of 666,300 shares. The cost of all these shares was initially met by direct borrowing from the Ambrosiano. But in July 1977 XX Settembre had another huge capital increase, lifting it from 900 million to 19.8 billion lire, by the issue of 1,260,000 new shares. All the new money came out of the pool of back-to-back lire in three instalments in the second half of 1977. As can be seen from the document reproduced on page 170, all XX Settembre's shares, old and new, totalling 1,320,000, were deposited with the IOR.

It is clear that the IOR kept an eye on the affairs of XX Settembre.

Although D'Andrea continued to manage the company, on 15 July 1977 a new president replaced Landra, Giulio Pacelli. He was a nephew of Pope Pius XII, often used by the Vatican to represent its interest.

The establishment of the XX Settembre back-to-back account at the end of June 1977 was quickly followed by the opening of account "RED", no 001 6 02553. To see what that represented we must return to the affairs of Rizzoli, and the coup that was to give P2 its prize, the *Corriere della Sera*.

On 16 July 1977 the Rizzolis were due to pay the Agnellis the purchase price for their one third share of the *Corriere*. Under the formula which was agreed when the payment was deferred for three years, the sum now amounted to some 20 billion lire (about $23 million). The Rizzolis might have tried to borrow the money, but the company was already overwhelmed with debt, much of it owed to Montedison.

The answer was to find someone willing to put up new equity capital. Rizzoli's capital was 5.1 billion lire, divided into 600,000 shares of 8,500 lire each, of which 210,000 were registered in Andrea's name, 48,000 each in the names of his sons, Angelo and Alberto, and the rest in the name of Rothschilds of Zürich, acting for the family. A plan, mainly devised by Ortolani, was drawn up: 20.4 billion lire would be raised by the issue of 2.4 million new shares. But who would put up the money?

On 11 July 1977 the Ambrosiano advanced 12.5 billion and the Cattolica 7.5 billion to Rizzoli for the "increase in capital", thus enabling the company to pay the Agnellis on time. On the same day the Ambrosiano granted Rizzoli a further overdraft facility of 2.5 billion lire. All this new credit was to be secured on unquoted Rizzoli shares. The overdraft facility could be made to look like normal banking business, but the 20 billion lire for the capital increase could not, unless it were just a temporary measure. Another solution had to be found.

Calvi had one at hand. On 29 July Andrea Rizzoli sold the 2.4 million new shares; they went first to the brokers Giammei, then to the Credito Commerciale and finally to a nominee company, Compagnia Fiduciaria Nazionale. The last-named turned out to be acting for Giammei. That same day the IOR, drawing on eight different bank accounts, paid 20,524,240,000 lire to Giammei. Giammei paid 20.4 billion lire to Andrea Rizzoli, which he paid to the company, enabling it to repay the 20 billion lire owing to the Ambrosiano and the Cattolica.

That same day two Milan lawyers, Gennaro Zanfagna and Giuseppe Prisco, joined the Rizzoli board at Calvi's request. They were told that they were to represent the "institution" financing the capital increase, but were never told, according to their later testimony, what that institution was.

Some later investigators thought it must have been the IOR, putting up the money on its own account.

But it is now clear from Calvi's papers that the money came from the pool of back-to-back lire. On 27 June that pool had been swollen by the opening of the IOR's sixth debit account, no 12498 at the Credito Varesino, with the withdrawal of 25 billion lire. On 10 July a further 10 billion lire was debited to account 188 B at the Cattolica. Most of this money was designated for the new "RED" account, and the rest of it was used to finance the XX Settembre operation, taking place at almost the same time. Calvi's notes indicate that, in addition to the 20.4 billion lire plus costs, needed for the Rizzoli shares, a further 1.5 billion lire was put through the "RED" account at its inception. This cannot be traced. Presumably someone was being paid a commission for something.

The result of the transaction was that 20 billion lire of direct debts of Rizzoli to the Ambrosiano and the Cattolica were replaced by 22 billion lire of indirect debts to the Ambrosiano group banks by way of the IOR, with the IOR in turn owed a notional matching amount. This differed from some of the other deals, in that the IOR had some idea of when and how the loans might be repaid. On that crowded day, 29 July 1977, the Credito Commerciale addressed a letter to Andrea Rizzoli. Raffaello Bartolomasi, the man at Credito Commerciale who handled the IOR's business, was in charge of the matter. But he did not draft the letter. That was done by Ortolani, who, according to Angelo Rizzoli, typed it himself in a room in the Hotel Palace in Milan. It informed Andrea Rizzoli that he could reclaim the 2.4 million new shares on payment of certain sums on or before certain dates: 35 billion lire before June 1981, 45 billion before 30 June 1983 and 55 billion before 30 June 1985.

It must have been clear to everyone, including Andrea Rizzoli himself, that only a miracle would enable him to meet these terms unaided. He was, in effect, handing over future control of the company. This also meant that the IOR could hardly rely on the letter as security that the "RED" account would eventually be cleared. It would be better to have the share certificates.

What did happen to the share certificates? They were sent to Giammei, and the IOR put its stamp on them. But, at some unknown moment, the IOR's name was blacked out again. Nevertheless, the letters remained visible. Four years later, when the certificates were returned (in what circumstances we shall see) Angelo Rizzoli saw them. He disclosed this to the P2 commission in March 1982. Press and TV seized on his words. Had the Vatican secretly financed and controlled the country's leading newspaper for four years?

Marcinkus agreed to be interviewed by *Panorama* in May 1982, and was naturally asked about the IOR stamp on the Rizzoli share certificates. He replied: "The IOR has never owned any shares of the *Corriere della Sera*." (Presumably he meant Rizzoli.) "It was proposed to us that we should provide some finance: an interlinked operation. We would have financed a third party, via a bank, and the recipient of the loan would have given as security shares of the *Corriere*. For this reason, as a first step, the stamp of the IOR was placed on the shares of the publishing company, without, however, any signature or endorsement. In the end the operation was never carried out. At no time were the shares of the *Corriere* at our disposal."

This implied that the IOR *had* considered financing Rizzoli with its own money. Calvi's papers, and the other evidence that has come to light, show that it was never expected to be anything but an intermediary. Marcinkus could hardly be expected to explain the back-to-back arrangement to *Panorama*.

Under that arrangement it would have been standard procedure for the Rizzoli shares to have been held by the IOR, or in an IOR account at the Credito Commerciale. But the list of securities shown on page 170 contains no reference to Rizzoli shares. It shows that against the "RED" account the IOR held two "plichi chiusi" – closed, or sealed, packets. Perhaps they contained the Rizzoli share certificates. But why in sealed packets? Was there someone within the IOR from whom they had to be concealed? And who tried, ineffectively, to black out the IOR's stamp? And when?

The final lira back-to-back account, "RED-B", was not opened until late 1977. But, before we examine that, we must return to the IOR's role in Calvi's operations outside Italy.

SEVENTEEN

Way Offshore in Nicaragua

We have to go back to July 1976, when Compendium became Banco Ambrosiano Holding, the Luxembourg holding company for the legal part of Calvi's foreign empire. I have mostly called it BA Holding, to avoid confusion.

As it was legal and open, it had to have a legal, open source of funds. On 27 October 1976 the Ambrosiano wrote to the Mincomes, asking for permission to make a further investment of 292 million Swiss francs (about $117 million) in BA Holding.

This was needed, the Ambrosiano explained, because BA Holding intended to treble its capital, and the Ambrosiano would have to subscribe 72 million Swiss francs on its existing holding. In addition, the Ambrosiano wanted to increase its stake by buying more shares, or the right to subscribe for more shares. These acquisitions it expected to cost a further 220 million Swiss francs "at most". The Ambrosiano would not have to spend the money all at once; BA Holding's capital increase would be staged over six years. In the meantime, however, it would need financing by the issue of stand-by credits.

The letter contained a further request: the Ambrosiano would like to swap its 40 per cent stake in the Gottardo for BA Holding's shares in La Centrale, which it reckoned were equally valued at about 260 million Swiss francs.

The P2 member Firrao, though in charge of all such matters at the Mincomes, must have had some trouble in getting this past his minister, Rinaldo Ossola. Firrao telexed the Ambrosiano for more details, such as the number of BA Holding shares the Ambrosiano intended to buy "from third parties". Calvi could have answered this one precisely, because the "third party" was the apex of his secret network, United Trading, which held 25 per cent of BA Holding's capital. However, he stonewalled, by answering other questions instead. He said the Ambrosiano would not have to commit more than 100 million Swiss francs in any one of the six years which it was expected to take to effect the capital increase.

Two days before Christmas the Mincomes authorised the Ambrosiano to invest a total of 292 Swiss francs in BA Holding over six years, but with no more than 100 million in any one year. At once the Ambrosiano advanced 100 million Swiss francs to its Luxembourg associate.

It also swapped the Gottardo shares for the La Centrale shares. The point of this was to bring the Italian part of the Ambrosiano empire inside Italy, and concentrate the foreign part with BA Holding. It made perfectly good sense, but it had somehow been left out of the official authorisation. Later the Bank of Italy inspectors decided that this transaction was a breach of exchange controls, and sent the details to the public prosecutor. This charge against Calvi, however, was dropped.

As always, the granting of Mincomes authorisations was followed by an enormous payout. On 18 January 1977 Calvi caused United Trading to pay 6 million Swiss francs to Ortolani's account 594 427 PG 60 R at the Union Bank in Geneva. Ortolani transferred 2 million Swiss francs to an account in the name of his own bank, Bafisud. He paid 1.5 million to Gelli, another 1.5 million to the same unidentified recipient as before and 1 million to a Panamanian company, Calodria. This – again, the smallest share – was almost certainly Calvi's. The evidence shows that Calodria was a nominee company of Lombard Odier, which was handling Calvi's personal affairs at the time.

Lombard Odier is one of the great private banks of Geneva. Half a dozen of these traditional establishments, all run by Protestants, form the great attraction of Geneva for the man who wants his money handled discreetly. They announce their presence in the quietest of eighteenth-century streets by the most modest of brass plates, bearing only their initials. If you don't know that L.O. & Cie means Lombard Odier, you have no business to be there. Inside, the rooms are so arranged that the client going in will never see the client going out. Only the bank knows who its clients are.

To be part of the *Groupement* which represents these banks in Geneva, you must be an unlimited partnership. That is, each partner is liable, to the whole extent of his personal fortune, for the fortunes of the bank. A strict legal and moral code governs the partners' relations with each other, and with the world. These Geneva banks boast that not one of them would accept, as a client, the Dominican dictator Rafael Leonidas Trujillo.

At the time, of course, no one knew that Calvi was conducting a major fraud. No doubt, like many other people, the bankers of Geneva thought his law-breaking consisted only in smuggling money out of Italy, and in tax evasion. They have never considered this wrong. If other countries were to conduct themselves properly, like Switzerland, their currency would be as strong as the Swiss franc. If, instead, they are foolish enough to have currency laws, what business is that of the Swiss? And, if other countries have penal taxation, why should the Swiss enforce that?

On 28 January 1977 the Ambrosiano invested another 46 million Swiss francs in the acquisition of 25,810 BA Holding shares, taking its stake to nearly 69 per cent. Of these, 18,000 were bought from a new subsidiary of Manic, Starfield, which had bought them from the Gottardo just before the end of 1976. At the same time Starfield paid a 10.5 million Swiss franc "commission" to BA Holding itself, enabling it to record a small profit for the year. The Ambrosiano bought the other 7,810 shares from United Trading. These secret names were not to be found in the records in Italy, where the Cisalpine appeared as the seller.

On 25 March 1977 the Cisalpine was assured of a substantial increase in its resources, when the Mincomes granted permission for the Ambrosiano to double its credit line to $100 million. Another payout followed. On 5 April the Cisalpine lent $2.6 million to United Trading by way of the IOR, and on 6 April United Trading paid $2.5 million to yet another Ortolani account at the Union Bank in Geneva, 596 926 TB 60Q. Calvi, again, seems to have got a minor share, with $358,000 paid into Calodria. The rest was divided, as usual, between Gelli, Ortolani and account 591 969 PE. This payout may have reflected two Mincomes authorisations; on 6 April permission was granted for the $60 million loan to Genghini. (The one for a construction project in Saudi Arabia, part of which was diverted so that Genghini could buy Pantanella).

In July 1977 BA Holding began to increase its capital, with the issue of 75,000 new shares at par value of 1,000 Swiss francs, to bring its capital to 165 million Swiss francs. There were effectively only three subscribers to the issue: the Ambrosiano, which invested another 51 million Swiss francs in 51,510 new shares; the IOR, which increased its holding by 3,600 shares to 4,900 at a cost of 3.6 million Swiss francs; and United Trading, which subscribed some 20 million Swiss francs and brought its holding to about 40,000 shares.

On 13 July 1977, Calvi wrote to the IOR as chairman of the Cisalpine. He said that the Cisalpine would pay 71,645,000 Swiss francs (nearly $30 million) to the IOR, and that this money was to be used by the IOR to buy, on behalf of the Cisalpine, 34,265 shares of BA Holding (see Appendix B).

On 22 July this sale took place. It was in fact another back-to-back loan. But why did Calvi not simply leave the shares in United Trading, which could have borrowed the money to take up the rights issue?

Part of the answer is that the shares were sold at more than 2,000 Swiss francs each, a wholly artificial price, so that United Trading made a profit of more than $10 million. But it is also possible that Marcinkus was becoming alarmed at the size of the sums he was passing on to United Trading. The total was now some $205 million, and for this the IOR held no security at all. Now the 34,265 BA Holding shares were sent to an IOR account at the Gottardo, and 50 million Swiss francs of the payment were used to reduce United Trading's debt to the IOR.

Once this was done, however, Marcinkus was still entitled to point out that the IOR held no security for the other back-to-back loans.

This is where we come back to Calvi's letter of 26 July 1977, later produced by the IOR to the joint commission. Calvi asked the IOR to acquire and hold the 500 shares of United Trading on its behalf. He added: "It is agreed that the possession of these shares (and they constitute the entire capital of United Trading) will be held by the Institute solely as a fiduciary for the account of the Ambrosiano." Then followed the assurance, so characteristic of Calvi's "parallel" letters, that the Ambrosiano would be responsible for any consequences for the IOR that might result from its appearing to be the owner so far as third parties were concerned. The letter looks as if it had been written at the request of Marcinkus.

Yet Marcinkus cannot have been in a hurry for reassurance. It was not until seven months later that the United Trading share certificates were sent to the IOR. According to the memorandum Marcinkus wrote for the joint commission, this followed the February 1978 request from Calvi, made in some manner not specified by Marcinkus, that the IOR should sign the United Trading management contract with the Gottardo – the one which, Marcinkus alleged, was mysteriously backdated four years, without his making any protest about it at the time. We have touched on these events before; now we can see them in the context of what else was going on. The "parallel" letter of 26 July 1977 went to Marcinkus just as the Rizzoli and XX Settembre operations were being carried out. The United Trading shares actually reached the IOR soon after a second increase of capital for BA Holding. This time, 65,000 new shares were issued. On 6 February 1978 Calvi wrote to the IOR asking it to acquire a further 18,867 BA Holding shares, representing both the subscription rights on the block it had already "bought" and more shares from United Trading's holding. In fact the IOR took up 18,868 shares and the cost was 22,720,000 Swiss francs, again to be provided by the Cisalpine. Probably it was during discussions of this deal that Marcinkus pointed out that the IOR had not yet actually got the United Trading certificates. Even then, Calvi seems almost to have overlooked them, posting the Gottardo's management contract to the IOR on 27 February and the United Trading certificates not until ten days later.

. The Ambrosiano itself took up another 45,331,000 new BA Holding shares, bringing its total new investment since the Mincomes authorisation to more than 145 million Swiss francs. The Ambrosiano's direct loan had been reduced to 16.2 million Swiss francs, but it had guaranteed third party credits to BA Holding of more than 122 million Swiss francs. This was why the Bank of Italy inspectors soon afterwards concluded that Calvi had failed to comply with Mincomes conditions.

The IOR also subscribed to the capital increase of February 1978 in respect of the shares it held on its own account, bringing its investment to 11,016 shares, which had cost a total of 14.25 million Swiss francs.

It held a further 53,133 shares as a result of Calvi's letters, which clearly stated that the IOR was to hold the shares for the account of the Cisalpine.

Either Marcinkus believed this or he did not. If he did believe it, it was his duty as a director of the Cisalpine to make sure that the investment was recorded in its books.

If he did not believe it, then he thought the shares belonged to some part of Calvi's secret network, and was helping Calvi to conceal the network's existence.

Marcinkus attended a Cisalpine board meeting on 20 October 1977 in the Bristol Hotel, Paris, and another on 2 March 1978 in Zürich. He did not mention at either that the Cisalpine had invested some $50 million, about one tenth of its own resources, in the unquoted shares of its own parent company. He allowed Calvi to go on recording this money as a deposit with the IOR.

The IOR's reward for making this deception possible was quite small – one thousandth of the sum involved every six months, a total of some 188,730 Swiss francs a year, or about $100,000. It was paid out of a special account at the IOR, set up to receive dividends on the BA Holding shares and to pay interest to the Cisalpine.

One reason why BA Holding needed more money in 1977 was that Calvi had plans for it to launch another overseas bank for the group, in Managua, the capital of Nicaragua.

Calvi came to know Nicaragua through Mario Genghini, the construction boss who had so obligingly bought Pantanella. Genghini had a paper mill in Nicaragua, and some good contacts. Calvi met Bosco Matamaros, the Nicaraguan representative at the United Nations offshoot, the Food and Agriculture Organization, which has its headquarters in Rome. Matamaros organised a big dinner for Calvi, graced by the presence of the dictator of

Nicaragua, Anastasio Somoza. Calvi bought an estate in Nicaragua and obtained a Nicaraguan passport. When it ran out Matamaros was able to renew it for him, wearing his other hat as Nicaraguan ambassador to the Vatican. Calvi showed his gratitude at the expense of United Trading.

The Cisalpine began to make loans to Nicaragua. The sums were not large. The Calvi banks do not seem ever to have committed more than about $8 million. Most of the loans were for genuine commercial projects – a fishing fleet, for example, and an aluminium extruder. But some of the companies, with loans of $3 or $4 million, were controlled by the Somoza family.

There are enough real conspiracies in this book, without the imagined conspiracy between Calvi, P2 and the Vatican to finance right-wing régimes in South America. Their actions may have had that effect, insofar as the bribes they paid went to those in power. There is not much point in bribing people out of power. But only about a quarter of the Cisalpine's loans were to South American countries. The bank's efforts on that continent were largely directed to extracting bank deposits, which could be used for the ever-rising costs of Calvi's share manipulations and the demands of Gelli and Ortolani for "commissions".

Argentina proved a fertile source of deposits. In 1982, while the press resounded with stories that Gelli had financed the purchase of exocet missiles used by Argentina against the British in the Falklands, Argentinian depositors were queueing up at the British interests section of the Swiss embassy, to swear their claims on the Cisalpine in front of a British diplomat.

Marcinkus himself showed no enthusiasm for South America. At the Cisalpine board meeting in Paris on 20 October 1977, at which the establishment of the new bank in Nicaragua was raised, he expressed concern about the loans the Cisalpine had made in Nicaragua. He wanted a wider spread of risk, and a limit on the total. At the next Cisalpine board meeting, on 2 March 1978 in Zürich, he pointed out that it was a high-risk area. (It was indeed; the Sandanistas were already fighting Somoza with some success.) He suggested that the Cisalpine should look more to Mexico, which was safer because of its closeness to America.

Boosting the economies of South America was no part of Calvi's intention in setting up the Banco Comercial in Managua. The use to which he put it proves that. It got its banking licence from the Nicaraguan authorities at the end of September 1977, the path being smoothed, no doubt, by the Somoza loans. It had a small local office, and Calvi appointed a relative of Somoza's, Joaquin Sacasa, as his representative, but the bank was in reality run from Nassau. Its first loans were to three Panamanian companies recently formed by the staff of the Cisalpine. All three were technically subsidiaries of Manic, the main Luxembourg holding company of the secret network. Manic was itself, in Calvi's scheme, a subsidiary of United Trading, although its capital of $45 million was still being wholly financed by the IOR. The three Panamanian companies, and the loans to them, were there to create profits for the secret network, and to solve the problem of the huge numbers of Ambrosiano shares that Calvi had accumulated in various pockets.

The smallest borrower, with loans of some $9 million, was Ariana. It used the money to buy shares in the Cisalpine. The shares were bought either from the grandly named Ambrosiano Group Promotion Consulting Representative and Trading Company (whose main purpose, as we shall see, was to rig the profits of its parent, BA Holding) or from United Trading, which made a profit on the deal, though an illusory one.

The next largest loan, of $25 million, was to Belrosa. It used this money to buy shares in a Nassau-based investment company, Capitalfin International. This had been set up in 1971 by four Italian industrial groups: ENI, Montedison, Banca Nazionale del Lavoro and Fiat. It made a number of investments, but by the mid-1970s the dominant one was a half-interest in a British company, Navcot Shipping. The other half was owned by a shipping magnate of Russian origin but Italian connections, Boris Vlasov. Navcot had acquired Shipping Industrial Holdings, a ship-owning and insurance-broking company once chaired by the former British Home Secretary, Reginald Maudling. The broking interests were hived off into a separate company, H. Clarkson, three quarters of whose capital was subscribed by Capitalfin. Navcot was severely hit by the shipping crisis of the early 1970s, and by June 1977 had accumulated losses of more than $50 million.

The Ambrosiano joined the Capitalfin consortium at the end of 1976, when the Cisalpine acquired 980,000 shares, or some 16 per cent. By this time the reader may have formed the impression that Calvi could pick up the scent of a bad investment, and go straight for it, like a pig nosing out the truffles. It is fair to say that, at the time he joined it, Capitalfin was still recording a profit. But the troubles at Navcot were already apparent. Calvi thought the investment worthwhile, none the less, because he was helping two institutions which were to be useful to him, ENI and the Banca Nazionale del Lavoro. That bank's managing director, Alberto Ferrari, was chairman of Capitalfin at the time. One of the board members was Leonardo Di Donna, a senior executive of ENI. Both were members of P2.

Ortolani later claimed that he was responsible for the deal; he and Gelli received a substantial commission on it, in the following way. In February 1977 Capitalfin issued new shares at par value of $1 each. The Ambrosiano, this time through Promotions, was to take up 3,920,000. The initial subscriber, however, was a secret Panamanian company, Pueblo, which immediately resold the shares to Promotions for $6,272,000, giving Pueblo a profit of $2.3 million. Of this, $1.2 million was paid to Ortolani, who shared it with Gelli.

In November 1977, when the disaster at Navcot was fully apparent, Belrosa used its $25 million loan to buy both the 980,000 Capitalfin shares from the Cisalpine and the 3,920,000 from Promotions. The Cisalpine made only a small profit, but Promotions made $12.4 million. Of that nearly $6.4 million, or 14 million Swiss francs, was paid to BA Holding. Without this money, Calvi's great new holding company would have lost more than 9 million Swiss francs in 1977. Instead it was able to reveal to the world, in its brief but glossy accounts, a profit of nearly 5 million Swiss francs. Within a year Capitalfin's shares were worthless.

Of the three new Panamanian companies, much the largest borrower from the Banco Comercial was Astolfine. This was where Calvi decided to concentrate the accumulated Ambrosiano shares. In November 1977 Astolfine was lent $110.3 million, with which it acquired nearly 2.6 million shares – about 12 per cent of the bank's capital.

Astolfine bought the shares from three sources. One block came, indirectly, from Suprafin in Milan. It had again been buying shares throughout 1976 and 1977, when the market in them remained depressed, but it had also acquired a large block from Anna Bonomi. By the autumn of 1977, it held nearly 2 million shares, financed by the Ambrosiano itself. So Calvi had to do something, yet again, to relieve Suprafin of its burden. He arranged for a company called Zeffiro to buy 1,020,000 shares from Suprafin for $18.3 million – equivalent to 15,750 lire a share, when the market price was 13,000. The shares were registered in the names of Panama companies: Cascadilla, Lantana, Marbella and Orfeo. Where did Zeffiro get the money? By borrowing from the Cisalpine. But this could be only a temporary solution; if the loan were to remain on the Cisalpine's books for the year-end accounting questions might be asked. Therefore, the shares were resold for $18.6 million to Astolfine, which borrowed the money from Banco Comercial to repay the Cisalpine with interest. Banco Comercial was even less supervised than the Cisalpine, and in any case its first accounts were not to be produced until 31 October 1978.

The second block of shares acquired by Astolfine also numbered 1,020,000, but this time the price was $22.7 million, or the equivalent of

19,000 lire a share. It paid this amount because the theft of $7 million had to be covered up.

These shares, registered in the names of Sansinvest, Finkurs, Finprogram and Lafidele, were the shares that had been sold to the Rizzolis, or rather to their Luxembourg holding company Rizzoli International, at the end of 1975. In September 1977 Calvi said he would buy them back. They had doubled in number because of a rights issue, and there had been some complex restructuring in the way they were held. Essentially their total original cost, $23.4 million, was financed by two Cisalpine loans of $10 million and $14.5 million. The Rizzolis apparently expected the shares to be bought back at a price that would at least cover their cost. Calvi, who by this time would not deal directly with Angelo Rizzoli, refused. According to one account, he said he was not going to do them any more favours, as they just squandered his money. They would be paid only the market price.

This worked out at about $15 million, and a sum of $15.3 million was duly paid over. That was enough for the $14.5 million loan to be repaid with interest. But Rizzoli International could not repay the $10 million loan to the Cisalpine (transferred, meanwhile, to the Banco Comercial). The Rizzolis asked for permission to export funds from Italy to cover the deficit of Rizzoli International but the P2 man at the Mincomes, Firrao, refused. This was convenient for Calvi, because the money did not have to be found. Rizzoli International was later put into liquidation, and the loan was never repaid.

Angelo Rizzoli was bitter against Calvi, especially as he had caught a glimpse of documents suggesting that a further $7 million had been paid for the shares. He was right. Calvi arranged for yet another Panamanian company, Azalea, to buy the shares. Where did it get the money? Why, from the Cisalpine, which lent it $22.3 million. Out of this $15.3 million went to the Rizzolis, so that they could repay the $14.5 million loan.

The extra $7 million was paid into a bank account at Rothschilds in Zürich. This money was almost certainly divided between Ortolani, Gelli, Calvi and probably Tassan Din. By this time Tassan Din, though still employed by the Rizzolis, was hand in glove with Calvi.

Again, the money borrowed from the Cisalpine had to be restored before the auditors came in. In November the shares were resold to Astolfine, which borrowed $22.7 million from the Banco Comercial, to repay the Cisalpine with interest.

The third block of Ambrosiano shares acquired by Astolfine came from the apex of the secret network, United Trading. Like its subsidiary Suprafin, United Trading had continued to buy Ambrosiano shares that were circulating outside Italy, and now had 554,880. In November 1977 these, too, were transferred to Astolfine. The shares were "sold" by United Trading for $69 million, equivalent to more than 100,000 lire a share. No real money changed hands, however, since the financial arrangements were quite circular. Astolfine borrowed the $69 million from Banco Comercial and paid the money to United Trading, which immediately redeposited it with Banco Comercial, through a nominee company, Nordeurop, which was interposed to ensure that nobody should hear of United Trading.

The effect of this manoeuvre was to raise the average value of Astolfine's 12 per cent holding in the bank to $42.5 a share, nearly three times the market value. Why Calvi did it can only be a matter of speculation. By late 1977 United Trading's deficit was approaching $200 million. The outflow of money to Ortolani, Gelli and others, together with the interest that had to be paid on the IOR back-to-back loans, heavily outweighed its income from dividends. The deficit had been slightly reduced by the sale of BA Holding shares to the IOR at an inflated price, and by the sale of Cisalpine shares to Astolfine. But the huge transaction in Ambrosiano shares, yielding a "profit" of nearly $60 million, made a bigger impression.

But on whom? Calvi himself knew that none of the shares had really been sold; they still belonged to the secret network. Was he trying to reassure Marcinkus?

The creation of yet another layer of secret network companies must have been designed to confuse someone. But perhaps the person most confused, by now, was Calvi himself. Probably he had convinced himself that 12 per cent of the Ambrosiano was worth over $110 million, against a market value of about $35 million. If the market was right, then, clearly, the whole operation was bankrupt. By late 1977 Calvi had entered the world of fantasy.

EIGHTEEN

Two Scorpions in a Bottle

One fantasy Calvi could not sustain was that Sindona had vanished from his life. Sindona's lawyer in Milan, Rodolfo Guzzi, approached him in the autumn of 1977 with a suggestion. Calvi should "buy" a villa owned by the Sindona family, which would not really change hands. It was just a way of sending his old friend $500,000.

This was three years after the Sindona crash. Emerging from Taiwan, Sindona returned to the United States in December 1974. Although the Federal Reserve Bank of New York had been obliged to put in $1.7 billion of public money to shore up the Franklin National Bank, Sindona reckoned that his American friends were powerful enough to keep him out of prison. He did remain at liberty for years, living in the Pierre Hotel, New York. But the net had been closing since the Watergate scandal. Sindona's friends were friends of Nixon, and Nixon was finished.

Sindona thought he might be better off in Italy. There, the amount missing was about $386 million. If that were replaced, Sindona would not face a charge of fraudulent bankruptcy – only charges of balance sheet and tax irregularities. The case might drag on for years, and meanwhile he would have "provisional liberty".

But who could replace $386 million? Only the Bank of Italy. Gelli and Sindona's other friends tried to sell the proposal to the authorities. They got a sympathetic hearing from several politicians, including the Prime Minister, Giulio Andreotti. Three men stood out against this illegal use of public money. One was Giorgio Ambrosoli, the official liquidator of Sindona's Italian empire. The other two were in the Bank of Italy: Paolo Baffi, the Governor, and Mario Sarcinelli, head of the inspectorate.

In the spring of 1977 Calvi, under pressure from Sindona, tried to convince Baffi and Sarcinelli. He got nowhere. Sindona thought Calvi could have tried harder. At least he could contribute to the legal expenses. Hence the demand for half a million dollars.

Calvi prevaricated. On 13 November 1977 Calvi's employees, on their way to work, found the walls of Milan plastered with posters, accusing him of "fraud, issuing false accounts, unjustified appropriation, export of currency and tax swindles". Moreover, Calvi had "demanded and received the payment of tens of millions of dollars" in relation to tax transactions with Sindona. The two Swiss bank accounts Calvi had opened in false names were described, accurately.

Calvi sent his staff out to tear the posters down. But the weekly *L'Espresso* got there first, and published the accusations.

The man Sindona had hired to write the posters, and put them up, was Luigi Cavallo, known as *il provocatore*. He brought out an occasional publication, *Agenzia A*, which he circulated to journalists and politicians.

Cavallo wrote to Calvi threatening that further material would be sent to Ambrosiano shareholders and employees, should he not "reconsider the possibility of honouring the undertakings so freely made by you some years ago".

At the instigation of Gelli, Calvi met the lawyer Guzzi on 13 December 1977. Guzzi had one great merit in the eyes of Italian justice. He tape recorded many of his conversations. When the magistrates seized the recordings, they had the entire story of the blackmail campaign. "I was only helping my client," Guzzi pleaded, when he stood in the dock beside Sindona in the autumn of 1985. He was found guilty of extortion, however.

For all Guzzi's phone calls and Cavallo's posters, Calvi hesitated to part with $500,000. Just before his Christmas holiday, Cavallo sent him a letter which began: "In the tribes of Uganda there is a well-known tale of two scorpions in a bottle. They embark on a battle to the death which inevitably has a lethal outcome for both contenders."

The letter ended: "Do not make the mistake of putting your trust in your instincts of survival, or on the mercy of the first scorpion. It has been decided: either agreement and respect of your undertaking, or a fight to the death. Therefore, if you prefer to look forward to Christmas peace and your usual sea fishing trip, telephone to whom you must and make an appointment. Refinding an old friend, and normality, is certainly more enjoyable than finishing up like the second scorpion in the bottle."

Cavallo kept it up into the new year, 1978. Before the annual meeting of La Centrale in February he accused Calvi of publishing false balance sheets. (The accusation was true; the details wrong.) Cavallo's diatribe was published by the blackmailer Mino Pecorelli in his scandal sheet *OP*.

Gelli, too, put pressure on Calvi, who caved in. He met Guzzi in the Caffè Greco in Rome, a great place for plotters. Before 1870, people who dreamed of a united Italy used to meet there, and it has been kept as it was then, with marble tables and little plush-lined alcoves for intimate conversation. There Calvi told Guzzi that he had found a client willing to pay $500,000 for the villa, and Guzzi gave him the number of the bank account to which the money was to be paid.

Or so Guzzi told the parliamentary commission which was inquiring into the Sindona affair, in January 1982. Calvi, questioned by the same commission, said: "I've never entered the Caffè Greco. I don't know the place." Nevertheless, he made United Trading pay $500,000 to the bank account indicated by Guzzi, 461 954 at the Union Bank in Chiasso, at the end of March 1978. A piece of paper with the number and bank in Sindona's writing was among the papers in Calvi's safe.

Guzzi's pretence that Sindona was selling a villa was his undoing later, because the pretended sale left so many traces that Guzzi could not deny what had happened.

Sindona's later extortions were more direct. He made no secret to me, and others, that in the end Calvi paid him a great deal more than $500,000. Sindona put the figure as high as $5 million. He claimed Calvi owed him the money for Ambrosiano shares he had bought on Calvi's behalf. The later payments were almost certainly made through Gelli, but the accounts to which Gelli paid the money have never been traced.

Probably Sindona renewed his demands in early April 1978, when he met Calvi face to face. Calvi, who hated parties and by now Sindona too, attended a party given for Sindona at the Capitol Hill Club in Washington. The host was the Italian-American Philip Guarino, director of the senior citizens' division of the Republican National Committee.

Calvi told the parliamentary commission that he had met Sindona twice in New York. "He asked me for a job, but I hadn't got anything suitable."

Calvi could not admit that Sindona was blackmailing him, without admitting that the accusations were true. Nor could he admit in public that he thought Sindona might kill him. But Carlo Calvi, who was living in Washington in 1978, remembers a visit from his father, a few weeks after that party in Sindona's honour. Calvi had booked into the Hyatt Hotel, but then moved twice, first to the Madison and later to a suite at the Mayflower. Even then, because the windows were at ground-floor level, Calvi moved his bed into the kitchen. This was not paranoia. Calvi knew that Sindona was capable of hiring killers, and events proved him right.

Calvi's use of United Trading to pay that first $500,000 to Sindona was exceptional. For nearly a year, from the autumn of 1977, the secret network was used only occasionally for underhand payments, and then only for relatively small amounts. Calvi was running short of money outside Italy, and what he had he needed mainly to meet United Trading's interest bill, now some $15 million a year.

This was when he began to use the international money markets in a legal, open way. Early in 1977 BA Holding raised its first term loan of 50 million Swiss francs from a consortium headed by Crédit Suisse. But the main sources of money for the Ambrosiano's activities abroad, both legal and illegal, were the IOR and the group's own banks in Italy. By early 1978 these had been used to their limits.

Indeed, the Ambrosiano banks were well over their limits. With the second stage of the BA Holding capital increase, the Ambrosiano had committed nearly 284 million Swiss francs in just over a year, when its six-year limit was 272 million Swiss francs. The Ambrosiano, the Cattolica and the Varesino had deposits with the Cisalpine totalling nearly $167 million, also well over their limits. As long as Calvi had only the Mincomes to worry about, he could rely on Firrao to make things all right for him. He had, besides, the help of the IOR.

Apart from its shareholdings in the Ambrosiano banks, the IOR was financing the group in three direct ways:

1. Its deposits with the Cisalpine. At the end of 1977 these totalled $113.6 million, but of this $29.6 million represented back-to-back deposits from the Banca del Gottardo, made through the IOR to fool the Swiss authorities. Thus, only $84 million was the IOR's own money.
2. The "contango" loans of $20 million on the shares of Zitropo and $45 million on the shares of Manic.
3. The 85 million Swiss franc loan to BA Holding.

This did add up to about the $200 million mentioned in Sindona's attacks as coming from a mysterious source. However, at the end of January 1978 Calvi had to repay the 85 million Swiss francs. Repayment was due; it was a five-year loan made at the end of January 1973. But the Zitropo and Manic loans were due every six months, and they were regularly renewed. Why did the IOR not renew this one? It was doing well out of it; though the Ambrosiano books recorded the interest rate as 5 or 5.5 per cent, the IOR had been secretly guaranteed 7.25 per cent. Thus, over the life of the loan, the IOR had earned more than 30.2 million Swiss francs, though BA Holding itself paid out only 23.3 million. The secret premium of 6.9 million Swiss francs was paid by United Trading, swelling its deficit still further. The only inducement for the IOR to put an end to such a profitable investment was that during the five-year period of the loan the Swiss franc had risen by almost 75 per cent against the dollar, so that in dollar terms the IOR would make a profit of nearly $22 million.

The need to repay the IOR dictated the timing of the second stage of the capital increase for BA Holding. As we have seen, the IOR agreed to hold shares, but did not put up any money of its own, apart from the 3 million Swiss francs necessary to subscribe for its own entitlement. The rest was found either from the Cisalpine – and here the IOR did give temporary help, by increasing its deposits there to the record level of $130 million – or from the Ambrosiano in Italy. This was why the Ambrosiano broke through the limits imposed by the Mincomes.

Calvi was now desperately looking for new sources of funds for BA Holding. But, for the time being, his Italian banks remained the prime source. Getting the money out without further breaches of the limits was the problem, and in solving this the IOR was as helpful as ever.

Since late 1975 (if not earlier) Calvi had used the back-to-back arrangement with the IOR to take money out of Italy. It went through the IOR subsidiary in Lugano, Svirobank, and the Crédit Suisse. Most of this money had gone to subsidise the bankrupt Zitropo, but some was also used for the minor bribes of Palmetto. All this money was irretrievably lost from the moment it was paid, but it had to be added to the notional debts owed *to* the IOR to achieve at least a near balance with the amounts owed *by* the IOR to the Ambrosiano banks.

For the first couple of years of this arrangement, Calvi seems to have added the sums arbitrarily to the Setemer, CIM or XX Settembre accounts. But, late in 1977, when Calvi's disposable funds outside Italy were running short again, there was a huge rise in the sums being taken out of Italy by the IOR route. In the seven months from November 1977 more than 20 billion lire ($24 million) got smuggled out. The last of the lira back-to-back accounts listed on page 162, 001 6 02559 RED-B, appears to have been opened specifically to deal with this huge increase. It can be deduced from Calvi's notes that it was first used in late November 1977, and that between then and the end of the year over 10 billion lire went through the account, for despatch to Switzerland and conversion into about $11.5 million.

Of this, $6 million was paid to Zitropo and then sent back to Italy. Zitropo had to subscribe to a rights issue made by its ill-fated investment Pacchetti, as part of a reconstruction to keep the conglomerate from collapsing completely. If it had collapsed, Calvi would have had to admit that the IOR's $20 million loan was irretrievably lost.

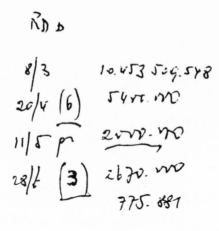

What happened to the other $5.5 million is not clear. Probably much of it was paid to Ortolani and Gelli, possibly to minimise the damage caused by Sindona's blackmail campaign. But, since it was known as "RED-B", it may have had some connection with Rizzoli – a commission, probably, for the capital reconstruction in the summer.

To meet this outflow there was still plenty of spare capacity in the credit lines extended to the IOR by the Cattolica and the Varesino the previous summer, but in December 1977 the last payment was due on the capital increase of the property company XX Settembre, which was also being financed through the lira back-to-backs. A further 5 billion lire was advanced by the Cattolica on the IOR's account no 188, or B. By the end of the year, when interest had been added to the IOR's six debit accounts at the Ambrosiano banks, it owed over 114.2 billion lire (more than $130 million).

The outflow through "RED-B" continued in the first half of 1978. Reproduced above is a handwritten note showing that three items, totalling 10,070 million lire, were debited to that account. Of this, 5.4 billion lire were converted into $6 million – the figure in brackets on the note – and removed via the IOR's Svirobank/Crédit Suisse route. I do not know who was the ultimate recipient of this money.

Then, on 11 May, 2 billion lire were debited to the account. This money did not leave Italy, and there is good reason to believe that it was paid to Anna Bonomi.

What happened between Calvi and Anna Bonomi has been gradually coming to light, though the full story may never be known. As we have seen, Calvi had lent her $5 million through Radowal, just before it became United Trading. Anna Bonomi had provided security, including the jewels at Bulgari, for lira loans ostensibly made to her front man Marinoni. These overdrafts totalled some 5.5 billion lire, or nearly $7 million, at the time of the Bank of Italy inspection.

Notes and papers found when Gelli's office was raided in March 1981 indicated that Anna Bonomi believed, for reasons not spelled out, that she was not responsible for these debts. It was not until 1988 that she claimed, under interrogation, that this was because Calvi had promised to pay her half the profits made on the speculation on Credito Varesino shares in 1972 – which, she said, came to 20 billion lire, so that Calvi owed her 10 billion lire, a debt he had not honoured. The magistrates were sceptical of this story, because she said that, although Calvi had written this agreement down at the time, the paper had been subsequently destroyed. What is clear is that, by 1978, they were at daggers drawn. Then, through Cosentino (the politician who resigned after the Lockheed scandal) she met Gelli. He offered to intercede with Calvi on her behalf. On 16 May Gelli persuaded Calvi and Anna Bonomi to sign a cooperation agreement. The same day, Anna Bonomi signed a receipt for 2 billion lire. She later said that she had got the money from Gelli, and that she did not know whether he had reclaimed it from Calvi. Gelli himself scoffed at the idea that he would have paid, and there is every reason, therefore, to believe that the money came from Calvi, who countersigned the receipt. But the magistrates, who did not understand the lira back-to-backs, were unable to trace the source.

In June 1978 2,670 million lire were converted into $3 million and taken out of Italy by the usual route. It was paid to Ortolani. This may well have been a reward to the the P2 bosses for the Bonomi peace treaty. But another peace treaty was needed, as we shall see.

While "RED-B" had become the primary account for the illegal export of money, Calvi continued to put occasional payments through other lira back-to-back accounts. His notes indicate that in January 1978 2,670 million lire were debited to the Setemer account at the IOR, which converted them into $3 million, again probably for the benefit of Ortolani and Gelli. In the first half of 1978 the CIM account was debited with various sums, totalling nearly 5 billion lire. Most of this disappeared in Italy, but 500 million lire, converted into dollars, went to Palmetto.

Calvi's papers indicate that the IOR was to get a quarter of a percentage point as its "turn" on the interest on the "RED-B" account. The IOR's main reward for helping Calvi to export money illegally remained its premium on the exchange rate – about 30 lire to each dollar. Its profit in seven months was about $750,000.

We now come to the letters which the IOR wrote on 3 January 1978 – or else wrote much later, and backdated (which would account for the Bank of Italy men not finding them). The letters were certainly written to mislead somebody. They described the accounts as "deposits" with the IOR, thus creating the impression that this was ordinary, sound interbank business. They said that "on average" the deposits were 50 billion lire from the Ambrosiano, 35 billion from the Cattolica and 25 billion from the Varesino. In fact, on the ostensible date of the letter these amounts were all well above their "averages". They rapidly increased. By the end of June the IOR owed a total of 140 billion lire, or about $170 million.

Though Calvi had paid Sindona his blackmail money, Sindona's man Cavallo wrote to the Bank of Italy about Calvi's Swiss bank accounts. On 17 April 1978 a Bank of Italy inspector, Giulio Padalino, arrived at the Ambrosiano at the head of a team of 50. They inspected the Cattolica and the Varesino, too. None of these men belonged to P2. None of them could be corrupted. They had been trained and organised by Mario Sarcinelli.

This patriotic man, determined to bring new standards of honesty to Italian life, had inspired his inspectors with his own ideals. "He is, quite simply, the finest man we've ever had here," one of them said. They were proud of their part in bringing down Sindona.

The huge loans to the foreign associates, and to the IOR, were bound to attract their attention. Calvi could not go on feeding his foreign network – even the legal part of it – from his Italian banks. Yet the demands of the network were still rising. Not nearly enough real profits were being earned to cover interest payments, let alone bribes. Quite apart from the money removed from the IOR through the lira back-to-backs, United Trading's dollar loans continued to rise in the first half of 1978. Besides the $500,000 to Sindona, it provided $4.9 million for Rizzoli operations in Argentina. The money went via Ortolani, who no doubt took a commission on his usual scale. By late June 1978 the Cisalpine's loans to United Trading, by way of the IOR, had risen by about another $23 million. The whole operation might have collapsed four years earlier than it did, if rescuers had not been found.

The rescuers were the state-owned oil corporation, ENI, and the largest nationalised bank, Banca Nazionale del Lavoro. Both were in the sphere of the Socialist Party.

For the non-Italian reader, this has to be explained. How can a bank or an oil company be socialist? The Italian word *lottizzazione* can only be translated as "jobs for the boys". The representatives of the political parties meet at least once a year to decide which party gets the top jobs in the nationalised industries. The Christian Democrats are the most numerous; they get such plums as the Banco di Napoli, and many of the richer savings banks. But the Socialist Party is strong too; it can claim ENI and the Banca Nazionale del Lavoro. The Bank of Italy has managed to remain outside the system; one governor after another has been appointed for the sole reason that he knows how to do the job. This makes the Bank of Italy an object of suspicion to many Christian Democrats.

In 1978 everybody knew that the president of ENI, Giorgio Mazzanti, and one of his directors, Leonardo di Donna, were Socialist Party men. The managing director of the Banca Nazionale del Lavoro, Alberto Ferrari, was assumed to be a Socialist Party appointee. What nobody knew then was that these three people were in P2.

ENI had formed a bank in Nassau, Tradinvest, at about the same time as the Cisalpine, and Cisalpine representatives sat on the Tradinvest board. They had drawn closer through the Capitalfin venture, in which the Banca Nazionale del Lavoro was also a partner, and of which Ferrari was chairman.

ENI's first loan to BA Holding was $10 million, put up by Tradinvest in January 1978. It helped to repay the loan from the IOR. In June 1978 the Banca Nazionale del Lavoro came forward with a much needed short-term loan of $20 million.

This money helped Calvi to restructure the secret network at the end of June 1978. To judge from the number of diagrams and notes about this among Calvi's papers, he regarded it as an important operation. Why? Was the secret network by this time a thing in itself, a work of art whose complexities made it more beautiful?

What it had long ceased to be was a way of making money. The restructuring required an increase of $52.75 million in the dollar back-to-back loans passed through the IOR – an increase that was to prove almost fatal, for two separate reasons which we shall come to later.

There were two aspects of the restructuring. First, the Cisalpine lent $19.75 million to Astolfine, by way of the IOR and United Trading. This helped Astolfine to repay its huge direct loan from the Banco Comercial – over $110 million, plus interest – which it had incurred in 1977 when it took over the secret holding of 2,594,880 Ambrosiano shares, or 12 per cent of the capital. Astolfine now resold 1.6 million of these shares to Anli, one of the three main Luxembourg holding companies in the secret network, at $50 a share. The proceeds helped Astolfine to repay the Banco Comercial. That enabled the Banco Comercial to repay the deposit made by United Trading (via Nordeurop) when it had sold its Ambrosiano shares to Astolfine for the outrageous price of $69 million.

There were a dozen book entries in this operation. As a work of art, it must have looked wonderful to Calvi. But it made no difference to his problems. The secret holding of Ambrosiano shares had been split in two. But it was all still owned by the secret network. What Calvi had done was to increase the value he put on the shares from about $42.5 each to nearly $50, but Astolfine's remaining shares were now "cost free". That is, the sum it had received for those it had sold covered the cost of those it still held. In the real world, the share price remained about $15. But in Calvi's world the revaluation provided "cover" for the siphoning off of another $19.75 million to United Trading, by way of the IOR, to meet its growing real cash deficit.

The other aspect of the restructuring was easier to follow. Calvi had to hide his disastrous investment in Capitalfin.

Capitalfin's main problems arose from two British companies, the shipowner Navcot and the broking business H. Clarkson. To keep Navcot afloat, Capitalfin poured in money during the first half of 1978. Calvi's share was $8 million, in the form of loans to Capitalfin from the Cisalpine and Banco Comercial, to add to the original investment of $25 million. By the summer of 1978, however, Capitalfin had decided that it should cut its losses in both concerns and get rid of them as best it could – but without forcing them into bankruptcy.

The cost was enormous. Navcot was handed over to Capitalfin's partner in it, Boris Vlasov, with Capitalfin taking a loss of over $80 million. The future of Clarkson was covered by a more curious arrangement. ENI was apparently willing to take over the shareholding, for a nominal $1, but for some reason this was kept secret and BA Holding ostensibly took its place. To accomplish the deal, Capitalfin was to give Clarkson $20 million. Before this deal had been worked out, however, it was apparent that the Capitalfin shares were worthless. Calvi's investment – the original $25 million and the later $8 million – was lost. The Banco Comercial and the Cisalpine ought to have written off the money.

Instead, Calvi decided to hide the loss through the back-to-back arrangements. A new loan of $33 million was arranged for Belrosa, the Panamanian company which had made the original investment. This enabled Belrosa to repay its existing loan to Banco Comercial, and to "buy" the worthless $8 million loan to Capitalfin. The name Belrosa was not recorded in the books of the Cisalpine; the loan appeared merely as an interbank loan to the IOR. So the huge commitment to Capitalfin was hidden. However, in order to accomplish the Navcot deal, Banco Comercial had to lend Capitalfin yet another $10 million.

As a result of the Belrosa and Astolfine operations the apparent debts of the IOR to the Cisalpine jumped to more than $330 million. The magnitude of these loans, and the manner in which they were made, were to have serious consequences for Calvi. But in July 1978, as the Bank of Italy inspectors pulled out of the Ambrosiano offices to write their report, he must have had a feeling of relief. It was at this moment that money from ENI began to flow in. In July and August ENI's bank in Nassau, Tradinvest, made two five-year loans totalling $60 million to BA Holding. Another ENI offshore bank, Hydrocarbons, advanced $20 million. Then, in October, Hydrocarbons lent BA Holding 100 million Swiss francs, equivalent to another $60 million.

The financial support given to the Ambrosiano by ENI was to cause uproar even before the crash. Most of the controversy centred on a $50 million loan made in December 1980, and this was investigated by Rome's senior magistrate, Ernesto Cudillo. The P2 commission also investigated, when they found that Giorgio Mazzanti and Leonardo Di Donna were P2 members.

According to their testimony, neither Mazzanti nor Di Donna initiated the loans. The financial manager, Florio Fiorini, said that was his doing. He was answerable to Di Donna, but had considerable authority. He was not a P2 member and denied that he had been influenced by P2. He had never met Gelli and had met Ortolani only once, at a cocktail party.

Fiorini explained: "There were always relations between the Banco Ambrosiano and ENI. I would say, however, that there was a big development in the relationship in 1978 for a very simple reason. We found ourselves in 1978 in the position of having concluded an important financial agreement with a producing country which would give us large liquid resources for some years, in fact for five years, although in reality a permanent liquidity, since this agreement would be renewed in the fifth year. With this prospect, in 1978 we were faced with the problem of how to invest these liquid resources ..."

The oil-producing country, Fiorini explained, was Libya. "For particular Libyan reasons, the funds were deposited with our bank so that the Libyans could account for it as interbank deposits. As a result we found ourselves with a quite significant growth in our bank in Nassau ... We looked in turn where to place part of these funds. Among the banks the one which would realise the most important conditions was the Ambrosiano..."

By "realise the most important conditions" Fiorini no doubt meant that the Ambrosiano paid the highest interest rates. He did not mention the Capitalfin disaster, which may have left the directors of ENI feeling that they owed Calvi something.

Nor did Fiorini explain why, under the deal with the Libyans, they were prepared to deposit so much money – figures of up to $500 million were mentioned – with ENI. Di Donna did this, though not very clearly. "The price of Libyan oil was a little higher than oil coming from others. The Libyans let it be known that, although they were prepared to make available financial facilities which would have the practical effect of lowering the price, they would not, for commercial reasons, make a direct discount."

This appeared to mean that some of the money ENI had to pay the Libyans would be left on deposit in ENI banks, so that they could earn interest on it.

So it was Libyan money that came to Calvi's aid in 1978. ENI lent the money to BA Holding, which passed it on to the Banco Comercial in Nicaragua. Out of ENI's initial $80 million, a very small part was used to make a few genuine commercial loans. A relatively small amount was used by Banco Comercial to acquire from the Cisalpine some of the loans made to Nicaraguan companies, including those to the Somoza family. Calvi used most of the money for two purposes: to get a grip on the Rizzoli group and to finance a huge, incestuous share deal to rig the Ambrosiano group's profits.

Rizzoli was in desperate straits in 1978. We shall see later how Calvi and his P2 friends forced Andrea Rizzoli out of the company. When that happened, in the autumn of 1978, Cisalpine came up with the $17.2 million balance of the $29 million Rothschilds' commitment of late 1976. But, before it could do this, something had to be done about the $10 million loan to Rizzoli International, (made to enable the Rizzolis to buy the Ambrosiano shares in 1975). Rizzoli International could not repay, because Firrao had refused permission for them to export the money. The loan should have been written off. Instead, it was "sold" at full value to Banco Comercial in Nicaragua. This bank also lent a further $8.8 million to Rizzoli International because it was forced to put up a guarantee for some of the loans Montedison had provided in 1975. And Banco Comercial made further loans to finance Rizzoli operations in South America.

The biggest single use to which the first ENI loans were put was the creation of artificial profits for La Centrale, now the holding company for Calvi's Italian subsidiaries – the Cattolica, the Varesino and the Toro insurance company. La Centrale had recorded a loss in 1977, and Calvi had decided that this must not be repeated in the financial year ending on 31 October 1978.

In 1978 La Centrale held nearly 20.7 million shares of Credito Varesino, valued in the balance sheet at about 3,700 lire each, rather more than the market value. It was arranged that Ortolani's Uruguayan bank, Bafisud, should buy 4.5 million of these shares at nearly 6,000 lire each, giving La Centrale a profit of more than 10 billion lire. This enabled it to declare profits for the year of over 6.5 billion lire. Nearly half was paid to the Ambrosiano in dividends.

Bafisud could not afford the shares, which cost more than $32 million. At the time its capital was $2.5 million and its total resources about $50 million. But Banco Comercial lent it $37 million to make the purchase. Probably there was a secret agreement that Calvi would buy the shares back at some future date.

By October 1978 all but $15 million of ENI's first three loans had been used up. But Calvi found he urgently needed well over $100 million. The auditors of the Cisalpine were asking too many questions.

This crisis in Calvi's affairs, never before described, was as serious a threat to him as the Bank of Italy inspection. But the story is important for another reason. It shows Marcinkus helping Calvi to deceive the auditors, and enabling him to continue his fraud.

NINETEEN

Enter Graham Garner Asking Questions

The Nassau office of the accounting firm Price Waterhouse continued to audit the books of the Cisalpine after the Zürich branch ceased to be auditors for Compendium/BA Holding in the spring of 1972.

We have seen that the first Cisalpine set of accounts must have dismayed Price Waterhouse because of its loans to mysterious Liechtenstein companies. But, since then, the back-to-back arrangements with the IOR had made the balance sheets look quite presentable. The auditors had not insisted on any notes of consequence, though they had expressed their concern at the scope of Calvi's powers.

By 1976, however, Price Waterhouse was worried. It was not being allowed to check confidential deposit accounts.

Many customers of banks in the Bahamas like to have their names known only to the bank's management. Accounts can be opened in code names. The Cisalpine had a number of such customers, including South Americans in search of discretion and Italians breaking the currency laws.

Bank auditors like to do random checks on deposit accounts, to make sure that the customers agree with what is in the bank's books. This is not possible if they do not know the real names and addresses of the customers. Price Waterhouse wrote to Calvi about this and other matters. At a board meeting of the Cisalpine, held on 22 February 1977 in the Ultrafin offices in Zürich, Calvi spoke of the auditors' "negative attitude". (Marcinkus was there, as usual.) Calvi seems to have indicated that the auditors could not have the names.

In May 1977 the board of the Cisalpine decided to replace Price Waterhouse with an equally renowned firm, Coopers and Lybrand. The final cause of the break with Price Waterhouse is unknown. The partner in charge then, Leslie Cropper, is dead. Certainly he had not discovered the back-to-back arrangement. In the usual exchange of correspondence with the firm replacing them, Price Waterhouse wrote that they knew of no professional reason why Coopers should not take on the account.

Coopers accepted the account at the end of June 1977, but it was not until the autumn that the two partners concerned, Peter Evans and Graham Garner, began to look closely at their new client. They saw the importance of the IOR to the bank's business. Garner, who did the detailed work, became curious about this secretive institution.

The new auditors' first step, in October, was to get the Cisalpine to write to the IOR, to confirm the total of its apparent debts at 30 September of $164,750,000 and 126,345,000 Swiss francs. The IOR returned the letter appropriately signed, giving Coopers no reason to suspect that the debts were not its own.

Garner also discussed the IOR with Siegenthaler and with Giacomo Botta, of the Ambrosiano's foreign department, who was in Nassau in late November 1977. They told Garner that the Ambrosiano had had a close relationship with the Catholic Church ever since its foundation, that the IOR was the Vatican central bank, that the IOR had provided considerable support for the Cisalpine and that Marcinkus, who was a director, was also president of the IOR.

Garner then sought information from the Coopers office in Rome, and was informed that the IOR was the Vatican central bank, that it conducted a full range of banking activities and that it was reputed to be very wealthy.

Thus the auditors had no reason to doubt the IOR's solidity on 20 December 1977, when they wrote to the Cisalpine defining their task, and safeguarding themselves with the usual provisos. "Because the examination is conducted primarily to enable us to express a professional opinion on the financial statements, it is not designed and cannot be expected to disclose defalcations and irregularities other than those which would have a significant effect on our opinion."

By the second week of February 1978 work on the balance sheet for 1977 had been substantially completed. The Cisalpine's assets stood at nearly $515 million. Of these, $291 million were composed of cash and deposits with other banks, broken down as between "affiliates" at $37 million and "others" at $254 million. On the other side of the balance sheet, liabilities included deposits with the Cisalpine of $466 million, of which $254 million came from "affiliates" and $212 million from "others".

Of the Cisalpine's deposits with "other" banks, $236 million, or 93 per cent, was with one bank – the IOR; of the deposits received from "other" banks, $114 million, or nearly 54 per cent, came from the IOR. The preponderance of one customer on either side of the balance sheet on such a scale could warrant a special mention, so that other customers can see how vulnerable a bank is, either to one customer's inability to pay what it owes, or to one customer's sudden decision to withdraw its money.

Garner and Evans considered whether there should be a note in the accounts about this. There was no accounting standard in force specifically requiring it. They consulted a Coopers partner in Canada, Peter Aspinall, and agreed that a note was not necessary if they were satisfied that the debt was fully recoverable.

Before approving the accounts, they obtained a letter from Calvi and Siegenthaler containing this assurance: "All transactions entered into between the Bank and the IOR were on normal commercial terms, and there were no factors included in such transactions which required disclosure in the accounts."

The auditors did not know that the IOR owned 25 per cent of the Cisalpine. They were led to believe that there was no common interest between the two. When they made specific inquiries about Cisalpine Inc, the Panamanian company in whose name the IOR shares were registered, the answer implied that the shares in its name belonged to BA Holding.

In spite of having signed the accounts without a note, Coopers were not entirely happy, and on 20 February 1978 they wrote what is called a management letter to Calvi which, among other things, set out their concern about the IOR. They had, they wrote, "been able to satisfy ourselves that the bank is considered to be of sufficient size to be able to repay" the sums it owed. However "we have had difficulty in obtaining any specific financial information about this bank. We should be grateful if, for our files, you could let us have a letter, with as much detail as you are able to give, letting us know why directors are satisfied to make advances of this size to this bank".

Coopers then asked for information on another aspect of the IOR relationship that puzzled them, though they appreciated that it was not directly their concern as Cisalpine's auditors. "IOR is both a borrower and a lender of Cisalpine. Cisalpine obtains a turn on this money which conversely means that IOR is suffering this turn. We would appreciate knowing why IOR does not merely borrow or lend the net amount since it would undoubtedly cost them less."

Coopers also indicated in the management letter that, in spite of their decision that a note had not been necessary, they were still concerned about the presentation of the IOR business in the accounts. They asked for their client's comments on whether the accounts represented a "normal spread of third party banks and that the deposits could be replaced without difficulty in the event that an individual bank might wish to repay or withdraw its deposits."

This letter had not been answered by the time of the Cisalpine board meeting on 2 March 1978 in Zürich, when it was the directors' turn to approve the accounts. All the directors turned up: Calvi, Marcinkus, Count Luciano della Porta, Garzoni of the Gottardo and Antonio Tonello, who was chairman of the Toro insurance company and of Credito Varesino, besides being a director of La Centrale. This was the meeting at which Marcinkus expressed some concern about the bank's lending to South American countries. Pierre Siegenthaler was there too, in his capacity as general manager of the bank. It is not clear whether the management letter from Coopers was seen by all the directors, but the letter from Calvi and Siegenthaler was before the meeting. Therefore Marcinkus knew of the auditors' concern about the transactions between the IOR and the Cisalpine. He knew of Calvi's assurance that these were normal commercial transactions. The fact that they were not normal could hardly have slipped his mind. Only a month earlier, he had received at the IOR the letter from Calvi asking him to to take up the second batch of BA Holding shares on behalf of the Cisalpine. And, the day before the meeting (according to his own later account) an envelope turned up at the IOR with the United Trading management contract, mysteriously backdated, inside. The articles of association of the Cisalpine made it clear what his duty was. The directors "shall cause true accounts to be kept". Marcinkus said nothing.

Calvi did not reply to Coopers and Lybrand until 29 May 1978. His answer was rather vague. He wrote that over the years the IOR had developed into a fully fledged commercial bank and was entitled to issue cheques; that it performed all the functions of the central bank of the Vatican and had a direct relationship with the Federal Reserve Bank of New York, but that, like many other central banks, it did not publish accounts; however, throughout the Cisalpine's long association with the IOR, it had not considered that it posed any credit risk and had consistently granted the facilities it required, and had recently been able to obtain very attractive rates from deposits with it.

Calvi had other reasons to worry. The Bank of Italy inspectors were troubled by two things. One was the Ambrosiano's role as a share dealer. When they produced their report an appendix was devoted to analysing the deals, some of which they could not understand because of the part played by the IOR.

What troubled them much more was the financial network the Ambrosiano had constructed overseas, beyond the reach of the Italian authorities. On 7 June the leader of the inspection team, Giulio Padalino, wrote to his superior at the Bank of Italy, Sarcinelli, examining at length the bank's financing of BA Holding, against the terms of the authorisations granted by Mincomes. Padalino added: "Much perplexity has arisen about the real nature of an acquisition, effected on 18 October 1977, of 1,020,000 shares of Banco Ambrosiano Holding (5.1 per cent of the total) by four Panamanian companies, through Cisalpine Overseas Bank Ltd, Nassau, a bank which is itself controlled by Banco Ambrosiano Holding. It has not been possible to obtain useful information about these Panamanian companies, although there is no doubt that Banco Ambrosiano knows the real owners of these shares, since it approved the transfer of the shares to them."

These were, in fact, the shares Calvi had bought back from the Rizzolis.

Coopers wrote again to Calvi on 5 July 1978, repeating their questions and pointing out that the net exposure to the IOR had risen to $155 million. This was an increase of $33 million since they had first raised the issue. They suggested that the whole matter should be discussed at a meeting.

This meeting took place in Nassau in August, when Calvi was on his way to South America. Siegenthaler was there. According to Garner, Calvi said that he himself was not aware of the financial position of the IOR, but was satisfied that it was good for its commitments. He suggested that Garner should get a reference from the Swiss Bank Corporation. He did not know why the IOR did not set off its deposits against its borrowings, but he assumed that a number of the IOR's deposits might be made in a fiduciary capacity, for its clients.

Garner said his firm now thought it would be good accounting practice to put in a note about the preponderance of business with one institution. Calvi said he thought this would jeopardise the relationship with the IOR. But he invited the auditors to draft a note for the board to consider.

It was a typical stonewalling performance. In fact Calvi was rattled. The auditors' letter had figures a month out of date. In July the net exposure to the IOR was not $155 million but about $215 million. The back-to-back loans had soared to over $330 million, largely because of the $52.75 million destined for Astolfine and Belrosa. Calvi knew they had to rise further, if only because more money would have to be borrowed to pay the interest on the existing loans.

Calvi's desperate search for a solution can be seen by the quantities of notes in various hands to be found among his papers. So far as Calvi ever had confidants, he consulted them now. If the gap between what the IOR had on deposit and what it appeared to owe could be cut back to the same level as in the 1977 balance sheet, then surely Coopers, having once accepted that figure without a note, would not change their minds? The solution is in the handwriting of Giacomo Botta. After two pages of frantic juggling with figures, he wrote: "If it were possible to feed the IOR via

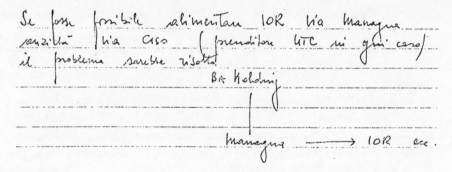

Managua rather than via Ciso (the recipient being UTC in any event) the problem would be solved." These words are followed by a little diagram indicating how the money would flow, as shown in the original reproduced above.

It was a simple answer. If the back-to-back operation could be shifted to the Banco Comercial, it could advance money to United Trading through the IOR, and United Trading could use that money to reduce its borrowings, through the IOR, from the Cisalpine; thus the IOR's apparent debts to the Cisalpine would be reduced at a stroke. Coopers and Lybrand would never know, because they were not the auditors of BA Holding, nor of Banco Comercial (which, as we shall see, had found a more pliable auditor).

But would the IOR accept the change? The IOR did not have the same relationship with the Banco Comercial as with the Cisalpine. Marcinkus was not on the board and had no deposits with it. Indeed, Marcinkus had expressed concern about the risky state of Nicaragua. Even more to the point, as Botta was drawing his diagram, in August 1978, the affairs of the IOR had once more become a matter of hot debate.

On 6 August Pope Paul VI died. He was 80, had been ill for months, and, unlike his successor, died amid scores of witnesses. His death nevertheless threw the Vatican into confusion, because he had arranged that his successor should be free to change all senior appointments.

Marcinkus was more exposed than most people in the Vatican. As he had told the FBI agents in April 1973, his rise had caused a certain amount of hard feelings. He had been very much the personal protégé of Paul VI. And the personal secretary of Paul VI, Monsignor Pasquale Macchi, was a close friend of Marcinkus. Carlo Calvi remembers once bumping into them by chance at Nassau airport. He thought they seemed annoyed at being seen together. Calvi, too, was friendly with Macchi, who collected modern paintings. Calvi gave him some. The Calvi family received gifts in return from the Vatican.

Macchi left the Vatican immediately after the death of Paul VI. So Marcinkus lost an important ally just when hostile criticism of the IOR was coming to the surface. Cardinal Egidio Vagnozzi was head of the Prefecture for Economic Affairs, set up by Paul VI in 1967. He was responsible for all the Vatican's financial bodies *except* the IOR, and the exception had long rankled. He is said to have put together a file on the way the IOR was conducted. The file later turned up in the safe of a Swiss lawyer; we shall deal with that story in due course.

As the cardinals gathered to elect a new pope, Marcinkus must have known of the Bank of Italy inspection of the Ambrosiano. It is possible that the Italian cardinals, at least, had also heard something.

According to Benny Lai, a writer on Vatican affairs, the man who raised the issue of the IOR amid the assembled cardinals was Cardinal Pietro Palazzini, a traditionalist who had not been close to Paul VI. He questioned the accountability of the IOR, and its apparently autonomous status, and asked whether it should be answerable to Cardinal Vagnozzi.

According to Lai, Cardinal Jean Villot, the Vatican Secretary of State, set up a hurried investigation into the constitutional status of the IOR, which ruled that the IOR was rightly independent. In theory, the IOR was answerable to a commission of five cardinals, chaired by Villot himself.

On 22 August *The Times* published the long article by Paul Horne, already quoted, in which Marcinkus denied all business dealings with Sindona and all currency speculation.

The IOR's critics could not have found themselves with a better potential champion than the surprising new Pope, Albino Luciani, who was elected on August 26 and took the title of John Paul I. He had spent much of his career in the region covered by the Banca Cattolica del Veneto, having been Patriarch of Venice since 1969, and before that, for some years, Bishop of Vittorio Veneto. We have seen that he protested when the IOR sold the Banca Cattolica to Calvi – or, rather, when the sale became public. We have also seen that there is a direct conflict of evidence about the way Marcinkus received his protest.

Whether, on that occasion, Marcinkus had been courteous or rude, he must have been aware of the new Pope's willingness to hear pleas for a more spiritual attitude to money. The most famous of these pleas was in the financial weekly *Il Mondo* on 6 September. The editor, Paolo Panerai, headlined his open letter to the Pope: "Your Holiness, is it right?"

Panerai called on the Pope to reintroduce "order and morality" into the

Vatican finances. "Is it right that the Vatican should operate on the markets of the world like an ordinary speculator? Is it right that it should own a bank which in reality encourages Italians to export capital and evade taxes?"

What Panerai did not know was that Calvi was financing the owners of *Il Mondo*, the Rizzolis, with billions of lire, many of them channelled through the IOR itself.

In the open letter, neither Calvi nor the Ambrosiano was mentioned. The closest Panerai got to what was really wrong with the IOR at the time was his mention of the position of Marcinkus at the Cisalpine. "He is the only bishop to sit on the board of a lay bank, and, what is more, one which is based in one of the paradises of capitalism."

But there was no personal attack on Marcinkus, whom Panerai described, perhaps surprisingly, as "very calm and cordial". He mentioned the involvement of Marcinkus with Vetco, and his consequent troubles with the American Securities and Exchange Commission, but his attack was more directly aimed at Luigi Mennini, on account of his dealings with Sindona. "Foreign exchange dealers around the world know that Mennini is one of the most skilful, one of the wizards of the currency markets, even more skilful than Carlo Bordoni, the former right-hand man of Sindona, today in jail in the United States."

At the time, Panerai heard that his "open letter" had been read by the Pope, and had reinforced his attitude to the Vatican's involvement in financial matters.

On 25 September 1978 *Newsweek* published an article in which "top Vatican officials" were reported to have discussed the way Marcinkus ran the IOR. One was quoted as saying: "There's some movement to get him out of there."

This was gossip, but so is much that comes out of the Vatican. There are two solid facts: that on the morning of 29 September Pope John Paul I was found dead in bed, his rule having lasted thirty-three days, and that somebody decided not to hold an autopsy. For the conclusions many people drew from that, the Vatican has only itself to blame. The first circumstantial stories that the Pope was poisoned came from within the Vatican. As there was no autopsy, there was no hard evidence to refute them.

The theories which later arose, culminating in David Yallop's book *In God's Name*, assume that all the people who profited from Calvi's fraud were in one conspiracy. We have seen that Calvi was conspiring with Marcinkus, and that he was conspiring with Gelli, but there is no evidence that Gelli and Marcinkus were conspiring with each other.

Nor is it true, as David Yallop says, that Gelli then took to using the name "Luciani" as an exclusive code between himself and Calvi. He had been using the name for years. Another P2 member, General Raffaele Giudice, told official interrogators that he was first introduced to Gelli as Luciani in 1975.

In August and September Calvi was with his wife and daughter in South America, where he was preparing for the opening of a subsidiary in Argentina the following year. He also had Rizzoli problems there, and back in Italy. His notes, so full of his anxieties about Coopers and Lybrand, show no concern about the Pope. If there was anyone he wanted to murder at that point, it was probably Garner.

Clearly, Marcinkus could not know who the next Pope was going to be, nor whether he himself would be confirmed in his position at the IOR. There are signs that Calvi, on his return to Italy, helped Marcinkus to clear up some things that would be difficult to explain. They must have reached an oral agreement just before 10 October, when Calvi, as chairman of the Cisalpine, wrote Marcinkus two letters (see Appendix B). Both were about the contango loans the IOR had made to finance the capitals of Zitropo ($20 million) and Manic ($45 million) in the early 1970s. The Manic loan had been three times renewed in writing, and was due to mature on 30 October. The last written renewal of the Zitropo loan had been to 5 October 1975, so the subsequent renewals must have been agreed orally. Now both loans were being renewed for what turned out to be a final six months.

Marcinkus let slip in his written memorandum that the Zitropo loan had always been renewed at Calvi's request. Indeed, it is hard to imagine Calvi ever offering to repay money if he did not have to. It seems probable that Marcinkus now said he wanted the IOR's $65 million back, but that when Calvi pointed out the difficulty of repaying at once he agreed to a final extension.

If Marcinkus had lost his job at this point, he would have had to explain to his successor, and perhaps to some unsympathetic Pope, how the IOR had come to lend such huge amounts to two obscure Luxembourg companies. Both were in dire straits. Zitropo, in its early days, had made a few profitable deals, but since 1974 its only investment had been its holding in the ill-fated Pacchetti. Calvi had given up trying to manipulate the Pacchetti balance sheet with dealings in Ambrosiano group shares, and its portfolio now consisted of a rag-bag of investments. Its shares were languishing at less than 50 lire each, and minority shareholders were threatening to sue.

As Zitropo was a Luxembourg company, an appearance of solvency had to be maintained for the cursory examination of the balance sheets which the authorities there were likely to make. To achieve this, the Pacchetti investment was valued at cost. If it had been entered at market value, it would have been obvious that Zitropo was bankrupt and that the Vatican's $20 million investment had been lost. So had the $12 million back-to-back loan made by the Cisalpine through the IOR in 1974 to finance the capital increase to 5.5 million shares (all but ten of which resided in the IOR's account in the Kredietbank in Luxembourg). Calvi had also lost the loans made to Zitropo by United Trading and Manic, besides the $16 million poured secretly into Zitropo from his Italian banks.

Did Marcinkus know that Zitropo was bankrupt? It is hard to believe he did not, unless he did not know that Zitropo owned Pacchetti. And that, at least, was a matter of public record in Italy.

The position of Manic was not much better. Its main investments were in two Bonomi companies, Beni Immobili Italia and Saffa. It had acquired these shares for some $40 million – about twice what they were now worth. Manic had also lent $7 million to Zitropo, and $12 million to a ghost company, Starfield, the one which had taken over the Cisalpine's loan to Sindona's old company Edilcentro. These investments were financed primarily by the IOR's $45 million, and by loans from United Trading and the Cisalpine.

So, as with Zitropo, it would have been sensible for the IOR to ask for its money back. Perhaps it had no idea of Manic's true state, since the Gottardo had stopped sending balance sheets after 1976. It is also possible that Calvi was not telling Marcinkus the truth about Manic.

The first non-Italian pope for four centuries, Karol Wojtyla, was elected on 16 October 1978 and took the name John Paul II in homage to his predecessor. Just after that event, Calvi secured the cooperation of Marcinkus in dealing with Coopers and Lybrand. On 24 October Calvi wrote to the IOR, as chairman of the Cisalpine, to say that Banco Comercial would be making back-to-back payments to the IOR and that the IOR was to make matching payments to United Trading. The terms were to be the same as for the Cisalpine back-to-backs; the IOR was to get a sixteenth of a percentage point, and the arrangement could be ended at fifteen days' notice. (See Appendix B(vi))

Two days later the Banco Comercial made its first loan to the IOR, advancing $15 million of what was left of the original funds from ENI. The IOR lent the money to United Trading and United Trading paid it back to the IOR, enabling the IOR to repay $15 million of its debts to the Cisalpine.

But this was a mere nibble at the problem. To get back to the figures Coopers and Lybrand had passed at the end of 1977, more than $110 million had to be repaid. Calvi's circular book-keeping would not do for the legal part of his empire. He needed yet more money from outside sources. His friends at ENI and the Banca Nazionale del Lavoro came to the rescue. At the end of October 1978 ENI, using its Hydrocarbons bank in the Cayman Islands, came up with a loan of 100 million Swiss francs (nearly $60 million) and the Banca Nazionale del Lavoro, through its London branch, produced a $50 million three-year loan.

This was lent to BA Holding, which passed it on to Banco Comercial, which lent it to the IOR. The IOR then lent about $68 million to United Trading, which passed all but $6 million back to the IOR, to enable it to reduce its debts to the Cisalpine by a further $62 million. (The $6 million was used by United Trading to repay money it owed to the Gottardo, its only other source of loans.)

This was still not enough. The IOR's debts to the Cisalpine were not just composed of the United Trading back-to-backs; there was also the $12 million loan made to finance the Zitropo capital increase in 1974 (which, since it was later transferred to United Trading, will no longer be treated as a separate item). And there were the two Swiss franc loans of 71,645,000 and 22,720,000 made by the IOR to acquire the BA Holding shares. It was now decided that the first of these should also be switched to the Banco Comercial. On 6 November 1978 Calvi wrote a second letter to the IOR – another of the joint commission's "parallel" letters – which confirmed that the new agreement also covered loans for the BA Holding shares.

Thus, by early November, the IOR debts to the Cisalpine were down to little more than $226 million. The net exposure, about $116 million, was a few million dollars less than it had been at the end of 1977.

While getting this fixed, Calvi also had to deal with the Bank of Italy's requests for information. On 18 October he told an Ambrosiano board meeting that the Bank of Italy inspectors were asking for information about BA Holding and its investments. The board agreed with him that they should not divulge more than was legally available to shareholders.

Calvi met the leader of the inspection team, Padalino, on 30 October. Padalino suggested to Calvi that it would be in his own interest to be more open about his affairs, because that would make it possible to develop his bank to the point where it could play a part in international banking. Calvi told him that the operations of BA Holding covered by Ambrosiano guarantees, and conducted in the context of the Mincomes authorisations, were "exceptional and extraordinary". He had had to provide extra funds because Crédit Suisse, which had lent BA Holding 100 million Swiss francs, was under pressure from the Swiss National Bank to get it back. He promised to reduce the lending of the Ambrosiano to its overseas associate by the end of the year.

Marcinkus had not yet come to terms with the new Pope. It was on 9 November 1978 that Calvi wrote him the letter about the lira back-to backs, and it can now be seen that this was intended to strengthen his position. The IOR's debit accounts at the Ambrosiano, the Cattolica and the Varesino had been explained to Calvi's fellow-directors, as we have seen, by the three grossly misleading letters the IOR wrote on 3 January 1978 (or wrote later, and backdated).

But what looked like enormous debts to the three Italian banks might also have to be explained to the new Pope, or to a new head of the IOR. So Calvi wrote the IOR the "parallel" letter already referred to on page 163. Later the joint commission was allowed to see it, and to make notes, but not to photocopy it.

Writing as chairman of the Ambrosiano, not of the Cisalpine, Calvi referred to the IOR's six debit accounts – R, R-1 and S at the Ambrosiano, R and B at the Cattolica and 112498 at the Varesino. He explained that all these were for the Ambrosiano's purposes, and that the IOR was just an intermediary. It could cancel the arrangement at fifteen days' notice.

We have already seen that this was not true. The lira back-to-back operations which these accounts covered were, at first, for the IOR's benefit. From the summer of 1974 onwards, Ambrosiano group money met the losses of CIM, a company the IOR controlled. The XX Settembre operation, too, was initially for the IOR's benefit, although, as we have seen, the precise financial gain has been hard to assess.

True, the IOR was a mere intermediary in the Setemer operations, the Rizzoli deal done through the RED account and the illegal export of capital through the RED-B account.

There is no evidence that Wojtyla had taken any interest in the IOR before his election as Pope. According to Benny Lai, he did not immediately give his full support to Marcinkus. However, the fact that they were both outsiders in a Curia dominated by Italians apparently established a bond. Marcinkus was confirmed in his position as president of the IOR in late November 1978. He had every reason to be grateful to Calvi. We shall now see what he did in return.

TWENTY

Disaster Postponed

The lies of Calvi to protect Marcinkus are understandable, considering the advantages he gained from his association with the IOR. The advantages Marcinkus gained from association with Calvi were less obvious, but he too was prepared to lie in defence of that link. Up to this point Marcinkus had not done a great deal of outright lying; his way was to mislead people by keeping his mouth shut or telling the truth in small doses. Now he had to be prepared for more than that, because of the persistence of the Cisalpine auditors, Coopers and Lybrand.

Once Marcinkus was confirmed in his post by the new Pope, nobody in the Vatican asked why the IOR owed nearly $125 million to the Banco Comercial in Nicaragua. Taking this into account, the IOR's apparent debts to the Cisalpine and the Banco Comercial had increased slightly, by $6 million. Not all these loans had been put through by the time the Banco Comercial drew up its first balance sheet, on 31 October 1978. But already nearly 85 per cent of its "liquid" assets were tied up in the IOR back-to-backs. These supposed deposits with the IOR provided the required balance for the loan portfolio of more than $120 million, which was mostly tied up in Ortolani's Bafisud, enabling it to hold Varesino shares. There were also some loans to other Ortolani-related companies, and to Rizzoli's ventures in South America.

The sudden and large expansion of the Banco Comercial was understated in the Ambrosiano's communications to the outside world – wisely, as outright civil war had begun to rage in Nicaragua in September 1978. Later, in his written memorandum, Marcinkus recorded that the IOR's "relations of banking intermediary" were transferred to the Banco Comercial, and did not say why. The new Pope clearly did not ask why.

As a result of the switch to the Banco Comercial, the gross exposure of the Cisalpine to the IOR was down to $230 million, the net exposure to $116 million. Both figures were slightly lower than they had been on the 1977 balance sheet, which Coopers and Lybrand had passed. Calvi probably felt he had solved the problem. Why should these niggling accountants need any more information?

Garner had been making further checks on the IOR. He had followed up Calvi's suggestion of contacting, through Coopers' Zürich office, the Swiss Bank Corporation. It could provide no figures, but gave the opinion that the IOR was as good as the Vatican itself; the world's 800 million Catholics stood behind it. Garner also asked the opinion of Coopers in London and was told that, although the IOR's accounts were not published, it was considered good for large sums. The controversy in Italy that autumn over the IOR's conduct was not, however, drawn to his attention.

As Calvi had suggested, Garner drafted a note for inclusion in the next Cisalpine accounts. The note would not have named the IOR; it would simply have drawn attention to the substantial proportion of the Cisalpine's assets and liabilities accounted for by a single institution. To the world at large this might not have meant a great deal, but it might have raised a question in the mind of the Bahamian banking authorities.

Garner sent the draft note to Siegenthaler in late November. In subsequent discussions, Siegenthaler told him that the directors did not want the note in the accounts. He appears to have said this shortly before he went to Zürich for a board meeting, and it is not clear which directors he consulted, if any, apart from Calvi.

At the board meeting on 4 December, Marcinkus was present as usual. The question of the auditors' note does not seem to have been discussed. The main business was the retrospective approval of the $29 million loan to Rizzoli (see below, page 244), and the voting by the directors of a 20 per cent increase in their own pay.

On 6 December Garner wrote to Siegenthaler about the auditors' reaction to the news that the directors did not want a note. Calvi kept a copy of this letter in his safe (see Appendix E). It was important to the legal actions which began in 1986, when the liquidators of the Cisalpine sued Coopers for damages, alleging negligence, and Coopers in their turn sued the Calvi estate, the IOR and Marcinkus personally for fraudulent and/or negligent misrepresentation.

After referring to their discussions the previous week, Garner wrote: "You are aware that we consider it would be good accounting practice for a note along the lines previously forwarded to you to be included in the financial statements. You have advised us that the Directors do not wish such a note to appear in the financial statements.

"I am accordingly writing to advise you that in these circumstances, provided we can satisfy ourselves on the recoverability of the debt due by your customer to the bank, we will not insist on disclosure. This position applies not only to this year but to subsequent years, provided:

"a) The situation between the customer and your bank does not alter materially, and

"b) Future accounting standards do not require us to make a disclosure."

Coopers had little alternative but to back down on the matter of the note, as there was no accounting standard requiring it, and the figures had gone down to about the level of 1977, when they had not insisted on a note.

The more important matter was that the auditors' desire to learn more about the IOR and its relationship with the Cisalpine had not yet been satisfied. Garner wrote: "There remains the problem of our being able to satisfy ourselves as to the recoverability of the debt due by your customer to the bank. As we have discussed with you previously, whilst all indications are that your customer is good for its commitments, we have been unable to see such underlying financial information as would normally be available to us to satisfy ourselves on a debt of this magnitude. In the circumstances, I would appreciate it if a meeting could be set up for me with Dr Marcinkus next time I am in Rome or, alternatively, if there is to be a Cisalpine board meeting in Nassau during 1979, at that time. As you know, I am likely to be in Rome sometime prior to the end of June next year on other business and can advise you of the specific dates in advance."

This must have caused Calvi considerable further annoyance. Cooper's having conceded the question of the note, Calvi might well have felt that it would have been logical for them also to have dropped their requests for more information about the IOR, since they seemed to have accepted that it was good for its debts. But to deny them access might only have increased suspicions, and the easiest way out was to comply with the request. On the copy of Garner's letter in Calvi's files, Siegenthaler has scribbled in Italian: "His Excellency has been told and would agree to receive Mr Garner."

Marcinkus, when he agreed to see Garner, was clearly accepting that the question of the IOR's creditworthiness was a legitimate one for an auditor. He was not arguing, as he did after the crash, that the debts were not his and that he was purely an intermediary.

To judge from the scrawl on the Coopers and Lybrand letter, Marcinkus agreed to meet Garner quite quickly, probably before the public had heard anything of the conclusions reached by the Bank of Italy's inspectors.

Their massive report was completed on 17 November 1978. A short section at the beginning was made available to the Ambrosiano for its comments. But the crucial part was confidential and headed simply: "Not entirely favourable." The confidential part pointed out, among many other things, that, after the Ambrosiano had received authorisation from the Mincomes to extend credit to the Cisalpine, and to finance the capital of BA Holding, it had exported more capital than the permitted amount, and breached the terms. It had also sent money to the Banco Comercial without any permission at all. Padalino recommended a further investigation, and suggested that the export permits should be withdrawn. The inspectors of the Cattolica and the Varesino, who had concluded their report the previous month, had also drawn attention to the role of these subsidiary banks in financing the foreign associates. So if Padalino's recommendation had been carried out, it would no doubt have applied to the Cattolica and the Varesino too. This would have been disastrous enough for Calvi. But the inspectors also found evidence of criminal infractions of exchange controls in the three big share deals which involved the Toro insurance company, the Varesino and the swap of Gottardo for La Centrale shares, involving a total of more than 50 billion lire.

All this remained a secret; secrecy is a rule of life to Bank of Italy inspectors. On 14 December Padolino wrote to the public prosecutor of Milan outlining the breaches of the law he had found, and enclosing the files of evidence. Once the documents reached the prosecutor's office, the leaks began. A few days later the pre-Christmas issue of *L'Espresso* published a well-informed article, outlining the charges, and pointing out that the situation would require extremely delicate handling in the light of the possible international repercussions, and the "diplomatic" consequences arising from the fact the Vatican was involved.

At 8.50 a.m. on 20 December, Calvi telexed Baffi at the Bank of Italy about the confusion and anxiety this article had caused the Ambrosiano board. The board, he said, knew nothing of the "conjectures" and the "events conjured up" were "totally irrelevant to us in the way they are presented". The board's concern was all the greater, Calvi went on, because he himself had had a "normal and cordial" meeting with Sarcinelli in Rome, the previous day, and nothing had been said about the alleged offences.

How much of the article in *L'Espresso* was really new to Calvi is not known. He must have known about the Bank of Italy's concern over the financing of BA Holding, since he had discussed this with Padalino on 30 October. And the meeting with Sarcinelli had hardly been "normal and cordial" to judge from Sarcinelli's evidence at the trial of Calvi's associates in 1991. Though the meeting ended politely – any conversation with Sarcinelli would – there had been "moments of tension". So the telex was clearly written for the benefit of the other directors, and the Ambrosiano staff. To the staff, Calvi issued a communiqué.

A copy of this telex is among Calvi's papers, and so is a copy of a formal letter to Marcinkus, whom he addressed as "Eccellenza". Writing on behalf of the board of the Ambrosiano, Calvi declared: "I consider it my duty to send you a series of documents which outline the position taken by our board following the news published by the weekly *Espresso* in Milan today." (Among the documents, presumably, was the telex to Baffi.)

The charges mentioned in *L'Espresso* may well have been news to Marcinkus, but since Marcinkus already knew that Calvi was violating exchange controls with his help, Calvi can hardly have thought the article would shock him. The letter must have been intended for Marcinkus to show to anyone in the Vatican who was concerned that the chairman of a bank so closely associated with the IOR was under investigation for violations of the currency laws.

This is the only letter to be found which is personally addressed by Calvi to Marcinkus. There is, as usual, no record of any reply. There is one clue, though. The following day, 21 December, the Banco Comercial made a $10 million back-to-back loan via the IOR to United Trading, which desperately needed the money to pay the interest due on the other loans. This brought the back-to-back loans (including both the Cisalpine and the Banco Comercial) to more than $360 million, their highest level. But the $10 million loan was for only two months, and it was duly repaid on 21 February, out of the proceeds of the sale of some Cisalpine shares held by United Trading.

This was the very last back-to-back loan made through the IOR. And it was repaid, not renewed. These facts may suggest that Marcinkus had decided, perhaps as part of an overall review of his relations with Calvi, that there should be no further increase in the level of back-to-back loans. But he seems to have been willing that they should continue at their existing level. And he was still prepared to help Calvi with the Coopers and Lybrand problem; he did not back out of seeing Garner.

As far as Garner was concerned the meeting with Marcinkus was not urgent. The letter in which he asked for it implicitly conceded that Coopers would be prepared to approve the Cisalpine's end-1978 accounts, on the basis of the figures as they then stood, *before* he saw Marcinkus.

Garner did, however, make further inquiries about the IOR at the Coopers and Lybrand office in Rome. He was told that it functioned like a bank, administered property entrusted to it which was destined for religious and charitable institutions and earned interest on its deposits with other banks, passing on this interest to the Pope. The office in Rome added that it had thousands of clients, and, crucially, that it held $2 billion "between deposits and accounts". Again, there was no mention of the controversy about it the previous autumn.

Unknown to Garner, a more immediate crisis loomed over the Cisalpine. The executives preparing the annual accounts had failed to resolve a problem that went back to the previous summer, about the $52.75 million back-to-back loans to finance the Panamanian companies Astolfine and Belrosa. The Cisalpine executives had no knowledge of United Trading, whose accounts were run in Lugano by the Gottardo. Calvi kept the nature of the IOR loans secret by ensuring that neither the Cisalpine nor the Gottardo had the full picture. So the Cisalpine had issued instructions that the IOR's account should be first credited with $52.75 million and then debited again at once in favour of Astolfine and Belrosa, rather than (as Calvi had clearly intended) in favour of United Trading, which would pass the money on to the Panamanian companies..

However, the IOR executives who had to authorise the credits and debits had no back-to-back agreements covering Astolfine and Belrosa. Sticklers for form, they refused to accept the transfers. This impasse went on for seven months. Twice, in July and August, the IOR refused to process the loans. Later in the year, as work on the accounts started, the matter had to be resolved. Either the Nassau executives would have to resort to outright falsification of the books, or they would have to record the loans as having been made directly by the Cisalpine to Astolfine and Belrosa. This would have removed a large part of the bank's apparently liquid assets, and rung loud alarm bells at Coopers and Lybrand.

A couple of years earlier, the Cisalpine had established an office in Monte Carlo. This was a convenient place, outside Italy, for keeping the records of the relationship between the Ambrosiano and Cisalpine. There was a telex line between Monte Carlo and Nassau; messages to and from Milan went by scrambler phone. In October 1978 telex messages about the $52.75 million started to fly backwards and forwards. Yet the Ambrosiano still could not get the instructions right, and in November the IOR again refused to process the loans.

The matter had still not been resolved by 15 December, when Coopers made the Cisalpine write to the IOR to secure confirmation of the figures for its borrowings from the Cisalpine. The IOR drafted a note to say that it could not confirm the figures, because it had not had any confirmation from the Gottardo. Coopers did not hear about that, however. On 7 February 1979, having not yet received the confirmation, they telexed the Cisalpine saying that they must have the confirmation by 15 February.

That finally secured some action. Botta telephoned de Strobel at the IOR to explain that the money was really for United Trading. The IOR at last agreed to put the loans through its books and to send the confirmation to Coopers – again with no indication that they were not the true borrowers.

So, at the very time when Calvi was enlisting the help of Marcinkus to deal with the threat of exposure posed by the auditors, bungling by himself and his executives nearly gave the whole game away.

Afterwards, the months of altercation over the $52.75 million were regarded by the three Vatican appointees to the joint commission as important evidence of the IOR's innocence. They argued that it showed the IOR was merely an intermediary. Moreover, they said, it showed that others at the Ambrosiano besides Calvi were aware of the nature of the back-to-back operations. That is, the IOR was fully entitled to assume that Calvi was acting with the full knowledge and approval of his colleagues.

This reasoning ignored the role of Marcinkus as a director of the Cisalpine, where he was representing the IOR not as an intermediary, but as a shareholder and creditor. The episode of the $52.75 million may well demonstrate that some of Calvi's executives knew that the funds placed with the IOR were not ordinary interbank deposits. But Marcinkus unquestionably knew it, and helped to ensure that Coopers and Lybrand did not.

Furthermore, the story of the $52.75 million undermines the Vatican's claim that the IOR knew little of Calvi's secret network before the summer of 1981. The wrong instructions they had been given informed them of the existence of Astolfine and Belrosa. They certainly could not help knowing of United Trading, Manic and Zitropo, whose share certificates were in their possession.

With the IOR's confirmation, the Cisalpine's 1978 accounts were duly drawn up on 14 February 1979 and signed by Coopers and Lybrand. The amount "due from banks" totalled nearly $336 million, divided between $67.8 million from Ambrosiano affiliates and $267.8 million from "others". There was no note to say that this last figure included $230 million, or 42 per cent of the bank's total assets, from one "other" – the IOR. The bank's total deposits were $472 million, again divided between affiliates, with $218 million, and "other", with $254 million. Again there was no note to say that $110 million, or 23 per cent, of this came from the IOR.

What Coopers did not know was that the IOR's own deposits with the Cisalpine had actually increased during the year by a few million dollars. This rise had been more than compensated for by a fall in the deposits made via the IOR by the Gottardo, which had dropped by $9.6 million to $21 million during the year. The Gottardo's back-to-back arrangement, though done to deceive the Swiss authorities, was not so damaging to the

Cisalpine as Calvi's other deceptions. At least the money was coming in, not going out.

The board meeting to approve the accounts once more took place at the Ultrafin offices in Zürich, on 15 March 1979. All the directors were there again, and so was Siegenthaler. Garzoni asked whether the bank should publish a profit-and-loss account. There was no legal requirement for it to do so, and the Cisalpine, like other Bahamian banks, did not. After discussion it was "generally agreed" that it would not be done, though the information could be given in a "confidential and selective manner to certain banks if management deemed it appropriate".

Coopers had again required a letter from Calvi saying that the IOR business was on normal commercial terms. Whether that was before the meeting is not recorded in the minutes. But that year's "management letter" from Coopers was read. It said: "We have had various discussions during the year on IOR in relation to the points raised in last year's management letter, dated 20 February 1978, and we have now accepted the situation on the basis laid down in Mr Garner's letter to Mr Siegenthaler dated 6 December 1978."

Once more Marcinkus kept his mouth shut. All the minutes record is that the board "duly took note of the comments made by the auditors".

The contents of the management letter had previously been discussed by Garner with Siegenthaler. Coopers had originally wanted to include the following two sentences: "However, we still wish to obtain any further information on the IOR to support the recoverability of the amounts placed with them, and to obtain a better understanding of the nature of the transactions. In this respect we believe that a meeting with Dr Marcinkus would be useful."

Coopers, however, had agreed to leave the this part out at the request of Siegenthaler, who was presumably acting on Calvi's instructions.

Garner agreed to the deletion because he knew that Marcinkus had agreed to a meeting. In the event, there was no Cisalpine board meeting in Nassau, and Garner's visit to Europe was postponed. It was not until December 1979 that Garner and Marcinkus at last met face to face. By that time, some other strange events had overtaken Calvi.

TWENTY-ONE

Financing the Casino Wars

> Let me issue a warning to anyone who is tempted to settle for
> a peaceful life on what is called the Côte d'Azur. Avoid the
> region of Nice which is the preserve of some of the most
> criminal organisations in the south of France: they deal in
> drugs; they have attempted with the connivance of high auth-
> orities to take over the casinos in the famous "war" which left
> one victim, Agnes Le Roux, the daughter of the main owner
> of the Palais de la Méditerranée, "missing believed mur-
> dered"; they are involved in the building industry which helps
> to launder their illicit gains; they have close connections with
> the Italian Mafia.
>
> GRAHAM GREENE, *J'Accuse* (Bodley Head, 1982).

It was almost certainly not the fault of Marcinkus that the Cisalpine financed
one of the shadiest participants in the casino war of Nice. That was the
doing of Gelli and Ortolani.

At the beginning of the 1970s there were two casinos in Nice. One was
a place of faded grandeur on the Promenade des Anglais, the Palais de la
Méditerranée. The other was a cheaper place for smaller gamblers, the
Casino-Club. Ownership of the Palais was divided in three; half the capital
was owned by a family called Le Roux. The forceful Renée Le Roux had
managed the family fortune since the death of her husband, Henri, in 1967.
The other half of the casino was divided between two shareholders, one
being the man who ran it, Maurice Guérin.

The Casino-Club was owned and run by Jean Dominique Fratoni, known
as Jean-Do, a middle-aged Corsican. He had been in small-time gambling
in France for much of his life without any great success. But when gambling
was legalised in Britain Fratoni crossed the Channel and made so much
money working at the Victoria Sporting Club that he was able to buy
the Casino-Club. He had a powerful friend in Nice, the mayor, Jacques

Médecin (who in September 1990 fled to South America, as the French authorities prepared corruption charges against him).

Médecin wanted to turn Nice into a great gambling centre, and decided that Fratoni was the man to do it. The old Hotel Ruhl on the Promenade des Anglais was redeveloped as the Méridien, with a casino underneath which retained the old name, Ruhl.

The Casino Ruhl, run by Fratoni, was opened at the end of 1974. The great inauguration party at the beginning of 1975 was attended by Médecin, the film star Alain Delon and some other actors and actresses who happened to be making a film nearby. Right from the start there were rumours about the sources of Fratoni's money. The Ruhl was owned by a company called SOCRET – Société de Créations et Exploitations Touristiques – ostensibly controlled by Fratoni himself, as he had 51 per cent of the shares.

Who owned the other 49 per cent? Fratoni had three Italian collaborators in SOCRET: Antonio Pistilli, Cesare Valsania and Arrigo Lugli. They seemed respectable enough; Pistilli was an accountant, Valsania a retired senior officer of the Italian air force and Lugli a stock and currency broker in Rome.

Later, investigators in France and Italy looked into suspicions that the Ruhl had been used to launder kidnap money. There seemed to be a link with two crooks in Marseilles, Alberto Bergamelli and Jacques Berenguer – the same pair suspected of planning the kidnapping of Amedeo Ortolani in 1975. A thug called Francesco Russello appeared at the Hotel Méridien, and was later found with kidnap money in Italy, before being murdered by repeated stabbings in the face. But it was never proved that the owners of the casino had any connection with kidnapping.

There might have been perfectly normal commercial reasons for the Italians to go into partnership with Fratoni. In Italy, as in America, gambling is legal only in a few places. The Ruhl took to flying in planeloads of Italians, as British casinos at the time were flying in Americans.

But a major attraction to Italians was that casinos provided a cover for breaking the currency laws. By what became known as a "compensation" deal, those who could make foreign currencies available to Italians abroad, in exchange for lire in Italy, could demand an exchange rate very favourable to themselves – just as the IOR did. Through the casino it would have been simple for the Italian partners to advance expensive francs to Italians on a trip to Nice – whether for gambling or for other purposes – in exchange for cheap lire back in Italy.

The impact of the Ruhl was soon felt by the other casinos. Renée Le

Roux had for some time been unhappy with her manager, Maurice Guérin. Matters came to a head on 8 July 1975, when a group of gamblers, including some known criminals, descended on the Palais and, in a single evening, won 4,850,000 francs, or the equivalent of nearly $1 million. Three days later Guérin resigned. Renée Le Roux took over the management of the casino.

She had taken on a tough opponent. Fratoni wanted an outright monopoly of local gambling. In September 1975 it was the turn of the Sun Beach Casino at Menton to suffer misfortune. A group of gamblers, including three Italians and a Frenchman who had been at the Palais on 8 July, made a killing of nearly 3 million francs. The Sun Beach had to be bailed out, and Fratoni provided the money, thereby getting effective control. (That casino went into liquidation later.)

For a time, after Renée Le Roux took over the running of the Palais, it survived side by side with the Ruhl. But she made a bad mistake; she decided that she, too, would go after the Italian market. Her "operation charters", based on a deal with a Sicilian travel agency, proved a disaster. Eight out of ten Italians did not gamble at all, and those who did gambled on credit, so that their losses had to be collected from them in Italy – no easy task. There was also a curious gap, never accounted for, between the number of invoices for gamblers issued by the casino and the much larger number actually booked on to the flights and into the local hotels. In seven months, from November 1976 to June 1977, the Palais lost 10 million francs.

The underlying position of the Ruhl was not much better, but it was stronger than its rival for one reason. In September 1976 it raised a $5 million loan from the Cisalpine.

The detailed arrangements for the loan were negotiated by Pistilli, the accountant. But there can be little doubt that the man who provided the link between the Ruhl and the Ambrosiano was Arrigo Lugli, the currency broker, who later admitted that he owned part of the mystery 49 per cent stake in the Ruhl.

Lugli, in the 1970s, was very close to Gelli and Ortolani, who used his services to transfer large sums out of Italy (and, sometimes, back in again). A large part of Ortolani's illicit profits on the speculations conducted through Rizzoli Finanziaria in Rome passed through the hands of Lugli. When Gelli's office was searched in 1981, cheques were found bearing the names of Lugli and Ortolani. In 1978 and 1980 Gelli lent Lugli a total of $4.5 million – much of it destined for a client of Lugli, rather than Lugli himself. The loans were never fully repaid. After the P2 scandal had broken, Gelli, a fugitive from Italy, nevertheless launched a legal action in Rome to recover the money – which he had got from Calvi in the first place.

So deeply interested were the P2 bosses in the loan to Casino Ruhl that a $1 million tranche of it was sold by the Cisalpine to Ortolani's Bafisud. The source of the money was well concealed; it was channelled through two banks, one in Holland and the other in Switzerland, before it reached Casino Ruhl. By Ambrosiano standards it was quite well secured. The shares of SOCRET and another Fratoni company were pledged; moreover the Cisalpine took a mortgage on the Ruhl building and the Casino-Club. Fratoni, Valsania and Lugli all gave personal guarantees.

Fratoni and his colleagues, thus backed, were able to bring off the startling coup that gave the Ruhl a dramatic, if short-lived victory over the Palais – and led to the disappearance of Agnès, daughter of Renée Le Roux.

Not one character in this book has admitted to making a simple commercial misjudgement. No more did Renée Le Roux. As the full extent of the disaster emerged, allegations of conspiracy began to cloud the story of "operation charters". The Ruhl was sabotaging the operation, through the agents recruiting the gamblers in Italy. Or, as there was an agreement between the shareholders that they would not sell to outsiders without first offering their holdings to one another, was an attempt being made to depress their value?

The two holders of the half share of the Palais not in Le Roux family hands became convinced that she must be ousted. The showdown would be at the annual meeting scheduled for 30 June 1977. But, since the two sides were evenly balanced, how could she be outvoted?

However, the family was not united. For months there had been friction between Renée and her daughter Agnès, who controlled ten out of the 7,000 Palais shares in her own right. Renée tried, and failed, to have her daughter's shares frozen. At the crucial meeting she was voted out of office by 3,510 to 3,490. Agnès had gone over to the other side.

It emerged later that Agnès had become the mistress of her lawyer, Jean Maurice Agnelet. He had persuaded her to sell the votes on her shares to Fratoni. The price was 3 million Swiss francs, or about $600,000. This deal, done in May 1977, must have been facilitated by the Cisalpine loan the previous autumn.

The betrayal of her mother appears to have aggravated the already disturbed and unhappy life of Agnès. In early October 1977 she twice attempted suicide. At the end of that month she disappeared from the face of the earth. Behind Nice are mountains with crevasses deep enough to hide a woman's body, but they would also have to hide her Range Rover, which disappeared at the same time.

The lawyer Agnelet was charged, years later, with various offences connected with the purchase of her vote. Some of the 3 million francs were traced to a Swiss bank account of his. But the protracted inquiries have never produced any evidence that the disappearance of Agnès was not her own doing.

After the dismissal of Renée, the Palais continued to lose money, and on 14 April 1978 it closed its doors. A prolonged sit-in by its employees did not prevent its demolition.

The writing was on the wall for Fratoni and the Ruhl as well. In May 1977 a tax inspector began a rigorous inspection of its books. He spent a year poring over them, and called in his colleagues from the customs to help. As a result of their reports, the authorities decided to close the Ruhl in November 1979.

Fratoni and his friends had been remarkably inept at concealing their illicit financial dealings. Huge, unexplained sums of money had been paid out by the Ruhl, much of it just before the tax inspector arrived. The private accounts of Fratoni and the air force officer Valsania had become intermingled with those of the casino. What most aroused the suspicions of the authorities were lists of clients to whom the casino had made loans. The French authorities alleged that these represented illegal financial activity, the money then being laundered through the gaming tables. Much can be hidden under the guise of winnings and losses; the French suspected that this was kidnap or drug money. Although many of the borrowers were Italians, it was never proved that the racket being operated was anything worse than a breach of Italy's currency controls. However, the loans were in themselves a breach of French regulations.

Shortly after the Ruhl was closed, and before Fratoni could be formally interrogated on a charge of tax fraud, he disappeared from Nice. Unlike Agnès Le Roux, he soon gave evidence of being still alive. He proclaimed his innocence from Switzerland, which will not extradite people wanted for tax or currency offences. The Ruhl was allowed to open under new management, though it was suspected that Fratoni still pulled the strings. It closed again, finally, in January 1982, when SOCRET was put into liquidation.

As for its $5 million debt to the Cisalpine and Bafisud, SOCRET had defaulted on the repayment terms even before the first closure in 1979. It is not clear whether all the Cisalpine directors heard of this bad loan at the time. But Marcinkus knew of it in October 1981. That was when a Cisalpine board meeting, attended (for reasons which will emerge later) only by Marcinkus and Count Luciano della Porta, decided to foreclose on the mortgages held as security. Nothing had been achieved by the time the Ambrosiano crashed, but the liquidators managed to recover some $800,000 from the properties. Neither Lugli or Valsania were keen to honour their personal guarantees. (I tried to interview Lugli, but was turned away at his door.) Fratoni, still a fugitive, was hard to pin down. He was tried in his absence, in Nice, for tax evasion and other offences, and sentenced to various terms of imprisonment.

On the list of those to whom the casino had made loans, one name stood out because of the size of the sum against it – 95,813,000 francs, or about $19 million. The name was Andrea Rizzoli.

Since the early 1970s, Andrea Rizzoli had spent much of his time at his villa in Cap Ferrat, near Nice. His first wife had left him when he began a liaison with a young model, Ljubia Rosa, whom he married in 1973. His son Angelo publicly said that he came completely under her influence. "She brought him to the casino – he lost," Renée Le Roux said afterwards. She presumably meant that he had lost at the Ruhl, not the Palais.

Gelli, too, had a villa at Cap Ferrat, bought with $2 million he had taken from the Ambrosiano. His son Raffaello developed "a much accentuated feeling" for Andrea's young wife – her own phrase when interrogated. But she maintained that this did not happen until later. Already, however, Andrea's gambling was providing the P2 bosses with an excellent opportunity to tighten their hold on his company. Angelo afterwards told *L'Europeo* that he believed his father had lost 30 billion lire, or $35 million, in 1978 alone. Andrea did not have that sort of ready money – he used to write out dud cheques for some of his losses – and Ortolani, Gelli and Calvi knew this. That was why the Ambrosiano had to finance the Rizzoli capital increase (via the IOR) in 1977.

Even if Andrea was allowed to become indebted to the Ruhl, he was costing a great deal of real money, much of it illicitly provided by the Rizzoli company; he was reckoned to be drawing well over 1 billion lire a year in "expenses". Tassan Din (by now in the P2 camp) said that Andrea's gambling not only interfered with the management of the company, but began to affect its image with the outside world, "and above all with those institutions which were providing the credit".

Through the first nine months of 1978 Rizzoli Editore was desperate for money to keep going. Minutes of the executive committee of the company record repeated reports from Tassan Din that 10 billion lire was needed to pay the bills. Various proposals were put forward, including the idea of going to London and trying to raise a loan there. The minutes also record (with a hint of puzzlement) that Tassan Din was urged to secure the balance of the $29 million apparently promised by the Rothschilds at the end of 1976, since all the relevant permissions had been given.

Tassan Din did not explain why that money was not forthcoming. There had been sweeping changes at Montedison, the real source hiding behind Rothschilds. The extravagant Cefis, the instigator of Rizzoli's acquisition of the *Corriere*, had been ousted. A new austerity had been imposed. "Austerity" was a fashionable word in Italy in the summer of 1978. "We use the English word," a Bank of Italy man explained to *Euromoney*, "because it reminds us of your great period of austerity under Attlee."

The mild economies which the Italian Government succeeded in making had little in common with the régime of Attlee and Cripps. But they did curb the grosser absurdities of the nationalised industries, Montedison among them. The new bosses there not only refused to put any more money into Rizzoli; they wanted to get back the money already lent. At this point the Rizzoli group's losses, though slightly reduced from their peak in 1977, were still running at nearly 20 billion lire a year. Nobody would take that on as a commercial proposition. There was only one solution: Calvi.

Ortolani went to work on Calvi. But Calvi, whose whole life was one long gamble, disapproved of people who went into casinos. That was why he had refused to do the Rizzolis any more favours in 1977, when he bought back the Ambrosiano shares from them at the strict market price.

Calvi's attitude helped the P2 men to get rid of Andrea. In September 1978, while the headlines were filled with the startling succession of popes, Montedison effectively pulled out of Rizzoli, and the Ambrosiano took over the burden. The Cisalpine bought the $11.8 million loan Montedison had made via Rothschilds in 1976, and simultaneously made available the $17.2 million balance of the $29 million commitment. No one in the Rizzoli company noticed the change, as Rothschilds continued to act as a front for the loans. Much of this money must have been used at once, to repay the credits Montedison had made available to the Rizzolis to buy the *Corriere* in 1974. Indeed, the Banco Comercial put up the further $8.8 million which guaranteed the repayment of these credits.

At the same time negotiations were conducted with Andrea. He resigned as chairman in October 1978. Angelo took over the chairmanship, while Ortolani himself stepped into the vacant position on the Rizzoli board. Gelli was given responsibility for Rizzoli's dealings with foreign governments and agencies, particularly in Argentina, where Rizzoli's expanding operations were in deep trouble.

Andrea went quietly, once assured of money enough to continue his extravagant way of life. The arrangements then made, however, provided yet another opportunity for money to be fraudulently siphoned off. What Andrea needed, to replace his "expenses" from the company, was an assured income. In spite of the casinos, he still had assets – some shares in a property company, a private plane and two estates. One of these was the Villa Rasca in Italy; the other was Las Acacias, a ranch in Argentina. These assets were to be transferred to the Rizzoli group, which in exchange would cancel some outstanding debts, and issue him with 8 billion lire of debenture stock carrying 12 per cent interest, thus providing him with an income of nearly 1 billion lire a year.

The Rizzoli group, however, did not need real estate. It needed cash. Conveniently, Gelli wanted to buy the ranch in Argentina. A price of $3.15 million was agreed. Gelli was duly provided with the money by Ortolani, who got it from Calvi, who stole it from the Ambrosiano by the device of selling to the Banco Comercial, at an inflated price, a building in Buenos Aires.

But that was only half the fraud. The $3.15 million never reached the Rizzoli group. It was first paid to Rothschilds in Zürich and then disappeared into a bank in Lugano. Who pocketed the money has not been established.

Andrea was still the titular owner of Rizzoli's three million shares, apart from a block of 96,000, divided equally between Angelo and his younger brother Alberto, who was joint managing director of the company.

Not that Andrea had possession of the shares he nominally owned, except for a block of 210,000, kept for him in Italy. Rothschilds in Zürich held 294,000 of Andrea's shares as security. As for the 2.4 million shares issued in July 1977, they were probably in sealed envelopes at the IOR, as security for the back-to-back lira account 001 6 02553, known as RED, on which the debt now stood at nearly 25 billion lire with rolled-up interest.

These shares Andrea had the right to reclaim, if he could turn up at the Credito Commerciale in Milan before the end of June 1981 with 35 billion lire. The letter in which he agreed to this arrangement said that, if he died before that date, the retrieval rights would devolve equally on Angelo and Alberto. It seems to have been Andrea's intention that his two sons should inherit equal stakes in the family firm. On ceasing to be chairman, he divided the 210,000 shares he held in Italy equally between the two, although he kept the right to enjoy any income from them during his life. He also gave 105,000 shares each to his two daughters, Annina and Isabella, from the holding at Rothschilds. The remaining 84,000 of this holding were split equally between Angelo and Alberto.

Angelo, however, insisted that he should have the sole right to reclaim the 2.4 million shares. He wanted sole control of the family firm. Besides, Alberto did not get on with Tassan Din. So Alberto, too, had to go. But this meant providing for him financially as well. The agreed price was more than 5 billion lire. It was Angelo who personally acquired Alberto's interest in the shares, but it was the company that paid. The company also transferred to Alberto the estate in Italy, the Villa Rasca. Angelo said that he would get the money to repay the company from Calvi, but he never did repay.

The negotiations over the shares took some six months. It was not until May 1979 that Alberto, too, resigned from the company. The Credito Commerciale issued a new letter giving Angelo the right to reclaim the 2.4 million shares on the same terms as his father had had. Alberto's place on the board was taken by Tassan Din.

Angelo was now alone with the P2 men. He was a figurehead, wholly dependent on Calvi for money, and on Tassan Din for the daily management of the group. He lived well enough; when Rizzoli went into controlled administration, it was discovered that some 29 billion lire had disappeared from the company without being properly accounted for, and Angelo admitted that, of this, 11 billion lire was his debt.

But, as he was later to recount, he was continually being made to sign personal undertakings and guarantees for huge sums. "I signed these undertakings because I was up against the wall," he said. "I ran the risk of being thrown out at any time, with the threat, made to me on several occasions, of being held liable for the undertakings I had signed."

The P2 men were planning the coup that would give them control of Italy's most important publishing group. Their deadline was June 1981, the first date when the 2.4 million shares could be redeemed.

TWENTY-TWO

Catastrophe Befalls the Bank of Italy

Calvi's fraud was gathering pace. Between November 1978 and July 1979 over $20 million disappeared out of the Ambrosiano group. What happened to much of that remains a mystery. But the great bulk of it passed through Ortolani accounts, and it seems likely that this was intended for the benefit of Ortolani and Gelli. It may have been a reward for the ousting of Andrea and Alberto Rizzoli. We know that $3 million went to Gelli, enabling him to buy the ranch in Argentina, and Ortolani's share was probably larger. Even Calvi got $1 million, paid by Ortolani into his Butric account at the Roywest in Nassau.

Most of the money was removed in two operations. One, mentioned in the last chapter, was relatively crude. In March 1979 a Panamanian company called Montreal Holding acquired an office building in Buenos Aires, occupied by the local offshoot of the Olivetti company. The cost, with expenses, was about $7.1 million. Montreal itself was then acquired by the Banco Comercial in Nicaragua for $10,789,000, the difference of $3,689,000 disappearing through an account in the name of an Ortolani family company, Ducador. Shortly afterwards, Banco Comercial paid a further $5 million to another Ortolani account. To cover the hole this left in the Banco Comercial accounts, the Olivetti building's value was simply lifted to $15,789,000. So, altogether, $8,689,000 had been removed.

The other operation has to be reconstructed from odd jottings in Calvi's notes. The amount was $10 million. Of this, $5.3 million came from the Ambrosiano banks in Italy, in the form of 4,621,600,000 lire. It would seem that this was removed by way of the RED-B account at the IOR, and then through the IOR's Lugano subsidiary, Svirobank. As usual the exchange rate used by the IOR was about 30 lire above the market rate, and so the IOR's profit on this illegal export of currency was about $190,000.

The $4.7 million balance of the $10 million came out of United Trading, in the form of 8 million Swiss francs. There is one oddity about this payment. Calvi recorded it as an asset in his private United Trading balance sheets – a loan apparently due for repayment on 30 April 1979. No previous payments to Ortolani had been entered in this way. The only other personal payment recorded as a United Trading asset was the $5 million loan to Anna Bonomi, made by United Trading's predecessor, Radowal, in the autumn of 1971.

The 8 million Swiss francs never were repaid. There were to be further payments to Ortolani which Calvi again entered as "assets". If Calvi regarded part, or all, of the $10 million as a loan, he left few clues about its purpose. Against the 8 million Swiss francs he wrote: "Ecfsa". In most countries with Latin languages the initials SA after a firm's name indicate that it is a limited company. But if there was a company with the initials ECF, in which Ortolani was investing, nobody has found it, although it may have been an incorrect reference to the Ortolani holding company in Liechtenstein, Electronic General, which controlled Voxson.

The 8 million Swiss franc payment out of United Trading marks a turning point in the relationship between Calvi and the IOR. Although United Trading borrowed the money from Banco Comercial, it was not channelled through the IOR back-to-back arrangement.

We have seen that the curiosity of the auditors forced Calvi to switch the back-to-back operations from the Cisalpine to the Banco Comercial. Loans of $65 million and 30 million Swiss francs were put through the Banco Comercial in the autumn of 1978. Then there was only one further loan: $10 million in December 1978, quickly repaid the following February.

From that point onwards no new foreign currency back-to-back loans went through the IOR, either from the Cisalpine or the Banco Comercial, though loans already outstanding were renewed.

It was not that United Trading needed less money; on the contrary, it needed more. The interest burden was growing all the time. There is no obvious reason why the new money was not put through the IOR; as we shall see, Calvi had no problems with the auditor of the Banco Comercial.

It is possible that the initiative came from the IOR, as a result of the overall review of their joint operations which, I believe, must have taken place between Calvi and Marcinkus in October 1978. We have seen that, because of a bureaucratic muddle, the IOR did not approve the $52.75 million of Cisalpine back-to-back loans destined for Astolfine and Belrosa until February 1979, though the loans had in fact been made in 1978. Once that had been done, the total outstanding from the Cisalpine and the Banco Comercial put together came to $345 million. It is possible that Marcinkus decided to call a halt because of the sheer size.

And yet it was at this very moment that the IOR allowed a further increase in the lira back-to-back loans. It borrowed a further 8 billion lire from the

Archbishop Paul Casimir Marcinkus at his desk in the Istituto per le Opere di Religione, 1983 (*Photo: Vittoriano Rastelli*)

Calvi with his wife Clara, seated between Senora Mennini and Luigi Mennini of the IOR, with eleven of the Mennini's fourteen children (*Photo courtesy of Clara Calvi*)

Pope Paul VI, the man who appointed Marcinkus *(Photo: Agenzia Ansa)*

Cardinal Casaroli, who as Vatican Secretary of State found himself at loggerheads with Marcinkus in the aftermath of the collapse of the Banco Ambrosiano *(Photo: ADN Kronos)*

Right: Pelegrino de Strobel, the IOR's accountant who kept the record of the deals with Calvi *(Photo: Carlo Carinso)*

A celebratory lunch at the Ambrosiano: opposite Calvi, Carlo Canesi proposing a toast, with Ruggiero Mozzana (partially obscured) on Calvi's left *(Photo courtesy of Clara Calvi)*

Roberto Rosone, the Ambrosiano general manager who was shot in the leg, shown here at the funeral of Gabriella Corrocher, Calvi's secretary *(Photo: Agenzia Ansa)*

Alessandro Mennini, son of Luigi Mennini: the IOR connection got him his job at the Ambrosiano *(Photo: Agenzia Ansa)*

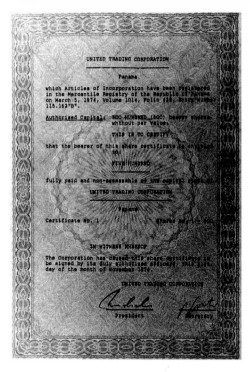

Graham Garner of Coopers and Lybrand,
around the time of his encounter with
Marcinkus in the Vatican
(Photo courtesy of Graham Garner)

Above right: The United Trading
Corporation share certificate which
was held at the IOR

Right: A share certificate for
Manic, one of the key companies
in Calvi's secret network

The Palazzo di Vetro, which housed
the CIM store owned by the IOR

From left to right: Carlo Calvi, Michele Sindona, Clara Calvi and Rina Sindona, in Calvi's rented villa in Lyford Cay, Bahamas *(Photo courtesy of Clara Calvi)*

Anna Bonomi with her lawyers *(Photo: Agenzia Ansa)*

Mario Sarcinelli, on his release from prison in Rome in 1979 *(Photo: Agenzia Ansa)*

Licio Gelli, the head of P2, taken in his garden at Arezzo in 1989, after talking with the author *(Photo: Philip Willan)*

Umberto Ortolani, the financial brains in the partnership with Gelli *(Photo: Agenzia Ansa)*

Angelo Rizzoli (seated left), with Bruno Tassan Din on his left, the man who helped Gelli and Ortolani plan the "Sistemazione" Rizzoli *(Photo: Agenzia Ansa)*

Francesco Pazienza, the "warrior" Calvi hired in 1981
(Photo: Agenzia Ansa)

Inset: Flavio Carboni, the property dealer who
organized Calvi's last trip to London in June 1982
(Photo: Agenzia Ansa)

Silvano Vittor, the smuggler from Trieste who was
Calvi's last companion, with his girlfriend Michaela
Kleinszig *(Photo: Agenzia Ansa)*

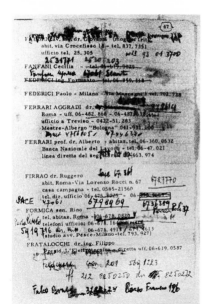
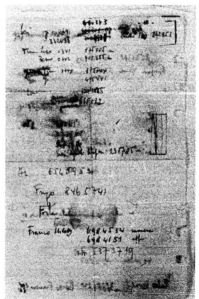

The page from Calvi's address book which was found in his suit after his death:
the printed side includes the name Firrao; the verso the name and phone numbers of
Mons. Hilary Franco

Above: Calvi's body lying
on Waterloo pier. The line
between the soaking feet
and lower legs and the rest
of the suit is clearly visible

Right: A scene from one of
the reconstructions of
Calvi's death, showing the
walkway under Blackfriars
Bridge, the ladder and the
scaffolding, with the river
below *(Photo: Ray Victor)*

group's Italian banks. This was to finance the illicit export of the 4,621,600,000 lire, and a further 3 billion capital increase by the property company XX Settembre. As a result, the IOR's liabilities to Calvi's Italian banks rose to 155 billion lire, or about $182 million.

The lira back-to-backs were nearer home and more likely to be discovered by the Bank of Italy inspectors than the foreign currency operations. So the fact that the lira operations rose, while the foreign currency ones did not, suggests that the change was not caused by a sudden onset of caution at the IOR.

It happened, more probably, because Calvi discovered that he no longer needed the IOR to channel new money to United Trading. The auditors of the Banco Comercial, a local Nicaraguan firm, named after its principal, one Federico Cossio, turned out to be quite free of those tiresome scruples which troubled Coopers and Lybrand. Not only did these new auditors not question the creditworthiness of the IOR; they were happy to accept huge loans to Panamanian and Liechtenstein companies of no apparent means. Calvi now found that he could feed his secret network directly, saving the IOR's commission of one sixteenth of a percentage point.

Federico Cossio looked respectable. The firm was part of an international group operating under the aegis of the American Horwath and Horwath, a group which also contained the British accountants Stoy Hayward. Initially Calvi seems to have taken the trouble not to present them with anything too outrageous. The operations of the summer and autumn of 1978, including the switching of the back-to-backs from the Cisalpine to Banco Comercial, appeared to strengthen greatly the first Banco Comercial balance sheet, dated 31 October 1978, which the auditors had to approve. The initial huge loans to Astolfine and Belrosa were eliminated, and the "deposits" at the IOR appeared to provide the bank with a cushion of strong liquid assets.

Federico Cossio was a Cuban who fled to Nicaragua after the Castro revolution, and formed strong links with the Somoza régime. By 1979 Calvi discovered that generosity could induce great flexibility in Cossio's attitude. During the following two years Cossio earned very substantial fees for various vague "consultancy" services, over and above his function as auditor. Cossio also received a $300,000 loan to buy a house in Miami, which had not been repaid when he died in 1984.

Not that Calvi ever trusted Cossio so far as to let him know of the existence of United Trading. Banco Comercial did not lend to it directly. The 8 million Swiss francs which United Trading needed to borrow to make the payment to Ortolani in January 1979 were first passed through the bank account of Nordeurop. This was the Liechtenstein company which had been formed some years before and which had, from time to time, been used as a nominee for United Trading.

The next loan by Banco Comercial under the new system was made in March 1979. It enabled Calvi to buy a block of more than a million shares in La Centrale. Most of these had been acquired by the Zanon family in 1973 as part of the deal with Calvi over the Toro insurance company. At that time Calvi signed an undertaking that he would buy the shares back at the end of 1978, either at the value put on them at the time of the original deal, equivalent to 20,000 lire, or at the market price – whichever was the higher. In spite of Calvi's operations to rig the profits of La Centrale, the shares had gone down to about 5,000 lire. But Calvi stuck to the spirit of the original deal and bought them back at 17,750 lire a share. To pay for them, United Trading had to borrow more than 36.5 million Swiss francs ($21 million) from Banco Comercial. This loan was initially made to a Panamanian company called Commotion. (That Calvi's knowledge of English was patchy may be deduced from the names he chose as likely to inspire confidence. *Commozione* in Italian means emotion, often of a tender kind.) It is clear from Calvi's United Trading balance sheets that this loan was treated as a Nordeurop back-to-back loan from the start, and Commotion was soon replaced by Nordeurop as the channel.

Such loans were not the only drain on the resources of Banco Comercial. We have seen its acquisition, at an inflated price, of the Olivetti building in Buenos Aires. Then, at the beginning of April 1979, Banco Comercial made a loan of 26 million Swiss francs, or about $15.7 million, for the benefit of the Rizzoli group. (This was when P2 had got Andrea Rizzoli out of it, and was about to get rid of his younger son Alberto.) The money bought a controlling interest in a popular TV weekly, *TV Sorrisi e Canzoni*. To conceal this further huge commitment of the Rizzoli group to Calvi, the loan was made to a Panamanian company, Worldwide Trading, which was part of Calvi's secret network. The Rizzoli company agreed to repurchase *TV Sorrisi e Canzoni* from Worldwide before 31 May 1981. Presumably Angelo Rizzoli hoped that somehow, by then, the group would have enough money to pay for it. It never did. Worldwide was left with the shares in the magazine, but, as they were eventually sold for $13 million, it was one of the less disastrous loans.

Much the heaviest call on Banco Comercial came when Calvi had to repay to the IOR the $65 million of "contango" loans on the capitals of Zitropo and Manic. We have seen that the two loans had been renewed for six months in letters from Calvi, dated 10 October 1978 – when John Paul

I was dead and it was not yet known who the next pope would be. If Marcinkus decided then that this would be the last renewal, he got his way. Calvi had to produce $20 million on 5 April 1979 to repay the Zitropo loan, and $45 million on 30 April to repay the Manic one. The two sums duly appeared "on the instructions of the Banca del Gottardo", as Marcinkus wrote in his memorandum to the joint commission, implying that the money came out of the blue.

The money was lent by Banco Comercial to United Trading, by way of Nordeurop, and then sent from Nordeurop's account at the Gottardo to the IOR's account at Manufacturers Hanover Trust, New York. Marcinkus may well not have known its route. But the subsequent behaviour of the IOR has never been explained.

With the repayments, Zitropo and Manic had reverted to their true owner, United Trading. If the IOR had legally owned the two companies while the loans were outstanding, this was no longer the case. From April 1979 onwards, the IOR owned them only in the sense that it could be said to be the legal owner of their parent, United Trading. Nobody seems to have grasped this in the confusion that followed the crash.

But the confusion was caused by the IOR's own action, or rather inaction. In spite of the repayment of the loans, it allowed the Zitropo and Manic share certificates to remain in its deposit account at the Kredietbank in Luxembourg. Is this proof that the IOR was just an absent-minded inno-cent? No. The IOR sent clear instructions to Kredietbank in May 1979 that six Manic shares, out of 45,000 in its account, were to be sent to the company itself, to be held as directors' and shareholders' qualifying shares. Clearly the IOR knew that the shares were still in its account. Kredietbank, it seems, continued to believe that the two companies were directly owned by the IOR. The presence of the certificates in the account at the time of the Ambrosiano crash led everyone else to share this view, apparently including Cardinal Casaroli.

In his written memorandum, Marcinkus maintained that, as far as he was concerned, the secret network companies belonged to the Cisalpine. He could make out a good case for believing that, since all the letters written by Calvi undertaking to buy back the Zitropo and Manic shares were written in his capacity as chairman of the Cisalpine, and specifically state that the Cisalpine would pay for the shares – not that it would arrange for the payment.

However, Marcinkus was a director of the Cisalpine. If he believed that it was taking over these investments, he should have ensured that they were recorded in the Cisalpine's books. Before that event, he should have ensured that the contingent liability to acquire them was recorded. Either Marcinkus was failing in his duty as a director of the Cisalpine, or he knew quite well that the Cisalpine was neither buying the shares nor paying for them.

Over the years, the IOR had earned a substantial income on these curious loans. Final interest instalments of $900,000 and $2,025,000 were paid to the IOR when the loans were repaid. That brought the total interest paid to the IOR on the Zitropo loan to nearly $11.2 million, and on the Manic one to nearly $23.2 million. In addition, the IOR had been paid three *una tantum* commissions in the early years of 200 million lire each, or a total of about $1.2 million.

Since neither Zitropo nor Manic had ever earned income of anything approaching this amount, virtually all the IOR's interest had come out of new loans, concealed by the back-to-back arrangements, and had thus gone to swell the United Trading deficit. So that United Trading could make the two final payments and pay interest on existing back-to-back loans, it had to borrow a further $10,025,000, via Nordeurop, from Banco Comercial.

But where did Banco Comercial get the money? By April 1979 Calvi was once more running desperately short of funds outside Italy, and the repayment to the IOR must have been just as inconvenient to him then as the previous October, when he was first given notice of it. Indeed, his apparent lack of preparation for the repayment suggests that he may have been expecting the IOR to renew the loans yet again. To meet other demands for money, early in 1979, Calvi had already resorted to ad hoc financing of the Banco Comercial by the insurance affiliates of the Ambrosiano group, Toro and two smaller insurance companies, Risco and Vittorio. To repay the IOR, he had to fall back on the most reliable source of funds, his three Italian banks. In April 1979 the Cattolica and the Varesino each lent Banco Comercial $10 million, while the Ambrosiano itself, which had already advanced $5 million, poured in another $15 million.

Most of the rest of Banco Comercial's needs were provided by the Cisalpine, which more than doubled its advances, to over $50 million. The Cisalpine was already borrowing nearly $175 million from Calvi's banks in Italy, and the extra funds came from the Gottardo. Clearly the Cisalpine's resources were stretched to the limit. The last $2,025,000 needed on 30 April 1979 to pay the IOR its final interest instalment on the Manic loan was financed *by* the IOR itself, which temporarily increased its deposits at the Cisalpine by a similar amount.

In using the resources of his Italian banks to repay the IOR, Calvi was defying the Bank of Italy inspectors. But by April 1979 he knew he could do this. On 24 March 1979 Paolo Baffi and Mario Sarcinelli were arrested. The charge against them was that they had failed to volunteer information to magistrates investigating a presumed fraud.

Sarcinelli's inspectors had, a year earlier, dealt with Italcasse, the central bank of Italy's 90 savings banks. They discovered a "black fund" of $90 million, most of which had gone to the Christian Democrat party. Some $320 million went to a firm in Sardinia, Società Italiana Resina. Its boss, Nino Rovelli, had fraud charges pending against him. (He was never convicted.)

The Bank of Italy had handed over its report on Italcasse to the magistrates. What it had not handed over was another report, on the Credito Industriale Sardo, a bank founded to promote the industrialisation of Sardinia. This too had made concessionary loans to Rovelli. The Bank of Italy had concluded that its actions were unwise, not criminal.

Italy had two laws which contradicted each other. One said that a public servant who, in the course of his duties, discovered an offence, must report it to the magistrates. However, the statutes of the Bank of Italy, which had the force of law, said that an official of the bank who discovered an offence must report it only to the Governor – that is, to Baffi – and that the Governor must report it only to the Treasury Minister. It was for the Minister to decide whether the magistrates should see it. Sarcinelli had in fact given the information on the Credito Industriale Sardo to Baffi. And Baffi had given it to the Treasury Minister, Filippo Pandolfi, who decided that no legal action should be taken.

Pandolfi at once explained this, and declared that both men had acted properly. His remarks had no effect whatever on the magistrates, who allowed the 68-year-old Baffi to remain at liberty "because of his advanced age" but kept the 42-year-old Sarcinelli in the grim, damp Regina Coeli prison.

The political storm that followed shook all Italy. Only the neo-fascists applauded the arrests. Italy's great newspapers, right-wing and left-wing alike, defended the reputation of these two honest men. There was one exception: the *Corriere della Sera*. On some days it gave the impression of being on both sides at once. Those respectable journalists who still worked for it pointed out the absurdity of the charges against Baffi and Sarcinelli. And yet a front-page headline went so far as to accuse Sarcinelli of embezzlement – an allegation completely unsupported by the story underneath. The editor, Franco Di Bella, had secretly joined P2 the previous year.

The other newspapers, hunting for clues to the intrigues behind the arrests, did not find this one. They soon established that one of the magistrates who had ordered the arrests, Antonio Alibrandi, was a neo-fascist. He had a son, several times accused of possessing arms, but always released. (The son's right-wing terrorism brought him into association with Danilo Abbruciati, whom we shall meet again.)

The other magistrate, Luciano Infelisi, was regarded as *cattolico integralista* – more Catholic than the Pope. Four days before the arrests, he had a long talk with the blackmailer Mino Pecorelli. In his scandal sheet *OP*, Pecorelli had been running a campaign against Sarcinelli, whom he called "the red functionary". It was assumed that somebody paid him to do this. Gelli, perhaps? But, according to the report of the P2 commission, Pecorelli had turned against his old friend Gelli, and was beginning to publish material made available to him by the security services, about Gelli's betrayal of his fascist friends at the end of the war. What Pecorelli was telling the magistrate is not known. A few hours later, as Pecorelli was getting into his car, a young man on a motorbike shot him dead.

Looking for more light on the events which led up to the arrest of Baffi and Sarcinelli, some journalists found out about the attempts to rehabilitate Sindona, and the firm stand which Baffi and Sarcinelli had made. If the arrests represented Sindona's revenge, they were counter-productive indeed. Until then, the attempt to pay Sindona's debts out of public money had been a secret, as closely guarded by the Bank of Italy men as by P2. But the shock of seeing Sarcinelli marched off to prison induced some important officials to talk. So the story of the mounting pressure on him became known.

Six months earlier, in September 1978, Sarcinelli had been approached with the Sindona project by Franco Evangelisti, who was the right-hand man of Giulio Andreotti. Sarcinelli told him that the plan was impossible. He then got a series of threatening phone calls. So did the liquidator Ambrosoli, and Sindona's old enemy Cuccia, who had nothing directly to do with the matter, but was supposed, rightly, to have great influence. Sindona's lawyer Guzzi phoned Sarcinelli, hinting at a bribe. Sarcinelli flatly refused to see him. But he could not refuse to see the Minister of Public Works, Gaetano Stammati, a P2 member. Stammati, who had been talking to Gelli, produced an elaborately worked out plan. Sarcinelli pointed out that it required the Bank of Italy to hand out public money, in exchange for nothing whatever.

According to the friends of Sarcinelli, he told one of the people who were pestering him: "The government is the government. If it wants to spend public money on paying Sindona's debts, then it has every right to put this plan before Parliament." The mere hint that the matter might be publicly debated put an end to the conversation. In the furore that raged while Sarcinelli was in prison, the plan to bring Sindona back to Italy became public, and therefore impossible.

However, nobody could get Sarcinelli out of prison. Italy has no Habeas Corpus Act. Only the magistrates who had ordered his imprisonment could order his release, and they extracted their price. Baffi was forced to suspend Sarcinelli from his post. He came out of prison on April 5, but he never ordered the inspection of another bank.

Soon afterwards Baffi, worn out and humiliated by these events, resigned. Sarcinelli lived to tell the tale, and to give evidence when Sindona was tried in Italy for blackmail and murder. In 1980 a court established that the charges against Sarcinelli were groundless, and that, even if they had been well based, they could not have constituted a reason for sending him to prison. He has had a successful career at the Treasury, and representing his country internationally.

But, at the time, the Bank of Italy was so terribly shaken that its normal work was disrupted. On the face of it, there seemed to have been a failure of nerve among some of its officials at least. On 10 May 1979 the Bank's "administrative currency nucleus", consisting of Cesare Avoli and Odoardo Bulgarelli, in consultation with a lawyer, Vincenzo Mezzacapo, presented a report contradicting everything the inspector Padalino had said about the financing of the foreign associates. Calvi, they concluded, had not broken the terms of the Mincomes permissions. This report was entirely secret until the P2 commission published it, and even then it went unnoticed, being among a mass of other documents.

And on 22 June 1979 Calvi had another stroke of luck. The Guardia di Finanza which had been asked by a Milan magistrate to look into the criminal exchange control charges against Calvi, reported that he had done nothing wrong. The head of the Guardia, Raffaele Giudice, belonged to P2. The investigating magistrate to whom this report was made was Luca Mucci. The magistrate who had received the report made by the Bank of Italy inspectors the previous December, Emilio Alessandrini, had been murdered by terrorists of the Red Brigades.

So the immediate threats to Calvi would seem to have been removed. It is probable that he knew of the Guardia di Finanza report, but it is not known whether he knew of the apparent backtracking in the Bank of Italy. Possibly not; he may have known only about Padalino's original recommendation, for his private papers make it quite clear that he regarded it as urgent to reduce, or even to eliminate, the loans from his Italian banks to the foreign subsidiaries. It looks as if he feared that the Mincomes authorisations would not be renewed. There are a number of notes of schemes from this period, designed to remove the loans to the Cisalpine and the Banco Comercial from the Italian banks' books before they drew up their year-end balance sheets.

One way was to raise more money outside Italy, and use it to repay the Italian banks. Calvi was able to raise substantial short-term loans from various foreign banks in May 1979, but he needed long-term loans. So, at the end of May, he turned to his obliging friends at ENI, whose Nassau bank Tradinvest came up with a five-year loan of $37.5 million, $25 million of which was to the Cisalpine and the other $12.5 million to the Banco Comercial. If ENI ever asked to see the financial statements of the Banco Comercial, what did it make of a balance sheet total which had swollen in a matter of months to more than $400 million, a quarter of which was lent to a Liechtenstein company called Nordeurop?

Much of the Cisalpine's $25 million seems to have been used to repay the Italian banks, but Calvi had other plans for most of the $12.5 million lent to Banco Comercial. At the end of June 1979, $9 million was advanced to United Trading by way of Nordeurop, but then it was paid to Ambrosiano Group Promotion and Consulting, which passed it on to its parent, BA Holding. There it was described in the books as a dividend, equivalent to more than 15 million Swiss francs. The purpose of the payment was, yet again, to rig the profits of BA Holding.

We have seen that this was first done in 1977. The profits were rigged again in 1978, by Promotion paying a dividend of more than 11 million Swiss francs to BA Holding, out of fabricated "fees and commissions" paid to it by Astolfine. As a result, BA Holding was able to show a profit of 6,337,000 Swiss francs in 1978, rather than a loss, and to start paying dividends. The 1978 dividend was 25 francs a share; the IOR received 275,400 Swiss francs on the 11,016 shares it held on its own account. The 1979 operation was even cruder. It enabled BA Holding to show a profit of 8,280,000 Swiss francs rather than a loss of 6.75 million. Again it paid 25 francs a share in dividends, enriching the IOR by another 275,400 Swiss francs (about $172,125) of embezzled money. The IOR also received the dividends on the 53,133 shares it held for the Cisalpine and the Banco Comercial, but most of this was paid out again in interest, after the IOR had deducted its semi-annual fee of one-thousandth of the sum outstanding.

The IOR's benefit, however, was far from Calvi's main motive in rigging the BA Holding profits. In June 1979 BA Holding had to be seen as profitable, so that Calvi could begin to exploit a new source of funds – the syndicated loan.

As we have seen, this merely means a loan made by a number of banks acting in concert. The one which does the organising is called the lead bank. It has no legal responsibility to the others if the loan is not repaid. The arrangement is not now so fashionable as it was then.

For the first syndicated loan, in the middle of 1979, the lead bank was the Gottardo. It was not then appreciated abroad that it was wholly dominated by Calvi. Although it was known to be part of the Ambrosiano group, the Gottardo gave the appearance of a certain detachment, and it had built up a business unconnected with the Ambrosiano. It looked solid, Swiss and respectable. By leading first one and then two more syndicated loans for Calvi it enabled him to persuade other banks to do the same.

Nobody knew then that the Gottardo was a vital part of Calvi's illicit network. It was technically the manager of United Trading. It knew it was supposed to be managing that on behalf of the IOR. But, as the managing director of the Gottardo, Francesco Bolgiani, admitted to the joint commission, what Calvi said went. All the foreign currency back-to-backs went through its books. Fernando Garzoni, who in 1979 became chairman of the Gottardo and was also a director of the Cisalpine, was perhaps as near to getting the whole picture as Calvi ever allowed his associates to be.

This first syndicated loan was for 50 million Swiss francs for five years, and it reached BA Holding in July 1979. But this was the equivalent of only about $30 million. Clearly, it was not going to be enough. There was $200 million or so still owing to the Italian banks. There was the interest cost of United Trading's debts, running at about $50 million a year. And there were the ever-increasing demands of Gelli, Ortolani, Sindona and others.

Before there was even time for BA Holding to pass on the new money to Banco Comercial, where it was needed, Calvi had to rethink the schemes which now gave a central role to the Nicaraguan bank. On 19 July 1979 the dictator Somoza was overthrown, and the communist-backed Sandanistas, led by Daniel Ortega, took over Nicaragua.

TWENTY-THREE

Back-scratching in Peru

A week before the overthrow of Somoza, Giorgio Ambrosoli, liquidator of Sindona's Italian empire, was murdered outside his home in Milan.

When I interviewed Sindona in 1984, he was awaiting extradition to Italy for this murder. Courteous, but tense, he assured me of his innocence. What motive could he have, after all? It was of no advantage to him, he said, that Ambrosoli should be murdered.

This was true. But hardly anything Sindona did was to his own long-term advantage. It was not to his advantage to antagonise Hambros Bank, or to trust Bordoni, or to make an enemy of the influential Cuccia. It was not to his advantage to be seen by FBI men with the go-between who found him the assassin, or with the assassin himself.

Sindona was not found guilty of this murder until 1986. But the magistrates of Milan immediately began work on the indictment. The press became aware of this and printed stories about the clues that pointed to Sindona.

The magistrates had been recording the phone calls made to Ambrosoli by men with Sicilian accents. These calls began in December 1978. "You've been to America and you've told lies," said the voice on the phone. Ambrosoli had indeed been to America; his evidence enabled the authorities there to establish that Sindona had bought the Franklin National Bank out of money diverted from the clients of his Italian banks. The calls continued, alternating threats with offers of a bribe. ("Una bella busta" – a beautiful envelope – was the phrase used.)

Ambrosoli wrote to his wife: "Whatever happens, I'll certainly pay a high price for taking on this job. But I knew that before taking it on and I'm not complaining, because it has been a unique chance for me to do something for the country."

The terror that Sindona inspired was widespread. The previous autumn Nicola Biase, a former employee of Sindona who had agreed to testify about his frauds, was visited by two men who said: "We did have orders to take your legs off. That's been postponed, but we're going to kidnap someone in your family."

According to Clara Calvi, at some time during the first half of 1979 Calvi was staying at the Carlyle Hotel in New York. Two men threatened him, saying that he still had to pay Sindona. Calvi telephoned Sindona, who came to the hotel and collected the money in person.

After the arrest of Baffi and Sarcinelli, Cuccia went to see Sindona in New York. The Sicilian voices on the phone had been threatening to kidnap Cuccia's daughter, and she had indeed seen menacing figures in a car following hers.

Sindona told Cuccia that he had read Ambrosoli's confidential reports, and proved this by quoting from them. (Who passed them on has never been established.) He said that his son, Nino, had been intending to kill Cuccia, and that only he, Sindona, had prevented this. Then he said that Ambrosoli would have to disappear.

At Sindona's trial, Cuccia was closely questioned about this. Why hadn't he reported Sindona's threats to the magistrates? Cuccia said that it was only his word against Sindona's. He suggested that Sindona might have sued him. Perhaps Cuccia had allowed his lifelong habit of silence to get the better of him.

The assassin Sindona hired, William Aricò, was not well chosen. In spite of his Italian name he did not speak a word of the language, and had to take an Italian-speaking gangster, Giuseppe Scuccimarri, with him. Aricò himself was killed in 1984. He was trying to escape from an American prison when an improvised rope broke and he fell to his death. But he had already confessed, and his deposition was read at Sindona's trial. This was the crucial evidence on which Sindona was convicted.

Sindona himself died mysteriously, by poison, in March 1986, just after he had been found guilty of murder. The evidence was overwhelming that he had taken the poison of his own accord. But who smuggled it in to him? He had been almost six years in custody, and repeatedly searched.

Well before the murder of Ambrosoli, Calvi was insisting on a bodyguard, paid for by the Ambrosiano. His second-in-command, Roberto Rosone, protested that this was becoming more expensive than the bodyguard of the Shah. Calvi pointed to the Red Brigades, gangsters with left-wing pretensions who were then kidnapping and murdering capitalists. But it was not the Red Brigades he feared. His will, a hastily scrawled document leaving everything to Clara, is dated the day before Ambrosoli's murder.

Sindona was due to be tried in the United States in the autumn of 1979, on charges arising from the collapse of the Franklin National Bank. But on

2 August 1979 he vanished from New York, having staged his own kidnapping. Later, in a rambling and largely fictitious letter to President Reagan, Sindona admitted that the kidnapping was faked. But he explained that he had done it, not because he feared to be tried for fraud – of which he was, he protested, completely innocent – but because he had to organise a revolt of Sicilian separatists. He is probably the only person accused of fraud who has ever maintained that he could not have done it because he was too busy committing high treason.

One of those who helped him to stage the kidnapping, Miceli Crimi, later admitted that they both had links with a movement for an "independent and anti-communist Sicily". Crimi was a doctor, and, to make the kidnapping look real, carefully shot Sindona in the leg, having given him an anaesthetic first.

Sindona's visit to Sicily, though illegal, was not very secret; he stayed with a Mafia boss, Rosario Spatola, and went to restaurants to dine with other Mafia bosses, including his old friends and backers, the heroin-smuggling Gambino family. Sindona seems to have spent his time, not so much on Sicilian separatism, as on his campaign of extortion.

On 15 September Cuccia got a threatening phone call, ordering him to give money to Sindona's family. Four days later he received a letter, posted in Rome the previous day, purporting to come from Americans of Sicilian origin. "We are repeating and completing the telephone call . . . It's your fault that our New York friend has been ruined and that his life is now in danger. If they kill him we'll destroy first your family and then you . . . Make the agreement at once with the Banco di Roma and the Bank of Italy. Have the warrant for our friend's arrest withdrawn at once . . . The family is in grave financial difficulties. Help them at once, and not with words, with money . . . Don't resign, don't leave your job in the bank until you have regularised our friend's position; we will begin the punishments at once. If you tell the police and the judges and the lawyers about the telephone call, or about this letter, we shall destroy your family and you . . . You have now understood very well that we are not joking . . ."

This was typed, as the authorities afterwards established, on a machine which Crimi had lent to Sindona.

On 22 September Sindona wrote to his daughter and his son-in-law, Magnoni: "With calm, but decisively, it has been made clear to him by various means, including written ones, that he can, and therefore has the duty to . . . regularise everything in Milan and Rome . . . If he doesn't move he'll feel it quickly . . ."

If the letter to Cuccia was written "with calm", what did Sindona do when he got excited? One thing he did, also on 22 September, was to send Crimi to Arezzo with a message for Gelli. He must get more money from the "Conte", as Calvi was called by his P2 associates.

On 5 October two of Sindona's friends from Sicily, Rosario Spatola and John Gambino, tried to set fire to Cuccia's house. (It was the second such attempt.) Immediately afterwards Cuccia's daughter got a phone call: "Tell your father that if he doesn't do what we want we'll burn you all alive; we're friends of the gentleman in New York that he knows."

Cuccia sought the protection of the authorities, but Calvi was in no position to do that. He paid. Sindona later made no secret of the fact that Calvi had contributed to the cost of his defence. He said that the money went through Gelli's Swiss bank account. It has not been traced. But it must have been sufficient, for on 8 October John Gambino smuggled Sindona over the Brenner Pass into Austria. On 16 October Sindona reappeared in New York, with money to pay the lawyers who, he still hoped, would keep him out of prison.

Because Ambrosoli was murdered, the depositions he had been making to the American investigators in the last three days of his life were leaked to the press. He alleged that, after the Pacchetti-Zitropo deal, $6.5 million had been divided between "an American bishop and a Milanese banker". This did Calvi's reputation no good. But the foreign bankers, now lending to BA Holding, failed to notice it.

Ambrosoli knew about Calvi's Swiss bank accounts in the names of Ehrenkreuz and Ralrov, because these were in the posters put out by Sindona's hired blackmailer. It is evident, from the papers Calvi kept, that Ambrosoli was looking for proof. A letter from the Kredietbank in Luxembourg, dated early in July 1979, asked the Gottardo how to deal with Ambrosoli's persistent requests. "Monsieur Ambrosoli est revenu à charge pour nous demander des nouvelles." (Mr Ambrosoli is chasing us again for news.) On 30 July the Gottardo replied that there was no need to give the liquidator the information he wanted. But by then Ambrosoli was dead.

The magistrates took over the inquiries, which were eventually to produce the proof that Ehrenkreuz was a Calvi family company. After Calvi's death the liquidators of BA Holding sued the Calvi family in Canada, suggesting that the Ehrenkreuz money had helped to buy the property Calvi acquired there.

Even while Ambrosoli was still alive, and investigating one crooked payment, another one was being set up in a way which threw suspicion on Calvi. In June 1979 ENI announced a deal with Petromin of Saudi Arabia to supply crude oil for the next two and a half years. What was not announced was that ENI had simultaneously made a deal with a Panamanian company, Sophilau. It was to receive payments for "consulting services" amounting to 7 per cent of the total paid for the oil. The first instalment of this, more than $17 million, was paid into Sophilau's Swiss bank account on 18 July. This export of currency was legal; the Mincomes had authorised it. Perhaps the P2 member Firrao would not have got it past the minister, if the minister had still been Rinaldo Ossola. But he had lost his post in March 1979. The new minister was the P2 member Gaetano Stammati.

The ENI president, Mazzanti, had to go, when, in the autumn of 1979, the press uncovered the scandal of the $17 million payment and the Mincomes authorization for it. A parliamentary commission of inquiry failed to discover who got the money. This one has never been pinned on to Calvi. But it emerged that Ortolani and Gelli were involved, as was their man at the Mincomes, Firrao.

Ortolani remained proud, years later, of another deal he fixed in 1979, a peace treaty between Calvi and Carlo Pesenti. Pesenti had inherited a cement works in Bergamo, at the foot of the Alps. It was a perfectly sound business, but Pesenti over-extended himself. Though Italy has laws forbidding a bank to own an industry, it has no laws forbidding an industry to own a bank. Pesenti's main company, Italmobiliare, effectively controlled two banks, the Banca Provinciale Lombarda and the Istituto Bancario Italiano, both much used by the IOR. A third bank, the Credito Commerciale, also used by the IOR, was to slip from Pesenti's hands that autumn, as we shall see.

Pesenti also owned one of Italy's leading insurance companies, RAS. Calvi and Pesenti were not on good terms because Calvi's Toro insurance company had built up an unwelcome stake in RAS.

In July 1979, at the Hotel Dolder in Zürich, they made a secret agreement, pledging themselves in general terms to cooperation and consultation. The idea, according to Ortolani, was that, ultimately, they should merge. Calvi said later, when pressed by official interrogators, that it was Ortolani's idea, and that, for the sake of the "aura of Masonic sacredness", both Ortolani and Gelli had signed it, as well as the two principals, and that it had been given to Gelli to keep.

It was one of those deals, always ecstatically greeted by the people concerned, in which two almost bankrupt firms try to prop each other up. It was considered important to the image of the Ambrosiano group when Pesenti joined the board of La Centrale in October 1979.

In fact Pesenti's troubles were just coming to a head. In November 1979 he had to repay to the IOR the seven-year loan contracted in 1972. It was indexed to the Swiss franc; therefore it had quadrupled, from 50 billion lire to more than 200 billion lire (about $154 million). When the 1979/1980 balance sheet for Italmobiliare showed this immense loss (which had obliged Pesenti to sell his third bank, the Credito Commerciale) the shareholders were up in arms.

"I made a mistake, that's all," Pesenti said. He thereby becomes the first character in this book ever to admit that. He went on: "Anyway, there's an illustrious precedent; President Giscard d'Estaing has just had to repay a loan indexed to the price of gold."

Two small shareholders demanded proof that the loan had ever existed, and began a legal action which was still dragging on when Pesenti died in 1984. Meanwhile a court in Milan declared the 1979/1980 balance sheet invalid on other grounds.

Calvi seems to have lost more than he gained from the pact with Pesenti. Ortolani later claimed that it was achieved by his "valuable consultancy and mediation". Such words, from the lips of Ortolani, meant that he thought he deserved a lot of money. Almost certainly, this was one pretext for huge payments, totalling $12.5 million, handed out by United Trading to Ortolani in the second half of 1979, in four instalments, beginning in August. About a quarter of this was passed on to Gelli. The other pretext for these payments was that Gelli had arranged a peace pact between Calvi and Anna Bonomi, which we shall examine in the next chapter. These payments worsened Calvi's ever-growing problem, the United Trading deficit.

Now that Somoza had fallen, Calvi could not rely on Banco Comercial and its helpful auditor. For a year he had been planning the opening of another bank in South America. This one was in Gelli's favourite country, Argentina. It was to be grandly called "Banco Ambrosiano de America del Sud". That suggests that it was intended to supplant Banco Comercial as the spearhead of Calvi's drive into Latin America.

But it is evident from Calvi's papers that he found the banking authorities of Buenos Aires less pliant than he would have liked. They objected to his original choice of local directors because they lacked banking experience. Corrupt as General Galtieri's government may have been, it was not corrupt in the way that suited Calvi. So, although the Buenos Aires bank did open towards the end of 1979, it never played an important role in Calvi's fraud. As for the story that he financed the exocet missiles used by Argentina in 1982, by that time he needed some secret weapon to finance him.

The fall of Somoza did not mean that all was lost in Nicaragua. Calvi's banks had lent generously to Somoza family companies, but they had not neglected the opposition. Among Calvi's papers is a list of the ministers in Ortega's government, with brief notes about each. Against the name of the minister for agriculture, it is noted that he was president of a slaughterhouse company, IGOSA (Industria Ganadera de Oriente). Banco Comercial had lent the company $1 million the previous October. Simultaneously, $125,000 from IGOSA had been credited to Calvi's bank account at the Roywest.

Calvi was not thrown out by the new régime. He never again visited Nicaragua, but he continued to own his ranch there, and to carry a Nicaraguan passport. And Banco Comercial kept its licence. Ortega announced that Nicaragua would honour its debts, except for those regarded as having been corruptly obtained.

So Calvi could have continued to feed his secret network through the Banco Comercial. To judge by various projections among his notes, he thought for a time that he would have to do so.

The difficulty was in Europe. BA Holding was now raising international loans. This meant publishing a synopsis, at least, of the balance sheets of its subsidiary banks. Banco Comercial's second set of accounts had to be drawn up on 31 October 1979. The auditor, Cossio, could be relied on to make this as uninformative as possible. But the total would have to appear, and the total was now about $450 million. International bankers might be alarmed to see such a huge amount, nearly half the Ambrosiano's international business, channelled through a bank in Nicaragua, whose new rulers were regarded as hostile to capitalism.

But, in the late summer of 1979, Calvi hit on a remarkably convenient solution. He found a new South American haven, Peru.

He already had good contacts there. Ortolani afterwards claimed that he was responsible for these contacts, as he had introduced Calvi to the Peruvian ambassador in Rome. These services, Ortolani claimed, had brought him "an important reward" from Calvi. Then Calvi helped the Peruvian Government with a timely loan in 1978, when it was having difficulty in paying for a naval frigate it had ordered from an Italian shipbuilder. Calvi's particular friends were Javier Silva Ruete, the minister of the economy, and Alvaro Meneses Diaz, president of the Banco de la Nación – the central bank.

The arrangement these three people made was carried out almost at once, though a formal "cooperation agreement" was not signed until some months later. The essence of it was that the Italian currency laws allowed Italian banks to place short-term deposits with foreign banks, provided that these foreign banks were genuinely independent. What could be more

independent than the central bank of Peru? Instead of having to pay back
the loans that his Italian banks had made to the foreign parts of his empire,
Calvi could now switch the money to this perfectly legal use. And the central
bank of Peru would then secretly pass the money on, just as, for so many
years, the IOR had done.

What the central bank of Peru got out of it was a "turn" of one quarter
per cent – considerably better than the IOR's one-sixteenth. Besides, Calvi
agreed that in due course his banks would deposit some extra funds, which
would not have to be passed on.

Calvi was later to make a further dozen or so back-to-back arrangements
with respectable international banks, including Williams and Glyn's of
London. These, however, were isolated deals, not continuous arrangements
like those he made with the IOR and the Banco de la Nación.

The vital part of the agreement with the Peruvians was rushed into use
even before the rest of the arrangements had been worked out. In August
and September 1979 the Ambrosiano, the Cattolica and the Varesino
deposited $55 million with the Banco de la Nación. The Gottardo chipped
in with a further $5 million. All this was passed on to the Cisalpine, which
was thus enabled to reduce its borrowings from the Italian banks to about
$105 million.

On 11 October the second part of the agreement with the Peruvians was
put into effect. The Banco Ambrosiano Andino of Lima received its licence
from the superintendent of banks, brother-in-law of the president. It had
a capital of $12.5 million, mostly subscribed by BA Holding. The Banco
de la Nación took a 2 per cent stake, and Meneses Diaz was made a director.
So were three senior executives of the Ambrosiano, but not Calvi himself.
The new bank blossomed; by the end of the month its balance sheet total
exceeded $435 million.

The reason for this sudden growth was simple. On 26 October, five days
before the end of the Banco Comercial's second financial year, the great
bulk of its business was transferred to the new Peruvian bank. All that was
left was a handful of the smaller loans, totalling about $15 million. So
Calvi could say publicly: "In connection with the events which occurred in
Nicaragua, the Bank decided to reduce its activity."

Everything else in the Banco Comercial was transferred lock, stock and
barrel to the new Banco Ambrosiano Andino. There was very little genuine
business in these assets. Among the loans were $42 million owed by World-
wide Trading – that is, the Rizzolis. This included the 26 million Swiss
francs lent to them to buy *TV Sorrisi e Canzoni* earlier in the year. It also
included a loan of $24.1 million made to Worldwide to enable it to acquire

the unpaid debts and interest owed by Rizzoli International, now in liquidation, to the Cisalpine and the Banco Comercial. Also switched was the $37 million loan made to Ortolani's Bafisud, when it bought a block of Varesino shares in order to rig the profits of La Centrale.

Much the largest part of the "assets" transferred to the new bank, more than $270 million, was money that had been channelled into United Trading through the IOR and Nordeurop. Since June 1979, over $19 million more had been poured into the secret network through Nordeurop. Of this, $5.55 million had gone to the disastrous Nassau-based investment company Capitalfin. Then $5.5 million had been paid to Ortolani, in the first two instalments of the $12.5 million he received in the second half of 1979. Another $4 million had been needed by the secret network to subscribe for a new issue of Ambrosiano shares. The rest was required for interest and other financial charges.

The total debt of Nordeurop/United Trading to Banco Comercial had reached just under $131 million. This was now replaced by three new loans from Andino: one for $62 million, another for $65.5 million and a third for 28 million Swiss francs. These totalled $144.5 million. The excess was used to capitalise unpaid interest, a further $13,625,000 thus being added to the hidden deficit.

The IOR element in the back-to-back loans to United Trading had remained constant since the beginning of 1979, apart from exchange rate fluctuations, and now stood at $126 million. This was made up of dollar loans of $65 million and Swiss franc loans of 101,645,000, of which 71,645,000 Swiss francs were financing one of the two blocks of BA Holding shares which the IOR had agreed to hold secretly on Calvi's request.

According to the written memorandum which Marcinkus put before the joint commission, the switching of the IOR back-to-back loans to the new bank was done without the prior permission of the IOR. Allowing himself a brief note of indignation, he wrote: "The transfer was suddenly ordered and executed, without the knowledge of the IOR, by the heads of the Banco Ambrosiano spa." (The Italian initials SPA stand for Società per Azioni, meaning that it is a company with shareholders.)

Marcinkus continued: "The nature of such relations was subsequently confirmed in the letter of 17 December 1979 sent by the president of the Banco Ambrosiano spa (i.e. Calvi) who also fulfilled the function of 'special advisor' of BAA (i.e. the Andino)." As we shall see, it is significant that the words "special advisor" appear in English in the original Italian text.

The letter of 17 December 1979, to which Marcinkus referred, was one of the "parallel" documents produced by the IOR for the joint commission.

(See Appendix B(vi)) It was not really a letter, but a note typed on the bottom of copies of the two letters Calvi had written the previous year, when the back-to-back operation had first been extended from the Cisalpine to the Banco Comercial. The note merely states that the obligations assumed in these letters are also valid for operations with the Andino.

Marcinkus did not say whether the notes were produced by Calvi only after the IOR had raised objections. But he did try to explain the IOR's acceptance of the new situation: "The absolute lack of operational autonomy of the BAA, which was in reality managed exclusively by the heads of BA spa, did not make it seem strange that this bank, after having ordered the transfer of the deposits on its own initiative, should confirm the under-takings of its foreign associates, all of whose interests it, in fact, looked after."

By the time Marcinkus wrote this, in 1983, it had become clear that the Andino was Calvi's creature, but that is not how it was presented publicly in 1979. Yet Marcinkus was arguing that he knew it *at the time*. If he did, it could only be because Calvi had explained to him that the formation of the Andino was a cosmetic operation. This part of the memorandum amounted to an admission of what the Vatican had tried to avoid admitting – that Calvi had told Marcinkus a good deal about his activities. The English words "special advisor" – introduced by the IOR to justify its acceptance of an undertaking on behalf of the Andino by Calvi, who was not a director – look like a direct quote from the minutes of the first Andino board meeting, held not in Lima but in Lausanne, on 22 November 1979. A resolution was passed giving Calvi that title, spelt in that way. So it looks as if the IOR had been given a copy of that resolution, at least. But had they, in that case, not seen the full minutes? If they had, they would have seen the complete list of the loans transferred from the Banco Comercial, as well as the details of the deposits with the IOR and the advances to Nordeurop.

The IOR might not have known that Nordeurop was really United Trad-ing. If it did know, or if it had any idea of the enormous increase in the debt burden of United Trading, its rational response would have been to inquire what assets it had to cover the debts. After all, the IOR held United Trading's share capital, as a kind of security for the back-to-back loans. It is possible that Marcinkus did seek assurances from Calvi. Perhaps Calvi convinced him that United Trading was solvent, and that everything would be all right in the end. There is evidence that Calvi had by now convinced himself of this.

We have come to the point where fantasy was beginning to take over.

TWENTY-FOUR

Fantasy and Reality – Marcinkus v Garner

The evidence is in the private balance sheets that Calvi kept in his safe at the Roywest. In the autumn of 1979 he started presenting the assets of United Trading in a new way. It was an extraordinary blend of realism and fantasy.

In the mid-1970s, Calvi had written off the loans to Edilcentro and La Centrale Finance, at a cost of about $25 million. He had, since then, recognised no further losses. All loans were entered at the full amount owed. And he had made no attempt to value the investments; all shares were entered at their cost.

Under this accounting method the growing gap between assets and liabilities was clear, though the causes of that gap were not. One cause – the handouts to Ortolani, Gelli and others – was not entered at all. The other cause – the need to borrow more to pay the interest on existing loans – was also not entered, because Calvi kept no profit and loss account. Now Calvi completely reassessed the assets (as can be seen from his private balance sheet reproduced opposite).

We begin with the realism. Zitropo, recently wholly reacquired from the IOR at a cost of $20 million, was rightly judged to be worthless. Calvi put a couple of dashes against the letter Z. The market value of its Pacchetti shares, at $15.1 million, was far outweighed by its borrowings. Over $115 million had gone into Zitropo over the years, and Calvi now accepted that this was lost.

Manic (shown as M) was given a value of $8.5 million, reached by taking the market value of its Beni Immobili Italia and Saffa shares of $22.5 million, and deducting a $14 million loan from the Cisalpine. But this value was not enough to cover another loan to Manic, of $10 million, made by United Trading itself. In effect, Calvi was recognising that the $45 million he had so recently paid to the IOR to reacquire Manic was also lost. The Beni Immobili and Saffa shares were eventually sold in 1980 and 1981 for $25.3 million.

Calvi also put a couple of dashes against Belrosa (Bell). So he realised

268

24/10/79

```
    4963    BAH                              1250/    3,8 x 3 =        11,4
1.056.084    L.C.                           5930/    7,5 x 5 =        37,7

5.500.000    Su                                        x 1 =          6,6

Ast. 1.231.944                              18100/   26,9 x 5 =      134,3

Bell. Cap                                                             ==

A/    2.222.222 x 18100 x 5 =  242,3
         45.000 x   850    =   23,1
                              265,4 -
                               42
                              223,4                                 223,4


M/    45/m
      10/m 17/3/80  13 1/2% // per

      15.390.666 B x 515=       9,5
       1.857.000 S x5810=       13
                               22,5-
                               14
                                8,5                                  8,5


Z/    8/m
      25m frs 30//11/79 2%
      30/m    30/11/79 11 1/2% // per

      172.228.778 x  73         15,1                                 ==


AB/  18/11/75 5.518.670                                              ==

Eofsa    30/4/79 3% B/frs                                            4,8
                                                                   426,7

      53137 BAH     1250/ 40,2 x 3 = 120,6
                     - 71,645
                       22,720    =   57,1
                                     63,5
                                    ====                            63,5
                                                                   490,2
                                                                ==========

c/  Drs/Frs 1,654
    Drs/lit 830
```

that the $40 million it had poured into Capitalfin (Cap) was lost. Capitalfin
went into liquidation in September 1981.

There were only two loans to outsiders left in the United Trading balance
sheet by October 1979. One was the debt of Anna Bonomi (AB), secured
by her promissory note for $5,518,670. Calvi had been entering this regu-
larly at face value in the balance sheet. Now he gave it a value of nil.

This would appear to be the result of his second peace treaty with Anna
Bonomi, made on 9 October 1979. The first one, made in May 1978,

brought little improvement in their relationship, although at the end of that year the Ambrosiano released the jewels and other security it held against the lira debts, taking instead only a personal guarantee. Anna Bonomi's story is that she still wanted the rest of the 10 billion lire which, in her opinion, Calvi owed her. She got Gelli to back her in this.

Calvi gave way. Not only did he write off the promissory note, to judge from his balance sheet – though what happened to it has never been established – but on 18 December he paid out $7.9 million to a Swiss bank account in the name of Anna Bonomi's front man, Marinoni. This was equivalent to about 6.4 billion lire, so that, with the 2 billion he had paid her in May 1978, he had paid her 8.4 billion of the 10 billion she claimed. Moreover the cancelled promissory note was worth about 4.5 billion lire and Anna Bonomi still owed the Ambrosiano nearly 5.7 billion lire. Yet she insisted that the $7.9 million had not fully paid off Calvi's debt. Shortly before his death Calvi was to pay her another $2 million.

The other loan in the balance sheet was the 8 million Swiss francs (shown as $4.8 million), advanced to Ortolani in January 1979 under the mysterious heading: "Ecfsa". The loan had apparently been due for repayment on 30 April 1979. Yet Calvi went on entering it at its face value, as if he expected Ortolani to pay it one day. Here we have already left realism behind.

Fantasy was in full flight when Calvi came to value the shares of Ambrosiano group companies held by United Trading. As a result of the new issue of Ambrosiano shares in 1979, United Trading owned 3,454,166 – 2,222,222 through its subsidiary Anli and 1,231,944 through Astolfine, another subsidiary. There were altogether 30 million Ambrosiano shares in existence. The Milan stock exchange quotation in October 1979 was 18,100 lire. Judged by the market, then, the holding in United Trading was worth $75.3 million, and the whole bank theoretically worth $654 million. Calvi now inserted the Ambrosiano shares in the United Trading balance sheet at five times their market value, so that the holding adds up to $376.6 million. This would have made the whole bank worth $3,271 million.

Similarly, the holding of 1,056,084 shares in La Centrale, principally composed of the block bought back from the Zanon family at about three times the market level, was also valued at five times the quoted price, to make them "worth" $37.7 million.

United Trading's other major investment in the Ambrosiano group was in BA Holding. It now held 4,967 BA Holding shares on its own account. There were also the 53,133 shares held by the IOR in its account at the Gottardo, and financed by back-to-back loans from the Cisalpine and the new Andino, now totalling 94,365,000 Swiss francs. Marcinkus afterwards claimed to believe that he thought the IOR was holding these shares on behalf of the Cisalpine. But they were treated by Calvi as part of the portfolio of United Trading, which thus, in effect, owned 58,100 shares. (Calvi got the total right, although, for some reason, he put four shares too many in the IOR's holding, and four too few in United Trading's.)

BA Holding's shares were not quoted on any stock exchange. Earlier in 1979, United Trading had bought 100 shares at 1,525 Swiss francs each. But now, for the balance sheet, Calvi took a nominal value of 1,250 Swiss francs – and multiplied it by three, making each share worth 3,750 Swiss francs. So he valued the whole package at $132 million.

By these fantastic valuations Calvi succeeded in wiping out the true deficit of United Trading, which was at least $300 million by this time. Indeed, he showed it with a surplus of nearly $50 million. Who was he kidding? The IOR? Most of all, I think, himself.

The market in Ambrosiano shares in Milan had stabilised by now. The dealing firm Suprafin had been as active as ever, but now Calvi no longer had to hide the shares it bought in the secret network; genuine buyers could be found. (However, he reduced the value he had put on Suprafin by $3 million from its original cost, to a more realistic value of $6.6 million.)

He must have believed that Ambrosiano shares were going to rise, because at about this time he personally invested some $240,000 in the shares for the benefit of his family, principally his daughter. The investment was not made with Ambrosiano money through a company in Panama or Liechtenstein, but through a company registered in Milan, Ridal.

At first sight it looks as if Calvi had found someone else to share his fantasies. He succeeded in selling some BA Holding shares at a price even higher than the one he had put on them; 4,963 shares owned directly by United Trading, which he had valued at 3,750 Swiss francs each, were sold at the end of October for 4,000 francs each – a total of more than $12 million.

The buyer, however, was not an objective third party. It was Calvi's Peruvian partner, the Banco de la Nación. This was part of the gigantic agreement with the Peruvians. Another part of it was that Calvi had agreed to develop a huge tract of the hinterland of Peru for agriculture and mining. Clearly he believed in this, for he made it a personal venture through a private company, Central American Services.

While Calvi was cooking his secret balance sheet, he still had problems with the public ones. In the first place, there were the loans from his three Italian banks, which still totalled $125 million. Calvi's respite from official

questioning, brought about by the arrest of Baffi and Sarcinelli, and prolonged by the friendly attitude of the *Guardia di Finanza*, was now at an
end. The magistrate Luca Mucci did not accept the assurances of the
Guardia that Calvi had done nothing wrong. On 16 October 1979 Mucci
wrote to the UIC, asking it to check whether Calvi owned various companies
registered in Liechtenstein and Panama. And on 25 October Mucci summoned Calvi himself for questioning. It was a polite occasion, with Calvi at
his stonewalling best. He knew nothing of a company called EPI, he said.
(This was Etablissements pour les Participations Internationales, a nominee
company of the Gottardo.) *L'Espresso* heard about this interview with Mucci
and reported it. But *L'Espresso* did not have the text of the Bank of Italy
report. It said the inspectors had concluded that the whole Ambrosiano
board was responsible for "secret export of capital, violation of the banking
laws, issuing false balance sheets and statements and illegal appropriation
of profits".

The inspectors had not written those words. The Bank of Italy immediately said so. "There are no documents of ours containing the passages
referred to in the article." So Calvi now had an authoritative denial to show
to potential lenders.

However, he had a new problem with Coopers and Lybrand. During the
hasty rescue by the Peruvians, the vast portfolio of assets the Andino
acquired overnight was financed mainly by loans of nearly $360 million
from BA Holding. Its resources were thus stretched to the limit. It had to
borrow from the Cisalpine. Seeing from the books of the Cisalpine that BA
Holding now owed it $150 million, Coopers and Lybrand began to worry.
They asked if they might send a questionnaire to the auditors of BA
Holding. These auditors, Fiduciaire Générale, had just become part of
Touche Ross. This could have meant that two great international firms
of accountants were comparing notes.

To avoid this, Calvi decided that BA Holding's debts to the Cisalpine
would have to be eliminated. As much business as possible would be concentrated in the Andino. Calvi knew that he would not have any trouble
with auditors in Lima. In the first place, Andino would not produce a
balance sheet for public consumption until the end of 1980. Even then, its
auditors were the local firm attached to the Horwath and Horwath group,
and these local men called on the services of their Nicaraguan colleague,
the man who had bought a house in Miami with Calvi's help, Cossio.

In November 1979 the original $60 million of back-to-back loans from
the Italian banks to the Cisalpine, via the Banco de la Nación, were rerouted
to the Andino. On top of that, another $90 million of loans from the Italian

banks were switched to Andino, via the Peruvian central bank. So direct advances to the Ambrosiano foreign associates were removed from the balance sheets of the three Italian banks.

This rerouting enabled the Andino to repay some of its advances from BA Holding, and therefore BA Holding was able to reduce its debts to the Cisalpine. But the debts of the Andino were still enormous, and BA Holding still owed nearly $40 million to the Cisalpine. Furthermore, the outflow of cash from United Trading continued. Calvi had not only to pay the $7.9 million to Anna Bonomi, but a further $7 million to Ortolani and Gelli, for the last two instalments of the $12.5 million "commission" – almost certainly their reward for arranging the Pesenti and Bonomi peace treaties. Pesenti took his place on the board of La Centrale on 30 October, and with him came another industrialist, Luigi Lucchini (later invited by the magistrates to explain accounts they had found the family held at the Cisalpine; he said they had done nothing wrong). Lucchini was asked by the press whether he was going to buy more Ambrosiano shares. He would say only that he did not exclude a closer collaboration between Brescia (where the Lucchini family had a steelworks) and Milan. All this support by industrialists helped Calvi to keep up the price of Ambrosiano shares.

To meet his cash commitments, Calvi got Andino to lend United Trading a further $27.3 million, via Nordeurop, in November and December 1979. He had been relying on a new five-year syndicated loan of 50 million Swiss francs, organised by the Gottardo for BA Holding, and this was duly paid over in December. Calvi also managed to tap, though only for the time being, a huge new pool of money.

Ultrafin, the Ambrosiano's Swiss investment banking offshoot in Zürich, had also organised a syndicated loan, not for the Ambrosiano but for the Nigerian state of Imo, to finance a glassworks. The loan was guaranteed by the Italian Government, since Italian firms were to export the plant. The money, $150 million, was to be deposited by SACE, the official export credit guarantee organisation, with a "leading" bank until the exporters were paid. And the exporters would be paid gradually, over many months. In December 1979 Ultrafin chose, as its "leading" bank, the Andino. Only a month later, Firrao became director general of SACE.

The sudden appearance of $150 million was a godsend to Calvi. It enabled the Andino to bring down its debts to BA Holding to less than $200 million, and BA Holding repaid all but a nominal sum of its debts to the Cisalpine. In fact, there was enough left over for Andino and BA Holding to lend over $50 million *to* the Cisalpine. This enabled the Cisalpine to window-dress its balance sheet over the year-end. It would, otherwise, have shown an embarrassingly large fall by comparison with the previous year. By hijacking the Nigerian loan, Calvi had solved most of his 1979 balance-sheet problems. But not all. The auditors were worrying again.

That summer the Pope had announced that there would be an extraordinary meeting of cardinals. On Monday 5 November 1979 all 123 cardinals of the Church gathered in the Vatican. The previous day the *Sunday Telegraph*'s Rome correspondent, Leslie Childe, wrote: "I understand that priority has been given to the Vatican finances, now believed to be heavily in the red." This was spotted by Graham Garner of Coopers and Lybrand. He had already noticed an article by Childe the previous August, which mentioned the Vatican's "unwise investments" and "soaring pensions bill". Though the August article did not mention the IOR, it first raised in Garner's mind fresh doubts. Did he really know enough about the IOR's financial position to conclude that it was good for its debts to the Cisalpine?

While the conclave of cardinals continued, Garner's doubts were strengthened by a further article by United Press International in the *Nassau Guardian*. It reported that Cardinal Vagnozzi had outlined the Vatican's precarious economic situation. Finally, an article in the *Economist* at the end of the week reported that the Vatican's annual deficit was estimated to be running at £6 million to £9 million a year.

This estimate was on the low side. In the Pope's closing address to the cardinals he said that the deficit would reach 17 billion lire that year – nearly $21 million, or more than £9 million at the existing exchange rate. Income from the Vatican's property, investments and other sources of revenue were "quite insufficient to cover the costs of the central government of the Church, and for administering the universal charity of the Pope". The deficit would be even larger in 1980. This year it had been covered only by St Peter's Pence, the annual voluntary contribution of the faithful.

Garner was now worried, not only by the question of the IOR's ability to meet its commitments, but by the possible impact of the Vatican's financial crisis on the IOR. He was still mystified by the IOR's dual role as depositor with and borrower from the Cisalpine. His promised meeting with Marcinkus had not taken place.

Later in November, Giacomo Botta of the Ambrosiano's foreign department was in Nassau. Garner now renewed his request to see Marcinkus. In a report written by Botta, among Calvi's papers, the first item reads: "We will attempt to arrange an interview for Mr Graham Garner in Rome."

With the 1979 audit coming up, there was no time for delay. A board meeting of the Cisalpine was due on 4 December 1979 in Zürich. By coincidence Garner was due there that day, on the business of ENI's bank Tradinvest, which he also audited. A number of Ambrosiano executives were in Zürich at the same time, and a large lunch was arranged for them all. Siegenthaler invited Garner to join them, so that he could meet Marcinkus.

They had only a brief exchange; Marcinkus told Garner that he would see him at nine the following morning in the Vatican. After lunch Garner went off to find himself a flight to Rome, while the directors of the Cisalpine held their meeting, which was, as usual, banal and unrevealing. They agreed to increase the general provision against losses on bad loans. They also agreed that the bank's name be changed to Banco Ambrosiano Overseas Ltd the following year. The IOR issue was not raised. Marcinkus must have caught a late flight to Rome the same evening.

Garner went to the IOR's office the next day, 5 December 1979. Up to now Marcinkus had conveyed a misleading impression to his fellow-directors of the Cisalpine by simply keeping his mouth shut about the arrangements between himself and Calvi. He might perhaps have pleaded that he thought they all knew. But now he was face to face with Garner, and he knew that Garner did not know.

Garner was hoping to gain a better understanding of the IOR and its business relationship with the Cisalpine, and now also to find out what effect the Vatican's deficit might have on it. He had previously accepted that the IOR could repay its huge debts to the Cisalpine, but further information to support this would be welcome. That they might not be the IOR's debts at all had never occurred to him.

Marcinkus greeted Garner in his office and then took him into another room to meet two other IOR officials, almost certainly Mennini and de Strobel. They did not speak English well and Garner gained no significant information from them. He returned to talk to Marcinkus alone.

Marcinkus told him that the IOR was very large. It was not in business to make profits. Marcinkus said that he wished to keep its balance sheet secret because, if its financial position were known, this would lead to pressure on him to finance the Vatican's losses, for which, as it was, the IOR had no responsibility. He wanted to create funds for pensions. The only people at present aware of the IOR's financial position were the Pope and five cardinals.

By the five cardinals, he presumably meant those on the supervisory commission of the IOR. There were three long-serving members, two Italians and a Dutchman. Cardinal Agostino Casaroli, who had succeeded

Jean Villot as Vatican Secretary of State early in 1979, had also taken his place on the IOR commission. The fifth member was also new: Cardinal Bernadin Gantin of Benin, an African, believed to be a strong supporter of John Paul I's attitude to the Vatican's wealth.

Marcinkus then made some general remarks about the IOR's assets and liabilities. The liabilities consisted of deposits from various branches of the Catholic Church; the assets consisted of cash with banks and investments for religious works. The IOR often made payments for these investments all over the world, always provided they were classified as religious works, as it was often easier for it to do this than for local Church bodies.

Garner asked why the IOR did not use its credit balances with the Cisalpine to reduce its borrowings. Marcinkus said that the sums, which were not particularly significant in relation to the IOR's total assets and liabilities, were not netted because the transactions related to separate and distinct matters which the IOR did not want to mix, the destination of all funds being specific.

Garner left the meeting having been given no hint that the debts were not the IOR's, and having been told nothing of the back-to-back arrangements. Far from having been informed that the money was being sent to an obscure Panamanian company, Garner was given the impression that it had been used for investment in religious works.

More than six years after this interview, Coopers and Lybrand, when sued for negligence by the liquidators of the Cisalpine, sued Marcinkus and the IOR, claiming damages "by reason of misrepresentations made fraudulently or otherwise wrongfully to the Plaintiffs as or in the course of the Plaintiffs acting as auditors of Banco Ambrosiano Overseas Limited". Not until the autumn of 1990 did the IOR file a defence. It said that it did not admit Garner's version of the interview, but offered no other version. Garner wrote his account of the interview on 10 December 1979, from the notes he made on the plane going home; if Marcinkus made notes, then or since, the world has yet to see them.

Either Marcinkus was deliberately misleading Garner, or he thought that the IOR would be liable for any debts United Trading failed to meet. In that case they would have been the IOR's debts, the IOR being the ultimate guarantor. Did Marcinkus think this at the time? Was it only after the crash that he decided (perhaps on the advice of his lawyers) to repudiate the claims? This does not seem possible. Calvi's letter of 24 November 1976, setting out the terms of the *conto deposito* arrangement, did not specifically relieve the IOR of all responsibility for the debts. But this was effectively done in the all-important letter of 26 July 1977, requesting the IOR to hold the capital of United Trading. At least from the time he received that letter, Marcinkus must have thought the IOR was a non-liable intermediary.

Why did Marcinkus conceal the truth from Garner? If Marcinkus had told Garner of the arrangements between himself and Calvi, the auditors would have wanted to know all about United Trading. They would hardly have been impressed by Calvi's rough balance sheets, with the values of Ambrosiano shares multiplied by five. They would have qualified the accounts by saying that they could not express a view on the recoverability of the United Trading debts. This might have led to a run on the bank, bringing the whole operation to a halt.

But, by not blowing the whistle, Marcinkus was not necessarily acting in the best interests of the IOR. It had nearly $100 million at stake in the Cisalpine, in deposits and shares, which it stood to lose. So, in the short run, it might have been sensible for Marcinkus to cover for Calvi while he sought to retrieve this investment. But he left the money at risk. His action makes sense only if he believed, as apparently Calvi did, that the investments of United Trading would ultimately prove fantastically valuable, and that only nit-picking accountants would be so short-sighted as not to realise this.

But the IOR had no direct interest in the possible future profits of United Trading. Its only evident reward was its one-sixteenth of a percentage point on the back-to-back loans – hardly sufficient inducement to put that sort of money at risk. Was the one-sixteenth really the only reward? Correspondence has been found which suggests that, shortly before the meeting between Marcinkus and Garner, the IOR had asked for higher interest rates on its deposits at the Cisalpine. Siegenthaler refused this, but agreed instead to pay the IOR a rebate in advance of 1 per cent on the interest due on some of the back-to-back loans. The sum totalled more than $600,000, but this money never reached the IOR. It ended up in a bank account controlled by Siegenthaler himself. (So did a series of other large sums, many of them since repaid to the liquidators. Fraud charges were brought against Siegenthaler in Switzerland and he was convicted in 1991.) As the IOR's executives were always careful to collect any money due, it may be that the request to Siegenthaler was never really made.

Other payments, however, remain unexplained. A special account was set up at the IOR, 053 6 00645, to receive the dividends on the BA Holding shares the IOR held. Out of this account was paid the interest on the two back-to-back loans financing these shares, plus the IOR's one-thousandth six-month commission. There remained a surplus, and a statement of the account among Calvi's papers indicates that $500,000 was paid out of it on

053 6 00645 (Rif. BAH)

31.10.1979	saldo a CREDITO	FR.SV.+	729.709,74
29. 1.1980	bonifico $usa 500.000	FR.SV.-	810.315,==
29. 1 1980	saldo a DEBITO	FR.SV.-	80.605,26
24. 4.1980	commissione rinnovo BAH 1	" -	71.645,==
24. 4.1980	commissione rinnovo BAH 2	" -	22.720,==

24. 4.1980	saldo a DEBITO	FR.SV.-	174.970,26

29 January 1980. Only if the IOR were to open its books could the recipient be identified. (Reproduced above).

Payments not accounted for were also made out of the lira back-to-backs. It can be seen from Calvi's notebooks that some of these were huge amounts in round figures, from half a billion lire to 4 billion. The total seems to be about $20 million. Probably some of this money could have been traced if the IOR's accounts at the three Italian banks had been thoroughly analysed. This was not done because the Italian investigators did not fully understand the workings of the lira back-to-backs.

If Marcinkus had kept the truth from Garner, he had nevertheless failed to satisfy him completely. In his file note of 10 December 1979, Garner wrote: "We still do not have any specific information on IOR, although there are certain areas in which we now have more knowledge." He was pessimistic about the possibility of learning much more, but decided that he would get in touch again with the Coopers office in Rome. This time, besides asking once more whether the IOR was good for its commitments, he inquired if they could confirm that the Vatican's publicised losses did not relate to the IOR. They could not. But the Rome office added that, although the Vatican's financial situation was not considered to be as good as in the past, the IOR was a Vatican department which operated as a commercial bank under the Pope's ultimate control, and it was thus unlikely that he would allow it not to recognise valid debts.

That was the situation as the 1979 accounts were being prepared in early 1980. The figures worried the auditors. The amount of the loans had remained unchanged, though there had been a small rise in the dollar total as a result of the weakening of the dollar against the Swiss franc. But the net exposure to the IOR had increased by some $22 million, because the IOR had removed a 40 million Swiss franc deposit. Nobody knows why. It may have been part of a general reduction in its commitment to Calvi. With the repayment of the Zitropo and Manic loans, the IOR had reduced its backing of Calvi by $85 million during the year. And yet Calvi's papers show that at this time the IOR had exceptionally high credit balances with the Ambrosiano and the Cattolica, totalling more than 35 billion lire ($40 million).

Were the auditors, then, to renew their request for a note? They might have treated the increase in the net exposure as a "material alteration". Instead, they did two things. First, they got Calvi and Siegenthaler to give them a further written assurance about the IOR. "The directors are satisfied that the gross amount due from the IOR at 31 December 1979 of $228,771,000 is fully recoverable in the normal course of business and that the net exposure at that date, of $137,252,000 is reasonable, particularly when it is considered that the IOR is a Central Bank."

Second, they wrote a management letter to Calvi. "During this year's audit we met with certain officials of the IOR to ascertain what information we could about the financial position of this entity. Whilst we did obtain a considerable amount of general information about the activities of the IOR we were advised that it was not possible for us to be informed of the financial condition of this entity as this information was only available to a very limited number of individuals. It is our understanding that none of the directors of Cisalpine, other than Bishop Marcinkus, are aware of the current financial condition of this entity."

The letter then gave the figures of the gross and net exposure to the IOR. It concluded: "From the facts available to us, we believe that consideration should be given to limiting the Cisalpine's exposure to this one single entity, particularly in the light of the matters referred to in the first paragraph of this section."

Both these letters were dated 14 February, as were the accounts. The board meeting to approve the figures took place in Claridge's Hotel in London on 21 February 1980, and all the directors were there, including Marcinkus. Only a few days earlier, he had had a sad interview in the Vatican with Sindona's American lawyers. Sindona was at last on trial in the United States, for offences connected with the Franklin National crash almost six years earlier. The Cardinals from APSA, Caprio and Guerri, still grateful to Sindona for buying their embarrassing investments, had promised to go to the American Embassy and give video-taped testimony to Sindona's good character.

It was Cardinal Casaroli who, at the last minute, forbade these two character witnesses to make their movie. But it was Marcinkus who had to break the news to Sindona's American lawyers.

At this time Sindona had not been formally charged with the murder of Ambrosoli. But the press was already full of the evidence which the magistrates were amassing. Andreotti had not given up all hope of getting Sindona's debts paid in Italy; he had a dozen interviews with Sindona's Italian lawyer Guzzi, two of them after the murder of Ambrosoli. It was Guzzi who broke off these talks, by announcing that he would no longer act for Sindona. But at least Andreotti was trying to keep his involvement a secret. (It came out later, in the report of the parliamentary commission on Sindona.) Cardinals Caprio and Guerri had almost brought the Vatican into public association with a fraud.

Now Marcinkus, by his silence, involved the Vatican in fraud more directly than Sindona had ever done. At that board meeting in Claridge's, the new assurance to Coopers was presented to the board and signed by Calvi. Marcinkus raised no objection, either to the clear implication that the IOR was the borrower, or to the statement that the loans had been made and were recoverable in the normal course of business. He knew that the recoverability of the money depended on United Trading's ability to pay. If, as the Vatican afterwards claimed, he knew nothing of United Trading's activities, how could he allow the assurance to be made?

The board went on to discuss a new group structure for the Ambrosiano's overseas banks. Marcinkus carefully recommended that the auditors should be consulted before anything was done.

To judge from the minutes, the management letter was not presented to the board. Calvi may have deliberately kept it from his fellow directors. But he could not ignore the recommendation in it – that the Cisalpine should reduce its exposure to the IOR. Calvi took that recommendation seriously. He carried it out in a manner all his own.

TWENTY-FIVE

Sistemazione Rizzoli

Calvi first reduced what the IOR seemed to owe the Cisalpine by increasing what it seemed to owe the Andino. On 11 March 1980 he transferred to the Andino the $12 million loan the Cisalpine had made five years before to finance the last capital increase of Zitropo. As the IOR remained the intermediary, its apparent debt to the Andino now rose to $135.5 million.

Next, on 25 April 1980, the Andino made loans to United Trading via Nordeurop, totalling $153 million. Of this, $126 million was first directed to Belrosa, which used it to buy most of United Trading's holding of La Centrale shares at ten times the market price – another of Calvi's fantasy deals to deceive himself that there was no deficit. United Trading used the money to repay seven back-to-back loans from the Cisalpine, totalling $121.6 million, and most of the remainder was needed to pay outstanding interest.

As a result of these two operations, there remained only four apparent loans to the IOR in the Cisalpine's books: a dollar one for $70 million, two Swiss franc loans for 10 million and 6 million and the 22,720,000 Swiss franc one made to finance the BA Holding share issue. These came to about $92 million, and were nicely balanced by the IOR's deposits with the Cisalpine, of $91 million – of which $70 million was the IOR's own money and $21 million came, dodging Swiss banking regulations, from the Gottardo.

The whole operation still further inflated the United Trading deficit, but only Calvi knew that. The IOR was losing income of $76,000 a year because of the one-sixteenth per cent it was no longer earning, but presumably that was worth while if it kept inquisitive auditors away. Coopers and Lybrand made no further efforts to assess the IOR's creditworthiness, although they continued to require a letter of assurance from the Cisalpine directors.

There was, however, an odd incident in May. Siegenthaler approached Garner and told him that Calvi wanted one sentence deleted from the management letter: "It is our understanding that none of the directors of the Cisalpine, other than Bishop Marcinkus, are aware of the current financial condition of this entity." (That is, the IOR.) Since Coopers' recommendation had now been met, why should Calvi have wanted this? The most likely explanation is that Marcinkus had seen the letter, and did not like to have the entire responsibility pinned on him. Garner agreed to drop the offending sentence, as long as the words: "in the Vatican" were added to the previous one. Thus, it stated that the financial condition of the IOR was "only available to a very limited number of individuals in the Vatican".

For Calvi, the removal of one problem created others. BA Holding once again appeared on the Cisalpine's books as a borrower of some $70 million. Calvi knew the auditors were not going to like that. He had to raise more money from outside sources.

So far in 1980 Calvi had raised nearly $100 million. Of this, $30 million had been channelled out of the Italian banks through the Banco de la Nación. The Gottardo had raised another syndicated loan of 70 million Swiss francs (about $42.5 million). A small group of German-owned banks in Luxembourg had come up with $25 million. Calvi was looking further afield, and had began to negotiate another loan with a syndicate led by the French subsidiary of the Midland Bank.

All the money he raised that spring was immediately used up. Besides keeping up with the interest payments of United Trading, he was finding his friends expensive.

As part of his new friendship with Pesenti, he had to buy an option on a block of 392,000 shares, or 9.8 per cent, in Pesenti's holding company, Italmobiliare. This cost $28 million, financed by a loan from the Cisalpine, and the shares were hidden away in a Panamanian company, Intermarket.

An even heavier burden was the Rome-based construction group, Genghini. By the end of 1979 its head, Mario Genghini, had debts of more than 300 billion lire. The Ambrosiano was much the largest creditor, but Genghini also owed large sums to the Banca Nazionale del Lavoro and the Banco di Roma.

The phrase: "Throwing good money after bad" might have been made for Calvi. In February and March 1980 he made two loans to Genghini outside Italy, one for $17.3 million and another for $25 million. The first, intended for construction work in the Middle East, disappeared into banks there. The second was channelled through an Austrian bank back into Italy, where it was used to pay some of Genghini's huge lira debts to the Ambrosiano. Calvi used the dormant Banco Comercial for these two loans, perhaps because Genghini had connections with Nicaragua. The loans were part of last-ditch negotiations to keep the group alive. They failed, and in June it was declared bankrupt. Genghini fled from Italy, pursued by charges of fraud. Calvi, to hide the fact that the money was lost, transferred the loans to Erin – not a poetic name for Ireland, but one of the companies in his secret network.

Another loan that Calvi made in early 1980 was kept secret at the time. But over a year later, on 2 July 1981, when Calvi was on trial for currency offences and had been in prison for 42 days, Gaetano Pecorella, a lawyer then representing Tassan Din, told the Milan magistrates that Calvi had something to say to them. At once three magistrates went to Lodi prison. They arrived just before 10 pm and interrogated Calvi until three the next morning.

Calvi told them that the Socialist Party had been borrowing heavily from the Ambrosiano. The debt totalled, he thought, about 15 billion lire. Ortolani had come to him at about the end of 1979, to say, on behalf of that party, that it was having difficulty in repaying. The Socialist Party would like its debts to the Ambrosiano not to appear so high. Ortolani had, therefore, proposed that an overseas subsidiary of the Ambrosiano should lend $21 million to Ortolani's bank, Bafisud. Part of that would be used to reduce the socialists' debt to the Ambrosiano in Italy, and Calvi said that this debt had in fact been reduced after the loan was made. Calvi added that he believed this because of the attitude of some leading members of the Socialist Party to him. Only $6 million of the $21 million loan had been repaid, he said.

The story is mysterious. It is true that, early in 1980, the Socialist Party owed the Ambrosiano about 9 billion lire, much of it already overdue. But these loans were not repaid. On the contrary, the debt remained outstanding, with unpaid interest accumulating. Letters from the Ambrosiano's Rome office to party headquarters went unanswered for another two years, and by the time of the crash the Socialist Party owed nearly 14 billion lire.

If any of the money had been repaid, Calvi would not have had to take Ortolani's word for it. He could simply have asked his own staff.

It is possible that Calvi made up the allegation about the Socialist Party in the hope of securing his release from prison. If so, it did not work. He later withdrew the whole story. Or it is possible that Ortolani had found a new pretext for extracting money from Calvi. The Cisalpine did in fact lend $21 million in early 1980 to an Ortolani company – not Bafisud but Sudam. Of this loan, $6 million went to Voxson, the Ortolani family electronics company in Italy, which was in trouble and needed to repay debts to the Ambrosiano. This $6 million was, rather surprisingly, repaid at about the time that Calvi was telling his story in Lodi prison. (The repayment was almost certainly made out of even larger sums that had been paid to Ortolani in the meantime.) But the other $15 million was never repaid. In 1981 that loan was switched from the Cisalpine to the Banco Comercial – after Marcinkus had queried it at a board meeting.

Later Ortolani alleged that this $15 million made its way to Calvi, to help him pay for a 10 per cent stake in Bafisud and a resort development in Argentina. But, while Calvi did have a personal stake in Bafisud, his papers show that it had mostly been acquired in 1978 and 1979, and had a book value of only $640,000. No evidence has ever emerged that he bought a further interest, or the land in Argentina. It is much more likely that most of the money stuck to Ortolani and Gelli. It may have been their "commission" on the Genghini negotiations, which were taking place at the time.

Among the papers taken from Gelli when he was arrested in September 1982 in Geneva was a chart, or table, which became known as the *tabella* (reproduced opposite). It appears to show how he and Ortolani, and occasionally others, divided the huge sums paid to them by Calvi in 1980 and 1981. Many of the entries are cryptic. The Italian authorities had no chance to question Gelli about them while he was on the run from the supposedly secure Swiss prison where he had bribed a warder. He made a sensational reappearance in Italy in 1988. By that time he had forgotten – or claimed to have forgotten – what most of the figures were about.

But some of them can be reconciled with known payments. One entry reads: "Da Robe sistemazione Gengo 15,000." That seems to mean: "From Roberto Calvi 15 billion lire (or $15 million) for the Genghini settlement." The money is divided between "U" – Umberto Ortolani – "L" – Licio Gelli – and an unidentified "Marco". If this does refer to the Sudam $15 million, it is curious that Calvi treated it as a loan from the Cisalpine, in whose books it would be recorded. If he thought he was not going to get it back, it would have been paid out of United Trading, like the other "commissions". This adds to the evidence that he, Ortolani and Gelli did not always agree which payment was a loan and which a bribe.

The $15 million was extortionate, considering that Mario Genghini was conspicuously not "systematised" – except in the sense used as a threat by Italians in street brawls: "Io ti sistemerò!" (I'll sort you out.)

If the $15 million is added to all Calvi's other payments to Ortolani, Gelli and others since 1975 it brings the total to some $75 million. Calvi's new, international banker friends were now eagerly lending to him. But $25 million here and there could not keep pace with the greed of Gelli and Ortolani. Between the summer of 1980 and the spring of 1981 another $200 million was to be removed under one guise or another. One deal

COM. GALLO-FIORI-DALOJA
DI MARCO - 400

TEDESCHI 235 -
65 -
30 -
30 -
85

U	L
500	1.500

ACQUISTO VIAFINI 3000

	L
500	1.500

PREMIO UMBERTO 10.000

	L
5	500
0	4.500

2ª RATA NOMINE 15.000

	L
0	7.500

SECONDO

3.000 - RIAMISTIMENTO

DA ROBE - CIN 4.000

U	L	B.
2.000	2.000	Parte ria.prev.Da.

DA ROBE - OPERAZIONE 10% ITALINDOS.
20.000 -MILIMO -

U	L
10.000	10.000

DA ROBE : OPERAZ. ENI 1.500

U	L	P
750	750	
25	125	125
775	875	

DA ROBE : TRASFERIMENTO ESTERO 10%
BANCO VARESINO 9.500

U	L
4.750	4.750

DA ROBE : OPERAZIONE TORO-MAN 2.500

U	L
2.500	2.500

DA ROBE - SALVATORIA PRATICHE 300

U	L
150	150
150	

DA ROBE - SISTEMAZIONE RIZZO

I° FASE

F	U	L	ROB	TAS
150	8.000	8.000	4.000	7.000
	150	150	4.000	7.000
150	8.150	8.150		

II° FASE

| 5 | 30 | | | 30 |

BADIO - ROBE 400

U	L	BAD
100	100	200

ACCREDITI

DA ROBE - SISTEMAZ. UMBERTO 15.000

U	L	MARCO
2.000	2.000	3.500
2.000	2.000	
	2.000	
	1.500	
4.000	7.500	3.500

A UMBE 7.000 - A MARCO 5.000

DA CETO - CONTROLLO 81 - 150

U	L	ZAFFER
50	50	50

500 - ZAFFERANO

DA ROBE - OPERAZIONE 217.000 AZ.
ITALINDOS. SERV. ITALIA
5.000 + 4.000

U	L	ORA	SER.I
RIZZO	16,2%	TAS	2,5%

20/415
F.

ANTICIPI

15-12-80 - TEDESCHI
24-3-84 - BATTELLI
29-3-84 - ANT.OPER.Poliz.
4-5-84 - Emilio L.
5-5-84 - Angelo

dwarfed all others. Gelli's table calls it the *sistemazione Rizzo* – the Rizzoli deal.

By the beginning of 1980 Calvi had poured over $200 million into the Rizzoli group. In Italy Rizzoli had short-term debts with the banks of the Ambrosiano group totalling more than 80 billion lire (some $95 million). In addition, these banks were still secretly financing the 1977 capital increase through the back-to-back account 001 6 02559 RED at the IOR. With rolled-up interest, the amount due on that account had reached nearly 30 billion lire, or about $35 million. Abroad, the Cisalpine had lent Rizzoli $29 million. Another $40 million was owing to the Andino, from the Panamanian company Worldwide. This represented the debts of the bankrupt Rizzoli International, and the acquisition price of *TV Sorrisi e Canzoni*.

Yet newspapers and books, on the whole, make money in Italy. Though the group had been mismanaged since the death of old Angelo ten years before, and had lost about 25 billion lire in 1978, it was expected to break even in 1980 – except for the crippling interest cost of its debts. In early 1980 Gelli, Ortolani, Tassan Din and Calvi planned a great financial reconstruction.

They seem to have had three aims. The first was genuinely commercial. To replace the debt with equity capital would at once reduce interest costs and improve profitability. But where could investors be found to buy equities which would pay no dividends for years? There was only one candidate: Calvi.

The second aim was to wrest a majority shareholding away from the Rizzoli family. Although the dependence of the group on Ambrosiano funds gave Calvi and his friends effective control, they owned no shares. Since Andrea had been packed off to the casinos, and young Alberto bought out, Angelo owned all but 210,000 of the three million shares. He could not take possession of the 2.4 million held as security for the RED account, unless he could turn up at the Credito Commerciale in Milan with 35 billion lire before June 1981, and he had no hope of finding that out of his own resources. Of his 390,000 other shares, 306,000 were held in Italy, and 84,000 were at Rothschilds in Zürich. The remaining 210,000 shares were held in trust for Angelo's sisters, Annina and Isabella. (Isabella, Andrea's child by his second wife, was still a minor.)

The third aim of the P2 faction was to generate large sums of money for themselves. Their greed progressed as the plans did. An early draft scheme from March 1980 shows that at that stage total commissions were expected to reach only 11 billion lire, or about $13 million. By June 1980 the figure had risen to $30 million. Most people think of the excesses of capitalism in terms of the Guinness-Distillers affair, when "commissions" of $25 million were paid out. But by September 1980 the P2 group were planning to pay themselves ten times this – 224 billion lire, or more than $260 million.

The amount in fact fell short of that, principally because Calvi took only a small part of the share allotted to him. Again we find evidence that Calvi was not at one with his three partners over these gigantic commissions. After all, he was finding the money. There is a document headed "Schema Calvi" among Gelli's papers. Calvi's plan involved making a further $21 million loan to Rizzoli via Rothschilds in Zürich, while the recapitalisation would be carried out by means of Calvi's old favourite, the back-to-back. A major European bank would be found to act for the Ambrosiano in putting up new capital for Rizzoli. The *schema Calvi* makes no mention of commissions.

But the only part of Calvi's scheme to go ahead was the further $21 million loan, agreed in May 1980. What happened the following month seems to have deprived Calvi of whatever sense of proportion he had left. He became putty in the hands of Ortolani and Gelli.

On 12 June 1980 the *Guardia di Finanza*, which a year before had produced an inconclusive report about Calvi, filed a new one, by Captain D'Aloia. It was much tougher; although it questioned whether Calvi could be prosecuted for the Toro deal under the 1976 currency laws, it suggested that the deal was fraudulent. Captain D'Aloia had tracked down the sale to La Centrale, at inflated prices, of Toro insurance company shares which Calvi already possessed.

This was plain robbery of La Centrale shareholders. This was an offence the Swiss police should help to unearth. On 25 June Mucci wrote to the Swiss authorities pointing out that this was a fraud investigation, and asking for their help. He then brought a charge of serious fraud against Calvi and on 3 July took away his passport.

The news was reported in the Italian press in early July 1980, but it scarcely seems to have spread outside Italy. The $40 million syndicated loan from fifteen international banks, led by the Midland Bank in Paris, duly reached BA Holding that month. But Calvi needed more, and bigger loans. He had at all costs to keep up his prestige with international bankers. At the end of September he was due to make his annual visit to the International Monetary Fund meeting, to be held that year in Washington. If he was not there, other bankers would notice, and make inquiries.

In a panic over his passport, Calvi seems to have let his life be dominated by the need to get it back. He was, as we shall see, successful at the last minute, in very strange circumstances.

Meanwhile Ortolani, Gelli and Tassan Din continued to "systematise" Angelo Rizzoli. They had kept him on a tight string; now they could tighten it, because he wanted to get married. In early July he signed a preliminary agreement. He did not agree to hand over formal control of Rizzoli, but it was the first step down the path. The agreement envisaged the introduction of unnamed new shareholders. It outlined proposals for recapitalising the company, either by the middle of September or by the end of the year. The price of Angelo's acceptance was to be $5 million.

Naturally it was Calvi who paid, or rather United Trading. The $5 million went into an account at the Union Bank of Switzerland, in the name of a company called Badacan, controlled by Tassan Din on 8 August – six days after the bombing at the Bologna railway station. Only $3 million reached Angelo. Tassan Din kept $1 million for himself and paid $1 million to an Ortolani account. Angelo afterwards said he had been told he could not have the full $5 million, because the money was needed to pay some Rizzoli debts in South America. At the time he took the $3 million without complaining, and left Italy for a long honeymoon.

The same day – 28 July – as Calvi ordered the payment to Badacan he also sent $2 million to the Swiss bank account of a friend of Gelli's: what this was for remains a mystery. United Trading got the $7 million in the usual way, in a loan from Andino via Nordeurop. Calvi's overseas banks were not badly off, because of the arrival of the $40 million loan led by Midland. But he now faced another difficulty. One rule the Luxembourg authorities enforce strictly is that a holding company's loans must not exceed a certain ratio of its capital. So BA Holding could not lend any more money direct to Andino. Instead, the money was used to repay BA Holding debts to the Cisalpine, which could then increase its loans to Andino. But that was going to mean more trouble with Coopers and Lybrand. So Calvi began persuading banks to lend directly to Andino. That was trickier. If they had asked to see a balance sheet, they would have realised that Andino's loans to Nordeurop now totalled more than $250 million. And yet Calvi managed to persuade the syndicate of Luxembourg-based German-owned banks, which had lent BA Holding $25 million in the spring, to make a loan in August, another $25 million, directly to Andino.

Much of this money went straight into accounts controlled by Ortolani. In August and early September 1980 the P2 bosses began to take advantage of Calvi's new vulnerability. Not only did they vastly increase the "commissions" promised when the Rizzoli deal was completed, but they began to demand huge sums in advance. Their pretext was probably that they needed to pay bribes to get Calvi's passport restored. On 22 August United Trading paid out $10 million, on 15 September $15.65 million, to three new Swiss bank accounts opened by Ortolani in Old Testament names: Noè 2 at the Trade Development Bank in Geneva, Elia 7 and Sem 2 at the Union Bank. What made Ortolani think of himself as Noah, Elijah and Shem?

The details of the Rizzoli deal were left to Gelli and Tassan Din. They worked them out together at Arezzo in early September 1980. Tassan Din told Angelo – now back from his honeymoon – to meet Gelli at the Excelsior Hotel in Rome a few days later. According to Angelo, the meeting lasted only fifteen or twenty minutes. Gelli had a sheaf of papers with him. He read aloud to Angelo the parts that concerned him. Angelo initialled each page, but said later that he had not been able to read the contents carefully.

The documents Angelo had signed came to be called the *pattone*, or great pact. It was the plan for a coup which was to enrich Ortolani, Gelli, Tassan Din – and Calvi – on a scale that made their previous depredations look puny. According to an introductory paragraph dated 18 September 1980, it was the only copy. It was entrusted to Gelli for safe keeping, and was found in the raid on his house. (The covering paragraph is reproduced in Appendix F(i).)

This was no ordinary business document, drafted by lawyers and meticulously typed. It consisted of eleven irregular and roughly typed pages, whose contents are often vague and cryptic. Many people have tried to unravel what it meant. But now, with the help of Calvi's papers, the main provisions can be established.

First, the capital of Rizzoli would be increased from 25.5 billion lire to 178.5 billion. Two new shares would be issued for each existing one, bringing the total up from 3 million to 9 million. Each new share was to cost 25,500 lire.

Before the issue, Angelo was to sell half the 2.4 million block of shares – the block which was to be redeemed from the Credito Commerciale. Who was to buy them the *pattone* did not say. Nor did it stipulate a price. It would have to be some 116 billion lire – enough for Angelo to pay the 35 billion lire to redeem the shares, pay off certain debts and subscribe to the new issue on his remaining 1.2 million shares.

Angelo was then to make over his remaining shares – the 306,000 in Italy and the 84,000 in Switzerland – to companies which would be specified by the "institution", as Ortolani, Gelli, Tassan Din and Calvi collectively referred to themselves. He was to do this for nothing. The Italian block, representing 10.2 per cent of the capital, would have a special significance, because it would represent effective control between the 40 per cent which would be left to Angelo and the purchaser of the other 40 per cent. Finally, Angelo was to be paid 10 billion lire to procure the sale of the remaining 210,000 shares held in Switzerland for his sisters, but only part of this money would be passed on to them.

We now come to the sums these people proposed to pay themselves. The unnamed buyer of Angelo's 1.2 million shares was to pay a *premio* of 50,000 lire on each of them, and also on each of the 2.4 million new shares for which the buyer would subscribe. (The relevant page of the *pattone* is reproduced in Appendix F(ii).) This would add up to 180 billion lire, or more than $210 million. The *premio* was not going to go back into the company. It was going to the four people setting up the deal.

The *pattone* did not say who got what, but a hand-written note by Tassan Din, found in Gelli's villa, shows that three participants were to get 35 billion lire each, while the fourth, called simply C, was to have 75 billion lire. Clearly the first three were Ortolani, Gelli and Tassan Din; the fourth was Calvi.

These figures are remarkable enough, but they do not show the full extent of what these four had decided to award themselves. Although it was not mentioned in the *pattone* – probably to keep it secret from Angelo – they intended to pay themselves a *premio* on the 294,000 shares to be acquired from the Rizzolis in Switzerland, and on the new shares this would enable them to subscribe for. This would make a further 44.1 billion lire, or nearly $52 million. So the total would be 224.1 billion lire, or nearly $264 million.

The size of the *premio* seems to have been related to a theoretical value that had been placed on each Rizzoli share of 100,000 lire, making the company "worth" 300 billion lire, or over $350 million.

What were the shares in fact worth? The Rizzoli director Gennaro Zanfagna, who did not know what was going on, wrote a worried letter to Calvi on 26 September 1980, eight days after the signing of the *pattone*. He told Calvi that the management committee of Rizzoli had considered it unwise formally to enter in the minutes of their meeting what had been noted informally – that the company was in a state of bankruptcy. Zanfagna wrote later that the shares, at this point, "had no economic value".

So no rational buyer of the company would have contemplated paying 25,500 lire for each new share, and no buyer would have paid a 75 per cent commission to anyone for arranging such a sale. Nor, indeed, could any of the legal, respectable companies in the Ambrosiano group. The only possible source of such sums was Calvi's secret network, and the conspirators knew this. The *pattone* was a plan to steal huge sums through this network, a plan that could work only because of the Vatican's role in keeping the network secret.

Calvi's own role in this giant theft is, once again, enigmatic. According to Angelo, the idea that Calvi should be given a share of the *premio* was Gelli's and Tassan Din's, not his own. Moreover, Calvi never took his 75 billion lire, though the others took amounts even larger than they had first envisaged.

Calvi may not even have been informed, at first, of the plan to pay the huge *premio*. Among Gelli's papers there was a draft version of the *pattone*, with a covering note saying that it was a copy prepared for Calvi. The date is 15 September, three days before Angelo was summoned to the Excelsior Hotel. The draft is similar to the final version but it has three pages at the end marked: "Confidential", including one outlining the *premio*. A copy of this draft is among Calvi's papers in the Bahamas, and the page referring to the *premio* is missing.

So it is possible that Gelli, Ortolani and Tassan Din had not yet broken it to Calvi that they were expecting a quarter of a billion dollars. According to Angelo, when he signed the *pattone* in Rome Calvi's signature was not on it.

But Calvi's signature was on all the pages of the *pattone* when it was found six months later. So at some point Ortolani and Gelli must have induced Calvi to agree to these outrageous payments – even if he decided that he would not take the 75 billion lire he had been allotted.

I put this to Gelli. Flatly contradicting Angelo Rizzoli's account, he insisted that they had all signed the *pattone* together. He went on to say that they had all been given ten days to make up their minds.

Calvi had already taken what, by the standards of normal frauds, was a large sum. On 12 September $3.7 million was paid into his account at the Roywest in Nassau. The money had come, via New York, from the Ortolani-controlled account Elia 7 at the Union Bank in Geneva, which had got the money from United Trading in the first place. It was much the largest sum Calvi received from Ortolani, and again it has to be noted that he did not steal it directly for himself. The Gelli *tabella* on page 285, with 4,000 entered under "ROB", makes it reasonably clear that the payment was connected with the Rizzoli deal. It may have been an advance on the commission the P2 men wanted Calvi to take. But it was all – barring, possibly, another $200,000 or $300,000 – that Calvi took.

The *pattone* contained a confused clause which seemed to say that a sum of 18 billion lire, or its equivalent, had been agreed as consideration for its completion before the end of the year. This may correspond to the $5 million paid in July (of which Angelo got $3 million) plus the $15.65 million paid out to Ortolani accounts on 15 September. Ortolani appears to have paid about two-thirds of this to Gelli.

The *pattone* envisaged that the deal might not be carried out by the end of the year, because of new laws on publishing companies. These laws forbade banks to own newspapers. (They were forbidden in general, by the Banking Law of 1936, to own any industrial enterprise, but it was now made clear that this included newspapers.) So there was no possibility of the Ambrosiano openly acquiring Rizzoli. A much greater difficulty was that the beneficial owners of publishing companies had to be disclosed. So it was not possible to use a company from the secret network to own the shares. At about the end of November it was decided to postpone the Rizzoli plan.

On 18 December, though, the participants reaffirmed the *pattone*, with a new deadline of 31 March 1981. A note was added to the agreement, saying that the money "already paid" was intended to ensure that the obligations of the agreement would be kept. On 1 December United Trading had paid out a further $15 million to Ortolani-controlled accounts. One called Antonino 13 at the Trade Development Bank got $10 million, half of which Ortolani passed on to Gelli. Yet another new account at the Union Bank, this time called Crizia 3, got $5 million, split in two and passed on to Tassan Din and Angelo.

Since the end of August 1980, United Trading had paid out a total of $40.65 million to Ortolani accounts in Switzerland. The extraordinary thing is that Calvi was expecting Ortolani either to repay this money or, at least, to keep it available to the secret network.

That Christmas Calvi went to his house in the Bahamas, having got his passport back. It was his last visit; his passport was taken away again the following spring. So there are no documents in his safe later than December 1980. This was when he added the drafts of the *pattone* to the vast pile of Rizzoli documents already there. He also made out a United Trading balance sheet, dated 17 December 1980 (reproduced opposite). In it are the seven payments to Elia 7, Noè 2, Sem 2, Antonino 13 and Crizia 3, with their dates, and the $40.65 total has been added to United Trading's assets.

And still there, as an asset, was the 8 million Swiss francs paid to Ortolani's Ecfsa in 1979. There is no clue how, or when, Calvi expected to recover this money. None of it was ever repaid. None of it was deducted, even, from the full *premio*. On the contrary, United Trading paid a further

17/12/80

300 BAO x 2200	0,6
36.000 LC x 22050	0,8
21.000 LC x 22050	0,5
5.500.000 Supr	5,8

Ast./ 1.231.946 x 41.400=   (53,7)

M./   1.892.777 $\begin{cases} 281.667 \times 41.400 & = \\ 1.611.110 \times 41.400 & = \end{cases}$ 12,3   (70,2)

      43.500 x 610   14,5

Er./   4.500.000   x   10.710 =   (50,7)

Bell./ 1.020.084(Zwill) x 22.050   =   (23,7)

      17.900 x 610   =   (6)

Z/ 172.228.778 x 99,50   # 18   5,2

AB   18/11/75   5.518.670   ==

Ecfsa 30/4/79 3% 8 frs   4,4

22/8/80   5   U/El   7
        5   Tr/N   2

15/9/80   6   Tr/N   2
        6   U/ S   2   25,65
       3,65 U/E 7

1/12/80 10 Tr/   13
       5   U/Kr   3   15
                          ————

                          289,05

      53.037 BAH 1210/   =   35,2   35,2
           - 71.245
           (22.720   V.pass.°)   ————
                          324,25
                          ============

Frs/Drs 1,824
Drs/Lit 950

Tot. cost. a pav BAA ⬭ = 204,3

$13.45 million to Ortolani accounts in early 1981, over and above the *premio*.

Clara Calvi said after her husband's death that he had been the most blackmailed man in Italy. Does blackmail account for the size of the sums extorted from Calvi? When he entered these payments as loans, was he concealing from himself the humiliating truth that he had yielded to black-mail, and that there was going to be no end to it? Or did he expect some of the money, at least, to be repaid?

TWENTY-SIX

A Restaurant-owner from Florence

Even Sindona got into the act again. In March 1980 he was found guilty
in the United States of various offences in connection with the collapse of
the Franklin National Bank. The hardest point against him was that he
had lied to the Securities and Exchange Commission. The sentence was
twenty-five years.

Sindona was furious with his lawyers, for not letting him testify in court.
He wanted new lawyers for his appeal. He wanted more money.

When the briefcase that Calvi took on his last journey to London came
to the surface in 1986, there was in it a letter from Luigi Cavallo, the
provocatore who had organised Sindona's blackmail campaign against Calvi
in 1977. The letter was dated 9 July 1980 – the time when Calvi, desperate
to get his passport back, seemed to offer a soft target to extortionists. Cavallo
wrote that Walter Navarra, who had also taken part in the 1977 blackmail
campaign, was trying to "resell" Sindona to Calvi. Cavallo has since alleged
that Calvi started paying Navarra. It has been discovered that, in 1980 and
1981, United Trading paid him a total of $860,000 through a Swiss bank
account. At Sindona's Milan trial, in the autumn of 1985, documents in
evidence showed the payment of some of this money. When I saw Navarra
in 1986, I showed him one of these documents. He reacted as if it meant
nothing to him. But Calvi kept in Nassau a tape recording of a phone call
from Navarra, demanding money. Navarra was acquitted, however, in the
Sindona trial, and the magistrates investigating the Ambrosiano crash did
not charge him.

Sindona's renewed extortions were a trifle compared with what the P2
bosses continued to demand. Gelli's *tabella* (see page 285) suggests that, in
addition to the sums that Calvi paid out for the Rizzoli *premio*, he had to
pay Ortolani, Gelli and occasionally others more than $95 million. About
$25 million of this may have had something to do with Rizzoli. It has
not been possible to identify every item. But some of the entries refer to
transactions known to have taken place in 1980.

One entry reads: "Da Robe: trasferimento estero 10% Banco Varesino

9,500." This is divided equally between U and L. (Umberto Ortolani and Licio Gelli.) A block of Credito Varesino shares had been sold to Ortolani's bank in Uruguay, Bafisud, in 1978. In the summer of 1980 Calvi bought the shares back and placed them with his secret company, Erin. The entry seems to refer to a "fee" for this operation, though it is hard to see what Ortolani and Gelli could have done to justify a payment of 9.5 billion lire, or $9.5 million. (At the end of 1980 the lira had depreciated, and was almost exactly 1,000 to the dollar, which was bad news for the currency but good news for those without a pocket calculator.)

Two other entries suggest that Ortolani and Gelli were to share 5 billion lire for "operazione Toro-Ras" and 20 billion lire for "operazione 10% Italimmob". The latter sum is marked: "Minimo" – at least. These appear to be the deals with Pesenti, already described. The 392,000 shares that Calvi acquired in Italmobiliare early in 1980 proved useful. In the autumn he switched them between companies in the secret network in such a way as to create an artificial capital gain of $17.5 million. This was paid as a "dividend" to BA Holding, to rig its profits, which were then declared to be $24 million. So BA Holding could go on raising money from its new friends, the international bankers.

The *tabella* also shows that Gelli and Ortolani were to get "2,000" each for something to do with CIM. This was the big store which had been the tenant of the Palazzo di Vetro in Rome. CIM had gone into liquidation, so how could it form an excuse for any commission payments? Gelli explained to the magistrates that he was supposed to mediate in the sale of the company, but that the deal had been abandoned. This would hardly have been surprising as CIM had little left but debts. Gelli also said that "2,000" meant only 200 million lire. But this would have been inconsistent with other items in the *tabella*, which have been positively identified. It must have meant 2 billion lire, or $2 million.

But, if the CIM sale fell through, what could have prompted the payment? An important deal which took place in late 1980 might have led to a claim for a commission by Gelli and Ortolani; the owner of the Palazzo di Vetro, the company XX Settembre, was bought by the Toro insurance company, part of the Ambrosiano group. Toro paid 80 billion lire, which made its way into the lira back-to-back pool, and the IOR used 60 billion to repay the Ambrosiano group banks. Shortly before the deal the lira back-to-backs had, with rolled-up interest, reached a peak of more than 180 billion lire.

It is improbable that the P2 bosses did much to earn their 4 billion lire. Gelli later admitted that they had no influence with the IOR. And yet they took another $1.5 million each when the IOR sold the Rome-based construction company, Vianini, to a company in Calvi's secret network.

Vianini was an international company, with a turnover of about $50 million. The IOR was known to control it; the IOR accountant de Strobel was its deputy chairman. Only 35 per cent of the capital (3 million shares) was openly held by the IOR, but it seems to have controlled at least another 3 million shares through nominees. On the Rome stock exchange the shares were quoted at about 6,250 lire each.

Calvi agreed to pay much more than this. On 1 December 1980 de Strobel and the IOR secretary Donato de Bonis signed a contract to sell six million shares at $10 each, a total of $60 million. But only $20 million would be paid to the IOR at once; a further $20 million had to be paid one year later, and the final $20 million by the end of 1982. These deferred sums would carry interest, so that the IOR would get about another $10 million. All the 6 million Vianini shares would remain with the IOR until the final instalment had been paid.

The contract the two IOR officials signed was with a Panamanian company called Laramie. This proved embarrassing to the IOR later; far from knowing nothing of Calvi's secret network, it had done a substantial deal with one of its constituent parts. Calvi may have told Marcinkus that Laramie was acting for the Cisalpine (which had changed its name to Banco Ambrosiano Overseas). A memorandum written by Siegenthaler and signed by Calvi says clearly that "Banco Ambrosiano Overseas Limited has entered into an agreement with IOR" to buy the Vianini shares.

And yet there was no mention of the impending deal at a board meeting of the Cisalpine held in Zürich on 14 October 1980 and attended by Marcinkus. Such a large acquisition would have required board approval, which is, perhaps, why the Cisalpine did not make it. To pay the IOR its initial $20 million, Laramie borrowed the money from the Cisalpine (I shall go on using the old name for the sake of clarity) but the loan was immediately transferred to the Banco Comercial of Nicaragua. Throughout 1980 Calvi was using this bank more and more, in order to relieve the pressure on the Andino.

Why the Vianini deal was made we shall inquire later. But there is no reason to think that Ortolani and Gelli did anything useful in it, let alone anything that would justify commissions totalling $3 million. It looks as if most of the sums listed in the *tabella* represented outright blackmail and bribery.

Calvi may well have been aware that much of the money he paid to Ortolani and Gelli was used for such purposes and had to be "written off".

But the treatment of the $40.65 million as an asset in the United Trading balance sheet suggests that he may have agreed to the outrageous Rizzoli *premio* because he expected that the money would either be repaid or kept available for future use by United Trading. No doubt Ortolani and Gelli took a different view; hence the list of "commissions" on the *tabella*. They clearly thought the money was theirs.

Here we have to look at the circumstances in which Calvi got his passport back. When the Milan magistrates raided Gelli's office and home on 17 March 1981, the great mass of papers they seized had to be carefully studied before they became intelligible. But a few documents were clear at once. There was a bank advice from the Union Bank of Switzerland's Geneva branch, dated 14 October 1980. It showed that $800,000 had been debited to account 596 757 K J 60 T. In the box for "details of payment" had been typed two names: Marco Ceruti and Ugo Zilletti.

The name of Ceruti meant nothing at first, but Zilletti was famous. He was vice-president of the Consiglio Superiore della Magistratura, the supreme body which regulates the activities of Italy's magistrates. Its president was Sandro Pertini, President of the Republic.

The Milan magistrates also knew that Zilletti had taken a personal interest, the previous summer and autumn, in Calvi's passport. He had been in touch with the senior Milan public prosecutor, Carlo Marini, about it. He had been so insistent with the prosecutor handling the Calvi case, Mauro Gresti, that Gresti had flown to Rome to talk to him about it on 25 September 1980. Zilletti had expressed great concern that Calvi could not travel. (It was later to emerge that he had also expressed the same concern to governor Ciampi of the Bank of Italy at a meeting on 23 September. At the Ambrosiano trial in 1991 Ciampi and Zilletti clashed over the importance of this episode at the meeting.) Gresti later testified that he nevertheless returned to Milan that evening not intending to give Calvi back his passport. But when he arrived he found Calvi hanging round his office, pleading for it. Gresti and the examining magistrate Luca Mucci then, apparently, gave in.

The appearance of the bank advice was therefore acutely embarrassing. Gresti and Mucci were taken off the Calvi case, which was handed to Gerardo d'Ambrosio and Ovilio Urbisci (the latter a veteran of the Sindona case).

The affair of the passport was turned over to the magistrates of Brescia, since those of Milan were too much involved in it. News that Zilletti was under investigation leaked out in mid-April 1981 in *L'Espresso*. He immediately consulted President Pertini about his position. Pertini apparently urged him to stay at his post, but he decided to resign, while maintaining his innocence.

The first step of the Brescia magistrates was to ask for the help of the Swiss authorities. Bribery, like fraud, is an offence which the Swiss take seriously – in theory, at least. In practice, though, they have often proved dilatory. After the Ambrosiano crash they became more helpful. However, when the magistrates investigating the crash, Antonio Pizzi and Renato Brichetti, wrote their report in 1988, they had still not had all the information they requested. Still, Sindona said, shortly before his death in 1986, that people who wanted to keep their bank accounts secret had better not use Switzerland, and by that time it was good advice.

In 1981 the Brescia magistrates got a somewhat patchy response. They asked the Swiss for the owner of account 596 757 KJ 60 T, and who had received the $800,000. They asked for all details of the account, including the names of people, organisations or companies that had had dealings with the owner, and for information about any accounts held by Gelli, Zilletti or Ceruti at the Union Bank or any other bank.

The Swiss appear to have asked only the Union Bank, which replied in mid-April that account 596 757 60 T belonged to Gelli, and that he also owned account 525 779 X S 60 R. He had two further accounts, one containing a "certain number of kilos of gold" and the other some shares, denominated in Swiss francs. (The number of kilos of gold, about which the Swiss were so coy, was later to be revealed as 250.)

What the Swiss also failed to reveal was that Gelli had been tipped off about the Italian inquiries, and was in the process of closing the first account mentioned, which had been his main one, and transferring the money in it – nearly $17 million – to a new account, 527 397 GL 60W, in the name of Luciano Gori (Gori being his mother's maiden name).

Marco Ceruti, the Swiss revealed, had had two accounts, 525 366 BW 60 A and 525 367 B X 60 D, but these had been closed in favour of his wife a month before. Zilletti did not have an account. Then the Swiss sent bank advices of some, but not all, movements in and out of Gelli's first account for September and October 1980, and they did the same for Ceruti's accounts.

These showed that Gelli had indeed paid Ceruti $800,000 on 14 October 1980, though the bank's copy of the advice did not have the names of Ceruti and Zilletti on it. Even more startling, the advices showed that Gelli had paid Ceruti a previous $4 million on 1 September 1980, and $800,000 on 8 October 1980 – a total of $5.6 million.

The advices also showed that Gelli had received $5 million from the

Trade Development Bank in Geneva on 1 September 1980, and another $2.6 million from the same bank on 15 October, and that he had paid $2.4 million to an account in the name of Ortolani's Bafisud at the Union Bank, and $2.4 million to his own second account, 525 779 X S 60 R.

Incomplete though the details were, the Italian investigators did get a picture of enormous sums going through Gelli's account. They could not question him about them, because he had fled the country. But they could and did question Ceruti.

Who was Ceruti? He turned out to be part-owner of a famous restaurant in Florence, Doney's, in via Tornabuoni. That's the glittering street where Gucci hands out handbags, and Ferragamo scarves wave from the windows of a palace built in Dante's day. Zilletti, who was professor of law at Florence University, liked to eat at Doney's, and was friendly with Ceruti.

Ceruti was a protégé of Florence's former masonic dignitary, Alessandro Del Bene, the man who received the British freemasons in 1973. Del Bene, Zilletti and Ceruti were all at one time or another involved with a travel agency, Acitur. Del Bene's principal business interest had been a transport firm, although in 1983 *Panorama* magazine reported that he was involved in international arms dealing with a Jersey company, Independent Trading. Ceruti also had an interest in a cargo airline business, Alha, run by his brother Gianpaolo. Before he bought his interest in Doney's he had been an antique dealer and he still maintained an interest in objets d'art, in particular items from Turkey: he had married a Turkish woman, Nadia Kürkcü, who ran her own public relations business in Florence.

It turned out that Ceruti had been in Rome on 25 September 1980, the day when Gresti went there to talk about Calvi's passport, and that Ceruti had tried to phone Gelli that day.

At this stage the Brescia investigations were brought to a halt. The magistrates of Rome were demanding that all investigations into P2 and its crimes should be transferred to their jurisdiction. When the appeal court ruled, at the beginning of September 1981, that Rome should take over, Calvi made no secret of his relief. Other Italians heaved cynical sighs. It was widely believed that the magistrates of Rome were more open to political pressure than those of the northern cities. The two Rome magistrates who had put Sarcinelli in prison – illegally, as it proved – were still at their posts.

The Rome investigators found both Zilletti and Ceruti innocent. The bank advice with Zilletti's name typed on it had been an obvious fabrication to discredit him; his intervention in the passport affair had been quite proper.

But Ceruti? The senior investigating magistrate, Ernesto Cudillo, argued: "Such huge transfers of sums cannot but be connected with underlying Ceruti-Gelli economic relations, quite unlike the price of the presumed corruption . . ."

Was he saying that the rate for bribing magistrates was a lot less than $5.6 million? If not, what was he saying?

Cudillo was working with only part of the picture. It is now clear that the money paid to Ceruti by Gelli had come from Ortolani, who had paid it out of the $40.65 million Calvi had caused United Trading to hand over in the last four months of 1980. It has since emerged that Ceruti was paid another $500,000 from this money, and yet another $3.5 million by Ortolani from the money paid to him by Calvi in early 1981. So Ceruti had received at least $9.6 million, suggesting that he might have been the unidentified Marco in the Gelli *tabella*. Gelli later told the Milan magistrates that he was certain this was not so, but could not explain what made him so certain. Gelli also said that the Robe in the *tabella* was not Calvi!

Gelli's only explanation to the Milan magistrates of the money he had paid to Ceruti was that he had lent him $6 or $7 million, which, he claimed, Ceruti afterwards repaid with "a very beautiful precious stone". Nobody has ever seen the stone. A handwritten note found among Gelli's papers suggests that Ceruti was probably paid yet another $1 million in cash in September 1980. The note (reproduced on page 302) suggests that the money was paid for "Pollaio – Alloia", or, perhaps, the madhouse resulting from the report of Captain D'Aloia.

On page 303 is another piece of paper found on Gelli when he was arrested, headed – for reasons that have never become apparent – "Bologna", followed by the number of one of Gelli's accounts. This turned out to be a schedule of the payments to Ceruti. Apart from the correspondence of the sums, this was apparent because of the name "Bukada" which was the code for one of Ceruti's accounts at the Union Bank; he had another account named "Tortuga". The money Gelli paid him in 1980 was marked: "Dif. Mi" and this has been taken to mean: "Difesa, Milano." (Defence, Milan.) The table indicated that Gelli and Ortolani were paid $2 million for the same service. This would seem to refer to Calvi's legal problems in Milan. In addition to the currency investigations and the fraud inquiry, he was also under investigation for the Pacchetti/Zitropo deal of 1972. The table then has a section headed "Dif. Roma" (Defence, Rome). This is more difficult to interpret. It suggests that the "Bukada" account received a sum of $2 million in early 1981: in fact, as we shall see, it got $3.5 million direct from one of Ortolani's accounts.

A. M. C.

CONSEGNATO CONTANTI
~~5.000.000~~ ~~3.000.000~~ 1.000.000 –
~~604.00~~ – RELATIVO AL 20%
DAL 20-7-80 AL 30-7-80

─ ─ ─ ─

ACCREDITATO $ 4.000.000
U.B. AI GENEVRA. DALLA SIGNA.
AGNOLINI

1-9-80 . ore 11.30

POLLARO-ALLOIA . ore 15.30
CONSEGNA $ 1.000.
DALLA SIGNA
AGNOLINI. NELLA
SUA SEDE A PERSONA
SCON- CREDO CAP – (piccolo incontri
1-9-80   INTERNAZIONALE - Bigna
                       NESLARGO - CURT, per
                       LA .... s.p.a.

But why had the names of Ceruti and Zilletti been typed on the bank advice? Gelli's own explanation was that this was done to remind him that Ceruti was Zilletti's secretary – or, at least, had made himself out to be. There is no reason to believe this. One theory was that Gelli had done this to convince Calvi that he could influence the highest level of the magistracy. It is quite possible that Gelli and Ortolani might have conned Calvi into paying them huge sums by falsely claiming that Ceruti could influence his friend Zilletti. But would they do that by typing two names on a bank advice? Calvi, after all, was a banker, and would surely have spotted the crude doctoring of a bank advice. And why should Gelli and Ortolani have paid

BOLOGNA - 525779 - I.B. -

DATA	MOTIVO	IMPORTO	VERB.CONTO	NOTE
3.9.80	DIP.MI	8.000.000		
3.9.80	10.000 - 20%	1.956.000	BULADA	
3.9.80	2.000 - U.L.	2.044.000	BULADA	
6.10.80	8.000	800.000	BULADA	
14.10.80	6.100 -SPESE-	800.000	BULADA	RICEVUTO 6.100.000
5.11.80	1.900 -dare a saldo	500.000	BULADA	A-SALDO----400.000
15.2.81		=========	BULADA	A-SALDO-4.600.000
15.2.81	DIP. ROMA	3.500.000		
12.2.81	2.000 - 30%	2.000.000	BULADA	DA RESTARE 1.900.000
	1.500 - U.L.		7.10.80	MILL. LIT. 850.000
12.2.81	3.500 - SALDATO		15.12.80	FINESCHI ANTIC.20.000
				DA SALDARE 1.030.000

DIPES. ROMA
5.000 - MENO
IL 30% PER G
IL COSTO I'

BALDATO

DATA	NOTE	IMPORTO
9.4.81	DEPOS."48 ORE" U.D.E. -	635.000
20.4.81	BON.M.T.D.C/o 855	600.000
ESTINTO	14.5.81 -	75.000

BON. TEMPORANEI COPERTI c/c 855

AL 12.2.81 TOTALE 9.600.000

Ceruti so much? Was he kidding *them* he could influence magistrates? Ceruti himself was interrogated by Cudillo twice, on 2 February and 19 February 1982. He denied receiving the $800,000, which was the only sum Cudillo knew about then. The bank advice was a crude forgery, Ceruti said. He had not even known of Calvi's existence, much less that he wanted his passport back.

Ceruti was summoned for interrogation by the P2 parliamentary commission; at that point he quietly disappeared. He went to Brazil, apparently by way of California. A warrant for his arrest was issued in Italy in 1987 but, unlike all the other major defendants at the Ambrosiano trial, he did not return, voluntarily or involuntarily, to Italy: and Pizzi and Bricchetti, in their report, did not take Cudillo's inquiries any further, and offered no theories as to why Ceruti should have been paid the money.

After his arrest warrant was issued, however, Ceruti did offer an explanation for the money, but according to his lawyers the Italian magistrates would not go to Brazil to hear it. It was only in the autumn of 1991 that it came to light, together with elaborate documentation to support it.

On 29 October 1991 Ceruti's Italian lawyer wrote to the Milan court to say that he had received the money in payment for a "very valuable collection of artistic goods and antique jewels" that Ceruti had bought in London in order to resell to Gelli. Attached to the lawyer's letter was an impressive list with 93 entries under the headings "Fabergé Collection", "Ancient Art", "Jewels" and "Enamels". Also attached were what purported to be a contract dated 12 May 1980 giving Ceruti the option to buy the collection and letters purporting to show that he had started to exercise the option in August 1980 and that subsequently $8.82 million and 2,164,000 Swiss francs (a total of just under $10 million) had been paid in various instalments up to July 1982. The contract said that Ceruti's patron, Alessandro Del Bene, would guarantee payment and the correspondence indicated that much of the money had been paid by him.

The contract and correspondence were with a Channel Island company called Merlin Writers (Jersey) whose principal was an accountant of Irish origins called Christopher Delaney. It was, however, impossible to verify the story with him since a month before the evidence was presented to the Milan court Delaney had disappeared from Jersey leaving over £1 million of unpaid debts.

The documents, however, indicated that another man, Frank Hogart, was involved; and Hogart, traced to his home in London's Belgravia, volunteered to give evidence.

Hogart's story, as he repeated it directly to me, was that he had been asked to sell the hoard on behalf of three Iranians, two of them former ministers in the Shah's government. Hogart, an international wheeler-dealer born in Morocco of a Swiss father who had operated from Paris before settling in London, had long known Del Bene, he said. Del Bene had extensive business interests in the UK and it was he who introduced him to Ceruti as a potential buyer of the artwork collection. Ceruti had come over to see the collection a couple of times – Hogart had entertained him at Annabel's nightclub – and on one occasion he had also met a friend of Ceruti's, Romano Calamassi, who had been asked to inspect the goods.

Calamassi also gave evidence to the Milan court saying that he had indeed been to London to look at the collection at Hogart's apartment in West Halkin Street and also in a nearby gallery. But he had met Ceruti in a pub off the Portobello Road, where Italian antique dealers in London were in the habit of gathering.

Hogart also said that on a couple of occasions Ceruti brought the intended final buyer to see the collection. This man was not identified to him, but later, when he saw Gelli's picture on television, he was certain it was him. He could not remember when these visits were or when the collection was handed over, although he said this was done before full payment had been received. Payment was in cash and the goods were taken away in a Mercedes, he said.

Hogart's story was received with considerable scepticism by the Milan court – and not without justification since the police and others investigating Delaney's affairs in Jersey quickly established that some of the documents purporting to evidence the deal had been prepared on a computer acquired by Delaney's office in 1987, years after the events they allegedly recorded. Then, in late January 1992, Delaney turned up again in Jersey and admitted to the police that the documents were all forgeries and that his company had never been involved in such a deal. He, Hogart and another intermediary, an unidentified woman living in Marbella who had introduced Ceruti to Hogart, had prepared the documents for a fee of $150,000. Delaney confirmed his statement directly to the Milan court when it travelled specially to Jersey to take evidence from him.

Hogart, however, continued to insist that the nub of the story was true and that he had indeed sold a collection of objets d'art to Ceruti, although he told me the total paid was of the order of $5 to $6 million, rather than the $10 million indicated by the forged documents.

The collection of works of art, however, has not been produced; and even if there was a deal, the forged documents themselves indicate that Del Bene, who died in 1984, put up much of the money. This would suggest that most of the money paid by Gelli – and Ortolani, as we shall see – to Ceruti stuck with him, as the details of his bank accounts also suggest. Nevertheless, the possibility that Gelli and his friends may have had contacts with the world of Italian antique dealers in London brings a new significance to events that will be recounted in later chapters; and the story could explain why some sums of money paid by Calvi to Ortolani in 1981 found their way, via intermediary accounts, to a Surrey-based shipping firm run by Italians.

Another matter Pizzi and Bricchetti did not get to the bottom of was the first item on the *tabella*, which also suggested attempts to divert the course of justice. It listed Colonel Gallo, the man in overall charge of the Guardia di Finanza investigations into Calvi, and Captain D'Aloia, the man who had made the report.

An even more inconclusive investigation followed the finding of another startling piece of paper in Gelli's villa. It read: "UBS – Lugano c/c 633369 'Protezione' Number corresponding to the Hon. Claudio Martelli for account of Bettino Craxi at which on 28.10.80 there was credited from Dr Roberto Calvi for the initialling of the agreement with ENI made by Dr Fiorini the sum of $3,500,000.

"On the signature of the contract which will take place on 20/11/1980 and which will be done between Dr CR and DDL there will be paid another sum of $3,500,000."

Martelli was deputy secretary of the Socialist Party; Craxi its leader. (He became Prime Minister in 1983.) Dr CR meant Calvi. Fiorini we have met before in these pages; he was the finance director of the state oil company ENI, and not a P2 member. DDL stood for Leonardo Di Donna, vice-president of ENI, who was a P2 member. By the strange Italian system, ENI top jobs were in the gift of the Socialist Party.

We have seen that Calvi borrowed heavily from ENI in 1978 and 1979, at moments when he was particularly desperate for money. At the end of 1980 he was, yet again, in dire need of outside funds, and had turned to these friends, who made a five-year loan of $50 million directly to the Andino. Here, it seemed, was evidence that the Socialist Party leaders had been bribed to induce ENI to make the loan.

Also among Gelli's papers was a copy of a letter apparently written by Di Donna to Calvi at a company called Ultrafin Canada in Edmonton, Alberta. This entrusted Calvi with dealing with local institutions and authorities on behalf of ENI "for the expansion of our interests and projects".

At first the investigation of the ENI affair was the job of the Milan magistrates. They asked the Swiss if there was indeed an account number

633369 called *Protezione* at the Union Bank in Lugano. If so, they wanted to know in whose name it was registered, the names of all those entitled to use the account and copies of all documents concerning it. They also asked for all banking documents relating to any account that Calvi, Di Donna or Fiorini might have with any bank in the Ticino – the Italian-speaking part of Switzerland, whose centre is Lugano.

The Union Bank responded promptly, in its way. It sent the Swiss authorities a sealed envelope containing the details of the account, but simultaneously filed a complaint in the appeal court, with a lawyer's letter asking that the order should be withdrawn. The lawyer's letter was, for the time being, all the Italians got. It was verbose, muddled, and even self-contradictory. But the vehemence of the response made it clear to the Italians that they had hit a sensitive nerve. They notified Martelli, a Member of Parliament, that he was under investigation.

Martelli at once denied everything. Nevertheless, the Milan magistrates wrote to the Swiss appeals tribunal repeating their request for details of the bank account, and this time naming Martelli as well as the other three. Craxi himself was never named in these proceedings.

Before there was any official response, in the summer of 1981 Martelli, Di Donna and Fiorini all wrote to the Union Bank asking it to declare that they were not the owners of account 633369 *Protezione*. The bank duly replied that they were not.

At this point all investigations linked to P2 were moved to Rome. Cudillo took over the investigation. At the end of November 1981 he wrote to the Lugano appeals tribunal. He seems to have had no reply. In January 1982 he wrote again, this time asking if the Union Bank's letter to Martelli saying that he did not own the account had ever been formally confirmed to the Swiss authorities.

That stirred the Swiss into action. In February 1982, nearly a year after the raid on Gelli's villa, a formal deposition was taken from the manager of the Union Bank at Lugano. He confirmed that none of the three – Martelli, Di Donna or Fiorini – owned the account. But he did at last confirm that there was an account number 633369 *Protezione*. It had been opened in July 1979.

Cudillo did nothing about this for a year. Then, in early March 1983, he reminded the Swiss that they had never replied to the earlier request for information. Without waiting for a reply, on 17 March he produced his report, ruling that the bank manager's letter had clearly shown that Gelli's note was false and that Martelli had no case to answer.

In June 1983 Cudillo also ruled that there was no case for Di Donna or

Fiorini to answer either. He gave two main reasons: first the confirmation that neither owned the *Protezione* account; second, that an independent financial investigation had found nothing abnormal or uncommercial in the terms of the $50 million loan from ENI to the Ambrosiano.

Cudillo also argued that a $7 million bribe would have been out of proportion for a $50 million loan. So it was, but the Rizzoli *premio* was also somewhat out of proportion.

As for the ENI-Ultrafin letter, this turned out to be similar to a genuine letter Di Donna had sent to Calvi. Gelli told the Milan magistrates that Di Donna had telexed the text to him. Di Donna, he said, had contacts with him for the purpose of strengthening the ENI-Ambrosiano relationship.

The Milan magistrates organised a confrontation between Gelli and Di Donna, who already admitted sending the letter to Calvi. At the confrontation Di Donna denied sending a telex to Gelli, and repeated his denial of having anything to do with *Protezione*. Di Donna had already explained that Calvi was offering to help ENI secure mineral concessions, which were hard to come by, in Alberta. Nothing had come of it, Di Donna suggested. Calvi himself, while still alive, told investigators that Ultrafin Canada had never been active.

My own inquiries indicate that negotiations over a joint project between Ultrafin Canada and ENI were more serious and had progressed further than either Calvi or Di Donna admitted. It was not known at the time that Calvi had bought a ranch and made a substantial property investment in Alberta in the mid-1970s. He had good contacts among Canadian businessmen and expatriate Italians, including a former chairman of ENI who had a home there. Discussions on this project between Calvi's local associate Jack Kennedy, a director of Ultrafin Canada, and an Italian businessman associated with ENI, went on at least until Christmas 1980. The project may have failed because of these very investigations.

Cudillo did write to the Swiss again, pointing out that he had still not been told who owned account *Protezione*. In March 1984 the Swiss ruled that the original request was no longer operative, and that if the Italians wanted to pursue the matter they would have to start all over again.

Cudillo never did. And he never asked the simple question: did *Protezione* receive the two lots of $3.5 million mentioned in Gelli's note?

Pizzi and Bricchetti, however, did ask the Swiss this question, and the Swiss confirmed that United Trading paid the first $3.5 million into that account on 30 October 1980 (the same day, incidentally, that Calvi made a $200,000 payment to Navarra) and the second on 2 February 1981.

Who got it? The Swiss have still not told anyone. By their own rules, they ought to tell the Ambrosiano creditors; the money was clearly embezzled, and some of it may be recoverable. But this remains one of the unsolved mysteries of the crash. The only clue is that Calvi did not kid himself this was a loan. The first *Protezione* payment is not in his 17 December 1980 balance sheet for United Trading. He had clearly kissed the money goodbye.

Calvi badly needed the $50 million ENI loan, because, as December 1980 approached, he could see the familiar year-end balance-sheet crisis ahead. By the end of November the $65 million of syndicated loans raised during the summer had been used up, and the internal group debts were mounting. Andino's debts to the Cisalpine had risen to nearly $119 million; BA Holding's to nearly $35 million. The Cisalpine had even had to resort to borrowing $30 million directly from the Ambrosiano in Milan to keep its books in balance. All these group debts, Calvi knew, would have to be paid off by the end of the year if the accounts were to be passed by Coopers and Lybrand without embarrassing inquiries. So the ENI five-year loan was a godsend, as was a $40 million temporary loan ENI made to the Andino over the year-end.

And in December 1980 Calvi turned to another old friend, Marcinkus.

TWENTY-SEVEN

The P2 Scandal Erupts

In that one month, December 1980, the IOR poured $65 million into the legal part of Calvi's empire. It bought promissory notes issued by the Ambrosiano's overseas associates. The Andino issued a note for $25 million, due for repayment on 30 June 1982. BA Holding issued two notes, one for $15 million, due on 30 June 1984, and another for $25 million due one year later. The Cisalpine also issued two notes, one for $25 million to be repaid on 30 June 1983 and one for $10 million, due in mid-1984.

That adds up to $100 million. But only $65 million of this was new money; the notes to the Cisalpine merely replaced existing deposits. What the Cisalpine owed to the IOR remained at about $90 million. All the notes were kept in Nassau, not in the Vatican.

Apart from its subscription to Ambrosiano share issues, this was the first time the IOR had provided new money for Calvi since the early 1970s, when it put up some $200 million. Indeed, in 1978 and 1979 it had cut its commitment by more than $100 million.

Probably the decision of Marcinkus to reinvest in Calvi was tied up with the Vianini deal, which took place at the same time. Calvi (through Laramie) had agreed to pay $20 million down and $40 million over two years for the construction company. This not only gave the IOR a huge capital gain; it greatly improved its income. The $20 million down payment, reinvested in Ambrosiano promissory notes, would alone have produced some $3 million a year, more than double the total income in dividends on all the 6 million Vianini shares. And the IOR was earning interest on the deferred $40 million too.

Marcinkus must have known that the purchase by Laramie, a Panamanian company whose directors were employees of the Cisalpine, was not a genuine commercial transaction. Like CIM, XX Settembre and Setemer, Vianini was being consigned to a legal limbo, rather than to a commercial owner.

So far, we have been pointing out how much Marcinkus must have known of Calvi's operation. Now we can see that he did not know it all. If he had, he would not have accepted the promissory notes. The entire $65 million was lost in the crash. Indeed, from the moment the IOR paid the money over, some of it went straight into the pockets of Ortolani, Gelli, Tassan Din and Angelo Rizzoli. It was $15 million of the IOR's money that Andino lent to United Trading (via Nordeurop) on 1 December 1980, and which United Trading immediately paid to the Ortolani accounts Crizia 3 and Antonino 13. There is no evidence that Calvi told Marcinkus he was making these enormous payments to the heads of P2. We shall see more clearly, from this point on, how far this was from being one coherent conspiracy. Though Calvi was conspiring with Marcinkus to rig the balance sheet of the Cisalpine, and conspiring with P2 for many other purposes, Marcinkus and P2 were not, apparently, conspiring with each other.

Thanks to the IOR, and ENI, Calvi was able to rig his balance sheets just before the end of the year. But there was one balance sheet he did not attempt to rig in December 1980 – his private one, for United Trading.

During the year its debts had soared by over 50 per cent, to more than $771 million. The IOR back-to-back loans now accounted for only about $172 million of this. On the other side of the balance sheet, the contrast with the year before was even more startling. In spite of the acquisition of the 4.5 million Varesino shares from Bafisud, and the inclusion of the $40.65 million paid to Ortolani as if it were a loan, the total assets had dropped by more than 35 per cent, to only $324 million. (See page 293.)

Calvi had abandoned his fantasies. In this, the last known balance sheet of United Trading, dated 17 December 1980, he used market values for those shares which were quoted on a market, and nominal values for those which were not.

He had not been wrong in thinking that Ambrosiano shares would rise in 1980. They had more than doubled, to about 42,000 lire, or $44 a share. But this was not the fivefold gain he had assumed, in his valuation of the year before. United Trading now held 3,124,723 shares, or 10.4 per cent of the capital. Of these, 1,231,946 were held by Astolfine in the Bahamas. Two days after making out his secret balance sheet, Calvi put these 1,231,946 shares into a new creation, the Astolfine Trust, set up by the bank which handled Calvi's personal affairs, Roywest. Why he did this has never been explained; he was heard to talk about these shares as if they belonged to him personally, and perhaps he intended to appropriate them as his reward for the Rizzoli operation. They were worth about 50 billion lire, as against the 75 billion lire he had been allotted by the P2 men. However, if this was his plan, he was overtaken by events, and these shares never really left the ownership of the secret network.

The secret network's other 1,892,777 shares were now held by Manic, which had acquired Anli's holding of 2,222,222 shares in September and had then sold 329,445 shares in the market. Anli, one of the original companies in Calvi's network, had been put into liquidation in the autumn of 1980. It had once had some outside shareholders; Calvi may have wished to eliminate a name other people might know. Or Anli may simply have been superfluous; all its functions were now duplicated by Manic.

Calvi was now valuing the United Trading holding of Ambrosiano shares at the market rate, so that they totalled $136 million, as against more than $400 million in the fantasy valuation of the year before. There were similar reductions in the value of La Centrale and BA Holding shares.

So the deficit of United Trading was revealed at more than $447 million. Had Calvi, then, given up fooling himself? Had he agreed to the huge Rizzoli *premio* as a last outrageous fraud, to be perpetrated while he could still fool others?

If Calvi had taken his agreed share of the *premio* in cash, and decamped with Gelli and Ortolani in the spring of 1981, this interpretation might fit. But he did not. The twists and turns in all he did, from the autumn of 1980 onwards, suggest he knew, and yet refused to know, that his situation was hopeless.

In early February 1981, Ortolani told Tassan Din that the money was in place, and that they could set in motion phase one of the Rizzoli operation – the acquisition of the shares held by Rothschilds at Zürich. On 12 February they went together to Rothschilds to effect the transfer.

The P2 men were not getting quite as much as they had hoped. Andrea Rizzoli had come out of the casino, long enough to decide that he was not going to sell one block he still controlled – the 105,000 shares held in trust for his younger daughter Isabella. This meant that only 189,000 shares were available: the 105,000 belonging to the elder daughter, Annina, and the 84,000 owned by Angelo. This made little difference to the control of the company, but it meant that the P2 men would have to forgo 15.75 billion lire of the *premio*.

The readjusted figures worked out like this: the cost of the 189,000 shares would be 18.9 billion lire. The *premio* was 50,000 lire a share on these 189,000, plus another 50,000 lire on each of the 378,000 new shares that would have to be subscribed for under the recapitalisation plans. The total, then, was 28.35 billion lire. The total cost of acquiring the 189,000 Rizzoli shares would, therefore, be 47.25 billion lire.

Calvi was footing the bill, this time in the guise of a Panamanian company called Bellatrix, which had been formed in 1979. Some Ambrosiano executives knew of its existence, and thought it was owned by the IOR. But in fact it was a subsidiary of Manic, and therefore, indirectly, of United Trading.

By this time the pocket calculators were needed again. The lira, which had stood at 1,000 to the dollar when the *pattone* was renewed in December 1980, was weaker. The 47.25 billion lire were equivalent to only about $46.5 million. Two days before Ortolani and Tassan Din went to Rothschilds, Calvi had arranged for the Andino to lend Bellatrix $46,537,683. Andino had borrowed the money from the Cisalpine, which could lend it because the balance sheet for 1980 had just been passed, and the men from Coopers and Lybrand were no longer looking into the books. The group had now used up nearly all the money advanced by ENI and the IOR. So the Cisalpine had once again to resort to the Ambrosiano group banks in Italy.

What happened to the Mincomes authorisations after 1979? As we have seen, in that year Calvi made every effort to reduce, or even to repay entirely, the loans from his Italian banks to the Cisalpine. But in 1980 he no longer seems to have been concerned about it. According to the evidence of Botta, the authorisations for the credit lines remained in place, and monthly reports of the amounts went to the Bank of Italy. So Padalino's recommendations had clearly not been carried out.

Did this mean that he had been over-ruled as a result of the report of 10 May 1979 by the administrative currency nucleus of the Bank? Attempts to find an answer to this question finally resulted in a meeting at the highest level of the Bank of Italy in September 1991. I was referred to evidence that governor Ciampi and Sarcinelli had given to the Ambrosiano trial the previous June. Ciampi had assured the court that the Bank of Italy had not lost its nerve as a result of the arrests of Baffi and Sarcinelli. The latter provided the answer to the question in his evidence. Even before his suspension he had decided that the Bank of Italy could not act on Padalino's recommendation. "You cannot put a bank into extreme difficulty," he said. "It's a different matter not to grant an authorisation . . . that only puts a brake on expansion." To take away the good name of an Italian bank on world markets, he added, might have led to "earthquakes".

Clearly Calvi had heard neither of Sarcinelli's decision nor of the 10 May 1979 report by the administrative currency unit by the summer of 1979. But, some time later, he must have discovered he would be able to continue to use his Italian banks to finance his overseas ones. I have now established that the Mincomes authorisations were not formally renewed. But Calvi seems to have been allowed to act as if they were.

So it was the depositors of the Italian banks who financed the $46.5

million. It had been paid into an account at Rothschilds in the name of Telada. Ortolani and Tassan Din set about distributing it.

According to the *pattone*, Angelo was to get $10 million for delivering his sisters' 210,000 shares, while his own 84,000 were supposed to be handed over for nothing, though he had already received $5.5 million in "advance" payments. He was now paid another $5 million, since he had succeeded in delivering only one sister's holding. So the Rizzoli family had now received a total of $10.5 million. Angelo afterwards complained that he never had been paid all that he had been promised. At the time, though, he seemed happy. He passed on $1.75 million to Annina and Isabella, and used the rest to buy a villa on Capri. Andrea had insisted that Isabella should get her slice, although her shares were not being sold. Later Angelo said that some of the money paid to Isabella had been used to finance the escape of Gelli from Champ Dollon prison, Geneva, on 9 August 1983. Angelo accused his stepmother, the ex-model Ljubia Rosa, of planning the escape with Gelli's son Raffaello. Later investigation did not substantiate this, however.

The balance of what had been set aside for the purchase price, a little more than $13.9 million, was transferred to another account at Rothschilds, called Recioto. Out of this, $7 million was smuggled back into Italy, and actually went where it was needed – to the Rizzoli company. This had to be done because, over the years, a similar sum had been illicitly removed. Ortolani and Tassan Din feared that this hole would be discovered in any audit of the company that might have to be done for the recapitalisation. Some $4 million was sent to South America to cover outstanding Rizzoli debts; Gelli's ambitious attempts to build up the Rizzoli empire there had proved expensive. The last $3 million was left in the Recioto account for the time being.

Although the fall of the lira had somewhat reduced the *premio* in dollar terms, there was still $27.25 million left. The Gelli *tabella* on page 285 carries an entry headed: "Da Robe Sistemazione Rizzo 1 fase." It shows that Ortolani and Gelli were to get $8 million each. But it looks as if Ortolani was to get an extra $150,000 as well. An unidentified "F" was getting another $150,000. Tassan Din was to get $7 million and Calvi himself $4 million.

According to the letter of the *pattone*, less than half should have been paid out at this point, the remainder being paid only when the new Rizzoli shares came to be issued. But Calvi had decided – or had been persuaded – not to defer any of it. The whole $27.25 million was now distributed.

But it was not distributed as in the *tabella*. Tassan Din got his $7 million;

it was paid to a bank account in the name of a company he controlled, Harrods Investments, at Lloyds Bank International in London. All the remaining $20.25 million was paid to Ortolani accounts. His Antonino 13 account at the Trade Development Bank got $10.25 million; his Crizia 3 account at the Union Bank got $10 million.

Of the $10 million in the Crizia 3 account, $8,150,000 was paid on to Gelli's main account at the Union Bank, 596 757 60T. That seems to have been his share of the *premio*. The other $1,850,000 was paid into a Bafisud account at the Union Bank, probably for Ortolani's benefit.

Of the $10.25 million in the Antonino 13 account, $6 million was paid to personal Ortolani accounts, bringing his share of the *premio* to at least $8,137,000. He may also have reaped some benefit from three sums, totalling $463,000, paid into three other accounts. It was also money from the Antonino account that made its way indirectly to a recipient in England.

There is no evidence that any of this money reached Calvi. His Butric account in Roywest, Nassau, had been credited with $280,000 in January and early February. This may have had something to do with his position as chairman of the Cisalpine. From the *premio*, he got nothing beyond the "advance" paid to him the previous September. His share, however, was not now returned to United Trading, but used for other P2 purposes – such as paying Ceruti.

For the last $3.5 million from the Antonino 13 account was paid to the restaurant-owner from Florence, Marco Ceruti. It was paid on 16 February 1981 and telephone records of the Excelsior Hotel in Rome show that Gelli had rung the numbers of Ceruti's wife and his brother's airline office in Florence a few days before. Was this connected with the alleged deal in objets d'art in London?

Even if Frank Hogart's revised story has some truth in it, Ceruti had already received enough to pay for the collection. And what about the table marked: "Bologna" found on Gelli when he was arrested in Switzerland? This had "Dif. Roma" marked against the sum, and also indicated that Ortolani and Gelli were to be paid a further $1.5 million for the same reason – whatever that was. (See page 303. The $2 million entry in the table appears to have been an error since no such sum was credited to the "Bukada" account.)

At this point Calvi had no immediate legal problems in Rome, and therefore it is a mystery what the three of them could have done to deserve the money, unless it was one more reference to the supposed influence of Ceruti with the top levels of the magistracy.

What Calvi did face in Rome was the parliamentary commission investigating the Sindona affair. This was the inquiry at which Calvi denied that he had ever paid blackmail money to Sindona – indeed, that he had ever entered the Caffè Greco.

In late 1980, the Sindona investigations had the benefit of an important new witness, Carlo Bordoni, former general manager of Banca Unione and Sindona's number one currency speculator. He had lost millions on the speculations, but not before prudently putting aside a few millions for himself. Just before the Franklin National crash he fled to Venezuela, but was arrested and extradited to stand trial with Sindona. He turned state evidence and was rewarded by a lighter sentence. Now, extradited back to Italy, he gave evidence which speeded up the inquiries. On 5 February the Milan magistrates arrested the 71-year-old Luigi Mennini, not for anything he had done as second in command of Marcinkus at the IOR, but for his activities as a director of Sindona's Banca Unione. The charges were fraudulent bankruptcy and illegal currency dealings.

The magistrates did not know of some illegal currency dealings which had taken place only the day before. Ortolani's Antonino 13 account had received $600,000, embezzled from the Ambrosiano group and exported from Italy by way of the IOR-Svirobank-Crédit Suisse route. Calvi seems to have resorted to this method of paying Ortolani at that point because United Trading was short of funds, as a result of the second $3.5 million payout to the account *Protezione*. That's the one whose ownership the Swiss never have revealed. *Protezione* is all the more mysterious because these payments did not go through Ortolani. Was somebody making a joke about "protection"? Two days before the first payment into that account, Bordoni had been given the benefit of the American "protection programme" which gives a new identity to witnesses whose lives may be in danger.

The arrest of Mennini must have been a severe embarrassment to the IOR – and not only because of the consternation among the faithful. Later that month Marcinkus, too, had to be away, escorting the Pope on a tour of the Far East. So the IOR was without its two guiding spirits.

Mennini did not obtain "provisional liberty" until 1 April. Marcinkus, still escorting the Pope, had to miss a board meeting of the Cisalpine in London on 17 February – the only meeting he did miss during his time as director. Calvi presided. The most important decision taken was the approval of the acquisition of 20 per cent of another Bahamian bank, Artoc Bank and Trust. It was run by the British financier Peter de Savary, but owned by Arabs. Calvi was always hoping for access to oil money. This time he did not stay at Claridge's, but at the St James Club, a place with a superbly vulgar exterior, said to be refined at heart. The attraction was that Peter de Savary owned it.

In late February Calvi ordered United Trading to pay out further huge sums to Ortolani accounts in Switzerland. Antonino 13 got $5 million. Ortolani opened a new account at the Union Bank, Mazut 66, and Calvi paid in $1,950,000, about half of which went to Gelli. The excuse for these payments is not known. They coincided with the making of a $40 million loan by Andino, intended to enable an Italian, Giovanni Fabbri, who controlled a paper-making empire, to buy the 392,000 Italmobiliare shares held by Intermarket. But the deal was never completed, and the loan was repaid at the end of March. Ortolani and Gelli repaid nothing.

Two of the Milan magistrates on the Sindona case, Giuliano Turone and Gherardo Colombo, were looking into the links between Gelli and Sindona. They already knew something about P2; in 1976 the Florence magistrates had suspected that its activities might shed some light on the murder of a magistrate, Vittorio Occorsio. In the files for 1976 was an affidavit Gelli had sworn in support of Sindona's attempts to avoid extradition from the United States. Gelli expressed admiration for Sindona's anti-communist stand, and said that this would prevent him from getting a fair trial in Italy. Now Bordoni was talking about the links between Gelli and Sindona. But the first hard evidence came from Miceli Crimi, the Sicilian doctor who had given Sindona an anaesthetic, before shooting him in the leg to make the faked kidnapping look real.

Crimi, a careless conspirator, had not destroyed the evidence. When he was arrested he had on him a book with Gelli's addresses and telephone numbers. He had railway tickets to and from Arezzo – the proof of his journey there on 22 September 1979. He also had the typewriter on which Sindona had typed the threatening letter to Cuccia.

On 12 March 1981 the magistrates issued a summons to Gelli to appear as a witness, and simultaneously issued orders for the search of his offices in Castiglion Fibocchi and Frosinone, his villa at Arezzo and his suite at the Excelsior in Rome.

The raid took place on Tuesday 17 March 1981. The documents found, when eventually published by the P2 commission, took up some 3,000 pages. While the magistrates were going through them, listing them, numbering them and writing out a description of each one, the public did not know that the raid had taken place.

But Gelli did. He rang up his secretary from South America while it was going on. He came back to Italy as soon as he could.

Two days after the raid, United Trading paid $6.5 million into Ortolani's

Crizia 3 account at the Union Bank. He passed it all on to Gelli's account, and Gelli transferred all but $500,000 to an account he had at Ortolani's bank, Bafisud, account 855.

The same day, 19 March, United Trading paid $435,000 to the Swiss bank account of Sindona's henchman, Walter Navarra.

Since the previous August, Calvi had paid $75.95 million into Ortolani accounts. Some of this had been passed on, as we have seen, but the bulk of it was shared between Ortolani and Gelli, and each was now richer by at least $25 million. This was before the main part of the *premio* on the Rizzoli deal.

The first news of the Gelli raid filtered out at the weekend. Many people thought that what had been seized was a list boasted of by Sindona, but never yet seen – the names of 500 important people who had smuggled out currency. Nobody thought of P2, though the freemasons were already discussing it. A two-day meeting of the Grand Lodge of Italy, with representatives of all 554 constituent lodges, was starting in Rome on Sunday, 22 March. It was thought likely to abolish P2. On Monday, however, the Grand Lodge decided on a compromise. P2 would not be "demolished", and Gelli could keep his title of Venerable Master, but the Grand Lodge nevertheless ruled that certain P2 methods were not consistent with proper masonic behaviour. The Grand Lodge did not know what was about to hit it.

Gelli was supposed to give evidence before the magistrates that week. But on 26 March his lawyers announced that he would not be appearing, "because of the impossibility of returning to Italy in time, for Gelli now lives in Montevideo". They also started legal actions for defamation over the first reports of the raid.

In fact Gelli had returned to Italy, and had left it again only the day before, travelling to Nice on a false passport in the name of Luciano Gelli. The day his lawyers made the announcement he was in Monte Carlo. There he bought some antiques for his villa at Cap Ferrat. He paid for them with lira bank drafts, representing deposits withdrawn in the previous few days by his wife, Wanda Venucci, his son Raffaello and one of his employees. That evening at 7.30 he took a flight for São Paulo in Brazil, via Geneva.

The lira drafts had to be taken back into Italy to be cashed. The antique shop employee who did this, Louis Noguères, was afterwards murdered by another employee. In the subsequent investigations, Gelli's illegal export of lire came to light. He was convicted of this in his absence by a San Remo court in 1985 and sentenced to a year and two months in prison.

When did Gelli last see Calvi? Some time in February, according to himself. But he made sure of completing the Rizzoli deal. On the very day of his flight from Italy, 25 March, he met Angelo in Rome to talk about it. Gelli did not dare go to the Excelsior, where his suite had been searched, but he did not go far away. He told Angelo to meet him at the Ambasciatori, on the other side of the Via Veneto. It is not quite possible for the doormen of one hotel to recognise the people arriving at the other, but any bellhop sent out on an errand from the Excelsior might have seen Gelli at the entrance of the Ambasciatori.

The Rizzoli operation should have been completed by the end of March 1981, but there had been difficulties. The only part of Calvi's empire that might legally own Rizzoli was La Centrale. Even that might prove to be politically difficult. According to Tassan Din, both he and Calvi were at this time sounding out the political parties. He thought all parties seemed to favour the idea, though the Communists were dubious at first. Only dubious? Well, Calvi had just arranged some secret financing for the Rome evening paper they owned, *Paese Sera*.

According to Tassan Din, another reason for the delay was that Mennini had taken with him into prison the only key to the IOR safe where the Rizzoli shares were. But in fact the problem was money. La Centrale, being legal and open, could not pay any secret commissions, let alone one the size of the *premio*. That would have to be met by the secret network, and in March the secret network had no money.

Calvi was planning to get it some. In February he opened negotiations with the National Westminster Bank in London for BA Holding's largest international loan yet – $75 million for five years. The ostensible purpose of the loan was to finance Italian exports. The talks were proceeding at a bankerly pace. You cannot tell bankers to hurry up because you need the money. They take alarm at once. Even less can you tell them to hurry because, at any moment, the papers the authorities have seized may prove to compromise you.

There luck was on Calvi's side. For the last few days of March and the first ten days of April the Sindona affair continued to take the attention of the newspapers. Bordoni was telling his story to the parliamentary commission.

Nobody knew that, at the end of March, the Brescia magistrates had begun to investigate whether Calvi had bribed Zilletti to get his passport back. Nobody knew that Calvi's currency offences, unearthed two years before by the Bank of Italy men, were now being vigorously investigated by two magistrates new to the case, D'Ambrosio and Urbisci, or that the fraud charges were also being pursued.

On 8 April the National Westminster Bank and 26 other international banks committed themselves to lending $75 million to BA Holding before the end of the month. The following day the $3 million left in the Recioto account at Rothschilds, after the first stage of the Rizzoli operation, was paid out to Tassan Din. What was he doing to earn it? This remains obscure.

On 13 April *L'Espresso* ran the story that Gelli had procured the return of Calvi's passport by putting pressure on Zilletti. It did not mention Ceruti, or the bank advice, but said, inaccurately, that a letter from a brother mason to Gelli was the source of the information. It did, however, mention the transfer of Calvi's case to two new magistrates. Then it speculated about the importance of Ortolani, his connections with Sindona and the suspicion that he had been involved in the ENI affair. It also mentioned that he was a director of Rizzoli.

Other papers took up the story, and Ortolani decided that he, too, had better leave Italy. But, like Gelli, he first took steps to ensure that the Rizzoli deal would be completed. According to Angelo, a meeting between himself, Ortolani and Tassan Din took place on Wednesday 15 April, in Rome. This was not a matter of moving to the hotel across the road. This was serious. Ortolani said they had to meet him at 5 p.m. by a newsstand in the unfashionable Corso di Francia, which runs north from the Flaminio Bridge. They arrived by car to find him waiting nervously. According to Rizzoli, he said he was about to leave because some of Gelli's papers might compromise him. He then said that Calvi had decided to comply with the plan for the recapitalisation of Rizzoli. (Tassan Din's version is that Ortolani said he had "convinced" Calvi.) Both versions agree that Tassan Din was told to contact Calvi, also then in Rome, to tie up the final details.

According to Tassan Din, Ortolani said nothing more. According to Angelo, Ortolani and Tassan Din moved away, so that he could not overhear them, and talked for a few minutes more. When they returned Angelo asked whether he could take part in the negotiations. (He was still managing director of the company, besides being its legal owner.) Ortolani said no. Gelli had entrusted him, Ortolani, with the negotiations with Calvi. But as he now had to leave Italy, he was handing the job to Tassan Din.

Angelo and Tassan Din got back into the car. Tassan Din called Calvi on the car phone, and arranged to go at once to the Ambrosiano office in the Via del Tritone.

The previous day, all the Rizzoli papers found in Gelli's office had been sent to the public prosecutor. But they were so hard to decipher that, at first, the investigators concentrated on the documents about Rizzoli

Finanziaria, the share-juggling operation in Rome. These had lists of payments to Ortolani, and bank advices, which were clear enough.

Even if Calvi did not know exactly what had been found, he must have known that the Rizzoli deal was full of danger for him. What did Ortolani do to "convince" him that it should go ahead? Did Gelli come back to Italy in secret to help with the convincing? Among the documents later published by the P2 commission is a report by the CIA in Uruguay to the Italian secret services, that Gelli had arrived in Montevideo on 10 April 1981 on a Varig flight from Rome, carrying an Italian diplomatic passport. Gelli has denied that he made any such secret return. The CIA report seems inaccurate; Varig, the Brazilian airline, does not fly direct to Montevideo, and the diplomatic passport Gelli carried was an Argentine one.

Ortolani's timing was good. On the day he fled from Italy, the authorities searched Zilletti's office and his two homes, in Rome and Florence. This was what convinced everyone that *L'Espresso* was on to something. The P2 scandal had begun in earnest.

On 16 April 1981 Calvi's passport was withdrawn. This time he was not going to get it back.

TWENTY-EIGHT

Calvi Hires a Warrior

It is time to introduce Francesco Pazienza. "I am an exceptional *manager*," he said (using the English word) when he was on trial in Bologna in 1987. "I am not an adventurer."

Calvi hired Pazienza as a personal assistant in the spring of 1981. As Calvi never explained his motives for doing so, we have only Pazienza's own story.

Pazienza was thirty-five in 1981. He had a medical degree from Rome University; by his own account he specialised in "deep sea physiology and behaviour". One of his first jobs was with Cocean, a company associated with the French oceanologist Jacques Cousteau. He then became an international business consultant, working mainly on marine projects in the Middle East and South America, among other places. ("I have mastered five languages," he told the court in Bologna.) In the mid-1970s he worked for the construction company Condotte d'Acqua. Then he started his own company, Techfin, registered in Luxembourg but operating from Paris. One of his clients was a rich businessman of Greek origin, Theodore Ghertsos. He got to know the former Nato commander, General Alexander Haig.

According to Pazienza, his clients had a particular need for information and security services, and he began to specialise in these. General Giuseppe Santovito was a member of P2, and when Pazienza faced the court in 1987 back to Rome early in 1980, as a consultant specialising in French affairs. Santovito was a member of P2, and when Pazienza faced the court in 1987 it was to answer allegations that he had joined in a P2 cover-up of the right-wing terrorists responsible for the bombing of Bologna railway station in the summer of 1980. Pazienza denied this. He did not belong to P2, he said; he had already joined another masonic lodge. He joined for the sake of the contacts, he told the court, and certainly not for the "little apron and the hood", which he found ridiculous. He was found guilty on the cover-up charge, but an appeal court reversed the verdict.

Separate legal proceedings against Pazienza were concerned with his part in the Ambrosiano crash. About this he was interrogated in 1986. He told the magistrates he was first introduced to Calvi at a meeting of the International Monetary Fund in Washington in the late 1970s. But, according to Pazienza, their association began in early March 1981, at a meeting arranged by the Christian Democrat politician Flaminio Piccoli. Pazienza had arranged a meeting for Piccoli with Alexander Haig in America. Piccoli then asked Pazienza to see Calvi, and they met in the office of a lawyer.

Pazienza thought Calvi would want his help in making contacts with the new Reagan administration. But Calvi wanted something quite different. He knew about a mission Pazienza was engaged on for SISMI.

This mission, Pazienza said, began when Monsignor Luigi Celata, acting on behalf of Cardinal Casaroli, asked General Santovito to dig up the dirt on Marcinkus. (There is no other evidence that Casaroli made any such request.) Santovito gave the job to Pazienza. He got in touch with a right-wing senator, Mario Tedeschi, whose magazine, *Il Borghese*, ran a regular column on Vatican affairs. Tedeschi introduced Pazienza to a man who supplied information for it, Giorgio Di Nunzio.

What Di Nunzio had got (Pazienza alleged) was the file on the IOR, assembled by Cardinal Vagnozzi in 1978, when John Paul I was elected Pope. Vagnozzi was dead by this time. Di Nunzio had left the papers with a Swiss lawyer, Peter Duft.

Di Nunzio wanted money for the papers, but neither General Santovito nor Monsignor Celata wanted to pay. Celata revealed that they already had the file; Vagnozzi had left a copy in the Vatican.

It was these papers Calvi wanted to question Pazienza about. From this it would appear that Calvi already knew about Di Nunzio and his papers. Pazienza and Calvi met at least twice more in the first half of March 1981, the meetings becoming "very heavy", in Pazienza's words, when Calvi discovered that Celata already had the documents.

At one of these meetings, Pazienza told Calvi he was tired of working for SISMI. Calvi said he should work for the Ambrosiano. Pazienza said he did not want to work for a big organisation, and it was agreed that he should work for Calvi personally. Calvi was worried about his battles with the Bank of Italy and the Milan magistrates. He told Pazienza: "I have need of a warrior like you." So Pazienza left SISMI and went to work for Calvi.

His first job for Calvi, he said, was to cope with the Vatican expert Di Nunzio. This man was also an expert on Mario Genghini, the constructor so "systematised" by Gelli and Ortolani that he immediately went bankrupt.

Di Nunzio knew about a loan Calvi had made to Genghini secretly through the Zentralsparkasse in Vienna, and about the financing of projects in the Middle East, which was supposed to have resulted in a $10 million payment to Calvi at a French bank. (Nobody has ever found this one.) Di Nunzio was threatening to send his information to the public prosecutor, and Calvi was terrified.

According to Pazienza, Di Nunzio wanted $3 million, but Pazienza negotiated him down to $1.2 million. Part was to be paid in Italy and part in Switzerland. The receipt of the Swiss part would be handled by the lawyer, Peter Duft. To make arrangements for the payment Pazienza sought out an old acquaintance, Alain Aboudaram, a Swiss money broker of Middle Eastern origin, based in Lausanne. He agreed, for a 2 per cent fee, to make a Swiss bank account available to Pazienza to receive the money that Calvi would provide to settle with Di Nunzio.

Here there is corroboration. On 16 March 1981 United Trading, acting through the nominee company Zus, paid $1.5 million to an account at the Swiss offshoot of the Banque Nationale de Paris in the name of Finanzco, an Aboudaram company. A few days later the Finanzco account was debited with $333,000, which was credited to an account at the Union Bank in Geneva, with the reference "Duft".

Aboudaram cooperated with the Italian authorities, and confirmed Pazienza's story, except that he spoke of meeting Pazienza in Geneva on 23 March, which would be a week too late for the date of the first payment. He might have been wrong, or the bank advice might have been backdated. A much more serious discrepancy, which Pazienza had to explain to the magistrates, was that far larger sums than those he mentioned had gone through accounts made available to him by Aboudaram. On 7 April 1981 United Trading paid $800,000 into an account at the Banque Bruxelles Lambert in Lausanne in the name of Realfin, another Aboudaram company. On 5 May $2 million from United Trading went into the same account. Of this, $600,000 also made its way to a Duft-denominated account, this time at the Handelsbank in Zürich, though not until 27 May. (Duft, of course, was not told of the true source of any of the money.)

So, within a few weeks of going to work for Calvi, Pazienza had received $4.3 million from him. Of this, $933,000 had been paid to Di Nunzio outside Italy. What happened to the rest? Pazienza explained – and it was confirmed by Aboudaram – that much of the money had been brought back into Italy by a Swiss specialist in "compensation deals". The equivalent of about $300,000 would have been paid in lire to Di Nunzio to make up his $1.2 million.

And the rest of the money? It was needed for expenditure, mainly on Calvi's behalf, Pazienza explained. He had warned that battles cost money.

The magistrates could not ask Di Nunzio for his version of these events, because he had died in 1982, of a heart attack, while on his way to a Swiss bank. Among the things they might have asked was why Ceruti had passed on to Di Nunzio some quarter of a million dollars out of the money he got from Gelli and a further $200,000 to the Duft account at the Handelsbank from the $3.5 million he got from Ortolani.

The magistrates did ask Pazienza why, if these were blackmail payments, Calvi did not get the incriminating papers in return. Pazienza explained that Calvi was protected against further demands because he, Pazienza, had made a tape recording of the meeting at which the deal had been done. What happened to the tape is not known.

I went to see Pazienza in the Metropolitan Correctional Centre in New York, before he was extradited to Italy in the summer of 1986. He had on the table in front of him a number of documents relating to the IOR and the Ambrosiano. These were part of the sample supposed to have been produced by the lawyer Duft in the early stages of the blackmail negotiations. They all seemed familiar to me, and Pazienza never has produced anything very startling from them. Vagnozzi, if he was collecting information about Marcinkus up to the summer of 1978, was probably concentrating on the IOR's links with Sindona – as, indeed, Pazienza said at the start of his interrogation. The back-to-back operations between Marcinkus and Calvi were not known then, and could scarcely have been pieced together from the documents available.

Pazienza's story is that, after coping with Di Nunzio, his next job for Calvi was to introduce him to the Casaroli faction in the Vatican. They met Monsignor Silvestrini, under-secretary to Casaroli. Calvi used the meeting to explain what a good thing it would be for him to own Rizzoli. Silvestrini replied only in general terms.

This appears to have happened in the week before Easter. And it was just before Easter that the Treasury Minister, Beniamino Andreatta, told Cardinal Casaroli of his concern about the relationship between the IOR and the Ambrosiano. Andreatta said he was afraid it was leading to something like the relationship between the IOR and Sindona. (Andreatta told the Milan magistrates about this conversation after the crash, on 19 November 1982.)

That week, Pazienza seems also to have been in contact with Marcinkus. Pazienza had a little company of his own in Rome, Ascofin. A list of telephone messages left at Pazienza's office was subsequently published by the

P2 commission. They showed that Marcinkus called Pazienza twice, on one occasion leaving the message that he wanted to talk to him "with some urgency".

Pazienza explained this to me by saying that as soon as he left SISMI it began to bug his phone, leaving fake messages. He gave similar explanations to the court in Bologna. He was asked why, if he had nothing to do with P2 and had never met Gelli, he had Gelli's ex-directory phone numbers in his notebook. "The result of the manipulations of SISMI," Pazienza replied.

Pazienza told the magistrates, too, that he never met or spoke to Gelli. The right-wing senator Tedeschi, the one who edited *Il Borghese*, had asked him to meet Gelli in the Grand Hotel in Rome, early in March 1981. But Pazienza replied that, if he were going to meet Gelli, it would be in his own office. That Tedeschi knew Gelli is certain; on Gelli's *tabella* (page 285) is a note of what appears to be a loan of 100 million lire to Tedeschi on 15 December 1980.

Pazienza said that Calvi, too, had asked him to join P2. If so it must have been very early in their acquaintance, because the raid on Gelli's premises made P2 an unsafe thing to join after 17 March 1981.

What does seem probable in Pazienza's story is that Calvi, obsessed with his acquisition of Rizzoli, could talk to Monsignor Silvestrini about nothing else. Beset as he was with blackmailers and with legal troubles, Calvi showed extraordinary determination to complete the Rizzoli deal. He spent Good Friday at his Alpine home in Drezzo, talking to Tassan Din. Angelo was banished to his nice new villa on Capri.

From Drezzo, Tassan Din rang Angelo and told him to be at the Hotel Excelsior in Naples on Easter Sunday, 19 April. Tassan Din then left for the Mediterranean resort Cecina, south of Livorno. From there he rang Zanfagna, the Rizzoli director and lawyer who was needed for the technical side of the agreement, though he did not know its full details. Zanfagna had just returned to Milan from a trip abroad, but Tassan Din told him to hire a plane at once to fly to an urgent meeting in Naples, picking him up at Pisa airport on the way.

At the Excelsior in Naples, Tassan Din presented Angelo with the new agreement, already typed. This was when Angelo discovered that La Centrale was buying the shares. The agreement contained little else that was new to him. He was to get 115.8 billion lire – the 35 billion he would need to reclaim his block of 2.4 million shares from the Credito Commerciale, plus the amount he would need to subscribe for the rights issue on the 1.2 million shares he would retain, plus expenses. Angelo's final 306,000 shares, which would constitute the crucial controlling block of 10.2 per cent, were, as previously agreed, to be handed over for nothing. To whom? That remained vague. He also had to sign some onerous personal undertakings, guaranteeing the financial state of the Rizzoli company.

Angelo accepted. He had little choice. There had been talks with other potential buyers, notably Bruno Visentini, president of the Republican party. But only Calvi had come up with the money.

According to Angelo, he was told in Naples that there would be no *premio* for anyone, because La Centrale was a public company and could not make "black" payments. Tassan Din and Zanfagna flew back to Milan the same day.

The following evening, 20 April, Tassan Din showed Zanfagna Calvi's written assent to the purchase. He had done rather more, that day, than get Calvi's signature. The mechanism had been set in motion for the payment of the *premio*. Whatever Angelo had been told, this remained the heart of the operation. The amount payable on the second stage, according to the *pattone*, was 180 billion lire. Of this, 35 billion lire each was to go to Ortolani, Gelli and Tassan Din, plus the 75 billion allotted to Calvi. But it was not all due from the moment that Angelo signed. Calvi should have paid out 84 billion lire, and the rest when the recapitalisation was complete. In fact he arranged for the payment of $95 million. At the exchange rate of about 1,100 lire to the dollar (as against 850 when the *pattone* was drawn up) this was equivalent to about 105 billion lire. This suggests that Calvi had decided – or been persuaded – to drop any idea of taking 75 billion in cash for himself, and to pay out the whole 35 billion apiece to the other three, without waiting for the recapitalisation.

The payment could not take place until the money from the National Westminster loan arrived at the end of the month. This must have dictated the timing of the deal. That same day, 20 April, the Cisalpine despatched a telex to Bankers Trust in New York, where it held an account, with instructions to pay $95 million to Rothschilds of Zürich on 30 April. The following day Rothschilds was advised to expect the money, which was to be credited to an account in the name of a Liberian corporation, Zirka.

On Wednesday 22 April Tassan Din publicly released the news that Angelo Rizzoli had sold 40 per cent to La Centrale. That was the first Michel Leemans had heard of it, though he was managing director of La Centrale. Astounded, he rang Calvi, who said: "Oh yes, I forgot to tell you. I was going to."

Tassan Din's statement declared that La Centrale, "in the context of a majority agreement" was willing "to collaborate even by means of placing these shares with Italian industrial and financial groups for the purpose of making a contribution to the maintenance of objective information in the democratic evolution of the country".

If that was meant as a guarantee of editorial freedom, it did not look a very convincing one. The public uproar, loud at first, got louder. The authorities had not yet released the list of 962 P2 members found among Gelli's papers. What was already known was that several charges were pending against Calvi, and that Zilletti was under investigation over the return of Calvi's passport. He resigned on 24 April. That same day Gelli's lawyers announced that he would be staying in Montevideo for his safety. And, still on 24 April, Calvi did something which was, for him, unheard of. He summoned a journalist to his office for an interview.

The journalist, Giampaolo Pansa of *La Repubblica*, rang the Ambrosiano for a statement about the new ownership of the *Corriere*, and got a secretary with what he described as "the gentle voice of an elderly governess" – presumably Graziella Corrocher. Then Pansa heard what he described as "a suffocated snarl". The snarl said: "I'm Calvi. What do you want?"

Pansa said he wanted to hear Calvi's point of view about the *Corriere*. Calvi continued to snarl. "You! And your paper! You've been attacking me for years . . ." Then the snarl calmed down and Calvi said: "Come and see me at half past four."

Scarcely believing his luck, Pansa went to the Ambrosiano and was ushered into a lift, which appeared to go only to the third floor. But, when a special key was turned, it went to the fourth floor, which had nothing on it but Calvi's huge, almost empty office "at once monastic and luxurious", Pansa reported. (The arrangement with the key, quite common in other countries, was regarded in Milan as intolerable ostentation.)

One wall of the office was glass, and gave on to a fantastic roof garden, full of rare plants, which Calvi enumerated for his visitor. Then, looking sidelong from eyes which, Pansa said, were "the colour of steel", Calvi declared that the acquisition of Rizzoli was "a completely normal operation". He went on: "There was this firm in difficulty, and we thought we'd give it a hand . . . You ask me why? Simple: to get it going well. If companies are going well, that's an advantage for everyone, isn't it?"

Pansa noticed that while Calvi talked he was grimacing, so continuously that it looked like a nervous tic. Talking faster, Calvi went on: "Look, we're not here for nothing. We're here to work. We've carried out a financial operation, and we hope to gain by it. As to that, we'll see . . ."

Pansa asked who would be Calvi's men on the new board of management. Calvi muttered: "My men? None of my men. Not for now, at least. Old balance sheet, old directors. It's up to them. First I want the auditing, then ... I don't put my own people on the board if I haven't found out how things stand."

Pansa thought he was lying, and wondered whether this was from necessity, or from a banker's habitual reticence. Calvi, as if reading his thoughts, snorted: "What ought I to do, in your opinion? You expect me to tell you my business? Would you trust a banker who talked and gabbled? As long as I'm sitting here, I'll respect the rules of the game."

Pansa asked what use a newspaper was to a bank. What use was the *Corriere* to Calvi?

Visibly controlling his irritation, Calvi said: "Use to me? I repeat, I've carried out a financial operation. Anyway, La Centrale did it, not the Banco Ambrosiano. Don't bring the bank into this; the bank's got nothing to do with it."

Pansa asked whether the operation had cost 200 billion lire. "I don't know," Calvi said. "We haven't reckoned it all up yet."

Pansa then asked him whether it was true that he was frightened and had bought a gun. "A gun?" exclaimed Calvi. "What gun? And why should I be frightened?"

And his legal troubles? Calvi, with a strained smile, said: "These are normal battles. For people in my position, it's to be expected. These things happen even in other countries. In fact, in other countries, they declare war on you for much less." He asked Pansa to get back to the subject of the *Corriere*. He was welcome to ask about that. But those questions Pansa did ask annoyed him. "I repeat to you once more – we have carried out a normal financial operation, which is usually called an investment."

Pansa needled him sufficiently, however, to provoke a diatribe against the newspapers. They attributed to him "facts which do not exist", Calvi said. He would like the *Corriere* to take a middle line, with no extremism. "It ought to be a paper that the workman or the clerk can open in the morning and understand at once how things are. Today, on the contrary, the papers don't make anybody understand anything."

Calvi suddenly seemed to grow tired, and dismissed Pansa, not before assuring him: "I'm a director here; not an owner. I've never possessed a share in my life. Even now, I don't own a single share." Illogically, he added: "Look at my desk! It's empty."

The desk was indeed clear, with not even an ashtray. Nobody was allowed to smoke in Calvi's presence. As he said goodbye to Pansa, Calvi muttered through clenched teeth: "Remember, we're not philanthropists."

None of this throws much light on what was really in Calvi's mind –

except, perhaps, the diatribe on newspapers. Did he see himself as issuing orders to editors? If so, he was very soon to be disillusioned.

By 29 April the National Westminster loan money had reached BA Holding, and the deal with Angelo could be completed. With Tassan Din, he went to Credito Commerciale in Milan, to redeem the certificates for the 2.4 million shares. Raffaello Bartolomasi, the man who looked after the IOR's business, was ready for them with the certificates under his arm. The 35 billion lire had already arrived from La Centrale.

Angelo and Tassan Din then took the certificates back to Zanfagna's office, where, on Calvi's instructions, they were to be destroyed, and new certificates issued. Zanfagna, another lawyer, and two Rizzoli accountants were there as witnesses. Before the old certificates were destroyed, they were held up to the light, so that those present could examine the various endorsements. On the backs, blacked out but still visible, were the stamps of Giammei, the IOR stockbroker, and the IOR itself.

The old certificates were then consigned to an undignified end. It was suggested that they should be burned. But there were eleven of them, made of rather heavy paper, and Zanfagna feared they might set his office on fire. So the other lawyer tore them into pieces and flushed them down the lavatory – which became blocked for two days.

That day Angelo signed two contract notes. The first was for the sale of 1.2 million Rizzoli shares to La Centrale for 115.8 billion lire. The other was for the transfer of his other 306,000 shares to Italtrust, a trustee company owned by La Centrale, technically for their nominal value but in reality for nothing. This 10.2 per cent block, allied to La Centrale's 40 per cent, would represent control. From Gelli's papers it seems that the intention was to divide it equally between Ortolani, Gelli, Tassan Din and the mysterious F. It was generally assumed that the fourth member of the syndicate was to be Calvi. But Gelli told me in 1989 that the fourth participant was to be Angelo Rizzoli. However, the *tabella* shows the fourth share being divided between Gelli and Ortolani. If the fourth share had been intended for Calvi, this could suggest that they had hoped to appropriate it after his death. But once the liquidators took over, Gelli and Ortolani had no hope of getting their hands on any part of the 10.2 per cent block, and there was a long dispute over it between Angelo Rizzoli and Tassan Din.

It was also on 29 April that the National Westminster loan money, which had just reached BA Holding, was transferred from there to the Cisalpine's account at Bankers Trust, together with another $20 million raised from general funds and loans from the Kredietbank. The following day, the $95 million was transferred to the Zirka account at Rothschilds. As far as the books were concerned, BA Holding lent the money to Andino, which then lent it to the secret company Erin. A few weeks later this was retrospectively cancelled, and the loan was deemed to have been made to Bellatrix instead.

On 30 April the Ambrosiano lent $80 million to the Cisalpine. Later the liquidators of BA Holding in Luxembourg and those of the Ambrosiano in Milan argued over whose money had been illicitly removed. The Ambrosiano loan to the Cisalpine was repaid the same day; it was mere overnight juggling with the books. The main source of the $95 million was, clearly, the loans from the National Westminster and Kredietbank.

On 4 May $60 million was paid out from the Zirka account. This was the share of the *premio* that went to Gelli and Ortolani – $30 million each. Gelli's *tabella* on page 285 suggests, however, that $9 million was deducted from each share. This must refer to $18 million of the $60 million paid at J. Henry Schroder in New York to an account in the name of Executive Consulting. Nobody has ever found out what that was for.

Gelli's remaining $21 million was first credited to an account at the Union Bank in Geneva, in the name of an Ortolani company, Ducador Inversiones – also confusingly labelled Mazut 66. From there Gelli transferred $7 million to his account 525 779 XS at the Union Bank in Geneva, and $11 million to his account at Bafisud.

Ortolani divided his $21 million in two, sending $5 million to a Ducador account at the Union Bank, which had taken over the Crizia 3 label, and the remaining $16 million to an account at the Crédit Suisse in Geneva in the name of Waston Trigas Teverest – not a company but a name disguising Ortolani's wife. This $16 million all went to New York: $6 million to the National Bank of North America, in the name of Belgrasp, and $10 million to Schroders, in the name of Vaducroi.

On 6 May in Milan there was a change in the arrangements for the 10.2 per cent of Rizzoli which formed the controlling block. The shares were still held in the name of Italtrust, but their ownership was vested in a specially formed investment company, Fincoriz, which was to be managed by Tassan Din. La Centrale was given the right of first refusal if the shares were sold, and Italtrust had a power of attorney for six months to handle the sale of the shares at the lira equivalent of not less than $100 each.

The same day, Tassan Din went to Zurich to meet Ortolani at Rothschilds. His $30 million of the Zirka money was transferred to a company named Telford, made available by Rothschilds. That was in Guernsey, but later the money made its way through Panama and New York. A lady friend of Tassan Din, Gabriella Curi, deposited it with Ansbacher in Dublin. Tassan Din had been denying he had this money, until, in 1983, the liquidators found it, and got the local courts to freeze it. Tassan Din then resorted to an ingenious explanation. Angelo Rizzoli, he claimed, had given him personally the 10.2 per cent of Rizzoli in gratitude for his services at Rizzoli. Calvi, however, had insisted that Tassan Din should resell the shares to him for $30 million, so that La Centrale could exercise full control.

Although there was evidence that La Centrale had been given the right to buy the shares, there was no evidence that it had actually done so. Moreover Angelo Rizzoli denied that he had given them to Tassan Din in the first place. Litigation continued in Dublin and in Milan. By the summer of 1989 the Dublin sum had reached $50 million. The liquidators then did a deal with Tassan Din; he was allowed to keep $7.5 million.

On 6 May 1981, the day Tassan Din moved his money, the government of Arnaldo Forlani appointed three senior judicial figures to inquire into P2. Everybody now knew that the government had Gelli's list of 962 names.

TWENTY-NINE

This Trial Is Called IOR

Now that reporters and magistrates alike wanted to question Gelli, he might have been been expected to stay in the safety of Montevideo. But he had business so urgent that he returned, not, indeed, to Italy, but to Switzerland. On 12 May Gelli met Ortolani and Angelo Rizzoli at the President Hotel in Geneva. What Angelo was there for is not clear. Ortolani and Gelli had made up their minds that he was not going to get any of the $5 million still in the Zirka account. They were keeping that for themselves. On 13 May it was paid to Ortolani's Ducador accounts, Crizia 3 and Mazut 66, at the Union Bank. Then $1.5 million was paid on to Gelli's account 525 779 XS.

It seems to have been at this point that Gelli discovered that the Union Bank had been obliged to disclose the numbers of his two accounts there. We have seen that the bank obligingly allowed him to close those two accounts and open a new one in his mother's maiden name, Gori. The new account had investment and safe-keeping sub-accounts, into which Gelli transferred his shares and his gold.

The same bank had been obliged to disclose the accounts of Ceruti, the Florentine restaurant-owner suspected of bribery. But he had taken the precaution of closing them in April, transferring much of his money to a new account opened by his Turkish wife, Nadia Kürkcü.

Gelli transferred nearly $17 million to his new account. Most of this represented earlier payments from Calvi, but more than $4.2 million had just come from his share of the *premio*. Another $4.3 million he had taken in cash or paid into a bank in Monaco.

Why Calvi had handed over $95 million, even earlier than Gelli and Ortolani envisaged when they drew up the *pattone*, and without deducting any of the money paid in 1980, remains a mystery. According to Angelo, Gelli once told him that, if Calvi did not do as he was told, Gelli would publicise his Swiss bank accounts. But Sindona had already done that, and Calvi had survived. As the Swiss would not cooperate with the Italians over currency offences, there would be no proof.

333

Much more serious, surely, was the possibility that Gelli would denounce Calvi as an embezzler. There the Swiss would cooperate. There Calvi's guilt would be patent, because he could not have saved millions of dollars out of his salary. It must have been for this reason that Gelli and Ortolani had compromised Calvi by insisting that he should take some of the money paid to them.

The Milan magistrates knew nothing of the millions Calvi had removed through the secret network and the IOR, but they had spotted the $56.6 million which La Centrale paid for the Toro insurance company. When Calvi made La Centrale buy the shares, on 20 November 1975, the market price was about 14,000 lire a share. Calvi made La Centrale pay 35,000 lire. This was fraud, since he owned the shares already. The difficulty was to prove that he did own them. The shares had been registered in the name of Manic, but the Italian authorities had never heard of Manic, though they did know the names of some nominee companies. They knew that the sale had been handled by the Gottardo, and the magistrate Mucci had asked the Swiss authorities to make the Gottardo disclose who the real seller was. But the Gottardo appealed against this to the court in Lugano, saying that the principal behind the selling company had "no legal link" with Calvi or La Centrale. They pleaded that the Italians were trying to get information for a currency case under cover of a fraud charge. The Lugano court had not come to a decision by the middle of May 1981.

The Gottardo was telling the truth, in its way. At the time of the Toro transaction, the IOR was financing Manic with the loan of $45 million, and the shares were in its name at the Kredietbank as security. In that sense, it owned Manic.

But it had never identified itself as the owner in writing. Early in 1975, when the Gottardo asked the IOR to ratify the conduct of the company, it did not reply. On 13 May 1975, in one of his "parallel" letters, Calvi had assured the IOR that it was acting for the Cisalpine as far as Manic was concerned. After that the Gottardo sent the next two balance sheets of Manic to the IOR "for your information". But it had ceased to do even that after the spring of 1977.

Suddenly, on 18 May 1981, a package reached the IOR from Luxembourg. It contained copies of documents about the statutory annual meeting of Manic, which had taken place on 28 April, and a copy of the 1980 balance sheet. There was a covering letter, dated 11 May, signed by two nominee directors, P. and E. Schmit. The latter was a manager at the Kredietbank. They wrote, in French, that they were sending the documents to the IOR "in your capacity as shareholder of our company". Three days later P. Schmit sent the IOR a second set of documents, with a covering letter clearly designed to correct an omission from the first. "We would be glad if you would return these documents signed to show your agreement." The second package reached the Vatican on 25 May.

If the IOR had signed the documents and returned them, it would have been admitting it owned Manic. That would have been of great help to Calvi. So was Calvi hoping that the IOR would for once (even if inadvertently) sign the documents and return them, giving him evidence he could produce in court?

The IOR, as so often before, sent no reply. But, if the IOR wanted nothing to do with Manic, why did it not send the papers back to Luxembourg, explaining that it had no shareholding in the company, and no interest in it, since the repayment of the $45 million loan?

Did anyone at the IOR read the 1980 balance sheet? It was more detailed than the bare minimum ones that the IOR had been sent in the mid-1970s. It showed that Manic owned shares valued at $102 million. Much the largest element was made up of 1,892,777 Banco Ambrosiano shares – 6.3 per cent of the bank's capital – worth just under $86 million at the current market price. It also showed that Manic had borrowed $33 million from Nordeurop (ie United Trading) and $22 million from the Andino. Thus, even if the IOR had had no previous inkling of what Calvi was doing, the sight of this balance sheet would have made it clear that he was recycling borrowed money into the bank's own shares. When the IOR produced these papers for the joint commission, it was providing evidence against its own contention that it knew nothing of the secret network companies before July 1981. But the three Vatican-appointed members of the joint commission were so anxious to support the IOR case that they failed to note the 1980 balance sheet of Manic, and wrote: ". . . only the balance sheets up to the financial year 1976 were sent to the IOR. Thereafter they were sent no further information."

The Milan magistrates thought La Centrale owned the nominee companies that appeared to have sold the shares. If the Toro deal were not outright robbery of La Centrale shareholders – and they could not prove this without the information from Switzerland – it must be an ingenious way to get money out of Italy. So, they thought, was the acquisition of the Varesino shares from Anna Bonomi.

On 20 May Calvi was arrested, and the charges against him were of illegal export of currency, stemming from these two deals. The charge relating to Toro was the more important, because it alleged that 23.6 billion lire had been spirited away into Switzerland. In the Varesino deal, the amount was only 2.2 billion lire.

Calvi was charged, not as chairman of the Ambrosiano, but as chairman of La Centrale. Also arrested were all the other directors of La Centrale at the time of the Toro and Varesino deals (including Prince Massimo Spada) and the former general manager. Carlo Bonomi (son of Anna) was arrested and imprisoned briefly. So was a co-director of the Bonomi family company Invest.

Because of the scandal about the return of his passport, there could be no leniency for Calvi. He was refused "provisional liberty" and sent to Lodi prison, outside Milan. Prince Massimo Spada escaped imprisonment because of his advanced age. Giuseppe Zanon, the original owner of Toro, also remained at liberty, by staying outside Italy.

Many people thought Calvi was finished. *La Repubblica*, which had been sitting on Pansa's interview for a month, published it the next day with a sarcastic conclusion: "What a pity that such a fine career should be cut short!"

Calvi's arrest coincided with a climactic row in Parliament over P2. Members demanded that the government should publish the P2 list. The government refused. But the chairman of the parliamentary commission on Sindona, De Martino, had obtained the names in the course of his inquiries. He released them to the press. The names appeared in the papers on 22 May.

The same day, a special general meeting of Rizzoli (which had no outside shareholders) approved its takeover by La Centrale. The staff of the *Corriere*, meeting that night, took a very different view. "We've got 40 per cent of our owners in prison, and the other 60 per cent in P2," one of them cried. In fact *all* their owners were in P2, except Angelo's little sister. But that Calvi, chairman of a Catholic bank, should be a Freemason, was so improbable that people could not take it in.

The journalists had just learned that, not only had their employer been saved from bankruptcy by a secret masonic lodge, but their editor, Franco Di Bella, belonged to it too. They had long been worried about some of the curious things they found in their own paper. There had been, for instance, on 5 October 1980, a completely uncritical interview with Gelli, who aired his neo-fascist views at length. It now turned out that the journalist who did the interview, Maurizio Costanzo, was a P2 member. The staff of the *Corriere* demanded that the editor should resign. He tried to tough it out, but soon he had to go. So did the Forlani government.

Meanwhile, Calvi was being interrogated in prison. The magistrates suggested to him that he must have had good relations with the directors of the Gottardo. Once he knew he was facing the serious charge of fraud, surely he could have asked the Gottardo, even if only in confidence, who the seller of the Toro shares was. Calvi replied: "The bank showed me the reply it had sent to the Swiss authorities – that is, that behind the operation was neither myself, nor La Centrale, nor linked organisations, but a foreign resident. Afterwards I received personally, from a Swiss judge, a notification of the said reply."

On 29 May, Calvi's trial opened with a preliminary hearing, at which the defence lawyers argued that the public prosecutor had acted improperly, and that the case should therefore be dismissed. This was rejected by the three judges. The trial was fixed for 10 June, and meanwhile Calvi had to stay in prison.

Also on 29 May, Alessandro Mennini went to the Gottardo. Was he asking whether the IOR could be named as the owner of Manic? It would seem so, since he next went to the Vatican, where he met his father Luigi Mennini, Marcinkus and de Strobel. Apparently Marcinkus told him that the IOR could not let itself be named.

Alessandro Mennini must have told Calvi this over the weekend. On Monday, 1 June, Calvi wrote to the Lugano tribunal, urging it to accept the Gottardo appeal for secrecy. He was being tried, he pointed out, for currency offences, not fraud. Clearly, if Marcinkus was not going to come forward and testify for him, he did not want the Gottardo to reveal any details about Manic.

Clara Calvi and her daughter Anna were lobbying for Calvi in Rome, with the help of Pazienza and Giuseppe Ciarrapico, a right-wing businessman who was a friend of Andreotti. The women succeeded in seeing Andreotti, who recommended a certain lawyer, and warned them that the Bank of Italy would want to put commissioners in to run the Ambrosiano. Andreotti suggested, as a possible friendly commissioner, Orazio Bagnasco. (He was known, for reasons which will appear, as "the door-to-door financier".)

When the women went to Lodi prison to see Calvi on Saturday 31 May, they found him weeping, scarcely able to look them in the face. He told them he no longer believed in politicians. They finally persuaded him to listen to Andreotti's message. He said that if commissioners came into the bank he was finished.

The following week, in Rome, the women succeeded in seeing Craxi. They flew back to Milan on Saturday 6 June. Alessandro Mennini met them with the Ambrosiano's armour-plated car, and they all drove to Lodi. Clara and Anna went in to see Calvi, while Mennini waited outside.

Calvi asked the women to go personally to plead with Marcinkus. They knew virtually nothing of the relationship between the Ambrosiano and the IOR, but they gathered that it was in the power of Marcinkus to come forward with evidence to help Calvi. Anna made a note headed: "This trial is called IOR." When they came out of the prison Alessandro Mennini tried to grab the note from her, saying that the name must never be mentioned "even in confession". Anna foiled him by sitting on the note. She and her mother drove to their country house in Drezzo.

To judge from Pazienza's rather disjointed account of these events, on that same Saturday he went to see Marcinkus on Calvi's behalf. It is hard to believe Pazienza when he claims that this was his second visit to Marcinkus within a month. A Turk shot and wounded the Pope in front of St Peter's on 13 May, and Pazienza, according to himself, was called in to give his advice on security. Marcinkus, who had been responsible for guarding popes amid crowds for nineteen years, does not seem likely to have asked Pazienza's advice. Perhaps he got it unasked.

Pazienza's efforts on Calvi's behalf sound more probable. On his own admission, he knew little about the Ambrosiano's dealings with the IOR, and when he saw Marcinkus he pretended to know more than he did. Marcinkus, he said, gave him a hard time. This is understandable if Pazienza's earlier story was true, and he had been employed to spy on Marcinkus by the faction hostile to him in the Vatican.

Nevertheless, Pazienza said, Marcinkus did say that someone – Pazienza thought he meant Luigi Mennini or de Strobel rather than Alessandro Mennini – had been to Lugano to see if there were papers there that could help Calvi. Pazienza was left with the impression that the IOR was going to help. In one account of the meeting, he said that Marcinkus told him to calm Calvi because "we are doing what we have to do". Pazienza claims to have sent Calvi a telegram saying: "Have visited Paul. He sends greetings. All well. Embraces."

On Sunday Calvi sent a message by the prison chaplain to his wife and daughter. They were not to try to see Marcinkus.

In Washington, however, Carlo Calvi had other ideas. On Sunday night he flew to Nassau, and the following day he opened the safes at the Roywest, using the combinations his father had given him for use in emergency. He spent two or three days hunting through the piles of paper for evidence of connections between the IOR and the Ambrosiano. To work out his father's cryptic notes would require a great deal more than two or three days. He found the letter Coopers and Lybrand had written about their problems with the IOR, and some papers about the back-to-backs.

Carlo then tried to ring Marcinkus, but could not get through. So he drove into Nassau and sent Marcinkus a telex asking him to ring. He was woken in the middle of the night by the phone.

Carlo, who was bleary with sleep, cannot recall much of what was said. But he remembers Marcinkus telling him not to worry, because a solution would be found. As we shall see, what Marcinkus seems to have had in mind was that he and his lieutenants would not make a public statement, or present themselves to be cross-examined in court, but that they would allow the Gottardo to try to persuade the court in Lugano to make an impressive declaration of Calvi's innocence.

A day or two later Pazienza turned up in Nassau. Clara Calvi had sent him to calm Carlo down. In Carlo's presence Pazienza phoned Marcinkus, who did not seem pleased. Carlo wanted to consult lawyers in the Bahamas, but his mother persuaded him to drop the idea.

Life was difficult, not only for the Calvi family, but for the leaderless executives of the Ambrosiano. The international banking community had at last got the message that something odd was going on there. Sources of credit began to dry up. A $25 million syndicated loan, led by Midland Bank International, was postponed and then cancelled.

The executives wondered about the $95 million loan, which at this point was moved from Erin to Bellatrix. What was that for? But their main concern was the IOR. Was it or was it not responsible for these secret debts?

Leoni, now general manager for overseas operations, was deeply worried. It is not clear how far Calvi confided in him. As a director of the Andino, he was naturally aware of the huge loans that bank had made to the secret network companies. He thought they could repay because they all came under the IOR umbrella. So he was unnerved when he got a phone call from the Gottardo, after Calvi's arrest. He was told that the "formalisms" between the IOR and these companies were inadequate. That is, there were no documents to pin responsibility for them onto the IOR. This news, Leoni testified later, was like "a bolt from the blue".

Botta, at the time of Calvi's arrest, was in the Bahamas, on a tour of the Ambrosiano offices there and in Latin America. Leoni rang him to ask if he could find any documentation in Nassau. All Botta could find were some letters from Manic, in which it took responsibility for the debts of its seven subsidiaries administered by the Cisalpine: Astolfine, Belrosa, Bellatrix,

Erin, Laramie, Starfield and Worldwide Trading. Botta took a copy of one of these back to Milan. But it was no consolation; it did not prove that the IOR stood behind the companies.

And there was trouble in Calvi's great haven, Peru. Alvarez Meneses Diaz, president of the Banco de la Nación when Calvi concluded such favourable deals in the second half of 1979, had been obliged to resign in the summer of 1980, after a change of government. He continued to work for the Ambrosiano as executive director of the Andino, and he was, briefly, a director of the Cisalpine. It was months before his successors at the Banco de la Nación unravelled the remarkable arrangements he had made with Calvi. But in the spring of 1981 they started to complain.

They did not so much mind the back-to-back deals, by which they passed on loans from the Ambrosiano's Italian banks to the Andino, concealing them from the Italian authorities. But they thought they were not getting enough of the "free" or "surplus" deposits, which they did not have to pass on. By May 1981 it was less than a tenth of the total, and the Peruvians thought it had been agreed at a third.

More serious was the sale of 4,963 BA Holding shares to the Banco de la Nación in 1979 at more than five times their market price – a total of $12.5 million. In April 1981 a parliamentary commission of inquiry was set up to examine the deal. The Banco de la Nación telexed Calvi, asking him to buy back the shares. Calvi had to appease the Peruvians by increasing their "surplus" deposits to some $50 million – though this kept them happy only for a couple of months – and agreeing to buy back the shares for $13 million, thus giving the Peruvians a satisfactory profit.

One of Botta's tasks on his South American tour was to carry out this deal. He was in Peru at the beginning of June, and telexed the Cisalpine to ask that a "clean" Panamanian company should be found to hold the shares.

Just at that time, however, the Peruvian press made the connection between their local Ambrosiano scandal and what was going on in Italy. Headlines appeared such as: "Italian Mafia linked with Peruvian high circles". On 9 June there was a meeting of the Andino board in Lugano, attended by Leoni, Botta and the third main executive in the Ambrosiano's foreign department, Carlo Costa. They clearly decided that they had to discover the true position. The general manager, Giorgio Nassano, was appointed to the board. So was a Luxembourg-based executive, Angelo de Bernardi, managing director of a BA Holding subsidiary, Ambrosiano Services. He was now asked to collate information about the group's

BANCO AMBROSIANO OVERSEAS LIMITED

MEMORANDUM

TO: Roberto Calvi   DATE: June 10,1981

FROM: Pierre W. Siegenthaler   NO.: PWS:72/81

SUBJECT: Ambrosiano Group Banco Comercial

Our affiliate Ambrosiano Group Banco Comercial has requested us to make a short term advance in their favor for an amount of $13,013,000.00 for a period of one month. We expect to receive full repayment together with interest on July 13th, 1981. A spread of 2% above Libor is suggested based on the current market rates.

Approved

---

overseas activities. Nassano and de Bernardi immediately set in train a review of Andino's activities, and called a halt to the making of new loans for the time being. Meneses Diaz resigned shortly afterwards.

The repurchase of the BA Holding shares from the Peruvians went ahead. The Banco Comercial of Nicaragua was resurrected to provide the money. It lent the $13 million to Promotions, which passed it on, interest free, to Transnational, which bought the shares. This was not quite the clean company Botta had asked for, since it had already been used to hide one of the Rizzoli International loans.

But where did the Banco Comercial get the money? Why, from the Cisalpine. Siegenthaler drew up the memorandum to Calvi reproduced above, dated 10 June, which constituted the formal record of the Banco Comercial's request for a loan. It was formally approved by Marcinkus – one of the very few Cisalpine documents on which his signature appeared. It is unlikely, however, that he signed it at the time. He may have approved the loan retrospectively at a board meeting on 27 October in Zürich, which Calvi could not attend because he had no passport.

That second week of June 1981, with Calvi's trial starting in earnest on 10 June, was traumatic for the Ambrosiano. Various documents dating from that week were later to come to light; they must have resulted from the meeting of Leoni, Botta and Costa in Lugano on 9 June.

First, a new balance sheet of Manic, dated 8 June, was drawn up in Luxembourg. There had been some juggling with the Andino loans that day, Manic having borrowed $95 million, of which it used $33 million to repay Nordeurop, while it lent $55 million to Belrosa to enable it to repay some of its $126 million. The effect was to increase Manic's total liabilities by $60 million, since the 1980 balance sheet sent to the IOR in May. But it represented no real change in the underlying debts of the secret network. Manic had, however, taken up a new issue of Ambrosiano shares, and now held 3,155,919.

Then a letter dated 10 June was written by Siegenthaler and Sue Anne Dunkley, secretary of the Cisalpine, to Manic. They asked Manic to "confirm your agreement with and acceptance of all actions taken by us" in respect of the seven Manic subsidiaries they managed. Attached were financial statements for five of them, with the same date. The Cisalpine executives wanted them signed and returned. The statements showed that these five companies – Belrosa, Bellatrix, Erin, Laramie and Worldwide Trading – owed a total of $351 million. The most heavily indebted was Bellatrix, whose two loans, with rolled-up interest, came to $144 million. There were no financial statements for Starfield, which was dormant, nor, oddly, for Astolfine. There was a note to show that Astolfine held 2,063,132 Ambrosiano shares in trust at the Roywest in Nassau, and a copy of the trust deed was attached. But no mention was made of Astolfine's liabilities, which totalled $62 million. Siegenthaler and Dunkley also wrote: "For the avoidance of any doubt we wish to state that in the case of necessity we will consider ourselves free and fully authorised to arrange for the disposal of any of the above companies' assets . . ."

Finally two letters dated 10 and 11 June were written by Nassano of the Andino and his assistant manager, Alcide Portocarrero, to Nordeurop. The first letter listed the 9 June total of term loans recorded in Andino's books as having been made to Nordeurop – that is, to United Trading, of whose existence the Peruvians were unaware. The second letter gave the total of call loans at the same date. The loans totalled almost $379 million – and this was without a 13 million Swiss franc loan which Nassano and Portocarrero appear to have overlooked. The loans had risen by $131 million in the previous year, largely in order to finance the huge sums United Trading had paid out to Ortolani accounts, the *Protezione* account, Pazienza and others.

All these papers were sent to the Gottardo. The executives in Milan did not want them to be where the Italian authorities might find them.

After hearings on 10 and 11 June, Calvi's trial broke until Monday 15 June. That Monday session was dramatic. The same day, the appeal court in Lugano produced its judgment on the Gottardo appeal. This was rushed to Milan by Alessandro Mennini, and produced at Calvi's trial.

The Lugano court agreed with the Gottardo that only currency offences were alleged at Calvi's trial, and that by Swiss law, therefore, the Gottardo need not hand over information. But, before reaching this conclusion, the court said that Gottardo had produced documents which proved that the seller of the Toro shares in 1975 "had and has absolutely nothing to do with Roberto Calvi or with the purchaser". The court added that "the principal, the counterparty of La Centrale, is a foreign company, neither Italian nor domiciled in Italy, in which neither Signor Calvi nor any other director of La Centrale holds any legal office", and that this principal "had acted *through other Luxembourg company*, which it wholly owned, and then through nominee companies belonging to the Banca del Gottardo". The italics are mine. This is a literal translation of the Italian phrase: "tramite altra società lussemburghese". This looks like a suggestion that the first company mentioned was also a Luxembourg one. But it might mean any other foreign company.

The Lugano court also declared: "The price paid for the purchase of the Toro shares was paid in favour of the Luxembourg company, in whose balance sheets it appears for 1975 and successive years."

Nobody knows what documents were shown to the Swiss court. By "the Luxembourg company" it could only have meant Manic. It was not, however, true that the proceeds of the Toro sale remained identifiable in Manic's balance sheet; they were quickly removed for other purposes. But who did it think owned Manic? It could hardly have been another Luxembourg company, as some may have believed because of the ambiguity of the wording, unless the court had been completely misled into thinking it was owned by the Kredietbank, because the shares were kept there. There were only two candidates for Manic's owner: United Trading and the IOR. Did the Gottardo tell the Swiss court that United Trading owned Manic? In that case, how could the court have accepted that Calvi had nothing to do with it, since all the directors of United Trading were directors of the Gottardo? Or did the Gottardo tell the court that the IOR owned it? It would have been curious to describe the IOR as a company. And what documents could have been produced, if the Gottardo officials themselves were unhappy at the lack of "formalisms"?

This tantalising half-disclosure looks like the solution Marcinkus had in mind, when he tried to reassure Carlo Calvi. Calvi's lawyer, amplifying the Swiss judgment, described the seller of the Toro shares as a "friend" of La Centrale, which, while independent, was bound by an agreement (unspecified) to sell the shares to La Centrale. Did not this imply that Calvi must have known the identity of the seller, when in the pre-trial interrogations he had clearly suggested he did not? And, if the "friend" was under an obligation to sell, how could the price have been freely negotiated, as Calvi had maintained?

One of Calvi's lawyers, Valerio Mazzola, was heard to exclaim during the trial: "How can you defend a client who has two brains?" Calvi became known as "the man with two brains" to the newspapers, and also to his business associates, who felt that it summed up their experience of him.

"Brain number one is good," said a stockbroker who knew Calvi well. "That's the brain which has built up Banco Ambrosiano into a big, solid, prosperous, well-run bank. Brain number two has no relation to the first. It's the brain of a man afraid to look in the mirror in case his reflection should learn his secrets. Brain number two thinks the world is run by conspiracies."

In Italy many things had been run by conspiracies, as the public was now aware. The P2 scandal had brought down the government, and on 28 June Giovanni Spadolini, of the Republican Party, became Prime Minister. The Christian democrats, who had dominated every government since 1945, now had to share power.

If the Bank of Italy, after the arrest of Baffi and Sarcinelli, had lost its nerve, it had now started to recover under its new governor, Carlo Ciampi. On 30 June 1981 it aimed a direct blow at the Ambrosiano, by spelling it out that banks must divest themselves of any interests, direct or indirect, in publishing companies. Moreover, they could not own overseas banks through holding companies. The days of BA Holding were numbered.

Calvi, still on trial, still in prison, went on believing in conspiracies. He could not consult his P2 conspirators. There was only Marcinkus, and the task of convincing Marcinkus he now had to leave to others.

THIRTY

What de Strobel Found in Lugano

It is hard to disentangle what Calvi's executives were doing to please Calvi from what they were doing to safeguard themselves. They were in fact going through a dress rehearsal for the eventual collapse. Some of them had a story ready by the time of the crash, and were willing enough to talk to the investigators. But everything they said was coloured by a wish to exculpate themselves. There are therefore some outright conflicts of evidence.

During June 1981 Leoni, Botta and their number three, Carlo Costa, decided to resign from the board of the Andino. The man from Luxembourg who had been trying to straighten things out, Angelo de Bernardi, took over Leoni's position as chairman. The influence of the Andino's general manager, Nassano, was strengthened when the bank's Peruvian lawyer, Jorge Carrera, joined the board.

Botta went to Lodi prison to tell Calvi of these changes. According to his later account, Calvi did not seem greatly concerned. But he wanted Leoni to go and see Marcinkus.

On 30 June Leoni visited Marcinkus with Carlo Olgiati, Ambrosiano general manager and deputy chairman. Luigi Mennini and de Strobel took it in turns to attend this meeting. Leoni's account is that he gave Marcinkus the facts, "like a pupil to his teacher". He said the Ambrosiano executives were worried by the debts of various companies to the Andino, and by the question of the formal relationship of the IOR to these companies. He asked that the IOR should at least start paying the interest on these loans. He did not, however, go into detail. Nor did Marcinkus ask for specific information; he merely said that the situation would have to be brought up to date and examined, after which they would decide what to do. Leoni said he did not yet have all the documentation to do that. Marcinkus then suggested that another meeting should take place, to study the relevant papers.

When Leoni returned to Milan he was, according to Botta, in no doubt that the IOR owned the companies with the debts. But did he also believe that their operations were carried on for its benefit?

345

Besides contradicting other witnesses, Leoni sometimes contradicted himself. At first he told investigators that only after the meeting with Marcinkus did he ask Botta to get Siegenthaler to organise the information about the companies managed in Nassau. But that information was all dated 10 June – 20 days before the meeting with Marcinkus. It was almost certainly provided as a result of the Andino board meeting the previous day. Later Leoni admitted that these papers had been sent to the Gottardo in an envelope marked for the attention of himself and Botta, and that he, Leoni, had gone to Lugano to open this envelope.

The Gottardo had yet to put together the information on the companies that it managed, as it believed, for the IOR. This task was completed by Friday 3 July. That morning de Strobel arrived in Milan by the night train from Rome. Leoni met him and drove him to the Gottardo in Lugano. There he introduced him to Garzoni and Bolgiani, whom he had not met before.

In the early hours of that morning, Calvi had made his extraordinary statement to the magistrates about the payment to the Socialist Party. But nobody knew that yet.

The clearest account of the meeting in Lugano was given by Bolgiani, in a letter to the joint commission, written in July 1983. He said all four men met in Garzoni's office, where de Strobel was shown a memorandum prepared by the Gottardo and dated 2 July.

This began by naming the companies "administered directly or indirectly on account of IOR". These were divided into two categories. The first listed eleven companies owned by United Trading. These were nominee companies, used by United Trading to conceal its identity. They included Nordeurop, the front for its loans from the Andino, Inparfin and Teclefin, through which it owned Suprafin in Milan, and Zwillfin and Chatoser through which it owned its stake in La Centrale.

Manic and Zitropo were listed separately, as being administered by the Kredietbank in Luxembourg.

There followed brief statements of the assets and liabilities of United Trading and its eleven nominee companies. It conveyed a strangely misleading picture. Ten of the nominee companies were shown, correctly, as having no debts, although the investments held in their names were listed as their assets. The only one stated to have debts was Nordeurop. Attached were the letters dated 10 and 11 June from the Andino, listing its loans to Nordeurop. These were in reality loans to United Trading; it is possible that the Gottardo executives did not know that. But how could they have then shown United Trading itself as having no debts? Apart from its borrowings through Nordeurop, it had $217 million of debts owed directly to the IOR, all of which had been processed through accounts at the Gottardo. (This $217 million was only $213 million at the time of the crash, not because any of it had been repaid but because the Swiss franc was stronger against the dollar.)

Also attached to this memorandum were the balance sheets of Zitropo and Manic at 31 December 1980. (The Manic one, as we have seen, had been twice sent to the IOR in May.) There was also the 8 June 1981 balance sheet for Manic.

According to Bolgiani, de Strobel examined these papers showing little surprise and making little comment, except an occasional remark such as: "Ah, yes, that I know." He might have said that when he saw the 1980 Manic balance sheet, or the Laramie statement showing that it owned the 2 million Vianini shares. He also mentioned that the debts of United Trading to the IOR were missing. They asked him what he meant, but he did not reply.

When interrogated in 1987 by the Italian magistrates, Bolgiani was asked why these debts had been omitted from the summary. He said he had always considered the payments by the IOR to United Trading as being "on capital account". Only after the crash, he said, did he realise what de Strobel was talking about. But he was a director of United Trading, and must surely have known that it had never issued more than 500 shares.

Bolgiani wrote that, at this first meeting, de Strobel was not shown the documents that Siegenthaler had sent from Nassau. He conjectured, however, that these had been discussed at a subsequent meeting between Leoni and de Strobel, at which he and Garzoni were not present.

Leoni, at first, gave quite a different account. He said he left de Strobel with Garzoni and Bolgiani, who already had the documents from Nassau, and that they went into a separate room. Leoni claimed he had not seen either the papers from Nassau or those prepared in Lugano. Later, when he admitted that he had gone to Lugano on purpose to open the package from Nassau, it became apparent that his earlier account was wrong. But he maintained that he had not seen the Lugano papers.

Bolgiani later admitted that he and Garzoni had seen the documents from Nassau. The Gottardo men had been alarmed by the revelations about the Manic subsidiaries, which, they said, had been operating without authorisation. They also claimed that they had known nothing, until then, of Nordeurop's debts to the Andino, since they had never drawn up any balance sheets for Nordeurop. They made up their minds that the Gottardo must withdraw from any involvement with the IOR companies, though they realised that it would have to be done gradually.

A secretary who accompanied Leoni, Elice Ghiggi, later gave evidence that she had seen Leoni and de Strobel working together in a room. Marcinkus, in his memorandum to the joint commission, implied that de Strobel was shown all the available papers.

De Strobel, it seems, did not take away any copies of documents from Lugano. With Leoni, he returned to Milan. By Leoni's account, he said little on the journey. He did remark that the position was not "so disastrous", in his view, but that he would have to discuss what he had seen at the IOR. At lunch at the Ambrosiano – where Olgiati joined them – he did not say much, but expressed sympathy for Calvi.

The memorandum of Marcinkus to the joint commission maintained that only after this visit of de Strobel's to Lugano did the IOR learn that Manic had seven subsidiaries managed by the Cisalpine. Yet he was a director of the Cisalpine. He also contended that only then did it learn of the existence of the debts of all the companies said to be "of pertinence" to the IOR.

On the evidence of the documents produced before the joint commission by the IOR itself, the position before 3 July 1981 was this:

The IOR had known of United Trading since at least early 1975, and of its debts, via the IOR, to the Cisalpine, the Banco Comercial and the Andino;

The IOR had known of and financed Zitropo since 1972, and Manic since 1973;

The IOR had known since May 1981 that Manic held a large block of Ambrosiano shares, financed in part by loans from the Andino and Nordeurop;

The IOR had known of the existence of Nordeurop since early 1978, because the name had appeared on the bank advices of a number of payments to the IOR, the most important of which were the two totalling $65 million which repaid the Zitropo and Manic loans in April 1979;

The IOR had entered into a contract to sell Vianini to Laramie in December 1980, though there is no evidence that it knew Laramie was owned by Manic;

The IOR knew of the existence of Astolfine and Belrosa, because of the attempts to place back-to-back loans of $52.75 million with these companies in 1978, though there is no evidence that it knew them to be subsidiaries of Manic;

The IOR had known of Suprafin since at least early 1975, and knew that it dealt in Ambrosiano shares, though there is no evidence that it knew Suprafin to be owned by United Trading.

All this contradicts the Vatican statement of November 1982, that an innocent IOR had suddenly discovered that it "juridically controlled", through no fault of its own, a chain of secret companies of whose existence it had had no previous inkling.

The facts listed above are those the IOR itself disclosed. If we also take into account the early dealings between the IOR and Radowal and its associates, it is impossible to avoid the conclusion that the IOR was aware, right from the start, of Calvi's secret network, even if it did not know all the companies' names. It also knew that an important function of the network was to hold and deal in Ambrosiano shares. It had itself bought a block of these shares, along with the nominee companies Ulricor and Rekofinanz, in 1975.

What Marcinkus almost certainly did not know was the size of the sums Calvi had handed out to Ortolani, Gelli and others.

How much did he know after de Strobel had returned from Lugano and reported to him? According to his own memorandum: "The complete extraneousness of the IOR to these companies and bodies was at the opportune moment confirmed the following Monday 6 July to Dr Bolgiani and Dr Leoni with the specification that the Institute could therefore give in their regard neither confirmation nor support."

This statement was put to Bolgiani by the joint commission and he replied: "I am not aware of any communication (by letter, telex or telephone) of 6 July; I never had any further communication with Dr de Strobel after his visit."

This conflict of evidence was ignored by the Vatican-appointed members of the joint commission. The members appointed by the Italian authorities accepted Bolgiani's version.

Leoni told his interrogators in 1985, more vaguely, that everything the IOR representatives had said on the matter was false. Whether or not he spoke to anyone from the IOR on 6 July, he decided to seek another meeting with Marcinkus on 9 July. This time he took not only Olgiati but Roberto Rosone, the general manager responsible for domestic affairs. As before, de Strobel and Mennini came and went during the meeting, which was brief.

Again, there is a conflict of evidence. According to the memorandum of Marcinkus, the three executives were told that, as far as the entities attributed to the IOR were concerned, the IOR "neither knew about them nor was their principal, and could not therefore assume ownership". The memorandum went on: "The general managers, having taken note of the situation, demonstrated the necessity of finding a formula to get out of the situation, relieving the IOR of all responsibility in their regard."

Rosone, on the contrary, said that he came away "confident", because of the importance of the debtor. Olgiati went so far as to say that Marcinkus had recognised responsibility for the debts. But both, on their own admission, knew virtually nothing of the facts.

Leoni, who was better informed, may have been listening more carefully to what Marcinkus said. By his account, Marcinkus used a curious phrase. He said he was willing to continue cooperating with the Ambrosiano, "with the necessary confidentiality, which, however, does not have to be concealment". Leoni understood Marcinkus to be saying that he believed in the relationship and its continuance, and this was a great relief to him.

Leoni also recalled an odd incident. Mennini tried to interrupt Marcinkus, starting to mention some letters from Nassau which were in the IOR's possession. Marcinkus brusquely told him to be quiet, and Mennini "withdrew into himself". Had Mennini been about to mention the parallel letters? In the one dated 13 May 1975 Calvi had written that the Cisalpine took full responsibility for Manic, and thus, by implication, for the subsidiaries whose debts were causing his executives such anguish. Both this letter and the one Calvi wrote on 26 July 1977, in which he took responsibility for United Trading, would have provided good evidence that the debts had nothing to do with the IOR. It looks as if Marcinkus did not want them mentioned, until he could have the matter out with Calvi. According to Leoni, his main message at the meeting was that he wished to leave matters until he could talk directly to Calvi.

Leoni has claimed not to know whether Calvi was aware that the three Ambrosiano managers were going to see Marcinkus on 9 July. But Carlo remembers that, about this time, he got a message from his father, asking him to ring Marcinkus and tell him that he would receive a visit from Ambrosiano officials that would please him. He also asked Carlo to ring Marcinkus again after the visit, to find out his reaction.

Why did Calvi think Marcinkus would be pleased by the visit of the three executives? Perhaps he thought Marcinkus would be convinced by it that not a soul in the Ambrosiano, apart from Calvi himself, had known what was really going on.

Not one of the people at the meeting seems to have heard that Calvi was in the prison hospital, having attempted suicide during the night.

It was not a serious attempt, the family later maintained. Clara Calvi said he had taken "some drugs" and made "a superficial cut" on the inside of one of his wrists. "The doctor told me that he was never in any danger of dying." But she said this after he had died, and the family wanted to prove it was murder. At the time the attempt looked real enough.

And, for once, we have the words of Calvi himself. The following year he gave an interview to *La Stampa*, in his lawyer's office, on condition that he should see the text before the interview was printed. When he disappeared, *La Stampa* felt itself released from this undertaking, and printed the interview on 15 June 1982.

The journalist Giuseppe Zaccaria asked Calvi: "In Lodi prison you attempted suicide: why?"

"From a sort of lucid desperation," Calvi said. "Because there was not a trace of justice in what was being done to me. And I'm not speaking of the trial."

The journalist led him on. "You, in short, continue to consider yourself persecuted. I ask you again: by whom? For what motives? For what specific sector of your activity?"

Calvi replied: "The motives – I think they're all in my work, and in the work of the Ambrosiano. The drop that made the vessel overflow, perhaps, was our intervention in the Rizzoli-*Corriere della Sera* group. And this is very worrying, because we guaranteed the survival of a great newspaper, without trying in the least to interfere with editorial policy . . ."

So Calvi said nothing about the attempt not being serious. He had tried to kill himself because other people were being so unreasonable. The journalist suggested that perhaps they didn't like his belonging to P2. The interview concluded with Calvi's ringing lie: "I have never been in P2."

There is a theory that most people who kill themselves are hoping to be rescued just in time, and get sympathy. If that was Calvi's aim on this occasion, it worked quite well. Bettino Craxi, leader of the Socialist Party, made a speech in Parliament asking why Calvi was being pursued so ruthlessly by the judiciary. Craxi did not then know that Calvi had been suggesting the Socialist Party got a secret subsidy from him through South America.

Calvi had an easier time after his attempted suicide, because he was now in the prison hospital. Carlo was able to ring him there, and report that Marcinkus had sounded reassured by the meeting with the Ambrosiano executives.

At the Gottardo, Garzoni, Bolgiani and another executive, Otto Husi, continued as directors of United Trading. Bolgiani said afterwards that he rang Marcinkus to ask who would now be giving them instructions, and was told that it would be Calvi, as in the past. But the Gottardo men took the first step to distance themselves from the situation. They got their sole nominee director of Nordeurop, Bruno Guggi, to resign, with the result that Nordeurop was soon forced into liquidation.

There was more trouble from Peru. Calvi's 1979 agreement with the Peruvians to develop a huge area of the Peruvian hinterland, Madre de Dios, at a cost of $10.5 million, had been suspended early in 1981. The Peruvian authorities had introduced new regulations to limit the amount of land that would be made available. Then, in May 1981, in spite of the scandal over the sale of BA Holding shares, it seemed possible to start on a more limited scale.

But now there were protests from environmentalists. One ecologist wrote to the Roywest in Nassau to complain. At the same time it was discovered that the private company which Calvi had created to run the scheme, Central American Services, had not repaid a loan of $1 million from the Cisalpine for a feasibility study. Carlo Calvi had to return to Nassau from Washington to deal with these problems. On 20 July he told the Roywest that Calvi was abandoning the project. As a result the $5 million capital of Central American Services remained safely in the Roywest. (Of this money, $3.7 million had come from Ortolani's Elia 7 account the previous September. That was, almost certainly, all Calvi got for himself out of the *premio*.) A few months later $1 million was used to repay the Cisalpine loan.

Considering Calvi's inability ever to admit that he had made a bad investment, it is most unlikely that he would have abandoned the project, if he had been in Nassau that day. But he was in Milan, hearing the verdict of the court.

The half-disclosure from Lugano had annoyed the judges. They ruled that the "unusual" statement of the Swiss court was of no use in the Italian proceedings. Perversely, perhaps, they went on to use it against Calvi. If, as the Lugano court had said, the proceeds of the Toro sale could be seen in the balance sheet of an unnamed Luxembourg company for 1975 and succeeding years, that was evidence that the money had stayed abroad.

Calvi was found guilty on both charges, sentenced to four years in prison and fined 16.5 billion lire, equivalent to nearly $14 million. Simultaneously, though, the court remitted two years of the prison term and 2 billion lire of the fine. He at once appealed and was released pending the appeal.

The verdicts on his co-defendants were odd. La Centrale's former general manager, and two of its directors (including, in his absence, Giuseppe Zanon) were found guilty, while the other directors and Carlo Bonomi and his colleague were acquitted.

Many people expected Calvi to get off on appeal. Some of those with most reason to hate him conceded that the evidence against him was purely circumstantial. The judges had been acting on the misapprehension that the sale of the Toro shares at more than double their price was designed to smuggle money out of the country, whereas it was in fact designed to enrich the secret network. Fraud was the proper charge against Calvi.

There was no suggestion at the trial that Calvi had drawn any personal benefit from the missing money. On the less important charge, relating to the Varesino shares, Calvi might have made things easier for himself if he had disclosed that Anli had paid 10,000 lire apiece for the shares, rather than the 8,100 that the documents before the court showed, so that the secret network's profit was only 600 million lire, not the 2.2 billion which appeared. Somebody else had pocketed the rest, and there is no reason to think it was Calvi. He could not have explained this, however, without explaining the workings of the secret network.

For the time being, he had been found guilty only of breaking the currency laws, which were universally hated and universally broken. The Bank of Italy suggested to him that, until his appeal was heard, he should step down from the chairmanship of the Ambrosiano. Calvi refused, and the Bank of Italy had no legal power to depose him. While he was in prison, Rosone had put forward a plan that he should be temporarily replaced by his predecessor Mozzana, who was now 78. The Bank of Italy had shown no enthusiasm for that idea; perhaps they had their suspicions of Mozzana. So, on 28 July, Calvi once more took his place at the head of the Ambrosiano board, which expressed its faith that his appeal would be upheld. He showed no resentment against Rosone – at least, not then. Rosone became general manager and deputy chairman, replacing Olgiati, who had had the sense to leave.

One person with misgivings was Graham Garner of Coopers and Lybrand. From Nassau, he got in touch with the Coopers and Lybrand man in Milan, and was assured that Calvi's conviction was considered to have political motives. The Milan firm had just been appointed auditors of La Centrale, and Garner accepted the firm's assurance that Calvi's conviction had not affected his or the group's reliability.

In early August, the Bank of Italy wrote personally to Calvi, demanding answers to a series of questions about the Ambrosiano and its foreign associates. This was closely followed by a ruling from the Treasury that the

Rizzoli capital issue could go ahead only on condition that the new shares issued to La Centrale carried no votes. The effect would be to leave Angelo Rizzoli in control of the company – not the result for which Calvi had paid Ortolani, Gelli and Tassan Din over $125 million.

Calvi's most pressing task, however, was to deal with his restless executives, particularly those from Lugano and Lima. Siegenthaler in Nassau avoided the issue by deciding to take a year's holiday. In early August Garzoni and Bolgiani came to Milan to tell Calvi of their decision to withdraw from the management of IOR-related business. Garzoni also said that he intended to resign from the boards of the Cisalpine and Ultrafin. Calvi was "in a state of low morale", Garzoni said later. Perhaps he had expected more loyalty from his Gottardo henchmen. He told them that the IOR situation would soon be tidied up. This did not change their minds, but they gave Calvi time to make other arrangements.

The Peruvians, Nassano and Carrera, presented a more serious problem. Their bank had the biggest exposure to the so-called IOR companies. Unlike the Swiss, they had not spent years working with Calvi. They had a simpler outlook. They wanted to know why, if the IOR stood behind the companies, it should not say so directly, in writing. On 3 and 4 August they had meetings with Calvi and the executives of the foreign division in Milan. Calvi seems to have explained, in general terms, that the loans had been made for the purchase of group company shares, to ensure control. But the Peruvians asked for precise details of the circumstances in which each loan had been sanctioned. The Peruvians and Angelo de Bernardi then retired to Luxembourg – where Calvi could not go, as his passport had not been restored to him. In Luxembourg they held a meeting of the Andino board, at which their demands were formally ratified.

This put Calvi on the spot. If he did not pacify the Peruvians, they might resign, leaving him with the task of finding more amenable directors. Or they might do something more drastic, such as declaring the recoverability of the loans to be in doubt. That would reveal the Andino to be insolvent.

What Calvi needed, not for the first time, was the cooperation of the IOR.

THIRTY-ONE

The Priests Are Going to Make Me Pay

There is nothing to show where, when or how Calvi got in touch with Marcinkus. The first date we have is 20 August 1981, a month after Calvi's release from prison. That was the day when Bolgiani of the Gottardo sent Marcinkus two complete sets of the papers de Strobel had been shown – the documents from Nassau, the summary prepared by the Gottardo and the list of loans to Nordeurop prepared by the Peruvians.

Why hadn't de Strobel simply taken photocopies on July 3, the day he was in Lugano, and brought all the papers back to the Vatican with him? Because his return journey was on Italian soil. Calvi was on trial; new charges were being prepared; Leoni's car might have been stopped and searched.

Such inconveniences were avoided on 20 August, by sending the papers via the Papal Nuncio in Berne, Monsignor Giordano, who forwarded them under diplomatic protection.

In a covering letter Bolgiani asked Marcinkus to sign one set of the documents and return them to indicate his acceptance, and also to sign an enclosed mandate authorising the sale of the Varesino shares, and part of the La Centrale holding. Marcinkus ignored the request. This enabled him to argue later that he took no responsibility for the figures.

In his letter to the joint commission, Bolgiani wrote that he had telephoned Marcinkus to get confirmation that he had received the package, and also to ask him who was going to give the Gottardo instructions, but on other occasions Bolgiani has said that his one and only phone conversation with Marcinkus took place earlier in the summer.

The package sent by way of the Papal Nuncio was produced by the IOR for the joint commission. To judge from a date written on the top document in what looks like Mennini's handwriting, it was received by the IOR on 25 August. At this time Calvi was on holiday. Pazienza had recommended the Costa Smeralda, the most fashionable part of Sardinia. Calvi stayed there in a villa lent him by Giuseppe Cabassi, a rich businessman with whom he had been negotiating secretly. Cabassi's interests ranged from the Rinascente store group to the Ausonia insurance company. Calvi hoped Cabassi might buy a block of shares in the Rizzoli group.

Calvi spent much of his holiday on the phone to Milan, where his executives were drafting the documents he wanted the IOR to sign. He had entrusted the task to Costa of the foreign department, de Bernardi from Luxembourg and a lawyer, Roberto Truffi.

When he was not on the phone, Calvi allowed Pazienza to introduce him to a set of exciting new friends. Pazienza brought his girl friend, Marina de Laurentis, to stay at the Cabassi villa. On holiday nearby was Maurizio Mazzotta, friend of Paul Getty's niece Claire Getty. Another holiday-maker was Pazienza's old acquaintance, and provider of Swiss bank accounts, Alain Aboudaram. Pazienza now introduced him to Calvi. Another friend who joined them was Alvaro Giardili, a builder, whose business card was later to be found on Calvi's body. He also had a business which dealt in small aircraft.

Pazienza also arranged for Calvi to meet a more recent acquaintance, a 49-year-old Sardinian property dealer, Flavio Carboni.

Pazienza had first met Carboni earlier that summer, in the office of a Rome police official, Francesco Pompo. Carboni said later that he distrusted Pazienza from an early stage. But, at the outset, they clearly found they had much in common, such as a taste for expensive cars and a talent for insinuating themselves into the confidence of the rich.

Carboni was no great property magnate. What his main business was remains, in spite of repeated interrogations, obscure. He operated a string of companies, several of them registered in Trieste, since that, for a time, gave him tax advantages. His right-hand man in managing these companies was Emilio Pellicani, of whom we shall hear more. Carboni used to borrow money at usurious rates from a Rome businessman, Domenico Balducci. (Someone, soon afterwards, found Balducci's rates too high; he was murdered in October 1981.) Although Carboni has maintained he never met Calvi before 1981, they had had common associates. One was Professor Ley-Ravello of Lausanne, the same man with whom Calvi had made property deals in the early 1970s. Calvi and Ley-Ravello parted in 1976, with Calvi claiming that Ley-Ravello owed him 4 billion lire. Ley-Ravello had helped Carboni to finance an agricultural property investment at Porto Rotondo, Sardinia. Another associate of Carboni was a Rome accountant to whom Calvi had paid a smallish sum, through United Trading, in 1978.

Carboni had a wife and two mistresses, a mature one in Rome and a very young one in Austria. The young one, Manuela Kleinszig, was on holiday with him, at a hotel in Porto Cervo, some twenty kilometres along the coast from Porto Rotondo.

Carboni was in the habit of arranging holidays for his friends, through a business associate, Ernesto Diotallevi, who owned several holiday apartments. Among the friends Carboni was expecting to see was the neo-fascist senator Giorgio Pisanò, and the Venezuelan ambassador to Italy, Nestor Coll. Also enjoying a holiday in Sardinia was a specialist car dealer from Rome, Fausto Annibaldi. Carboni was a good customer of his, and Pazienza had just bought an armoured Mercedes from him, using $45,000 of the money Calvi had paid into the Realfin account earlier in the summer.

Of all Carboni's acquaintances, the person who most interested Pazienza was a civil servant, Carlo Binetti. He was an assistant to the new Treasury Minister, Beniamino Andreatta.

Andreatta never has been primarily a politician. He was a professor of economics at Bologna university. His inclusion in the government was a tribute to his great talents, rather than to any political influence. He had chosen, as his right-hand man at the Treasury, Mario Sarcinelli. If Carboni and Pazienza thought Andreatta could be influenced through Binetti, they had a considerable obstacle to overcome. Whether they did think this, whether Binetti himself had any idea of what they thought, or was simply trying to enjoy a holiday, has been much investigated. Nobody has proved anything.

According to Pazienza, Carboni had expressed a desire to meet Calvi, and he thought there might be some reciprocal advantage, because of Carboni's acquaintance with Binetti. Carboni came over briefly one evening to the villa where Calvi was staying. Pazienza introduced them and arranged a further meeting, at which Binetti would be present. It was to be at sea, off the island of Budelli, in the La Maddalena archipelago off the north coast of Sardinia. Why at sea? Perhaps merely because Calvi liked to speed around in a new, powerful boat that Pazienza had just bought from Magnum Marine of Miami, at a cost of $360,000 – paid for, naturally, out of the money in the Realfin/Finanzco accounts.

Amid pleasure-loving people who were showing off their cars, boats and mistresses, Calvi seems to have become disoriented. "I must say I found this holiday, so different from usual, rather fun," Clara Calvi confessed afterwards. "Even Roberto laughed with us, and it seemed to me almost as if he was back at the university."

But she added that he had to interrupt his holiday to fly to Rome. She recalls this as happening frequently, but Pazienza has spoken of one particular trip. Calvi went to Rome in a Lear jet recently acquired through United Trading. To judge by the dates on the documents, this happened on Wednesday 26 August – the day after Marcinkus received the package from Lugano. Calvi flew back to Olbia, Sardinia, the same evening.

What happened that day can be reconstructed from the documents produced before the joint commission. Calvi wanted the IOR to sign the letters drafted in Milan, afterwards known as the letters of patronage. These were two brief letters in English, one addressed to the Andino in Peru, the other to the Banco Comercial in Nicaragua (where Leoni was still president, and Botta vice president, though they were shortly to be replaced by local nominees). The IOR was merely to confirm that it directly or indirectly controlled the following ten companies: Manic, Astolfine, Nordeurop, United Trading, Erin, Bellatrix, Belrosa, Starfield, Worldwide Trading and Laramie. It was also to say that it recognised their debts.

Attached to the letters was a schedule of the assets and liabilities of seven of the companies. For these seven, separate, brief, new financial statements were given. They conveyed a different picture from the documents Marcinkus had just received from the Gottardo. Manic's assets, composed principally of its 3,155,919 Ambrosiano shares, were now said to be worth $640 million, as compared with $182 million in the 8 June balance sheet. Nordeurop's debts of nearly $379 million were now said to be secured by assets worth $440 million – that is, by Astolfine's 2,063,132 Ambrosiano shares and the 4,933,194 La Centrale shares held in the names of Zwillfin and Chatoser.

Thus the companies' total assets were said to be worth $1.21 billion, against liabilities of just under $907 million plus 30 million Swiss francs, equivalent to a total of $922 million. But this total included Belrosa's $55 million loan from Manic. The total amount owed to the Andino and the Banco Comercial was thus $867 million. So it looked as if there was a substantial surplus.

A second look, and a few minutes with a calculator, would have revealed that Calvi had achieved this by returning to the world of fantasy and putting a value of some $200 each on the Ambrosiano shares. Furthermore, the IOR knew that United Trading, for which no financial statement was attached, had a further $217 million of liabilities – the back-to-back debts to the Cisalpine and Andino.

Did Calvi think such fantasies would woo Marcinkus into signing the letters of patronage? If he did, he was soon brought to earth by the conditions Marcinkus imposed.

358

To get the IOR signatures, Calvi himself had to draft and sign what became famous as the "letter of indemnity", dated 26 August 1981 (Appendix B(vii)). The letter is so damaging to the IOR, as proof that it conspired with Calvi to deceive third parties, that the joint commission was not allowed to take a photocopy. The IOR, however, did later let a copy out – possibly accidentally – to the Milan magistrates, but it remained unpublicised and its contents have never been fully revealed.

The letter, written by Calvi in his capacity as chairman of the Cisalpine, opened with the request that the IOR issue the letters of patronage "in the capacity of fiduciary" and the letters were then quoted. They did not say that the IOR recognised the debts. Instead, the formula used was: "We confirm our awareness of their indebtedness towards yourselves as of 10 June 1981 as per attached statements of accounts." To get even this, Calvi had to comply with six main conditions. The letter of indemnity stated them.

The first said that the Cisalpine indemnified the IOR against all damaging consequences that might arise from the issue of the letters of patronage. That is, it was saying that the letters of patronage were valueless.

The second said that the letters were to be used only within the banking organisation, and were not to be shown externally. (So the IOR knew that their purpose was to pacify the Ambrosiano executives.)

The third clause was that the companies were to undertake no further operations, except those designed to reduce or eliminate the debts they had at 10 June 1981.

It was the fourth clause that carried the sting for Calvi. It stipulated the "elimination" of the IOR's involvement in the companies and their operations by 30 June 1982. Could he ever have believed that he would meet this deadline?

The fifth clause extended this undertaking to four further companies: Suprafin, Inparfin, Zitropo and Intermax. The IOR was clearly concerned that it could be held responsible for the activities of these companies too. There were documents linking it with Suprafin, Zitropo and Intermax. Why Inparfin was named remains a mystery; it had been involved in early dealings in the shares of Sindona's Banca Unione, but Carboni has also said that the investment in "silos along the Mississippi" was made through this company.

The reason for the sixth clause is more difficult to understand. It said that the Cisalpine would assume the undertakings previously made in a number of the parallel letters. These letters were then listed.

There were the two letters written by Calvi as chairman of the

Ambrosiano on 26 July 1977, one of which asked the IOR to hold the capital of United Trading, while the other* was about the unidentified activities of Intermax.

There was the letter* of 9 November 1978, again written by Calvi as chairman of the Ambrosiano, which formalised the arrangements for the lira back-to-backs.

There was the letter of 24 November 1976, written by Calvi as chairman of the Cisalpine, which set out the main Cisalpine-IOR-United Trading back-to-back arrangement. (This entitled the IOR to "extinguish" the operations by giving 15 days' notice, as did the letter of 9 November 1978 in the case of the lira operations.)

There was the letter of 6 November 1978, also written by Calvi as chairman of the Cisalpine, in which the IOR's role in the financing of the capital of BA Holding was extended to the Banco Comercial, and the note at the bottom of that letter, dated 17 December 1979, extending it yet again to the Andino.

Finally, there was the letter* of 24 November 1976, in which Calvi confirmed the arrangements under which the Gottardo placed deposits with the IOR to be secretly passed on to the Cisalpine.

The odd thing about this list is what it left out. None of the letters about Zitropo or Manic were included; perhaps they were not considered relevant as the "contango" loans had been repaid. Then, although two of the letters about the IOR's role in the financing of BA Holding were listed, the two original ones were not.

Those were the letters of 13 July 1977, in which Calvi first asked the IOR to act as go-between in the financing of the capital increase of BA Holding, and the letter of 6 February 1978, in which he asked it to acquire a further block of shares. Also omitted was the letter of 24 October 1978, in which the main back-to-back arrangement was extended to the Banco Comercial.

Of those letters which were in the list, the most significant are those written by Calvi as chairman of the Ambrosiano. Their inclusion, taken in conjunction with the sixth clause of the letter of indemnity, meant that the Cisalpine, not the Ambrosiano, was being held responsible for United Trading, and, more oddly, for the lira back-to-backs.

Attached to the letter of indemnity was a schedule of the back-to-back loans outstanding on 30 June 1981. This showed that the IOR had

* These are the three letters the joint commission was not allowed to photocopy. It is hard to see why, as they were no more incriminating than the others.

borrowed $70 million and 38,720,000 Swiss francs from the Cisalpine, the latter being divided into three loans of 22,720,000, 10 million and 6 million Swiss francs. The IOR also owed $77 million and 101,245,000 Swiss francs to the Andino. Although in reality all of this money had effectively been passed on to United Trading, the Swiss franc loans originally made to the IOR to buy BA Holding shares were shown as being owed directly to the Cisalpine and the Andino. Why remains a mystery. (One hundred of the BA Holding Shares held by the IOR had been sold in late 1980 for $400,000. Curiously this money had been used to reduce the Swiss franc loan shown as owed to United Trading).

The Andino $77 million loan was due to expire on 27 August 1981 – the day after Calvi's meeting with Marcinkus. The 101,245,000 of Swiss franc loans were not due until 12 February 1982. The Cisalpine $70 million loan was due on 29 September 1981; the 22,720,000 Swiss franc loan on 12 February 1982; the 6 million Swiss franc loan not until 30 November 1982. The 10 million Swiss franc loan was due on 30 July 1981: it was renewed for six months. The subsequent renewals of these loans, as we shall see, show how determined Marcinkus was that his deadline should be met.

The schedule also showed the details of the reverse back-to-back operation, in which the IOR covered up the deposits of the Gottardo at the Cisalpine. That amounted to $6.8 million, 9 million Swiss francs and 11 million Deutschmarks.

These, then, were the terms Calvi had to accept before Marcinkus would agree to issue the letters of patronage. But why did Marcinkus do the deal at all?

His memorandum to the joint commission explained: "In the situation in which the IOR came to find itself as a shareholder directly or indirectly of all the investments through the holding companies UTC and Manic, but together with the extraneousness of all the operations carried out by these companies, as was recognised by the heads of the Ambrosiano, the Institute believed that the issue of the requested letters could, on the one hand, have effectively facilitated the elimination of the connections and, on the other, through the attachment to them of the statements of assets and liabilities as at 10.6.81, could have blocked all expansion of the indebtedness and thus third parties could not have been induced to provide further finance beyond that shown in the attached statements."

But the financial statements attached to the letters of patronage were not the same ones that de Strobel had seen in Lugano on 3 July, and had been sent to Marcinkus on 20 August. They were the new ones Calvi had provided, with fantasy valuations put on the Ambrosiano shares. As Marcinkus went on to point out in his memorandum, they showed a surplus of assets over liabilities. (The chart on page 363 shows the position of the secret network at this point.) Marcinkus must surely have known that this was due to the fantasy valuation, and that the secret network was in reality bankrupt. But a third party who did not know this might not have been discouraged from further lending.

And how could the letters of patronage have discouraged third parties from lending further money, if they were not to be shown outside the Ambrosiano group? In fact the IOR's action did not prevent Calvi from diverting money out of the Ambrosiano group. Even the debts of the ten companies named in the letters of patronage were to increase by over $170 million before the end of June 1982, because the IOR permitted further debts to be accumulated, representing the capitalization of interest.

What really happened on 26 August 1981? Marcinkus had every reason to reproach Calvi. If I am right in assuming that he knew nothing of the payments to Gelli and Ortolani, it would have been a shock to him to discover that the deficit of the secret network was so enormous that it could be covered only by the fantasy valuations. He was entitled to point out how easily the IOR could dissociate itself from the secret network. It could have given 15 days' notice to end the back-to-back arrangements; it is clear enough that this clause in the agreement entitled the IOR to override the maturity dates of the individual loans. Then it could have given back to Calvi the United Trading shares which it was holding as security. Calvi could have complied, if he had found another intermediary for the $217 million of back-to-back loans.

But there was no other possible intermediary; if he had shown some nominee company, or even United Trading itself, as the recipient of the loans, the balance sheets of the Cisalpine and the Andino would have been transformed, and it would have become obvious that these were not liquid assets. Coopers and Lybrand would have realised that the Cisalpine was bankrupt, and there would have been a new crisis with the Peruvian directors of Andino.

If Calvi was to repay the $217 million of back-to-back loans it had to be done with real money, not by further juggling with the books. Furthermore, that money could not come from any sales of the assets listed as held by the ten letters-of-patronage companies; the proceeds from the disposal of any of these would have to go first to the reduction of their $922 million of debts.

Marcinkus was obviously determined that the back-to-back arrangement

Table 3: The Secret Network at end June 1981

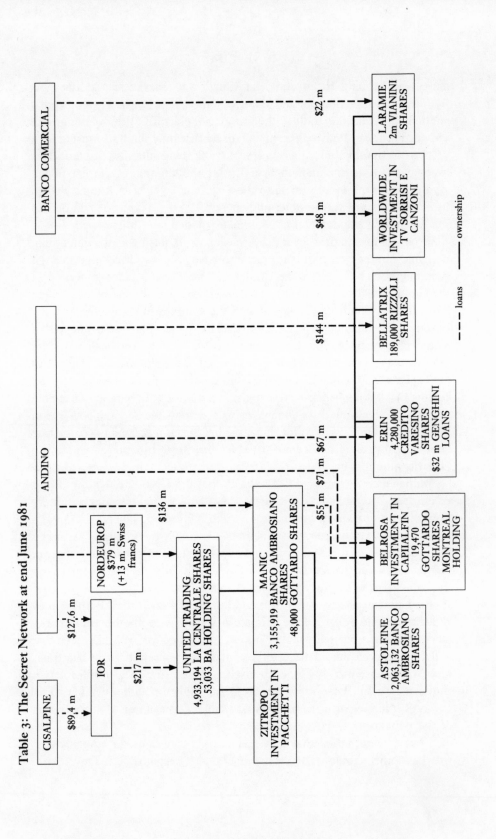

should be brought to an end. But Calvi's very weakness was his most powerful argument. He could point out that, if the arrangement ended suddenly, this would result in the immediate collapse of the whole group. He needed time to raise the money. During that time the IOR must at least pretend to stand behind the other debts. Otherwise the disquiet of Calvi's executives would threaten the survival of the group. Any threat to the Ambrosiano group was a threat to the $180 million or so that the IOR had invested in deposits, loan notes and shares. There was thus a great deal of self-interest in the decision of Marcinkus to give him time.

In the account of these events Marcinkus wrote for the joint commission, perhaps the strangest part is his claim to have only just discovered that the secret network belonged to the Cisalpine. "The circumstances emerging in the summer of 1981" in his words, showed him that the Cisalpine was the "holder of all interests connected with the complex of companies".

Clearly he did not want to admit that the whole purpose of the IOR's role, from the beginning, had been to enable Calvi to establish a parallel empire that did not, legally, belong to any part of the Ambrosiano group. But his explanation condemns his own conduct as a director of the Cisalpine.

If he had suddenly discovered, in the summer of 1981, that the Cisalpine owned a network of secret companies whose debts totalled almost a billion dollars, it would have been his duty as a director of that bank to ensure that this was properly disclosed to the other directors. Instead, as always, he kept his mouth shut.

And what had "emerged" to indicate that the Cisalpine was the owner of United Trading and its subsidiaries? Nothing in the documents that the Gottardo sent to Marcinkus made any such suggestion. The first document to say so was Calvi's letter of indemnity, in which the Cisalpine assumed the obligations of the Ambrosiano. The whole idea of placing the ultimate responsibility for the secret network on the Cisalpine seems to have arisen in the negotiations between Calvi and Marcinkus.

It is hard to see why either of them thought it a good idea. Perhaps they thought it would be safer if the ultimate guarantor were not the Ambrosiano, since that might bring the matter into the Italian courts. We have seen that Calvi considered the whole of official Italy to be prejudiced against him; and Marcinkus, with his long experience of refusing to give information requested by the Bank of Italy, knew exactly how the authorities felt about the IOR. Neither of them had any particular reason to distrust the courts of the Bahamas.

It must be supposed that they had the same reasons for agreeing that the Cisalpine should take over the ultimate responsibility for the lira back-to-backs, which Marcinkus did not mention at all in his memorandum. Theoretically the IOR could have withdrawn from these too, by giving 15 days' notice. In practice it could not be done, except (as with the dollar back-to-backs) by finding real money to enable it to repay its debts to the Ambrosiano's Italian banks.

At the end of August 1981 these debts stood at 122.4 billion lire. (About $100 million.) The IOR had at first retained the 35 billion lire that La Centrale had paid to its account at the Credito Commerciale for the Rizzoli shares in April, but on 31 August it repaid 32 billion lire of back-to-back debt: 12 billion each to the Ambrosiano and the Cattolica and 8 billion to the Varesino.

The 3 billion lire left in the pool was needed almost immediately for the payment Calvi made to Pazienza via the Swiss lawyer Gambazzi.

With the closing of the Rizzoli operation, there would have been only four remaining matching accounts in the IOR's books: the Setemer account 001 6 02505, the two CIM accounts 001 6 02535 and 02536 and the RED-B account 001 6 02559.

The total outstanding on these accounts would have been similar to the amount owed by the IOR to the Ambrosiano group. A large part of the debts represented rolled-up interest, and another substantial part lire that had been illicitly paid abroad, and debited mainly to the RED-B account. The investments held by the IOR as security would have fallen far short of covering the total. Since the CIM shares and debentures were worthless, the only security of any value held by the IOR was the block of 3,040,000 Setemer shares. The market price was then about 5,000 lire each, so the block was worth little more than 15 billion lire. Thus, even if the Setemer shares could be sold, over 107 billion lire (over $87 million) would have had to be found from other sources, if the lira back-to-backs were to be unwound.

Calvi's letter of indemnity did not, apparently, include the lira back-to-backs in the 30 June 1982 deadline. Marcinkus may have wanted them included. But here he had less to reproach Calvi with. He knew how most of the debts had been incurred, and why. Indeed, the CIM debts, which now probably stood at about 18 billion lire (about $15 million) had been accumulated for the benefit of the IOR. Calvi may even have argued that the IOR would have to find that money for itself. But that still left him with $82 million to find, on top of the $217 million he needed to repay the foreign currency back-to-backs.

So, to extricate the IOR fully, Calvi would need to raise nearly $300 million. With dollar interest rates at over 20 per cent, the total was increasing by some $5 million a month. And there was still the matter of the $867 million owed by the secret companies.

Calvi had only two possible ways to meet the deadline. One was to find someone to pay the fantasy $200 a share for the 10.4 per cent stake in the Ambrosiano, held by Astolfine and Manic. This would have brought in about a billion dollars, putting the total value of the Ambrosiano at four times the market value of Barclays Bank. The other way was to find the $300 million he needed to repay all the back-to-backs. Then he might have juggled the debts of the secret network for a little longer, because the letters of patronage themselves had no deadline written into them.

So the deadline of the letter of indemnity imposed a terrible burden on Calvi. When he returned to Sardinia that night he was devastated, according to Clara Calvi. She afterwards recounted that her husband said to her: "The priests are going to make me pay for having brought up the name of the IOR. In fact, they are already making me pay." He would say no more.

The night before his departure from Sardinia, however, he so far forgot his normal taciturnity as to entertain Carboni to dinner, and talk to him for half an hour about his troubles. Not that he mentioned his difficulties with Marcinkus. If the bank was to have a chance of survival, he must keep the IOR's deadline a secret. Whatever plans he was revolving in his mind to meet that deadline, it is hard to believe he did not know it was a death sentence for the bank – as it proved to be for himself as well.

THIRTY-TWO

Jogging Gelli's Memory

The draft letters of patronage that Calvi had included in the letter of indemnity had to be retyped on IOR-headed paper, and they were not stamped and signed by Mennini and de Strobel until 1 September 1981. They began as agreed with Calvi on 26 August: "This is to confirm that we directly or indirectly control the following entries . . ." (This last word was possibly meant to be "entities".) Because of the watered-down formula over the debts – the IOR confirming only its "awareness" of them – they were a long way from a binding commitment.

Mennini and de Strobel initialled each of the eight accompanying pages of financial statement, which could to be taken to indicate that they accepted the figures Calvi had provided, both for debts and assets, though the assets were based on his fantastic valuation of the Ambrosiano shares.

On the same day that he signed the letters of patronage, 1 September, Mennini phoned the IOR subsidiary in Lugano, the Banco di Roma per la Svizzera (Svirobank). He gave instructions for the transfer of two sums, $1,825,000 and $1,675,000, to account 304.026 at the Lugano office of Crédit Suisse.

This account was in the name of the Swiss lawyer Gambazzi, whom we have mentioned before, because he puzzled the Italian investigators so much by transferring the whole $3.5 million, the following day, to the Realfin account at the Banque Bruxelles Lambert in Lausanne. That is, it went to the benefit of Pazienza.

Even after the crash, the Italian magistrates discovered little about the lira back-to-back operations, and they concluded that the IOR must have known the money was for Pazienza. In the light of what we now know, it seems possible that Calvi did not tell Marcinkus the truth about that. However, he must have told him something, and made it sound convincing, to lure him in deeper just at the moment when he was trying to walk away. True, if the IOR charged its usual premium of about 5 per cent on the official exchange rate, its profit on the deal was about $160,000. Besides the 3 billion lire retained from the 35 billion Rizzoli payment, there were still plenty of lire left in the pool from the sale of XX Settembre the previous year.

Pazienza himself was later questioned about this money, all the more insistently because he had already admitted receiving $4.3 million from Calvi in the spring. At first he denied that the $3.5 million did come from Calvi. He said it was connected with transactions in gold, which he had acquired with money left him by Ghertsos, his former employer, who had died earlier in the year. It was pointed out to him that this could not be true, because the money came from the IOR. At this he gave up trying to account for it. Probably he had no idea that Calvi was putting the money through the IOR, any more than the IOR knew it was going to him. Only Calvi knew all the links in the chain.

Pazienza's influence over Calvi was at its height in the weeks following the Sardinian holiday. According to his account, Calvi gave him the task of finding a buyer for the Setemer and Vianini shares. Then Calvi began to discuss with him the question of selling the secret stake in the Ambrosiano. Calvi thought, or said he thought, that people should be willing to pay a billion dollars for 10 per cent of the bank, because it was a "controlling" stake.

Pazienza was also brought into the Rizzoli affair. After the government's decree that the new shares issued to La Centrale should carry no votes, Angelo Rizzoli wrote to Calvi to suggest they should discuss the situation. A meeting took place early in September, in an apartment Pazienza had recently acquired – no doubt with money from the Realfin and Finanzco accounts – in the Via del Governo Vecchio. This is the most beautiful and fascinating part of mediaeval Rome, and the most expensive to live in. Calvi had now seen for himself the car, the boat and the apartment on which Pazienza was spending Ambrosiano money. Instead of disapproving of this extravagance – completely unlike his own lifelong habits – he seems to have been fascinated by it.

According to Angelo, Calvi adopted a threatening tone to him at this meeting. He reminded Angelo of his heavy personal guarantees. Advantage had been taken of his arrest, Calvi said, to deprive him of the votes. He was determined to get some modification in the decree. Pazienza, he added, was to be a consultant to Angelo.

At this time events began to go Calvi's way. On 2 September the appeal court ruled that all the P2 investigations were to be handled by the magistrates of Rome. Calvi did not disguise his relief. He called Angelo to another meeting at Pazienza's apartment, and told him that he should contribute to a large payment that would now be made to deal with the consequences of the seizure of the P2 documents. He said much the same to Tassan Din in Milan. According to Tassan Din, Calvi spoke of raising $40, $50 or even $60 million to "influence" the investigations. He said he was going to approach Ortolani and Gelli as well.

Around 10 September Calvi had another, limited success. He seems to have threatened the Treasury that, if it did not modify its order depriving La Centrale of voting rights, he would withdraw all support for Rizzoli. The Treasury, legally, did not have a very strong case for what it had done. It reached a compromise with Calvi. The new shares could have votes, but these votes could not be used by La Centrale, because the shares would be deposited with the Bank of Italy until La Centrale could find a buyer for its whole stake in Rizzoli. This arrangement too was of doubtful legality, but everyone concerned was confronted with the absolute refusal of the journalists to work for P2.

The compromise, though not ideal for Calvi, at least meant that La Centrale would not be left with an almost valueless investment. In the financial statements attached to the letters of patronage, Bellatrix's assets, consisting of 189,000 Rizzoli shares, were valued at $2 million. Calvi had paid $46.5 million to get them.

On 14 September Pazienza met Angelo at a lawyer's office in Milan, to formalise his position as "consultant". According to Angelo, Pazienza handed him two envelopes. One contained the demand for the consultancy fee – 400 million lire a year, to be paid to Pazienza's company, Ascofin. The other contained a piece of paper on which were handwritten the words: "10 unités americaines (ten millions)" and then typed: "Realfin SA Banque Bruxelles Lambert Lausanne Switzerland".

Rizzoli was left in no doubt that he was expected to send $10 million to that bank for that account. This was where the worm turned. He sent the notes, and a report of the incident, to his lawyer. And he demanded to see Calvi.

The three of them met the following week, again in Pazienza's Rome apartment. According to Angelo, Calvi was extremely embarrassed, as well as confused and vague. He said that Pazienza's request referred to money "taken" by Ortolani and Gelli. It emerged that Calvi was talking about the money paid to Rothschilds in Zürich, in particular the $95 million he had transferred there at the beginning of May. Angelo, we now know, never had a cent of this money. So he may well have been telling the truth when he maintained that this was the first he had heard of it. But Calvi had already discussed the matter with Pazienza. According to Pazienza, Calvi had described this money as a "volano finanziario" – his own words, he said. A *volano* means a shuttlecock, or alternatively the flywheel or regulator of an engine. From this latter meaning, in financial terms it has come to mean a sum put aside for future use, and Pazienza understood Calvi to mean that this money was "a reserve" for "operations or black payments" – in short, for bribery. But Calvi told him, in extreme alarm, that this money had been "frustrated". Presumably this meant that he found he could not get at it. To judge from Pazienza's account, he appears to have believed – incorrectly – that the money was still in the Zürich bank. And yet he seems to have accused Ortolani and Gelli of cheating him out of it. Had he, then, believed that the *premio* was going to be set aside, not for the personal benefit of his P2 friends, but for objectives connected with Rizzoli?

At this point he had reason to be fed up with everyone connected with the Rizzoli transaction, Angelo included. The whole thing had gone wrong, and it would have been logical for Calvi to try to get back as much as possible.

If he said he wanted the money for bribery, that was surely only half the truth. He wanted to meet the IOR's deadline, which he could not mention to anyone. He was acutely conscious of the huge sums he had paid Ortolani and Gelli. He told Pazienza and Angelo that each of them must be worth $500 million. He was exaggerating, but he had paid them a gross total of some $250 million, nearly $200 million of it between August 1980 and May 1981.

We have seen that, on the evidence of Calvi's December 1980 balance sheet for United Trading, he regarded some part of this money as recoverable. This is all the documentary evidence we have. According to both Pazienza and Angelo, Calvi, though angry with Gelli and Ortolani, was still terrified of them, and wanted to avoid confronting them directly. But how did he know they had "made off" with the money? This can only mean that he had asked them for their help – and been refused.

It is useless to look to Ortolani and Gelli for the truth of the matter. Gelli, at the time of his arrest in Switzerland in September 1982, was confronted with the evidence that he had received $8.5 million from Calvi, and explained this as bona fide commissions. As for the rest of the $55 million frozen in his bank account then, he denied that it had come from Calvi. Ortolani took a different line; he has admitted that the money came from Calvi, but asserted that he deserved every penny, because of his brilliance as a financial mediator. But Ortolani, since his return to Italy in 1989, has refused to go into detail with journalists.

Gelli, on the other hand, has spoken freely since his return in 1988. But, as a source of information, he was worse than Sindona. In his very first interview, with Sandra Bonsanti of *La Repubblica*, he asserted that the money in his Swiss bank accounts was his own, and had not come from the Ambrosiano. "In fact, it was I who offered money to Calvi. When they asked me to place hundreds of millions of dollars, I said to Umberto: perhaps Calvi could use $200 million . . . But Calvi said no."

Gelli volunteered the same story to me, when I went to see him in October 1989. I asked when this offer had been made, and he replied that it was in 1980. I said I thought it curious that they should have made such an offer that year, as Calvi had little difficulty then in raising money on the international markets. Surely, I suggested, it would have been more appropriate for Gelli and Ortolani, as Calvi's old friends, to have offered him funds out of their own resources when he desperately needed it – that is, from the summer of 1981 onwards.

Gelli then changed his story. It was not his and Ortolani's personal funds that were on offer, but money from banks they represented. These banks would have been reluctant to lend money to Calvi after his trial. Besides, he, Gelli, represented a danger for Calvi, because he was a wanted man and could not be seen in any way to associate with him. And yet, by his own account, he had a phone conversation with Calvi at Christmas 1981.

Gelli has always maintained to official interrogators that the money he had did not come from Calvi. To me he simply denied that he owned account 593,607 ZC, opened at the Union Bank of Switzerland. In the face of the irrefutable evidence provided by the Swiss authorities, he denied the flow of funds from Calvi, via Ortolani, to this and subsequent accounts. He did not express himself to me quite so picturesquely as he did to Sandra Bonsanti: "I swear on my father and my mother . . ." Sitting in the Villa Wanda, looking the very picture of a contented elderly gentleman, he blandly denied the plainest evidence.

When I remarked that he had first met Calvi in 1975, he denied it. "No; it was 1976." I showed him a document (the one reproduced on page 148) in his own handwriting, published by the P2 Commission (but not understood by them) recording various deals with Calvi, all dated 1975. He looked at it without apparent emotion. Yet he put his finger on the most significant item, the commissions paid for the Mincomes permissions in October 1975, and read the name Cisalpine. "It means nothing to me," he said.

So there is not the slightest reason to believe his story that he and Ortolani offered Calvi $200 million, at a time when he was paying them huge sums. It is far more likely that, in the autumn of 1981, Calvi asked them for some of his money back, and they refused to give him any.

According to Pazienza, one of the tasks Calvi gave him was to retrieve the missing money. No doubt he went for Angelo first, as being apparently the easiest target. He tried to talk to Tassan Din about it, but Tassan Din avoided him. (Later, Tassan Din went on steadfastly denying to the liquidators that he had taken $30 million of the *premio* – until the liquidators traced the money to Dublin.)

Calvi's secret network, though still hidden from the authorities and from the international banks which had lent to him, was now no secret to his executives. He had to cope with the Gottardo men, Garzoni and Bolgiani, who wanted to distance themselves from anything connected with the secret network. Since they had taken their director off the board of Nordeurop, Calvi had been obliged by Liechtenstein law to wind it up. It appeared to be burdened with huge debts. In reality it was a front for United Trading. Calvi could simply have revealed this, and inserted the name of United Trading in the books of the Andino as the real borrower. But this would have shown his executives the true horror of the United Trading debts. Instead, he transferred Nordeurop's loans from the Andino to Astolfine. (The total was now $406 million, because some had been renewed with capitalised interest.) Astolfine was chosen because it had no direct debts of its own, but had apparently substantial assets, in the form of the Banco Ambrosiano shares held in the trust at Roywest. Pazienza has said that Calvi spoke of these shares as if they were his personal property. This may well have been his original intention; why else had he created the trust at the end of 1980? But he needed now to show them as belonging to the secret network, so as to create a semblance of solvency.

Because of the Gottardo men's attitude, Calvi decided that the management of all the companies would be handled in Luxembourg by Ambrosiano Services – that is, by de Bernardi. This involved him in further correspondence with the IOR. On 8 October Calvi wrote to the IOR, as chairman of the Cisalpine. This was another parallel letter which the joint commission was not allowed to photocopy. He confirmed the obligations of the letter of indemnity, written on 26 August. Presumably he wrote this letter in the IOR office; he asked the IOR to send a letter of the same date, 8 October, to Ambrosiano Services.

That letter, which the IOR duly despatched, was written in English. So were the letters of patronage, which were enclosed with this new letter. The letter authorised Ambrosiano Services to manage the "entities" named in the letters of patronage, specifying, among other things, that Ambrosiano Services was "to cause the sale of such assets and rights incidental thereto in whole or in part at such times to such nominal amounts and at such prices as you in your absolute discretion consider advantageous *in our interests* (my italics), it being understood that the net proceeds of any such sale as well as any monies arising from such assets shall have to be credited to the account of Starfield . . ." which was then to apply any such monies "towards the payment of interest and charges and towards repayment of principal" of the debts listed in financial statements accompanying the letters of patronage.

Ambrosiano Services was then instructed to account to the IOR on a six-monthly calendar basis, beginning with 31 December. The letter ended by instructing Ambrosiano Services to manage similarly a further list of companies, all of which were United Trading's nominee companies, with one exception. The list included Zitropo, which was thus, although not mentioned in the letters of patronage, effectively brought within their ambit.

It is possible that only when this package was received in Luxembourg did the Ambrosiano group executives see the letters of patronage for the first time. Not everyone was reassured. Nassano, wrestling with the problems of the Andino, pointed out that the wording did not demonstrate clearly that the IOR took responsibility for the debts. Calvi had to go back to Marcinkus, writing another letter as chairman of the Cisalpine on 15 October. This one, too, the joint commission was not allowed to photocopy.

In this letter, Calvi once more confirmed the obligations of the letter of indemnity. He then asked the IOR to comply with the requests contained in an enclosed letter (which, oddly, was dated 16 October) from de Bernardi of Ambrosiano Services.

De Bernardi first confirmed that Ambrosiano Services agreed with the IOR's letter of 8 October. Then he asked the IOR to do a number of things. First, it was to send a letter (a draft of which was attached) to Kredietbank in Luxembourg, informing it that it could accept instructions relating to Manic from Ambrosiano Services.

Then de Bernardi informed the IOR: "More recent statements than those attached to your letters of September 1 have to be supplied to our company, according to the enclosed drafts identified as annex b) and annex c)."

These were new financial statements, dated 10 September. The only change of any significance was that Nordeurop no longer featured, its huge debts to the Andino having been transferred to Astolfine. (The list of these debts overstated the total by $17 million, someone having inserted a 30 instead of a 13, but no one seemed to notice.) The important change was in the covering letters to the Andino and Banco Comercial which the

IOR was asked to sign. These read: "We refer to our letter dated September 1st 1981, and enclose herewith additional statements as of September 10th 1981, to update your records. We also confirm that we shall not dispose of our controlling interest in any of the above mentioned entities without your prior written approval."

De Bernardi's letter then continued: "Should you wish that any of the entities to be serviced by us assume any new indebtedness for principal amounts to be borrowed (interest accrued from time to time on existing indebtedness and remained unpaid being excluded) and/or to apply funds available to any such entity otherwise than for the purpose detailed in your above letter dated October 8, 1981, written instructions shall have to be given by you – or if more convenient for you by an attorney-in-fact duly appointed by you – to us, it being understood that you stand surety of our company in respect of the transactions to be so consummated."

This was a significant modification of what Marcinkus afterwards claimed as the merits of his August agreement with Calvi. It envisaged that the secret network companies might further increase their debts. The phrase in brackets implied that the debts would increase in any case, because of the continued capitalisation of interest. It also suggested that money raised from the sale of assets might not be used to reduce the debts.

Far from objecting, the IOR did all that was asked of it. On 26 October Mennini and de Strobel signed the letter to the Kredietbank, and the two new letters of patronage to the Banco Comercial and the Andino. This time Nassano was reasonably satisfied, though still unhappy that the IOR was not paying interest on the loans. The letters were also shown to Sue Anne Dunkley, secretary of the Cisalpine and a director of Astolfine. She had objected to the transfer of the debts from Nordeurop to Astolfine. She, too, was now placated.

Finally, in response to the specific requests in de Bernardi's letter, Mennini and de Strobel signed, also on 26 October, two notes at the foot of the letter:

"(a) with regard to 'surety' referred to on page 2, it will be guaranteed as in the past:

"(b) with regard to the 'attorney in fact', referred to on page 2, we advise you that Mr Roberto Calvi will act as 'attorney in fact' to all relevant purposes."

So the IOR formally empowered Calvi to act on its behalf, even to the extent of increasing the debts of the letters-of-patronage companies, and using the money for whatever purposes he saw fit.

In practice, though, it had become impossible for Calvi to use United

Trading or any of the other companies for illicit payments. Too many people were now watching their activities, quite apart from Marcinkus.

At the end of September Marcinkus was burdened with another major Vatican post. He was appointed to succeed Cardinal Guerri as pro-president of the pontifical commission for the State of the Vatican City. The job brought with it the title of archbishop, and the use of an apartment within the Vatican. However, Marcinkus continued as head of the IOR – and as a director of the Cisalpine, attending his nineteenth board meeting on 27 October 1981 in Zürich.

Only one other director attended – Calvi's brother officer from the cavalry, Count Luciano della Porta. Calvi could not come, as he had no passport. The other directors – Garzoni of the Gottardo, Antonio Tonello and the disgraced Meneses Diaz – had resigned or were about to do so.

The bank's management was well represented. Siegenthaler had interrupted his sabbatical year to attend. With him were Sue Anne Dunkley and the vice president, Calvin Knowles.

Marcinkus dominated the meeting, asking detailed questions of a type he had never asked before. He wanted to know about the loan to North Sound, the company which had acquired the block of shares in Pesenti's Italmobiliare; he asked whether the deposits were coming in from South America, and how the bank's new building in Nassau was progressing. On the recommendation of Coopers and Lybrand, he and della Porta decided to foreclose on the mortgages securing the loan to the Casino Ruhl in Nice, which had long been in default. They also decided that the Cisalpine should get rid of its stake in Ortolani's bank, Bafisud.

The directors also approved a long list of loans, which probably explains why the signature of Marcinkus appeared on the 10 June loan made to enable Calvi to repurchase the BA Holding shares from the Banco de la Nación. But two loans troubled Marcinkus and della Porta. One was the loan to Ortolani's company, Sudam. Of the original $21 million, $15 million was still outstanding and in default. Marcinkus wanted to know who had authorised it, and was told it was Calvi, although there was nothing in writing to this effect. The second was a total of almost $320 million in loans to the Andino. Again, the directors were told that this had been authorised by Calvi. Marcinkus and della Porta insisted that Calvi be telephoned then and there, and the conversation minuted. "We have spoken with Mr Calvi who confirms that he authorised and accepts full responsibility for both the loans. He further gives his full assurance that both positions will be settled before the fiscal year-end 1981."

This new, questioning attitude of Marcinkus is understandable, if he had only recently learned how big the secret network's deficit was. But the attendant Cisalpine executives might have wondered why he was so much concerned at the financing of the Andino. From the financial statements which accompanied the letters of patronage, it was obvious that the money was being passed on to Astolfine and the other secret network companies. Hadn't the IOR itself just guaranteed that these loans would be repaid? The executives would have been staggered if Marcinkus had announced what he afterwards told the joint commission – that he had just discovered all these companies to be owned by the Cisalpine.

Marcinkus did not say this, possibly because it was not true. He could have said a number of other things which would have been true, and of great interest to the other people present. The board meeting ended with a discussion: should the Cisalpine help the Andino by acquiring some of its Ambrosiano group investments? The suggested shares were those of La Centrale and Varesino, and a figure of $40 million was suggested. Marcinkus expressed a preference for Varesino shares, and argued that the $40 million figure was too high. What he did not say was that such internal deals would solve nothing; only genuine sales to independent parties would reduce the total debt.

Because the Gottardo men had not mentioned United Trading's $217 million back-to-back loans, there was nothing in the documents the executives had seen to arouse their suspicions that the IOR's debts to the Cisalpine were not the sound interbank deposits they seemed. Marcinkus could have told them. Instead, for the nineteenth time, he held his tongue.

THIRTY-THREE

One of those Two Is Making a Serious Mistake

Pazienza, by his own account, succeeded in finding an outside buyer in America for the construction company Vianini. How serious the buyer was cannot now be established. Calvi had stipulated a price of $100 million for the six million shares, or 73 per cent of the company, that Laramie had undertaken to buy from the IOR for $60 million less than a year before. Laramie had paid $20 million to the IOR in December 1980 for the first two million shares, having borrowed the money from Banco Comercial. It was scheduled to pay two further instalments in December 1981 and 1982. A quick resale at $100 million would be most useful to Calvi. But, as the IOR still held all six million shares, no deal could go ahead without its cooperation.

According to Pazienza, he went with Calvi to see Marcinkus about this, probably in early November 1981. It was the only time he saw Calvi and Marcinkus together. After initial greetings, the three sat in silence for three or four minutes. Then Pazienza spoke up: "Excuse me, Excellency; excuse me, Roberto, we have not come here for spiritual contemplation but to talk about the transfer of the block of Vianini shares."

At this Marcinkus said: "Vianini – what's that got to do with it?"

Pazienza, looking at Calvi, said: "Excellency, I believe you have been informed of the fact that we are here for the transfer of the IOR's Vianini shares to an American entity."

Marcinkus replied: "Never heard of this matter."

Pazienza, dumbfounded, turned to Calvi. Calvi said: "But, Excellency, don't you want to sell Vianini?"

Marcinkus replied: "If they pay well, I might think about it." At that Calvi began to stammer, and Pazienza bowed out. That, he said, was the end of the Vianini deal.

In his memorandum to the joint commission, Marcinkus made no mention of any proposal to sell Vianini to a third party. His concern was to justify his behaviour after Laramie failed to pay the second instalment, due in December 1981. (It could not have done so without borrowing the

377

money, and to burden the secret network with another $20 million of debt would have been contrary to the spirit of the agreement reached between Calvi and Marcinkus in August.)

The contract for the Vianini sale stipulated that, even if Laramie did not pay the full $60 million, it should nevertheless have delivered to it those shares it had paid for. Yet Marcinkus held on to all the shares, and the initial $20 million as well. In his memorandum he wrote that he did this because of the damage the IOR had suffered from the non-completion of the contract by Laramie.

Yet the obvious thing to do was simply to return the $20 million to Laramie. Why did he not do this? Possibly because he now foresaw that the Ambrosiano might crash. Still, he should have realised that $20 million, illegally detained, was not going to be particularly useful to him. Indeed, it proved useful only to the Ambrosiano creditors, since it gave them a basis for legal action, and therefore a means of putting pressure on the Vatican.

But there is another possibility. This I heard from the lips of Sindona, who told me that Calvi had paid the IOR $20 million for issuing the letters of patronage. I suggested to Sindona that he was talking about the Laramie $20 million, but he insisted that this was not so. He repeated his story to the Italian investigators after his extradition.

No other evidence of a $20 million payment to the IOR at this time has emerged, so the Vianini money may well have been intended as a fee for the letters of patronage. Calvi's own remarks, tape-recorded without his knowledge by Carboni, tend to support this. Discussing Marcinkus, Calvi said that there would be "enormous danger" if it were found that $20 million at a bank in New York had ended up "in a certain place". He added: "It would make the world explode."

Some people have concluded that Calvi was talking about $20 million paid to the Polish trade union Solidarity. It is true that Calvi had also mentioned Solidarity in his tape-recorded remarks, but he had not specified a sum. It is more likely that his remark about the $20 million referred to the Laramie money, and that he meant to accuse Marcinkus of making off with it.

Throughout the autumn of 1981 Calvi's morale was low. His appeal against the currency conviction had been set for the following spring. Although the P2 investigations had been successfully shifted to Rome, where he wanted them, and the fraud investigation on the Toro deal had run into the sands of the Lugano court, the inquiries into the Pacchetti/Zitropo/Varesino deals of 1972 were proceeding apace. He might soon be in prison again.

According to Pazienza, Calvi instructed him to prepare an elaborate escape plan. It was called "Operation Cigueña" – the Spanish word for a stork. (Why Spanish? Pazienza liked to show off as a linguist.) Pazienza's Magnum Marine motor boat had been berthed at Rapallo, between Genoa and La Spezia. Calvi was to board it in the middle of the night and be driven by a champion power-boat driver, who had been retained, in an hour and a half to Corsica, which is French territory. On the small island of Cavallo, off the southern tip of Corsica, a team of journalists and photographers accredited to a South American magazine would have been assembled. To distract attention from Calvi, they would take pictures of a Calvi lookalike, specially prepared by a make-up artist from Hollywood. Calvi himself, meanwhile, would board a Cessna plane and be flown to a military airfield in Morocco, which Pazienza could arrange because he knew the then head of the Moroccan general staff. From Morocco Calvi would be flown in a military aircraft with supplementary fuel tanks directly to Panama, where Pazienza would join him. They could stay there or go to some other Latin American country.

This is a typical Pazienza story, in its precision over some details, such as the extra fuel tanks, and its dreamlike vagueness over others. (How was the Calvi lookalike to get there? In the same motor-boat? Was the make-up artist to be on the boat as well? Why should he or she come from Hollywood? Wouldn't a stage make-up artist be better?)

The story is worth mentioning because it shows that the people around Calvi went along with his fantasy that escape from Italy would be immensely difficult and complicated, costing millions of dollars. Yet we have seen how easily Gelli slipped over the frontier, with a slightly falsified passport. His route, through Ventimiglia to the French Riviera, is perhaps the easiest. On every market day, the housewives of Nice pour into Ventimiglia to do their shopping. In the afternoon they all pour back again into France. Anyone who mingles with them has only to wave something of approximately the right colour and shape at the frontier guards. Italy's other frontier towns all have their market days, when shoppers come in from France, Switzerland and Austria, and at some of these the checks are very casual indeed.

Calvi could even have walked it. There are mountain paths in the Alps where a frontier guard is a rare sight. Calvi was quite fit, and accustomed to outdoor exercise on his Alpine farm.

But his new friends never mentioned these cheap and easy routes. And Calvi had so lost touch with reality that he seemed not to be aware of them. He had, for many years, travelled only by plane; he was accustomed to the checking system at airports.

Perhaps he was not ready to run away. None of his known bolt-holes would have been useful. He had a ranch in Nicaragua, but that had a left-wing government. He had a ranch in Canada, but Canada extradites people.

Calvi was still looking for solutions within Italy. He showed this by making an extraordinary move. On 19 October he met Francesco Micheli, a business associate of Italy's number two capitalist, Carlo De Benedetti. (Number one is Giovanni Agnelli of Fiat.) Micheli had come to talk about some of that real banking business which, in spite of everything, was keeping the Italian part of Calvi's empire prosperous. There were convertible debentures to be placed: some for the great computer firm Olivetti, the jewel in De Benedetti's crown, and some for his holding company, CIR. Calvi told Micheli he would like to meet De Benedetti himself. This was arranged for the end of that week in Calvi's Alpine house.

There Calvi made his proposition. He wanted De Benedetti to join the Ambrosiano board, with a view to taking over from him as chairman in a few months' time. We have only De Benedetti's account of what was said, and this may be incomplete, but it is unlikely to be fantastic. De Benedetti is outspoken, ruthless, ambitious and a hard bargainer. But he spoke to the investigators with remarkable frankness.

According to De Benedetti, Calvi explained that he had personal problems and was physically exhausted, mainly because of the legal action against him. The appeal against his currency conviction was due the following April. Calvi wanted to carry on until then. To leave beforehand would give a bad impression. But, shortly afterwards, he wanted De Benedetti to take over.

Calvi repeatedly extolled the financial position of the bank, saying that he had an expert opinion, a "document of appraisal" valuing the Ambrosiano shares at $250 each, against the market quotation of about $40. Perhaps Calvi was thinking of Mennini's initials on the documents that valued the shares at $200 each. Was he also thinking that he might eventually sell the whole secret network holding to De Benedetti?

De Benedetti let himself be tempted. He had every encouragement from the Bank of Italy to go in with Calvi. He said afterwards that Ciampi had assured him the Ambrosiano was sound. So he agreed to join the board as vice chairman, with a view to succeeding Calvi in some six to eight months. He bought a million Ambrosiano shares – 2 per cent of the total. He did not pay $250 each for them, or even $200, but about $43, or $3 more than the market price. (The total was 52 billion lire.) It was the sort of premium considered normal if there is some special advantage to be gained, and De Benedetti was getting a position as vice chairman.

The shares that Calvi sold him did not come from Astolfine and Manic, but from holdings inside Italy. De Benedetti paid partly in convertible securities of his group, but 27 billion lire was in cash, which he had borrowed from the Credito Commerciale. He obtained the money against the security of two notes totalling 32 billion lire, issued by Giuseppe Cabassi. Cabassi and De Benedetti had, earlier in the year, made a complex deal whose main purpose was that De Benedetti would eventually take up a large block of new shares in a Cabassi company, Brioschi. The new shares were expected to be issued in late 1982, when the notes would be redeemed. Now De Benedetti decided that he preferred the Ambrosiano investment to that in Brioschi, and as part of the deal he got Calvi to have La Centrale promise to place the Brioschi shares when they were issued. It was this part of the deal which was to lead to the conviction of De Benedetti in 1992 for being a contributor to the Ambrosiano bankruptcy.

At the weekend of 14 and 15 November 1981 De Benedetti returned to Drezzo with Micheli for final discussions with Calvi and with Rosone, who was now general manager of the Ambrosiano. Calvi wanted no publicity for the appointment. He was talking to the wrong person. Anyone who has seen De Benedetti surrounded by journalists, with microphones thrust into his face, cameras flashing and TV lights ablaze, has seen a man thoroughly happy.

They reached a compromise. De Benedetti would give one press interview, to Eugenio Scalfari, editor of *La Repubblica*. He would also call on the Treasury, the Bank of Italy and the Consob – the body responsible for regulating the stock markets. Then, in Milan, he would call on Enrico Cuccia of Mediobanca.

Calvi, when he eventually agreed to this, added that he himself would have to go to Rome, to inform some people of the appointment. Micheli understood him to mean important politicians.

Cuccia, when he saw De Benedetti, made no public comment. But someone overheard him say: "One of those two is making a serious mistake."

As it turned out, they both were. De Benedetti was co-opted to the board of the Ambrosiano on 18 November, and the following day *La Repubblica* published its interview. De Benedetti was typically outspoken. Hitherto, he said, Calvi's "dictatorship" of the Ambrosiano had been "absolute". After the recent legal and financial problems this dictatorship had been recognised as no longer "an element of strength but of extreme weakness".

He added: "Today begins a true and proper diarchy." And he stressed that he had the habit of getting behind his investments.

Shock waves went round Milan. It was not just that De Benedetti, who was Jewish, was accepting the number two position in a Catholic bank. He had a perfectly clean reputation, whereas Calvi's reputation was, by this time, murky.

Calvi was also shocked – but by De Benedetti's interview. The day it appeared, he made his trip to Rome. On his return he phoned Micheli. His tone, Micheli reported, was "absolutely ice-cold". All he did was to complain of the interview. But when he next saw De Benedetti, on 21 November, he said he had met with a "negative" reaction in Rome.

From whom? The investigating magistrates Pizzi and Brichetti wrote in their final report: "Who, then, was influencing Calvi? Whom did he meet on the trip to Rome of 19 November 1981 and what indications, or perhaps it would be more accurate to say directives, did he receive?" Their investigations never uncovered the answer.

There followed a campaign of harassment against De Benedetti. Pazienza boasted afterwards to *Il Mondo* (9 March 1982): "I said to Calvi, don't you give him so much as a chair to sit on! And he didn't get one."

Certainly De Benedetti did not get an office. When he asked for information, he was, in his own words, up against "a wall of rubber". De Benedetti's son, who was in Geneva, received a sinister phone call from someone claiming to be Ortolani. Then, at a committee meeting early in December, Calvi told De Benedetti to be careful because P2 was preparing a dossier on him.

Since De Benedetti, when he was keen on the deal, paid $43 million for 2 per cent of the bank, Calvi's secret 10 per cent might be worth five times that, or $215 million. Yet he still dreamed of raising a billion dollars. He sent Pazienza in search of customers.

According to a memorandum drawn up by Pazienza for the investigating magistrates, Calvi never precisely explained who was to be the seller of the shares, or how many were on offer. Pazienza was told that the "controlling stake" would be about 20 per cent, and that this would come from various Panamanian companies, and from a 3.5 per cent holding to be built up in the market.

In fact Manic and Astolfine held just over 5.3 million shares, or 10.64 per cent of the Ambrosiano capital. The 20 per cent figure implies that Calvi hoped to draw on another source of shares, and much the most likely one would have been the IOR's holding, amounting to just under 4 per cent. Pazienza alleged that Calvi invariably visited the Vatican before discussing this sale with him. Certainly, if the IOR wanted to cut its ties with the secret network, it might well have put its own holding in, so as to build up a block large enough to tempt someone wanting control of the bank.

Pazienza's story is that he was not instructed to ask for $200 or $250 a share. He was to try to sell them for about $400 million. If Calvi really meant to assemble 20 per cent, that would have been about the market level. But the buyers were also to be asked to put up a loan of $800 million. All this would have been needed to plug the hole in the Andino, Banco Comercial and Cisalpine accounts.

Did Calvi think such a device would fool a serious potential buyer? Pazienza enlisted the help of an American friend, Robert Armao, an economic adviser to the exiled Shah of Iran. He has claimed that together they succeeded in interesting a syndicate of investors from America and the Middle East.

The only document Pazienza has ever produced to back up this story is a telex from the Curaçao Banking Corporation, dated 9 December 1981, which shows that inquiries were still at a very superficial level.

Calvi's most immediate worry was to fund the commissions and bribes that he was accustomed to pay. He also needed "small change", as he described it, for various purposes in Italy. He could not use United Trading, now that its accounts were being watched. The $3.5 million paid to Pazienza at the beginning of September was clearly the last sum the IOR would allow him to sneak out by the lira back-to-backs. Pazienza was now expecting more money. He reckoned that Calvi owed him a commission even for his unsuccessful attempt to sell Vianini.

So a new system of removing money from the Ambrosiano had to be found. The plan was crude, by comparison with the sophisticated methods the IOR had made possible. Calvi would authorise the Ambrosiano to make a loan to an Italian borrower, who would then hand back some of the money – keeping enough, of course to make it worth his while.

Who was the pliant borrower to be? Here Carboni re-entered Calvi's life.

The idea seems first to have arisen in discussions between Pazienza and the car dealer Annibaldi, who was anxious for Carboni to repay the money he owed. Annibaldi then told Carboni about it. In late October a meeting was arranged with Calvi at the apartment he kept in Rome. Pazienza and his assistant Mazzotta were there too. Calvi explained that he needed money to settle his legal problems, and said he would guarantee the repayment of the loan. Carboni agreed to go along with the arrangement.

Credit facilities totalling 6 billion lire were authorised by Calvi for Carboni's company, Prato Verde. It was later established that less than 327 million lire went to the company. Carboni diverted nearly 3.3 billion to pay off his creditors, including Annibaldi and the man who owned the holiday apartments in Sardinia, Diotallevi. He also had to meet the expenses of his other companies. Then he allotted nearly a billion lire to cars, jewels, silver and a house for his brother Andrea.

The part supposed to be for Calvi's purposes, 1.4 billion lire, was paid in cash to Pazienza and Mazzotta. It was afterwards established that about 400 million lire went, in cash, to a lawyer Calvi had retained, Wilfredo Vitalone. (Vitalone was later accused of extracting huge sums from Calvi by pretending that he could influence magistrates, but he was acquitted by a Rome court in 1985.)

What happened to the remaining 1 billion lire? More than half of it was spent by Pazienza on a yacht, the Giulia VII. In late November Calvi paid Pazienza yet another $1 million abroad, to the Finanzco account at the Banque Nationale de Paris in Basle. As he could not use United Trading to make the payment, Calvi used an indirect subsidiary of BA Holding, Intermarket.

The total Calvi had paid into the Realfin and Finanzco accounts was now $8.8 million. Pazienza had already spent about half of it.

The Prato Verde loan gave Carboni his first experience of Calvi's largesse. When Calvi asked for his help again, Carboni was naturally willing to oblige. He knew a leading Freemason, Armando Corona, a fellow-Sardinian. Corona was president of the central masonic court, which, at the end of October, expelled the fugitive Gelli. He was also a member of the Republican Party secretariat. Calvi asked Carboni to effect an introduction.

There were long conversations between Corona and Calvi at Corona's room in the Colonna Palace Hotel, opposite the Parliament buildings in Rome. According to Corona, Calvi complained about his persecution by the press, and tried to find out more about the Republican Party's attitude to his ownership of the Corriere della Sera. (He could have asked De Bene-detti, who was the biggest single backer of the Republican Party, but by this time the two men were scarcely on speaking terms.)

At the end of Calvi's second meeting with Corona, in December 1981, there was an incident which perhaps began the supplanting of Pazienza by Carboni in Calvi's confidence. Carboni, having left Calvi and Corona together, returned to his home in Via Farnesina. Suddenly Pazienza appeared, in a great rush, demanding to be taken to see Calvi. Carboni took him to the Colonna Palace Hotel. There Pazienza, according to Carboni, was extremely rude to Calvi in his presence. The reason, it seemed, was that Calvi had gone to see a politician without first consulting Pazienza.

Carboni turned to go. Then Calvi quietly spoke to him, without Pazienza hearing, suggesting that they should contact each other directly. They exchanged telephone numbers.

Calvi now had to worry about the balance sheets for 31 December 1981. It was vital that such troublemakers as Garner of Coopers and Lybrand or Nassano of the Andino should not realise that the deposits the Cisalpine and the Andino had with the IOR were in reality the debts of United Trading. And there was now a good reason why the troublemakers should ask questions. Since the summer United Trading had stopped paying interest on its matching debts to the IOR. It had nothing to pay the interest with. In the past it had done it by further borrowing, but this was now impossible, because de Bernardi in Luxembourg was running United Trading's accounts.

As it was not receiving the interest due to it, the IOR had not paid the interest due to the Cisalpine and the Andino. It had failed to pay the Cisalpine either the 355,000 Swiss francs due in July on the 10 million Swiss franc loan, or nearly $10 million due on 29 September on the $70 million loan. It had failed to pay the Andino $7.2 million due on 27 August on the $77 million loan. Yet all the loans had been renewed, the Swiss franc one to the end of the year and the two dollar ones to 29 March 1982. Clearly, somebody was going to ask why.

Calvi had to find a way of getting money to the IOR so that it could pay the interest. In early December he devised a scheme which could not have worked without the cooperation of Marcinkus.

Zitropo had long been, in effect, bankrupt, its debts written off by Calvi in his private United Trading balance sheets. But it had no direct debts to the Ambrosiano group banks; from their point of view it seemed clean. Now it began to borrow from the Banco Comercial, paying the money it received to the IOR on behalf of United Trading, so that the IOR could pay the interest it owed to the Cisalpine and the Andino, less its one-sixteenth per cent turn.

Zitropo paid the money, not, as in the past, to the IOR's account at the Gottardo, but to its account at Chase Manhattan (in the case of the dollar loans) and to the Banco di Roma per la Svizzera for the Swiss franc loans. By the end of 1981, Zitropo had amassed debts of over $18 million to pay the interest and arrears. By the time of the crash this had risen to more than $46 million – of which $267,492 represented the IOR's profit.

Calvi also had to juggle the inter-group debts. The Banco Comercial had its year-end on 31 October. So there were two convenient months after its books had been audited, and before the books of the Cisalpine were audited.

This enabled Calvi to fulfil the promise he had made on the phone to Marcinkus and Count Luciano della Porta, that the Sudam loan would be removed from the Cisalpine portfolio. It was "sold" to the Banco Comercial. The Andino's loans to Astolfine were also reduced; some $217 million of them were transferred to the Banco Comercial.

But even this might lead to awkward questions; Nicaragua was known to be an unsettled country, and it seemed unlikely that the Banco Comercial was doing much genuine business. Calvi had also promised Marcinkus and della Porta that the Andino's $317 million of debts to the Cisalpine would be repaid by December 31. This could not be done by juggling with the Banco Comercial.

The ideal answer would have been to raise fresh funds on the international money markets. But Calvi was now finding that almost impossible, though Pazienza's friend Aboudaram found one or two minor banks willing to make small loans.

Calvi was forced once again to fall back on the resources of the Italian banks. He tried to hide this as best he could. He looked everywhere for banks prepared to take part in back-to-back arrangements, for the sake of a turn of one quarter or one eighth per cent on the interest rate. By late November he had been quite successful, having persuaded a dozen banks to channel some $145 million to the Andino and nearly $26 million to BA Holding, with commitments to transmit more.

But it was not going to be enough. To ensure that the Andino could repay the Cisalpine fully by 31 December, Calvi had to open up a direct credit line for the Andino with the Ambrosiano, and at the same time reopen one for the Banco Comercial. It shows how desperate he was that he went on doing what he knew would displease the authorities.

The Andino's credit line was $200 million, and by 22 December it had called on $145 million of that. But a late flood of back-to-back operations in the last week of December enabled Calvi to cut that back to $60 million.

By the end of the year, in addition to the Banco de la Nación, fifteen banks had been persuaded to act as intermediaries, passing a total of $243.3 million to the Andino or BA Holding. They included the Banco do Comercio e Industria, from São Paulo, the Banco de la Provincia, from Buenos Aires, the Luxembourg office of the Bank of Credit and Commerce International and (introduced by Pazienza and Aboudaram) the Arab African International Bank. There was also the Arab-owned Artoc Bank and Trust of Nassau, run by Peter de Savary, in which the Cisalpine had taken a 20 per cent interest earlier in the year. A small London bank which took part was AP Bank, formerly the Anglo-Portuguese Bank, owned at this time by the Norwich Union insurance group. AP had a link with Artoc; the deputy chairman of both was Leonard Walton. More famous banks also took part: the Cayman offshoots of J. Henry Schroder Banking of New York and of the Crédit Commercial de France, and, in London, Williams and Glyn's. The last-named was a partner of the Ambrosiano in a consortium finance house, Inter-Alpha Asia, which also agreed to be an intermediary.

After the crash, some of these banks were threatened with legal actions because they had helped Calvi's deception. They argued that they had no intention of doing any such thing. In the end the liquidators reached settlements with them all.

Calvi continued his search for outside money. On 17 December Arab Multinational Finance agreed to lend $30 or $40 million to BA Holding – but on conditions which, as we shall see, never were fulfilled.

Before the books could be balanced at the end of the year, De Benedetti had become suspicious.

THIRTY-FOUR

$100 Million – the Price of Salvation

De Benedetti had a fierce argument with Calvi on 21 December 1981. Then, as Calvi would not give him an office, he retreated to his own office at Ivrea, in the beautiful Alpine foothills north of Turin, where Olivetti has its headquarters. He invited Angelo Rizzoli there, because Angelo had been talking about a $600 million "hole" in the accounts of the Andino.

Angelo was understating it. Calvi's three Italian banks had poured $421 million into the Andino, in addition to the $60 million direct credit. This $421 million (plus another $26 million which had gone to the other foreign subsidiaries) was all concealed by the back-to-back arrangements, so that it appeared on the balance sheets of the Italian banks as normal interbank business. What could not be altogether concealed, however, was that the Andino now had debts of $679.5 million, as against $603 million the year before. Since he did not have to produce consolidated accounts, Calvi did not tell the Italian authorities this. But so many of his own executives now knew it that it had become a matter of gossip, and this was what Angelo had heard.

After talking to Angelo on 23 December, De Benedetti asked Olivetti's local office in Peru what was known about the Andino. The office telexed back that the Andino was essentially an overseas financial operation, and that its loans were "destined exceptionally to local public bodies, normally to various entities in countries like Chile, Argentina, Brazil, or else granted directly with foreign central banks, for example Nigeria". The telex concluded that it appeared "sound".

But De Benedetti remained suspicious, and asked Calvi about the debts, only to be told that it concerned the affairs of the men "in long skirts" – that is, the IOR. De Benedetti went to Rome, and talked to Monsignor Silvestrini. By his own early accounts, De Benedetti described Marcinkus as a thief. He asked how the Vatican could entrust its finances to a man like that, and suggested that the Curia should look into the IOR's relationship with the Ambrosiano.

But in an interrogation in 1990 De Benedetti added the information that he had proposed a direct deal with the IOR, to bypass Calvi, and had indicated that he was willing to buy some of the IOR holding – which he probably confused with the holding of the secret network.

Silvestrini replied, with a pained expression, that neither he nor Casaroli knew much about the activities of the IOR. He asked De Benedetti to send him a memorandum, so that they could discuss the matter with the Pope. As for Marcinkus, Silvestrini shrugged his shoulders and said he was a "lost sheep".

At Christmas, Calvi had a phone call from Gelli, who called merely to give him the season's greetings – or so Gelli now claims. According to Tassan Din, Gelli and Ortolani had been urging Calvi to sell Rizzoli to the Cabassi group. But Tassan Din opposed it, because Cabassi was supported by the Socialist Party. This was only one of many things Calvi might have discussed with Gelli. Surely he asked for some of his money back? If he did, it would account for this being the last call Gelli ever made to him, as Gelli insists it was.

That Christmas, Calvi rang Carboni and invited him to Drezzo. Carboni came at the beginning of January, bringing with him the civil servant Binetti. According to Carboni, Calvi spoke of his fear of Pazienza. At this time Calvi was frightened of many things; his bodyguard was costing the Ambrosiano a million dollars a year. But Pazienza?

Carboni and Calvi went for a long walk together. We have only Carboni's account of what Calvi said. He wanted Carboni to get the message through to the Vatican that, if matters were not amicably sorted out between him and the IOR, there would be a scandal. He wanted Carboni to put pressure on the Vatican directly, through people he knew there, and also indirectly, through his contacts among politicians and the press. It was to be done discreetly. Carboni asked whether the IOR had done anything wrong. Calvi said no – but neither had he. If he were brought down, though, the IOR would fall too. Carboni's reward for success in restoring the relationship would be $100 million.

The size of the commission sounds authentic, in view of the sums now known to have been paid to Ortolani and Gelli. It is likely enough, too, that Calvi was hoping to persuade Marcinkus to drop the 30 June deadline.

Was he hoping to go on as before? Piling up secret debts under the cloak of the IOR had ceased to be possible. Too many people now knew too much. And those who did not know were determined to find out.

The Consob, the stock exchange regulatory body, was demanding that the Ambrosiano shares should be quoted on the main Milan exchange, instead of the *mercato ristretto*. Calvi was resisting this because it meant that he would have to produce consolidated accounts for the whole group, including the foreign banks. He would also have to publicise the names of the ten biggest shareholders. Already, without waiting for the stock exchange listing, the Bank of Italy was bombarding him with demands for information.

Carboni, who did not know how bad things were, soon promised Calvi his help. They began to see each other regularly.

The showdown with De Benedetti came on 12 January 1982, at a meeting of the Ambrosiano finance committee. De Benedetti tabled three declarations: the first criticising the committee's way of working, the second saying that there were too many nominee companies among the bank's shareholders and the third repeating a request he had been making for some time, for a copy of the Bank of Italy's 1978 report.

The following day De Benedetti was summoned by the bank's lawyer, Luigi Chiaraviglio, and told that his name would not be put before the annual general meeting of shareholders for confirmation as a director.

A few steps from the Ambrosiano, at the head office of La Centrale, Calvi had been walking round and round the table, asking the manager, Michel Leemans, how they could find 52 billion lire, plus 2.4 billion interest, and expenses, to buy De Benedetti out.

Leemans could not understand why Calvi should make any concessions to De Benedetti. If De Benedetti now felt he had made a mistake in buying the shares, that was his worry. Leemans was not on the Ambrosiano board, and concentrated on his job in the Italian part of the empire – with only occasional interference from Calvi. He could not understand Calvi's desperate anxiety.

But Calvi was determined to make a clean break. He bought back De Benedetti's 1 million Ambrosiano shares for 54.4 billion lire (over $45 million). Calvi also said that La Centrale's undertaking to place the Brioschi shares would be honoured, but De Benedetti counter-proposed that, instead, he should hand over the 32 billion lire of notes convertible into Brioschi shares in exchange for 27 billion lire in cash. Calvi accepted, and thus De Benedetti got a total of 81.4 billion in cash. Calvi then sold the 1 million shares on to Carlo Pesenti's Italmobiliare.

Later the Milan public prosecutor Dell'Osso thought that De Benedetti should be prosecuted for extortion. But the investigating magistrates Pizzi and Brichetti concluded that this would be wrong. De Benedetti had not wanted to resign, and the terms were not a condition of his going, but had been conceded willingly once his departure was inevitable. He was the only Ambrosiano director who had refused to be a yes man. The extortion charge was not upheld by the Court of Appeal. However, on 12 March 1991 the Court of Appeal decided that De Benedetti should instead be charged with some responsibility for the Ambrosiano bankruptcy, because of the 27 billion lire. They also suspected that the transfer to Italmobiliare was not a genuine deal. So De Benedetti became a defendant at the trial in 1992.

Because of his departure, De Benedetti never sent the memorandum to the Vatican that Silvestrini had requested. But on 12 January 1982 a group of Catholic shareholders of the Ambrosiano sent a complaint directly to the Pope. They got a Polish priest in Milan to translate it for them, hoping that this would mean the Pope alone could read it. They never got a reply.

These Catholics had no inside information, except the 1978 Bank of Italy report. This had not been officially published, but it was not a secret, since it was among the documents produced at Calvi's trial. It went round the business world of Milan in duplicated form. The shareholders also had the most recent balance sheets, and the text of the various legal indictments against Calvi. This was enough to show them what was coming, though not how fast it would come. They saw the possibility "that IOR remains as partner and accomplice of Roberto Calvi, and thus, for at least ten years, is involved in a scandal not inferior to that of Sindona".

One of those who signed the letter was Amedeo Ancarani Restelli, a manufacturer of cycle chains. His father had been on the board of the Ambrosiano in its early days. After the crash, when the press got hold of the letter, Ancarani Restelli said of Marcinkus: "The problem is not that of a cleric who has behaved like a banker; the problem is that of a cleric who has behaved like a very bad banker, within a system which has no defence mechanism, because it is lacking in standards of correct financial management."

The letters of patronage were not keeping all Calvi's executives quiet. At the Gottardo Bolgiani and Garzoni, who perhaps knew more than most, resigned their directorships of United Trading. It remained without officers until after the crash. (Nordeurop, as a Liechtenstein company, was legally obliged to go into liquidation when it was left without directors, but United Trading was registered in Panama, and Panama is more tolerant than Liechtenstein of companies without directors.)

At the Andino, Nassano remained uneasy. He came to Milan at the end of January, and seems to have extracted from Calvi a promise that all the debts would be paid back before June was out.

This could have been done only if Calvi had sold the "controlling interest" in the Ambrosiano at the equivalent of $200 a share or more. According to Pazienza, he and his friend Armao met Calvi in Rome in January to talk about the sale. But the only figure that seems to have been discussed in detail was the commission these two expected for themselves.

There was a suggestion that, to help the sale, a "committee of international experts" would be appointed to establish the true position of the bank, including the IOR companies. No such committee ever was set up, or could be. Yet Calvi seems to have been deluding himself that he could sell the shares. On 28 January 1982 he started illegally buying yet more Ambrosiano shares on the market. He barely tried to conceal what he was doing. The buying was done by Ambrosiano employees in Milan, using Ambrosiano money. Rosone knew about it; he said afterwards that Calvi told him the shares would be resold in his "grand operation" at $200 each.

One day before the illegal buying began, Calvi and the Consob had issued a joint statement. Ambrosiano shares would be quoted on the main stock exchange. Calvi agreed to this only after the Consob threatened to use its compulsory powers, and have the shares listed whether Calvi liked it or not.

Even before De Benedetti's departure, shares in the Ambrosiano were being bought by the man who was to replace him as vice chairman, Orazio Bagnasco, the head of the firm Interprogramme. On 26 January Bagnasco's appointment was announced. He confirmed that an Italian firm he owned, Interpart, had over 1 per cent of the shares, and that he held another 1 per cent on behalf of his friend Luigi Lucchini, the steelworks owner. Bagnasco was reported to have spent something over $20 million on his 1.1 per cent – mainly, it seems, bought in the market.

Bagnasco's company, Interprogramme (with headquarters in Lugano) ran open-ended property investment funds, long recognised as a highly dangerous form of investment. He employed door-to-door salesmen to persuade small savers that they ought to invest in real estate. This became popular, because the price of buildings had outstripped Italian inflation, and at that time not much else had.

The weakness of the system is that the real value of a building cannot be tested until the building is sold.

The crash did not come until 1985. In early 1982 Bagnasco was doing well. But what was he doing on the board of the Ambrosiano? He had no previous experience of banking. When inquiries were made at his head office in Lugano a spokesman smoothly explained: "Calvi has realised that he needs to have a group of financial and industrial leaders to assist him in forming the philosophy and policy of the bank. Mr Bagnasco is going on the board to represent the entrepreneurial class."

Would he succeed where De Benedetti failed? Would he, for example, be given an office? "He will not expect to be given an office. He does not intend to play any part in the day-to-day running of the company. He will spend most of his time here in Lugano."

Clara said afterwards that Calvi had not wanted Bagnasco on the board. "He thought that the shadow of Andreotti was outlined there." But Calvi, she said, had to reconcile himself to a fait accompli.

The new accounting rules imposed by the Consob were not due to come into effect until 1983. But the Bank of Italy was already asking for details about the foreign subsidiaries. It was particularly interested in Calvi's plan to merge the Cisalpine with Artoc. The proposed loan of $40 or $50 million from Arab Multinational Finance to BA Holding was dependent on this merger.

Throughout January 1982, Calvi prevaricated. But on 5 February he and his executives were summoned to the Bank of Italy and told that they must provide the information. A few days later the Bank of Italy reminded him, by letter, that he had still not submitted a restructuring plan, including the sale of Rizzoli. A ruling by the Interministerial Commission for Credit and Savings meant that he must do this.

On 15 February the Ambrosiano began, for the first time, to disclose figures that meant something. It gave the details of deposits to and from its associates in the last six months of 1981 – and thus revealed to the authorities the opening of the $200 million direct credit line for the Andino.

The following day the Bank of Italy demanded a great deal more information: full details of the investments of BA Holding; details of the inter-group balances; the latest balance sheets of the overseas associates, together with the auditors' reports; more details about the proposed Artoc deal; a list of all shareholders owning more than 10,000 shares. The Bank of Italy knew from Bagnasco that Calvi had dealt with its previous letters by not showing them to the other directors. It demanded that this one should be submitted to the whole board, and that each director should confirm he was satisfied he had adequate information.

Calvi's actions at this time show such desperation that it is hard to make sense of them. He seems to have believed that handing out large sums of money would help. If he paid Carboni, perhaps Carboni would get the Vatican to be his friend again, although he had made little progress in this so far. Carboni afterwards said that he had asked Calvi not to pay him any of the $100 million in advance. He taped his conversations with Calvi, he said, to prove that he was not demanding money.

He got some, though. Calvi arranged a credit facility for a Carboni/Pellicani company, Etruria. The total came to 1.7 billion lire (about $1.4

million). Most of this was used for Carboni or his companies, although 267 million lire was passed on to Calvi for his "small change" expenses.

On 9 February 1982 Calvi sent an urgent telex to Calvin Knowles and Sue Anne Dunkley at the Cisalpine, instructing them to make the four following payments:

$4 million to account 677031 at the Union Bank in Lugano;

$2 million to the Banque de Dépôt et de Gestion in Lausanne for the attention of the president

$5 million to the Trade Development Bank, Panama, for Andros;

$3 million to the same bank's Geneva branch for Nertanic Assets.

The telex said that these were all "loans at sixty days' repayment at maturity". Knowles was away and Sue Anne Dunkley had to decide what to do. Each individual payment fell within Calvi's limit for sole authorisation for unsecured loans, but the total of $14 million did not. But Calvi pressed her. After informing Siegenthaler (still on his sabbatical) she did as Calvi ordered.

Account 677031 at the Union Bank belonged to Carboni. When the authorities found it, Carboni claimed that Calvi had owed him the money, for jewels. The investigating magistrates concluded that he was "lying shamelessly". Calvi's missing briefcase, which came to light in 1986, had a letter purporting to be from Calvi to Carboni, recognising a debt for jewels delivered. This was not thought to be authentic.

Much of the money was traced, such as the $100,000 Carboni paid into an account in the name of his Italian mistress, Laura Concas. An account controlled by Diotallevi got $23,400. Over $540,000 was withdrawn by Carboni in Swiss franc notes.

The money paid to Andros has never been traced, though Pazienza admitted that the account was his. He said Calvi had asked him for the name of an account to which he could pay some money for the benefit of an unidentified third party. Pazienza gave him the details of the Andros account, which was split, he said, into an A account – his – and a B account for the unnamed recipient. He claimed that, shortly after Calvi's death, he had himself been to Panama to find out what happened to the money. He was told that $1.5 million had ended up with General Bermudez, head of the National Guard. (No officer of that name has ever been traced.) He had no idea what happened to the rest.

However, Pazienza bought yet another boat, a 30-metre yacht, *Naque I*, registered in the name of Andros. It cost more than $1.7 million. Pazienza claimed that he bought it in partnership with Prince Ali Reza Pahlavi, but the prince denied this.

The $3 million paid to the Trade Development Bank in Geneva was not for "Nertanic"; this was an error. It went to an account for Mertanil Assets, which turned out to mean Pazienza's assistant Mazzotta. About $800,000 of the money was frozen in another Mazzotta account in Switzerland. He claimed that the money was paid to him for various tasks he had undertaken for Calvi, such as the resale of Rizzoli. Not only had Rizzoli not been resold; there was no evidence that Mazzotta had played any part in the abortive negotiations.

The most surprising recipient was discovered by the liquidators when they investigated the $2 million paid to the Banque de Dépôt et de Gestion at Lausanne. The money was credited to a Liechtenstein company, Kamus. Lawyers were appointed to negotiate with the liquidators of the Cisalpine, and reached an agreement, under which the name of the recipient would remain a secret, but half the money would be paid back. However, the Cisalpine had drawn on its credit line with the Ambrosiano to make the payments demanded by Calvi that day. So the Italian magistrates insisted that the Ambrosiano had been defrauded, and continued to demand the real name. The Swiss eventually revealed that it was Anna Bonomi.

She initially refused to answer questions. When she did give her version of events, she said she thought the $2 million had come from Calvi's personal resources. It was the final balance owed to her by Calvi under the agreement they had made under Gelli's aegis. That is, it was the amount outstanding from her share of the profits from their dealings in Credito Varesino shares in the early 1970s. The $7.9 million he had paid her in December 1979 had not been enough, and this was the final reckoning.

There were many things this explanation did not explain. Calvi had almost certainly expected her to use the $7.9 million to pay off debts she owed to the Ambrosiano in the name of her front man, Marinoni. But in late 1981 there remained some 7 billion lire outstanding. The Ambrosiano had written demanding repayment. Anna Bonomi then agreed to repay over five years – but presumably she had insisted that Calvi should first pay what he owed her.

The crudeness and haste with which Calvi made these four payments suggest that he turned to the Cisalpine as a last resort. Pazienza says that Calvi was in Rome when he asked for details of the Andros account, and that he told him he was going to the IOR to use its telex to order some movements of money, taking advantage of the fact that Mennini would not be there that day. Calvi said (according to Pazienza) that he had sometimes taken advantage of the Vatican communications system to make transfers of money.

Calvi may indeed have had a reason for going to the IOR; there must still have been about 10 or 15 billion lire in the back-to-back pool, and he may have hoped to use that. But, if he made the attempt, he failed. On 10 February the IOR repaid 12 billion lire to its back-to-back accounts at the three Italian banks, reducing its total debt, with rolled-up interest, to about 119 billion lire.

After ordering the four payments on 9 February, Calvi had to do something to give the "loans" some semblance of legitimacy. On 23 February he telexed Knowles and Dunkley to say that "Sig Bodan" would become director of a Panama company, which, as soon as it had been formed, would take over the $14 million liability.

Bodan – Harry Bodan-Shields – was a Nicaraguan, related to Somoza, who had been a director of the Banco Comercial, and was going to become involved in its affairs again, although he now lived in Louisiana. The Panamanian company which he subsequently produced for Calvi was called Inversionistas Dalavi.

Calvi promised the Cisalpine executives that he would give them "all other details" when they saw him at the beginning of March in Milan. But, when they did see him, he gave them no further information. It seems he persuaded them not to put the four loans forward for ratification by the directors, by promising them that they would be quickly repaid.

The executives went on to Zürich for the Cisalpine board meeting on 3 March. Again, the only directors there were Marcinkus and della Porta. But Siegenthaler, taking another break from his sabbatical, was made a director at the outset of the meeting.

According to one account, Marcinkus and della Porta were unofficially told of the $14 million "loans" before the meeting, and said that they would not have ratified them. But there, it seems, the matter was left.

Once more Marcinkus dominated the meeting. He asked about the Sudam loan. (It had been spirited off the Cisalpine's books.) He asked about the sale of the Bafisud stake. (It had not yet been completed.) The huge loan to the Andino had also been removed from the books, by what methods we have seen. Marcinkus and della Porta were taken aback to be asked to approve, instead, a $200 million credit line to BA Holding. They were told that the Cisalpine was the only overseas bank in the Ambrosiano group with credit lines from its Italian associates that had been approved by the authorities, and that it was important it should play its part in financing the others. They agreed to a limit of $150 million.

Marcinkus asked about the proposed merger with Artoc. He commented that Artoc's business sounded quite different from the Cisalpine's. He doubted whether it would really produce a flow of deposits from the Middle East. He and della Porta concluded that the merger looked risky and shoud be approached with caution. They were concerned at the prospect of changing "a successful and solid organisation which took eleven years to build".

Marcinkus knew all the reasons why the Cisalpine was not solid. Nor could they have escaped his mind; before the directors was a letter from Coopers and Lybrand. During 1981 the IOR had run down its deposits with the Cisalpine by nearly $7 million, to about $83 million. As a result, the gap between what it appeared to owe and what it was owed had grown again, to about $8.3 million. The gap would have been about $3 million wider, if there had not been, mingling with the IOR's own deposits, the back-to-back deposits of the Gottardo. But of this Coopers and Lybrand knew nothing. They wrote: "As in previous years, we have been unable to review the financial statements of the IOR, and because of the increased exposure we have therefore required specific representations from the Directors on the recoverability of this account."

Marcinkus was the only one aware how doubtful the recoverability was. For the twentieth time, he said nothing. The auditors' letter was "noted".

Marcinkus knew that United Trading, the recipient of $91.5 million of the Cisalpine's money via the IOR, had insufficient assets to cover the debt, and that the other assets of the companies covered by the letters of patronage were pledged to secure the debts to the Andino and the Banco Comercial. He had himself given Calvi until 30 June to find the money to enable United Trading to repay. Where did he think Calvi was going to get it?

THIRTY-FIVE

Calvi is Worthy of Our Trust

In Luxembourg, de Bernardi thought his position was this: he was manager of Ambrosiano Services; it was his duty to manage companies which belonged to the IOR; he had to accept any instructions Calvi gave him about these companies, because Calvi had been appointed by the IOR as its "attorney-in-fact". But he had to send financial statements for the companies to the IOR.

This he duly did on 19 March 1982. The statements, which gave the position up to 31 December 1981, were not very informative. Most of the investments were listed without any value against them, but there were some odd exceptions. The 189,000 Rizzoli shares held by Bellatrix were valued at 85,000 lire each, so that they totalled $1,336,608 – against Bellatrix's liabilities of $166 million.

The accounts for Manic were odd; they included only 2,492,956 of its 3,155,919 Ambrosiano shares. These were valued at $41 each, which was below the market price at the time – $42.5. (They had gone up when De Benedetti joined the board.)

Imperfect as these statements were, it would have been possible for any financially competent person to deduce from them that the gap between assets and liabilities now came to nearly $1.4 billion. De Bernardi had discovered the debts of United Trading to the IOR, which stood at $223.3 million. (The previous summer the total was $217 million, but the Swiss franc part of the debt was now worth more in dollars, because the dollar had fallen. The dollar was to recover in the coming months, so the figure was $213 million at the time of the crash.)

De Bernardi's balance sheet for United Trading was very different from the secret balance sheets Calvi prepared for himself – and which, no doubt, he was still preparing, though they have never come to light. De Bernardi did not show the consolidated position of the whole secret network. He had worked out that the 53,033 BA Holding shares in the IOR's account at the Gottardo in reality belonged to United Trading. He gave them, plus the remaining four held by United Trading, a value of $38.3 million, and put them down as one of its principal assets. United Trading's other main asset was the money owed to it by Zitropo, which totalled $39.3 million. Calvi had long since written that off as irrecoverable, but he did not tell de Bernardi, who put it down as an asset, along with Cisalpine shares, Gottardo shares and the Lear jet Calvi had bought the previous year. Even so, the deficit was nearly $153 million.

The debts of United Trading would not have surprised de Strobel. He knew they were the counterparts of debts by the IOR to the Cisalpine and the Andino. It could be only a matter of time before one of Calvi's executives worked out the back-to-back arrangement – if, indeed, this had not already happened.

When he sent the financial statements, de Bernardi asked de Strobel to return signed copies with his comments. He also told the IOR that the assurance it had given on 26 October, to the effect that it stood surety for any transactions carried out by Calvi on behalf of the IOR companies, was now "null and void". Had someone shown de Bernardi the letter of indemnity?

Calvi was at this time not without moral and political support. On 10 March another friend of Andreotti's joined the board of the Ambrosiano – Carlo Pesenti, the cement magnate, the man who had borrowed money indexed in Swiss francs from the IOR, and whose Italmobiliare had just bought De Benedetti's shares. But Pesenti, who was 75, shortly afterwards had a heart attack, and became so ill that he played no part in the events which followed. In any case he was in no condition to help Calvi with money.

Nobody could help him with the Bank of Italy, which was now forcing him into more and more damaging disclosures. On 17 March Calvi gave it information about several of the foreign subsidiaries, including brief details of the balance sheet of the Andino at 31 December 1981. It had made loans totalling $629 million. The Bank of Italy wanted to know more.

On 31 March Calvi told them that the Andino "promotes and participates in every type of banking activity connected to the financing of international trade, syndicated loans and the financing of projects in Peru, Latin America and other countries of the world". The Bank of Italy sent its own investigators to Peru, but they were rudely received and subjected to a body search. They discovered nothing.

In his letter of 31 March, Calvi also said that the proposed merger between the Cisalpine and Artoc had been shelved. He gave no reason, but the opposition of Marcinkus must have been the final blow.

Was Calvi, at this time, trying to persuade Marcinkus to think again about his 30 June deadline? If he did try, it was in vain. There is even evidence that the IOR was trying to secure an earlier repayment. The back-to-back loans, which had previously been renewed for six months, a year, or even longer, were now being extended only for short periods.

The two biggest Swiss franc loans, for 22,720,000 and 101,245,000, matured on 12 February 1982 after running for a full year. They were then renewed for only a month, and after that for two months, to 12 and 15 May. The 10 million Swiss franc loan, which had fallen due on 29 January, was extended to 29 March, and then again to 29 May. (Nothing could be done about the 6 million Swiss franc loan, which was not due for repayment until 30 November 1982.) The two dollar loans of $70 million and $77 million, which had both been renewed to 28 March, were extended to 28 May. At each renewal Zitropo borrowed from Banco Comercial to pay United Trading's interest to the IOR, which the IOR passed on to the Cisalpine, less its usual one-sixteenth.

By the end of March, therefore, there was no sign that Marcinkus had any intention of lifting his deadline. Carboni's task was becoming more urgent. He had managed to make some contacts inside the Vatican.

First he turned to a lawyer, Luigi D'Agostino, who introduced him to Cardinal Palazzini. He had led the criticism of the IOR just after the death of Paul VI. Now Palazzini agreed to listen to Calvi's story.

According to Carboni, who was present, Calvi told Palazzini that he had not always kept the IOR as fully informed of what he was doing in its name as he should have done. However, he argued, everything he had done had been in the best interests of both the IOR and the Ambrosiano. Palazzini heard him out politely, and apparently with sympathy. But he afterwards got in touch with Carboni to say that there was nothing he could do because, as far as he was concerned, the IOR was "impenetrable".

The lawyer D'Agostino then introduced Carboni to a rather less exalted figure, an American prelate of Italian origin, Monsignor Hilary Franco. He was a research assistant, second class, in the Sacred Congregation of the Clergy. He had lived in the Villa Strich at the same time as Marcinkus. There is no evidence that they were friends, but at least they knew each other.

When Calvi's missing briefcase came to light in 1986 it contained copies of letters from Calvi to Franco and Palazzini. The Calvi family has suggested that these letters may be forgeries. Carboni was (it emerged later) associating with a convicted forger, Giulio Lena. The letter in which Calvi acknowledged that he owed Carboni money may well be suspect, but the letter from

Sindona's man Cavallo is genuine; there is another copy in Calvi's safe in the Bahamas. So the Vatican letters may be genuine too, and certainly their contents accord with what we now know.

One of these, dated 18 April, was to Monsignor Franco, thanking him for his "valued intervention with the Vatican authorities, so that we should reach, as soon as possible, a satisfactory conclusion in my interests and those of the executives of the IOR". The letter concluded: "In order to obtain the documents which would be necessary for whoever undertook the verification, I would require notice of at least eight days."

It is possible that Calvi thought of showing someone in the Vatican the letters he had written to the IOR, and it is almost certain that he had not kept any copies of them in Italy.

On 24 April the IOR itself wrote one of its rare letters, this time to de Bernardi in Luxembourg. De Strobel had ignored de Bernardi's request that he should sign and return copies of the financial statements. But he did tell de Bernardi that the IOR continued to stand surety for any action carried out by Calvi; Calvi remained the IOR's "attorney in fact". This looks like an attempt to reassure Calvi's executives that all was well between him and the IOR.

A few days later Marcinkus conveyed the same message to the world at large. In his interview in the issue of *Panorama* dated 3 May (which would have first appeared a week before) Marcinkus declared: "Calvi is worthy of our trust. I have no reason to doubt him. We have no intention of selling the shares in our possession."

What shares were those? The interviewer suggested that the IOR controlled more shares than the 1.6 per cent in its name. Marcinkus replied that the precise figure was "as stated". He was concealing the 2.4 per cent in the names of Ulricor and Rekofinanz, just as Calvi concealed them in the prospectus the Ambrosiano had issued for its listing on the main Milan stock exchange.

In fact the IOR did not sell any Ambrosiano shares. The only sign of any loss of confidence was that in April it further reduced its deposits at the Cisalpine by about $6.5 million. (A reduction of some $5 million in March was only apparent; the Gottardo had repaid a back-to-back loan.) Another $18 million of deposits fell due on 27 April, and could have been withdrawn, but were renewed. Either the IOR did not recognise the huge deficit staring it in the face, or it was persuaded that, if Calvi was to have any chance of meeting the 30 June deadline, the IOR should not remove any more funds, and should do everything possible to maintain public confidence in the Ambrosiano.

Carboni was cultivating contacts outside the Vatican. His friends, the civil servant Binetti and the Venezuelan ambassador Coll, helped to look for banks willing to undertake back-to-back operations. But, after a visit to South America, they found that by now even the small banks were wary of Calvi, and unwilling to act as intermediaries.

Carboni tried to help politically too. He gave a reception attended by Corona, who had just been elected Grand Master of Italian Freemasons. Also present were the Christian Democrat leader Ciriaco De Mita, the owner of *La Repubblica*, Carlo Caracciolo, and Monsignor Franco. But it seems to have been an embarrassing occasion. Christian Democrats were no longer willing to be seen with leading Freemasons.

Carboni seems to have been more at home in less exalted circles. Calvi told him about his dealings with Professor Ley-Ravello in Lausanne, who, he said, still owed him money. Carboni had had more recent business dealings with the professor. He sent Diotallevi to see him. Ley-Ravello stood his ground and defied Calvi to sue. (Which he could not do without revealing that he had smuggled money out of Italy.) According to Ley-Ravello, Diotallevi left, saying he would "see about it with Carboni". The professor heard no more. Not everyone visited by a friend of Carboni was so lucky.

Whatever foreign banks now thought of him, Calvi emerged triumphantly from the annual meeting of Ambrosiano shareholders in April. He is said to have paid off some small shareholders who threatened to cause trouble. De Benedetti, who still held a few shares, could have turned up to challenge him, but did not. Nobody came publicly from among the 38,000 small shareholders to dispute Calvi's domination.

A few days later, on 23 April 1982, the *Financial Times* told its readers: "Banco Ambrosiano is doing fine." It also said that Calvi intended to open a representative office in London.

Any foreign bank can open a representative office in London. But there is no point in doing so, except as a preliminary to opening a branch, which can do normal, profitable, banking business. And this requires the permission of the Bank of England. Two years earlier, the Bank of England had told Calvi that he would not be allowed to open a branch. But such refusals are always made in strict secrecy. Even this one has never been officially disclosed.

On 27 April 1982 a Bank of England man was told: "This morning Roberto Rosone, Calvi's second-in-command, was shot in the leg outside his flat."

At this the Bank of England man was startled out of his reticence.

"Bankers gunned down in Threadneedle Street?" he said. "I don't think we'd fancy that."

One other place where the news of that shooting struck like a thunderbolt was Lugano. At Bagnasco's headquarters, the smooth-tongued spokesman who kept journalists at bay was reduced to stammering horror. Did Bagnasco himself, at this point, realise what company he had begun to keep?

The shooting of Rosone remains mysterious, but not so mysterious as it would have been, if the gunman had got away. He arrived on the back of a motor-bike, ridden by an accomplice, before 8 a.m. An Ambrosiano car was waiting to take Rosone to the bank. The gunman waited until Rosone appeared, and then shot him in the leg, at such close range that some people afterwards contended he must have been aiming to wound, not kill. The gunman jumped back on to the motor bike, which immediately sped away.

Whoever planned the attack had reckoned without one thing. Rosone lived over a branch of the Ambrosiano. Because of the Red Brigades, the bank branch had an armed security man outside. He fired at the fleeing gunman. The gunman turned on the pillion and fired back; the bullet went through the liver of Rosone's driver, and very nearly killed him. The security guard fired again, twice. Both bullets went through the gunman's head.

Whether this was good marksmanship, chance, or the hand of God, it hastened on the climax of the Calvi story. Once the gunman was lying dead in the road, the police could see who he was.

Calvi, on hearing of the shooting, hurried to Rosone's bedside, kissed him and cried: "Madonna, what a mad world!" Then he explained to Rosone that someone wanted to intimidate them both, so as to get hold of a group worth 20,000 billion lire. "And I believed him!" Rosone exclaimed later.

The police were examining the body of the gunman, who had in his pocket clear proof that he liked to live dangerously – a driving licence issued in Nigeria. He was dressed, very strangely for a pillion rider, in a made-to-measure silk shirt, an elegant grey suit and a camel coat. Somebody said: "That's *Er Baffo*. He always was the Beau Brummel of the Rome underworld."

Er baffo means "the moustache" in the dialect of Rome. The gunman's real name was Danilo Abbruciati, and he could afford to dress well because he was boss of a drug-peddling gang. In the underworld he was regarded as rich and successful – too rich and successful, surely, to be doing the job of an ordinary hit-man, unless as a special favour to a friend.

Who, then, were his friends? Several people already mentioned in this book. He was "linked with the clan of Berenguer and Bergamelli", said the *vice questore* of Milan, Antonio Pagnozzi. He was speaking of the master kidnappers from Marseilles, suspected of kidnapping young Ortolani, among others.

Another friend was Alessandro Alibrandi, the right-wing terrorist son of one of the magistrates who arrested Baffi and Sarcinelli. Young Alibrandi and Abbruciati had been on trial together for stealing hand grenades. But certainly that young man had nothing to do with the attack on Rosone; he had been killed the previous December, in a shoot-out with the police. (A policeman got killed, too.)

The authorities looked into the more recent friendships of Abbruciati. He had had business dealings with Diotallevi. He had been a partner in a company called La Costa delle Ginestre with the moneylender Balducci (murdered the previous October) and with Carboni.

The trial of Carboni and Diotallevi for complicity in the attack on Rosone has been many times postponed, but will no doubt eventually take place. Evidence about Swiss bank accounts will be important. Shortly before the attack, Calvi arranged a loan of $5 million to Inversionistas Dalavi. It came from Banco Comercial, whose board was now composed entirely of uninformed and unquestioning local nominees. The money was first paid into an account that had been opened for Inversionistas Dalavi at Crédit Suisse in the Bahamas. It was transferred to an account in the name of Carboni's Austrian mistress, Manuela Kleinszig, at the Geneva Airport branch of the Union Bank. There it ran into an obstacle. The manager was unhappy at such a large sum being credited to the account of a young girl, and demanded an explanation. After Carboni had consulted a lawyer, however, the credit was allowed to stand. The bulk of the money was then transferred to Carboni's own account at the Union Bank in Lugano, where he still had some $1.5 million from the February payment. The first payment he made out was one of $530,000 to Diotallevi, on 4 May 1982.

Both men have protested their innocence. Diotallevi's story is that Carboni's payment to him was in exchange for 690 million lire he paid to Carboni in Italy.

If Calvi ordered and paid for the wounding of Rosone, what was his motive? After the crash Rosone suggested that he had been inconvenient to Calvi. He had, he said, objected when large unsecured loans were made to Genghini, to the Ortolani firm Voxson, to Carboni's companies. There is little independent evidence that he made these objections, though Bagnasco has offered some support. But it is known that, when Calvi was in prison, Rosone had suggested that Mozzana should come out of retirement to take his place.

The net was now closing round Calvi. His appeal against the currency conviction had been postponed until 21 June. He may well have expected to win that. But he had now been twice investigated by the magistrates Cudillo and Galucci in Rome about the Rizzoli Finanziaria share manipulations, and other matters arising from the P2 investigations. Calvi may not have been much worried about this, as it was handled in Rome. The persistent Milan magistrates, however, were pursuing the charge of fraud over the Zitropo/ Pacchetti/Varesino deal. His co-defendants there would be Anna Bonomi and Sindona himself (then in prison in the United States). The evidence was going to be based on what Ambrosoli had discovered before his murder.

Calvi's lawyers contended that the two Milan magistrates in charge of the case, Gherardo Colombo and Giuliano Turone, were personally prejudiced against Calvi. Therefore the case ought to be transferred to Rome. The court of appeal heard Calvi's arguments on 3 May – and rejected them. The case would be heard in Milan.

On 18 May Calvi was discussing with Tassan Din and Angelo Rizzoli whether the payment of some more money to somebody would get that decision reversed.

The Milan magistrates, Colombo and Turone, were indeed implacable, not from personal enmity but because they were determined to find out what had been going on. The Bank of Italy was equally determined.

On 3 May Calvi wrote to the Bank of Italy with a plan for restructuring the group's investments. He proposed to form a new holding company, which would take effectively controlling stakes in both the Ambrosiano and La Centrale. He would carry out his promise to sell Rizzoli, but retain the investment in BA Holding – and, therefore, in the overseas network. The new holding company would have an initial capital of 200 billion lire, subscribed by unidentified "founding shareholders". This would soon be increased to 500 billion lire. Most of the money would be spent on the acquisition of Ambrosiano shares.

Perhaps Calvi imagined that this would enable him to dispose of the secret network's holding of shares. But, if he thought that the Italian investing public would have happily subscribed to a new holding company that proceeded to buy Ambrosiano shares at $200 each, he was dreaming.

When trading in Ambrosiano shares began on the main Milan stock exchange on 5 May, Calvi was there in person to see how the shares were doing. They did badly. They were quoted at 40,000 lire each (about $33). Investors' faith in Calvi was waning.

The IOR, too, was losing its faith in him. The two big Swiss franc back-to-back loans were falling due: the 22,720,000 from the Cisalpine on 12 May and the 101,245,000 from the Andino on 15 May. Telexes began to fly between Luxembourg, Nassau and Lima. On 19 May instructions were issued that they should both be extended, but only until 14 June.

Calvi was now desperately looking for some other body that might be prepared to lend him the money, so that he could repay the IOR. The second letter from him to Monsignor Franco, found in his briefcase, was dated 12 May. "I am, with this letter, requesting that you grant me a meeting as soon as possible, as I must speak to you on matters of the greatest urgency and importance. As I have already told you in fact, during our last talk, the need to find $250 – $300 million has become most necessary. Concerning this I would like to discuss with you some of my ideas, which I believe to be most useful in order to facilitate and speed up the finding of the above-mentioned funds."

Is this, as the Calvi family has suggested, a forgery? Calvi was hoping for support somewhere in the Vatican. Clara Calvi told the second inquest in London that her husband said he had spoken directly to the Pope about the repayment of the debt and the handling of the Vatican finances. He also told her that he was looking to Opus Dei to repay the debt. Anna Calvi repeated this.

There is no evidence that Calvi ever saw the Pope, though no doubt he would have liked to. Another suspect letter from his briefcase, addressed to Cardinal Palazzini and dated 30 May, asks for such a meeting. But the request was certainly ignored and Calvi resorted to drafting the Pope a letter. Did he also approach Opus Dei? Palazzini was supposed to be close to this rich and secretive society of Catholic businessmen. Opus Dei has denied that Calvi ever did approach it; certainly he got no money that way.

On 28 May three other back-to-back loans fell due: one from the Andino for $77 million and two from the Cisalpine, for $70 million and 10 million Swiss francs. No money arrived. The interest did; Zitropo borrowed another $4.2 million from Banco Comercial to pay that. There were no instructions about renewal. The sums just remained on the books of the Andino and the Cisalpine as being due from the IOR on demand.

According to Carboni, Calvi's relations with the IOR came to a head in late May. Something happened – but what? Carboni has frequently contradicted himself. In his early versions, he said that Franco had at last persuaded the IOR to talk to Calvi. Marcinkus was away, arranging the Pope's tour of Britain, which took place from 28 May to 2 June. But there was to be a meeting with Mennini and "those in charge" of the IOR. Carboni says this was fixed for 21 May; his friend Pellicani says 31 May. It was to be in the afternoon. Carboni and Calvi went to see Franco in the morning to discuss it. Franco advised Calvi to be open and truthful.

Carboni then had to leave for another appointment, but he arranged to call Calvi later in the morning. When he did, he was surprised to be told by Calvi that he had gone to see Mennini immediately after seeing Franco, and that it had been very brief and had not gone as he had expected, and that they would have to talk to Franco again.

In later versions the story became far more dramatic. The meeting fixed for the afternoon would have been not just with Mennini and those in charge of the IOR, but with a "commission of cardinals" who were to sit in judgement on the dispute between Calvi and the IOR. And Calvi, after he had seen Mennini on his own, was desperate and weeping, saying that he had messed everything up, that Mennini had been angry and had thrown him out of the office.

The "commission of cardinals" may sound unlikely – if the IOR's supervisory commission had been prepared to intervene, this has never been admitted by the Vatican – but that Calvi did go to see Mennini is likely enough. What he wanted is clear from the figures above: an extension of the loans. It is also likely that Mennini refused to listen.

Both Franco and Carboni were angry with Calvi for not having stuck to the original arrangement. In his later versions, Carboni even threatened to break off relations with Calvi; he relented, however, when Calvi pleaded with him.

Calvi had done rather more than plead. In mid-May he had ordered a further $7.5 million to be paid to the account at the Union Bank at Geneva airport in the name of Manuela Kleinszig. This time, however, the manager there sent it back to the Crédit Suisse in the Bahamas. Carboni, with the help of a Swiss friend, Hans Kunz, protested at the head office of the Union Bank in Zürich. On being told that the money was from the sale of tractors to Egypt, the Union Bank opened a new account for Carboni there. Calvi had by now increased the payment to $10 million – perhaps he regarded it as another *volano finanziario*, a reserve for his impending flight. This was credited to the new account at the beginning of June. (In the Banco Comercial it was retrospectively disguised as a loan to Inversionistas Dalavi.) But the Union Bank was again suspicious because Carboni had mentioned Calvi. Carboni was asked if the money came from the Vatican. He replied that it did in part, the remainder being "import-export operations". The Union Bank told him that they did not want the money.

This proves how bad Calvi's reputation had become. To find that no bank will lend you any money is bad; to have banks refusing even to act as intermediaries is worse; to have a Swiss bank refusing to accept your money is the end.

But Calvi was not acknowledging the end. Not yet. Carboni got over the immediate problem, by finding a little local bank, the Zürcher Kantonalbank, which seems to have accepted his money without question. And Calvi went on hoping for a change of heart on the part of the IOR. There is a story that he got in touch with Marcinkus, who had been in England with the Pope, and that Marcinkus told him he was wasting his time. If this is true, it must have happened on or after 2 June.

What, exactly, was Marcinkus planning to do if Calvi defaulted? Tell the world that the IOR no longer backed him? Denounce him to the magistrates? Either would have brought about the disaster which did in fact happen, but which Marcinkus was presumably still trying to avoid.

A much more effective threat would have been to reveal to de Bernardi in Luxembourg, and thus to Calvi's other executives, that the letters of patronage were not valid. This would in the end have had much the same effect as a public announcement, but it might have meant a slow collapse of Calvi's power, rather than a crash. Then the IOR might have had some chance of recovering at least a part of its investment.

And what did Marcinkus mean to do if Calvi did succeed in finding the money? Cover up for him as before? Keep up the charade of the letters of patronage? It was significant that they carried no maturity date. In his memorandum to the joint commission, Marcinkus implied that, even if Calvi had paid up, the IOR would have broken off relations. In that case, what incentive had he to pay up?

On 30 May Calvi's daughter Anna had lunch with him at Drezzo. (Clara had gone to Washington to stay with Carlo.) According to Anna's evidence at the second inquest, Calvi told her that there was a deal he had to close with the Vatican, and that it involved a large sum of money. "For that amount of money people can kill," he said. There were people who wanted to prevent the deal, and for that reason were ready to kill him.

Anna got the impression that it was the IOR which had to pay the Ambrosiano, which was true as far as it went. What she did not understand was that United Trading first had to repay the IOR. Calvi told her that Opus Dei was going to find the money for the IOR. Even if that had been true, which it was not, why should anyone have wanted to kill him? In front of Anna, he took a dismantled gun out of a cupboard, assembled it and said: "If they come I will kill them."

This may all have been put on for Anna's benefit. If Calvi thought he was going to be accused of organising the shooting of Rosone, he would not want his wife and daughter to believe him guilty. The best way to distract their minds was to suggest that he was himself in danger.

And yet he went to the trouble of taking the gun from Drezzo to Milan. When the family had the contents of the Via Frua apartment moved to Montreal, in one of the packing cases was the automatic and two boxes of ammunition.

But a gun was useless to him against his fellow-directors of the Ambrosiano.

THIRTY-SIX

Like the Devil He Has Disappeared towards Hell

On 31 May 1982 the Bank of Italy sent a stern letter to Calvi, commenting on his restructuring plan. It said the plan needed a "more concrete and exhaustive definition" for both the internal and the external holdings of the Ambrosiano.

The sting of the letter came when it pointed out that, by Calvi's own figures, the total exposure to "third parties" of the Cisalpine, the Andino and the Banco Comercial came to more than \$1.4 billion. The lack of adequate information about the nature of the risks meant it was impossible to value BA Holding's investments in these subsidiaries.

It is not clear exactly how much of the Bank of Italy's importunities Calvi had been keeping from his fellow-directors in recent months. In February the Bank of Italy had demanded that the directors and the auditors should be shown all the correspondence, and should declare, in writing, that they had all the information they required to carry out their statutory duties. It now reiterated this demand and called for a special board meeting, at which the directors and auditors should be shown the latest letter.

Then they were to hold another board meeting, in the shortest possible time, to approve a new restructuring plan, which would comply with the law.

Calvi had already strung the authorities along for eighteen months, and they were still not imposing a time limit for compliance. He may have hoped to keep stalling for a bit longer. However, he called a board meeting for Monday 7 June.

Calvi spent the previous weekend at Drezzo, where he wrote more letters. One, dated 5 June, was to the Pope himself. It was not in his briefcase but turned up in the course of investigations into the whereabouts of its contents. Carboni admitted that he had given it to a Czech bishop in the Vatican, in what circumstances we shall see. It was not publicised until April 1992, and, although there were allegations that it was a forgery, it sounds genuine enough.

Calvi wrote he had thought much in recent days and had concluded that his Holiness was "the last hope". He was, he wrote, having to carry the heavy burden of the "errors and faults committed by the present and previous representatives of the IOR". He had, on the orders of the Pope's "authoritative representatives", financed "many countries and politico-religious associations." He had created banks in South America to counter the penetration of pro-marxist ideology in concert with Vatican authorities and now he had been "betrayed and abandoned" by those he had always treated with the maximum "respect and obedience".

Since we now know the real reasons for the formation of Ambrosiano banks in South America, there is also little cause to believe the implications behind another claim Calvi made to the Pope, that many people wanted to know if he had supplied arms to South America and money to Solidarity. Was he hoping the Pope might yield to veiled blackmail? As a Vatican official said when denying that the Pope had ever received the letter, Calvi sounded a desperate man.

By some accounts Carboni turned up at Drezzo on 6 June, with pessimistic news from Monsignor Franco. That day Calvi wrote again to Franco. The letter begins: "The hope for clarifying in time my relationship with the IOR is now lost. Also lost is the hope of obtaining a loan of $300 million in the next ten days. Now I must try to arrange *not without risk* (my italics) and with all my strength, to repay the above-mentioned sum at least."

The letter is odd. It goes on to refer to the Vatican "commission" which, according to Carboni, was supposed to arbitrate between Calvi and the IOR. Was there ever any such commission? If not, Carboni may, as Calvi's heirs have suggested, have forged the letter. But why would he have forged the reference to "risk"? The suggestion that Calvi embarked on his last journey knowing it would be hazardous is no part of Carboni's argument. He has always maintained that whatever dangers Calvi feared were in Italy, not abroad.

That Calvi was now meditating flight is clear. Anna, who was at Drezzo that weekend, booked a hotel room at Morcote on Lake Lugano, just inside Switzerland. When Calvi got back to Milan that evening, he packed two suitcases and put them in a cupboard.

On the morning of Monday 7 June, Calvi met Angelo Rizzoli and Tassan Din to discuss the much-postponed sale of Rizzoli to the Cabassi group. They may also have talked of the investigations into the Rizzoli Finanziaria-Savoia-Banca Mercantile affair. The same day, Tassan Din wrote a long memorandum about that to the Roman magistrate Cudillo, countersigned by Rizzoli. He alleged that 1 billion lire of the illicit 3.9 billion lire profit had gone to the Ambrosiano on Calvi's direct instructions. With such friends as these, did Calvi need enemies?

In the afternoon the Ambrosiano board meeting had to consider the letter from the Bank of Italy. Calvi told his fellow-directors that other commitments had kept him away from Milan for nearly all the previous week. So the discussion would have to be postponed until the next board meeting.

A few months earlier, all Calvi's fellow-directors would have heard this in respectful silence. The director who now protested was the man brought in to make Calvi's life easier after De Benedetti went, the man who had not expected an office or any say in the day-to-day running of the bank – Orazio Bagnasco.

It was not a noisy protest. Nor did Bagnasco insist on an immediate discussion. All he wanted was that each director should be allowed to take home and study at leisure the Bank of Italy's letter and the preceding documents, copies of which had been prepared for them. A vote was taken. With Calvi and Rosone abstaining, the board voted by a majority for Bagnasco's proposal. Rosone afterwards explained his abstention by saying that, as managing director, he had no need to take the papers home to study them.

We now come to the many conflicting accounts of who last saw Calvi on which date. The people who contradict each other may not be telling lies; they were questioned days, weeks or months afterwards, and may well be mistaken.

It seems to have been on the same day as the board meeting that Carboni came to supper at Calvi's apartment in Via Frua. But it may have been the following evening; the accounts are inconsistent. Carboni's diary of phone calls made to his office (as later published by the P2 Commission) has no page for 8 June.

Whether it was on Monday 7 June or Tuesday 8 June, it was a cold meal, prepared by Anna. After dinner, over a whisky, Carboni and Calvi had a long talk. Calvi had recently started to give Carboni a fuller picture of his financial dealings, even telling him the names of the secret network companies. (Or so Carboni said afterwards, but he was interrogated when some of the names of the companies were already common knowledge.)

Calvi now told Carboni that his problem could be solved only if someone were to buy the secret holding of Ambrosiano shares. He had acquired a further million or so on the market, in the secret support operation begun in February, so that he had a total of nearly 6.5 million shares.

For this plan of Calvi's we do not have to take Carboni's unsupported word. A few days earlier, Calvi had phoned Botta at home early in the morning, to ask him the exact number of shares held by the secret companies and the precise size of their debts. Botta got the information from Luxembourg. Calvi then asked him to draw up a transfer form for the shares, for sale to an unspecified third party for $1.2 billion, the size of the debts.

Pazienza has claimed that he was still negotiating with an American/ Middle Eastern consortium (not one member of which he has ever produced). His story is that he last spoke to Calvi about it on the phone on 8 June. He was planning a trip to New York to see Armao about the sale the following weekend.

According to Carboni, Calvi talked as if the IOR had promised to buy the shares, but had then let him down. This can hardly have been true. But did Calvi, by this time, know truth from falsehood?

What emerges from Carboni's statements is Calvi's insistence that his priority was to find the $250 to $300 million to meet the immediate crisis with the IOR. That came before the sale of the shares. It must have been at this point that they discussed a plan for Calvi to go to Zürich, where it seems he thought he could get the money to pay the IOR. Did Calvi really think he had money waiting for him in Zürich? Did he believe the Bellatrix money was still in the account at Rothschilds? Was he thinking of striding into Rothschilds and demanding to know where it was? Or had he been in touch with Ortolani or Gelli, and got some promise out of them?

When Carboni left that evening, he took with him Calvi's packed suitcases. He left them, it seems, at an hotel.

This is where the timetable becomes tricky. At about nine in the morning of 9 June Anna went to Morcote. Calvi went to the bank as usual. At some time that day he was visited by Alvaro Giardili, one of the new acquaintances introduced to him by Pazienza the previous summer, in Sardinia. His visiting card was found on Calvi's body. The journalists Piazzesi and Bonsanti, in their book *The Story of Roberto Calvi*, say that Giardili told Calvi that his wife and children were under threat of death. Piazzesi and Bonsanti asked Giardili who told him about the threat. He replied: "Taboo."

Was it a real threat? It may have been. The following year Giardili was arrested during a round-up of suspected Mafiosi. It might also have been part of a plan to separate Calvi from anyone who, at this crisis, might have given him some sensible advice, or at least kept his feet on the ground.

At midday Calvi was in his apartment at Via Frua. His brother-in-law, Luciano Canetti, had lunch with him there, and found him in good health and spirits, according to his statement, read at the first inquest. In the same statement Canetti said he had a call from Calvi at 9 p.m. the same evening, and thought he was phoning from his office in the Ambrosiano. This is possible, because that evening Calvi had a dinner date at the Ambrosiano guest suite. His guests were Francesco Micheli, the man who had introduced De Benedetti to Calvi, the French banker Pierre Moussa, then head of Paribas, Karl Kahane, an Austrian businessman, and Florio Fiorini, the ENI finance director. Micheli had organised the party so that Calvi could discuss the possible acquisition by Moussa and Kahane of the Ambrosiano's foreign subsidiaries. It can only be assumed that they had not glanced at the books. At the dinner, Calvi talked in French about himself, his life and the Falklands War (then raging). Moussa said they were prepared to spend $200 million on the foreign operations of the Ambrosiano. Calvi prevaricated; it would, of course, have been impossible to disentangle the foreign subsidiaries from the group. Suddenly he walked out, almost before dinner was over. Micheli ran after him, but could not reach him; he was already in the lift, going down. Micheli said to his fellow-guests: "Like the devil, he has disappeared towards hell."

Calvi must have been in a great hurry to get to the airport. Who took him there has never come to light. The ride from the centre of Milan to Linate airport would take less than half an hour; the flight to Rome normally about 45 minutes. Carboni's right-hand man Pellicani was told to go to Rome airport to meet him at 9.30 pm. On finding that Calvi would not be there until 11.30, (as Pellicani remembered it, the plane had been delayed by a storm) Pellicani left Calvi's own chauffeur, Tito, to pick him up.

Calvi went straight to a flat Carboni had in Via Ignazio Guidi, in the southern suburbs of Rome. (He had another in Via Farnesina, on the other side of the city.) Carboni himself was out, entertaining guests at a night club. But Manuela Kleinszig was there; so was Pellicani, who was staying with Carboni although he had a flat of his own. (Pellicani has been much interrogated since, and has on the whole proved a better witness to times and dates than Carboni.) Calvi waited for Carboni to come home, and then spoke to him briefly. Carboni woke Pellicani, who had gone to bed, and asked him to drive Calvi to the flat which Calvi himself kept in Rome, in the Via del Collegio Capranica, in the old part of the city.

The following day, 10 June, seemed to be one of business as usual for Calvi. He went to the Ambrosiano's main Rome office, and rang up Rosone. He also went to see his Rome lawyers, Giorgio Gregori and Pietro Moscato.

Carboni had, he claimed in his early statements, a "nondescript" day. So nondescript, in fact, that he forgot it altogether, until the investigators jogged his memory. In his later accounts he said he had arranged to have lunch with Calvi. But Calvi rang his office in the morning to put it off, suggesting that they should meet in the evening instead.

They did meet that evening, but where and when is hard to make out from the conflicting accounts given by Carboni and Pellicani. At some point in the evening Carboni went to Calvi's flat. Then he left, but later he sent Pellicani to fetch Calvi and take him to Pellicani's own flat in Via Valperga, in the suburb of Magliana. Carboni joined them there and talked to Calvi alone, while Pellicani waited. Then Carboni and Pellicani left Calvi on his own and returned to Carboni's flat in Via Ignazio Guidi. It was now after 3 a.m. on a very warm night.

Calvi's move to the Via Valperga in the middle of the night of 10/11 June was the moment of his disappearance. Before he abandoned his own flat he left a short note, saying that he was tired and not feeling well, and was going away for a few days. There is only Carboni's word for what passed between Calvi and himself that night. He was no longer using a tape recorder when he talked to Calvi.

In his lengthiest account of that night's conversation, given in 1985, Carboni said that Calvi was worried about three things.

First, he had heard rumours that the president of the appeal court, due to hear the currency case on 21 June, would probably uphold his conviction.

Second, he was under pressure to pay some unnamed person 10 billion lire to secure the destruction of some incriminating document connected with the P2 investigations.

Third, Mennini was still insistent that the money owed to the IOR should be repaid. This was, apparently, what worried Calvi most. Mennini, with whom he had made an appointment at 8.30 in the morning, had demanded payment the following day. Otherwise he would "expose" Calvi.

It was primarily the threat from Mennini, according to Carboni, that made Calvi determined to go to Zürich. Carboni had by this time made arrangements for Calvi in Zürich, through his Swiss business associate Hans Kunz. Yet he claims he tried to dissuade Calvi from going abroad, suggesting that he could lie low in Sardinia for a time. Calvi did not want to do that. As Carboni left, Calvi was apparently still undecided. Should he go to Zürich at once, or should he keep the 8.30 a.m. appointment with Mennini, and make a final attempt to persuade him?

Carboni's various versions of the story have all stressed Calvi's difficulties with the IOR, but not until the beginning of 1984 did Carboni come out with the version that the aim of Calvi's last journey was to raise the $250 to $300 million he needed to meet the IOR's demands. However late, the story may be true.

None of this explains why Calvi should have left his flat in the middle of the night. The story that the IOR was going to expose him at once is most unlikely to be true. Although most of the back-to-back loans were now on call, the two biggest Swiss franc loans had been renewed until 14 June, not 11 June. The deadline Marcinkus had set was for 30 June. So the IOR was not going to do anything that night.

Even if Calvi was planning to travel to Zürich the following day, why should that mean leaving his own apartment for Pellicani's in the middle of the night? There is something missing from Carboni's account of the conversation. One explanation that makes sense is that Calvi feared immediate arrest. He may have been tipped off that the Roman magistrate Cudillo was about to issue warrants for the arrest of Tassan Din, Gelli, Ortolani and others involved in the Rizzoli Finanziaria-Savoia-Banca Mercantile fraud. The warrants were to be issued later that day, 11 June. In fact there was no warrant for Calvi's arrest; he was to be ordered only to appear before Cudillo and say what he knew about the matter. But even that prospect might have scared him into precipitate flight.

Another explanation may be that Carboni frightened him. Carboni may have known that the Milan magistrate Alfonso Marra was actively pursuing the trail suggested by the telltale body of the gunman in the road. Danilo Abbruciati had, after all, been Carboni's partner. If the trail led to Carboni, it was not going to stop there. (A week later, on 18 June, the magistrate Marra was breaking it to Rosone that all the connections of the man who had shot him were leading them back to Calvi.)

Treating Calvi like a goose which might lay more golden eggs, Carboni made careful arrangements to get him out of the country. He phoned Silvano Vittor, a 37-year-old smuggler in Trieste. They knew each other because Vittor's mistress, Michaela Kleinszig, was the sister of Carboni's mistress Manuela. Vittor, who had an adolescent son by his wife, had a small girl by Michaela. His legal job was working in the building business of a relative; his illegal one was smuggling clothes and coffee between Italy and Yugoslavia, and for this he owned three motor boats. He was always on the lookout for ways of making more money; he had already asked Calvi to employ him as a driver. Now he agreed to look after Calvi without (according to himself) making any stipulation about money.

Pellicani went to his flat at about 10.30 to give Calvi breakfast. Calvi was up, but had not been to see Mennini. Presumably he had decided that it was useless to ask for an extension of the IOR deadline. He did not know that, when he failed to turn up at the IOR, Mennini had phoned his Rome office, which thus learned of his disappearance.

Pellicani was due to fly to Venice that day to see his mother. Carboni arranged that Calvi should go with him, and that Pellicani should then drive him to Trieste. Pellicani booked two seats on the 2.30 p.m. flight to Venice. Then he picked Calvi up and took him to the airport, which they reached shortly after one.

From the airport, at 1.30, Calvi rang his office in Milan, and spoke to Gabriella Corrocher and then to Rosone. He learned that his driver had found the note he left, and had taken it to the Rome office of the Ambrosiano. His lawyers, Gregori and Moscato, had also been informed, and had gone at once to inform the magistrate Cudillo. Finding that Cudillo was out, they informed a senior magistrate, Domenico Sica.

Calvi's family has since suggested that the lawyers acted too hastily. Calvi had not then left the country. At the time, too, Calvi was annoyed by all the fuss. It seems not to have entered his head that people would think he had written the note under duress, and had been kidnapped.

He told Rosone that nothing had happened to him, and that he had changed his programme because an unexpected commitment had arisen. He said he would be back in his office on the evening of the next day, Saturday. He wanted Leoni and Botta to be there too.

Shortly afterwards he rang Rosone again, to ask for any further news, and to assure him once again that he was all right.

Calvi also rang Mennini, to apologise for missing his appointment. We know this not only from Pellicani, but from Mennini, who later said that Calvi promised to see him the following week.

On the flight to Venice was Tina Anselmi, who chaired the parliamentary P2 commission. Calvi had given evidence before her – and yet she did not recognise him. No more did Mariano Rumor, another politician who knew him, nor Guido Carli, who had been Governor of the Bank of Italy at the time of the Sindona crash. This is not so odd as it seems. Calvi was known behind his back as "the bank clerk", and he looked like one. Without his normal entourage of underlings and bodyguards, he was totally unremarkable.

At Venice airport they hired a car and drove to see Pellicani's mother. Pellicani drove Calvi on to Trieste, where they met Vittor, as arranged, at the Hotel Savoia Excelsior. They all went to Vittor's apartment.

Only at this point (according to Carboni) did Calvi make up his mind to leave Italy. Carboni told the British police that Calvi rang Mennini from Trieste, asking yet again for an extension on the time limit for repayment. Mennini said no.

Carboni's story is that, because of Mennini's refusal, Calvi rang Carboni (who was still in Rome) asking him to send a passport and some money.

Calvi's own Italian passport had been finally confiscated over a year earlier. Even before that, he had been collecting alternatives. His Nicaraguan friends had got him two passports, an ordinary one and a diplomatic one. They were in his own name, which was not useful if he wanted to leave the country unobserved. However, he had them with him. He had at least one false Italian passport; Clara Calvi saw him hiding it in the Milan apartment in April. Was this the passport that he asked Carboni to send?

According to Carboni, while they were talking in the night of 10/11 June in Pellicani's apartment, Calvi told him that an envelope containing a passport would be delivered to Carboni's home. And, after Calvi had left for Venice, an unidentified man turned up with it.

At this point Carboni's friend from the underworld, Diotallevi, re-enters the story. He had been in close contact with Carboni and Pellicani for some days. The telephone diary kept by the secretary at Carboni's office, which was afterwards published by the P2 commission, recorded numerous calls from him, some with cryptic messages, such as: "Time is running out; stay in the vicinity of the Via Veneto", and "Leave your address – very urgent – otherwise he will miss the train". There is no page for 8 June, but on the morning of 9 June Diotallevi rang to say that a "blond youth (SERGIO)" had arrived. At the moment the passport was delivered, Diotallevi happened to be with Carboni, asking Carboni to repay a debt of 160 million lire (about $125,000) to Diotallevi's mother-in-law, Filomena Angelini. This part of the story is curious because, of the $530,000 that Carboni had paid to Diotallevi on 4 May, some had already gone to Filomena. Diotallevi was also thinking of buying Carboni's private plane, a Cessna 210. Carboni was willing to sell because Calvi had offered to sell him the Lear jet.

It was now decided that Diotallevi would go in the Cessna to Trieste, so that he could see the plane's performance and at the same time deliver the envelope to Pellicani. Diotallevi took the blond youth with him. During the flight he discovered that the envelope contained a passport for Calvi. Whether he told the blond youth about it was not clear. But certainly one more person now knew that Calvi was about to leave Italy from Trieste. When Diotallevi arrived at Trieste he wanted to give the passport to Calvi personally, but Pellicani, who was waiting at the airport, persuaded him to hand over the passport and the money.

It is more likely that Calvi had brought a passport from Milan, and had given it to Carboni to have doctored, than that Carboni's friends had produced a completely new one in such a short space of time.

Once Pellicani had delivered the passport and the money to Calvi, he went back to Rome in the Cessna plane with Diotallevi and the blond youth. The youth has never been identified. Pellicani was told his name, and scribbled it on a piece of paper, but afterwards could not read his own handwriting. He said the name was "Mecalli" or "Mecarri" or maybe "Mecaki". They arrived back in Rome in the early hours of the morning.

Calvi, too, spent most of the night travelling. Vittor took him to the nearby harbour of Muggia, and then in a boat along the coast to Yugoslavia – a journey of only fifteen minutes. Calvi had nothing with him but a notebook, according to one account given by Vittor. In Yugoslavia Vittor entrusted him to two local friends, never identified, who drove him the 150 kilometres to Klagenfurt in Austria, where he was to stay with the Kleinszig sisters and their father. Manuela was still with Carboni in Rome, but Calvi was received by Michaela, mistress of Vittor. She had not been told Calvi was coming, and, at five in the morning, she was not pleased. She asked him to go to a hotel. He pleaded to be allowed to come in and wait for Carboni.

Vittor had returned to Trieste. He had to attend the confirmation of his son that day.

On Saturday 12 June, at about 8 a.m. Calvi rang Anna, who was still at Morcote. He told her that he was in Austria, and that he was all right, but tired. He said he did not think anyone had noticed his departure. (Yet he knew the magistrates had been informed of his disappearance.) He suggested that she should listen for it on the news. He also asked her to ring her mother and brother in Washington to reassure them – but not to reveal where he was, so that they could not accidentally drop any clues.

Clara and Carlo already knew about Calvi's disappearance. They had been rung on Friday evening by Pazienza, who said he had just learned the news from a senior policeman known to him and Calvi, Federico D'Amato. Pazienza was ringing from the Dorchester Hotel in London. He had come to London for the night, before catching the morning Concorde flight to New York, where (according to himself) he was due to discuss the sale of Ambrosiano shares with Armao. We have seen that no such sale was ever seriously in prospect.

THIRTY-SEVEN

Where Have We Landed Up?

The first news of Calvi's disappearance was published by the ADN Kronos news agency that Saturday at 12.22, under the headline: "Calvi has vanished; has he been kidnapped?" It was broadcast on news bulletins shortly afterwards. Calvi rang Carboni and asked him to come right away. Carboni's story is that he had not been expecting to see Calvi until the following Monday, when they were due to meet in Zürich. But, because of the publicity, Calvi wanted to discuss their plans at once.

Late that afternoon Carboni, Pellicani and Manuela left Rome in the Cessna plane. They flew first to Milan, where they dropped Pellicani and collected the two suitcases of Calvi's which Carboni had left at an hotel earlier in the week. Carboni and Manuela flew on to Klagenfurt. Calvi and Michaela met them at the airport, and they returned to the house for dinner. According to Carboni, Calvi was so delighted to see him that he gave him an expensive watch.

Calvi showed Carboni one of his Nicaraguan passports. He had used it, he said, in crossing from Yugoslavia to Austria. He did not use it again, though; the Kleinszig family produced it months after Calvi's death, saying it had been found behind the piano.

Late that evening Vittor, the smuggler, arrived by car from Trieste. Did he bring Calvi's briefcase with him? In early interrogations this was denied, but in 1990 Vittor admitted, apparently after some hesitation, at least that Calvi did have his briefcase in Klagenfurt.

The following morning, Sunday 13 June, Calvi was seen burning some papers in the fireplace. He may have burned his address book – with the exception of one page, which was found on him after his death (see photograph between pages 248 and 249). He kept seven other scraps of paper with addresses, phone numbers and other figures scrawled on them. But why that one page of the address book? It had names beginning with F. On one side the names were typed, but with many handwritten alterations and additions. On the other side were further handwritten telephone numbers, including at least two for Monsignor Franco. (These tragic events did not deprive Monsignor Franco of his interest in finance. In 1986 he was accused of illegally exporting currency to the value of $13.2 million, in partnership with an Israeli and two Americans. In his defence he said that Israelis often helped Catholic charities, and that he had been convinced of the "good and pious intentions" of his partners. He was acquitted.)

On the typed side of the page from Calvi's diary was the name of Firrao, the P2 member who, as a senior civil servant at the Mincomes, had played such a crucial part in Calvi's early dealings with Gelli and Ortolani. Firrao had since become head of SACE, the state export credit insurance body. Was Calvi planning to use him to put pressure on Gelli and Ortolani? Those dealings with the Mincomes are a sore point with Gelli to this day; when I asked him about them he resorted to blatant lies.

Calvi spent a great deal of time, that Sunday morning, on the telephone. Most of the calls were to his family. Carlo Calvi had been due to attend a computer conference in Los Angeles when he heard of his father's disappearance. Once Anna had phoned Washington with the news that Calvi was alive and well, Carlo and his mother decided to go to Los Angeles, but to leave their phone number with Anna. Calvi rang Anna, who gave him the number. He rang Clara in Los Angeles, where it was still Saturday night, and assured her that he was all right. She remembers him ringing her three or four times. What other phone calls Calvi made we do not know.

The whole party then decided to lunch at a restaurant at St Veit, a small town nearby. But outside the restaurant Calvi saw a car with Italian number plates, and feared that he would be recognised. So they all had lunch at the house in Klagenfurt.

After lunch Calvi and Carboni discussed their plans. According to Carboni, Calvi still wanted to go to Zürich, in spite of the publicity. He wanted to collect a sum of money, the delivery of which he had been assured, and to negotiate for the rest of the sum he needed to repay the IOR. According to one of Carboni's later statements, the sum Calvi was sure of collecting was $150 million.

Calvi asked Carboni to ring Franco and tell him not to worry about the stories in the newspapers, because Calvi was in the process of finding a solution to the problem.

What money could Calvi have meant? Carboni was clearly confused by Calvi's various references to sums of money, and did not distinguish between money which belonged to Calvi personally and money on which he had a claim as part of the Ambrosiano group. The sum of $150 million suggests that it was the Bellatrix money Calvi had in mind. One vital piece of evidence is missing. If we had the last balance sheets Calvi made out for

United Trading, we should know whether he regarded the Bellatrix money as an asset, or as gone for good.

Had Calvi already been in touch with Gelli and Ortolani, and had they promised to hand over $150 million?

Gelli has maintained that he had no contact with Calvi after Christmas 1981, and that Calvi would not have known where he was, though movements of money in his bank accounts suggest that he was in Europe, rather than in South America. Large sums went through his account at the Compagnie Monégasque de Banque in Monte Carlo, so Gelli may have been at his villa in Cap Ferrat.

Ortolani told *La Repubblica* in 1983 that he last saw Gelli in April or May 1982. Ortolani was almost certainly in Switzerland at this time. He was based in Geneva. A secret service memorandum, later published by the P2 Commission, records that he left Switzerland for São Paulo in Brazil, but not until 16 June. We have so far followed Calvi's movements only until Sunday 13 June.

On that day Tassan Din was still in Milan, apparently unaware of the arrest warrant signed by Cudillo in Rome two days before. (It had not been made public.) He was interviewed on television about Calvi's disappearance. But he quietly left Italy shortly afterwards, "on business", said a statement from Rizzoli, issued when the *Guardia di Finanza* tried to arrest him two days later. It was reported that he was in Switzerland – possibly in Lausanne, where his family lived. He was due to appear before Cudillo the following Friday, 18 June, on a separate charge – *violenza privata*, or the undue influence which he was supposed to have exerted over Calvi, when he was in prison the previous year, to make him say that the Sudam $21 million had been paid to the Socialist Party.

If Calvi was in touch with Tassan Din, he might have asked him for help in getting the Bellatrix money back. But there is no evidence that this happened.

That Sunday evening a board meeting of the Ambrosiano was held in Milan, at the insistence of the Bank of Italy. Bagnasco wanted to be chairman in Calvi's place. He was already vice chairman, after all. But Rosone was a vice chairman too, and he insisted that he was senior to Bagnasco. It shows how little they knew of what had hit them that they still thought the position desirable.

The board reached a compromise. Bagnasco was put in charge of a delegation to negotiate the restructuring plan with the Bank of Italy immediately. The directors expressed the hope that Calvi would make a "speedy return to his family and his work".

As they passed that resolution, their chairman was preparing to set out from Klagenfurt to Zürich, with a petty smuggler for company.

What did they find to talk about? At dinner, Calvi reminisced about his wartime experiences in Russia. Then, at about 10 p.m., he and Vittor set out in an Alfa Romeo belonging to Michaela. The rest of the party stayed at Klagenfurt for the night. The following morning, Monday 14 June, Carboni got a phone call from Calvi. He was at Innsbruck, which he had reached at about 5 a.m. He wanted to see Carboni urgently, because he had changed his mind about going to Zürich. Would Carboni join him as soon as possible?

In one of his statements, Carboni has said that this was most inconvenient for him, since he was planning to go to Lugano, where he had arranged to meet Diotallevi to discuss the money he owed to Diotallevi's mother-in-law. From there he had intended to go back to Rome, and then to Venezuela and the United States. But this is not consistent with his other story, that he had been expecting to meet Calvi in Zürich on 14 June.

Zürich was in fact where he went, in the early afternoon of that Monday, on a Crossair scheduled flight. Manuela went with him. So did Michaela, leaving her child with an aunt. The previous day he had sent the Cessna back to Italy. It needed servicing, he said. (Perhaps the movements of a private plane would have been too easy to trace. Or Carboni may not have wanted the pilot to know where he was going.)

Hans Kunz met them at Zürich airport, and they checked in at the best hotel, the Baur au Lac. Carboni then rang Calvi and asked him if he would mind meeting them in Bregenz, just on the Austrian side of the border, to save them the long drive to Innsbruck. Calvi agreed, and rang back a little later with the name of a hotel, the Centrale, where they could all meet. He also asked Carboni to bring some money for him. This Carboni could do, because he had in Zürich the $10 million that Calvi had recently paid him. Hans Kunz had signatory powers, up to a limit, on Carboni's account at the Zürcher Kantonalbank. Carboni says he got Kunz to collect $20,000 for Calvi. However, Carboni omitted to say that he also drew out money for his own use; altogether $60,000 and 30,000 Swiss francs were withdrawn from that account that day. And on the same day Carboni ordered $200,000 to be paid into Manuela's account at a bank in St Veit, where the girls' mother lived.

Calvi, at the Hotel Europa Tyrol in Innsbruck, was spending much of his time on the phone, according to Vittor. It may have been at this point that he telephoned his Rome lawyers, Gregori and Moscato. They were to say, after his death, that he had been in touch with them, and that he did not sound at all depressed, and certainly not suicidal. But the only call known for certain was one to Anna, who told him that she and her fiancé, Vittorio Senso, were leaving Morcote and going to Lucerne, because it was further away from Italy. When she knew where she was staying she would leave her number with a friend, from whom her father could get it.

That same day, Monday 14 June, the two back-to-back loans, totalling 123,965,000 Swiss francs, were due to be repaid to the IOR. They were not. And there are signs that at this point the IOR saw the coming catastrophe.

The first sign was what happened to the interest on the Swiss franc loans. Though the principal had not been repaid, the mechanism for the payment of the interest was still working. A last loan was made to Zitropo by Banco Comercial. From this 604,044.77 Swiss francs, representing the interest on both loans, was paid to the United Trading account at the Banco di Roma per la Svizzera. The IOR, if it had kept to the usual procedure, would have passed the money on immediately to the Andino and the Cisalpine, less its commission of one sixteenth per cent. This time, it hung on to the money for a time, waiting to see what would happen.

Next, Marcinkus notified the Cisalpine that he was resigning his directorship. He wrote to Siegenthaler that it was no longer possible for him to find the time to attend board meetings, in view of his many other commitments.

This news, it seems, did not at once filter through to the executives of the Ambrosiano group. If it had, it would surely have destroyed what faith they still had in the letters of patronage.

The executives, however, had other bad news. Six Bank of Italy inspectors arrived in Milan that day, bearing a letter from Ciampi, who demanded that they should be shown the minutes of the Ambrosiano board meetings, and other relevant documents. Rosone turned for advice to Michel Leemans, manager of La Centrale. "And then a few phone calls were enough," Leemans said, "to establish what a serious position the Ambrosiano was in."

This was when Leemans told Rosone that he would have to call in "Grandmother" – The Bank of Italy.

But what about all this money the IOR appeared to owe? De Bernardi soon arrived from Luxembourg, bringing the letters of patronage. Rosone and Leemans made an appointment with the IOR for the morning of Wednesday 16 June.

How much of all this did Calvi know? He seems to have had an informant in Milan, but nobody has ever come forward.

On the afternoon of Monday 14 June, at about four, Calvi and Vittor left

Innsbruck and took three or four hours to drive to Bregenz, where they checked into the Hotel Centrale. From there Calvi rang Anna in Lucerne, and told her to go to Zürich. Kunz would help her to find somewhere to stay, he said. Anna was uneasy; she did not know Kunz. It is not clear whether Calvi now told his daughter that he himself would not be in Zürich.

Carboni and Kunz had left the Kleinszig sisters in Zürich, and were having a difficult journey to Bregenz, because of Kunz's erratic driving. Calvi grew tired of waiting for them. He and Vittor went to a restaurant to eat. Carboni and Kunz found them there about nine. Vittor was sent back to the hotel; the others made it clear that they did not want him there while they talked.

Calvi explained that he did not want to go to Zürich, because he thought he might be recognised and arrested. He was a director of the Gottardo, a Swiss bank, and the Swiss authorities might want to detain him for their own reasons. He had decided to go to London instead.

Why London? Carboni told the British police: "He said that in London he could manoeuvre as if he was in Zürich, that in London he had all his deposits in gold and jewels, that he had many friends there in a position to help him, that it was the capital of masonry, that he spoke English perfectly and that he knew the city like the back of his hand."

The words of one proven liar, retailed by another, must be doubly unreliable. No evidence has ever emerged that Calvi had gold and jewels in London at the time. (Clara Calvi had jewels, which were afterwards found in the safe at Nassau.) There is no evidence that he had any contacts with English Freemasons, in spite of his own cryptic remarks about joining a London lodge. He understood English; he had learned it, as a necessary commercial language, when he was working his way to the top, but he seems to have been very shy of speaking it. As for friends – his reason for going to London would surely be that he was not known, outside Claridge's, the St James's Club and a handful of banks.

Calvi did have a small amount of money in London, managed for him by a subsidiary of Artoc, which had been set up by Ellsworth Donnell. He may have been comforted by the knowledge that he could get at this. (Although, in the event, he never did.)

Carboni has also suggested that Calvi chose London because it would be a convenient place to await developments and then make his next move, which might be to the Bahamas or America (either North or South). The one consistent part of Carboni's story is that Calvi's idea of going to London instead of Zürich arose only on 14 June, not before.

But Carboni's diary, taken from him on his arrest in Switzerland on

30 July 1982, provides one piece of evidence to the contrary. It was not systematically kept, and most days were left blank, but some carried entries of names, appointments and telephone numbers. For the day of Calvi's disappearance, 11 June 1982, the entry reads: "William Morris".

William Morris was married to the aunt of Carboni's Italian mistress, Laura Concas. The Morrises lived with their daughter Odette in modest circumstances in Heston, near Heathrow airport. They had met Carboni briefly a couple of times when they were on holiday in Italy, but they moved in different worlds. However, they were to play an important role when Carboni came to London. This entry in the diary, about which Carboni seems never to have been questioned, suggests that he foresaw their useful-ness on the day that Calvi left Italy. But nothing in this story is simple, and the telephone number which appears under the name is not that of the Morrises.

What about the money that Calvi had been hoping to get in Zürich? By Carboni's account, Calvi thought he could still get at it from London. But what money was it? Carboni's various versions bring in the "Banca Lam-bert", which he thought was in Zürich, and a sum of $150 million which Calvi could get at only if he had a power of attorney from his wife. He said that in the restaurant in Bregenz there was a discussion: should he or Kunz go to America and get this power of attorney from Clara Calvi?

This is the basis of the theory that Calvi could find a large part of the money he needed to repay the IOR from his own resources – that is, from the money he had successfully embezzled. Yet it is now clear that this was not so.

There is no "Banca Lambert" in Switzerland. Calvi may have talked of the Banque Bruxelles Lambert. At the Realfin account there he had paid in $6.3 million for Pazienza, all of which had now gone out again. But that was in Lausanne. It had branches in Geneva and Lugano, but none in Zürich.

Calvi's "own" money in Switzerland was managed by the Geneva private bank Lombard Odier. He would not have needed a power of attorney from his wife to remove it. We have seen that in early 1977 Ortolani paid some $1.3 million to a Lombard Odier company, Calodria, and that this money almost certainly represented Calvi's share of kickbacks he had paid out to Ortolani and Gelli. Calvi may also have transferred to Lombard Odier the $2 million previously paid by Ortolani to his Union Bank account. However shrewdly invested, the total could hardly have grown to $150 million. From late 1977 Calvi appears to have had all his illicit payments, amounting to about $8 million, paid to his account in the Bahamas. We have seen that his gains from his own fraud were petty by comparison with those of Gelli and Ortolani. On 30 March 1982 the Canadian property development he shared with another Ambrosiano director was sold for some $24 million – a profit of about $18 million; but all the proceeds had not yet been received and the evidence suggests that this money stayed in Canada, at least to begin with. In any event, he had no secret hoard in Switzerland, or anywhere else, of anything approaching the size necessary to repay the IOR.

Whatever else they talked about at Bregenz, Kunz certainly undertook to make arrangements for Calvi's trip to London. And Carboni gave Calvi the $20,000. (He told the British police that he gave Calvi $16,000 or $17,000 and Vittor $3,000 or $4,000.) Having settled that, they had quite a merry evening, by Carboni's account, with Kunz embracing and dancing with a large lady who owned the restaurant. Carboni and Kunz then had another hazardous trip back to Zürich.

Early the following morning Kunz got in touch with Lovat McDonald, a Scottish businessman living in Geneva, and asked him to arrange the visit to London of two Italians. McDonald rang his solicitor in London, Robert Clarke. Between them they organised a private plane to fly to Innsbruck to pick up two "directors of Fiat", as Clarke says he was told. A car was to meet them at Gatwick and take them to Chelsea Cloisters, a nine-storey block of 748 furnished apartments in Sloane Avenue, not far from the Thames. McDonald knew the place because his company, Draycott Finance, had an address nearby.

When Kunz had the details of the flight, he joined Carboni at the Baur au Lac. Together they rang Calvi in Bregenz, explaining to him that he would have to go back to Innsbruck to get the flight, and that the pilot would give him the address where he was to stay. Carboni also immediately authorised the payment from one of his accounts of $7,139 to Wood, Nash and Winters, Clarke's firm, to cover the cost of the flight (which was about £3,000) and a £100 deposit at Chelsea Cloisters, against the £565 price of the minimum let of 22 days.

Carboni then had another important conversation. Diotallevi was in Zürich. Why? And what did they talk about? Carboni's version makes even less sense than usual. He says that Diotallevi was asking him to repay the 160 million lire he owed to Diotallevi's mother-in-law. He told Diotallevi to wait until he got some money from Sardinia. Carboni was, no doubt, the sort of man who can always think of more amusing uses for money than repaying debts. But he still had nearly $10 million in the Zürcher Kantonal-bank; would he really have tried to bilk an associate who was given to hiring gunmen? If Diotallevi had business with Carboni, so urgent that he had followed him to Zürich to discuss it, it must surely have concerned Calvi.

That day, Tuesday 15 June, was when *La Stampa* published its interview with Calvi. The part about his attempted suicide we have already quoted. At the time, when nobody knew whether Calvi had fled or been kidnapped, what aroused the most interest was Calvi's reply when he was asked whether he had any idea who had ordered the attack on Rosone.

"Unfortunately, in these affairs there is no map to find one's bearings . . ." Calvi said. "Certainly, on reading all the theories put forward in the press about those responsible and their motives, I become truly frightened."

Asked whether he had received threats, he said: "We have received threats on the telephone which I have also reported. We were the object of a campaign of denigration in which Milan was inundated with posters. But I do not know from whom these warnings came, nor why they were made . . ."

So he was still denying that the posters of 1977 were put up on Sindona's orders, and that he had paid Sindona to stop. By this time these facts had been made clear in public, at hearings of the parliamentary commission on Sindona. But blank denials of the obvious had served Calvi well in the past, and he was not going to stop now. This was the interview in which, for the last time, he denied his membership of P2 – although he had admitted it to the P2 commission.

When he was asked about Gelli he said: "I have only had business dealings with Gelli, and certainly as a businessman he was very clever . . . Gelli was a person who put forward valid business propositions, worked on them and concluded them."

Why the praise? Did he want to put Gelli in a good mood, before he asked for some of his money back?

In Austria, Calvi and Vittor drove back to Innsbruck, where they met the pilot of their plane. Vittor did such talking as was necessary, in poor English. They left for Gatwick in the middle of the afternoon, without going through any customs or passport formalities. At Gatwick they seem to have had no trouble with immigration controls, in spite of Calvi's obviously doctored passport. (Or did he use his remaining Nicaraguan one? If so, he probably still had his briefcase with him.) They could not find the car that had been sent to meet them, and instead took a cab to Chelsea Cloisters. They arrived between eight and nine in the evening.

Calvi took an instant dislike to Chelsea Cloisters. He complained of the building even before he was inside. Flat 881, which they had been allotted with only one key between them, consisted of two small rooms, about 13 feet square, with a kitchenette and a little bathroom. The bedroom had two single beds and the sitting room a couch, chairs and television; everything was clean, but basic. "Where have we landed up?" Calvi moaned.

The telephone was in the bedroom. Calvi seized on it. He got hold of Kunz (whose phone numbers were on one of the scraps of paper found afterwards in Calvi's pockets) and complained bitterly of the rooms. He told Kunz that Carboni must come to London at once.

It was not easy for Kunz to get hold of Carboni. While Calvi was on his way to London, Carboni was telephoning his office in Rome, and a friend in the Rome police. He learned that Pellicani had been arrested for *reticenza*, which means failing to tell the police what you know. Pellicani had been seen travelling to Trieste with Calvi. Carboni, too, was wanted for questioning. He thought he would rather stay outside Italy. For some reason he decided to go to Amsterdam. He had never seen it, he said. The Kleinszig girls continued to tag along; Kunz organised another private plane for the three of them. The three arrived between seven and eight in the evening, went to the Amstel Hotel, dined and went to bed.

The following morning Carboni rang Calvi. (Kunz had given him the number.) Calvi forcefully expressed his disgust about Chelsea Cloisters, and insisted that Carboni should come to London at once, to find him something better.

Why? Didn't Calvi want completely anonymous quarters, where he was unlikely to be found? True, he was used to Claridge's. (He still had a small credit account there.) But he had put up with odd arrangements ever since leaving Italy. The Hotel Europa Tyrol at Innsbruck had even made him share a room with Vittor. To this arrangement he objected so passionately that Vittor was forced to spend their first night at Chelsea Cloisters on the sitting-room couch. (He afterwards dragged one of the beds into the living room.)

Calvi's extreme dislike of his quarters would be rational if he were not looking simply for a hiding place. Did he want an apartment in which he could negotiate with the phantom purchasers who were going to buy his secret holding of Ambrosiano shares? Or was he hoping to meet his P2 friends, and get some of his money back?

THIRTY-EIGHT

What the Telephone Records Did and Didn't Show

We have now reached the morning of Wednesday 16 June 1982. Calvi was insisting that he must be found better accommodation. Carboni and the two Kleinszig girls were reluctantly catching a plane from Amsterdam to London. Ortolani was leaving Switzerland for São Paulo. There was a warrant out for his arrest on a charge of fraud, in the Rizzoli Finanziaria case, and the Swiss might in theory have extradited him.

Gelli's whereabouts on that day are unknown. Tassan Din was in Switzerland. Pazienza, by his own account, was in America.

And three of Calvi's executives were in Rome, preparing to confront the IOR. They were Rosone, Leemans and de Bernardi. From Luxembourg, de Bernardi had brought the letters of patronage and the financial positions of the companies covered by them. Only Erin had been able to reduce its debts, by selling all its Credito Varesino shares. De Bernardi reckoned the total debt at nearly $1.3 billion. That included the back-to-back loans of United Trading.

Marcinkus was away again, in Switzerland with the Pope, but Mennini and de Strobel received Rosone, who at this first meeting was alone. He said he had come to put forward a plan concerning the debts of the various companies towards the Ambrosiano group banks. According to the memorandum of Marcinkus to the joint commission, Rosone was immediately told that the IOR had no responsibility for these debts, and that Calvi had given a precise undertaking to close the IOR position "in a definitive and complete manner" before 30 June. According to Rosone's subsequent report to the Ambrosiano board, they did not show him Calvi's letter of indemnity, but merely indicated that they had letters signed by Calvi. He said, however, that they proposed a "repayment in line of capital".

Rosone did not explain what this meant. Perhaps he did not know. At this point he asked if de Bernardi and Leemans could join them, to which Mennini and de Strobel agreed.

Leemans now took over. He said the Ambrosiano had been taken in by

Calvi, as much as the IOR. They ought to meet in a solution of the problem. He suggested that he could find international banks willing to raise a five-year loan of $1 billion, on concessionary terms, to help the Vatican. Once he had organised this loan for them, Leemans suggested, the IOR should take over all the debts and all the shares which were supposed to be security for them.

Mennini and de Strobel rejected this at once. It put all the risk on the IOR, which would be able to repay the loan only if it could resell the Ambrosiano shares at something like Calvi's fantasy figure of $200 each. They were by this time being quoted at less than $25 each.

Leemans thought of a modification. An "outside entity", by which he appeared to mean the IOR or a body backed by the IOR, would buy 5.2 million of the Ambrosiano shares for $1,275 million raised on special terms, but this entity would have an option to resell, and would receive a guarantee of repurchase of the shares. If the IOR did not want the whole block, it might perhaps acquire only half, with some other investor being found to take up the other half. For this other investor, Leemans had in mind De Benedetti.

The IOR did not immediately shut the door on this idea, but laid down two conditions. There would have to be a guarantee that the shares were bought back at the original purchase price, and the preferential interest rate would have to be no more than the dividend on the shares, so that the IOR would suffer no loss.

Rosone, Leemans and de Bernardi then left to consider the IOR position. Leemans flew to see De Benedetti in Ivrea. De Benedetti told him he would only consider taking an option on the Ambrosiano shares, with no firm undertaking to buy. That evening Leemans returned to Rome and sent a note to the IOR, to say that its terms could not be met.

Did Calvi know anything of these negotiations? According to Vittor, Calvi did not leave Chelsea Cloisters while he was waiting for Carboni to arrive in London. Vittor himself went out to get times of British Airways flights, and to buy food. Calvi could have learned what was going on only by telephone. So it is vital to know how many calls he made.

The telephone in this flat, like those of many in the block, was an extension of the main switchboard and all calls had to go through the operators. Incoming calls were put through without any record being kept, and there was thus no firm independent evidence of what calls Calvi received. Outgoing calls could be dialled from the flat after a line had been requested. Their cost was automatically metered, but the operators also kept a rough record, in case of a dispute, by jotting down each request for a line. These notes indicated only which operator, on which shift, got the request – not the exact times when the calls were made. It was not recorded where the call was to, how long it lasted or whether it even received an answer. It would have been unusual, but not impossible, for the operator to fail to make a note when someone asked for a line.

As there was no record of incoming calls, we have only Vittor's evidence. He said that Carboni and Kunz were the only people who rang Calvi. Vittor is not a very reliable witness, and he was not always there. But we know that Calvi would not give his number even to Anna. If anybody knew it, besides Carboni and Kunz, that person has never come forward.

According to the telephone supervisor, who gave evidence at both inquests, the operators' notes showed 17 requests for lines from 15 to 18 June. A total of 463 units had been metered. This was a high usage for a few days, she said at the second inquest.

Nobody ever questioned this. But I have analysed the figures. A great many local calls could have been made for that number of units – but not many long international ones. At the Post Office rate then, fifteen minutes' conversation during the day with America would have used 187.5 units, and a call of the same length to Switzerland or Italy 125 units, falling to 100 at the cheap rate after 8 p.m.

On the evening that Calvi and Vittor arrived there were five requests for lines, one of which was presumably the call to Kunz. Another may have been a call to Anna. Did Calvi use the other three in an attempt to track down Carboni? It is hard to see that Calvi could have used less than 50 units, representing 7.5 minutes of continental calls.

He rang Anna at least four more times in the next two days, and he spoke to his wife in America, a conversation which she recalled as lasting about a quarter of an hour. If this used 175 units, and the calls to Anna another 125 (which would have allowed a total of only 15 minutes to Switzerland) there would have been only 113 units left for the seven remaining unidentified calls from Flat 881, two on 16 June and five on 17 June, an average of barely two minutes each, even though at least one of the calls was made at the cheap rate. Even if most of the calls went unanswered, or were very brief, there cannot have been room for more than a couple of conversations with somebody in Italy lasting six or seven minutes. Unless Calvi made some of the known calls from some other phone in some other place, his information about events at the Ambrosiano must have been sketchy. However, on the evening of 17 June somebody in Milan did give Calvi some vital information, if Vittor is telling the truth.

It is possible that some of Calvi's calls were to people in London. Again, nobody has ever come forward to admit receiving such a call.

There is another possibility – that the meter at Chelsea Cloisters was unreliable, and that Calvi used more than 463 units. This is unlikely, considering how careful the management was to make a profit out of the tenants' phone calls. The supervisor mentioned that the charge was 9 pence a unit, as compared with the Post Office charge of 4.5 pence. In fact her figure was not quite correct; the Post Office charge at the time was 4.3 pence, excluding VAT.

According to the operators' notes, two lines were asked for between 8 and 9 a.m. on the morning of 16 June, one in the late morning and one in the early evening. What the early morning calls were we do not know. They may have been attempts to get hold of Anna or Kunz. The late morning call was almost certainly to Anna. She had moved from Lucerne to the Gothard hotel in Zürich. The wife of Hans Kunz was in touch with her, and seems to have passed her new number on to Calvi.

The early evening call, probably made at about seven, when Calvi was still waiting for Carboni to arrive, was almost certainly to Clara, now back in Carlo's rented house in Washington. (The address and number was on another scrap of paper found on Calvi's body.) Her memory of the conversation was a little confused. Asked about it at the second inquest, she said at first that Calvi told her: "The deal is going harder; we had a lot of troubles." Then, she said, the call was interrupted and he had to dial again. Then she recalled him saying: "It is blowing up; crazy, wonderful things for us that will change all our lives." He was very happy, he said. But he told her to stay where she was because there she was safe from "very, very important people". It was to be the last time she spoke to her husband.

It looks as if Calvi was simply trying to reassure his wife. If he had heard of the discussions Leemans was conducting with De Benedetti and the IOR, he might have had some grounds for believing that a crash could be averted, but it is hard to see how he could have known. Any other prospective deal could only have been with somebody in London. We have seen, from the tally of telephone units, that only a local call can have been of any great length.

Shortly after Calvi's conversation with his wife, he got a call from Carboni. It had taken him all day to reach London. With the Kleinszig girls, he had had to wait for hours at Amsterdam before they could get on a London plane. At Heathrow they took a taxi, whose driver chose the Hilton Hotel for them. As soon as they had checked in, Carboni rang Calvi.

Calvi said he would come immediately, but would not go into the Hilton, for fear of being recognised. Shortly afterwards, Calvi, Vittor, Carboni and the two girls met outside the Hilton in Park lane, on the edge of Hyde Park. Carboni insists that he was struck by the absence of Calvi's moustache; Vittor is equally insistent that he did not shave it off until the following morning.

All five went into Hyde Park. Calvi and Carboni talked at some distance from the others. Carboni is, once more, the only source for what was said. According to him, Calvi did not immediately launch into complaints about Chelsea Cloisters. Instead, he once more asked Carboni to speak to Franco, to see whether there was any news about the repayment of the IOR loans, and whether Franco had spoken to Rosone. Carboni was again to reassure Franco that Calvi's disappearance would not prejudice "the operation".

So Calvi had no idea of what had happened at the IOR that morning, or of the talks between Leemans and De Benedetti – if Carboni is speaking the truth.

According to Carboni, the conversation then turned to Calvi's dissatisfaction with Chelsea Cloisters, and his need to find something better. It was only at this point that Carboni remembered his Italian mistress, Laura Concas, and her aunt who lived in London. So he left Calvi in the park, returned to the Hilton and rang up Laura Concas to get her aunt's telephone number.

Unlike Chelsea Cloisters, the Hilton Hotel keeps detailed records of phone calls, including the number called, the the time the call was made, its cost, its duration and the number of units used.

Carboni's story was that he spoke first to Laura Concas and then to her aunt, Mrs Alma Morris. This would appear to be what happened; the first call to Rome was at 19.49 and the first call to the Morris home at 19.58.

But there is a difficulty. The call to Laura Concas was not to her home, but to the Clinica Sacra Famiglia, where she was visiting a patient. How did Carboni know she was there? Laura Concas herself turned up, a surprise witness, at the second inquest, and said that Carboni had first rung her flat and spoken to her mother or her maid.

But the Hilton records do not show any such first call to Italy. Carboni must have found out where she was before he arrived. There was no reason why he should not; he had plenty of time to ring her from Amsterdam airport. But why should he not say so?

Laura Concas told the inquest that she had rung the Morris family after speaking to Carboni. The Morris family also said they got a call from her. But the Hilton records show the call to the Clinica Sacra Famiglia as lasting 7.5 minutes. There would have been only 1.5 minutes before the end of that call and Carboni's call to the Morris family. It looks very much as if Laura Concas must have spoken to them earlier.

The Hilton record is consistent with one of Carboni's earlier stories; he said then that he had rung the Morris family immediately after speaking to Laura Concas. Later he changed his story, and said that he did not speak to them until later in the evening. He said the Hilton record of a call at two minutes to eight must have been wrong. It is true that the Hilton's figures are odd. The lengths of its units varied between calls and were different from the official lengths, the standard length being much shorter, but the cheap rate rather longer.

All these discrepancies, like the name "William Morris" in the diary, arouse the suspicion that Carboni's journey to London was not so completely unplanned as he later made out.

After making his phone calls, Carboni rejoined Calvi in Hyde Park, and told him that he would look for a flat the next day. They walked about for two hours or so. Calvi talked once more about the $250 million or so he needed to repay the IOR. Again, Carboni shows confusion about the money. Was Calvi talking about money he regarded as his own, or money he could get at? It is possible that the confusion was in Calvi's mind as well. Calvi said he believed he could find a large sum that "belonged" to him – the $150 million he had been talking about before. But others apparently had control over it, and might have removed it. "Let's hope," Calvi said, that it was still in Zürich. Again, the description fits the Bellatrix money – except that it had long since left Zürich. Calvi was quite close to a large slice of it, the $30 million Tassan Din had hidden in Dublin. Even if he had known that, his chances of getting it away from Tassan Din would have been poor.

In one of his early versions, Carboni said that Calvi was hoping to raise another $100 million from his contacts in London. Did Calvi really think so? He had raised syndicated loans, led by the National Westminster and the Midland; he had also persuaded Williams and Glyn's to take part in a back-to-back arrangement. But how could a fugitive, so much afraid of being recognised that he would not enter a hotel, approach banks like these?

Probably the last British bankers Calvi met were two from Artoc – Peter de Savary, the chairman, and Leonard Walton, the deputy chairman. They had been in Milan the previous December, to talk about the abortive merger between Artoc and the Cisalpine. Ellsworth Donnell, of Artoc, who was managing a small amount of money for Calvi, did not hear from him while he was in London.

There is another mystery here. On Calvi's body was the visiting card of Colin McFadyean, a senior partner in the City of London solicitors,

Slaughter and May. McFadyean was aware of Calvi's existence, and of his association with Artoc. But he had never met him and did not know how Calvi came to have his card. He, too, said that Calvi had not been in touch with him in London.

In one of his statements, Carboni said Calvi had told him he would be "finished" if he failed to find the $250 million – yet another indication that Calvi could not have heard about the visit of his executives to the IOR. There is no sign that he had seen the newspapers either. Italian newspapers then reached the West End of London in the afternoon of the day they appeared. If Carboni and Calvi had bought one they would have read that Calvi had been traced as far as Trieste, and that Rosone and Bagnasco were still rivals for his job, but had called a truce while Bagnasco went to the Bank of Italy to see Ciampi. They would also have read that Tassan Din could not be arrested because he was abroad, and that the authorities were looking for Carboni. This last news Carboni had already heard by phone, when he learned of Pellicani's arrest.

Calvi's fears of being seen apparently kept him away from Piccadilly and the stands with foreign papers. The television set at Chelsea Cloisters, on which Vittor incessantly watched the World Cup, would not have brought him much news from Italy. The bulletins were still full of the British victory in the Falklands, which had happened two days earlier, and the consequent resignation of the Argentine dictator Galtieri.

In Milan that day, when Rosone arrived back from Rome, there was one last moment of comic relief. The Bank of Italy denied that Bagnasco had been to see Ciampi, or, indeed anyone there. Bagnasco was not abashed. "A technical equivocation," he said. Rosone called a board meeting for the following morning, but Leemans, phoning from Rome, persuaded him to put it off until midday. Leemans was going to make a last appeal to Marcinkus, who had now returned to Rome.

At the end of the walk in Hyde Park, Calvi asked Carboni to look after his family if anything should happen to him. Or so Carboni says, though denying that Calvi was frightened for any specific reason. Carboni's account also has Calvi thanking him for all his help and saying that he did not know how he could repay him. But Carboni's various versions always leave out that he had already been more than amply rewarded for his troubles.

After the walk, Calvi and Vittor went back to Chelsea Cloisters, while Carboni and the Kleinszig girls went to their rooms at the Hilton. Calvi made no more phone calls that night; we do not know whether he received any. But Carboni, in the room he shared with his Austrian mistress, rang his Italian mistress Laura Concas four times after 10 p.m., speaking for just over 26 minutes in all. (Both mistresses, at the second inquest, expressed undying devotion to Carboni.) Then he rang the Morris household at 10.47. This was the call he admitted to. It was then, he said, that he arranged to go to their home the following morning. William Morris and his wife would help him to find a flat.

Nobody was monitoring the calls received by that family, but William Morris apparently remembered two calls. He said he talked once, briefly, to Carboni. He spoke little Italian and Carboni spoke virtually no English. Then a later call was taken by his wife or daughter. Carboni said he spoke to Mrs Alma Morris.

The next day, Thursday 17 June, at 8 a.m., Leemans had his last meeting at the IOR. He saw Marcinkus, Mennini and de Strobel. Leemans put forward a last-ditch proposal: that a $1 billion loan would be raised for the IOR, which would pass the money on to the Ambrosiano. But the IOR would have to pay the interest – about $150 million a year.

Marcinkus repeated that the IOR could not go along with a rescue plan like this. It was not responsible for the operations that had created the debts, and would assist in a solution only if it were guaranteed against loss.

Leemans persisted: "You realise what this means? When I leave this room I go straight to the telephone, and let the Ambrosiano board meeting know that there's nothing else for it; they'll have to call in the Bank of Italy. That means that everything about these letters of patronage will have to come out."

Marcinkus replied: "I realise I'm going to have to pay a high price for that, personally. I made a mistake. I was convinced of the validity of that friendship." He also said: "I did all this to help a friend and look where it's got me."

Leemans asked: "Don't you at IOR want to save your own faces?"

"Whatever happens to our faces," Marcinkus said, "We just don't have that kind of money."

In London it was one hour earlier. The Hilton records show a call to Chelsea Cloisters at 7.46 a.m.; this was the Kleinszig girls arranging to meet Vittor and go shopping. The Chelsea Cloisters telephone supervisor said that there were eight requests for lines from Flat 881 that day: six between 8 a.m. and 1 p.m., one in the "early evening" and a final one between 10.45 p.m. and midnight.

Anna Calvi said that her first call from her father that day was at 8.30 a.m., local time, in Zürich. That would have been 7.30 a.m. in London, so either she or the telephone supervisor is mistaken – unless Calvi did not ring from Chelsea Cloisters.

But the substance of the call she was not likely to forget. Calvi's tone had changed completely. He was patently worried. He told her that Pellicani had been arrested, which was true, and beaten up by police, which was not. He was concerned for her safety, and that of her fiancé Vittorio, and said that they must leave Europe and go to America. Something most important was happening, and there was about to be an uproar which would make things dangerous for them. He repeated the story that Opus Dei was repaying the IOR debt, and that there were people who wanted to stop this. Anna was not keen to fly at once to America. Calvi said she should think about it; he would ring back shortly.

What prompted this change of mood? If it was caused by the conversation with Carboni, then Carboni has left something out of all his various accounts. This is likely enough. The dead gunman, Danilo Abbruciati, is conspicuous by his absence from all of them. Anna herself had the impression that her father had heard some news directly from Italy.

In mid-morning Calvi rang Anna again. She started to explain that she did not want to go to America because Vittorio would not be able to go with her, as he had no passport. He had travelled to Switzerland on his identity card. But her father insisted; she was to go and Vittorio was to stay. She must go out at once to buy a ticket, and he would call back again to find out what arrangements she had made.

Calvi called back at 12 or 12.30. Anna was in the bathroom and Vittorio spoke to him first. Calvi repeated the story about Pellicani, and told him he should not return to Italy. Then he or Anna gave Calvi the details of the flight Anna had booked. It left Zürich at midday the following day. Calvi said he would ring again at eight the following morning, to speak to Anna before she left, and then again in the afternoon to speak to Vittorio, to make sure she had gone. He added that he would not have time to speak to her again that afternoon. This was an odd remark. Did he know that the Ambrosiano board meeting had already started? Was he waiting for someone to call him? Or had he some other engagement?

So three of Calvi's six calls that morning were to Anna. What about the other three? We have seen that, if they were to Italy, they must have been very brief. But we have no witness. Calvi was alone for most of that morning. Vittor had gone shopping with the Kleinszig girls. Carboni was out with Mr and Mrs Morris, looking for a better flat for Calvi.

At about midday, after shopping, Vittor brought the girls to a restaurant, La Brasserie, close to Chelsea Cloisters. They had checked out of the Hilton, and had their bags with them, as they were expecting to return to Austria that day. Vittor went back to see Calvi at the flat, and learned that Carboni had not yet been in touch. He returned to the restaurant and had lunch with the girls. Then he went back to Chelsea Cloisters, leaving the girls in the restaurant.

In the early afternoon Carboni rang. He had not yet secured a flat, but he told Calvi he had. No doubt he did not want to disappoint him. He even told Calvi to be ready to move by three. Calvi said his cases were already packed.

According to one of Carboni's statements, Calvi did not sound worried, but asked him if he had heard anything from Italy, or spoken to Monsignor Franco. If this were true, it would suggest either that Calvi had not got through to anyone in Italy that morning, or that the person he had spoken to knew nothing of the conversations with the IOR.

Carboni's description of Calvi as unworried conflicts with Vittor's account. He said Calvi was very different that day, more "troubled". He lay down to rest on the bed in the afternoon, as he had the previous day, but quickly jumped up again, and started to tell Vittor about the conversations he had had with Anna that morning. Vittor was more interested in the World Cup on television. Now and again he went to the restaurant to see the girls.

In Milan the Ambrosiano board meeting went on for five hours, with a brief break for sandwiches. A motion was passed at the outset which removed Calvi from his post "in the interests of the bank and of Signor Roberto Calvi himself – in case he could be constrained to commit involuntary acts". That is, they were giving him the benefit of the doubt. Some people still thought he might have been kidnapped.

The directors then went on to debate the proposition that they should dissolve the board and call in the Bank of Italy. Rosone reported, not very clearly, on his visit to the IOR. Leoni, who had been invited to attend though he was not a director, listed the debts and outlined how they had arisen. Rosone also told the directors of the illegal share support operation, which had been going on since February. The directors wanted to know why they had not been told all this earlier. Bagnasco kept calling on Rosone to resign. "I want more documentation," he demanded. To the other directors, $1.3 billion of debt was documentation enough. In the final vote, Bagnasco abstained.

The meeting ended at 5 p.m. Leemans was back in Milan before that. Once he knew the result, there was nothing more he could do, and he turned to go back to his own office. (La Centrale was not immediately affected by the crash.) Then he remembered that he had not spoken to Gabriella Corrocher, whom everyone loved and respected. He retraced his steps and said goodbye to this gentle spinster of 55, who was reputed to have a private life – a devoted lover of her own age – but who had given all her working life to the bank.

Gabriella Corrocher came out of her own office, went into the general office and read what the typists were typing out – the announcement of the board's decision to dissolve itself and call in the Bank of Italy. She wrote a brief note, cursing Calvi for bringing disgrace on them all, and jumped out of the window before the horrified typists could stop her. She died instantly.

What did Calvi know? Vittor told the second inquest that, because Calvi seemed so upset, he asked if there was anything he could do. Calvi replied "between clenched teeth" that he had telephoned the board of the bank. "In regard to what happened there" Vittor could be of no help to him.

Vittor was cross-examined closely about this. Why hadn't he said it in his earlier statements? Was he now trying to prove that Calvi had a motive for suicide? Vittor stuck to his story. And the telephone operator's notes bear him out to this extent at least – that Calvi made a call in the early evening. It was the first since lunchtime. Nobody in Milan has ever admitted receiving that call.

This is odd. To receive a call from Calvi, even to tell him what had happened at the board meeting, would not be a crime. There seems to be no reason why the person concerned should not come forward.

Unless it was Gabriella Corrocher. She was, after all, the first person Calvi phoned on the day of his disappearance. She had an office of her own and a direct line; she could receive calls without anyone else's knowledge. If he phoned her on the morning of 17 June, she would have been able to tell him that the board was meeting that day. If he phoned her later in the morning, she would have been able to tell him that the meeting was post-poned until noon. But she might not have known anything about the talks in the Vatican.

When did Calvi phone again? "Early evening" is a vague time. The board meeting ended about 4 p.m., London time. Gabriella Corrocher killed herself about two hours later. If Calvi spoke to her during these two hours, he may have vented all his anger on her. That would account for her bitter denunciation of him in the suicide note.

Carboni, meanwhile, had been negotiating for a new flat, with Mrs Morris acting as interpreter. The negotiations had fallen through, and they returned to Heston. At about 5 p.m. Carboni rang Calvi and again lied to him, saying he was about to settle new accommodation. Was this before or after Calvi learned the result of the board meeting? For much of that evening we have not even the evidence of Vittor, because he kept popping round the corner to see the Kleinszig girls. They had outstayed their welcome at the restaurant, and Vittor took them to a pub, the Queen's Arms, in a side road very close to the front door of Chelsea Cloisters. It must have been shortly after opening time, 5.30 p.m. The two girls resumed their wait, becoming more and more exasperated.

Calvi also popped out from time to time. Once he went into the Queen's Arms and spoke to Michaela Kleinszig. She afterwards said that he was nervous, and wanted to know if they had had any news from Carboni about the flat. He did not feel good where he was, he said. He asked if Carboni would be "punctual". The girls thought this happened about 9 p.m.

Michaela is the last witness, apart from Vittor, who admits to a conversation with Calvi. That leaves us with the mystery of the non-meeting.

THIRTY-NINE

Why Did Carboni not Go up?
Why Did Vittor Flee?

The telephone operator's evidence is that, on the last evening of Calvi's life, someone in Flat 881 asked for a line between 10.45 and midnight. We do not know whether it was Calvi, Vittor or someone else, nor whether the person asking for the line succeeded in making the call.

That evening, if Vittor is telling the truth, Calvi knew that he was no longer chairman of the Ambrosiano, and that the Ambrosiano itself was in the hands of a commissioner. This meant that all the secret network's shares in it, acquired with such ingenious illegalities, over so many years, were waste paper. If he had really hoped to sell them, he now had to wake from that dream.

On the other hand, there were worries he no longer had. He did not have to find $300 million for the IOR, or think about the IOR at all. For his own needs and those of his family, the $30 million or so he had in Geneva and in the Bahamas would be ample.

But how was he to get at any of it? He had not even tried, while he was in London, to take out the money he had there. Quite apart from the fraud charge already formulated against him, and the much greater fraud charges which obviously must follow, he had jumped his bail in Italy and was travelling on a false passport; the British police would soon have grounds for arresting him.

How much Calvi knew is a vital question. If he knew his real situation, he certainly had reason to kill himself. If his informant was Gabriella Corrocher, he did not know that she had killed herself shortly after the call.

Carboni and the Morris family spent the evening on the trail of another flat. But this one, too, seemed to come to nothing, and they returned to Heston, where Carboni had left his case. The time they arrived, was, it seems, about 10 p.m. Carboni said that they then received a call saying that they could, after all, have the flat the following day. Carboni at once rang Chelsea Cloisters with this news. Vittor answered the phone. His main concern was the discomfort of the Kleinszig girls. He told Carboni to come at once. It seems to have been shortly after this that Michaela rang the flat from the pub, to find out what was happening. Vittor told her that Carboni was on his way. The Morrises were later to say that he left them in a minicab for the Sheraton hotel at Heathrow at 11 p.m. or shortly after, but other evidence suggests that he must have left somewhat earlier. Moreover he did not go to the Sheraton Hotel; he went to Chelsea Cloisters.

What happened when Carboni arrived there is the strangest part of the story. Vittor, who gave himself up to the Italian authorities on 24 June, made a statement which was read to the first inquest. "Carboni rang from the porters' desk to tell us to come down. Calvi did not want to know and made me reply that he should come up. I went down and found Carboni, who had a taxi. I explained that Calvi did not want to go out and after having let the taxi go I went by foot to collect the girls . . ."

It would be natural for Carboni to let the taxi go and send Vittor the few steps round the corner to collect the girls, if he were going up to Flat 881 to see Calvi. But Vittor made it clear that Carboni came with him to the pub. Both Carboni and Vittor have insisted, in all their various versions, that Carboni did not go up to see Calvi.

When the first inquest was held Carboni was still in hiding in Switzerland. But he hired a lawyer to defend his interests and sent a statement to be read in court. This is his account of his non-meeting with Calvi.

"Vittor was not waiting for me outside. I entered the hall and saw him coming towards me. As soon as he saw me he said: 'Let's go to the bar to those poor girls.'"

So there was no ringing up from the porter's lodge? Interrogated in Lugano in August 1982, Carboni said he did not remember whether there had been a call from the porter's lodge or not. He told two British policemen in October 1983 that he had rung up and spoken to Vittor, who came straight down. This was the version he gave to Philip Willan, who went to see him for me in November 1984. Then he was interviewed in January 1985 by Kingsley Napley, the solicitors representing the Calvi family. He reverted to his original story; as he went to the porter's desk Vittor put a hand on his shoulder and hurried him out of the building. So Calvi might not even have known that Carboni had arrived.

To go back to Carboni's first version: "We arrived at the bar which was two or three minutes away, and met the girls who were seated in a corner. I had no time to sit down since the bar was closing. I believe I was with the girls and Vittor for about 15 to 20 minutes. After which I made it clear to

Vittor that the next morning I would let Calvi know the latest news on the apartment and I urged him in the meantime to tranquilise Calvi."

The man from Kingsley Napley pressed him on this point. Why didn't he now go up to see Calvi, who had been waiting for him all day? Carboni said that there was an incident outside Chelsea Cloisters, when two drunken young men and a girl started to bother them, trying to dance with the Kleinszig girls. As a result he did not want to leave the girls. But then, by his own account, a taxi turned up and the three drunken people got into it.

At that point, then, Carboni could have gone up to see Calvi, couldn't he? He explained that, by then, he was exhausted, and in no mood to start listening to Calvi's problems all over again. He was not employed by him and was therefore under no obligation to do so. His priority was to get the girls and himself to the Sheraton at Heathrow, where rooms had been booked for them by Mrs Morris.

Under no obligation? To the man who had just paid him $10 million? (Or did he know he was only supposed to be holding the money for Calvi's future use?) Clearly Carboni had been putting himself out, so far, in the expectation that there would be more money. For that, he could have stood another boring half hour. There was all the more reason for him to go and cheer Calvi up, since Vittor, in his evidence at the second inquest, said he told Carboni that Calvi had become very depressed.

How much did Carboni know at this point? To judge from the evidence of the Morris family, who were rather vague about times, Carboni was at their house briefly between 4.30 and 5 p.m., and again after 10 p.m. But they have said nothing about his ringing Italy on either occasion. Nor would he have had much time to do so while they were out looking for a flat. So Carboni may well have heard no news from Italy when he arrived at Chelsea Cloisters. The accounts of Vittor hustling him out suggest that Vittor had decided to waylay him and tell him what Calvi had said about the board meeting in Italy. If Carboni, at this point, heard this news for the first time, he would have realised there and then that there was no more money to come from Calvi. Indeed, Calvi might even want some of his own money back.

And had Vittor some other news for Carboni? Had he something to tell him about a visit to Calvi, late the previous evening, which he could not have told him until then without Calvi overhearing?

Either or both of these possibilities would account for Carboni's refusal to step into the lift.

When did Calvi (if it was Calvi) make his last phone call? "Between 10.45 and midnight" suggests that it may have been while Vittor and Carboni were fetching the girls from the pub. If the pub was closing it must have been about 11.15 p.m. Carboni was apparently allowed to buy a beer, but he was hungry and wanted sandwiches. Before going back to Chelsea Cloisters they stopped at a nearby restaurant, Le Suquet, to see if they could get something to eat, but they were told it was too late. It is hard to see, from the participants' published descriptions of what they did, that they could have been back at Chelsea Cloisters later than about 11.45 p.m. And yet Vittor has said that they were away for an hour and a half. If so, they must indeed have been discussing something of importance.

A taxi came by. Carboni and the girls got in, and gave the driver a piece of paper on which William Morris had written the name of the Sheraton Hotel. Carboni did not, it seems, tell Vittor the name of the hotel, but he promised to ring as soon as he got there.

When the others had left, Vittor, by his own account, went straight back to Flat 881. He knocked to be let in. Calvi always kept the one key they had been given, and always insisted that Vittor should knock three times and identify himself by his Christian name: "Silvano." This time, though, there was no reply.

If Vittor, Carboni and the Kleinszig girls had been telling the truth, it could not have been much past midnight. Yet it was not until about 1 a.m. that Vittor asked one of the night porters, Anthony Fernando, to help him get into the flat. Fernando spoke no Italian, but he remembered that the duty manageress, Dolores Calvelo, knew some. He rang her on the house phone, and she spoke to Vittor, who explained his difficulty. She wanted Vittor to show Fernando some identification, but he said it was in his room. So she told Fernando to go up with him, let him in and check his identification. She confirmed that the time was between 1 and 1.30 a.m.

When Vittor and Fernando went into Flat 881 the television was on but the screen was blank. Fernando provided confirmation that neither Calvi nor anyone else was there. According to Fernando's initial statement to the police, Vittor took two closed, packed cases from a cupboard, as if to look for his identification, but was unable to open them. Then Vittor appeared to remember he had an identity card in his wallet, and showed this; he would seem to have had it on him all the time. At the second inquest Fernando initially said that the wallet came from one of the bags, but then agreed that it looked as if it must have come from Vittor's pocket.

What was Vittor doing during the hour or so between midnight and his approach to Fernando? According to himself, after knocking on the door of Flat 881 and getting no answer, he went down to the hall and asked "two staff members" to ring the flat. When they got no answer either, he went upstairs again and did more knocking. He heard the phone ringing in the room, and assumed that Carboni was trying to get through, as he had promised. Vittor then went downstairs again, and wandered about among the local bars and restaurants, in case Calvi had gone out to get something to eat. He cannot have found many places open at that time of night. Vittor then returned, and only at this point spoke to Fernando.

There is no corroboration for this account. Vittor may have been hanging around outside the door of Flat 881, trying to make sure there was no one inside. He may have had the wallet in his pocket; he may even have had the key, but feared to enter without a companion. If he thought Calvi had been kidnapped, he may also have thought the kidnappers might come back for him.

But if that was what he feared, why did he wait so long before he fled? By his own account, Vittor lay down on the bed, but was too frightened and worried to sleep. In his own words: "I thought so many things, because he [Calvi] kept on changing." At about eight in the morning, he said, he left Chelsea Cloisters, took a taxi to Heathrow and caught the first available flight to Vienna, taking off at 10.10 a.m.

But if he really was in Flat 881 all night, why didn't he stay there a few minutes longer? He knew Carboni was going to ring. He knew his lover was still in London. He was to argue at the inquest that they could have rung him in the middle of the night; the fact that they did not added to his unease.

If we accept Vittor's own timetable, he can scarcely have left the flat when they began telephoning. According to Carboni, he and the girls got up between 8 and 8.15 a.m. and immediately rang Chelsea Cloisters. Carboni made a number of other calls, including one to Kunz. Thinking he would have completed the arrangements for Calvi's flat before the day was out, he asked Kunz to send a private plane to pick him up that evening.

Just before 7.30 a.m. that morning, Anthony Huntley, a postal clerk at the *Daily Express*, was hurrying to work along the walkway by the river, under Blackfriars Bridge. Other people must have passed that way, but this young man was over six feet tall. As he glanced over the parapet of the walkway towards the river, the angle of his vision took in the poles of some scaffolding, standing below the level of the walkway, in the river. He caught sight of a man's head. Momentum carried him past before he realised what he had seen. He turned back to take a proper look at the hanging body.

In Zürich Anna Calvi was already worried. Vittorio's father had told them, the evening before, about the Ambrosiano board meeting and the suicide of Graziella Corrocher. Anna was waiting for the call her father had promised to make at 8 a.m. Instead, she got a call from Kunz. He told her his wife would come to the hotel with 50,000 Swiss francs for her, and that he would himself be seeing her father that day. It is not clear what Kunz meant. He had, by now, arranged a private plane to collect Carboni from Gatwick that evening. Perhaps Kunz thought Calvi would be on the plane as well. Frau Kunz duly turned up with the money, and revealed to Anna, for the first time, that her father had gone to London. But Anna stuck to her plan to go to America. Vittorio remained behind, waiting in vain to hear from Calvi.

The River Police, called in by the City of London Police, had by now succeeded in recovering the body. The River Police had great difficulty in keeping their boat steady, while they got Calvi down. When the tide is coming in it conflicts with the downstream flow of the Thames, and the battle of currents is particularly violent where the water is compressed by the piers of a bridge. One policeman struggled to keep the powerful police launch in place, while two others took down the body and brought it into the boat. The body was all the heavier because Calvi's pockets contained eleven and a half pounds of bricks, taken from a building site a few yards away. They were also full of money in various currencies, totalling $10,700.

While the police were searching Calvi's pockets, and photographing his body, Carboni was taking a taxi to the Morris home, which he reached at about 9 a.m. He had left his bags at the Sheraton, and said goodbye to the Kleinszig girls. They were in a hurry to get back to Austria, and they went straight to Heathrow, apparently without making any further inquiries. Michaela, asked at the inquest whether she was worried at getting no answer from Chelsea Cloisters, said she had thought Vittor and Calvi must have been out having breakfast when they called. Once more, the girls just missed Vittor. They seem to have arrived at Heathrow just before his flight to Vienna took off. They left, also for Vienna, at midday in a private plane.

Carboni was on the phone again, from the Morris household. He spoke to an interior designer, Ugo Flavoni, to whom he owed money. Flavoni was in Geneva with some friends. Carboni told him about the plane that was coming to Gatwick later that day. Flavoni said he and his friends would come along for the ride, and he and Carboni could discuss their business on the way back. In his statement to the British police, Carboni said he also called another of his creditors, Diotallevi. He was now back in Rome, but Carboni told him to go, yet again, to Lugano. There Carboni would meet him and pay him the 160 million lire.

In between these calls, the Morrises were trying Flat 881 at Chelsea

Cloisters. Carboni was more and more worried that they got no answer. He asked the Morrises to postpone the arrangements for the new flat, while he tried to find out what had happened. Odette Morris told the first inquest that she did not work on Friday; at the second she said she took that day off to go with Carboni and act as interpreter. They left in a taxi which went to the Sheraton to pick up Carboni's bags, and then, at the driver's suggestion, to the Chelsea Hotel. They arrived at about 1.45 and took a room so that they could use the phone in private. Carboni rang Flat 881 again. He then sent Odette to Chelsea Cloisters to see what she could discover, and to put a note under the door of Flat 881. She wrote the note, in Italian, at his dictation. It was addressed to Silvano Vittor but cryptically signed: "Odina". It read: "I have telephoned so many times but I have not seen you. Tell me what I have to do to find you. Telephone Elde and Vitto immediately."

Carboni intended Vittor to understand that he was to ring the mother of the Kleinszig girls, Hilda, who lived apart from her husband but near Klagenfurt, in St Veit. Vittor might have understood the message, but it would surely have been completely baffling to Calvi. Carboni did not include any name or number Calvi would have known.

This might suggest that Carboni already knew Calvi was dead. But it could just as well be evidence that Carboni had ceased to care what happened to Calvi. Whatever Carboni had known the night before, that morning he certainly knew what had happened in Italy. If Calvi no longer had millions to hand out, why bother to find him? At this point all Carboni's anxiety seems to have been for Vittor, his friend.

While Odette was delivering the note and peering through the keyhole of Flat 881, Carboni rang the mother of the Kleinszig girls. She told him that she had heard from her daughters, who had arrived in Vienna, but not from Vittor. Carboni gave her the number of the Chelsea Hotel. When Odette returned, she and Carboni sat down to a late lunch. But he was not hungry, and returned alone to the room to make more telephone calls. In the three or four hours he had the room, he used 617 units on the meter. This puts into perspective the 463 units Calvi used on the first evening and the two full days that followed. If all Carboni's calls were to Europe, he could have spoken for nearly 75 minutes. His calls were dearer than Calvi's; Chelsea Cloisters charged 9p a unit, the Hilton 10p and the Chelsea Hotel, then part of the Holiday Inn chain, 13p.

When Odette had finished her lunch, Carboni went to see Chelsea Cloisters for himself. But he was afraid to go in, and asked Odette to go upstairs again. She also left a second note, much the same as the first, at the reception desk. Carboni himself wandered about outside, looking into shops, restaurants and pubs, including the Queen's Arms. Then he and Odette returned to the Chelsea Hotel. He rang the mother of the Kleinszig girls again. To his immense relief, she told him that Vittor had phoned her, and that she had asked him to ring Carboni at the Chelsea Hotel.

For some reason this made Carboni think that the flat for Calvi was likely to be needed after all. The Morris parents arrived at the Chelsea Hotel that evening. Carboni gave them $1,700 to change into sterling, to use as a deposit for the new flat for Calvi. The hotel could not change such a large amount, and the banks were closed, so they took the money to Heathrow to change. Carboni's version – the 1985 one – is that, as soon as they had gone, Vittor rang. He sounded anxious. He thought Carboni would be able to tell him what had happened, and seemed suspicious when Carboni said he did not know. Vittor told Carboni about going to Flat 881 and not finding Calvi, but he did not say where he himself was – only that he was "very far away". As this Carboni version was not available when Vittor appeared at the second inquest, Vittor was not asked why he himself, in the statement he made just after his arrest, said he did not speak to Carboni until the following morning, Saturday 19 June, when Carboni rang him. However, there is a mystery about what Vittor did when he arrived in Vienna. He said he took a train to Klagenfurt and went to the Kleinszig home, where both girls joined him at about midnight. But at the second inquest both Kleinszig girls said that they did not see Vittor until the morning of the 19 June. Michaela said he told her he had spent the night at her mother's house in St Veit. This inconsistency was not put to Vittor himself, when he later turned up to give evidence at the same inquest. But if he had gone to St Veit on the evening of 18 June, it makes Carboni's account of the phone call more plausible.

Carboni (according to his 1985 statement) was once more thrown into turmoil by Vittor's call. He had forgotten all about the plane that was coming to Gatwick to pick him up. He and Odette left the Chelsea Hotel and took a taxi to return to Heston. On the way, Carboni remembered about the plane, and diverted the taxi to Gatwick. The plane had four passengers: Flavoni, a woman friend, and her brother and his wife. It was due at about 8 p.m. Carboni and Odette had great difficulty in locating the right building. When they did, they were told that the plane had been obliged to take off again, in order to get back to Geneva on schedule. If his 1985 version is correct, and he now knew that Vittor was "very far away", he would no doubt have taken the plane and got out, without inquiring further what had become of Calvi.

Carboni and Odette returned to the Morris home, where Carboni had already been told he was welcome to stay the night.

Late that evening they rang Laura Concas in Rome. As Carboni was talking to her she was watching the news on television. It included an item about the discovery of a body with a passport in the name of Calvini. Carboni knew at once that it was Calvi.

This was also widely suspected in Italy. The senior magistrate Sica had spent the evening interrogating Tassan Din, who had returned to Italy to face the fraud charges over Rizzoli Finanziaria. As soon as Sica heard about the body he got on the next plane to London.

Carboni, so badly shaken that he had to be calmed down with a brandy, believed Calvi must have been murdered. He knew that he would be a suspect; the Italian papers had been full of his name, as the man who got Calvi out of Italy. The following morning, 19 June, he rang the lawyer Wilfredo Vitalone, who advised him to speak to Sica. He rang Sica's office, but Sica was already in London.

According to Vittor, Carboni rang him in Klagenfurt. It was only now, in Vittor's version, that he told Carboni what had happened at Chelsea Cloisters after they parted on Thursday night. Vittor said that Carboni asked him to come and meet him later that day in Innsbruck.

Carboni, according to his 1985 version, was now afraid he might be looked for at Heathrow. He talked Odette Morris into going with him to Gatwick, saying he would find her a job in Italy. They did not, however, fly to Italy, but to Edinburgh, where they booked two rooms at the George Hotel for the night.

In Austria, Vittor and the Kleinszig girls were spending the night in Innsbruck. They had gone there to meet Carboni, but when they got there they rang Kunz, who told them that Carboni would not be arriving after all. The following day, Sunday 20 June, they drove back to Klagenfurt in two cars, having picked up Michaela's Alfa Romeo from Innsbruck Airport, where Vittor and Calvi had left it the previous Tuesday.

That Sunday morning, in Edinburgh, Carboni and Odette Morris went back to Edinburgh Airport. Odette thought better of her adventure and returned to London. Carboni rang the invaluable Kunz, and asked him to come with a private plane to pick him up. He hung around the airport until Kunz arrived at about 3.30 p.m. On the way back, Carboni decided to divert the plane to Klagenfurt. The Kleinszig sisters were alerted by the pilot. Manuela joined Carboni on the plane, and they flew back to Zürich.

Carboni had been hoping that Vittor, too, would join him at the airport. But he seems to have been afraid of getting arrested there. He stayed in the house. Why did Carboni not join him there? Probably he was anxious to reach Zürich, so that he could make arrangements for the huge sums of money in his bank accounts there. The following day, Monday 21 June, $150,000 was withdrawn in cash from his account at the Zürcher Kantonalbank. Other measures were put in hand to relocate much of the money.

That day, Vittor and Michaela drove to Zürich, and all four were reunited. The fact that they were able to get together and decide on a story, before any of them saw the authorities, has been several times pointed out. (In the event, as we have seen, they contradicted each other, and Carboni incessantly contradicted himself.) Only the bank accounts tell a clear, unequivocal story.

The Italian papers were already carrying the first reports that the British police considered Calvi's death to be suicide. This was greeted with derision; it seemed to have become almost a matter of national honour that Calvi should have been murdered. The papers were full of conspiracy theories. The Vatican had put Calvi out of the way to hush up a scandal. (As we have seen, the day before Calvi's death, Marcinkus was admitting to Leemans that he knew a scandal was inevitable.) The Somoza family had done it, because Calvi owed them money. (In fact they owed him a good deal, as the creditors discovered.) The Freemasons had done it, *ritually*. This one didn't have to have a motive; the mere word "Freemasons" was enough.

Italian journalists crowded round the scaffolding where the body was found, and produced on-the-spot reports. They said that the place was unapproachable, except by a trained athlete. Or that the place was not approachable by anyone, except in a boat. Calvi must have been strangled somewhere else, and brought by water . . .

All these reports displayed the usual difficulty, shown by the peoples of the tideless Mediterranean, in grasping that the Thames at Blackfriars, twice a day, rises and falls fourteen or fifteen feet.

Michel Leemans came to London to see for himself. As a Belgian, he had no trouble in understanding the tides. On a fine Sunday morning, at low tide, he climbed over the parapet of the walkway, and went down the strong steel ladder, firmly attached to the wall. He had known Calvi well, and he knew that he was fit enough to do all this without difficulty.

The first inquest, held on 23 July 1982, heard expert evidence to much the same effect. But it left many questions unanswered.

FORTY

A Question of Time and Tide

Dr David Paul, coroner for the City of London, showed one great fault in his conduct of the first inquest. He was too keen on work. If he had taken the whole thing at a more leisurely pace, he would probably not have made the mistakes which led to the holding of a second inquest.

Dr Paul was said to dislike the thought of an inquest being turned into a theatrical event; hence his decision to hold it in a small courtroom at Milton Court in the Barbican complex, where there would be as few seats as possible for the press. This made the Italian reporters more determined than ever to get in. Dr Paul's insistence on a small court gave the press an unexpected bonus. The witness box, where the police photographers had to identify each picture, was so close to the reporters that most of them could see the pictures perfectly. Police photographs are not available to the press, but some of these turned up afterwards in an Italian magazine.

The most famous one showed Calvi lying dead on the damp boards of the River Police pier at Waterloo Bridge, the rope still round his neck, looking no less grim and tormented than in his final days of life. (See photograph between pages 248 and 249.)

Other pictures were views of the scaffolding, taken from various angles by a police photographer, Detective Constable Eatwell. These established how nearly invisible the scaffolding was. It had been put up five weeks before Calvi's death, on 10 May. Hardly anyone, even among those who passed it every day, knew it was there. Police Constable John Palmer, of Snow Hill Police Station, whose job was to patrol that part of London, said in court that he had not known of its existence. It was invisible from any motor road, hard to see from the boats on the river, and only just visible from one point on the platform of Blackfriars British Rail station, where commuters arrived from Kent. Sir David Napley, who was appearing for the Calvi family, had looked for it early on the morning of the inquest, and had failed to find it. Anybody less than six feet tall would be likely to see it only if he were walking slowly along the walkway close to the parapet, looking into the river.

One picture of the scaffolding, taken ten days after Calvi's death, showed flotsam clinging to it, including a length of rope. This rope was of great interest to John Blofeld QC, the barrister appearing for Carboni. The Italian newspapers had been asking where the rope round Calvi's neck had come from.

Now it was established that lengths of rope were often washed up on the scaffolding, and left there dangling at low tide. Blofeld said of the rope in this picture: "It would seem to be at any rate of equal, if not further, length to the piece of rope that we have seen retrieved from Calvi's body in photograph 16."

"Yes," replied Detective Constable Eatwell. "You know, it's very similar to that."

The man who supervised the erection of the scaffolding, a foreman fitter, Sidney James Hall, gave evidence in the solid way that might have been expected from his workmanship. He explained what it was there for. Workmen had to repair the doors of the storm drain which runs into the Thames at that point. (Although Hall did not say so, the drain is the River Fleet, which gave its name to Fleet Street.)

Sir David Napley, for the Calvi family, was as keen to find evidence of murder as Carboni's lawyer Blofeld was to find evidence of suicide. Clara Calvi, who was not present, had been telling the press that her husband must have been murdered. She denied that her reason for saying so was in any way connected with his life insurance.

Sir David questioned the foreman fitter about the difficulty of going down the vertical ladder, and of stepping from the ladder on to a board which was secured to the scaffolding (at the level of the fifth horizontal pole, it was afterwards established). Hall said that the board could be slippery when wet, but that the poles were not slippery. The workmen did not usually try to carry heavy weights up and down the vertical ladder. Any large piece of equipment they needed was lowered to them by a rope.

Sir David questioned Donald Bartliff of the River Police about the possibility that Calvi might have been brought to the spot by boat. Bartliff described the various difficulties caused by stages of the tide, and concluded: "So if you're taking a boat in there, you have to know what the River Thames is all about, sir."

Though it was by now high time for lunch, Dr Paul allowed only a 20-minute adjournment. To be late back would have been to miss the star of the show. Frederick Keith Simpson, professor of forensic medicine at the University of London, stepped into the witness box with a lightness and swiftness remarkable in a man of 75. He had been married for the third time a few days earlier. Dr Paul was concerned to make it clear that Professor Simpson was not employed by the police, but had been called in by himself as a consultant.

Professor Simpson said of Calvi: "Although only five foot nine in height, he weighed thirteen stones and two pounds."

Simpson did not say how much overweight that made him. By the standards of the Weight Watchers, the superfluous weight was only ten pounds – enough to slow a man down when he runs, but not enough to prevent him from walking long distances or climbing down ladders.

"He was a little obese, heavily built," Professor Simpson continued, "but in every other respect, in the course of my full examination after death, I found him to be a healthy person . . . I am unable to say what processes of thought were going through his mind, but I can say there was no disease of the brain. And there was no disease elsewhere to cause him pain or distress . . ."

Using coloured photographs, Professor Simpson elaborated his autopsy report. This had said that there was "no cause for suspicion of foul play". The professor explained why the marks on Calvi's neck were consistent with "self-suspension" and not consistent with strangling by another person. There were two marks around the neck, one indicating where the initial constriction took place and the second, higher up, where the body had settled into the noose. This was to be expected. If Calvi had been strangled and then hung up the marks would have been different. There was no major neck injury – that is, the body had not fallen from any height into the noose. Calvi had been alive when the rope went round his neck. There was no evidence of drowning, since there was no water in the mouth or lungs. There was no evidence of drink or drugs in the stomach, and no marks of violence which might suggest that Calvi had been pinned or held down, nor any signs of a struggle.

"Did you find any injection marks on the body?" Dr Paul asked.

"No, sir," replied Professor Simpson.

This question and answer reminded everyone that Professor Simpson was the man who spotted a tiny injection mark on a Bulgarian exile, Georgi Markov, and thereby established that he had been murdered by a hypodermic needle hidden in the tip of an umbrella.

Sir David Napley asked if the Professor was excluding the possibility of murder.

"No, sir," Professor Simpson replied. "I am not saying that this was not effected by some other person, only that I can find no evidence whatever to suggest that this was so."

Both men were speaking quietly. Both were polite. This was, nevertheless, a bout between heavyweights.

"Let me put a hypothesis to you," said Sir David. "Supposing that
someone came up behind this man, seized him, and pinned his arms to his
side, someone else put a chloroform pad on his mouth, would I be right in
thinking that there would be no post mortem signs to indicate whether that
had occurred or not?"

Quietly, almost regretfully, the Professor replied: "No, sir. I would expect
pinning, if there was any violence, to leave at least finger marks. Secondly
I would assume, and I would state to the court, that chloroform does not
cause instant unconsciousness. It causes struggling against such a position
of inhaling."

Sir David asked: "Are there any anaesthetics which could be applied,
which would render a man very quickly insensitive, but still alive?"

Here Dr Paul put in: "You are referring to inhalation anaesthetics?"

Sir David agreed.

"Certainly none that I know of," Simpson said.

Sir David asked about the time of death. Simpson said he had not been
able to take temperature as a guide; he had gone by rigor mortis. "I formed
the view that, because rigor mortis was well established in the upper part,
and not quite so well established . . . in the lower limbs, that his death had
taken place about eight to twelve hours before I made my examination.
Rigor mortis normally starts at about seven to eight hours and is complete
by twelve hours."

As Simpson had started his examination at 2 p.m. on 18 June, that put
the time of death at between 2 a.m. and 6 a.m. But Simpson added: "I
must say that rigor mortis is not mathematical. When estimating rigor mortis
I usually give several hours on either side, and one can be approximate but
not accurate."

"But you would regard it as fairly reliable between those two parameters?"
Napley suggested.

Simpson replied: "I think the only likelihood is that he died in the early
hours."

This fitted the time of low tide, already given to the court by Hall, the
foreman who put up the scaffolding, as 5.24 a.m. The board which the
workmen used to climb on to the scaffolding would have been fully visible,
and in daylight, from about 4 a.m. onwards. A point not made in court,
perhaps because it is obvious to English people, is that, at 4 a.m. in the
middle of June in London, it is light enough to see what you are doing. Just
as Italy has no tides, it has no midsummer dawns as early as this, and

455

Italian reporters did not grasp that the low tide that morning coincided with daylight.

The best evidence about Calvi's distress of mind was given indirectly, by Dr Ian William Daniel Campbell Wilson, principal scientific officer at the Metropolitan Police Forensic Science Laboratory. He listed the drugs found among Calvi's belongings.

There were 24 capsules of an antibiotic. There were two injection ampoules and one box of tablets, all for relieving muscular spasms. Two other anti-spasmodics were in injection ampoules. Yet more anti-spasmodics were tablets. An antibacterial, Bactrim, differed from another antibacterial, Urotractin, only in that the latter was advertised as more suitable for urinary infections.

Tablets labelled Pressamine appeared to be for blood pressure. There were capsules designed to promote the flow of bile, and an amino-acid called Polase, whose purpose was uncertain. There was a form of aspirin combined with vitamin C, some vitamin preparations without aspirin and a cold cure.

Then Dr Wilson started on the tranquilisers. The 53 capsules of Dalmadorm 15 seemed to be for promoting sleep. The eighteen tablets of Tavor were for tranquilizing; so were the twenty-two capsules of a valium preparation, the twenty-four tablets of a paracetamol preparation and the ten tablets labelled Reasec. The fifteen pink sugar-coated tablets were anti-depressants. Calvi also had one suppository and some unused 5 mm syringes.

It has often been pointed out that Calvi could have killed himself in comfort, by going to bed and swallowing all this. But that argument ignores the presence of Vittor, who might have been equal to getting Calvi to a hospital. There his stomach would have been pumped out. He might have come round to find a policeman beside the bed.

In fact he had taken very few pills. Dr Wilson found traces of Dalmadorm in his stomach, and residual traces of mild tranquilisers taken several days earlier. He had examined Calvi's blood and urine for traces of anaesthetics, and found none.

Sir David asked him: "Are you able to say from your examination that there is no possibility of this man having inhaled an anaesthetic of some sort?"

Dr Wilson, a serious young Scot, replied: "No, I would not go so strong as to say that there is no possibility whatever. What I have said is that I did not detect one."

Blofeld asked: "So you certainly have found ... no drug in your investigations that could account for anything more than a possibility of drowsiness?"

"That is my conclusion," Dr Wilson said.

Now, at last, at 2.15 p.m., Dr Paul allowed everyone to have lunch. His words to the jury were those of a dedicated workaholic.

"I don't want to see you again until a quarter past three, which will give you a chance to get some fresh air and stretch your legs. I have four other cases which do not require a jury, which I will be dealing with while you are eating."

If Dr Paul had taken time off for lunch, he would probably not have made his subsequent mistakes. When Lord Lane, the following March, quashed the verdict of suicide, and ordered a new inquest, it was entirely on account of things said and done after that lunch adjournment.

This, then, is a good place to look back at what the expert witnesses had established, five weeks after Calvi's death, while the whole thing was fresh in their minds.

Calvi had been found in a place which he could have reached on his own feet. The time given for his death was consistent with the falling tide and the growing light. He could not have been carried to the spot unless pinioned or drugged, and he had not been pinioned or drugged.

There was one discordant note, of which a great deal was to be heard later. Pc Bartliff of the River Police thought Calvi's clothes and the property taken from them were so wet that he must at some time have been submerged in the river. The witnesses differed among themselves about the position of Calvi's feet when the body was found; Anthony Huntley said they were dangling into the water; Pc Palmer of the City of London Police said they were just clear of the water; Pc Bartliff said: "The shoes and socks and about six inches of the lower trousers were covered by the rising tide."

Blofeld pointed out the obvious difference in the photograph between Calvi's wet feet and ankles and the less wet appearance of the rest of him.

"That is correct, sir," Bartliff replied. "But the length of the ebb tide is something like six hours." He meant that the clothing would have had that amount of time to dry out, before the rising tide submerged the feet again.

"All you can say," Blofeld suggested to Bartliff, "is that when you arrived the clothing and the contents were damp. That is the word you used."

"That is correct," Bartliff replied.

"How they came to be damp, you can't say, because you weren't there. Is that fair?"

"That is correct, sir."

If Calvi's body had been submerged up to the neck, it must have been hanging from the scaffolding shortly after 1.30 a.m. – that is, while the tide was still fairly high, and in total darkness.

Whether Calvi's clothing was damp or soaked was not a point at issue the following March, when Lord Lane quashed the verdict. One of his reasons for doing so was that Dr Paul kept the jury until 10 p.m., instead of adjourning the case at a reaonable hour and resuming it next day. In this Dr Paul was abetted by the lawyers, who did not want to work on a Saturday. But it is the coroner's duty to make sure that the jurors are not becoming too exhausted to follow the evidence.

And exhausted they must have been. The whole afternoon was taken up with wildly confusing accounts of comings and goings by shadowy figures with foreign names, not one of whom appeared in person. Mr Morris and his daughter Odette gave evidence, but, as the relationship between Carboni and Laura Concas was not explained, nobody could understand why the Morris family had been so helpful.

Another irregularity which led to the quashing of the verdict was that Dr Paul allowed the reading of a statement from Carboni. The reading of a statement by Vittor was legal, because he was in prison in Italy and could not attend the court. But Carboni, then in hiding in Switzerland, could have come forward to give evidence in person.

It is easy to see why Dr Paul permitted the reading of both statements. They did give some semblance of connected narrative to what was otherwise a jumble.

True, if it was physically impossible for anyone to have murdered Calvi, as the evidence of Simpson and Wilson suggested, then Carboni and Vittor had not murdered him. But evidence about their movements was nevertheless important, and it should have been given in such a way that the jury could follow it. Dr Paul himself does not seem to have followed it. In his summing up, he referred wearily to "... one of those girls from Austria who appear to have flitted lightly through the evidence you have heard".

Before his summing up, Dr Paul gave the jury a half-hour adjournment, with the words: "I will then sum up and send you out and, with any luck, we should be away from here soon after."

On those grounds alone, Lord Lane said afterwards, he would have quashed the inquest. A coroner is not allowed to suggest that a jury should hurry up. But Dr Paul committed another irregularity while summing up. He said: "... the open verdict may seem like a super open door to scuttle through ..."

This hint that an open verdict would be cowardly was considered by Lord Lane as extremely improper. In fact the jury took an hour and a half to make up its mind, not reaching the verdict that Calvi had killed himself until 10 p.m., and then only by a majority, not a unanimous decision.

There were exciting scenes around the Law Courts in March 1983, after Lord Lane quashed the verdict. Carlo Calvi was telling a group of Italian journalists: "I am more convinced than ever that my father was murdered." One of the pathologists engaged by the Calvi family was saying that the English did not understand about Carboni. His account of Carboni's underworld contacts may have been perfectly accurate. But he was talking about Calvi's chosen companion, and what he said conflicted with what Carlo was saying about his father's complete respectability. It is natural for a son to defend his father, and Calvi's family had very little inkling of the story I have now unearthed.

The financial details were still scarcely known when the second inquest opened, on 11 June 1983. It was conducted by Dr Arthur Gordon Davies, coroner for Inner South London, in a larger courtroom at Milton Court, and it ran for eleven working days. Carboni was represented by Richard Du Cann QC, and Sir David Napley had retained George Carman QC to represent the Calvi family.

By contrast with Dr Paul, Dr Davies gave every witness full scope. He was perhaps too tolerant of the methods of the heavyweight barristers. Technically, a witness at an inquest is not supposed to be cross-examined. But Carman treated some of them almost as if they had been accused of murder.

Clara, Anna and Carlo gave evidence in person; nearly all of what they said had already appeared in the newspapers. The real novelty was the appearance of the witnesses involved in Calvi's last journey.

Instead of "flitting lightly", both Kleinszig sisters gave evidence. They had to answer questions through an interpreter; sometimes this caused confusion. For the Calvi family, Carman fiercely attacked their credibility. This caused Manuela to make a passionate speech about her love for Carboni and his love for her. Three days later Laura Concas (who had been asked to give evidence about the calls from the Hilton) made a surprise appearance and said she had been Carboni's mistress for nearly fourteen years. She and Manuela maintained that they had not known of each other's existence. Yet Manuela also maintained that she had been in the room at the Hilton while Carboni was telephoning Laura Concas.

At the beginning of the inquest it was announced that neither Carboni nor Vittor could attend, because they were in prison in Italy. (Carboni had been arrested and handed over by the Swiss.) But on the eighth day Vittor, let out on bail, turned up. He quibbled over some odd points; he denied that he was a bodyguard. Just a companion, he maintained unconvincingly. Carman attacked Vittor's credibility, particularly when he said that Calvi had known the result of the board meeting at the Ambrosiano. There Vittor stood his ground.

The jury got a few flashes of insight into the background. They learned that Carboni had been charged with the attack on Rosone. One of the few financial transactions presented in evidence was the $530,000 payment Carboni made to Diotallevi. But that Calvi had first paid Carboni was not mentioned; such information as the Swiss had collected about the $19 million paid into Carboni's bank accounts was considered confidential, though it had appeared long before in the Italian papers.

Manuela Kleinszig was questioned about the account at the Union Bank in Geneva, opened by Carboni in her name. She professed ignorance. When Du Cann began to question her about it, she started talking about 100,000 Swiss francs that she had been asked to pick up from another account opened in her name, at the UTO bank in Zürich. This account had been fed with over 800,000 Swiss francs from the Union Bank account. But at that stage the two were not known to be connected, and the matter was allowed to drop. Manuela said nothing about the $200,000 Carboni had paid to the bank in St Veit in her name, on 14 June. Instead, when Carman asked her if Carboni had kept her for the past three years, she said: "I lived sometimes in Italy; sometimes Austria. In Italy I was supported by Flavio and in Austria by my father financially."

It was not the evasions of the Kleinszig girls which led the jury to return an open verdict, but the confusion over the expert evidence. We have seen that at the first inquest Pc Bartliff had said Calvi's body was so wet that it must have been totally submerged, but then agreed that he had only said it was "damp".

He repeated his opinion that the body had been submerged at the second inquest. This time the idea caught on. A fresh expert witness, Ralph Ekblom, a hydrographic surveyor from the Port of London Authority, provided detailed charts of the levels of the tide throughout the night. These showed that Calvi's body would have been submerged up to the neck at about 1.30 a.m., and completely clear of the water an hour and a half later. (The chart reproduced opposite is a modified version of Ekblom's.)

The point was not specifically put to the other members of the River Police who had helped to recover Calvi's body. But Carman did question

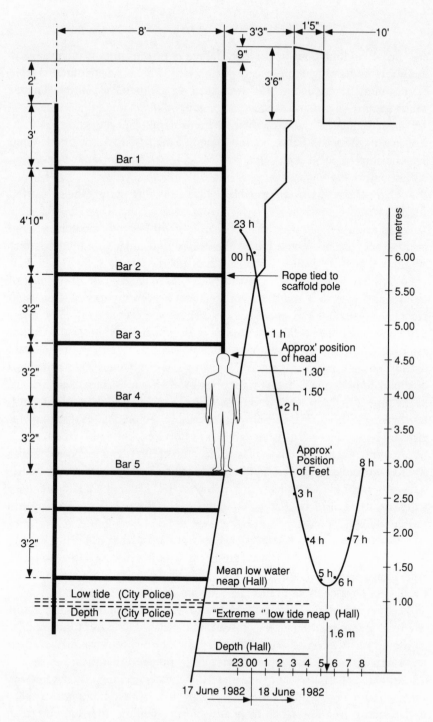

Table 4: Time and tide on the night of Calvi's death

the City of London policeman, John Palmer, who took out of Calvi's pocket the wallet containing the pieces of paper with names, addresses and telephone numbers on them. "Do you recall this – that the pieces of paper were sodden?" Carman asked.

Palmer replied: "Yes, they were certainly damp."

Carman insisted: "I did not say 'damp'. I said 'sodden': as if they had become immersed in water and had become sodden through immersion rather than damp?"

Palmer said: "Yes, quite wet." This was hardly a whole-hearted endorsement.

When Professor Simpson gave evidence, on the second day of the second inquest, the coroner asked him: "Were there any signs that the body had been immersed in water for any length of time?"

He replied: "No, sir. I asked to see the clothing, and the lower part of the trousers were wet and the rest damp, but the lower part of the trousers reaching up the leg had been in the water for some time."

We have seen that at the first inquest Simpson had been quite clear about rigor mortis; it indicated that death had taken place between 2 a.m. and 6 a.m. Now he repeated that rigor mortis was complete in the arms and less marked in the legs, but he went on to produce a more confused account of the time. He thought death had been "somewhere in the region of eight, ten or twelve hours" – meaning, presumably, before his examination at 2 p.m. The coroner then specifically asked how long before his examination he thought death had taken place. He answered: "Twelve hours. Rigor would be ordinarily expected to be complete in the region of twelve hours. This was not quite complete. If it followed the usual, likely and common rules, death would have happened about twelve hours before, but I would have to allow several hours on either side of that."

This was not quite the same as his previous answer, at which 2 a.m. had seemed to be the outside limit. He seemed now to be saying that death could have been considerably earlier than that. But his view that death could also have been several hours *after* 2 a.m. was not affected.

The coroner asked Simpson whether Calvi could have been hung somewhere else, and then taken to the scaffolding and rehung. Simpson said he supposed this was possible, but that the mark on his neck would have had to be exactly repeated. Surprisingly, nobody pursued this idea.

Carman, apparently accepting that Calvi had died on the scaffolding, questioned Simpson on the thesis that Calvi had been immobilised with an undetectable drug and taken by boat to the scaffolding, and hung there by others. Simpson clearly thought this far-fetched.

Then Carman started questioning Simpson on the absence of neck injuries, to see what could be deduced from this in relation to the tide. Simpson had earlier agreed that, if the body had fallen free more than two feet into the noose, he would have expected to find damage. Carman pointed out that, bearing in mind the length of rope between its fixture on the second horizontal bar of the scaffolding, and Calvi's neck – a distance of about four to four and a half feet – it would have been impossible for Calvi to fall free before about two to two-thirty, because he would have hit the water. Simpson agreed with this.

Carman put the point again in a convoluted way. "Therefore, it could not have been suspended from that point in the scaffold so as to fall free or it would need to have been suspended so as to fall free after quarter past, half past two, or something of that kind?"

"Yes," Simpson agreed.

Carman tried to pin him down to the time. "So we can almost safely operate, bearing in mind your rigor findings, that Calvi met his death by suspension at or about – and this is an approximate time – two o'clock or a little before?"

"In the early hours of the morning is much safer," Simpson said cautiously. "There is a bracket and there is quite a wide one."

"But the tide problem makes it look like two o'clock or before?" Carman said.

Simpson replied: "Yes."

With this answer, Simpson plunged himself into trouble. He must have become muddled. Certainly Calvi could not have fallen free *before* about 2.15 a.m. because of the water level, but it did not follow from this that if he had died long *after* two – as was consistent with the rigor findings – he *must* have fallen free, i.e. plunged several feet down. He could have hung himself later, when the tide had fallen, without either falling into water or falling free so far as to cause injuries to his neck.

Simpson had now fixed the time of death in people's minds at Carman's "two o'clock or a little before". But why was Carman wedded to the 2 a.m. time? The answer became apparent in his next question. "If I told you his wrist watch was stopped at 1.52 partially wound, with water damage, that might be the kind of time that would fit in with your rigor mortis findings and with the positions of the tide and absence of the neck injuries?"

"I suppose so," said Simpson. "It would depend on why it stopped."

Carman again provided the answer. "Partially wound and badly damaged by water."

What Carman knew was that some new evidence, not available at the first inquest, would shortly be produced. Calvi had been wearing a self-winding Patek Philippe wrist watch, of the kind which keeps going while the wearer is moving, as long as it is not damaged. It was not waterproof; water damage could have stopped it. Calvi also had on him a Patek Philippe pocket watch; this had stopped at 5.49½. An Omega wrist watch was found in his luggage. None of these watches had been examined before the first inquest, but the police had now repaired the omission, and sent all three to a police scientist, Roy Selzer, for examination. His report had said that the wrist watch was corroded and partially wound and had stopped at 1.52½. Carman was using this an an indication of the probable moment of death, on the assumption that it stopped shortly after Calvi had been hung, because at 1.52 in the morning his whole body, virtually up to the neck, would have gone into the water, wrist and watch included.

Carman went on to attack the suicide thesis, questioning Simpson on the difficulties that a somewhat overweight and unfit man of 62 would face in clambering around the scaffolding, tying up the rope and so on – all on the assumption that this would have taken place shortly before two, so that darkness would have increased his problems. Carman then returned to his thesis that Calvi could have been brought and hung up by others, and in the course of this he put it to Simpson that on these unknown person letting the body go it would naturally fall into the water, and that the water would come up to somewhere below the head.

Simpson was now in difficulties. Carman's thesis was undeniable: if the body was strung up shortly before two in the morning, then it must have fallen into the water and been submerged up to the neck. But Simpson simply did not believe this had happened. He now interjected: "That was not so from the clothing I saw. The water level had never been above calf level."

Simpson did not raise the matter again until some questions later, after the lunch adjournment, when Carman was dealing with the absence of marks of violence. "With your knowledge of marks on the body, quite clearly the body could be so positioned and left to trail in the water, so that you would not necessarily, on post mortem, find any marks of violence on the body?"

Simpson replied: "I cannot say that. I only found evidence of water rising up to mid-leg as far as the clothing was concerned."

Carman this time replied: "We know from other evidence that the wallet and contents were sodden and the wrist watch was badly corroded and damaged by water."

The coroner interjected that the court had not yet heard evidence about the watch.

Carman accepted this, but pressed on. "And you would accept, would you not, that to manoeuvre a body from the top of the boat, to tie it and leave it so that it floats into the water, need not necessarily leave marks which would be detectable at post mortem?"

Simpson said: "Yes, I accept that, but I do not believe from the appearance of the clothing that the body floated in the water. The clothing looked as if the water had risen only half way up the leg."

"We will hear other evidence about the clothing," said Carman – a promise which was scarcely fulfilled. "If you accept death occurred at about quarter past two" – Carman probably meant a quarter to two, the time he had previously been using – "it is manifest from the tide height that the body must have descended appreciably into water."

The answer to this was yes – if you accept the evidence deduced from the watch that death took place shortly before two. But Simpson now introduced a red herring that probably did much to influence the jury's decision against suicide. He said: "You are assuming it was where it was eventually found. It could have been sitting on the upper level. I have had people hang themselves sitting. That could happen too. The body need not be fully dependent."

Simpson was trying to reconcile his belief that Calvi's body had never been submerged with Carman's insistence, on evidence that Simpson had no independent knowledge of, that death took place shortly before two. He had resorted to the hypothesis that Calvi had hung himself in a sitting position on the second or third horizontal bars of the scaffolding, which were out of the water at the time, his head falling forward into the noose but his body only later slipping off the bar into a vertical position once the tide had gone down. But, if Calvi had not been submerged, the watch would not have been submerged either. So the theory did nothing to solve the dilemma.

The full implication of the Simpson hypothesis did not immediately sink in. The coroner intervened to suggest that Carman was perhaps pinpointing the time of death too closely, and Carman explained that he had chosen 1.45 because of the watch. When he returned to questioning Simpson, he asked whether Simpson had previously encountered cases of people hanging themselves over water, which he had not.

Carman's questioning ended lamely, with Simpson conceding only that there was nothing medically inconsistent with Calvi being undetectably drugged and his body then lifted from a boat on to the scaffolding.

For all Carman's efforts, it was not his questioning but the friendly examination of Du Cann which did most to shake the credibility of Simpson as a witness.

Du Cann returned to the question of the time of death. "The span of hours you gave us was twelve as the outside limit and eight as the inside limit?"

This was indeed what Simpson had said at the first inquest, and his initial answer to the coroner implied it. Now his answer was: "Between twelve and four. I said two or three hours in either direction from two o'clock. I think the span is two or three hours around two o'clock in either direction."

Du Cann was clearly puzzled. "Twelve to eight hours – can I examine that? – would mean between two o'clock in the morning and six o'clock in the morning?"

Simpson replied: "Yes."

"How ought we to record that time span of four hours?" Du Cann asked.

Simpson said it was "an estimate which is to be stretched several hours in either direction".

"It could take us back to 11 p.m.?" asked Du Cann.

"It could, I think, and on to five," Simpson said. "It is not a mathematical problem."

But that is what he had turned it into. He seems to have become confused by his own figures. Perhaps the confusion meant only that rigor mortis was a rough and unreliable guide. Du Cann put it to him that Calvi could have died at any time between high tide at 23.17 on 16 June and low tide at 5.24 on 17 June, so far as could be judged from rigor mortis. Simpson answered somewhat off the point: "I can say in my view, looking at the clothing, and in the absence of evidence of drowning, I do not think myself the whole body was ever submerged."

He then reverted to his thesis that Calvi had hung himself while sitting. "I am also bearing in mind, Mr Du Cann, the possibility that the man Calvi could have been sitting for some time with his neck in a noose – I have seen that – and only have dropped into the lower water at a later stage. That is a possibility."

This time the extraordinary scene he was conjuring up had its full impact. "I think the jury are having difficulty," commented Du Cann.

Simpson persisted: "If a man were to put a noose round his neck and still be seated, he may just fall into the noose without dropping off the bar. It is a possibility."

To the entertainment of everyone in court, Du Cann then tried a physical demonstration. This was probably a mistake. It was in the interest of his client, Carboni, that there should be a second suicide verdict, and the ridicule which now attached itself to Simpson did not help.

Most of the rest of the second day, the third day and the morning of the fourth were taken up with the dramatic appearances of the Kleinszig sisters. It was not until the afternoon of the fourth day that the examination of the technical experts resumed. Roy Selzer, the police expert, then explained about the watches. The wrist watch, he told the coroner, had suffered "considerable corrosion damage", which was "more consistent with immersion rather than rain or spray". The pocket watch, which had stopped at 5.49, also showed signs of rust, but the damage was "minimal" by comparison with that of the wrist watch. The pocket watch, when wound up, worked satisfactorily. The damage to it was more likely to have been caused by a humid atmosphere, or rain or moisture splashing on its surface, than by total immersion.

Carman went through the operation of an automatic watch with Selzer, and established that, in normal circumstances, if such a watch had stopped because it had naturally run down, it would have had to be immobile for some 12 to 24 hours beforehand. Carman then asked Selzer if the mainspring was partially wound, as he had said in his report. Selzer assented.

Carman then asked: "If the watch is in working order, it being partially wound, you would expect it to keep working until it became totally unwound. Do I state that correctly?"

"In fairness, I think that is an over-simplification," Selzer replied. "It was partially wound, meaning that there was some tension within the spring barrel, but obviously it cannot unwind completely so there is no tension. It was partially wound. It was almost completely unwound."

"There was some slack?" persisted Carman.

"Some slight tension," agreed Selzer, "which may or may not have been enough to keep it going."

With these answers he had destroyed completely the significance of 1.52. The watch might have been wholly immersed, but it might have stopped simply because it ran down. If it had stopped for this reason at 1.52 on the morning of 18 June, whether submerged or not, Calvi would have had to be immobile for some hours beforehand, a suggestion nobody had made. Whether Calvi had gone to the scaffolding under his own steam or been manhandled there by others, the movement would have been enough to ensure that the mainspring had substantial tension in it, if the watch had stopped as a result of being plunged into water. It must still have been ticking when it was taken off Calvi's body, and the time when it ran down, after that, was irrelevant.

Carman, a clever and experienced barrister, took in his stride the discovery that "partially wound" meant "almost completely unwound". The jury could not have told by his demeanour that it had destroyed his assumption about the time of death. He continued deftly to question Selzer. "Does it come to this: that it has either stopped by water invading it sufficiently thoroughly by 1.52 or it has stopped because it was sufficiently unwound?"

"Yes," Selzer said.

"And if it stopped because it is insufficiently wound, in normal circumstances it must have been on a non-active body for twelve to twenty-four hours because of the automatic function of the watch before 1.52?"

"Yes, assuming it was working properly beforehand," Selzer said.

"Let us take the time: 1.52 a.m. on 18 June," said Carman. "If the person wearing the watch at 1.52 on 18 June had been moving around the evening and afternoon of the previous day, apart from water, you would normally have expected the watch to continue to work after 1.52?"

"Yes," agreed Selzer.

"So if the wearer was wearing it normally and moving around in the afternoon and evening of the previous day, if it is 1.52 a.m. it should have continued to work?"

"Yes," replied Selzer.

"What then appears to have stopped it," concluded Carman triumphantly, "is water, if the wearer was wearing it in the afternoon and evening?"

Selzer said: "Yes." Like Simpson, he seems to have been confused by Carman's convoluted questions. He had been seduced into conceding the very point at issue, which was whether the watch had stopped at 1.52 a.m. on 18 June – not at 1.52 p.m., or at 1.52 the following morning, or whenever the spring unwound.

When Du Cann examined Selzer it emerged that it could not even be said that the corrosion had been caused by immersion. He established that Selzer had not been given the watch to examine until March 1983, eight months after Calvi's death, and that in the meantime it had been sealed in a plastic bag with its leather strap, the dampness of which could have caused the corrosion to take place.

On the ninth day of the inquest it became clear that the confusion about the watches was persisting. The coroner asked Detective Inspector White about the watches, adding: "The importance was not realised because at that time there was nothing to point to crime?"

"Nothing at all, sir," said White.

"It was, shall we say, not treated with the same care and concern as if there had been more obvious signs of crime?" the coroner asked.

"Quite right, sir," White agreed.

This was the only point at either inquest in which the police mentioned their natural reaction to finding a man hanging – that he must have done it himself.

A juror showed he was confused by asserting that Pc Palmer had said the watch had stopped at 1.52. The coroner asked White to check. The following morning White reported. When the watches were taken off the body nobody had looked to see whether they were going or not. The coroner commented that, therefore, 1.52 "has no validity, because it might just be when the watch went down, morning or afternoon or any time". "That is correct," said White.

That should have been the end of the watch as evidence of the time of death. But the misapprenhension persisted long after the inquest. For example, the journalists Paul Foot and Paolo Filo della Torre wrote in a 1984 part-work called "Unsolved" that "the time it had stopped and other evidence indicated conclusively that Calvi had died shortly before 2 a.m." Without the watch, what other evidence is there? There is the opinion of Pc Bartliff that the body had been immersed. There is Palmer's evidence that the wallet was wet. (Could it have got wet when Calvi's jacket was opened and the contents of the pockets removed on Waterloo pier?) White, too, thought that the body had been immersed, but he did not see it until the evening of 18 June. The further evidence on the clothing, which Carman had promised the jury, was that police scientists were unable to tell whether the moisture was water from the Thames or rain.

Anyone who looks at the photograph of Calvi's body, taken at about 9 a.m., can form an opinion about the clear and obvious line between wetness and dampness. Could a man's suit, once totally immersed, dry out in about six hours of a very damp night?

Nobody disputed that the clothes were very damp. There was speculation at the inquest that this might have been caused by spray, or by rain blown under the bridge. The most obvious explanation (though nobody gave it at either inquest) was that Calvi had been walking about in the rain.

According to a report produced by the London Weather Centre, there was no rain before 4 a.m. on the morning of 18 June. There was then "slight" rain. At 5 a.m. it was dry again. At 6 a.m. slight rain restarted, and at 7 a.m. it became continuous.

How slight was the rain? Calvi was not wearing a raincoat. If he had been wandering about all night, wondering whether to kill himself, a chilly drizzle on a grey morning might well have been enough to make up his mind for him. He must have been all the colder because he had not had a decent meal for several days. Wandering along the Thames with bricks in his pocket, looking for a good place to drown himself, he may have been as much perplexed as most Italians are to find the deep water replaced by a foreshore of slimy mud or very shallow water. To come by chance on a scaffolding, with a piece of rope left over from the last high tide, would solve his problem. Between about 2.40 and shortly before 8 a.m., horizontal bar five and the board attached to it would have been free of the water. He might have had to do some scrambling to fix the rope. But, by simply stepping off bar five, he would neither have fallen into the water nor have dropped far enough to injure his neck.

It is logical to suppose that Calvi, who had every reason to hang himself, did so. But, if he did, he started a legend, in which logic has no place.

FORTY-ONE

"Frank" and other Witnesses

The legend began, for me, even before the second inquest. In February 1983 a long article on the Calvi affair appeared in the *Sunday Times*. I was one of the authors. Soon afterwards a man called at the office and asked to see me. He would not give his name, but said he would tell me the secret of Calvi's death for £3,000. I told him that the *Sunday Times* was unlikely to pay that sort of money, and certainly not unless what he said could be proved.

Later the man telephoned and said I should call him Frank. He suggested that I ought to check up on an Italian antique dealer, Sergio Vaccari, who had been murdered in London about three months after Calvi's death.

Vaccari had indeed been killed in his flat in West London on 16 September 1982. The police suspected that the murder was connected with drug dealing. This hardly justified paying Frank any money. But he said that he would tell me what he knew in any case, leaving open the possibility that he would get some reward if the story proved to be true.

Frank had written his story down, graphically if illiterately. He first met Vaccari in an antique shop in the Portobello Road. Vaccari lived in a flat above the shop until shortly before the time of Calvi's death, when he moved to the more expensive one in West Kensington. Frank had interests in common with Vaccari; both were dealing in antiques and jewels, and they met occasionally.

One day in the summer of 1982 Vaccari asked Frank to come with him to collect a safe. They went in a hatchback car to a place in the Portobello Road area. Vaccari got out and asked Frank to stay in the car. Left alone, Frank opened a briefcase in the car, and found inside it a large black purse, the size of a handbag, and some flat paper packages. Frank opened the purse and found four packets, containing five photographs. One packet had two photographs of Calvi, which Frank recognised; the papers had been full of them that summer. Another packet, Frank wrote, contained a photograph of Calvi "wearing a dog collar". The last two packets had photographs of two different women. Frank did not recognise either of them then, but later realised that one of them was Jeannette May, the former wife of Evelyn de Rothschild, who disappeared in the Camerino region of Italy in 1980. Her remains, with those of her companion Gabriella Guerin, were found on a hillside in January 1982.

Before Frank had time to put the purse back, the rear door of the car was opened and he saw a man and a blonde woman with Vaccari. They slid some boxes into the back, while Frank slipped the purse behind the seat. Vaccari said: "Goodbye, Rosso," to the man, and got in, telling Frank that he had not got the safe after all. He then said that he wanted Frank to get him a silver frame for a photo. He picked up both purse and briefcase, took out the photograph of a woman and handed it to Frank. It is not clear whether this was yet another photograph, or the one of the woman who was not Jeannette May.

Vaccari, waving the purse, asked Frank if he had seen the other photographs. Frank admitted he had. He asked Vaccari whether he thought that Calvi had really hung himself. Vaccari replied: "I may as well tell you, as I do not think that you will put my life in danger. I have been asked to investigate the case. I did think that the lookalike photo of Calvi – you know, the one of him in a priest's collar – was a double for Calvi, but I was wrong. Roberto was definitely the fellow hanging under Blackfriars Bridge. Some horrible, ruthless men got him to do it by showing him some videos of Mafia torturing and by telling him that his daughter would be the star of the next video." Vaccari then added that he did not know whether the videos had been shown to Calvi in London or beforehand in Italy, but that he was going to try to find out when he himself returned to Italy the following week.

Frank asked Vaccari whether it would be dangerous for him to go back to Italy. "Very," he replied. "I wouldn't want to end up on a video myself, and what you now know is dangerous information." Frank wrote: "I felt the warning."

A few weeks later, while Frank was watching *Police Five* on TV, Vaccari's murder was described. "The hairs on my arm pushed through my shirt-sleeves," wrote Frank.

In view of all that has been written about Calvi's death, it is worth mentioning that Vaccari was not killed in some subtle way, or made to look as if he had killed himself. He was (like one of the people who frequented the Ruhl Casino) repeatedly stabbed in the face.

Frank's account was mingled with his own speculations – that Vaccari himself could have been the hit man, or Rosso, whom Frank saw with the blonde woman the day after he saw him with Vaccari.

There were plenty of reasons to doubt Frank's evidence. The idea of a Calvi double being photographed in a dog-collar seemed particularly far-fetched. But, four years later, I read Pazienza's story of Operation Cigueña, with his plan to hire a double to distract the reporters from the real Calvi. Frank could scarcely have known this at the time.

There were other things Frank was unlikely to know, such as the cryptic message about "Sergio", left by Diotallevi at Carboni's office. Sergio was Vaccari's first name. And Vaccari was fair-haired, which, in an Italian, is rare enough to cause comment. Could he have been the blond youth who flew in the plane from Rome to Trieste on 11 June with Diotallevi – the one whose name Pellicani remembered, vaguely, as something like "Macari"? He was not a youth, being 42 (although he looked young) and, according to details of his travels apparently compiled by the police from his passport, it would have been difficult for him to have been in Rome. He is said to have left London for Copenhagen on 9 June and to have returned from Copenhagen to London on 15 June. But the Italian investigators have never established the identity of this man, and, if by any chance it was Vaccari, he might well have been asked by Diotallevi or his associates to find out something about Calvi's death. Vaccari, though he came from a respectable and wealthy family in Milan, was a drug dealer, and probably a fence for stolen antiques; he was so thick with the Italian underworld in London that he was well placed to hear rumours.

It was easy enough to find Vaccari's antique shop, a rather shabby one in the Portobello Road. The owner told me that Vaccari had lived above it, and had introduced him to a man called Frank. He also said that he had found a file of cuttings and notes on Calvi in Vaccari's room when he left. He said he had thrown it away.

In mid-March 1983 stories began to appear in the newspapers linking the murder of Vaccari with the deaths of Jeannette May and Calvi. Sometimes journalists create news; there seemed to be nothing in the Calvi link beyond a feedback from my own inquiries. Frank assured me that he had not spoken to any other journalists.

Jeannette May's disappearance, however, happened shortly after a robbery at Christie's in Rome, and may possibly have been connected with it. She was herself in the antiques business. The police found photographs of jewellery and antiques in Vaccari's safe, and one of these showed a clock stolen in the robbery. Two Italian policemen came to London in March 1983 to make further inquiries.

The next development in the Vaccari saga took place in Trieste on 24 March 1983, though I did not learn of it for many months. The Trieste magistrate who was initially in charge of investigations into Calvi's flight questioned an acquaintance of Vittor, Eligio Paoli. Paoli claimed that one Riccardo Piazzesi, living in Chiasso, was a source of information on the whole Calvi affair, and in particular the role of Gelli and Ortolani. According to Paoli, he had said that Vaccari knew a great deal about Calvi's visit to London. Nobody has ever established whether Piazzesi existed. (Paoli had already been feeding the investigators with information. In January he had said that Calvi had been entrusted to the care of a man called Volpi in London; so he could have changed his story once the Vaccari name had been publicly touted around.)

Later Paoli amplified his story, claiming that Carboni was in league with Gelli and Ortolani, and that Gelli was in London at the same time as Calvi.

One of Paoli's versions was that Calvi had been invited to a supper, at which Vaccari had been present. A newspaper cutting about Vittor's evidence at the inquest was found, and on this Paoli had written: "Sergio Vaccari – Pier Luigi Torri, London, September."

Torri certainly existed; he was a leading member of the Italian underworld in London in the 1970s, when he was involved in a major fraud. But he was not in London in the summer and autumn of 1982; he had been sent back to Italy by then.

Paoli was involved in a bizarre allegation of fraud against Vittor, who was supposed to have tried to extract money from him for Calvi's briefcase. He was also suspected of being another blond young man in the Calvi story – not the one on the plane but the one who was originally thought to have driven him across the Italian border from Trieste. It was discovered, however, that Paoli had been somewhere else at the time. Then Vittor admitted that Calvi had left Trieste in a boat, with him. The men who drove Calvi to Klagenfurt never have been identified.

Paoli, when questioned by the P2 Commission, backtracked about Vaccari, and could not explain why he had written the name. Yet he stuck to his Vaccari story when Dalbert Hallenstein, a journalist based in Verona, interviewed him for me at the end of 1984. He even added that he had been told that Vaccari was trying to get Carboni and his associates on the phone before they went to London.

In a story of the underworld, one scarcely hopes for documents. Yet there are documents. The British police found two address books and a diary among Vaccari's possessions. I managed to obtain one address book, which contained nothing that I could see to provide a link. I was promised a sight of the rest, but the promise was not kept.

In Rome, however, I gave a statement summarising Frank's story to a policeman, Corsetti, and a magistrate, Jacoboni, who were investigating the death of Jeannette May. (Jacoboni repeated it in his inconclusive report on the affair, delivered in October 1989.) From them I learned that copies of Vaccari's papers had been sent to a magistrate in Rome, who was inquiring into the Italian end of his operations. In the autumn of 1987 he let me and my researcher Philip Willan look at them for about three-quarters of an hour. I was promised a longer examination of the papers, but this promise, too, was not kept. However, I was able to see the name "Frank" at the right sort of points in July and August 1982 and that Vaccari was in London while Calvi was; and I noted the name of at least one Italian living in London who had received money from an Ortolani associate in 1981. Only in early 1992 was I able to have a more leisurely look at the diary. The entries for the days Calvi was in London provide no evidence of any contact; nor do the entries for the previous days provide any firm corroboration of his whereabouts, although, in so far as anything can be gleaned from them, they point to Copenhagen rather than Rome. Still, according to Frank's story, Vaccari was not necessarily in personal contact with Calvi, but had only been told what had happened to him.

I also heard, independently, that customs officers investigating a gang of drug traffickers led by an Italian jeweller from Turin had been told by an informant of someone who was allegedly involved in Calvi's death; nothing concrete, however, has emerged to support this allegation. There were to be even more specific allegations of mafia involvement but so far there have been no more than tantalising glimpses of links between those who might have had an interest in Calvi's death and the world of Italian drug and antique hustlers in London.

Gelli, whose whereabouts at the time of Calvi's death remain a mystery, and Ortolani, who was probably in Brazil, were defendants in the Ambrosiano trial, but as they were being tried for their part in Calvi's fraud, not for any connection they may have had with his death, the facts about their movements on those vital days have not come out.

Another defendant in the trial was Pazienza. Where was he on those days? According to himself, in New York, talking to would-be purchasers of Ambrosiano shares. There is no evidence that these negotiations ever happened. After Calvi's death Pazienza travelled freely in and out of Italy, not fearing arrest; it was years before investigators got on to the trail of the $8.8 million that Calvi had paid him outside Italy, through the Realfin and Finanzco accounts. His weak point was the Prato Verde fraud, which he and Carboni had conducted entirely in Italy. The local investigators found it quite easily. They interrogated him in the autumn of 1982. After that

Pazienza decided it would be wiser to live in New York. Not until March 1983 did the Italians issue a warrant for his arrest.

By that time Pazienza was elusive. He had (he told me in 1986) set up in the fishing business with boats registered in Liberia. Using what for money? By that time there was little left in the Realfin and Finanzco accounts. Though he denied that the Andros $5 million had reached him, it seems probable that this was the money he used.

The fishing business does not seem to have been a success. In July 1984 Pazienza turned up in the Seychelles. The man in power there was Albert René; the *eminence grise* behind him was a bearded Italian, Mario Ricci. The Seychelles were then supposed to have great oil potential. Pazienza and his friend Armao became involved in an attempt to set up a Seychelles national oil corporation.

In New York, customs agents had become eager to talk to Pazienza. They were investigating the possibility that some Ambrosiano money had reached the United States. They asked Pazienza's lawyer, Edward Morrison, if he would talk to them. Pazienza asked for an assurance that he would not be arrested.

The Seychelles became uncomfortable. Pazienza's story is that Italian secret service agents had traced him there, and that an attempt was made on his life. He seems to have gone to Mexico, using his mother's maiden name, Donato. Wherever he was, he continued to negotiate with the US customs men. Finally he agreed to meet them in New York on 4 March 1985, having been assured that he would be allowed to go free after the meeting.

The customs men may have meant that assurance when they gave it, but they were overruled. The Justice Department issued a warrant for his arrest on behalf of the Italians. He was detained by the somewhat embarrassed customs officials. For over a year he fought extradition. In the end he saw he faced a losing battle, and agreed to return. In Italy he was imprisoned for another six months, before obtaining "conditional liberty" pending the trial.

The $933,000 Pazienza paid to the bank account in the name of the Swiss lawyer Duft, allegedly for the Di Nunzio blackmail, is still under investigation – and thus Duft found himself unwittingly entangled in the affair. In Italy, the authorities impounded the *Giulia VII* yacht bought with the Prato Verde money and a couple of Rolls Royces.

Duft himself, I have discovered, was connected with a Geneva company, Sasea. In 1984 it acquired a new managing director, Florio Fiorini – the former ENI man who was not a member of P2, just remarkably helpful when Calvi wanted a loan. Sasea began to expand very fast after the injection of new capital. Nobody has succeeded in proving that this was Ambrosiano money. Sasea became interested in the oil prospects of the Seychelles, but after Pazienza had left.

I talked to Pazienza in New York, while he was awaiting extradition to Italy. I found him reluctant to admit that he had done well out of Calvi. And yet that very fact was on his side; it showed how little motive he had for wanting Calvi dead.

What motive, indeed, did anyone have? At one time the Italian press was full of stories that Calvi had been murdered by someone who wanted to get at his briefcase. He was alleged never to be without it. It was full of documents compromising to . . . you could fill in the names at this point, according to taste. Some of the contents of this briefcase we have seen at the appropriate points in the narrative. It came to light in the spring of 1986. The neo-fascist senator Giorgio Pisanò, who had written a book called *The Calvi Murder*, said he had bought it from two unidentifiable men for 50 million lire. It was opened on television, allegedly for the first time, in the presence of a journalist, Enzo Biagi, and of Carboni, Pellicani and Vittor. The last three were there to vouch that it was the briefcase they had seen Calvi carrying. They were indeed experts. Whether Calvi had his briefcase in London, or it never left Trieste, it was probably Vittor who kept it.

Carboni had a friend with convictions for forgery, Giulio Lena. Hence the suspicions about the letter found in the briefcase, in which Calvi appeared to acknowledge that he owed Carboni money. In October 1989 Carboni and Lena were charged with attempting to extort money from a bishop in the Vatican, by selling him papers from the briefcase. This happened in the autumn of 1985 – some six months before the famous first opening on TV.

The bishop, a Czech, Pavel Hnilica, approached Carboni because he wanted help in improving the Vatican's image after the Ambrosiano scandal. According to Hnilica, Carboni said he was in a position to exonerate the Vatican, and that there were papers he would have "to collect from various friends of Calvi". Carboni also said he would need money. Hnilica told investigators the money was not to buy the papers, but to pay journalists to write favourably about the Vatican. Lena was brought in because, it seems, Carboni asked him to put up money so that he could get hold of the briefcase. Hnilica, who had between 20 and 30 million lire in an account at the IOR, gave Carboni two signed but blank cheques. He said that Carboni had asked him not to fill them in, but led him to believe they would be made out for relatively small amounts, such as half a million lire.

But the amount filled in on each cheque was 600 million lire (about $325,000) and they were made payable to Lena, who presented them to two commercial banks, in February and March 1986, and took the money. When the banks tried to clear the cheques with the IOR, it refused to honour them, saying the signature was incorrect.

According to Hnilica, the first he saw of the briefcase was on television. But he had been given some letters signed by Calvi, including the one Calvi wrote to the Pope. The briefcase did also contain Calvi's second Nicaraguan passport (the first was found at the Kleinszig home) and the keys to his Milan apartment. There was certainly nothing worth killing him for.

The Carboni-Hnlica affair was investigated by a Rome public prosecutor, Francesco De Leo, and an investigating magistrate, Mario Almerighi. Almerighi's report, dated 24 March 1992, only became available shortly before this book went to press. In addition to examining the dealings between Carboni, Lena and Hnlica, Almerighi reconstructs Calvi's flight with his eye on the fate of the briefcase and its contents. Almerighi reveals that, in addition to the letter to the Pope, Carboni handed over other documents to Hnlica which were not in the briefcase when it was formally opened. One of these was a long memorandum, unsigned, but no doubt drafted by Calvi, in which he wrote of his reluctance to meet the commission which was supposedly going to adjudicate between him and the IOR because he did not have the necessary documents since they were "kept abroad". Almerighi then postulates that Calvi's purpose in leaving Italy was not just to try to raise money but, more importantly, to get the material for "pressure and blackmail".

Almerghi's thesis is that Calvi was taken to Trieste and there persuaded to leave his briefcase while he was taken to Klagenfurt so that its contents could be photocopied. The briefcase was then taken by Vittor to Klagenfurt and Calvi then took it with him to London. Almerighi then suggests that after Calvi's disappearance from Chelsea Cloisters, the more important documents were removed and given by Carboni to Flavoni at Gatwick on 18 June to take back to Switzerland (Flavoni denies this). The briefcase itself was then probably taken back by Carboni himself via Edinburgh.

Although there is some circumstantial evidence to back this thesis, it seems unnecessarily convoluted. If Calvi took his briefcase with him to London, as he surely would have wanted to, it would seem much more likely that Vittor found it in the flat in Chelsea Cloisters and took it with him when he rushed back to Austria. The most significant items in it were likely to have been Calvi's up-to-date balance sheets for United Trading which would have shown how he regarded the Bellatrix $141.5 million, and up-to-date IOR accounts like the one on page 162. If Carboni and Vittor had found these they would have been most unlikely to have been able to make head or tail of them. They might even have thrown them away. They would also have been too cryptic for Calvi to have used to put pressure on the Vatican. He would have needed the parallel letters, of which some copies were in the Bahamas. Calvi may have kept other copies in the safe at Ultrafin in Zurich or the one at the Gottardo in Lugano, but they have never surfaced – although Almerighi believes that crucial papers were removed from the Ultrafin safe before it was officially opened by the Swiss authorities in December 1982.

The people most anxious to prove that Calvi's death was murder were his widow, son and daughter. Clara Calvi sued the insurance company Assicurazioni Generali, which refused to pay her 4 billion lire (plus interest) on various grounds, one of them being that Calvi's life insurance policy was invalid because he had committed suicide.

One of the Italian magistrates adjudicating on the claim watched an elaborate staging, on two consecutive nights, of what might have happened on the night that Calvi died. One of the possibilities enacted was the theory that Carman had put to Professor Simpson – that Calvi was tranquilised by some undetectable drug, and brought to the scene by boat. A dummy was used for this. The suicide theory was also enacted, by an actor of about Calvi's age and build. Another actor (who was also a stuntman) played the victim in other murder scenarios.

The scene under Blackfriars Bridge was the same, the tide conditions were the same – but the whole thing was made effectively irrelevant by the obsession that the time of death was about 2 a.m. on 18 June. Because it was tied to this time, the reconstruction took place when the tide was convenient for the approach of a boat but extremely inconvenient for the actor reproducing the suicide, who had to do a considerable amount of clambering on the horizontal poles. Nobody who looks at the pictures of the reconstruction could guess at the existence of the board at level five, where Calvi could have walked at low tide, with the growing daylight to guide him. This was in the most literal sense a cover-up, with water and darkness doing the covering.

The Italian judge seems to have been particularly taken with the enactment of Calvi being lured to the scaffolding as a passenger in a boat, to be met by a man who seemed to be there to secure the boat, but slipped a noose from behind over Calvi's head and quickly tightened it.

The watch turned up again in the judge's remarks, when he found in Clara Calvi's favour, pointing out that an expert had told him the watch would have stopped within minutes of being plunged into salt water. It provided, the judge said, "a more precise definition" of the time of Calvi's death. No, it didn't. But probably this one will run and run. Against some legends, argument is useless.

The judge also said that Carboni arrived in London on 15 June, the same day as Calvi. This was a serious mistake, because it led him to argue that Carboni's explanation of his reason for coming – that Calvi had asked him to find a better flat – was "unconvincing". There were, as the judge pointed out, many reasons to be suspicious about the account Carboni and Vittor gave of those last few days, but this particular allegation was ill-founded.

The judge then perversely argued that Calvi's clothes might have become wet because of rain or spray rather than immersion. But if the time of his death had really been 1.52 a.m. there would be no point in trying to prove that his body was not immersed up to the neck. The judge went on to say that there was no rust on Calvi's hands. But how could there have been, if he had been under water?

Then the judge argued that the bricks in Calvi's pockets would not have been heavy enough to keep him under water (assuming that he had first thought of drowning himself). As every sailor knows, your shoes can drown you, and few pairs of shoes weigh over eleven pounds – the total weight of the bricks and stones disposed about Calvi's clothing.

Even the judge's arguments *for* suicide were factually wrong. He accepted that Calvi must have known of the events in Italy on 17 June, because of the "large number" of metered units used on the telephone. It was not a large number, as I have shown. The evidence that Calvi knew is Vittor's evidence, which the judge was otherwise treating with caution.

In 1992 the Calvi family was still fighting hard for the insurance money: it had become a key negotiating point in any eventual settlement with the liquidators. Calvi left his family, by my estimate, a total of some $30 million, including the property in the Bahamas and the ranch in Canada. The question is how much of this was his to leave. No charges have been brought against any member of the Calvi family. It is not a crime for a woman to believe what her husband tells her, and there is no evidence that Clara Calvi or her children knew about the embezzlement and fraud.

The largest single liquid asset was the half share in the sale of the Rocky Mountain Plaza development in March 1982, for $24 million. It is not entirely clear how Calvi originally financed his overseas property investments, but, as we have seen, there is no evidence that he embezzled money on a vast scale until he came to know Gelli and Ortolani.

Apart from the few sums that Calvi took by way of Palmetto, the most contentious part of the family wealth was the $10 million or so that Ortolani paid back to Calvi as his share of the "commissions". Much of this went into the Butric accounts in Nassau, where some $8 million was frozen on the application of the Cisalpine liquidators. There was also over $500,000 in jewellery in Nassau. The family succeeded in keeping secret the whereabouts of some other investments. They have offered a substantial sum to the liquidators in Nassau, Luxembourg and Milan. But by the middle of 1991 there had been no agreement, because there is a belief, particularly in Italy, that the family is sitting on a crock of gold, far larger than the $30 million I have estimated. This is another legend against which argument may be vain. But in fact there are no vast sums unaccounted for; Calvi was a minor beneficiary of his own fraud.

The long legal fight over the insurance money has to some extent obscured the questions which remain to be asked even if Calvi took his own life. Why did he come to London? Vittor waited until 1986 before telling the *Corriere della Sera* that, "a little before the end", Calvi told him he was due to meet "two very important people, who, it seemed, were in a position to solve his problems".

Did he really meet anyone in London? In 1989 a new, independent witness emerged and swore an affidavit for the Calvi family. Cecil Coomber lived in Flat 834 at Chelsea Cloisters. He said that, two or three days before the news of Calvi's death was published – he thought on Thursday 17 June – two men came to his door between 7 and 7.30 p.m. The younger of the two, a man aged about 30, started to talk to him in Italian, saying he had heard he spoke the language. Coomber knew a little Italian, but it was not enough to hold a conversation. He tried to explain that they should speak to the manageress of the building, who did speak Italian. The men went away. Coomber later discovered that they had been trying to communicate with the receptionist about their flat, and had been directed to him, because it was thought he knew Italian.

Later that evening, at about 10 p.m., Coomber and a companion decided to go out for a meal. They went to the lift, where they saw a party of men waiting – Coomber thought three in all. As they waited for the lift, Coomber saw that two were younger men, who spoke together in Italian. The third was an older man in a suit, with a moustache, who looked thoughtful or concerned. When the lift arrived they all got in, and at the ground floor Coomber and his friend headed for the front door, while the others turned towards the back entrance. As Coomber walked towards the door, it dawned on him that one of the younger men and the older man were the pair who had knocked at his door.

Coomber was shown pictures of Calvi and was certain he was the older man, emphasising particularly his memory of the moustache. He was also shown photographs of Vittor and Carboni, but did not recognise either of them as one of the men he had seen with Calvi.

Why had Coomber not said so seven years earlier? He had known about the inquiries into Calvi's death, but had simply not thought that what he had seen was significant. It was by chance that he was passing the reception desk at Chelsea Cloisters just as an Italian journalist, Laura Bonaparte, who was pursuing her own inquiries into the Calvi story, had rung the reception-ist. The receptionist handed the phone to Coomber because of his reputed knowledge of Italian, and to her he mentioned that he had seen Calvi. She told Kingsley Napley. There may yet prove to be London taxi drivers, men who keep coffee stalls, or Smithfield butchers, who saw Calvi and did not mention it.

There are several odd things about Coomber's story. Calvi seems to have had a strong inhibition about speaking English, but if he wanted to complain he could. Was it really Calvi? We have seen that on the plane from Rome to Trieste three people who knew him did not recognise him, because he looked so commonplace.

If it was Calvi, we have the contradiction between Vittor and Carboni, about which day he shaved off his moustache. Coomber is certain about the mous-tache but vague about the day. Could it have been Wednesday? The Hilton telephone record shows that Carboni rang Chelsea Cloisters after his arrival from Amsterdam at 6.18 p.m. Calvi went at once to see him, and was thus unlikely to have been outside Coomber's door between 7p.m. and 7.30. But Coomber might be mistaken by an hour. Calvi would have been back by 10 p.m., when Coomber thought he saw him being taken away.

If it was Thursday, then Calvi would have gone off with some other people before Carboni arrived at Chelsea Cloisters. This might account for Vittor taking Carboni's arm and hustling him out, and for neither of them going up to see Calvi. But if Vittor knew that Calvi had been escorted away by two other people, he would surely have insisted that Carboni should come up with him to see whether Calvi had returned.

If, on the other hand, Vittor knew that Calvi had had an encounter the previous night, and that there were people in London who knew where to find them, that might account for his panic on Thursday night, and his decision to rush back to Austria.

*   *   *

Having found the new witness, Cecil Coomber, the Calvi family decided to hire the New York-based international firm of investigators, Kroll

Associates, to inquire again in detail into Calvi's last days and the circumstances of his death. At the time of going to press they were hard at work: Coomber's friend had been found and he was able to corroborate to some extent what Coomber remembered. Another resident of Chelsea Cloisters, Betty Fuchs, also provided some corroboration: she said that Coomber had come to her room after the first inquest and told her about the Italians who had come to his door. She said that he had told her that one of the men "looked ill, or he was frightened".

More dramatically, on 19 July 1991 a mafia supergrass in New York, Francesco Mannoia, said that he had been told that Calvi had been strangled by one Franco Di Carlo. He had been told this twice in Sicily by another mafioso, Ignazio Pullarà. The first time, in 1983 at the time of the second inquest, Pullarà said no more. The second time, in 1986 during the great mafia trial, Pullarà said he had been killed because he had seized "a large sum of money belonging to Licio Gelli and Pippo Calò". He added that before they had Calvi killed, Gelli and Calò had succeeded in getting the money – "tens of billions of lire" – back, but Calò had had him killed because he had shown himself untrustworthy.

There had, of course, been previous stories that Calvi had been killed by the mafia – and Tommaso Buscetta, the most famous mafia supergrass, has also alleged that mafia boss Calò had had Calvi killed – but the naming of Di Carlo gave the story a little more weight. For Di Carlo had been part of the Italian underworld in London, moving in the same circles as Vaccari and also with an interest in antiques and drugs. He is now serving a 25-year sentence for drug offences.

One of those who heard Mannoia's story was De Leo, the Rome prosecutor investigating the briefcase affair. He and Almerighi decided their investigations should be broadened into Calvi's death, working on the assumption that he was murdered. This was opposed by the public prosecutor in Milan, Pier Luigi Dell'Osso and the magistrate Matteo Mazziotti, who had always considered suicide most likely. The dispute went to the appeal court which ruled in January 1992 that the Rome team should be allowed to go ahead with their inquiries with the benefit of all the information collected in Milan.

If they or Kroll unearth anything, it may not be the answer to the question – who murdered Calvi? The lies, the contradictions, the evasions, the honest mistakes and the lapses of memory, which have dogged our steps throughout this book, may be obscuring the answer to quite a different question. Of all the scoundrels who battened on Calvi, which one pushed him over the edge into killing himself?

I have traced the life of a man promoted beyond his abilities, covering up his blunders with lies and frauds, paying blackmailers, grimacing as he speaks and packing his luggage with tranquilisers. This is not an exceptional story. What made Calvi extraordinary was that he operated on such an enormous scale, for so long. One man made this possible: Marcinkus. It was the defection of this confederate, the harsh deadline imposed by this former ally, that seems to have weighed most heavily on Calvi's mind.

Most of Calvi's other confederates have now been condemned by Italy's criminal courts: the 23-month Ambrosiano fraudulent bankruptcy trial ended in April 1992. Most attention focused on De Benedetti's 6 years and 4 months sentence. For his walk-on part, it was surely too harsh. The main beneficiaries of the fraud, Ortolani and Gelli, were given sentences even stiffer than those asked for by the public prosectuor: 19 years for Ortolani and 18 years and 6 months for Gelli. Their Rizzoli stooge, Tassan Din, got 14 years. The still-fugitive Marco Ceruti got 9 years and 8 months. The other main beneficiaries, Carboni and Pazienza, got 15 years and 14 years and 8 months respectively. Anna Bonomi was sentenced to 7 years and 6 months.

All the main Ambrosiano executives – Rosone, Leoni, Botta, Costa, Alessandro Mennini – also received stiff sentences, as did the directors, like Bagnasco, who got 7 years and 6 months.

Ortolani and Gelli face further sentences: in the summer of 1992 a trial over the Rizzoli affair began in which they, along with Tassan Din, Angelo Rizzoli and forty others, are defendants. But Ortolani and Gelli will never go to prison. They, like the others condemned in the Ambrosiano trial, remain at liberty until the appeal process begins. It cannot start until the detailed judgement is handed down later in the year, and by the time it is over they will be much too old to be incarcerated.

Most prominent of Calvi's associates to have escaped judicial condemnation are Marcinkus and his colleagues at the IOR, Mennini and de Strobel.

In February 1987 investigating magistrates Pizzi and Brichetti dramatically obtained arrest warrants for the three top IOR executives. The Vatican had claimed all along that they were immune from prosecution because the Concordat stated that the "central entities of the Catholic Church are exempt from all interference on the part of the Italian State". On 13 April 1987 a special court, the Tribunale della Liberta, denied this and ruled that the warrants were valid and Italy formally asked for their extradition. The Vatican refused and the IOR's lawyers took the case to Italy's Supreme Court of Appeal, which, on 17 July 1987, upheld the Vatican. Pizzi and

Brichetti tried to get this overruled by Italy's Constitutional Court but failed in June 1988 when it sidestepped the issue.

So Marcinkus was safe; and he did not even try to defend his actions in the case brought against him and the IOR in Nassau by Coopers and Lybrand after they were sued by the liquidators of the Cisalpine. He and the IOR were barred from defending the case on the facts when they failed to produce relevant documents. That trial ended in March 1992 but the judgement was still awaited in June: if the judge were to find Coopers and Lybrand negligent, then he could well order the IOR to recompense them for any damages awarded. To this day, however, the Vatican continues to assert that Marcinkus did nothing wrong.

LONDON 1983 - 23 JUNE 1992

APPENDIX A: The Letters of Patronage

ISTITUTO
PER LE
OPERE DI RELIGIONE

CITTA DEL VATICANO September 1, 1981

RIF. N.° 772662
VS. N.° 1120

CITARSI NELLA RISPOSTA

BANCO AMBROSIANO ANDINO S.A.
L I M A - Perù

Gentlemen:

This is to confirm that we directly or indirectly control the following entries:

- Manic S.A., Luxembourg
- Astolfine S.A., Panama
- Nordeurop Establishment, Liechtenstein
- U.T.C. United Trading Corporation, Panama
- Erin S.A., Panama
- Bellatrix S.A., Panama
- Belrosa S.A., Panama
- Starfield S.A., Panama

We also confirm our awareness of their indebtedness towards yourselves as of June 10, 1981 as per attached statement of accounts.

Yours faithfully,

ISTITUTO PER LE OPERE DI RELIGIONE

487

ISTITUTO
PER LE
OPERE DI RELIGIONE

CITTA DEL VATICANO September 1, 1981

Prot. N° 772663
Pos.: N.° 1120
SI CITANSI NELLA RISPOSTA

AMBROSIANO GROUP BANCO COMERCIAL S.A.
MANAGUA, Nicaragua
_____

Gentlemen:

     This is to confirm that we directly or indirectly control the following entries:
- Worldwide Trading Co., Panama
- Laramie Inc., Panama.

     We also confirm our awareness of their indebtedness towards yourselves as of June 10, 1981 per per attached statement of accounts.

     Yours faithfully,

ISTITUTO PER LE OPERE DI RELIGIONE

Below is a list in chronological order of the secret letters written by Calvi to the IOR. Those described by the joint commission as "parallel" letters are marked *. Those reproduced on the following pages are marked † and referred to in the text as (B(i)) etc.

†1. 30 November 1972 letter asking the IOR to pay $43.5 million to account "zeta" at the Gottardo. (B(i))

2. 27 January 1973 letter asking the IOR to take up 85 million Swiss francs of debentures issued by BA Holding.

† 3. 29 May 1973 letter confirming repayment of original $43.5 million loan plus interest and una tantum commission. (B(ii))

† 4. 29 May 1973 letter in which Calvi undertook, on behalf of the Cisalpine, to repurchase from the IOR 1,500,000 shares of Zitropo for $25.35 million. (B(ii))

†5. 10 October 1973 letter in which the terms for the IOR's initial financing of Manic are set out. (B(iii))

6. 29 May 1974 letter in which the IOR Zitropo loan is effectively renewed for a year at the reduced amount of $20 million.

*7. 28 October 1974 letter renewing the $45 million Manic loan for three years.

8. 13 May 1975 letter renewing the $20 million Zitropo loan for six months.

*9. 13 May 1975 letter in which the Cisalpine assumed full responsibility for Manic.

†*10. 24 November 1976 letter setting out the terms of the "conto deposito" arrangement between the Cisalpine and the IOR. (B(iv))

*11. 24 November 1976 letter setting out the terms of the arrangement under which the IOR passed deposits from the Gottardo on to the Cisalpine.

*12. 13 July 1977 letter from Cisalpine to the IOR saying it would provide 71,645,000 Swiss francs for the IOR to subscribe for shares in BA Holding.

†*13. 26 July 1977 letter from Banco Ambrosiano asking the IOR to acquire and hold the shares of United Trading. (B(v))

*14. 26 July 1977 letter from Banco Ambrosiano indemnifying the IOR for all actions and decisions taken in respect of Intermac (or Intermax).

*15. 4 October 1977 letter renewing the $45 million Manic loan for a further six months.

*16. 6 February 1978 letter concerning the IOR's subscription for further shares in BA Holding for 22,719,000 Swiss francs on behalf of the Cisalpine.

*17. 28 April 1978 letter renewing the Manic loan to 30 October 1978.

*18. 10 October 1978 letter renewing the Manic loan to 30 April 1979.

19. 10 October 1978 letter renewing the IOR $20 million loan secured on 1,500,000 Zitropo shares to 5 April 1979.

†*20. 24 October 1978 letter extending the IOR back-to-back operations to the Banco Comercial. (B(vi))

*21. 6 November 1978 letter confirming that the terms of the 24 October letter also applied to the loans to finance the shares of BA Holding.

*22. 9 November 1978 letter from Banco Ambrosiano setting out the lira back-to-back agreement with the IOR.

†*23. 17 December 1979 note extending the conto deposito operation to the Andino. The date comes from the Marcinkus memorandum. (B(vi))

†*24. 26 August 1981 "letter of indemnity" requesting the IOR to issue the letters of patronage. (B(vii))

*25. 8 October 1981 letter to the IOR requesting it to write to Ambrosiano Services authorising it to manage the companies covered by the letters of patronage.

*26. 15 October 1981 letter to the IOR asking it to comply with various requests from Ambrosiano Services, including that it sign further letters to Andino and Banco Comercial.

APPENDIX: B(i)

Questa Cisalpine Overseas Bank Limited prega codesto
Istituto per le Opere di Religione voler disporre quanto segue per la rela
tiva attuazione - per conto - quale anticipazione in Dollari U.S.:

- bonificare US$ 4,3,5(?. ?? - (*illeggibile manoscritto*)
- a Cisalpine Overseas Bank Limited
  c/ riferimento zeta
- presso la Banca del Gottardo, Lugano
- valuta: 4 Dicembre 1972.

La Kredietbank S.A. Luxembourgeoise, Luxembourg mette
rà a disposizioni certificati azionari Zitropo Holding S.A. No. 20.000 (venti-
mila) (19.989+11) che saranno ritenuti a credito di un deposito collaterale l'ope
razione di anticipazione in oggetto di questa Cisalpine Overseas Bank Limited.

L'operazione in questione sarà addebitata in conto anticipazio
ne intestato "Cisalpine c/fiduciario zeta".

L'operazione sarà regolata al tasso d'interesse debitore del-
l'8-1/4% annuo ed avrà la durata prevista di sei mesi con scadenza al 4 Giugno
1973, salvo rinnovo per un ulteriore periodo di sei mesi, previa intesa.

Questa Cisalpine Overseas Bank Limited, alla scadenza prevista
del 4 Giugno 1973, oltre a regolare gli interessi per il periodo decorso, verserà
inoltre un importo di Lit. 200.000.000 (duecentomilioni) quale commissione una
tantum ed attinente il periodo di attuazione indicato con scadenza 4 Giugno 1973.

I valori suindicati messi a disposizione dalla Kredietbank S.A.
Luxembourgeoise, Luxembourg, dopo l'estinzione dell'operazione di anticipazione
in oggetto in linea di capitali, interessi e commissioni, saranno messi a disposizione di questa Cisalpine Overseas Bank Limited.

li 30 novembre 1972 The Chairman

[firma manoscritta]

TELEPHONE: 2-5001-2-3/4

CISALPINE OVERSEAS BANK LIMITED
NASSAU   EAST BAY STREET, P. O. BOX 6347

lì 29 maggio 1973

Spett.
ISTITUTO PER LE OPERE DI RELIGIONE
        V A T I C A N O

    Con la presente Vi confermiamo che restiamo
impegnati irrevocalbilmente ad acquistare da V.SS. al
4 giugno 1974 num.1.500.000 (unmilionecinquecentomila)
azioni ZITROPO HOLDING S.A. al prezzo di US$ 16,90 ca=
dauna.

    Sull'importo corrispondente al prezzo indicato
di US$ 16,90 per azione ed ammontante a US$ 25.350.000,=
(venticinquemilionitrecentocinquantamila) Dollari U.S.)
verrà corrisposto a codesto Istituto l'interesse del=
l'8-1/2 % (otto e mezzo per cento) in ragione d'anno
sull'intera somma con valuta 4 giugno 1973.

    Codesto Istituto per le Opere di Religione
sottoscrive la presente a conferma del suo impegno ir=
revocabile a cedere a questa Cisalpine Overseas Bank
Limited le num.1.500.000 azioni ZITROPO HOLDING S.A.
al 4 giugno 1974 come sopra precisato.

    Con osservanza,

TELEX: NS 193   TELEGRAPH: CISOBANK   ANSWERBACK (TELEX): CISOBANK

TELEPHONE: 2-8001-23/4

CISALPINE OVERSEAS BANK LIMITED
NASSAU EAST BAY STREET, P.O. BOX 6347

lì 29 Maggio 1973

Spett.

ISTITUTO PER LE OPERE DI RELIGIONE

V A T I C A N O

Con riferimento al nostro impegno del 30 Novembre
1972 Vi bonifichiamo:

US$ 43.500.000,= valuta 4 Giugno 1973 per rimborso capitale,

US$ 1.814.312,50 valuta 4 Giugno 1973 per interessi liquidati, e.

Lit. 200.000.000 (duecentomilioni) dovuteVi per commissione una tantum

In relazione, le N.3.099.990 azioni ZITROPO HOLDING
S.A. restano a disposizione.

TELEX: NS 193   TELEGRAPH: CISOBANK   ANSWERBACK (TELEX): CISOBANK

APPENDIX: B(iii)

CISALPINE OVERSEAS BANK LIMITED

lì 10 Ottobre 1973

Questa Cisalpine Overseas Bank Limited prega codesto Istituto per le Opere di Religione voler disporre quanto segue per la relativa attuazione - per conto - quale anticipazione - c/ riporto in Dollari U. S.:
- bonificare US$ 45.000.000, = (quarantacinquemilioni Dollari U. S.)
a Cisalpine Overseas Bank Limited
in favore Manic S. A. Holding, 37 rue Notre-Dame, Luxembourg
presso la Banca del Gottardo, Lugano
valuta iniziale: 30 Ottobre 1973.

L'importo totale potrà essere rimesso alla Cisalpine Overseas Bank anche in più tranches.

Ai singoli importi relativi verrà applicata la valuta in relazione alla rispettiva data di ricezione.

La Kredietbank S. A. Luxembourgeoise, Luxembourg metterà a disposizione certificati azionari Manic S. A. Holding per il totale del capitale azionario ed obbligazioni della stessa per importo nominale complessivo di US$ 45.000.000, = (quarantacinquemilioni Dollari U. S.) che saranno ritenuti in relazione alla presente operazione di c/ riporto.

L'operazione sarà regolata al tasso d'interesse debitore del 10% (dieci per cento) annuo ed avrà la durata prevista di un anno con scadenza al 30 Ottobre 1974 salvo rinnovo, per un ulteriore periodo di sei mesi, previa intesa.

Questa Cisalpine Overseas Bank Limited, alla scadenza prevista del 30 Ottobre 1974, oltre a regolare gli interessi per il periodo decorso e rimborsare il capitale (US$ 45.000.000, =) se l'operazione non verrà prorogata, verserà un importo di Lit. 200.000.000 (duecentomilioni Lire ital. quale commissione una tantum ed attinente il periodo di attuazione indicato con scadenza 30 Ottobre 1974.

I valori suindicati (azioni ed obbligazioni Manic S. A. Holding) messi a disposizione della Kredietbank S. A. Luxembourgeoise, Luxembourg, dopo l'estinzione dell'operazione di c/ riporto in oggetto in linea di capital interessi e commissioni, dovranno restare a disposizione di questa Cisalpne Overseas Bank Limited.

The Chairman
Roberto Calvi

On.
stituto per le Opere di Religione
Città del Vaticano

494

M

TELEPHONE: 2-8601 - 2/3/4

CISALPINE OVERSEAS BANK LIMITED
NASSAU   EAST BAY STREET, P. O. BOX 6347

24.11.976

Spett.le
Istituto per le Opere di Religione
CITTA' del VATICANO
_____

   Con la presente confermiamo che eventuali bonifici ef=
fettuati da questa Cisalpine Overseas Bank Limited ,Nassau ,
in"conto deposito" presso codesto Istituto vanno accreditati
in favore di questa Banca.
   Questa Banca conferma a codesto Istituto le istruzioni
di voler eseguire in relazione a ciascun importo pervenuto in
"conto deposito" un bonifico bancario di rispettivo pari import
e valuta in favore di UNITED TRADING CORPORATIONS.A.,Panama
presso la Banca del Gottardo ,Lugano.
   Approva quanto fino ad oggi eseguito al riguardo.
   Sul conto creditore a nome di questa Banca verrà appli=
cato il tasso pertinente indicato,mentre sul conto debitore
a nome UnitedTrading Corporation S.A.,Panama ,verrà applica=
to il tasso debitore rispettivo di pari aliquota maggiorata
del 0,0625 %.
   Con riferimento a quanto sopra Vi autorizziamo irrevocabilmente con un preavviso di 15 giorni ad estinguere le citate operazioni addebitando il conto creditore diquesta Ban=
ca presso di Voi Signori a pareggio. del conto debitore del=
la United Trading Corporation S.A. ,Panama con impegno di regolamento da parte nostra nel termine indicato delle differenze emergentied attinenti in particolare il conteggio degli
interessi come stabilito.
   Distinti saluti
                    CISALPINE OVERSEAS BANK LIMITED
                         Il Chairman

TELEX: NS 193   TELEGRAPH: CISOBANK   ANSWERBACK (TELEX): CISOBANK

APPENDIX: B(v)

Banco Ambrosiano
VI-FONZATA NEL 1996 · SEDE SOCIALE IN MILANO · ISCRITTA AL TRIBUNALE DI MILANO N. 3173 · CAPITALE L. 33.000.000.000 · RISERVE L. 78.013.000.000
DIREZIONE CENTRALE

All'ISTITUTO PER LE OPERE DI RELIGIONE
CITTA' del VATICANO

     Questo Banco Ambrosiano S.p.a. prega codesto Istituto per le
Opere di Religione,Città del Vaticano, di voler acquisire ,in nome
e per conto di questo Banco e mantenere in possesso fiduciario l'inte=
ro capitale sociale della UNITED TRADING CORPORATION -Panama- costitui=
to da numero 500 (cinquecento) azioni al portatore senza valore nomi=
ale.

     Resta convenuto che il possesso di tali azioni(e quindi
dell'intero capitale sociale della United Trading Corporation)sarà ri=
tenuto da codesto Istituto unicamente a titolo fiduciario per conto di
questo Banco Ambrosiano,che resta e resterà interamente responsabile di
ogni conseguenza o pertinenza ,che ,in qualsiasi modo,possa collegarsi,
giuridicamente o anche solo di fatto,alla circostanza di essere codesto
Istituto,nei riguardi di qualsiasi terzo,possessore delle suddette cin=
quecento azioni(intero capitale della United Trading Corporation),non=
ché collegantesi a tutte le partecipazioni,comunque possedute o con=
trollate dalla United Trading Corporation-Panama.

     Questo Banco ,che si impegna a curare e seguire la gestione
la suddetta United Trading Corporation e controllate ,provvedendo
che sia svolta in maniera del tutto regolare,si obbliga formalmente
con la presente a sollevare codesto Istituto da ogni responsabilità
per tutto quanto come sopra convenuto e a tenerlo indenne da ogni onere
di qualsiasi natura ,che eventualmente venisse a gravare lo stesso
Istituto in conseguenza o in relazione al possesso fiduciario,ora ri=
esto,impegnandosi a rimborsare ,a semplice richiesta del medesimo
stituto,ogni somma che al riguardo,a suo insindacabile giudizio,
vesse sborsato.

     L'Istituto per le Opere di Religione ha in qualsiasi momento
scolta di ritornare ,nella forma che riterrà,a questo Banco il pos=
sesso del capitale sociale della United Trading Corporation e rinun=
are al mandato fiduciario conferitogli.

     Anche questo Banco Ambrosiano potrà richiedere all'Istituto
er le Opere di Religione di ritornare in possesso delle azioni della
United Trading Corporation -Panama- in qualsiasi momento, a condizione
che l'Istituto per le Opere di Religione sia stato completamente sod=
disfatto di ogni sua eventuale spettanza e garantito di essere
ibero da ogni responsanilità al riguardo .

     Distinti saluti

                    BANCO AMBROSIANO S/p.a.

26 luglio 1977

CISALPINE OVERSEAS BANK LIMITED
P. O. BOX 6347
NASSAU, BAHAMAS

24 ottobre 1978

Spett.le

ISTITUTO PER LE OPERE DI RELIGIONE

CITTA' del VATICANO

       Questa CISALPINE OVERSEAS BANK LTD,in nome e per con=
to dell'AMBROSIANO GROUP BANCO COMERCIAL S.A.-Managua-,dal qua=
le Banco é stata conferita a questa Cisalpine Overseas Bank Ltd
procura generale ("poder generalisimo") in data 7 novembre 1977
per atti del Dott.Italo Tarsia ,notaio in Milano,rep.n°182276
n°2721 di raccolta,con la presente conferma che eventuali boni=
fici effettuati dall'Ambrosiano Group Banco Comercial S.A. in
"conto deposito" presso codesto Istituto vanno accreditati in
favore di detto Banco.

       Questa Banca ,sempre in nome e per conto dell'Ambro=
siano Group Banco Comercial S.A.,conferma a codesto Istituto
le istruzioni di voler eseguire ,in relazione a ciascun importo
pervenuto in "conto deposito" ,un bonifico bancario di rispet=
tivo pari importo e valuta a favore di UNITED TRADING CORPORA=
TION S.A.-Panama- presso la Banca del Gottardo Lugano.

       Sul conto creditore a nome dell'Ambrosiano Group Ban=
co Comercial S.A. verrà applicato il tasso pertinente indica=
to,mentre sul conto debitore della United Trading Corporation
S.A. verrà applicato il tasso debitore rispettivo di pari ali=
quota maggiorata del 0,0625 %.

       Con riferimento a quanto sopra questa Banca ,in nome
e per conto dell'Ambrosiano Group Banco Comercial S.A.autorizza
irrevocabilmente codesto Istituto ad estinguere ,con un preavvi=
so di 15 giorni,le citate operazioni addebitando il conto cre=
ditore dell'Ambrosiano Banco Comercial S.A. presso di Voi
Signori a pareggio del conto debitore della UNITED TRADING COR=
PORATION S.A. ,con impegno di regolamento da parte dell'Ambro=
siano Group Banco Comercial S.A. nel termine indicato anche
delle differenze emergenti ed attinenti in particolare il con=
teggio degli interessi come stabilito.

       Distinti saluti

                 per AMBROSIANO GROUP BANCO COMERCIAL S.A.
                 CISALPINE OVERSEAS BANK LIMITED
                    il Chairman

Si conferma che le obbligazioni assunte con la presente lettera sono
valide anche in nome e per conto del BANCO AMBROSIANO ANDINO S.A. Lima
e per tutte le operazioni che riguardano detto Banco.

           BANCO AMBROSIANO S.p.a.

BANCO AMBROSIANO OVERSEAS LIMITED

IBM House P.O.Box 6347 Nassau, Bahamas

26 Agosto 1981

Questo Banco Ambrosiano Overseas Limited si pregia
richiedere a titolo fiduciario a codesto Istituto per le Opere
di Religione di volere, nell'interesse di terzi e per conto di
questo Banco, indirizzare le seguenti lettere rispettivamente
al Banco Ambrosiano Andino S.A., Lima, Perù, e all'Ambrosiano
Group Banco Comercial S.A., Managua, Nicaragua:

```
" to
" Banco Ambrosiano Andino S.A.
" Lima, Perù
"
" Gentlemen:
" This is to confirm that we directly or indirectly
" control the following entries:
" - Manic S.A., Luxembourg
" - Astolfine S.A., Panama -
" - Nordeurop Establishment, Liechtenstein -
" - U.T.C. United Trading Corporation, Panama
" - Erin S.A., Panama
" - Bellatrix S.A., Panama
" - Belrosa S.A., Panama
" - Starfield Inc., Panama .
" We also confirm our awareness of their indebtedness
" towards yourselves as of June 10, 1981 as per atta-
" ched statement of accounts.
"                           Yours faithfully,
"              ISTITUTO PER LE OPERE DI RELIGIONE
" encl.

" to
" Ambrosiano Group Banco Comercial S.A.
" Managua, Nicaragua
"
" Gentlemen:
" This is to confirm that we directly or indirectly
" control the following entries:
" Worldwide Trading Co., Panama
" Laramie Inc., Panama .
" We also confirm our awareness of their indebtedness
" towards yourselves as of June 10, 1981 as per atta-
" ched statements of accounts.
"                           Yours faithfully,
"              ISTITUTO PER LE OPERE DI RELIGIONE
" encl.
```

Questo Banco Ambrosiano Overseas Limited solleva codesto Istituto per le Opere di Religione da ogni responsabilità,
danno o molestia che potessero derivare in dipendenza delle di
chiarazioni esposte nelle citate lettere, il cui contenuto riguarda sostanzialmente operazioni, società ed enti vari di effet
tiva ed esclusiva pertinenza di questo Banco Ambrosiano Overseas
Limited che pro forma vennero collegate a codesto Istituto per
le Opere di Religione.

On.
ISTITUTO PER LE OPERE DI RELIGIONE
      CITTA' del VATICANO

Resta inteso che, con la presente, questo Banco Ambro
siano Overseas Limited si impegna comunque a tenere del tutto in
denne l'Istituto per le Opere di Religione in qualsiasi sede, an
che giudiziaria, da ogni conseguenza dannosa dovesse al riguardo
insorgere con l'obbligo di rimborsare, a semplice richiesta del
medesimo Istituto, ogni somma che a suo insindacabile giudizio
avesse sborsato.

Questo Banco Ambrosiano Overseas Limited si rende ga
rante che le lettere in parola saranno utilizzate dalle Banche
cui sono dirette unicamente all'interno dell'organizzazione ban
caria con esclusione di ogni esterna manifestazione.

Questo Banco si impegna ed assicura che al riguardo
nessuna operazione o variazione, se non di riduzione od estinzio
ne, verrà effettuata dopo il 10 Giugno 1981, data di riferimento
delle lettere e delle situazioni fornite.

Questo Banco Ambrosiano Overseas Limited si obbliga
inoltre a provvedere entro il 30 Giugno 1982 a che le società
ed enti contemplati nelle suddette lettere e le operazioni re
lative vengano eliminate anche formalmente dal collegamento con
codesto Istituto e rimangano nella forma e nella sostanza, come
lo erano e lo sono, ritenute da questo Banco Ambrosiano Overseas
Limited.

Tale impegno riguarda anche la Società Suprafin S.p.A.,
Milano, la Imparfin A.G., Vaduz, la Teclefin Etablissement S.A.,
Eschen, la Società Zitropo Holding S.A. e la Intermac Et.Financier,
Mauren, che ha modificato la ragione sociale in Timaring Finanz
und Beteilung Anst'esse formalmente figu-
ranti al nome di Istituto per le Opere di Religione, di cui agli
uniti elenchi e sostanzialmente concernenti il Banco Ambrosiano
S.p.A., il Banco Ambrosiano Overseas Limited, il Banco Ambrosia
no Andino S.A. e la Banca del Gottardo (Lugano e Nassau).

Questo Banco Ambrosiano Overseas Limited conferma an
che a suo carico con la presente tutti gli impegni assunti dalle
predette Banche rispettivamente con le seguenti lettere:
a) dal Banco Ambrosiano S.p.A. in data 26 Luglio 1977 (due lettere) e in data 9 Novembre 1978;
b) dal Banco Ambrosiano Overseas Limited (già Cisalpine Overseas
Bank Limited) in data 24 Novembre 1976, 6 Novembre 1978 e 17
Dicembre 1979 anche per Banco Ambrosiano Andino S.A.
c) dalla Banca del Gottardo in data 24 Novembre 1976.

Distinti saluti.

BANCO AMBROSIANO OVERSEAS LIMITED
Il Presidente,

499

APPENDIX C: The Contract for the Sale of the Banca Cattolica

COMPENDIUM
Société Anonyme Holding
27 luglio 1971
14, rue Aldringer - Luxembourg

All' ISTITUTO PER LE OPERER DI RELIGIONE
CITTA' DEL VATICANO

Con la presente ci pregiamo comunicarVi la nostra offerta a
fermo per l'acquisto fino al 50 % delle azioni costituenti
l'intero capitale sociale della BANCA CATTOLICA DEL VENETO,
Vicenza al prezzo di Lit. 1.600.- (milleseicento) per ciascuna
azione con godimento, da attuarsi con le seguenti modalità:
1° - per il 45% delle azioni costituenti il predetto capitale
sociale e cioé nr. 16.254.000. azioni, con applicazione contestuale
alla accettazione da parte Vostra di questa nostra offerta a fermo
e contro pagamento da parte nostra di $ 42.000.000.- (dollari USA
quarantaduemilioni) da versarsi come segue/:
- $ 12.000.000.- il 5/8/1971
- $ 10.000.000.- il 24/9/1971
- $ 10.000.000.- il 8/10/1971
- $ 10.000.000.- il 22/10/1971
2° - per le restanti azioni e cioè fino all'ulteriore 5% del
capitale, e cioè fino a nr.1.806.000.- azioni, con applicazione
alla data della "dichiarazione di intenti" concernente la suddetta
Banca Cattolica del Veneto, da determinarsi entro il 31 ottobre
1971, e contro pagamento di $ 4.500.000.- (dollari USA quattromilioni
cinquecentomila) il 29/10/ 1971 .
Inoltre Vi comunichiamo che assumiamo formale impegno di mantenere
inalterato sotto il profilo delle alte finalità sociali, morali
e religiose cattoliche lo svolgimento della attività della Banca
Cattolica del Veneto in conformità ancora all'art. IV della Banca
medesima. e dell' art. 3 dello Statuto del Banco Ambrosiano, Uplauo.
Vi preghiamo, nel caso di vostra accettazione, di voler tenere a
nostra disposizione le azioni suddette (secondo le modalità di
attuazione sopra indicate) mediante accredito delle stesse a dossier
seguito di lett. a Istituto Opere di Religione, città del
Vaticano all'oggetto : Banca Cattolica del Veneto.

COMPENDIUM S.A.
per mandato speciale

APPENDIX D: The IOR's letter "of pertinence" about Suprafin of 20 January 1975

All. n. 17

ISTITUTO
PER LE
OPERE DI RELIGIONE

CITTÀ DEL VATICANO   20 gennaio 1975

Prot. N.° 634792
Posiz. N.° 1120
DA CITARSI NELLA RISPOSTA

                    Spett.le BANCO AMBROSIANO S.p.a.
                    M I L A N O

        Con la presente ci riferiamo al dossier
titoli esistente al 31 dicembre 1974 concernente la Società
SUPRAFIN s.p.a. -Milano- di pertinenze di questo Istituto
e Vi preghiamo di voler procedere nella forma più opportuna
alla gestione e amministrazione del dossier in oggetto
provvedendo alle convenienti operazioni di investimento é
di disinvestimento.
        Vi preghiamo di volerci ragguagliare pe-
riodicamente della situazione del dossier sopramenzionato
e delle pertinenti operazioni.
        Distinti saluti

                                ISTITUTO PER LE OPERE DI RELIGIONE
                                      Città del Vaticano

COOPERS & LYBRAND

CHARTERED ACCOUNTANTS

NASSAU, FREEPORT

TELEPHONE AREA CODE (809)(32) 5106
TELEGRAMS COLYBRAND
TELEX NB 200

POST OFFICE BOX NSBG.
2ND FLOOR,
CHARLOTTE HOUSE.
CHARLOTTE STREET.
NASSAU. BAHAMAS

IN PRINCIPAL AREAS
OF THE WORLD

6th December 1978

Mr. Pierre Siegenthaler
Cisalpine Overseas Bank Limited
IBM House
P. O. Box ES 6347
Nassau, Bahamas

Dear Pierre,

ISTITUTO PER LE OPERE DI RELIGIONE (ICR)

I am writing to confirm our discussions last week with regard to a possible note setting out your bank's relationship with the above named customer. You are aware that we consider that it would be good accounting practice for a note along the lines previously forwarded to you to be included in the financial statements. You have advised us that the Directors do not wish such a note to appear in the financial statements.

I am accordingly writing to advise you that in these circumstances, provided we can satisfy ourselves on the recoverability of the debt due by your customer to the bank, we will not insist on disclosure. This position applies not only to this year but also to subsequent years provided:-

(a)   The situation between the customer and your bank does not alter materially, and

(b)   Future accounting standards do not require us to make such a disclosure.

There remains the problem of our being able to satisfy ourselves as to the recoverability of the debt due by your customer to the bank. As we have discussed with you previously, whilst all indications are that your customer is good for its commitments, we have been unable to see such underlying financial information as would normally be available to us to satisfy ourselves on a debt of this magnitude. In the circumstances, I would appreciate it if a meeting could be set up for me with Dr. Marcinkus next time I am in Rome or, alternatively, if there is to be a Cisalpine Board meeting in Nassau during 1979, at that time.

/Continued.

502

Mr. Pierre Siegenthaler
6th December 1978
Page 2

As you know, I am likely to be in Rome sometime prior to the end of June
next year on other business and can advise you of the specific dates in
advance.

Yours sincerely,

Graham C. Garner.

GCG/ash
GE 1430

Su Eccellenza e stata
preavvisata e sarebbe d'accordo
di ricevere il sig. Garner

L'entità in possesso del presente documento stilato in un
esemplare è da considerarsi investito dell'incarico di attua-
re le ipotesi di cui ai documenti allegati stilati su fogli nu-
merati a mano dall' 1 all'8 che fanno parte integrante dell'accordo e che sono tutti muniti di firme e sigle.
La controparte venditrice riceverà indicazioni circa i tempi
ed i modi per le esecuzioni suddette anche per definire ogni
particolare tecnico.
Tenuto conto delle alte finalità del progetto la controparte
venditrice accetta formalmente che eventuali varianti siano
proponibili e pertanto sin da ora accettate nelle more della
formale impostazione del programma, pur mantenendo il riferimento ai documenti allegati; quanto sopra anche in funzione
di esigenze di adattamento al rispetto sia di leggi esistenti
che di quelle nuove in fase di elaborazione.
La scadenza è quella indicata nel documento n. 8 e cioè 31
dicembre 1980.

Roma, addì 18 Settembre 1980

(ii) Page of the contract showing the commission
to be paid

Il mandato e gli accordi sottostanti firmati in data odier
na si intendono perfezionati con le seguenti modalità :

. l'acquirente di n° 1.200.000 azioni vecchie cedute dalla
parte venditrice provvederà a sottoscrivere l'aumento di
capitale pari a 2 (due) azioni nuove ogni 1 (una) vec-
chia per 2.400.000 azioni a Lit. 25.500 per azione ed a
versare a titolo di premio Lit. 50.000 per ogni azione
posseduta dopo aumento di capitale. Al momento della gi-
rata delle azioni vecchie l'acquirente verserà sulle 50.000
Lire per azione sopra indicate un acconto di Lit. 10.000
per ogni azione del nuovo capitale nelle modalità indicate
dall'Ente incaricato del mandato.

. La Società indicata dall'Istituzione e intestataria delle
azioni ex Rot si impegna a cederle all'acquirente alle
stesse condizioni e modalità di cui al pacchetto al prece
dente paragrafo.

. Al momento della firma del presente accordo il controvalore
stabilito a titolo di acconto per il completamento degli
stessi entro il 31 dicembre 1980 sarà di Lit. 16 miliardi
comprensivo dei diritti della parte venditrice per quanto
attiene le azioni ex Rot cedute franco valuta.

INDEX

INDEX

and Bonomi, Anna, 75, 76, 80, 91, 95, 109, 179, 405; her claims of half share of Credito Varesino profits, 95–6, 180, 211, 270, 395; friendly with, 89; paid $7.9m to, 269–70; paid $2m to, 395; relations with deteriorate, 180; second peace treaty with, 270; signs cooperation agrrement with, 211; writes off loan to, 269–70

and briefcase, 295, 394, 400–1, 406, 410, 420, 477–9

and Carboni; offers $100m to, 389; payments to, 394, 404, 407; tape-recorded by, 70, 100, 378. *See also* Carboni

charged with fraud, 287, 405

and Coopers and Lybrand, 220–2, 226, 234, 237, 272, 274, 279

and deals that led to currency charges, 154, 179–80, 287, 334–36

and Ehrenkreuz, 93, 152, 261

and foreign banks, 17, 19, 25, 29, 48, 256–7, 282, 288, 319

and Garner, 222, 226, 231–2, 353, 385

and Gelli and Ortolani, 10, 177, 210–11, 241, 262–3, 264, 283, 284–5, 306, 311, 480; C on, 139, 146, 149, 428; and claim to have offered money to C, 371–2; demands on C, 200, 178, 257, 295; early dealings with C, 147–51; flight, C in touch with on?, 413, 422; C frightened of, 370; hold over C, 151–3, 333–4; paid total of $250m by C, 240, 320; payments to C by, 151, 178, 196–7, 247, 291, 352, 426, 480; in Rizzoli deals with, 155, 157–9, 203, 216, 243–6, 286–7, 289–92, 312, 354, 370

and gun, 329, 408–9

and inquests, first, 452–8; second, 459–70

and IOR relationship, inherited by C, 62

and last days, 5–6 June, 410; 7, 8 June, 411–22; 9 June, 413–14; 10 June, 414; 11 June, 415–19; 12 June (in Austria), 419–20; 13 June, 420–3; 14 June, 423–5; 15 June (to London), 427–9; 16 June, 430–7; 17 June, 437–45; 18 June, 445–50; 19 June, 450–1. *See also* Carboni; Vittor

and letter to Palazzini, 400–1

and letter to Pope, 406, 410–11, 478

and letters to Mons. Franco, 400–1, 406, 411

and Ley-Ravello, 93–4, 183, 402

and Marcinkus, 3, 49, 50, 64, 70, 74, 81–2, 89, 94, 113, 118, 137, 166, 184, 187–9, 204, 217, 225, 226, 227, 230, 267, 275, 277, 309, 310, 325, 341, 343–4, 345, 352, 355, 367, 373, 375, 385, 386, 399, 401; meeting of 8/81, 358–66; discussion of back-to-backs, 131; deadline on C, 4, 5, 7, 359, 361, 389, 397, 400, 401, 416, 484; M not told of P2 payments, 3, 311, 362; no letters from, 45; overall reviews of operation, 234, 248; promises solution, 338, 339; refuses to testify for, 337; and United Trading contract, 130, 198; and Vianini meeting, 377–8; will only deal with C, 350

and Mozzana, joint accounts with, 73, 93, 99, 108, 152

and origins of secret network, 124–6, 202–4, 213, 215,

and P2, 9, 140, 147, 351

and Padalino, 228, 233, 255

and passports, 287, 295, 298, 319–41, 328, 336, 341, 418, 420, 428

and Paul VI, 70

and Pazienza; afraid of, 389; hires, 322; on holiday in Sardinia with, 355–8, 413; payments to, 174–7, 324–5, 342, 365, 367–8, 384, 394–6, 426, 475–6

and Peruvians, 264–5, 271, 340–1, 352, 354, 362, 373, 385, 391

and phone calls (15–17/6/82), 414, 415, 417, 419, 421, 437–9, 440, 442, 444, 481

and Price Waterhouse, 76–7, 94, 218

and private papers, 3, 42, 45, 50, 95–7, 100, 118, 132, 138, 160; on Banca Cattolica, 76, 78–80, 500; on Bastogi, 66–7; on Credito Varesino, 80, 89–90; Garner letter, 232, 502–3; on IOR/BA Holding, 277–9; on lira back-to-backs, 16 –3, 165–6, 169–70, 176, 183–5, 189–91, 193–4, 209–12; on Rizzoli, 158, 291 (C's copy of the pattone); on Suprafin, 134; on United trading, new method of financing, 222–3; on Zitropo, 85–6, 105. *See also* Radowal, United Trading accounts

and Ralrov account, 68–9, 73, 152, 261

reduces IOR debt, 281–2

reorganises secret network, 124–6, 202–4, 213, 215

rescued by ENI and Banca Nazionale del Lavoro, 213, 228

and Rizzolis, 155, 157, 192, 203, 243–6, 286–94, 320–1, 326, 330–2, 368–70

and shooting of Rosone, 403–4, 416, 428

and Socialist Party, 62, 283, 306, 308, 309, 346, and share of Rizzoli premio, 290–1, 311, 312, 314–15, 327, 352

and Sindona, 17, 26, 62, 66, 69, 78, 80,, 121, 122; and Bastogi bid, 66–7, 71–2; blackmailed by, 93, 111, 140, 205–8, 210, 212, 257, 259, 295, 316, 333; commissions from, 68–9, 73–4, 93; drops Radowal because of, 124; effect of S's crash on C, 119, 122–3, 124, 138–9, 174; meeting with, 65; $6.5m commission, 87, 88–9, 92–3; pays for the defence of, 261; pays premimum for Pacchetti to, 110; and Radiocar, 147; sells Finabank shares, 117; Zitropo, buys from, 88; Zitropo, finance for, 84–5

and Somoza dinner, 199–200

and wealth and gain from fraud, 5, 99, 151–3, 178, 196–7, 247, 352, 372, 425–7, 480. *See also* Calvi, Ortolani & Gelli payments to C; Sindona commissions; share of Rizzoli premio and will, 259

See also Garzoni; IOR, total backing for C; profits on special deals with C; Mennini, Luigi

Canesi, Carlo, *C's boss*, 63, 64, 70
Canetti, Luciano, *C's brother*, 413, 414
Capaldo, Pellegrino, *on joint commission*, 47
Capitalfin, 201, 202, 213–16, 266, 269
Caprio, Cardinal Giuseppe, *Secretary of APSA after 1969*, 59, 93, 120, 279, 280
Caracciolo, Carlo, *owner, La Repubblica*, 402
Carboni, Andrea, *Flavio's brother*, 384
Carboni, Flavio, *property dealer*, and associates,

509

INDEX

356-7, 384-5, 402; and briefcase affair, 477-9; and C's letter to Pope, 410; and C's flight: (last days in Italy) 412-19, (in Klagenfurt) 420-1, (to Zurich) 423, (Bregenz meeting) 425; (diary) 425-6, (back to Zurich) 427, (to Amsterdam) 429, (Calvi tries to contact) 432, (to London) 433, (walk in Hyde Park) 434-6, (and Italian phone calls) 434-6, (at Chelsea Cloisters) 443-5, (rang from Sheraton Hotel) 446, (leaves Edinburgh) 450, (withdraws $150,000) 451, (see also Vittor); and Etruria fraud, 393-4; exchanges telephone numbers with C, 385; on C's need to find money to repay IOR, 413, 415, 421, 426, 435-6; and help with IOR, 389-90, 400, 406-7, 411; and inquests (first), 453, 458, (second), 459-60, 467; and insurance judgements, 479; meets C in Sardinia, 357, 366; and Morrises, 426, 434-5, 437-8, 440, 442, 444-5, 447-50, 458; and Paoli, 474; and Prato Verde fraud, 383-4; and Rosone, attack on, 404, 460; sentenced, 484

Carli, Guido, Governor, Bank of Italy, 1960-1975, 114, 119, 417

Carman, George, QC, 459, 460, 462-9, 478

Carrera, Jorge, director Andino, 345, 354

Casaroli, Cardinal Agostino, 8, 9, 11, 34, 36, 37, 42, 159, 251, 275, 279, 323, 325, 389

*Cascadilla, 202

Casino-Club, 238

Casino Ruhl, 239-43, 375, 472

Catintours, 168

Cattaneo, Mario, Italian appointee to joint commission, 47

Cavallo, Luigi, Sindona's henchman, 206, 212, 295, 401

Cefis, Eugenio, head of Montedison till 1978, 156, 157, 244

Celata, Mons. Luigi, 323

Central American Services, 271, 352

*Centralfin, 117

Ceramica Pozzi, 52, 58

Ceruti, Gianpaolo, brother of Marco, 300, 315

Ceruti, Marco, restaurant-owner, 320, 333, 484; and Di Nunzio, 325; disappears, 304; offers explanation, 304-6; payments from G & O, 298-301, 315

Cerutti, Carlo, one of the "three wise men", 9, 35

Chase Manhattan Bank, 124, 385

*Chatoser, 346, 358

Chelsea Cloisters, 427-9, 431, 433, 43, 436-9, 442-6, 448, 449, 478

Chiaraviglio, Luigi, lawyer, 390

Childe, Leslie, journalist, 274

Chiomenti, Pasquale, mediator, 30, 31-4, 36, 47

Christian Democratic Party, 30, 34, 150, 213, 253, 344

Ciampi, Carlo, Governor, Bank of Italy, 29, 298, 313, 344, 380, 436

Ciarrapico, Giuseppe, friend of Andreotti, 337

Cicchitti, Marcella, O's daughter-in-law, 149

*Cimafin, 72, 76-78, 80, 83, 88, 124

CIM - Grandi Magazzini, 161, 167-70, 172, 175, 177, 184, 189, 209, 211, 310; ceased operations, 187; financed by Ambrosiano for IOR's benefit,

229, 365; and G, 285, 296; staff occupy Palazzo, 186; and start of lira back-to-backs, 166; to leave the Palazzo, 173

CIR, 380

**Cisalpine Inc, 67, 220

**Cisalpine Overseas Bank (Nassau), 26, 39, 41, 44, 72, 74, 76-7, 80, 84, 88, 99, 117, 122, 135, 136, 147, 151, 176, 201-2, 204, 213, 214, 229, 244, 256, 257, 268, 283, 284, 286, 311, 315, 327, 330, 339, 340, 341, 342, 352, 374, 399, 410, 480; and Argentina, 200; and auditors, 35-6, 133, 218, 223, 230-2, 234-7, 272-3, 274-80, 282, 288, 339, 353, 362; board meetings, 66, 68, 71, 74, 81, 89, 94-5, 104, 113, 121, 177, 199-200, 218, 220-1, 231, 242-3, 279-80, 284, 297, 316 (without M), 341, 375-6 (without C); financed by Ambrosiano banks, 68, 74, 138-9, 149, 153, 179, 197, 232-3, 265, 309, 313, 331, 395, 396-7; formed, 66; and G, 371; loans to BA Holding, 22, 282, 309, 396-7; loans to Somoza, 200, 216; and parallel and secret letters, 43, 96, 105, 108, 129, 136, 197-8, 334, 358-62, 372-3; position at crash, 19-22; profits rigged, 99, 157; and Ruhl, 238, 240-2; and $14m removed from, 394-6. See also back-to-back operations; IOR shares in and deposits at; M as a director of; Mincomes; Rizzoli Editore; Rizzoli International

Citibank, 58, 93

Clarke, Robert, solicitor, 427

Cocean, 322

Coffey, Joseph, NY policeman, 102, 103-4

Colias, 66, 71, 72

Coll, Nestor, Venezuelan ambassador, 357, 402

Colombo, Emilio, Treasury Minister, 1974, 116

Colombo, Gherardo, magistrate, 317, 405

Commission on sistemazione Rizzoli (premio), 286-7, 288-9, 290-2, 294, 295, 308, 312, 314-15, 318, 319, 327, 331, 333, 352, 370, 372

Commonwealth United, 59

*Commotion, 250

Communist Party, 142, 143, 319

Compagnia Fiduciaria Nazionale, 192

Compendium, see Banco Ambrosiano Holding

Concas, Laura, Carboni's Italian mistress, 394, 426, 434-436, 450, 458, 459

Concordat, 30, 34-7, 51, 58, 484

Condotte d'Acqua, 58, 323

Connolly, Michael, joint chairman, creditor banks' committee, 25

Consob, stock market regulatory board, 381, 389, 392, 393

Continental Illinois, 58

Coomber, Cecil, witness, 481-3

Coopers and Lybrand, 8, 218, 226, 227, 249, 272, 288, 313, 353, 362, 375; sued by liquidators, 35-6, 231, 485. See also IOR

Cornwell, John, author Thief in the Night, 15, 36, 41, 94

Corona, Armando, Freemason, 384, 402

Corriere degli Italiani, 145

Corriere della Sera, 156, 175, 192, 194, 244, 253, 328, 329, 336, 351, 384, 480

INDEX

Eisenberger, Irving, *speculator*, 101
Ekblom, Ralph, *hydrographic surveyor*, 460
Electronic General, 147, 248
Elia 7 account, 289, 291, 292, 293, 352
EMI, 145, 147
Emigrant Savings Bank of New York, 9
ENI, 33, 141, 156, 275, 311, 313, 414, 476; and
  Capitalfin, 201, 214, 216; largest creditor of
  BA holding, 26; loans to Ambrosiano group,
  213, 215–17, 227–8, 256; and Petromin, 261–
  2, 320; and Protezione, 306–9; used Libyan
  money, 215–16
Ense, Winfried, 102
Equity Funding, 104, 172
Ericsson, 38, 69, 161, 171
*Erin, 283, 296, 331, 339, 430
Etablissement pour les Participations
  Internationales (EPI), 63, 122, 123, 272
Etruria, 393
European Community, 33
Evangelisti, Franco, *Andreotti's right-hand man*,
  254
Evans, Peter, *partner, Coopers and Lybrand*, 219,
  220
Executive Consulting, 331

Fabbri, Giovanni, *paper magnate*, 317
*Fabiar, 83, 124
Falde, Nicola, *P2 member*, 145
Falez, Antonio, *friend of M*, 168, 173, 182, 184
Falklands War, 200, 414, 436
Fasco AG, 57, 59, 87
FBI, 54, 102, 103, 121, 181, 223, 258
Federal Reserve Bank, 117, 118, 205, 221
Fedigan, John, *friend of Marcinkus*, 181, 182
Feldman, Ned, *manager, Ultrafin, New York*, 66,
  95
Fernando, Anthony, *porter, Chelsea Cloisters*, 445,
  446
Ferrari, Alberto, *managing director, Banca
  Nazionale del Lavoro* 26, 147, 155, 201,
  213
Fiat, 156, 187, 201
Fiduciaire Générale, 25, 76, 272
Fiduciary Investment Company, 181, 182
Fiduciary Investment Services, 101, 181
Filo della Torre, Count Paolo, *journalist*, 469
Finabank, 56, 57, 67, 68, 74, 93, 100, 116, 117,
  120–2, 126
Finambro, 114–16
Finanzco, 324, 357, 368, 384, 475, 476
Fincoriz, 331
Finimtrust, 134
Finkurs, 155, 203
Finprogram, 155, 203
Fiorini, Florio, *financial director, ENI*, 26, 215,
  216, 306–8, 414, 476
Firrao, Ruggiero, *civil servant, P2 member*; at
  Mincomes, 150, 164, 195, 203, 208, 262; at
  SACE, 273, 421
First National City Bank, 85
Flavoni, Ugo, *friend of Carboni*, 447
Foligni, Mario, 102, 103, 104
Food and Agriculture Organisation, 199
Foot, Paul, *journalist*, 469

Forlani, Arnaldo, *Prime Minister, 1981*, 332, 337
Fornarsari, Mario, *Vatican lawyer*, 102, 103
Franco, Hilary, *Vatican official*, 400, 401, 406, 407,
  411, 420, 421, 434, 439, 478
Franklin National Bank, 80–1, 84, 87, 115–18,
  120, 205, 258, 259, 279, 295, 316
Fratoni, Jean Dominique, *casino owner*, 238–43
Fuchs, Betty, *witness*, 483

Galeazzi, Count Enrico, *chairman, SGI*, 51
Gallo, Colonel, 285, 306
Galtieri, General Leopoldo, 263, 437
Galucci, Achille, *prosecutor, Rome*, 405
Gambazzi, Marco, *Swiss lawyer*, 169, 175, 365,
  367
Gamberini, Giordano, *Freemason*, 142, 144
Gambino, Agostino, *Vatican co-chairman of joint
  commission*, 35, 36, 47
Gambino family, *mafiosi*, 260
Gambino, John, *friend of Sindona*, 261
Gantin, Cardinal Bernadin, 276
Garner, Graham, *partner, Coopers and Lybrand*,
  226, 234–5, 237, 281–2, 353, 385; letter to
  Siegenthaler, 231–2, 503–4; meeting with C,
  222; meeting with M, 274–8; misled by M, 8
Garzoni, Fernando, *chairman, Banca del Gottardo*,
  72, 95, 125, 135, 221, 257, 346; distances
  himself from C, 352, 372, 375, 391; visited by
  de Strobel, 346–7 visits Bahamas with C, 66
Gatti, Adolfo, *lawyer hired by M*, 10, 30, 35
Gelli, Licio, *Venerable Grandmaster of P2*, 3, 10,
  139, 155, 158, 160, 215, 225, 243, 254, 262,
  263, 323, 326, 332, 333, 369, 413, 421–2, 474,
  480; admits getting $8.5m, 370; arrest warrant
  issued for, 158, 416; arrested, 9; and Arrigo
  Lugli, 240; and author, 371; and Bologna
  bombing, 140; and "Bologna" note, 301–3;
  315; business career, 140–2; and Capitalfin,
  201–2; and Casino Ruhl, 238–40; and Ceruti,
  299–305, 315, 320; claimed last call to C, 389;
  claimed offer of money to C, 371–2; expelled
  from freemasonry, 384; and files, 147–9, 153,
  211, 306, 308, 320, 328, 332; flight, 318–19,
  321, 328, 379, 422, 430, 475; as Freemason,
  142–4; Gori, opens account in name of, 299,
  333; interview in *Corriere*, 336; keeps Rizzoli
  pattone, 289; and Las Acacias, 245, 247; meets
  O, 145; and Mincomes permissions, 149–51,
  164, 178–9, 371, 421; money received from O
  accounts, 151, 153, 178, 202, 247, 263, 292,
  301, 315, 318, 331, 333; premises searched, 9,
  317–18; and Rizzoli job, 244; schedule of early
  deals, 147–9, 157, 371; sentenced, 484; and
  Sindona, 120, 206–7, 261; and tabella, 10,
  284–5, 291, 295–7, 301, 306, 314–15, 329,
  330–1; used name Luciani, 225–6. *See also*
  Anna Bonomi; Bafisud; Calvi; lira
  back-to-backs
Gelli, Raffaello, *son of Licio*, 243, 314, 318
Geneva agreement, 5, 15, 16
Genghini, 189, 197, 282
Genghini, Mario, *head of a construction company*,
  189, 197, 282, 284, 323, 404; contacts with
  Nicaragua, 199; on tabella, 285,
Getty, Claire, 356